CARIBBEAN INTEGRATION

CARIBBEAN INTEGRATION

Uncertainty in a Time of Global Fragmentation

EDITED BY

Patsy Lewis

Terri-Ann Gilbert-Roberts

Jessica Byron

The University of the West Indies Press

Jamaica • Barbados • Trinidad and Tobago

The University of the West Indies Press
7A Gibraltar Hall Road, Mona
Kingston 7, Jamaica
www.uwipress.com

A catalogue record of this book is available from the National Library of Jamaica.

ISBN: 978-976-640-899-2 (print)
978-976-640-901-2 (epub)

Cover art: Stefanie Thomas, *Unanchored in Caribbean Blues*, 2021. (Artist's statement: "Its composition takes inspiration from the colours and spatial elements of CARICOM's flag. It presents a fishing boat, a relatable element of the Caribbean experience, perhaps run aground, unanchored, but still functional and beautiful at its core. CARICOM has the potential to be righted, especially if we pay attention to new areas like youth participation, language, climate change, gender and reparations".)

Contents

Part III Bringing the People In

Part IV Emerging Priorities for CARICOM

Figures

Tables

Acknowledgements

This book had its genesis in the work of the regional integration research cluster of the Sir Arthur Lewis Institute of Social and Economic Studies at the University of the West Indies (UWI), which was founded by Patsy Lewis as a part of the "Fifty-Fifty" project. That project, initiated by Brian Meeks in 2012 while he was University Director, provided opportunities for a variety of research clusters to reflect on the Caribbean region's experience fifty years after its first states gained their independence from Britain (beginning with Jamaica and Trinidad in 1962). Those discussions also gave attention to the challenges and opportunities for the next fifty years.

The regional integration cluster convened a conference in 2013 to commemorate the Caribbean Community's (CARICOM's) fortieth anniversary, which brought together scholars from across the globe to reflect on the CARICOM experience and the prospects for the future. This collection includes chapters based on the ideas presented at that conference, and developed for this collection, with a focus on aspects of the CARICOM experience which are not usually discussed. An earlier volume, *Pan-Caribbean Integration: Beyond CARICOM*, which focused on CARICOM's relations with the French- and Spanish-speaking Caribbean, was published by Routledge in 2018.

We are indebted to Brian Meeks for his insight in launching the broad research project, and we thank him, and subsequently University Director Aldrie Henry Lee, for making Sir Arthur Lewis Institute of Social and Economic Studies resources available to support the work of the cluster and conference. We thank the members of our research cluster for their support and exchange of ideas. We also thank the members of the conference organizing committee and the staff of Sir Arthur Lewis Institute of Social and Economic Studies, in particular Nadine Manraj-Newman and Richard Leach, for their support before, during and after the conference.

We are appreciative of the CARICOM Secretariat, which treated the conference as one of the official anniversary events, facilitating the attendance of then secretary general Irwin LaRocque, who delivered a plenary address during the conference, which has been published in this volume. The partnership with the Secretariat and the participation of its leadership in the dialogue speaks volumes about the intention of this academic work to inspire and influence policymakers and other stakeholders to translate the ideas into practice.

In the preparation and revision of the manuscript, we are grateful to Sebastian Salomon and Sarah Gault, Brown University graduates (2018) from the Watson Institute of International and Public Affairs Masters in Public Administration Program; and Alexandria Miller, a PhD student in the Africana Studies Department, Brown University, for their support.

Finally, we wish also to thank the anonymous reviewers of our manuscript proposal and each of our chapter contributors who have shared their intellectual insights in this collection. We are grateful to be able to include a chapter co-authored by our colleague Roland Craigwell, who sadly passed on before this volume could be published.

Abbreviations

ACCP	Assembly of Caribbean Community Parliamentarians
ACP	Africa, the Caribbean and the Pacific
ACS	Association of Caribbean States
ADF	augmented Dickey–Fuller
ALBA	Bolivarian Alliance for the Peoples of Our America
ALBA-TCP	Bolivarian Alliance for the Peoples of Our America People's Trade Treaty
ASEAN	Association of Southeast Asian Nations
ASV	annual sales volume
BBC	British Broadcasting Corporation
BLP	Barbados Labour Party
Brexit	British exit from the European Union
CADRES	Caribbean Development Research Services
CAFRA	Caribbean Association of Feminist Research and Action
CAHFSA	Caribbean Agricultural Health and Food Safety Agency
CAIC	Caribbean Association of Industry and Commerce
CANAS	Caribbean Air Navigation and Advisory Services
CARICOM	Caribbean Community
CARIFESTA	Caribbean Festival of Arts
CARIFORUM	Caribbean Forum
CARIFTA	Caribbean Free Trade Association
CARIWA	Caribbean Women's Association
CARPHA	Caribbean Public Health Agency
CARSEA	Caribbean Sea Ecosystem Assessment
CBI	Citizenship by Investment
CCA	CARICOM Committee of Ambassadors
CCCCC	Caribbean Community Climate Change Centre
CCJ	Caribbean Court of Justice
CCL	Caribbean Congress of Labour
CCRIF	Caribbean Catastrophe Risk Insurance Facility
CCSS	CARICOM Crime and Security Strategy
CCYD	CARICOM Commission on Youth Development
CDB	Caribbean Development Bank
CDEMA	Caribbean Disaster Emergency Management Agency
CDF	CARICOM Development Fund
CEDAW	Convention on Elimination of All Forms of Discrimination against Women
CELAC	Community of Latin American and Caribbean States

CEP	Caribbean Environment Programme
CEPR	Centre for Economic Policy Research
CET	Common External Tariff
CHG	Conference of Heads of Government
CMA	Caribbean Monetary Authority
CMU	Caribbean Monetary Union
COFAP	Council for Finance and Planning
COHSOD	Council on Human and Social Development
COTED	Council for Trade and Economic Development
CPA	Cotonou Partnership Agreement
CPDC	Caribbean Policy Development Centre
CRC	CARICOM Reparations Commission
CRFM	Caribbean Regional Fisheries Mechanism
CRNM	Caribbean Regional Negotiation Machinery
CROP	Council of Regional Organisations of the Pacific
CROSQ	Caribbean Regional Organisation for Standards and Quality
CRR	Centre for Reparation Research
CRYC	Caribbean Regional Youth Council
CSC	Caribbean Sea Commission
CSEC	Caribbean Secondary Education Certificate
CSM	CARICOM Single Market
CSME	CARICOM (or Caribbean) Single Market and Economy
CSN	CARICOM Skilled Nationals
CTO	Caribbean Tourism Organisation
CVQ	Caribbean Vocational Qualification
CXC	Caribbean Examinations Council
CYAs	CARICOM Youth Ambassadors
CYAP	CARICOM Youth Ambassador Programme
CYDAP	CARICOM Youth Development Action Plan
CYDG	CARICOM Youth Development Goal
DLP	Dominica Labour Party
EBM	ecosystem-based management
EC	European Commission
ECB	European Central Bank
ECCB	Eastern Caribbean Central Bank
ECCU	Eastern Caribbean Currency Union
ECLAC	Economic Commission for Latin America and the Caribbean
EEC	European Economic Community
EEZ	Exclusive Economic Zone
EMU	Economic and Monetary Union
EPA	Economic Partnership Agreement
FDI	foreign direct investment
FTAA	Free Trade Area of the Americas
GDP	gross domestic product
GSP	Generalized System of Preferences

GR	Golding Report
GRECO	Group of States against Corruption
HOG (or HoG)	CARICOM Heads of Government
IACC	Inter-American Convention against Corruption
ICT	information and communications technology
ICZM	Integrated Coastal Zone Management
IDPAD	International Decade for People of African Descent
IFIs	international financial institutions
IIRSA	Integration of the Regional Infrastructure of South America
IMF	International Monetary Fund
IMO	International Maritime Organization
IMP	Integrated Maritime Policy
IMP-MED	Integrated Maritime Policy of the Mediterranean Region
IOM	International Organization for Migration
IPCC	International Panel on Climate Change
LDCs	least (or lesser) developed countries
LDCs	less developed countries (CARICOM)
LFA	Logical Framework Analysis
LI	liberal intergovernmentalism
LME	large marine ecosystem
MARPOL	International Convention for the Prevention of Pollution from Ships
MDCs	more developed countries
MFN	most favoured nation
MOU	memorandum of understanding
MSP	Maritime Spatial Planning
NAARC	National African-American Reparations Commission
NAFTA	North American Free Trade Area
NBER	National Bureau of Economic Research
NCDs	non-communicable diseases
NDC	National Democratic Congress
NDP	New Democratic Party
NGO	non-governmental organization
NNP	New National Party
OAS	Organization of American States
OCA	Optimum Currency Area
OECD	Organization for Economic Cooperation and Development
OECS	Organisation of Eastern Caribbean States
OJR	Original Jurisdiction Rules
OLDESPECA	Latin American Organization for Fisheries Development (Organización Latinamericana de Desarrolo Pesquero)
OSPECA	Central American Organization of Fishing and Aquaculture (Organización del Sector Pesquero y Acuícola del Istmo Centroamericano)
OTEC	Ocean Thermal Energy Conversion
OTN	Organisation of Trade Negotiations

PAHO	Pan-American Health Organization
PANCAP	Pan Caribbean Partnership against HIV and AIDS
PFIR	Piarco Flight Information Region
PIROFISA	Pacific Framework for Integrated Strategic Action
PIROP	Pacific Islands Regional Ocean Policy
PLP	Progressive Liberal Party
PMEGG	Prime Ministerial Expert Group on Governance
PMSC	Prime Ministerial Sub-Committee on Reparations
PNC	People's National Congress
PNP	People's National Party
PP	Phillips–Perron tests
PROGOVNET	Principled Ocean Governance Networks
RSS	Regional Security System
RSYD	Regional Strategy for Youth Development
RTC	Revised Treaty of Chaguaramas
RTD	right to development
SDT	special and differential treatment
SMEs	small and medium enterprises
TCL	Trinidad Cement Limited
TNG	trade negotiations group
TPAP	Ten Point Action Plan
TWG	Technical Working Group
UNCLOS	United Nations Convention on the Law of the Sea
UNDESA	United Nations Department of Economic & Social Affairs
UNEP	United Nations Environment Programme
UNGA	United Nations General Assembly
UNIFEM	United Nations Development Fund for Women
UWI	University of the West Indies
UWP	United Workers Party
VAR	vector autoregression model
WBES	World Business Environment Survey
WCAR	World Conference against Racism
WCR	wider Caribbean region
WGEPAD	Working Group of Experts on People of African Descent
WIC	West Indian Commission
WICB	West Indies Cricket Board
WICP	Women in the Caribbean Project
WIF	West Indies Federation
WTO	World Trade Organization

Chapter 1

Caribbean Integration

Uncertainty in a Time of Global Fragmentation

PATSY LEWIS, TERRI-ANN GILBERT-ROBERTS AND JESSICA BYRON

These reflections on the Caribbean Community (CARICOM), one of the world's oldest regional integration organizations, come at a time when the world's most advanced scheme – the European Union – appeared to be in crisis. The United Kingdom's vote in June 2016 to leave the European Union had far-reaching repercussions not just for the integrity of the European Union and the future of the United Kingdom, but for schemes such as CARICOM, which drew inspiration from and modelled themselves off the European experience. Inspired by the campaign to disentangle Britain from Europe, and in fulfilment of an election promise reflecting the Jamaica Labour Party's disaffection with CARICOM, the new government, which came to power earlier that year, established a commission to assess Jamaica's membership in CARICOM. The United Kingdom's decision to leave the European Union, just weeks after Jamaica established its commission, stoked anxiety as to whether CARICOM itself would survive Brexit.[1]

The Jamaica Labour Party government's decision reflected longer-held dissatisfaction in some quarters of the Jamaica Labour Party and the private sector with Jamaica's engagement with CARICOM. Dissatisfaction with the Caribbean regional project was not confined to Jamaica, as the slow pace of implementation of regional decisions, as well as perceived uneven benefits and costs, were long-standing sources of discontent. The global recession, which began in 2008, two years after CARICOM launched its ambitious single market and economy (CSME), reduced countries' enthusiasm for the project, slowing implementation. Removing most barriers to conducting economic activity across the region, harmonizing policy across a wide field of economic activity, launching a single currency and allowing for limited labour mobility have either been stillborn (single currency) or have been advancing at an excruciatingly slow pace, jeopardizing the ambitious agenda.

CARICOM thus marked its fortieth anniversary in 2013 unsure of its future. The global recession, which took a toll on economies across the region, raised questions of member states' commitment to the process. The significant downturn in all regional economies created a crisis of funding for CARICOM's activities, leading to a restructuring of the secretariat and adoption of the first system-wide strategic plan. Long-standing concerns with the slow pace and seeming reluctance of members to implement decisions came to the fore, leading Heads of Governments to postpone the implementation of the "single economy" aspects of the agreement. Tensions over trade imbalances and hostility towards freedom of movement, to the limited extent that it existed, intensified. The crisis was also one of leadership, evident in the prolonged time frame taken to appoint a replacement for retired secretary general Edwin Carrington.

CARICOM was not the only regional scheme affected by the global recession and its aftermath of slow recovery. The European Union, the primary model for integration schemes worldwide, faced its own struggles to define itself as it expanded eastward to embrace most of the Eastern Bloc, including states of the former Union of Soviet Socialist Republics, extending liberalization beyond trade to include capital and the movement of people, with attendant tensions. The global financial crisis and recession exacerbated structural differences between Southern Europe (the so-called PIGS, in particular Greece) and their more affluent neighbours (in particular Germany), unveiling wide power imbalances within the organization. The refugee crisis in 2015, of refugees from the Middle East and Africa, aggravated by the European Union's inability to adopt a coherent, effective approach, also further weakened its cohesion. The Brexit referendum on leaving the European Union was the sharpest indicator of the crisis, revealing disaffection with the project across Europe, evident in the strong electoral showing of parties in support of their country leaving the European Union.

In Latin American, sharp political conflicts, in particular in Brazil and Venezuela, placed pressure on established schemes such as the Common Market of the South (MERCOSUR)[2] and more nascent, fragile schemes such as the Union of South American Nations (UNASUR), the Bolivarian Alliance for the People of Our Americas (ALBA) and the Community of Latin American and Caribbean States (CELAC). As Quilconi and Rhon (2020, 207) note, the success of post-hegemonic schemes, such as UNASUR, CELAC and ALBA, depended on ideological convergence and the role of states, in this case Brazil and Venezuela, willing to drive these new institutions. The CARICOM countries that are members of ALBA were already feeling its decline (Lewis, Gilbert-Roberts and Byron 2018a, 224–45). In addition, Venezuela's deep economic and political troubles tested CARICOM's unity, given the differentiated relationships of its member states with ALBA. With the collapse of its economy, deterioration of its political climate and large-scale migration of its population, including to CARICOM countries, Venezuela is no longer in the position to play the role it has done, especially in the Organisation of Eastern Caribbean States (OECS).[3] By extension, Cuba's role is also diminished given Venezuela's role in its economy. Cuba had already begun to move towards a policy of requesting remuneration for some of its services, although not from the OECS (Martinez Reinosa 2018). The Venezuelan crisis has also widened cracks in CARICOM's ability to project a cohesive foreign policy, as evident in the 2018 Organization of American States vote (see chapter 8).

Developments at the global level have also increased the region's precariousness. Although fears that the negotiations with Britain on a new trade agreement in the wake of Brexit would be on unfavourable terms were alleviated when the CARIFORUM–UK Economic Partnership Agreement (EPA) was signed in August 2019, very much along the lines of the CARIFORUM-EU EPA,[4] the region still faced a less than favourable environment within which to negotiate a post-Cotonou agreement with the European Union.

The novel coronavirus pandemic also emerged as a new challenge for regionalism as it threatened to reorder economic priorities, restructure production systems and processes, and realign economic partnerships. It had already exacerbated and foregrounded inequality along lines of gender, race, ethnicity and class across the globe. In the CARICOM region it significantly depressed economic growth, especially in tourism-dependent economies (ECLAC 2020; WB 2020), and was likely to reverse gains in debt reduction as governments were forced to borrow to fund initiatives to mitigate some of the more egregious effects of the economic shutdown. The Economic Commission for Latin America and the Caribbean (ECLAC) argues that its effects are likely to be longer term, affecting how businesses operate the role and use of technology and how countries produce and trade, among others.

Thus, this reflection on Caribbean regionalism occurs against the backdrop of deep global instability and increasing awareness of the immediacy of climate change and its multidimensional effects (Ashtine 2020). While these chapters were crafted before the Covid-19 pandemic, which has significantly slowed global economic growth, ravaged health systems and resulted in unprecedented loss of lives, the volume explores new challenges CARICOM countries were confronting even then, as well as new arenas for action.

CARICOM is not new to the upheavals that global developments present, as these have driven its major structural changes and reshaped its trade relationships.[5] Axline (1994), in one of the earliest efforts at theorizing regionalism based on the comparative approach, noted the challenges in generalizing about experiences given the unpredictability of exogenous variables such as the external environment, and the greater role they play in regional integration in developing countries (214). This is especially true for the small, highly open states of the Caribbean. The Revised Treaty of Chaguaramas, which launched the CSME and gave birth to the Caribbean Court of Justice (CCJ), was the region's response to the liberalizing ethos that birthed the European Single Market and Economy, World Trade Organization (WTO) and the North American Free Trade Area.[6] This shift also reframed traditional trade and aid relationships with Europe, in particular, the Lomé Convention, which gave way to the Cotonou Partnership Agreement[7] and, ultimately, the CARIFORUM–EU EPA. It also continued to threaten non-reciprocal trade relations with its other main trading partners, Canada and the United States. The Free Trade Area of the Americas, which was being negotiated between 1998 and 2004 among all the countries of North and South America, with the exception of Cuba, had it not been abandoned, would not only have ended the region's non-reciprocal access to the US market, but would have opened their markets, to one degree or another, to all the states of the arrangement.

The CARICOM Heads of Government meeting in Grenada in 1989, which heralded the CSME's formation, was one of two responses to the changing global environment recommended by the West Indian Commission (1992), established to advise CARICOM on the way forward. The CSME was meant to "deepen" the integration of members' economies by removing existing barriers to trade in goods, liberalizing trade in services and removing restrictions on the movement of capital. It also provided for a phased relaxation of restrictions on the movement of labour. The other response was to "widen" CARICOM's relations with its Caribbean and Latin American neighbours. The latter effort led to the formation of the Association of Caribbean States (ACS), a grouping of thirty-five states and territories that share the Caribbean Sea; the negotiation of a number of trade agreements with various countries in Latin America and the Caribbean; and the admission of Suriname and Haiti as members of CARICOM.[8] Thus, CARICOM's search for competitiveness did not emerge from an inherent desire to strengthen individual economies or even to construct a regional economy (not that there were not measures to facilitate these over the years), but as a defensive initiative to strengthen the private sector's ability to withstand increased competition that these liberalizing processes portended. These initiatives were not without tensions, as they served to aggravate imbalances among various member states, in particular between the OECS and the rest of CARICOM, and between Jamaica and Trinidad – where imbalances in trade that favoured the latter grew (see chapter 8). The implementation of limited provisions for freedom of movement also created new tensions, leading to at least one legal challenge and some high-profile cases.[9] As Söderbaum (2016, 24) notes, regional schemes such as CARICOM were not motivated by the desire to curb sovereignty to reduce conflict, but were a vehicle for "economic development and state formation", so it is no surprise that these measures to deepen the process aggravated national tensions.

Such tensions have not helped resolve the implementation difficulties that have dogged the CSME, the CCJ and now the EPA. The global recession, which weakened most economies, and International Monetary Fund (IMF)-monitored structural adjustment and/or poverty reduction programmes in the 1980s/1990s implemented in most also exacerbated tensions within the group. Challenges with implementing decisions within regional arrangements are not unique to CARICOM. While other regional agreements experience such challenges (Gray 2014), slow implementation has been particularly problematic for CARICOM, given the special role that regional integration is expected to play in shoring up the defences of these small Caribbean states.

Theorizing Regionalism and the CARICOM Experience

While this volume represents a deliberate focus on CARICOM's experience to reflect on its practice, challenges and possibilities, it is worthwhile to locate the volume in efforts to broaden the theoretical framework for assessing integration schemes outside of Europe. CARICOM is largely absent from attempts to theorize regional arrangements. As scholars justifying the comparative turn in the literature note, the field has been dominated by attempts to understand the workings of European integration with little reflection on the experiences of non-European arrangements and how an exploration of these could contribute to more robust theorizing (Acharya 2016). Thus the concerns of European-centred literature, in keeping with the underlying premise of overcoming nationalism and reducing conflict, were to understand the relationship between the state and supranational authorities, the role of interest groups and networks in furthering integration, the role of law in driving regional integration, and the role of integration in furthering competitiveness and integrating economies, inter alia.[10] This literature did not take account of the different contexts in which such schemes outside of Europe were formed, nor how their rationale – objectives and goals – differed from those of European integration. These regional groups were less motivated by the need to avoid interstate conflict than by the desire to shore up sovereignty and transform the structures of their economies.

The limitations of European approaches to understanding regional integration were identified earlier in the literature by Nye (1965), who noted that key underlying assumptions of European integration did not hold for developing countries (see also Wionczek 1966). Acharya (2016) in his critique of the Eurocentricity of attempts to theorize regionalism goes further in asserting that, given the diversity of regional movements and their different drivers, it is not possible to have a general theory of regionalism (126). More generally, attempts to understand various aspects of Caribbean integration on its own terms are largely absent from efforts to theorize regional integration.

The shift towards exploring "new regionalism" in the wake of the explosion of free trade agreements and the shedding of ideals of regionalism as a route to industrialization behind protected tariff walls and trade restrictions was also not particularly useful to understand CARICOM. Central to the conceptualizing of new or open regionalism was an acceptance of globalization, with success measured by openness to trade liberalization. Nor did much of this literature capture the coercion behind CARICOM's shift towards centring neoliberalism. Axline's (1994, 4) categorization of integration schemes into four generations – free trade areas, regional import substitution, collective self-reliance and "regional co-operation in the new world order" – is an attempt to capture the broad outlines of the experiences of regional schemes to allow for a comparative framework of analysis. His framing of these schemes in generational terms reflects a temporal approach to understanding the evolution of different forms of regionalism and the impetus behind them. As Söderbaum (2016, 17) observes, despite the value in historizing integration experiences and theorizing, there were important "continuities and similarities" between "old and new regionalisms". The challenge with attempts to find broad patterns here is that they can flatten the experiences of different schemes and mask the coercive elements of the external forces Axline identifies at work in the shift to the fourth generation of schemes. Rather than a joyful embrace of neoliberalism and optimism that its uptake would address trenchant problems of small size, weak competitiveness, inter alia, for CARICOM, the drivers of this turn are to be located in the forced liberalization of trade to meet the conditions for loans from the IMF and other international financial institutions who tied their financing to countries' fulfilling IMF conditionalities. They are also to be located in the formation of the WTO and the push by major trading and donor countries to restructure their trade relations along neoliberal lines rather than on non-reciprocal market access. Towards this end, the United States advanced the failed Free Trade Area of the Americas as the basis for its relationship with countries in Latin America and the Caribbean, for the Caribbean region would have replaced the non-reciprocal Caribbean Basin Economic Recovery Act (CBERA);[11] while the European Union significantly altered the trade protocols and aid provisions of the Cotonou Agreement in favour of reciprocal EPAs, among others. This shift was justified on the mantra that trade liberalization was the route by which these states would be "integrated" into the global economy, which was to be the answer to their development challenges. The European Union, in particular, claimed that the liberalizing of African, Caribbean and Pacific economies was a necessary condition for these countries to reap the benefits of the global economy (e.g. see Article 34(1) of the Cotonou Partnership Agreement). Against this backdrop, regional integration schemes were simply the tools for making this possible by locking in neoliberal reforms. It is not surprising that the European Union has directed significant proportions of its funding to the Caribbean to further the integration process and towards implementing the EPA, more specifically (EC 2015).

The turn towards a comparative frame to account for the absence of non-European schemes and to provide a stronger basis for theorizing regionalism has provided fertile ground for research, especially in Latin America and the Caribbean with a relatively long history of regional integration and large numbers of regional organizations. It utilizes a comparative methodology to assess aspects of regionalism from various disciplinary perspectives, which for the most part leaves underlying neoliberal assumptions unquestioned. Riggirozzi and Tussie (2012) are an important exception, as their exploration of new forms of cooperation across Latin America in the 1990s arising from the victories of left-wing parties interested in a more "solidarist" basis for integration was a deliberate attempt to push back at what they termed "American-led neoliberalism" as the analytical lens through which to assess the success of regional organizations. These groupings decentred trade and, as they observed, especially in the case of ALBA, forces a rethink of how the regional space is conceptualized, what regional governance can look like, how politics operating at both national and regional levels work, and what regions mean for state and non-state actors (Riggirozzi and Tussie 2012, 2). The *Oxford Handbook of Comparative Regionalism*, edited by Borzel and Risse (2016), in particular, represents an important illustration of the many different spaces that the framework opens up for comparative analysis across disciplinary perspectives and issue areas. As Borzel and Risse note, regions do not operate in isolation from one another, but there exists "ample evidence of interaction, mutual entanglement, and diffusion processes" (639).

Yet, this shift towards the comparative frame is not unproblematic for the study of Caribbean integration and, in particular, CARICOM. With a few exceptions, such as Axline's (1994) early advancement of a comparative frame in which Payne (1994) explores CARICOM; and Mace et al. (2016), which focuses on a particular issue, the role of summits in regional governance in the Americas; and in which Jessica Byron (88–105) has a chapter that speaks to CARICOM's experience, CARICOM is largely missing from the comparative frame. Its absence, in particular from the *Oxford Handbook* – aside from a brief historical reference to its formation – signals its perceived unimportance in attempts to theorize regionalism.[12] Even Riggirozzi and Tussie's important volume excludes the Caribbean, despite the attractiveness of these alternative forms of regional cooperation to CARICOM's smallest states and the challenges their participation posed for its coherence.

Gray (2014), who works within the comparative frame and draws on insights and methodologies from international relations and comparative politics to bear on the study of regional institutions, does include CARICOM and the OECS in her work. Her treatment of the region, however, suggests some of the challenges with the location of Caribbean integration in the literature. For instance, Gray's attempts to establish, through empirical methods, the importance of weak capacity in explaining the poor implementation track record of many integration schemes, does not reference any of the efforts of Caribbean scholars to understand CARICOM's experience. More egregious is her collaboration with Slapin (Gray and Slapin 2012) to understand the effectiveness of regional schemes, based on "expert surveys" of "24 different characteristics for PTAs" based on such wide-ranging issues as "perceptions of their capacity, including but not limited to how well they work as trade promoting instruments, how they deal with non-tariff barriers, how well their bureaucracies function, their perceived influence, the effectiveness of adjudication, and the match or mismatch between their ambitions and their actual competencies" (311). The survey was based on the insights of twenty-five "experts", assessing forty regional arrangements. Of the twenty-five, nineteen were from Europe, one from Africa and five from Latin America. None was from the Caribbean, even though CARICOM and the OECS were included in the survey (316). The majority of respondents assessed multiple regional agreements, in one instance, as many as fifteen. The largest number of individuals commenting on multiple agreements were among the European respondents, eight of whom commented on CARICOM and three on the OECS. The authors justified this approach on the basis that these experts worked with many arrangements around the world (317) "and thereby could apply a genuine comparison across several PTAs, whereas experts in developing countries tended to have direct experience with relatively fewer agreements" (316–17).

This example illustrates a weakness of the comparative approach, despite its laudable goal of bringing other schemes into the conversation and identifying the possible threads around which new theoretical frameworks can develop. The attempt to review large numbers of schemes, necessary for such work, can sacrifice exploring their complexity, which must be based on focused, in-depth research. This is particularly problematic when the underlying assumptions of the work do not hold for all schemes. The common assumption underlying the work of Gray (2014) and Gray and Slapin (2012) was that the primary role of regional arrangements was to facilitate trade and reduce trade barriers. This misses the various ways in which CARICOM has worked outside of trade, its weakest and most frustrating aspect to date, and across a wide range of non-trade issues to enrich the lives of its citizens and to strengthen its members' limited capacity. The real challenge is that while the trade liberalization assumption holds for preferential trade agreements, especially those created to embrace (and/or which have pivoted to embrace) trade as their raison d'être, it does not work to explain CARICOM's multifaceted agenda and challenges of reconciling the push to liberalize its markets while trying to bring benefits difficult to realize at the national level. It also does not account for CARICOM's role in a region comprising some of the world's smallest states. In other words, the comparative frame may well be comparing apples and oranges. An additional danger of this approach is that it can marginalize scholarship from the very regions being brought into the comparative frame.

The turn towards a comparative frame for theorizing regionalism represents an important effort to decentre the European experience and rebalance the scholarship to take account of other experiences. It allows for a keener appreciation of the underlying similarities, which is essential for theorizing, and offers exciting possibilities for bringing regional organizations within a comparative frame, widening the analytic scope for understanding these arrangements. The challenge is that it can lose sight of the complexities and peculiarities of particular arrangements that can complicate attempts at theorizing. For the Caribbean region, there is the more insidious problem of being given short shrift because of the small size of its members and their seeming insignificance, and of marginalizing the work of Caribbean scholars focused on understanding the arcane workings of CARICOM.

European Union as Model and Driver of Caribbean Regionalism

The literature also misses the tremendous influence that the EU model and the European Union itself continue to exert on CARICOM. One of the main goals of comparative regionalism is to move away from centring the European process as originator, model and measure of success of regionalism (Acharya 2016). Acharya (2016) argues that while the goal of European integration was to integrate European economies, for the post-colonial world the goal was autonomy or "the preservation of state sovereignty" (110). Contrary to this assertion, the European Union was very much the model for CARICOM integration, even as its member states were reluctant to give up any sovereignty to a supranational authority. The ambition to move from a free trade area to a common market, then single market and economy, alongside the creation of political, administrative, functional and legal institutions to support the process, was very much in keeping with the trajectory of European integration. This contradiction is at the heart of Caribbean integration and explains its excruciating slowness in pushing along key aspects of the CSME. This was compounded by the reality that at the start the assumptions of competitive economies and differentiated trade underpinning integration theory did not hold for CARICOM states. Jhinkoo-Ramdass (chapter 6), Maurin and Craigwell (chapter 5), Gordon and VanSickle (chapter 7), and Lewis (chapter 8) illustrate the challenges the region faces in achieving core regional integration objectives. CARICOM governments also recognized this when they retreated from the goal of creating a monetary union.

Nor did CARICOM have the means to compensate for the differential benefits from regional integration that might have smoothed over some of these difficulties that came to the fore in the Jamaica Commission on CARICOM and the OECS's response to it. These contradictions at the heart of the regional project are compounded by the shift to greater liberalization of international trade, which exacerbates these underlying tensions, as there are few tangible avenues for compensating the losers.[13] As the Inter-American Development Bank's (IDB 2020) report on CARICOM observes, "securing access to markets requires firms with the capacity to produce goods in sizeable volumes, and at consistent quality for large foreign markets" (91), which is challenging for most CARICOM economies, but particularly so for the tiny OECS countries. Rather than revisit its core objectives in the light of global shifts away from trade multilateralism and the challenges of achieving some elements of the CSME and the potential for deepening existing rifts, CARICOM governments have recommitted themselves to completing the CSME.

The EU involvement in shaping CARICOM's regional project is very much in evidence. The inclusion of Pascal Lamy, former EU trade commissioner and WTO director general, as a member of the restructured Commission on the Economy (see chapter 8) to chart a way forward for CARICOM is a clear indication that CARICOM will remain on the path to a particular type of regional integration, whether or not this exacerbates tensions among its members. In addition, the European Union continues to influence the direction of Caribbean integration through its trade and aid relationships represented in the CARIFORUM–EU EPA and financing through the European Development Fund, which prioritized integration.

Two factors might lead to a different way of thinking about CARICOM's implementation deficit – first, the European Union's continued engagement with the regional project with support for creating a single regional space inclusive of the Dominican Republic and aimed at facilitating the entry and smooth operation of EU firms; and second, the tensions inherent in pursuing both an agenda for deeper economic integration while being deeply committed to holding on to sovereignty. Understanding the deficit might lie beyond the various explanations offered in the literature – lack of political will; oppositionist politics at the national level (Lewis 2005; 2006); administrative deficiencies and limited resources (Mills et al. 1990; Stoneman et al 2012); the absence of mechanisms for transferring regional decisions into action at the national level (Pollard 2003); not being able to overcome the insurmountable wall of insularity (Best 1996); lacking strong mechanisms for implementation (West Indian Commission 1992) – to focus on the impracticalities of centring trade in integration, when the original conditions never favoured this type of integration. This observation brings into question the value of using trade liberalization to assess the success of Caribbean integration, a concern that Lewis (chapters 3 and 8) speaks to.

Locating the Collection in Scholarship on CARICOM

Outside of the comparative frame, there is a wide body of literature that has focused explicitly on CARICOM, ranging from attempts to understand its evolution to more focused efforts to understand its challenges, particularly in deepening the integration process and creating a more popular and less technocratic movement. These range from single-authored volumes (Axline 1979, Payne 2008, Boxill 1993, Gilbert-Roberts 2013, and Hinds 2019) to edited collections focusing on a diverse range of authors and concerns. These include[14] efforts at understanding the historical, socio-cultural and political evolution of the integration process, seeking to understand the drivers of integration and early tensions within the group (Axline 1994; Payne 2008; Boxill 1993; Mullerleile 1996); its implementation challenges (Pollard 2003; Lewis 2003, 2005; Hinds 2006; Brewster 2005; Best 1996); its model of governance (V. Lewis 2003; Thomas 2001; Grenade 2005; Gilbert-Roberts 2013; Hinds 2020); issues in law (Pollard 2003; Kaczorowska-Ireland 2014; Berry 2014); and challenges in furthering economic integration (Byron 2004; Ramsaran 2013; Constantine 2021); and as an agent of development (Girvan 2007; Brewster 2001; Demas 1997). A small group of authors have focused on understanding the subregional OECS and its relationship with CARICOM (Lewis 2001, 2002; Hendrickson 2006; Venner 2007; Byron 1999; Grenade 2011).

Most of the literature on CARICOM, especially within the last ten years or so, has been multiauthored edited volumes that explore different aspects of the integration experience. The edited volumes by Hall and Chuck-A-Sang (2012a, 2012b, 2013), Hall

(2012), and Benn and Hall (2006) have drawn on a wide range of scholarship to reflect on different aspects of the process. Hall and Chuck-A-Sang (2010), in particular, offer varying critical perspectives of scholars, regional technocrats and political leaders on several dimensions of the CARICOM integration process, focusing on traditional areas of trade, foreign policy and security.

There have also been a few attempts to explore CARICOM within a wider regional Americas context. The edited volume by Knight, Castro-Rea and Ghany (2014), which presents a dynamic look at changes in regionalism across the Americas, especially in the wake of the failed Free Trade Area of the Americas talks and EU efforts to reconfigure its relationship with the region, represents a rare attempt to take a cross-regional approach that includes CARICOM. This collection thus offers important reflections on CARICOM, especially on its external trade relations (Lewis 151–84, Kirton 69–82, Montoute 241–54), its general direction (Bishop), and possibilities and constraints of culture (Ghany 231–40, Girvan 255–62). The *Oxford Handbook of Caribbean Economies* (Looney (ed) 2020) also follows this vein of exploring broad thematic and individual country issues across Latin America and the Caribbean. And although not focused on regionalism, the collection does have chapters that look at CARICOM explicitly (Lewis 81–97) but more generally provides a regional take on a broad range of concerns such as drugs, crime and violence (Hinds 126–39; Sherill and Morris-Francis 108–25); climate change and natural disasters (Ashtine 21–8, Looney 140–58); debt (Henry 98–107); energy security (Goldwyn and Gill 11–20); and external relations (Greene-Dewasmes and Heron 182–92; Bernal 193–203), among others. The volume *Pan-Caribbean Integration: Beyond CARICOM* (Lewis et al. 2018b) focuses on CARICOM's relations with the French and Spanish Caribbean, and so presents CARICOM's attempt to widen its membership, reflecting on an entirely different aspect of the integration experience.

This collection, *Caribbean Integration: Uncertainty in a Time of Global Fragmentation*, contributes to the literature on Caribbean integration by presenting an updated, wide-ranging assessment of CARICOM nearly fifty years after its formation. It does not seek to explicitly locate CARICOM and the broader regional experience within theoretical frames, although there are attempts in various chapters to do so. In addition to exploring issues of central concern in the traditional literature with economic integration, and the feasibility of achieving key cornerstones of economic integration (monetary union, fiscal convergence, industrial programming, and policy convergence), it also reflects on CARICOM's engagement with its people and captures some of CARICOM's widening social agenda and concerns (climate change, gender-based violence, youth engagement) and newer fields of engagement (reparations), and explores new directions for CARICOM. It thus addresses the need for critical analysis of prospects for the future of the community, and is especially timely in light of concerns raised earlier as to the viability of integration projects in the wake of Brexit and widespread anti-EU sentiments across Europe; and instability in regional alternatives such as ALBA, which, as Quiliconi and Rhon (2020, 204) note, require "ideological convergence and regional leadership in order to succeed".

The book's strength lies in its centring of Caribbean scholars and practitioners in reflecting on key aspects of the integration experience, providing that deep dive into the working of the organization to which the comparative turn does not easily lend itself.

It goes beyond the scholarly community to include key participants in the regional project, such as the CARICOM secretary general and the chairman of the CCJ.

Structure of the Book

It is clear from the collected chapters that while the original impetus for the regional project can be located both within competing goals of competitiveness and meeting aspirations for a united region based on kinship, most of the developments since the CSME's formation have been driven by market integration goals, especially an acceptance that "development" lays in their "integration" into the global economy. The chapters in this collection reflect both on the challenges the region faces in pushing forward the market integration impetus of the CSME and a desire to expand CARICOM's remit to take account of broader non-market issues that confront the region. Of course, these goals are not always clearly distinguishable from one another. They also reflect the tug between international drivers of the process and national imperatives, the prevalence of governments in decision-making and the limited opportunities available for public participation.

The collection is divided into four parts. Part 1, "Reflecting on CARICOM", presents a broad overview and assessment of the integration process, laying the basis for the more in-depth focus on specific aspects of the project that are addressed in subsequent parts of the book. Part 2, "Completing the Internal Market", explores challenges in achieving an integrated economy, including policy formulation as well as economic and fiscal convergence. Part 3, "Bringing the People In", focuses on the more popular aspects of CARICOM: youth engagement, CARICOM's role in promoting legislation to combat domestic abuse and advance gender equality, the movement of people across the region, and the role of the CCJ. Part 4, "Emerging Priorities for CARICOM", explores novel areas in CARICOM's functional agenda, such as climate change, electoral financing reform and reparations, and proposes an expanded agenda for CARICOM beyond the CSME.

Part I: Reflecting on CARICOM

Former CARICOM secretary general[15] Irwin LaRocque's opening chapter (chapter 2), "CARICOM beyond Forty", sets the stage for understanding the twists and turns of the integration process and for the deeper analysis that follows in subsequent chapters. He succinctly traces the origins and evolution of the integration process and ongoing attempts to create a single market and economy. He assesses its successes and challenges in implementing the CSME and identifies a larger agenda that includes climate change, youth engagement and gender-based violence, with which CARICOM has to come to terms. He also presents his own perspective on CARICOM's agenda beyond its first forty years and initiatives undertaken by the secretariat to guide this agenda for change. In LaRocque's account, the CSME's formation was driven by the external environment (the formation of the WTO, and the likely erosion of preferential market access to Europe and North America), with governments scrambling to keep up. The slew of new organizations that emerged in tandem were all directed at meeting the requirements of the CSME. The primacy of the economy (and a particular variant at that) is evident in LaRocque's observation that although CARICOM has four pillars – the economy, human and social development, security cooperation, and foreign policy coordination – the focus of the Revised Treaty of Chaguaramas was on the economic elements of integration, representing a clear signalling of priorities. Ultimately, LaRocque's primary concerns are with the deficits of CARICOM's governance regimes and their ability to fully complete the CSME. Despite the chapter's heavy focus on the economy, LaRocque points to the so-called functional arrangements in the fields of health and education, suggesting that the regional integration process had much ground to cover in bringing citizens and their concerns closer to the centre of its agenda.

Patsy Lewis (chapter 3), "Whither Caribbean Integration? Recasting the Foundations of a New Integration Project", presents a less sanguine view of the integration process. She argues that rather than representing a route to the region's survival, its embrace of neoliberal goals of competitiveness, as represented in the CSME, has exacerbated existing fissures among member states, already deepened by the financial crisis and global recession. The chapter identifies the various ways in which CARICOM states' external arrangements with various Latin American regional schemes and trading arrangements, as well as with the European Union, hold the potential to fragment the region further. Lewis argues that CARICOM's salvation lies in prioritizing a development agenda, at the centre of which is the creation of a regional economy grounded in regional productive processes that take account of the particularities of its smaller members, and not in the pursuit of shallower competitive goals. Central to this shift in CARICOM's agenda is centring its people and their concerns in the regional process. This stands in contrast to the neoliberal measure of success that is at the heart of discussions around new/open regionalism and comparative regionalism. The question which this chapter does not answer is what scope, if any, CARICOM has to move away from a neoliberal trade agenda which is embedded in larger processes, such as the requirements of WTO compatibility and the European Union's larger–than–life role in moving CARICOM in this direction.

Tamara Onnis, in chapter 4, "Applying the Theory of Liberal Intergovernmentalism to CARICOM: The CARIFORUM-EU EPA", assesses the EPA between CARIFORUM and the European Commission (EC) and its Member States, CARICOM's most extensive trading agreement with countries outside of CARICOM. She employs the theoretical perspective of liberal intergovernmentalism (LI) – developed to explain aspects of European integration – to EPA negotiations. She focuses on negotiating and bargaining processes among CARICOM members, in particular the competencies of the bargaining institutions, the interplay between the latter and heads of government, and on member state preferences. She uses LI's three-step approach and analysis, namely the formation of national preferences, bargaining and negotiation, and the creation of functional institutions, to explore the bargaining dynamics that shaped the EPA.

Onnis's chapter is an attempt to understand the extent to which LI, an approach developed to better understand European integration, was adequate to explain aspects of Caribbean integration, especially its negotiations with the more powerful EU. Her account challenges LI's assumptions of the primacy of the state in shaping negotiating priorities, arguing that it was the regional institution, the Regional Negotiating Machinery, that led CARICOM's (and the Dominican Republic's) negotiations with the

European Union. She argues that rather than reflecting state priorities, which LI would lead one to expect, the negotiating stances reflected the positions of various participating groups, largely from the private sector and the Regional Negotiating Machinery itself. Further, rather than the Regional Negotiating Machinery functioning as the institutional arm of member states, its role was mostly independent of these states. Nevertheless, the LI framework did reflect the role of the more dominant European Union in shaping the negotiations and their outcome. But even so, CARICOM's refusal to budge on key issues, such as greater EU control over the offshore financial sector, suggests that there were limits to compromises that even weak states were willing to make when vital interests were threatened. Further, CARICOM, though the far weaker partner, was able to wrest some concessions from the European Union, affirming LI's assumption that states sign agreements when there is some benefit to them. Nevertheless, the chapter underscores the European Union's important role in embedding trade liberalization at the heart of CARICOM, suggesting that it plays a major role in influencing the direction of Caribbean integration, despite whatever minor victories CARICOM might have scored in the negotiations. It would also suggest that despite claims of the European Union's waning influence on integration schemes, it continues to play an important role in shaping the direction of CARICOM.

Together, these three chapters frame the rest of the discussions that follow: the limited role of civil society/popular engagement; the limitations of CARICOM countries and the regional organization itself to steer the integration process when measured against the strength of global neoliberalizing processes and the role of core states; and the limitations of CARICOM's focus on trade and market integration.

Part II: Completing the Internal Market: The Limitations of Economic Integration

The four chapters in this part explore some of the challenges inherent in achieving core economic integration goals, such as coordinating fiscal policies, creating a monetary union and increasing CARICOM's role in national economies. Common concerns of all are challenges in completing key elements of the CSME, especially the elusive goal of fiscal harmonization and monetary policy, the balance between national priorities and regional policy coherence, and the ability of the integration project to bring benefits. Drawing on literature on the EU experience, the chapters present original research meant to address the gap of a dearth of studies on the CARICOM region, while highlighting the peculiar challenges that make achieving these goals possible. They also suggest that CARICOM has been less than successful in its core task to create a regional economy, ending with Lewis's reflection on whether CARICOM should not pay more attention to the transformation of economies and protecting its resources.

Alain Maurin and Roland Craigwell (chapter 5), "A Study of Economic Cycles in the CARICOM Free Trade Area: Situation, Challenges and Lessons", seek to fill a perceived gap in the literature on short- and medium-term economic fluctuations and the terms of convergence of CARICOM economies. On the assumption that synchronization of business cycles was necessary to attain the deeper levels of integration required to complete the CARICOM Single Market and Economy, they explore cyclical similarities and dissimilarities among Barbados, Jamaica and Trinidad and Tobago to examine the degrees of business cycle synchronization across Caribbean economies, the determinants of these movements, and the roles institutions should play in the economic regulation and coordination of growth policies. Using an extended version of the Bry–Boschan procedure, they built the chronologies of business and growth cycles of these three largest Caribbean economies for which there was sufficient data. They show that while these countries are characterized by generally divergent economic business cycles, as well as growth cycles, they are highly synchronized with the cycles of the industrialized countries. This leads them to conclude that CARICOM's regional integration policy has not been successful in furthering the convergence of economic cycles and to argue for a more explicit focus on understanding business cycles based on increasing the availability of data across the region and stronger initiatives to accelerate integration, especially in the direction of harmonizing fiscal and monetary policies and implementing a monetary union. While not commenting on whether a monetary union is a worthwhile goal to pursue, it does speak to the challenges inherent in achieving this goal.

Julia Jhinkoo-Ramdass (chapter 6), in "Fiscal Convergence: Is It a Necessary Criterion for a Caribbean Monetary Union?", picks up this concern in her efforts to understand why the Caribbean has been unsuccessful so far in achieving a monetary union, by exploring the specific challenge of achieving fiscal convergence among CARICOM countries. She focuses on a number of configurations of groups of countries, including the underresearched Eastern Caribbean Currency Union (ECCU), whose monetary policy is controlled by the Eastern Caribbean Central Bank. Her specific areas of enquiry are whether monetary policy has facilitated the fiscal convergence of ECCU member countries and whether fiscal convergence has occurred in the absence of monetary policies in countries operating outside of a common monetary framework. Her tests for fiscal convergence are based on cross-correlation, dispersion and cointegration tests of annual data for government net lending, and total current revenue and expenditure. She argues that fiscal convergence was unlikely to be achieved within the group given the high levels of volatility in their external environment, suggesting that a monetary union need not rely on convergence to occur. Rather, what was important was the imposition of strong fiscal rules on members of a monetary union. She does not explore the political mechanisms that would need to be in place to do this.

Ronald M. Gordon and John J. VanSickle (chapter 7), "CARICOM Policy Formulation Process: Review and Reconfiguration", explore CARICOM's role in the performance of the private sector across the region. The multi-country study that informs this chapter sheds light on the structure of the regional private sector, in terms of firm size and focus of business and geographical scope of operation. They find a wide divergence in economies, which leads them to argue for differential policies and strategies at the regional level to take account of these divergences. This recommendation is based on the findings from a business survey that forms the basis of their analysis that national policy was far more important than regional policy in the performance of firms. The chapter argues for a reconfiguration of CARICOM policy formulation to incorporate the distinctiveness of countries' economic and business environments, and for the more active engagement of the private sector, especially small- and medium-size firms in regional policy formulation.

Patsy Lewis's chapter 8, "CARICOM beyond the CSME", focuses on Jamaica's dissatisfaction with the CSME represented in the *Report of the Commission to Review Jamaica's Relations within the CARICOM and CARIFORUM Frameworks* (the Golding report). The report provides a window to explore Jamaica's perspective on challenges confronting the integration process, such as macroeconomic convergence, freedom of movement, and the divide between CARICOM's designated lesser developed states (LDCs) and more developed states (MDCs). For Lewis, Jamaica's dissatisfaction represents an opportunity to reflect on competing visions of the regional integration process represented by the Golding report, the Landell-Mills report and CARICOM's Strategic Plan for the Caribbean Community 2015–19 (CARICOM Secretariat 2014a, 2014b); CARICOM's response in the St Ann's Declaration (2018); and the report of the restructured Commission of the Economy (2020). She argues for a more expanded agenda for CARICOM beyond narrow objectives, such as completing the CSME, to consider more fundamental issues of economic transformation and protecting citizens' rights.

Part III: Bringing the People In

An important criticism of the regional integration project is the limited avenues it provides for popular engagement (Lewis 2003; Best, cited in Lewis 2003; Gilbert-Roberts 2013; Hinds 2019), or even with the private sector as Gordon and VanSickle (chapter 7 in this volume) have suggested. The project has been critiqued as a top-down process privileging heads of governments (Gilbert-Roberts 2013). Specific initiatives, such as the Assembly of Caribbean Community Parliamentarians, and civil society forums have also been criticized as ineffective (Lewis 2005; Hinds 2019). Key elements introduced with the CSME, namely limited provisions for freedom of movement and the CCJ, while located as measures to strengthen the regional private sector, nevertheless represent initiatives that more directly affect ordinary people. The five chapters in this part engage with different aspects of popular engagement, critiquing efforts towards this end as well as underlining the importance of popular involvement to CARICOM's success. They explore very different instances of the possibilities and limitations of the regional space for broadening citizens' rights, and tensions between the national and regional spheres with different and sometimes unexpected results. These include the exclusion of youth from the regional project (Terri-Ann Gilbert-Roberts, chapter 9); challenges of transforming national legislation to protect women against interpersonal violence, in keeping with regional model laws (Halimah A.F. DeShong, chapter 10); national challenges to CARICOM's already limited regional movement regime (Natalie Dietrich Jones, chapter 11); the CCJ's potential to strengthen the rights of ordinary citizens (Adrian D. Saunders, chapter 12); and the dangers of promoting regional industrial projects that ignore popular perceptions, increased awareness of the environmental effects of such programmes, and the experiences of local populations (April Karen Baptiste and Hubert Devonish, chapter 13). They speak to often-neglected aspects of the Caribbean integration process that extend beyond its economics and functional integration agendas. Importantly, these various chapters illustrate the importance of the national arena in either furthering or restraining the regional project.

Terri-Ann Gilbert-Roberts, in her chapter "Is CARICOM Politically Sustainable? Assessing the (Youth) Participation Deficit", shifts the conversation from the challenges of achieving economic integration to question the very viability of CARICOM's political model, which provides inadequate opportunities for popular engagement, especially of youth, one of its most critical constituencies. She focuses on the exclusion of citizens from the regional framework in what she terms the "participation deficit", which she locates within the existing national ethos of representative politics that minimizes the importance of active participation at the regional level. Her particular focus is on youth engagement with the regional project, exploring CARICOM's measures since 1973 to include youth, as well as youth surveys and consultations, to document a gradual process of rhetorical regional "citizenisation" of youth alongside constrained youth engagement. She warns that failure to engage youth and their concerns more centrally could lead to their withdrawal from the project, with deleterious effect on CARICOM's survival. In observing that young people of the region were interested in a more political union, she raises fundamental questions about the efficacy of CARICOM's privileging of a limited economic agenda.

In the chapter that follows, "CARICOM Model Legislation on Domestic Violence: Negotiating Love, Intimacy and Abuse in Caribbean Law", Halimah A.F. DeShong explores regional efforts to advance the agenda of female empowerment through legislation. She explores the extent to which the CARICOM Model Legislation on Issues Affecting Women, introduced between 1989 and 1991, has influenced member states' practice and philosophy in attempting legislative and policy change. She analyses the successes and slippages that characterize the introduction of and failures to introduce such legislation from the perspective of regional organizing and governance, and how these processes interface with national imperatives. She argues that the introduction of domestic violence and sexual offences legislation in several member states, as well as ongoing policy and legislative reform in the areas of citizenship rights, equal pay, sexual harassment and inheritance in these countries, need to be understood in a context of regional governance, feminist and other social justice-oriented organizing, and national imperatives. She argues that despite the regional push for legislation, ultimately, laws are interpreted and implemented in national contexts, subject to attitudes that persist at the local level.

In the chapters that follow, Natalie Dietrich Jones and Adrian D. Saunders explore new innovations introduced with the Revised Treaty of Chaguaramas which potentially open the door to more popular engagement with the process. Jones's chapter, "A Failure to Comply? Explaining Dissonance between Regional and National Migration Policy in CARICOM Using the Case of Barbados", explores what she views as an apparent disconnect between treaty provisions, which encourage hassle-free travel and skilled migration within CARICOM, and member governments' national migration policy. She focuses on Barbados, where this has been most contentious, concluding that governments' interpretation of their treaty obligations responds to national imperatives rather than regional commitments, with deleterious effects on the mobility component of the integration project. As is the case with many integration agreements, mobility regimes are introduced to advance market integration goals, limited to a specific group of people, namely skilled workers, rather than in response to philosophical goals about regional belonging. Jones's exploration of the disconnect between national immigration and regional policy reflects the latter's inability to address longer-standing patterns of migration, mostly illicit, that fall outside of the neoliberal impetus of the CSME. It also suggests the limitations of a regime based on market integration considerations to address the long-standing desire (and the resulting conflicts it generates) for migration as an avenue to belonging,[16] considered necessary to the legitimacy of the regional project. Jones's exploration of the tensions between the regional and national regimes for managing migration accords well with Lavenex et al.'s conclusion from reviewing a number of regional schemes that "highlights the prevalence of sovereignty concerns as a limit to deeper integration" (in Borzel and Risse 2016, 458).

Adrian D. Saunders, president of the CCJ, in his chapter, "New Hope for Caribbean Integration: The Revised Treaty of Chaguaramas and the Jurisdiction of the CCJ", reflects on the CCJ's importance to the sustainability of the regional project, detailing its jurisdiction, institutional underpinnings and jurisprudence. He notes that most of the cases brought before the CCJ were from private individuals and non-state entities seeking to assert their rights arising from the CSME, in particular, the right of movement within the CARICOM. He focuses on several rulings by the court on non-state entities that have forced states to comply with treaty provisions, and argues that by enforcing the regional treaty and forcing national governments to abide by their regional commitments, the CCJ has fundamentally altered the CARICOM landscape, elevating the role of law.

The final chapter in this part by April Karen Baptiste and Hubert Devonish, "Weighed and Found Wanting: Global, Regional and Local Scales in a Caribbean Environmental Discourse", presents an instance of the failure of a key element of regional economic integration – the development of cross-national industrial projects, arising from the exclusion of people from the conversation and the failure to take account of environmental concerns. They explore the implications of the absence of popular engagement in efforts to kick-start a regional industrial initiative, a long-held goal of CARICOM, with the implementation of an aluminium smelter project between Trinidad and Tobago, Jamaica, and Guyana in the mid-2000s. The smelter, which was to be located in the southwest peninsula of Trinidad, was eventually abandoned when it ran afoul of concerns related to health and the physical environment from residents of surrounding communities. The chapter focuses on newspaper reports to establish public discourse around the project in an effort to understand why it failed. It suggests that four themes of rights, economic effects, ecological consequences, and concerns for health and safety were central. The authors, using a politics of scale framework, locate the project's failure in the inability to reconcile the four scales (local, national, regional and international) in which the topic was discussed, leading to a breakdown in communication. They conclude that for regional projects of this nature to be successful, there needs to be a negotiating of meaning across these scales. The failure of this initiative underscores new considerations with which extant goals of integration schemes should contend: the strength of public engagement and the increased avenues of expression now available to them; and the growing salience of environmental concerns in determining the success or failure of such schemes.

Part IV: Emerging Priorities for CARICOM

The final part of the collection explores a range of areas which are either new or absent from CARICOM's agenda or require a stronger regional approach. These include climate change, electoral financing reform and reparations. Jay R. Mandle (chapter 14) takes on the timely challenge of climate change and its role in the integration process, while Cynthia Barrow-Giles (chapter 15) and Verene A. Shepherd (chapter 16) enrich the discussion by reflecting on new arenas of engagement for the regional project. Shepherd speaks to an emerging arena of action, the task of pursuing reparatory justice as a regional pursuit, while Barrow-Giles highlights an area of national politics, electoral reform, that confronts all CARICOM member states but remains largely in the domestic domain.

Jay R. Mandle in his chapter, "Climate Change and the Integration Project", argues that despite CARICOM states' continued reluctance to concede political sovereignty, they have been generally favourable to deepening functional cooperation in areas such as health, disaster preparedness, security and education. He suggests that climate change, and the challenges it presents to key economic sectors, in particular tourism, is likely to strengthen support for deeper functional cooperation but argues that CARICOM needs a more technological approach to combat its effects. Mandle reflects earlier concerns in the political literature on federalism and regionalism with identifying likely catalysts to propel further integration, especially the conditions under which countries would cede sovereignty. Although there is some literature suggesting the likelihood that such catalysts were likely to come from external factors (Wheare 1968, military threats; Lewis 2002, economic shocks and loss of international support), Axline (1994, 190) argues that the role of external factors has been largely absent from the theory of economic integration. Yet, any account of CARICOM's journey shows the important role that exogenous shocks have played in its evolution, despite Axline's reflection that their unpredictability, especially those originating from the external environment, makes it challenging to generalize across integration schemes. Mandle's addition to this debate is his identification of climate change as the new external exogenous catalyst likely to promote deeper integration.

Cynthia Barrow-Giles's chapter, "Second-Generation Reform: Political Party and Election Financing in the OECS", shifts the focus to the need for a regional approach to address a challenge that resides squarely in the domestic domain: electoral reform, and in particular the control of election financing. She argues that despite the critical function that money plays in democratic politics, regional policies have not been developed in this realm. She notes that this is an area that has elicited a regional approach from regional organizations in Europe (the European Union) and Latin America, but has failed to make it onto the regional agenda in the Caribbean. The broader implication of the exclusion of the regional project from national political structures and legislation is that this misalignment has already had implications for the implementation of CARICOM's agenda, most notably extending the role of the CCJ as the final court of appeal for its members.

In her chapter, "The Reparatory Justice Movement in the Caribbean: The Role of CARICOM since 2013", Verene A. Shepherd explores CARICOM's entry into the reparations debate. The 2013 adoption of a Ten Point Action Plan, crafted by the members of the CARICOM Reparation Commission (chaired by University of West Indies vice chancellor Hilary Beckles), marked the organization's formal entry into claims for reparations. Shepherd discusses CARICOM's rationale for joining the struggle for reparatory justice for native genocide, African enslavement and the legacies of colonialism; tracks the actions of Heads of Government of CARICOM since 2013; and assesses the impact and implications of such actions. This is an example of the more political rationale for CARICOM integration beyond the narrow confines of the economy, where joint political action is considered essential to pressing a common case that would be less effectively pursued at the national level. It also has the potential to address, not just the historical origins of CARICOM countries' present-day challenges, not least of which are size and their structural insertion into the global economy, but deeper psychological wounds. A project for reparations for the harms of the colonial past, especially of slavery, would be limited if it does not also shine a light on the ways in which anti-black racism, the legacy of slavery, is manifested at the national level and a recognition of the importance of taking a regional approach to tackling these common challenges.

Conclusion: What Is the Future for CARICOM?

Borzel critiques the traditional theoretical approaches to regional cooperation and integration as being state centric, arguing for a centring of "governance" as a concept that can help "overcome … statist and formal institutionalist bias" as it gives "equal status to state and non-state actors and does not prioritize formal over informal institutions" (in Borzel and Risse 2016, 41–42). While seeking to decentre states as the primary driver, actor and embodiment of aspirations of integration can offer exciting ways of thinking about integration and raises questions about the underlying assumptions of traditional integration theories, this book's primary focus is on the formal processes of Caribbean integration, speaking to both its frustrations and potentials, especially in pursuing agendas that more directly align with popular concerns. In the Caribbean, where analysis of integration beyond the formal state-driven processes, especially in migration and the economy, are neglected, and the underlying philosophical grounding of the process in European-derived integration theories does not necessarily reflect the aspirations of ordinary Caribbean people, the relevance of another book centring CARICOM and its challenges can be legitimately questioned. Nevertheless, a continued critical focus on CARICOM's formal mechanisms, especially their limitations and the outsized role of governments in the process, remains relevant, even as scholarship to widen the ambit of how we conceptualize regional integration and what subjects we allow to enter the conversation are important.

Despite the opening of approaches to decentre European experiences, the peculiar role that CARICOM plays in trying to augment the small size of its members is largely missing from the literature. This, however, is crucial to understanding why centring analysis on the organization itself, its relationship to states and its challenges are important to understand not just the integration process, but the very nature of these states and their challenges, some of which are uniquely experienced. The role of size, and how it opens and forecloses possibilities, is not a central theme of regionalism studies, outside of considerations of firm competitiveness. Yet, for the Caribbean region, CARICOM and its various institutions and associations are considered essential to the functioning, even survival, of these largely small and micro states whose viability as independent states is always in question with each twist and turn of the global economy.

This collection offers critical perspectives on the CARICOM project, including possible directions it might take. It asks us to consider whether CARICOM's success should rest on its ability to complete the CSME (which draws heavily on the European experience and traditional customs union theory), especially when it threatens the group's coercion. It invites us to consider which of the CSME goals were worth pursuing given changes in the global environment, the limits of trade and the possibilities (and dangers) that exist for the exploitation of minerals and seabed resources, and the absence of regional policy and regulations. Relatedly, it raises the question of whether CARICOM's focus on completing the CSME may not be distracting it from new challenges arising from the identification and exploitation of new resources, such as oil and the deep seabed, that require stronger regulatory frameworks as well as a regional approach for exploitation and management.

It asks us to consider how the absence of consistent measures to enhance the engagement of important groups such as young people and women, as well as the ordinary citizens of CARICOM countries, reduces confidence in the arrangement, but also denies it access to new energy and ideas that might help to dynamize the integration project. It asks us to consider new avenues for CARICOM involvement and to improve its effectiveness in existing areas, so as to increase its impact on people's lives.

Suggestions of an expanded agenda for CARICOM, even at the expense of the CSME, still raise the important question of the availability of limited resources for CARICOM, compounded by the economic downturn experienced as a result of the coronavirus pandemic. This makes it all the more urgent for CARICOM Heads of Government to focus attention on new challenges that offer both threats and opportunities for the region. In light of these difficulties, the question that CARICOM faces after nearly fifty years is whether it still has a robust and meaningful role to play in the social and economic lives of its members. The main thrust of all the chapters in this collection is that it remains important. Yet, in seeking to understand the challenges in implementing the more formal economic elements of the agreement, against the backdrop of global uncertainty, the collection raises questions as to the relevance of the neoliberal model of the regional project. This volume goes beyond considerations of the feasibility of achieving economic integration to reflect on a broader range of challenges CARICOM must confront, including new areas which have expanded its scope, and other arenas for possible action. Its presentation of a larger platform or range of issues connects to broader aspects of the lived reality of Caribbean people that invites reflection on the possibilities of the regional project if it were viewed in a more wide-ranging way beyond what is now viewed as the urgent task of completing the CSME.

The question of the relevance of all elements of the CSME or, at least, an ordering of priorities for implementation, raised in chapter 8, has become more urgent in the wake of the coronavirus pandemic and needs to be addressed. The need for regulatory frameworks to govern the exploitation of resources (see chapter 8) and ECLAC's advocacy of a new model of development which underscores the role of regional organizations suggest that despite its failings CARICOM continues to have an important role in its members' ability to address these new challenges. Amitav Acharya (2018) envisages a central role for regional organizations in what he sees as the development of a "multiplex world" (139), characterized by different poles of power. For Acharya, the relevant regional organizations are ones that bring together large and increasingly powerful countries, such as the Association of Southeast Asian Nations (142), grounded in open regionalism, countering antiglobalization and populist forces in Europe and the United States, thus rescuing the liberal order. His regionalism centres power and is concerned with world order. His concerns and perspectives on regional organizations are thus not particularly relevant to the Caribbean for whom regionalism is a survival mechanism. In viewing regionalism's potential for what amounts to rescuing the liberal order, Acharya does not address the question of who wins and loses from this order. As the chapters in this collection show, the Caribbean states in CARICOM have found this world difficult to navigate on their own. Trade liberalization has not made them more competitive nor has it increased their standard of living nor expanded their opportunities and horizons. The region, with Latin America, remains among the most unequal in the world. ECLAC's executive secretary, Alicia Barcena (ECLAC 27 May 2020), noted that the pandemic laid bare "structural problems and the failings of social protection systems" across Latin America and the Caribbean and called for a rethink of the current model of development pursued across the region. Central to this reconceptualization was a rethink of the region's role in development that would allow countries to take advantage of some of the global trends accelerated by the pandemic such as the breakdown of global supply chains nearshoring[17] and the accelerated use of additive manufacturing (3D printing) and artificial intelligence and robotics (driven by the need to create social distance conditions at work), in order to create a "more inclusive and sustainable development" (20). This required the region to "achieve productive trade and social integration" and "coordinate on macroeconomic and production matters in order to negotiate the conditions for the new normality" (20). Central to this vision was the region's ability to leverage its sizeable population of 650 million people to mitigate against supply and demand shocks, provide the economies of scale needed for new industries, and "foster shared production and research networks" (10). ECLAC makes no suggestion as to how CARICOM states, most of which, with the exception of Guyana and Belize, were physically separated from the rest of the region, with narrow economic bases and small populations, could be feasibly integrated in this vision. Notwithstanding, what ECLAC points to is the increased importance of regional approaches, mechanisms and structures to combat global challenges. The consolidation of global trends and the emergence of new challenges underscore the role of CARICOM and other regional institutions. They require CARICOM governments to take stock of these new challenges, craft strategies as to how the region should respond and to examine the adequacy of regional institutions to address these. CARICOM's relevance is not based on its ability to engage in global power dynamics, but in its ability to remain relevant to these Caribbean small states and to help chart a collective approach to common threats.

Notes

1. "Brexit" is the term widely used to refer to Britain's referendum-based decision to leave the European Union.

2 Venezuela has been suspended from the bloc, which includes Argentina, Brazil, Paraguay and Uruguay.

3. The OECS includes as full members Antigua and Barbuda, Dominica, Grenada, St Kitts and Nevis, St Lucia, St Vincent and the Grenadines, and Montserrat; and as associated members the British Virgin Islands and Martinique, with Guadeloupe's membership bid under consideration. All of its independent members are categorized, along with Belize, as lesser development countries of CARICOM.

4. A successor agreement to replace the Cotonou Partnership Agreement (between the African, Caribbean and Pacific group of countries and the European Union), which expired in 2020, was finalized in April 2021.

5. For a detailed discussion of how external influences drove the early evolution of Caribbean integration up to 1991, see Payne, in Axline (1994).

6. It was also the impetus behind the negotiations of the Free Trade Area of the Americas, which were eventually abandoned.

7. This was expected to give way to a new successor agreement in 2021.

8. For a more focused discussion of CARICOM's widening project, see Lewis, Gilbert-Roberts and Byron (2018b, 3–14).

9. These include the case of Shanique Myrie, a Jamaican woman denied entry to Barbados (discussed by Saunders in chapter 11 of this volume), and Eddy Ventose, a St Lucian national resident in Barbados denied the right to vote in the 2018 elections (discussed by Lewis in chapter 8 in this volume).

10. See Söderbaum (2016) for a brief discussion on the different theoretical approaches to understanding European integration and regionalism.

11. CBERA was passed by the United States in 1983. The Caribbean Basin Initiative and the Caribbean Trade Partnership Act (CBTPA) operate within the CBERA framework. The WTO waiver governing the CBTPA, which expired in September 2020, was renewed up to September 2025. See IDB (2020, 79).

12. This discussion is not meant to be read as an exhaustive account of CARICOM's appearance in the comparative frame, but to attach some significance to its absence from one of the main efforts to bring attention to the comparative analytical frame.

13. The CARICOM Development Fund was established to provide compensation for dislocations within and among countries arising from the application of the CSME. It is grossly underfunded, however, so it is not expected to have much effect as a compensatory mechanism.

14. This is by no means an exhaustive list, as CARICOM has preoccupied a large number of academics and practitioners since its formation. Absent from this list are works that focused on CARICOM's location in the international system and its foreign relations, most notable among these, former OECS director and prime minister of St Lucia, Vaughan Lewis.

15. Irwin LaRocque held the position from 2012 to 2021, when Carla Barnett was appointed as CARICOM's first female Secretary General. She took office in August 2021.

16. While the Revised Treaty of Chaguaramas does provide for full movement, this is ultimately left in the hands of individual states, without a time frame for implementation.

17. "Nearshoring" refers to the shift to securing supplies nearer to production bases, in this case away from China.

References

Acharya, Amitav. 2016. "Regionalism beyond EU-Centrism". In *The Oxford Handbook of Comparative Regionalism*, edited by Tanya A. Borzel and Thomas Risse, 109–30. Oxford: Oxford University Press.

———. 2018. *The End of American World Order*. 2nd edn. Cambridge, UK and Medford, US: Polity Press.

Ashtine, Masao I. 2020. "Impact of Climate Change on Caribbean Economies". In *Handbook of Caribbean Economies*, edited by Robert E. Looney, 21–38. London and New York: Routledge.

Axline, Andrew. 1979. *Caribbean Integration: The Politics of Regionalism*. London: Frances Pinter; New York: Nichols Pub. Co.

———. 1994. "Cross Regional Comparisons and the Theory of Regional Cooperation: Lessons from Latin America, the Caribbean, South East Asia and the South Pacific". In *The Political Economy of Regional Cooperation: Comparative Case Studies*, edited by Axline, Andrew, 178–216. London and Madison: Pinto Publishers; Fairleigh Dickinson University.

Benn, Denis and Kenneth Hall, eds. 2006. *Production Integration in CARICOM: From Theory to Action*. Kingston and Miami: Ian Randle Publishers.

Bernal, Richard L. 2020. "China's Increasing Influence in Central America and the Caribbean". In *Handbook of Caribbean Economies*, edited by Robert E. Looney, 193–203. London and New York: Routledge.

Berry, David. 2014. *Caribbean Integration Law*. Oxford: Oxford University Press.

Best, Lloyd. 1996. "Independence and Responsibility: Self-Knowledge as an Imperative". In *The Critical Tradition of Caribbean Political Economy: The Legacy of George Beckford*, edited by Kari Levitt and Michael Witter, 3–18. Kingston: Ian Randle Publishers.

Bishop, Matthew. 2014. "Whither CARICOM?" In *Re-mapping the Americas: Trends in Region-making*, edited by W. Andy Knight, Julian Castro-Re, and Hamid Ghany, 185–202. London, England and Burlington, VT, USA: Ashgate.

Börzel, Tanja A. and Thomas Risse, eds. 2016. *The Oxford Handbook of Comparative Regionalism*. Oxford, UK: Oxford University Press.

Boxill, Ian. 1993. *Ideology and Caribbean Integration*. Kingston, Jamaica: Consortium Graduate School of the Social Sciences, University of the West Indies.

Brewster, Havelock. 2001. "New Vistas for the Caribbean Community". In *The Caribbean Community: Beyond Survival*, edited by Kenneth O. Hall, 64–68. Kingston and Miami: Ian Randle Publishers.

———. 2005. "Mature Regionalism and the Rose Hall Declaration on Regional Governance". In *Caribbean Imperatives: Regional Governance and Integrated Development*, edited by Kenneth O. Hall. Kingston and Miami: Ian Randle Publishers.

Byron, Jessica. 1999. "Microstates in a Macro-World: Federalism, Governance and Viability in the Eastern Caribbean". *Social and Economic Studies* 48 (4): 251–86.

———. 2004. "CARICOM at Thirty: New and Old Foreign Policy Challenges". *Social and Economic Studies* 53 (4): 147–80.

———. 2016. "Summitry in the Caribbean Community: A Fundamental Feature of Regional Governance". In *Summits and Regional Governance: The Americas in Comparative Perspective*, edited by Gordon Mace, Jean-Philippe Thérien, Diana Tussie, and Olivier Dabène, 88–105. Oxfordshire and New York: Routledge.

CARICOM Secretariat. 2014a. *Strategic Plan for the Caribbean Community 2015–2019: Repositioning CARICOM*. Volume 1. The Executive Plan. https://caricom.org/documents/11265-executive_plan_vol_1_-_final.pdf.

———. 2014ab. *Strategic Plan for the Caribbean Community 2015–2019: Repositioning CARICOM*. Volume 2. The Strategic Plan. https://caricom.org/documents/11853-the_strategic_plan_vol2-final.pdf.

Constantine, Collin M. 2021. "Whither CSME? A Reply to the Golding Report". Kingston: *Social and Economic Studies* 69 (3&4): 27–54.

Demas, William. 1997. *Critical Issues in Caribbean Development—West Indian Development and the Deepening and Widening of the Caribbean Community.* Kingston: Ian Randle Publishers.

ECLAC. 2020. "Measuring the Impact of Covid-19 with a View to Reactivation". Special Report Covid-19", April. Accessed 4 June 2020. https://www.cepal.org/en/publications/45477 -measuring-impact-covid-19-view-reactivation.

European Commission. 2015. *Caribbean Regional Indicative Programme 11th European Development Fund (EDF).* Ref. Ares(2015)3671530 – 07/09/2015. Accessed 6 July 2020. https://ec.europa.eu/international-partnerships/system/files/rip-edf11-caraibes-2014-2020 _en.pdf.

Ghany, Hamid. 2014. "The Constitutional and Political Aspects of Strategic Culture in Trinidad and Tobago". In *Re-mapping the Americas: Trends in Region-making*, edited by W. Andy Knight, Julian Castro-Re, and Hamid Ghany, 231–40. England and USA: Ashgate.

Gilbert-Roberts, Terri-Ann. 2013. *The Politics of Integration: Caribbean Sovereignty Revisited.* Kingston: Ian Randle Publishers.

Girvan, Norman. 2007. "Towards a Single Economy and a Single Development Vision". In *CARICOM Single Market and Economy: Genesis and Prognosis*, edited by Kenneth Hall and Myrtle Chuck-A-Sang, 409–65. Kingston and Miami: Ian Randle Publishers.

———. 2014. "Caribbean Integration: Can Cultural Production Succeed Where Politics and Economics Have Failed? (Confessions of a Wayward Economist)". In *Re-mapping the Americas: Trends in Region-making*, edited by W. Andy Knight, Julian Castro-Re, and Hamid Ghany, 255–62. England and USA: Ashgate.

Goldwyn, David and Cory Gill. 2020. "Caribbean Energy Security: Regional Profile and Challenges to Integration". In *Handbook of Caribbean Economies*, edited by Robert E. Looney, 11–20. London and New York: Routledge.

Gray, Julia. 2014. "Domestic Capacity and the Implementation Gap in Regional Agreements". *Comparative Political Studies* 47 (1): 55–84. First published 14 June 2013 research article. https://doi.org/10.1177/0010414013488535.

Gray, Julia and Jonathan B. Slapin. 2012. "How Effective Are Preferential Trade Agreements? Ask the Experts". *Review of International Organizations* 7 (3): 309–33. Doi:10.1007/s11558-011 -9138-1.

Greene-Dewasmes, Ginelle and Tony Heron. 2020. "The External Economic Relations of the Caribbean: A Comparison between the USA and the European Union". In *Handbook of Caribbean Economies*, edited by Robert E. Looney, 182–92. London and New York: Routledge.

Grenade, Wendy. 2005. "An Overview of Regional Governance Arrangements within the Caribbean Community (CARICOM)". In *The European Union and Regional Integration: A Comparative Perspective and Lessons for the Americas*, edited by Joaquín Roy and Roberto Domínguez. Miami: University of Miami.

———. 2011. "Regionalism and Sub-regionalism in the Caribbean: Challenges and Prospects- Any Insights from Europe?". Jean Monnet/Schuman Paper Series, 11, no. 4.

Hall, Kenneth O., ed. 2012. *The Pertinence of CARICOM in the 21st Century: Some Perspectives.* Bloomington: Trafford (self-published version of earlier works).

Hall, Kenneth O. and Myrtle Chuck-A-Sang, eds. 2010. *CARICOM: Policy Options for International Engagement.* Kingston: Ian Randle Publishers.

———, eds. 2012a. *Managing Mature Regionalism: CARICOM in the Twenty-First Century.* Bloomington: Trafford (self-published version of earlier works).

———, eds. 2012b. *Regional Integration: Key to Caribbean Survival and Prosperity.* Bloomington: Trafford (self-published version of earlier works).

Hall, Kenneth O. and Myrtle Chuck-A-Sang, eds. 2013. *Coping with the Collapse of the Old Order: CARICOM's New External Agenda*. Bloomington: Trafford (self-published version of earlier works previously published by Ian Randle).

Henry, Lester. 2020. "Debt and Fiscal Constraints". In *Handbook of Caribbean Economies*, edited by Robert E. Looney, 98–107. London and New York: Routledge.

Hinds, Kristina. 2006. "Domestic Non-Cooperation and Regional Integration: Problems of Caribbean Regionalism". *Social and Economic Studies* 55 (3): 32–48.

———. 2019. *Civil Society Organisations, Governance and the Caribbean Community*. Switzerland: Palgrave MacMillan.

———. 2020. "It's Complicated: The Caribbean's Relationship to White-Collar Crime". In *Handbook of Caribbean Economies*, edited by Robert E. Looney, 126–39. London and New York: Routledge.

IDB. 2020. "CARICOM Report: Progress and Challenges of the Integration Agenda", by Samuel Braithwaite, 14 May 2021. https://publications.iadb.org/publications/english/document/CARICOM-Report-Progress-and-Challenges-of-The-Integration-Agenda.pdf.

Jones-Hendrickson, Simon. 2006. *Essays on the OECS Economies: Selected Writings of a Caribbean Economist*. New York, Lincoln and Shanghai: iUniverse, Inc.

Kaczorowska-Ireland, Alina. 2014. *Competition Law in the CARICOM Single Market and Economy*. London: Routledge.

Kirton, Mark. 2014. "CARICOM's Engagement with Latin America: The Community of Latin American and Caribbean States (CELAC), Its Promise and Challenges". In *Re-mapping the Americas: Trends in Region-making*, edited by W. Andy Knight, Julian Castro-Re, and Hamid Ghany, 69–82. England and USA: Ashgate.

Knight, Andy W., Julian Castro-Rea, and Hamid Ghany. 2014. *Re-Mapping the Americas: Trends in Region-making*. The International Political Economy of New Regionalism Series. Surrey, England; Burlington, USA: Ashgate.

Lewis, Patsy. 2002. *Surviving Small Size: Regional Integration in Caribbean Ministates*. Barbados, Kingston, Trinidad and Tobago: University of the West Indies Press.

———. 2003. "Political Union: The Road Not Traveled by the West Indian Commission". *Global Development Studies* 3, nos. 1–2 (Winter 2002–Spring 2003): 1–24.

———. 2005. "The Agony of the Fifteen: The Crisis of Implementation". *Social and Economic Studies* 54 (3): 145–75.

———. 2014. "Assessing the Development Potential of the FTAA and EPA for Small Developing States". In *Re-mapping the Americas: Trends in Region-making*, edited by W. Andy Knight, Julian Castro-Re, and Hamid Ghany, 151–84. England and USA: Ashgate.

———. 2020. "CARICOM and That Vexing Issue of Size and Viability". In *Handbook of Caribbean Economies*, edited by Robert E. Looney, 81–97. London and New York: Routledge.

Lewis, Patsy, Terri-Ann Gilbert-Roberts, and Jessica Byron. 2018a. "Confronting Shifting and Economic and Political Terrains". In *Pan-Caribbean Integration: Beyond CARICOM*, edited by Patsy Lewis, Terri-Ann Gilbert-Roberts, and Jessica Byron, 224–45. London and New York: Routledge.

———, eds. 2018b. *Pan-Caribbean Integration: Beyond CARICOM*. In *The International Political Economy of New Regionalisms Series*, edited by Timothy M. Shaw. London and New York: Routledge.

Lewis, Vaughan. 2001. "The OECS and Closer Political Union". In *The Caribbean Community Beyond Survival*, edited by Kenneth O. Hall, 301–04. Kingston and Miami: Ian Randle Publishers.

———. 2003. "Regional Integration Institutional Arrangements: Underlying Assumptions and Contemporary Appropriateness". In Kenneth O. Hall and Denis Benn, *Governance in the Age of Globalisation*, 509–26. Kingston and Miami: Ian Randle Publishers.

Looney, Robert E. 2020. "Caribbean Natural Disasters and Country/Regional Responses". In *Handbook of Caribbean Economies*, edited by Robert E. Looney, 140–58. London and New York: Routledge.

Mace, Gordon, Jean-Philippe Thérien, Diana Tussie, and Olivier Dabène. 2016. *Summits and Regional Governance: The Americas in Comparative Perspective*. Oxfordshire and New York: Routledge.

Martinez Reinosa, Milagros. 2018. "Cuba's Cooperation with CARICOM: From Grant Aid to Compensated Development Cooperation". In *Pan-Caribbean Integration: Beyond CARICOM*, edited by Patsy Lewis, Terri-Ann Gilbert-Roberts, and Jessica Byron, 153–61. London and New York: Routledge.

Mills, Gladstone E., Carlisle Burton, J. O'Neil Lewis, and Crispin Sorhaindo. 1990. *Report on a Comprehensive Review of the Programmes, Institutions and Organisations of the Caribbean Community*. Georgetown: CARICOM Secretariat.

Montoute, Anita. 2014. "From Engagement to Influence: Civil Society Participation in the EPA Trade Negotiations and Regional Integration Processes". In *Re-mapping the Americas: Trends in Region-making*, edited by W. Andy Knight, Julian Castro-Re, and Hamid Ghany, 241–54. England and USA: Ashgate.

Mullerleile, Christopher. 1996. *CARICOM Integration: Progress and Hurdles: A European View*. Kingston: Kingston Publishers.

Nye, J.S. 1965. "Patterns and Catalysts in Regional Integration". *International Organization* 19, no. 4 (Autumn 1965): 870–84. https://doi.org/10.1017/S0020818300012649.

Payne, Anthony. 1994. "The Politics of Regional Cooperation in the Caribbean: The Case of CARICOM". In *The Political Economy of Regional Cooperation: Comparative Case Studies*, edited by W. Andrew Axline, 73–104. London and Madison: Pinter Publishers; Fairleigh Dickinson University Press.

Payne, Anthony J. 2008. *The Political History of CARICOM*. First published in 1980 by Manchester University Press, revised and published in 2007 by Ian Randle Publishers, Kingston, Jamaica.

Pollard, Duke, ed. 2003. *The CARICOM System: Basic Instruments*. Kingston and Miami: Ian Randle Publishers.

Quiliconi, Cintia and Rivera Rhon. 2020. "Regional Cooperation in Latin America and the Caribbean". In *Handbook of Caribbean Economies*, edited by Robert Looney, 204–18. London and New York: Routledge.

Ramsaran, Ramesh. 2013. *The Financial Evolution of the Caribbean Community (1996–2008)*. St. Augustine: Caribbean Centre for Money and Finance.

Riggirozzi, Pía and Diana Tussie, eds. 2012. *The Rise of Post-Hegemonic Regionalism: The Case of Latin America*. United Nations University Series on Regionalism Volume 4. Dordretch, Heidelberg, London and New York: Springer.

Sherill, V.C. Morris-Francis. 2020. "Crime, Violence and Drugs in the Caribbean". In *Handbook of Caribbean Economies*, edited by Robert E. Looney, 108–25. London and New York: Routledge.

Söderbaum, Fredrik. 2016. "Old, New, and Comparative Regionalism: The History of the Scholarly Development of the Field". In *The Oxford Handbook of Comparative Regionalism*, edited by Tanya A. Börzel and Thomas Risse, 16–37. Oxford: Oxford University Press.

Stoneman, Richard, Duke Pollard, and Hugo Inniss. 2012. "Turning Around CARICOM: Proposals to Restructure the Secretariat". Landell-Mills Development Consultants. Prepared for CARICOM Secretariat. https://caricom.org/documents/9400-restructuring_the_secretariat_-_landell_mills_final_report.pdf.

Thomas, Clive. 2001. "The Community Is a Big Paper Tiger". In *The Caribbean Community: Beyond Survival*, edited by Kenneth O. Hall, 27–31. Kingston and Miami: Ian Randle Publishers.

Venner, Dwight K. 2007. *A Development Agenda for the Caribbean: Financial and Economic Approaches*. Kingston and Miami: Ian Randle Publishers.

WB. 2020. The Economy in the Time of Covid-19. Semiannual Report of the Latin America and Caribbean Region. Accessed 17 April 2020. https://olc.worldbank.org/content/economy-time-covid-19.

West Indian Commission. 1992. *Time for Action: Report of the West Indian Commission*. Black Rock, Barbados: West Indian Commission.

Wheare, K.C. 1968. *Federal Government*. 4th edn. London and New York: Oxford University Press.

Wionczek, Miguel S. 1966. "Introduction: Requisites for Viable Integration". In *Latin American Economic Integrations: Experience and Prospects*, edited by Miguel S. Wionczek, 3–18. New York: Frederick A. Praeger.

Part I

Reflecting on CARICOM

Chapter 2

CARICOM beyond Forty

IRWIN LAROCQUE

The development of the Caribbean Community (CARICOM) has as its primary objective the improvement of the lives of its people. This has been the beacon that has guided this process since the labour leaders in the 1920s and 1930s set us on the path to self-governance. It was organized labour that went as far as drafting a constitution for a united Caribbean in 1932 with the assistance of a young economist, Arthur Lewis (Will 1991; Basdeo 1997).

Although the intervention of World War II delayed the progress, a seminal conference, Towards the Closer Association of the British Colonies, held in Jamaica at Montego Bay in 1947, set the integration project right back on course. The focus at that time was for independence from Great Britain as a unit, and this eventually led, eleven years later, to the short-lived West Indies Federation, which provided some common services such as a supreme court and a shipping line. With independence in mind, a plan for a customs union was prepared, but free trade was not introduced among the islands (Demas 1960; Wallace 1962).

The end of the federation in 1962 brought a close to this approach to integration. In many ways, however, its end led to the beginning of another chapter in the integration process which would evolve into the forming of the CARICOM. The need to maintain and possibly expand the common services that existed during the federation was the catalyst for the 1963 Conference on Common Services. Then in 1965, the premiers of Barbados and British Guiana and the chief minister of Antigua and Barbuda – Errol Barrow, Forbes Burnham and Vere Bird, respectively – agreed to establish the Caribbean Free Trade Association (CARIFTA). It was the first attempt at economic integration through trade. The other territories joined this initiative, and CARIFTA was launched in 1968 along with the Commonwealth Caribbean Regional Secretariat, which became the CARICOM Secretariat (Hope 1974).

Eight years later, recognizing that CARIFTA could only carry the region so far, the leaders deepened the integration arrangements by establishing a community and common market on the basis of economic integration, foreign policy coordination and functional cooperation. This came into being in 1973 with the Treaty of Chaguaramas. It included a common external tariff, which, incidentally, required member states to give up some sovereignty (CARICOM 1973). However, decisions were largely unenforceable and dispute settlement arrangements were weak.

In 1989, the region was faced with a changing global economic environment, while the performance of the regional economy was sluggish. The traditional markets for its commodities were threatened with the advent of the European Single Market, and discussions continued on the global trading arrangements, which later became the World Trade Organization. Both these developments resulted in preference erosion for the commodities the region had come to rely on so heavily. Grant assistance was also declining (Mitchell 2006; Cashin, Mlachila and Haines 2010). Leaders recognized that the region needed to become more self-reliant for its development. At Grand Anse, Grenada, they agreed that a deeper form of integration was the logical answer to those challenges and decided to establish a single market and economy (CARICOM Heads of Government 1989). To achieve this, the treaty had to be revised significantly. The Revised Treaty of Chaguaramas was completed and signed in 2001.

The objectives of the revised treaty include improved standards of living and work; full employment of labour and other factors of production; accelerated, coordinated and sustained economic development and convergence; enhanced coordination of member states' foreign policies; and enhanced functional cooperation. That last objective promoted more efficient operation of common services and intensified activities in areas such as health, education, transportation and telecommunications (CARICOM Secretariat 2001). The single market became operational in 2006, with an official ceremony to mark the event at the Mona campus of the University of the West Indies. By 2013, twelve of the fifteen member states were single-market compliant, with Haiti and Montserrat working towards effectively being so.

Work in Progress

In revising the original Treaty of Chaguaramas to reflect the transition to the CARICOM Single Market and Economy (CSME), the important dimension of the services sector was added (chapter 3). This was a clear recognition that the regional economy was being oriented more towards services while not minimizing the continued importance of agriculture and other sectors. There was, as well, a deliberate effort to address some of the shortcomings of the earlier treaty. Provisions were included to shift from unanimity in decision-making and to establish a rules-based system. The dispute settlement mechanism was strengthened (chapter 9), and the Caribbean Court of Justice (CCJ) was established as a means of ensuring the rights and obligations under the treaty are observed (CARICOM Secretariat 2001).[1]

The revised treaty created or gave rise to the establishment of certain institutions, such as the CCJ, the CARICOM Competition Commission, the CARICOM Development Fund, the Caribbean Regional Organisation for Standards and Quality, and the Caribbean Agricultural Health and Food Safety Agency. However, CARICOM's integration architecture is not limited to those, as there are some twenty institutions, all of which have important tasks to undertake in delivering its objectives. The Caribbean Development Bank and the University of the West Indies are also integral parts of that architecture.

The CARICOM rests on four pillars: economic integration, human and social development, security cooperation, and foreign policy coordination. All four pillars are crucial to the integration arrangements, although the treaty focuses heavily on the creation of the CSME.

The ultimate goal of the CSME is the creation of a single economic space encompassing all member states. It has the following core regimes: free movement of skills, goods, services and capital, as well as the right of establishment (chapter 3). It also includes the abolition of exchange controls, free convertibility of currencies, an integrated capital market, convergence of macroeconomic policies and harmonized company legislation. A critical element is the harmonization of laws and administrative practices (CARICOM Secretariat 2001).

Attention has focused on the single market aspect of the CSME, probably because it is more clearly defined in the treaty and is the simpler part of creating a single market and economy. Progress towards the single economy impinges more and more on national sovereignty, and brings into question governance issues and the possible deepening of integration even further.

The Single Development Vision adopted in 2007 envisioned the completion of the single economy by 2015 (Girvan 2007). However, once again, the CARICOM had overreached in its ambitions just as it had done at Grand Anse in 1989, which had put the operation date of the CSME at 1993. The fact is that the revised treaty was completed and signed twelve years after Grand Anse, and the single market took a further five years before becoming operational in 2006. These overambitious and unrealistic targets, by their very nature, doom CARICOM to apparent failure when they are not met.

I am not suggesting that the region sets targets that allow for a leisurely pace. The world is not waiting on us. I am suggesting that setting targets should take into account not only the necessity and urgency of achieving the goal but, equally important, what it takes to get there, and the resources and capacity of the entire community to do so. In all of this, prioritization is of paramount importance.

This is not to say that the region has not made progress in its economic integration arrangements. All of the core regimes under the single market are operating, although there is still work to be done in some areas. Regional policies have been approved or are advanced in areas such as agriculture and food and nutrition security, energy, industry, and information and communications technology. Work has also commenced on a policy with respect to small- and medium-sized enterprises and is well advanced on the creation of a regulatory framework for financial services and an investment code.

However, the true test of the CSME is if it has helped in solving the economic problems of the member states. The CARICOM Secretariat has been looking at the construct of the CSME to see if in its present form, it can address the immediate concerns of member states, particularly with respect to growth.[2] I am of the view that we need to recalibrate and focus more on the productive sector and making our economies more competitive. We probably have adopted a too theoretical model of economic integration, and the time may have come to heed the call of our regional economists for us to focus more on production integration and on competitiveness.

The major element in any move to production integration has to be the full involvement of a competitive private sector. There is also an urgent need to address the ease of doing business across borders and within the CSME as a whole. In my missions across the region, there have been common concerns expressed by the private sector, for example, about the lack of harmonization of business procedures within the community, thereby adding to the cost of doing business.[3]

For CARICOM, enhancing competitiveness and expanding trade are crucial for advancing the development of the region. However, small, developing economies like ours have to struggle against characteristics which affect the process of economic growth, constrain ability to compete internationally, increase vulnerability to external events and limit capacity for adjustment. These include small population, geographical dispersal, minimal export diversification, inadequate infrastructure, economic rigidity with high adjustment costs, high transport and transit costs, and difficulties in attracting foreign investment. These constraints have been made even more stark by the effects of the global economic and financial crises on Caribbean economies.

While other countries have been able to respond to the situation by introducing countercyclical fiscal policies, the ability of CARICOM countries to apply such policy measures is constrained by the lack of fiscal space made worse by a severe debt burden. CARICOM's debt stock in 2013 stood at approximately US$19 billion, while the debt-to-gross domestic product ratio ranged from 60 to 144 per cent for most member states (World Bank 2018).[4]

This debt situation was aggravated by the diminution of the region's access to concessionary financing due to the international financial institutions and the donor community insisting on using gross domestic product per capita as the major criterion for deciding whether a country qualifies for development support. This concept of "graduation" or "differentiation" has adversely affected most CARICOM member states, as they have been categorized as middle-income countries and are therefore not eligible for such concessionary funding and development assistance. The community has been vigorously lobbying for quite some time against this concept, which ignores the vulnerabilities faced by small economies such as ours.

Faced with those realities, there is a tendency for some to look inward for solutions, but there is little doubt that those challenges would be better met by strengthening the integration arrangements. The path to regional development is based on the commitment by member states to pursue increasingly coordinated policies and the combined use of the region's resources and capacities. Regional integration is the vehicle that the community has chosen to pursue with the CSME as the engine.

In looking back at the first seven years (2006–13) of the operation of the CSME, it is clear that the revised treaty and its governance arrangements may be limited as a tool to advance the integration movement. Further, the governance arrangements have become untenable, and more time and resources are spent discussing the same issues rather than making decisions that can be effectively implemented.

Fundamental questions about the efficacy of the governance structures of our community must be asked. Are they, as they exist in the revised treaty, adequate for the next phase of our integration arrangements?

This issue is among the areas of priority being considered by the reconstituted Inter-Governmental Task Force, which is working towards making recommendations for further revising the treaty.[5] Two of the areas are governance and related issues, and the working methods of the various organs and bodies. The goal is to realign the regional architecture for integration to strengthen its capacity to assist in the growth and development of member states and to have a positive impact on the lives of our citizens.

The basis of CARICOM's governance arrangements is that CARICOM represents a community of sovereign states, as stated a decade ago in the Rose Hall Declaration of 2003 (CARICOM Secretariat 2003). The fundamental issue in going forward is how to balance that reality against the need for an effective system of governance to allow for efficient and timely implementation of decisions.

The region has not been short of ideas in this regard, particularly after the 1992 Report of the West Indian Commission, *Time for Action* (West Indian Commission 1992). That report delved into the prospect of supranationality by suggesting a system of commissioners empowered to enforce decisions. Most recently, the idea of a permanent committee of CARICOM ambassadors, comprising individuals of sufficient rank and influence to drive the implementation process at the national level, was put forward at a special session of the Conference of Heads of Government, convened in 2011.[6]

That concept envisages each member state establishing a regional integration unit led by an ambassador, who would be the country's representative on the committee. The Organisation of Eastern Caribbean States (OECS) Commission is fashioned broadly along similar lines and presents an opportunity to observe the workings of such an arrangement. While the Committee of Ambassadors may not be the ideal option, it is the best that can be achieved in the short term.

In that context, key to the functioning of any formulation is the role of the secretary general, the secretariat and community institutions established to assist in the development of the community.

There is already in place, by way of the CCJ, an institution which has compulsory and exclusive jurisdiction with respect to the interpretation and application of the treaty. The court, as its 2013 judgment in the case of Shanique Myrie and the Government of Barbados has shown, will cause a shift in the way the community's affairs are conducted (CCJ 2013).[7] It has also cemented the community's rules-based system and continues to engender a high level of confidence.

The judgment is far-reaching, addressing decision-making in the community, the nature and effect of community law, obligations of member states and rights of community nationals. It reinforced the critical role of the CCJ in the integration movement as a court, which will ensure that the community's decisions are adhered to and will provide guidance and certainty for member states, nationals and the secretariat in the application of community law.

The CARICOM Secretariat has reviewed the judgment to assess the implications for the CARICOM and its organs. The judgment will likely be a historical contribution to the development of the community integration arrangements. The eminent judges have issued a judgment which should give a considerable fillip to the movement for making the CCJ the final court of appeal for all member states, thereby completing the circle of sovereignty in the region. Many around the region seem to be pleased with the judgment on this particular matter in the court's role in its original jurisdiction. It should be borne in mind that it is the same court and the same judges who would be empanelled to consider matters in its appellate jurisdiction. Hopefully, this would remove any doubts about the capacity of Caribbean jurists to render judgments of the highest calibre.[8]

Achievements

One of the unintended side effects of the concentration on trade and economic aspects of the integration process has been the tendency to judge the success of the entire movement by the efforts in those areas. In some quarters, CARICOM's effectiveness is judged on issues related to the movement of persons or merchandise trade balances. This view is at odds with the economic reality, given the important contribution that trade in services is making to the region. While these issues need to be addressed, it is unfortunate that these are the criteria often used in the court of public opinion, since so much else has been achieved in the past forty years. It has also had the effect of minimizing the important role of human and social development. In health, education, disaster management and relief coordination, foreign policy coordination, and security cooperation, to name just a few, integration has made a significant and positive difference in the overall development of the CARICOM and has benefited its people.

The importance of health to CARICOM's development led Heads of Government to set up the Caribbean Commission on Health and Development. It was that commission's report in 2006 which alerted all to the serious effects of non-communicable diseases on people and on the economy of member states (PAHO and CARICOM Secretariat 2006). The findings engendered greater awareness of healthy lifestyles and were used by CARICOM to lead the international community into staging a UN high-level forum on the issue in 2011.

In order to more efficiently address the region's public health concerns, five regional agencies were merged to form the Caribbean Public Health Agency (CARPHA). CARPHA was established to address the surveillance and management of communicable and non-communicable diseases and public health response to disasters, among others.[9] Previously, faced with the threat posed by HIV/AIDS (to the youth population in particular), the Pan Caribbean Partnership against HIV and AIDS was established by CARICOM in 2001 and has made a critical impact on reversing and stabilizing the spread of the AIDS epidemic in the Caribbean. The Caribbean was aiming to be the first region in the world to eliminate mother-to-child transmission of HIV by 2015.

In education, the Caribbean Examinations Council, a CARICOM institution, which also celebrated its fortieth anniversary in 2013, continues to provide regionally and internationally recognized examinations and curricula relevant to the needs of the region. The community has also developed the Caribbean Vocational Qualification to establish standards and to provide artisans and tradespersons with a qualification recognized throughout the community. The Caribbean Vocational Qualification has the potential to ensure that the community has available to it a regional pool of certified skilled persons and puts the opportunities of the CSME within reach of many, given its inclusion in the free movement of skills regime in certain specified fields.

Responding to the increasing frequency and intensity of natural disasters in the region, CARICOM has established a mechanism to coordinate preparedness for and relief in the event of a natural disaster. The Caribbean Disaster Emergency Management Agency has proven its value both in the preparation for disasters and in the aftermath, with its coordination of relief efforts. Further, CARICOM has created the first multi-country disaster insurance scheme in the world, through the Caribbean Catastrophe Risk Insurance Facility. This not-for-profit entity is owned, operated and registered in the Caribbean for Caribbean governments. In the wake of natural disasters, it provides Caribbean governments with quick short-term liquidity when a policy is triggered.[10]

Well before climate change became a global issue, CARICOM began to address the need to mitigate the effects of and adapt to this phenomenon. The work of the Caribbean Community Climate Change Centre has made the CARICOM very influential in the global response to climate change, including in the formation of the Green Climate Fund.[11] Its provision of policy advice and guidelines to CARICOM member states has been so outstanding that it lends advice and assistance to other threatened regions.

The region's youth deserve special attention. Following the report of a CARICOM Commission on Youth Development in 2010, a five-year CARICOM Youth Development Action Plan has been designed to implement the six goals recommended by the commission. These goals were arrived at following consultations with youth throughout the community. The action plan includes education and economic empowerment and the establishment of integrated programmes providing employability skills, transition skills and entrepreneurial skills for youth in and out of school.

The CARICOM Secretariat collaborates with the CARICOM Youth Ambassadors and international development partners in initiatives designed to engage, motivate and inspire entrepreneurial interest and action among youth, and to increase livelihood opportunities and employability for economically and socially marginalized youth. The region's youth is making a significant contribution in the areas of sports, music and culture in particular, all of which contribute to employment and development of the regional economy.

Culture is also central to the promotion of regional identity and unity, and an important component in the regional integration construct. The region does have a comparative advantage in culture, due to the creativity for which it is known and respected internationally. In that context, therefore, CARICOM has identified the development of cultural and creative industries as one of the priority areas for job creation and growth. There now exists a Regional Development Strategy and Action Plan for the Cultural Industries.

Recognizing the challenges of crime and security, Heads of Government added security cooperation as the fourth pillar of the integration construct. To address the important area of combating crime and enhancing security in the region, the CARICOM has approved the CARICOM Crime and Security Strategy. The strategy provides a platform from which the region can advance the fight against a range of threats. These include illicit trafficking, transborder crime, gang and youth violence, and terrorism and cybersecurity. It also addresses issues of crime prevention and improving intelligence sharing among security forces.

The CARICOM is also addressing the serious issue of gender-based violence through the work of CARICOM's advocate for gender, justice and gender-based violence, Rosina Wiltshire. That work has informed legislation and policy on this issue in member states.

In the area of foreign policy coordination, CARICOM has continued to demonstrate that its influence in international affairs far exceeds its size. Experience has shown that when member states act in concert, their collective voice in the international community is greater than the sum of its parts. Foreign policy coordination addresses regional and national problems and helps to secure the election of CARICOM candidates for positions in international organizations in order to influence the international agenda.

The benefits of that collective voice in recent times are evident in the placing of non-communicable diseases and the plight of small, highly indebted middle-income countries on the global agenda by CARICOM. They are now components for consideration in the post-2015 Development Agenda. The adoption of the Arms Trade Treaty at the United Nations, in which CARICOM played an influential role, was in consonance with the region's deep concern about the prevalent use of firearms by criminals in these societies and with efforts to improve citizen security (United Nations 2014).

Foreign policy coordination is also the medium which provides recognition of CARICOM as an international actor. This has led to an increasing number of states seeking closer ties with the CARICOM. The CARICOM has taken advantage of these developments to establish technical cooperation agreements which redound to its benefit. These initiatives demonstrate that the pooling of skills and resources to bring about improvements in the region's circumstances and the lives of its citizens stands as testimony to the benefits of integration.

Roadmap to the Next Forty

Notwithstanding its many achievements and plans, there are serious challenges which need to be addressed if the integration process is to be advanced and made more meaningful to the people. These matters include sustainable economic growth, transportation, hassle-free travel, the high cost of energy and equitable distribution of the benefits of integration, which if not adequately addressed could lead to discontent. This requires the recognition that national growth and development are inextricably tied to regional growth and development. Regional policies and national policies must be so intertwined as to be almost indiscernible. It is in that actualization that citizens will feel most acutely that sense of being part of a community.

So what's next for CARICOM? Once again, we are at a crucial juncture in the progression of the regional integration movement, and what we have to accept and act upon in going forward is that the new situation demands not only that we change the way we operate but more importantly the way we think about integration. Vital in that process is the need to refocus and prioritize the work of the CARICOM, especially given the current economic and fiscal constraints of member states.

We have begun to make that change as the CARICOM is engaged in a reform process that encompasses every facet of its operations. In short, we are changing the way we do business. The Heads of Government agreed in March 2012 that since "form followed function", it was necessary to re-examine the future direction of the community and the arrangements for carrying this forward. This includes the role and function of the CARICOM Secretariat and the institutions of the CARICOM (CARICOM Heads of Government 2012).

A Change Facilitation Team has been recruited to assist me with this process of change. The team is currently undertaking consultations in member states on the first-ever all-encompassing strategic plan for the CARICOM, which is expected to set out a common vision and identify areas of priority focus over the period.[12] These country consultations provide an opportunity for nationals of each member state and associate member to influence the CARICOM's strategic direction. Critically, it will also address issues of implementation, including the roles and responsibilities of all participants in the CARICOM architecture, institutional and operational arrangements, and monitoring and evaluation mechanisms.

The strategic plan will not start with a blank slate. It will draw on approved policies and programmes. These include the 2007 Single Development Vision; the Strategic Plan for Regional Economic Development (on which there was close collaboration between the secretariat and the University of the West Indies); the priorities articulated by the Heads of Government at their May 2011 retreat held in Guyana; and approved policies and action plans in a range of areas, such as agriculture, energy, industry, security, health, youth, information and communications technology, and climate change (Girvan 2007; Applewhaite 2011).

Some common themes emerged from the consultations. These included

- the need to address economic recovery and growth as a core strategy over the next five years;
- the need to strengthen governance and decision-making arrangements, beginning with the Heads of Government Conference, to secure a more effective community;
- the need to solve the challenges with interregional transport, and the free movement of persons, including hassle-free travel as critical success factors for regional integration;
- the need to secure the region's future through targeted interventions in agriculture for food security, energy security, education, health, and information and communications technology;
- the need to reignite the fire of regionalism among Caribbean people, through shared understanding and building of a sense of community; and
- the need to communicate fully and consistently with the people on the issues of integration.

It is clear from the consultations that the people of CARICOM remain committed to realizing the potential of our integration movement.[13]

On the basis of the strategic plan, the review and restructuring of the secretariat and institutions of CARICOM will be addressed to enable better delivery, in a much more focused and effective manner to the people of the community. We must be able to meet the expectations of member states by providing the level and mode of service they require to overcome their challenges.[14]

Membership and Associate Membership

In respect of the issue of widening the integration movement, I will limit my comments to what might be the minimum criteria for membership.[15] The revised treaty provides that "membership of the Community shall be open to any other State or Territory of the Caribbean Region that is, in the opinion of the Conference, able and willing to exercise the rights and assume the obligations of membership" (CARICOM Secretariat 2001, 6). It is therefore necessary for the community to review and agree on the rights and obligations of membership, which would have to be accepted by any applying country should it wish to be a member or associate member of CARICOM.

The revised treaty by itself does not represent the entirety of the obligations and benefits of a member of the CARICOM, nor is it only limited to the CSME. The community has not yet codified a CARICOM *acquis communutaire*, which is made up of the collection of rights and obligations that the prospective member would have to adhere to, including prior decisions, legislation, court decisions and the evolving community law. The secretariat is facilitating the work of a Technical Working Group looking at the issue of membership and associate membership.[16]

Conclusion

The future of this regional movement is bright. I am guided by the optimism and enthusiasm for CARICOM, by our youth in particular. Their desire for integration and their impatience for it to become a lived experience are an inspiration. I look forward to the results of the national consultations from which a free flow of ideas is emanating and which allow the people to seize a stake in the integration movement.

CARICOM will continue to evolve, as development is an ongoing process. There may be twists and turns. But through it all, we are positioning that vehicle of integration to drive the development of our countries and give our people as smooth a ride as possible on the road to a secure and prosperous life.

Acknowledgements

This address was delivered at the SALISES Regional Integration Conference as a part of the CARICOM fortieth-anniversary celebrations in 2013. It reflects the secretariat's thinking and priorities for CARICOM at forty – a critical juncture in the institution's history. While this volume was in preparation, minor updates have been included in the footnotes to place LaRocque's remarks in context of an evolving environment. However, it has been left largely in its original form and tone as a special point of reference for reflecting on CARICOM's strategic priorities. The perspective of a former secretary general takes on even greater significance in 2021, as a new secretary general – Carla Barnett – begins the process of reorienting the implementation of the strategic plan.

Notes

1. The CCJ was inaugurated in 2005.

2. In 2017, the Conference of Heads of Government received a report on a review of the status of the CSME, which had been mandated in its 2016 regular meeting in Grenada. The report showed that implementation is still uneven across member states (CARICOM Heads of Government 2017).

3. As the secretary general, I undertake periodic visits to member states to meet with all stakeholders including governments, opposition, private sector, youth and representatives of the media.

4. In 2019, data from CARICOM's internal statistical database estimated the debt stock at US$27 billion.

5. The Inter-Governmental Task Force, comprising officials from all member states, has not met since 2016 due to funding constraints.

6. The CARICOM Committee of Ambassadors (CCA) was established in March 2015, as a body of the Caribbean Community. It serves in an advisory capacity and as the main interlocutor between individual member states and the main organs and bodies of CARICOM.

7. Shanique Myrie, a Jamaican, brought the Government of Barbados before the CCJ for refusing her entry to the country and mistreating her at the port.

8. Currently, four member states – Barbados (2005), Belize (2010), Dominica (2015) and Guyana (2005) – have adopted the appellate jurisdiction of the CCJ, making it the final court of appeal.

9. CARPHA's first significant test was addressing the outbreak of the H1N1 influenza in at least three countries of the region. It has since had to respond to the regional outbreak of the Chikungunya virus and the coronavirus (Covid-19) in 2020.

10. Payments are triggered according to the policies bought and generally are tied to the extent of the damage suffered.

11. The Green Climate Fund was established in 2010 as a financial mechanism under the United Nations Framework Convention on Climate Change to provide funding for climate change mitigation and adaptation in developing countries.

12. That process led to the adoption of the Caribbean Community Five-Year Strategic Plan 2015–2019: Repositioning CARICOM, which was approved by the CARICOM Heads of Government at its thirty-fifth meeting in Antigua, 1–4 July 2014 (CARICOM Heads of Government 2014).

13. At the time of this address, consultations had been conducted in only eight of the fifteen member states.

14. The secretariat later established in 2016 a Change Management Office within the Office of the Secretary General.

15. For a discussion of the DOMs bid for membership in CARICOM, see Jessica Byron and Patsy Lewis, "Responses to the Sovereignty/Vulnerability/Development Dilemmas: Small Territories and Regional Organisations in the Caribbean"; and Karine Galy, "The Stakes of Admitting the French Caribbean Territorial Authorities to CARICOM and the OECS" in Lewis, Gilbert-Roberts and Byron (2018).

16. The Technical Working Group submitted a report on its work to a meeting of the Committee of Ambassadors in January 2018. The committee recommended that further work be done by the Technical Working Group. By 2019, the secretariat reported that negotiations had begun with Curacao, St Maarten and Aruba towards associate membership.

References

Applewhaite, Lolita. 2011. "Statement by Ambassador Lolita Applewhaite, Secretary-General, Caribbean Community at the Opening of the Sixth General Meeting of CARICOM, Its Associated Institutions and the United Nations System", 28 July 2011. https://caricom.org/media-center/communications/speeches/statement-by-ambassador-lolita-applewhaite-secretary-general-ag-caribbean-c.

Basdeo, Sashadeo. 1997. "The 'Radical' Movement towards Decolonization in the British Caribbean in the Thirties". *Canadian Journal of Latin American and Caribbean Studies* 44: 127–46.

Caribbean Court of Justice – CCJ. 2013. "Shanique Myrie v. The State of Barbados". CCJ Application No. OA 002 of 2012. http://www.caribbeancourtofjustice.org/wp-content /uploads/2013/ 10/2013-CCJ-3-OJ.pdf.

CARICOM. 1973. "Treaty Establishing the Caribbean Community", 4 July 1973. https://caricom .org/documents/4905-original_treaty-text.pdf.

CARICOM Heads of Government. 1989. "Communiqué Issued at the Conclusion of the Tenth Meeting of Heads of Government of the Caribbean Community", 8 July 1989. https:// caricom.org/media-center/communications/communiques/communique-issued-at-the -conclusion-of-the-tenth-meeting-of-the-conference.

———. 2012. "Communiqué Issued at the Conclusion of the Twenty-Third Inter-Sessional Meeting of the Conference of Heads of Government of CARICOM", 9 March 2012. https:// caricom.org/media-center/communications/communiques/communique-issued-at-the -conclusion-of-the-twenty-third-inter-sessional-mee.

———. 2014. "Communiqué Issued at the Conclusion of the Thirty-Fifth Regular Meeting of the Conference of Heads of Government of CARICOM", 4 July 2014. https://caricom.org /media-center/communications/communiques/communique-issued-at-the-conclusion -of-the-thirty-fifth-regular-meeting-of-the-conference-of-heads-of-government-of-the -caribbean-community-1-4-july-2014-dickenson-bay-antigua-and-barbuda.

———. 2017. "Communiqué: Thirty Eight CARICOM Heads of Government Meeting", 7 July 2017. https://caricom.org/cochog/view/communique-thirty-eighth-caricom-heads-of -government-meeting.

CARICOM Secretariat. 2001. "The Revised Treaty of Chaguamaras Establishing the Caribbean Community Including the CARICOM Single Market and Economy". https://caricom.org /documents/4906-revised_treaty-text.pdf.

———. 2003. "The Rose Hall Declaration on Regional Governance and Integration Development". Adopted at the Twenty-Fourth Meeting of the Conference of Heads of Government of CARICOM. Montego Bay, Jamaica, 2–5 July. https://www.intradebid.org /data-repository/DocsPdf/Acuerdos/CARICOM%20-%20Rose%20Hall%20Declaration.

———. 2014. "Caribbean Community Five-Year Strategic Plan 2015–2019: Repositioning CARICOM". http://cms2.caricom.org/documents/11265-executive_plan_vol_1_-_final.pdf.

Cashin, Paul, Montfort Mlachila, and Cleary Haines. 2010. "Caribbean Bananas: The Macroeconomic Implications of Trade Preference Erosion". Working Paper 10/59, International Monetary Fund. https://www.imf.org/en/Publications/WP/Issues/2016/12/31 /Caribbean-Bananas-The-Macroeconomic-Impact-of-Trade-Preference-Erosion-23688.

Demas, William. 1960. "The Economics of the West Indies Customs Union". *Social and Economic Studies* 9 (1): 13–28. Sir Arthur Lewis Institute of Social and Economic Studies, University of the West Indies.

Girvan, Norman. 2007. "Towards a Single Development Vision and the Role of the Single Economy". Barbados: Heads of Government of CARICOM. www.caricom.org/jsp/single _market/single_economy_girvan.pdf.

Hope, Kempe. 1974. "Carifta and Caribbean Trade: An Overview". *Caribbean Studies* 14 (1): 169–79.

Lewis, Patsy, Terri-Ann Gilbert-Roberts, and Jessica Byron. 2018. *Pan-Caribbean Integration: Beyond CARICOM*. London and New York: Routledge.

Mitchell, Donald. 2006. "Sugar in the Caribbean: Adjusting to Eroding Preferences". Policy Research Working Paper, World Bank. https://doi.org/10.1596/1813-9450-3802.

PAHO (Pan American Health Organization) and the CARICOM Secretariat. 2006. *Report of the Caribbean Commission of Health and Development*. Caribbean Commission on Health and Development. Kingston, Jamaica: Ian Randle Publisher. www.who.int/macrohealth /action/PAHO_ Report.pdf.

United Nations. 2014. "The Arms Trade Treaty". https://unoda-web.s3-accelerate.amazonaws
.com/wp-content/uploads/2013/06/English7.pdf.

Wallace, Elisabeth. 1962. "The West Indies Federation: Decline and Fall". *International Journal:
Canada's Journal of Global Policy Analysis* 17 (3): 269–88.

WIC (West Indian Commission). 1992. *Time for Action*. Report of the West Indian
Commission. Kingston: University of the West Indies Press.

Will, W. Marvin. 1991. "A Nation Divided: The Quest for Caribbean Integration". *Latin
American Research Review* 26 (2): 3–37.

World Bank. 2018. *World Bank Open Data*. Online Database. https://data.worldbank.org/.

Chapter 3

Whither Caribbean Integration? Recasting the Foundations of a New Integration Project

PATSY LEWIS

This chapter[1] argues that the Caribbean Community (CARICOM) integration project has lost its way, largely due to its embrace of competitiveness goals within the neoliberal framework, which has robbed it of its theoretical foundations, tenuous as those were. This has the potential to exacerbate tensions already present. The chapter looks at what it considers to be some of the main fault lines along which the integration movement could disintegrate. These include uneven benefits from CARICOM, divergence in interests and the lure of competing integration projects in Latin America. The chapter argues that despite its current problems, the post-independence challenges of its member states, aggravated by a global recession, makes a regional framework for addressing common challenges even more urgent.

Introduction

> Many stakeholders are deeply pessimistic about the future of CARICOM integration; and most – although not all – view this as a matter of grave concern. Even when respondents saw greater opportunities in extra-regional association the vast majority were nonetheless unhappy at what is considered to be a huge missed opportunity for the Caribbean, due to lack of vision, weak implementation of decisions, mistrust and poor leadership. There was a real sense that the optimistic era of Caribbean integration may well have passed, ironically just at the time when it is perhaps most desperately needed. (Bishop et al. 2011a, 5)[2]

This sombre assessment of CARICOM was made in 2011 by a team of consultants assessing the challenges the organization was facing in the face of the global recession. In January 2012, another consultancy report, this time focused on restructuring the CARICOM Secretariat, declared CARICOM to be in "crisis", arguing that

> the crisis is sufficiently severe to put CARICOM's very existence in question. This is because many of its Member States are highly indebted with the result that a further downturn in 2012 could compromise their ability to fund the construct. The Secretariat and CARICOM institutions are not strong enough to cope with any major shortfall in funding. Notwithstanding the immediate dangers, there is evidence that, without fundamental change, CARICOM could expire slowly over the next few years as stakeholders begin to vote with their feet. (Stoneman, Pollard and Inniss 2012, 7)

On the surface, the CARICOM integration project seems well on its way. It has deepened the process from the goal of achieving a common market to the creation of a single market and economy. A common external tariff with compliance for the most part has been implemented, and countries have made strides in removing or significantly reducing barriers to persons wishing to establish businesses and supply services, and on capital movement, the latter with a few exceptions. Further, the category of workers eligible to move under the Revised Treaty of Chaguaramas has been expanded to nine, from the original five. Yet perceptions of failure persist.

Despite the liberalization of most intraregional trade, trade within the region remains low, with most of the region's goods traded outside. This can be largely explained by the nature of regional production, which remains geared for external markets, with economies often in competition with one another. There are real questions as to the extent to which production integration remains viable given important changes in the global economy and Caribbean economies, in particular, the increased liberalization of economies and the relegation of governments to facilitators of the private sector rather than development agents in their own right; the centring of competitiveness as the raison d'être of economic activity; and the shift to services over manufacturing in most economies. Further, there are no mechanisms for integrating production structures across the region to effect real rationalization and economies of scale, nor is it clear that this is a major goal of the movement.[3] Opportunities for production integration are also limited by changes in production structures that privilege global value chains based on specialization. The challenges for Caribbean small states, especially those of the Organisation of Eastern Caribbean States (OECS), to integrate into these global value chains are not very different from those inhibiting production integration. While challenges vary across different sectors, they include the high costs of transportation and energy, limited possibilities for economies of scale, small internal market size, low levels of skills, limited access to finance, quality of infrastructure, standards compliance systems including sanitary and phytosanitary methods, inter alia, although proximity to the US market is considered an advantage (Lanz and Werner 2018, 20–21).

Moreover, the region has not made many strides in bringing into effect the elements of the agreement that would result in the creation of a single economy, namely the harmonization of policy across a wide range of areas – trade, agriculture, industry, incentives to investment, transportation and tourism – which were to have been completed by 2015. Thus, sentiments that CARICOM is running out of steam can be attributed to an acknowledged deficit in the implementation of measures necessary to bring the CARICOM Single Market and Economy (CSME) into being and an apparent floundering of the region in the face of global recession.[4] A reported 50 per cent of measures necessary for the implementation of the CSME has not been achieved (Girvan 2009, cited in Bishop et al. 2011b, 19); and, even where measures are implemented on paper, in some cases the spirit of agreements is not adhered to. This is felt most widely in the area of intraregional travel, given credence by the highly publicized treatment of nationals from other Caribbean states by Barbados immigration and the widespread sentiment against intraregional travel in Barbados. Nowhere is the crisis more evident, though, than in the prolonged failure to agree on a CARICOM secretary general in 2011, which suggested a lack of consensus by regional leaders. Furthermore, the CARICOM

Heads of Government (HOG) announced in May 2011 at a special retreat in Guyana its decision to postpone the completion of the single economy, which was scheduled for 2015, while consolidating the single market (CARICOM Secretariat 2011).

Stoneman, Pollard and Inniss (2012) endorsed this decision, urging a significant curtailment of CARICOM's goals to a few feasible areas and relaunching the regional project around these. Bishop et al. (2011a) identified leadership as one of the challenges impeding the process, suggesting that there needed to be a change in the nature of political leadership of the integration scheme. They also located CARICOM's implementation deficit in an ineffective secretariat, arguing that reform of the secretariat was necessary to maintain its relevance and effectiveness. They also called for a focus on sectoral development that would draw on the region's "productive capabilities" and the location of a regional infrastructure to facilitate integration at the forefront of the regional agenda. This regional infrastructure includes information and communications technologies, education, transport, and healthcare. It further called for more academic input into the integration process. The authors of the Stoneman, Pollard and Inniss (2012) report were specifically charged with reorganizing the secretariat to make it a more effective implementation machine, in keeping with the widely held perspective that a failure to implement decisions taken by HOG was the main challenge confronting the regional process. The report did, however, acknowledge in passing that political leadership was also a part of the problem.

The common approach to the implementation challenge, evident in these two reports as well as other analyses of CARICOM's functioning, is to view the problem as one of organization that requires putting effective mechanisms in place; hence the West Indian Commission report's (1992) proposal for a commission to implement CARICOM decisions, which was picked up by the Rose Hall Declaration in 2003 (CARICOM Heads of Government 2003), with some modification, and reinforced by the PMEGG (2005) and TWG (2006) reports. The 2010 decision of the HOG meeting in Grenada to establish a Permanent Committee of Ambassadors as CARICOM's implementation mechanism was but a further modification of this theme.[5] Other analyses have looked more broadly at the decision-making process as well as the politics that drives, or should drive, the process. Thus, Pollard (2003) and the PMEGG (2005) and TWG (2006) reports have called for automaticity in decision-making, which would give regional decisions immediate legal effect in national law. The model for this is the European Union. Attempts to locate the challenges more broadly in the philosophical realm include Brewster (2001) and Lewis (2003), who argue for a more cultural and less economistic approach to the process.[6] More specifically, Lewis (2005) locates the failure to implement in political dynamics at the national level that hamper implementation of regional decisions, which require structural changes in the relationship between the national and regional levels in order to address this (see also Hinds 2006).

Why has CARICOM lost its way? An understanding of the problems facing the integration movement requires a broader enquiry into the underlying goals and philosophy underpinning the process, and how developments in the international sphere have affected these. This chapter argues that the global shift towards neoliberalism since the formation of the regional project has elevated competitiveness as the raison d'être of the movement, thus limiting its scope to achieving global competitiveness by way of the protected regional space.

Neoliberalism and the CSME

From its beginning, CARICOM was considered as a platform from which to engage with the world. On the economic front, it was to provide a protected space for the development of the private sector by furnishing a stable regional market for member states' goods as an end in its own right, not as a cradle for developing global competitiveness. The process was always contentious, as it tried to reconcile the varying interests of its member states, especially accommodating the microstates of the OECS in the development process.[7] It was also meant as an instrument for pooling resources in the functional sphere to achieve greater efficiencies. At the political level, it was to be a mechanism of solidarity from which to engage the world.

The evolution of the process from CARICOM to the CSME has been driven by developments in its external environment, particularly the end of the Bandung project and the consolidation of neoliberalism (as part of a broader package of globalization) as the new development paradigm within which to locate national and regional policy. The main drivers were the creation of the World Trade Organization (WTO), the formation and consolidation of large regional trade blocs such as the North American Free Trade Area, negotiations towards the creation of a Free Trade Area of the Americas (FTAA), and the intensification of the European integration process in the creation of a single market and economy. These had a profound effect on reshaping the development paradigm which CARICOM states had adopted after independence and upon which the regional integration movement was based. Central to this was unilateral preferential market access to their main trading partners – the United States, the European Union and Canada – as well as aid and concessionary international financing.

Neoliberalism, the paradigm which underpinned this shift, elevated the market and the private sector as key drivers of development, in the process diminishing the role of the state as well as its capacity to engage in the development process. The curtailing of the state's role in the economy was affected through systematic programmes of privatization and wage controls, directed by international financial institutions, primarily the International Monetary Fund, World Bank and donor countries. Underlying this was the view that a large state sector crowded out the private sector as it drew resources, particularly skills, away from the private sector. A diminished state, with lower-salaried workers, would release talent to the private sector on more favourable terms. For the private sector, the global embrace of neoliberalism privileged firms competitive enough to withstand global competition, signalling an end to or severe reduction in national and regional protection.

Thus, the embrace of the CSME was a direct response to these developments. Central to the CSME was the goal of creating regional firms competitive enough to withstand the challenges of open competition, which were expected from a devaluation of preference regimes in their trade with the United States, Canada and the European Union. The most immediate instance of this was the FTAA, which was to be negotiated between 1998 and 2005, and which was to replace preferential access to the US market. This was expected to be followed by negotiations with Europe for a WTO-compliant trade regime to replace the scheduled expiration of the trade protocols of the Cotonou Partnership Agreement. This drive for competitiveness was evident in the CSME's provisions, the most important of which were removal of restrictions on factors of production – goods, capital and some labour; the inclusion of services for liberalization as well as a wide range of beyond-the-border issues believed to affect competitiveness; and a commitment to harmonize policy across a wide range of areas. Chapter 3 of the Revised Treaty of Chaguaramas thus provides for the rights of persons to establish businesses and to provide services across the region without restriction. It also provides for the free movement of capital with the abolition of capital controls. While the movement of goods, services and capital was treated expansively, a more limited approach was taken to the movement of people. The latter was treated on a phased basis, with five categories identified initially – university graduates, musicians, artistes, sports and media personnel – expanded further in 2009 to include teachers, nurses, and persons who hold vocational certificates and associated degrees. There is no timeline for the full liberalization of movement, although the charter (Article 45) has this as a goal, providing for governments to effect this on a bilateral basis.[8] Despite this attempt to further liberalize labour movement, it continues to be severely restricted, with countries continuing to engage in restrictive practices in contravention of these agreements.

One can argue, therefore, that the global shift towards the neoliberal development paradigm lies at the heart of the challenges that confront CARICOM. The curtailment of the region's already limited economic vision to facilitator of competitiveness has exacerbated tensions already present. At the popular level, it restricts benefits to a relatively small group of business people and individuals considered as having specified desired "skills". This has moved it further in the direction of an elitist movement which privileges a few. Even within the private sector, it is most likely to facilitate the progress of larger, more "efficient" firms, while marginalizing small and micro firms. These tensions are likely to be manifested at the country level, as the firms most likely to be successful and the individuals most likely to benefit from limited movement are more likely to be in a small group of countries. OECS countries, but also Guyana, Suriname and Belize, who are at the margins of the integration process, are least likely to benefit from these developments. What follows is a discussion of some of the main fault lines of the regional integration process which threaten its survival.

Fault Lines in the Regional Integration Process

Sources of tension within CARICOM emerge in CARICOM–OECS relations, uneven gains from trade and geographical dynamics which continue to see some countries existing on the margins. Other challenges emerge from the tug of integration processes in Latin America, which draw, or have the potential to draw, individual member states with the possible effect of further weakening CARICOM's coherence. These are explored in the following.

Intra-CARICOM Tensions

CARICOM's competitiveness focus has served to exacerbate existing tensions within the movement between the OECS group and the rest. The OECS comprises some of the smallest states of the CARICOM grouping which, historically, have feared marginalization in the broader integration process, to which they have responded by deepening their own integration process in an effort to further carve out a clearly defined space. This is embodied in the decision to create an economic union building on already strong institutions of cooperation. These include a single currency; a common supreme court; a regional security system with Barbados; a stock market exchange; a civil aviation authority; some pooled diplomatic representation;[9] and their own trade negotiations group and mechanism for coordinating trade policy, the Trade Policy Unit.[10] The additional elements are a new treaty, which takes a more inclusive approach by providing, since January 2011, for free movement of all people, not limited to any category, and the abolition of discrimination with respect to "employment, remuneration, and other conditions of work and employment" (OECS 2010, para. 12.2). It also strengthens the framework for implementation by enhancing the role of the OECS Authority, which comprises heads of government, by giving it the power to legislate in well-defined and selected areas (OECS 2008, 9) with binding effect on member states (OECS, 2010, para. 8.8). It also strengthens the role of the OECS Secretariat by transforming it into the OECS Commission with commissioners responsible for preparing legislation for the authority's approval, in a clear borrowing of the recommendations of the West Indian Commission and the Rose Hall Declaration which proposed this as the mechanism for strengthening CARICOM's implementation ability.

The OECS integration process has been driven to some extent by dissatisfaction with the integration process and its inability to fully address their concerns, which have been expressed at various stages in the development of the broader regional process. Gonsalves (2012) identified dissatisfaction with the movement as

> the limited capitalisation of the CARICOM Development Fund; the veritable collapse of the discretionary CARICOM Petroleum Facility . . . ;[11] the decline of the manufacturing sector . . . , occasioned, in part, by unfair competition from at least one other CARICOM exporting country and the absence of a proper enforcement of the relevant CARICOM rules regarding protection of certain manufactured commodities from the OECS; the unresolved challenges in air transport, including competitive subsidies granted to one airline;[12] and Trinidad and Tobago's illegitimate monopoly, through the Caribbean Air Navigation and Advisory Services (CANAS) of all the resources derived from the Piarco Flight Information Region (PFIR), which includes the airspace of the OECS countries and Barbados. There is, too, a prevailing sentiment in the OECS, including among state officials and the social partners, that CARICOM's service to, and sensibility towards, the OECS member-states are less than desirable. (Gonsalves 2012, 6)

CARICOM's cohesiveness is also threatened by differential interests among the non-OECS Member States. Intraregional trade is the ground on which some of these tensions play out. Trinidad is the main beneficiary of intra-CARICOM trade,[13] accounting for 83 per cent of intraregional exports in 2010 but only 5.6 per cent of intraregional imports. This contrasts starkly with most of the other CARICOM states. Jamaica and Guyana, for instance, account for 43 per cent and 21 per cent of intraregional imports, respectively, but for only 2.4 per cent and 5.7 per cent, respectively, of intraregional exports. Likewise, the OECS group was the second highest importer of intraregional goods at 21.5 per cent but accounted for only 3.5 per cent of intraregional exports. Of the remaining member states, Barbados and Belize accounted for 6.9 per cent and 0.7 per cent of intraregional imports and 4.2 per cent and 0.7 per cent of intraregional exports, respectively.[14] For Jamaica, its huge trade deficit has been a source of great dissatisfaction.[15] In particular, it has accused Trinidad of having an unfair advantage in cheap oil which, it believes, is the basis of Trinidad's greater competitiveness. Jamaica has argued that Trinidad should make its oil available to the region at national prices.[16] In dollar terms, in 2010, Jamaica spent over US$822 million on regional imports, while earning only US$57 million for its exports to the region. Jamaica's dissatisfaction is also fuelled by Trinidad's greater role in its economy with the purchase of several Jamaican companies, including Air Jamaica,[17] as well as some highly publicized trade disputes. This sentiment was expressed by then minister of industry, investment and commerce Karl Samuda in this comment: "Look at the companies that have been bought out by members of the Community. What is the Jamaican ownership of the insurance industry? What is the Jamaican ownership of our banks, et cetera? People just come in and almost do with us as they wish. Well things have changed. [We] have to put a stop to it" (Reid 2009).

Barbados's engagement with CARICOM has also been problematic. There has been well-publicized hostility to the free movement components of the CSME. Guyanese nationals, in particular, have borne the brunt of this hostility. Barbados has also run afoul of Jamaica arising from the negative treatment accorded to some of its female nationals by immigration officials (See Gayle 2012).[18]

Haiti remains outside of the CSME, so Haiti is not able to benefit from its provisions, particularly free movement of skills. This is due to its economic challenges, aggravated by the 2010 earthquake, but may also be attributed to an unspoken fear of Haiti's full engagement in the regional project, particularly the free movement elements of the CSME. The Bahamas, although more integrally involved with CARICOM in the functional sphere, continues to maintain its distance from the economic elements of the process, refusing to sign on to the CSME.

Diversification of Relations with Latin American Countries

The region's engagement with its Latin American neighbours has also been a source of tension within CARICOM. Integration initiatives in Latin America have exerted a pull on some CARICOM states, which has the potential to diffuse the regional movement. Belize and Suriname, which remain marginal to the regional integration process, are increasingly, along with Guyana, becoming more drawn towards integration initiatives in Latin America, given their geographical location. Central to Belize's concerns continues to be its relationship with Guatemala and initiatives to weaken the tensions that exist between them. Migration movements between the two have resulted in a significant cultural and linguistic shift that integrates them more firmly into Latin America. Suriname and Guyana are participants in the Integration of the Regional Infrastructure of South America project, which has the potential to integrate them more physically within the South American mainland.[19] The geographical challenges most felt in Belize and Guyana are summed up by Stoneman, Pollard and Inniss (2012, 19): "however well integrated CARICOM becomes, it will always be quicker, easier and cheaper to drive a truckload of goods across the border to Mexico from

Belize than to export them anywhere in CARICOM". Challenges of geography affect the entire CARICOM as it is based on member states that are separated by water; this is aggravated by the failure to develop regional infrastructure to provide safe, reliable and affordable transportation.

Venezuela's attempt to expand its relations with CARICOM states had also placed some stress on the integration project. Its Petro Caribe initiative, which offers oil to a number of Caribbean and Latin American countries on concessionary terms, created some tension between Trinidad and other CARICOM member states, all of which, with the exception of Barbados, are signatories. Patrick Manning, Trinidad's prime minister at the time of the signing of the agreement, was unhappy with their decision.[20] Of more concern to the regional project is the participation of a number of OECS countries in Venezuela's Bolivarian Alliance for the Peoples of Our America People's Trade Treaty (ALBA-TCP) initiative. Dominica, St Vincent and the Grenadines, and Antigua and Barbuda are full members, while Haiti, Suriname and St Lucia have formally notified their intention to join.[21] The message here is that some of CARICOM's most vulnerable and disengaged members are finding ALBA a pole of attraction. Severe curtailment of concessionary trade regimes, shrinking aid, high debt levels and the aggravating effects of the global recession have increased ALBA's attractiveness as a source of resources.

ALBA presents several challenges for the regional movement, however. In the economic realm, it offers a wide range of economic initiatives such as the construction of oil refineries and a barter-type arrangement which permits trade in oil and commodities. These appear to offer more concrete gains than CARICOM's trade liberalization focus seems to afford, offering alternative economic activities in the face of the severe shrinkage of the traditional agriculture sector and acknowledging the challenges in procuring foreign exchange in the face of reduced foreign exchange earnings. ALBA also proposes a development bank and a common currency, the Sucre (Sistema Unitario Compensación Regional De Pagos/Unitary System of Regional Compensation of Payments).[22] ALBA's inclusion of foreign policy coordination also presents a challenge to CARICOM's coherence in light of its limited success in this sphere. Venezuela's and Cuba's support for the construction of an international airport in St Vincent, and Venezuela's commitment to help fund an international airport in Dominica are considered crucial for the development of the tourism sector of both countries,[23] especially in light of the collapse of their agriculture and manufacturing sectors. The failure of the regional integration project to assist in procuring resources to underwrite such high-cost infrastructural projects highlights CARICOM's impotence in addressing these crucial development challenges.

The formation of the Community of Latin American and Caribbean States (CELAC), which embraces all the member states of the Organization of American States, including Cuba, but excludes the United States and Canada, also holds the potential for integrating CARICOM more closely with Latin America, with the possibility of diluting its distinctiveness as a regional integration initiative. CELAC's goals include increasing coordination and synergy among existing integration groups, promoting the integration of Latin America and the Caribbean, political coordination, and enhancing the region's presence in international bodies (Heads of Government of the Latin American and Caribbean Countries 2010).

The Latin American and Caribbean market also exerts a pull on Trinidad and Tobago. Trinidad's major trading partners are Colombia, Brazil and Argentina (Government of the Republic of Trinidad and Tobago, Central Statistical Office 2012). Trinidad's trade competitiveness and its sanguinity in exploring market opportunities have played a role in driving the region's trade relations with Latin America. The most recent instance of this is Trinidad's signing of a memorandum of understanding with Panama to "facilitate export of propane, butane, bitumen, natural gas, cement, ceramic tiles, clay tiles, steel products" (*Gleaner* 2012). Gonsalves (2012, 3) has accused Trinidad under the government of Prime Minister Kamala Bissessar of having "all but abandoned leadership responsibilities in Project CARICOM".

EC–CARIFORUM EPA

The transfiguration of trade between CARICOM and some of its closest trading partners has also put pressure on the coherence of the integration movement. The Economic Partnership Agreement (EPA) signed in 2008 between the European Commission and member states of CARICOM and the Dominican Republic has the potential to weaken the movement. The differing economic structures and strengths that exist in the region suggest that countries are likely to be differentially affected by the EPA. Countries with more developed trade in goods and developed tradable service sectors are more likely to benefit. The OECS countries, in particular, with uncompetitive micro firms, primarily agriculture bases and services sector heavily based on tourism are unlikely to gain much from access to the European market. These diverging interests in trade, which in the negotiating phase of the agreement exposed tensions among member states, are likely to deepen as successive such agreements are negotiated.[24] The inclusion of the Dominican Republic as a partner in negotiations with CARICOM states also moved the Dominican Republic from the periphery of CARICOM closer to its centre. Specifically, the agreement's inclusion/acceptance of regional preferences, which provides for benefits extended by CARICOM to the European Commission to be available to members of Caribbean Forum, is likely to be a fillip to deepening the stalled free trade agreement between CARICOM and the Dominican Republic. It also brings the prospect of the Dominican Republic's entry into CARICOM that much closer. The Dominican Republic has already taken the initiative to seek formal membership in CARICOM, although CARICOM has not acted on this and there does not appear to be much enthusiasm.[25]

The governance structure of the EPA has also been identified as an area that is likely to weaken CARICOM. It already provides sanctions for non-compliance that are absent from the CARICOM agreement.[26] Further, the EPA's implementation ethos, driven by EU financing which now prioritizes EPA implementation, holds the possibility of a greater urgency in effecting EPA implementation than completing the CSME.

What challenges do all these developments hold for CARICOM integration? One can argue, and as the tone of this chapter so far suggests, that these developments could well prove inimical to CARICOM's coherence. These could lead to further divisions within CARICOM, compromising its integrity along existing fault lines: the more developed country–less developed country divide, tensions among more developed countries arising from differential perceptions of benefits and the tug of competing integration schemes.

OECS/More Developed Country Divide

The trend towards greater coherence among the OECS could weaken the broader movement. It is possible that a stronger OECS could act as a pole of attraction for other Eastern Caribbean states such as Barbados and, possibly, Trinidad and Tobago. This is not far-fetched, as governments in both countries have shown an inclination both towards closer relations with the OECS group as well as more pointed interest in regional integration that goes beyond the economic to embrace political union. Specifically, Barbados's prime minister, Owen Arthur, had proposed a confederation between Barbados and the OECS in 1995. Trinidad's prime minister, Patrick Manning, issued a call for a political union with Grenada, St Lucia and St Vincent in 2008, which led to an OECS endorsement of a union of the group with Trinidad.[27] Barbados is already a member of the Regional Security System, which includes all OECS members. Barbados's and Trinidad and Tobago's interest in a more political integration movement, moreover, was evident in their request to their fellow CARICOM HOG to consider moving towards political integration.[28] It was out of this request that the Rose Hall Declaration on Regional Governance and Integrated Development was adopted and the Technical Working Group on Governance was formed. Trinidad could also pursue a more independent path with a broader range of partners in keeping with its own economic interests, which are more divergent than the rest of CARICOM. Trinidad's inclination one way or the other, as experience suggests, can vary with changes in the political directorate. Gonsalves (2012, 5) sees the possibility of closer integration among the OECS, the French Overseas Territories (Department d'outre Mer), Guyana, Suriname, and Trinidad and Tobago, with the latter playing a leadership role. Dominica and St Lucia already have developed trading ties with Guadeloupe and Martinique, and the OECS has more formal engagement with the Department d'outre Mer than does CARICOM.

A weakened CARICOM is likely to see Jamaica maintain a greater distance from CARICOM as it pursues its own interests. Jamaica's market interests in both goods and services lie outside of CARICOM, as its negative trade balance with the region reflects. There is a possibility, although the material base for this is still relatively weak, for closer integration between Jamaica and its northern Caribbean neighbours: Cuba, Haiti and the Dominican Republic.[29] These fault lines could lead to a disorderly disintegration of the regional movement or a more managed process around the identification of a narrower definition of interests pursued within the regional sphere. The HOG's decision in 2010 to halt the CSME's implementation and the Stoneman, Pollard and Inniss report (2012), which advocates a narrowing of goals and a relaunch of a less ambitious CARICOM around these goals, suggest this to be the likely direction.

A more optimistic perspective on these developments is possible, however. The OECS economic initiative, rather than entrenching divisions, could act as a unifying device, showing what is possible from a more ambitious integration scheme. The latter would be based on strengthening of functional cooperation and a renewed focus on issues central to CARICOM. Their engagement in wider Latin American integration processes, which holds the danger of their marginalization as a group, could serve as an impetus for a stronger integration process with more clearly defined and articulated goals, but this requires a deliberate rethinking of the role of regional movement given these developments.

Is CARICOM Worth Saving?

CARICOM's challenges in finding coherence and relevance at a period of economic instability in the region raise the question of whether it is worth saving; or, put differently, does it have relevance given the challenges the region currently faces? I would argue that CARICOM remains more relevant than ever given the challenges small states face in a restructured global economy. This, however, requires a stronger and more engaged organization rather than the current trend towards a weaker, less engaged organization.

Shifts in the global economy, already mentioned, have made it more difficult for small states to forge an independent path. Their push for resources in the face of their economic challenges, high debt levels, weak competitiveness, creeping crime rates, high levels of skills migration, inter alia, begs a regional response now more than ever. Their need for resources has already led to arrangements with questionable entities in some states and foreign policy decisions driven by short-term expedience.[30] The inconsistency in diplomatic relations with respect to China and Taiwan exhibited by some OECS members is one instance of this. Taiwan's action against Grenada, which plunged this country into crisis and threatened its very survival, required a regional response. Such a response was weak at best.[31] The real question is not whether a regional integration scheme is needed, but how such a scheme should be constructed to be relevant in the face of current challenges. For CARICOM to become such a scheme, a deeper rethink than suggested by Stoneman, Pollard and Inniss (2012) is needed. Unfortunately, CARICOM has become a largely reactive body, responding to external stimuli as they arise. Developments such as the WTO and the FTAA and EPA influenced movement towards the CSME, while trade arrangements such as the EPA affect its implementation and dilute its focus.

What Would Be Needed to Rescue CARICOM?

What is required for CARICOM to fulfil a truly developmental role is to become a more engaged organization centred on addressing the main development challenges of its member states. This calls for a more holistic approach based on an expanded economic agenda beyond the competitiveness focus of the CSME, and the centring of human development. Central to this is a clearer definition of its role, which must be based on a vision of the possibilities of Caribbean people and its responsibility in realizing this. Put differently, the region's people and their capabilities would be at its centre. This would be reflected in a development agenda that is grounded in the post-independence challenges that its small states have experienced and a vision of how a regional agenda, rather than the current national focus, can address these. There is evidence that there is some appreciation of the need to centre people in the process. The mission statement of CARICOM's regional development agenda, defined by Girvan (2007), appears to recognize this, as it speaks to human rights, social and economic justice, and the banishment of unemployment.[32] Practice does not necessarily bear this out. Gonsalves (2012, 5) speaks to the failure to centre people, arguing that CARICOM's focus has been on "integrating state institutions and trading regimes, and not on the people themselves".[33]

The economic element of a regional developmental agenda would move beyond the current preoccupation with trade, which has exhausted its limits, to focus on the development of a regional economy. Central to this would be a reorganization of production processes on a regional level. In other words, the production, marketing and shipping of goods would be organized as a regional, rather than national, enterprise.[34] Such a strategy should create an enabling environment for small and medium economic and agricultural enterprises to flourish, given their predominance in the region. This is particularly important for the OECS, whose small firms and small farming systems are not likely to withstand competition within the CSME, far less the EPA.

The collapsed Windward Island banana industry provides a model for the development of an industry that was not viable on a national scale. This could be the basis for harnessing raw material for more competitive value-added enterprises. This raises the thorny issue of how to treat mineral raw material produced in some member states. A key element in the competitiveness of the regional economy would be energy, which would suggest the treatment of oil as a regional good[35] available at the same price throughout the region. This would remove one of the main points of tension in the region arising from the perception that Trinidad's dominance of regional trade is attributable in no small measure to its cheap oil. This raises the even thornier issue of how to harness oil, which is largely in foreign private hands, for the benefit of such a regional economy. Another element would be to foster intersectoral linkages at the national and regional levels as the basis for strengthening and diversifying economies, making use of whatever flexibilities are still allowed in the global arena to do this.

Central to a renewed regional project is the identification of specific issues for treatment at the regional level. The PMEGG (2005) sought to navigate between the need for regional action and the HOG's acceptance of CARICOM as a community of sovereign states by embracing the principles of proportionality and subsidiarity.[36] Proportionality limits regional institutions to actions necessary to complete the Revised Treaty of Chaguaramas, while subsidiarity curtails regional action to areas where national action cannot achieve the goals of community (cited in TWG, 2006), although the Technical Working Group recognized the need for expanding the arena for regional action.

Expanding the remit for regional action requires strengthening functional integration. The Treaty of Chaguaramas designated functional cooperation as a pillar of CARICOM, along with trade and foreign relations. Security was added later as the fourth pillar. Attempts to rethink the role of functional cooperation, especially as a necessary element to fulfil the CSME, are evident in the 2007 HOG Declaration on Functional Cooperation and the report of the committee on functional cooperation, which was established to consider the role of functional cooperation in the integration process (CARICOM 2007). The report on functionalism draws on the Single Development Vision (Girvan 2007) which argues: "Functional Cooperation in the economic field has a direct economic benefit in helping to realize the potential of market integration. In social, political and environmental matters, functional cooperation supports economic development by improving labour productivity, systemic competitiveness and sustainability. Just as important, functional cooperation speaks to other aspects of development, helping to provide integration with a 'human face' and facilitating broad stakeholder involvement" (Girvan 2007, 9).

Functionalism should therefore be treated as a "cross-cutting" issue underpinning all integration activities.

The Declaration on Functional Cooperation identified eight broad areas for strengthening functional integration: health, human and social security, labour, communication, crime and security, environment, energy, and agriculture. Its goal in health is to ensure "equitable access . . . to adequate health care" (CARICOM 2007). Its human and social development agenda includes social welfare, culture, education and training, and vocational qualification. Its goals for social welfare include the portability of pensions and other social security benefits. This, however, is unambitious, given the weak social provisioning that exists across the region. The costs to individual countries of effecting strong social protection systems suggest it as an area that would benefit from regional action. Not only is this important in its own right, but it is necessary to facilitate mobility within the region. Its goal for culture is equally limited, restricted to "foster[ing] collaboration among national cultural entities and ensur[ing] that CARIFESTA [the Caribbean Festival of Arts] plays its critical role in developing the region's cultural industries" (CARICOM 2007). A more relevant goal would be integrating culture more centrally in economic development. Its role for education and training is also limited to "equitable access", when what is needed is the alignment of education goals with national and regional development strategies. This is necessary to address high levels of skills migration, the misalignment of training with skills needed and the region's low competitiveness. Ambitions for labour include creating a regional labour market information system to facilitate the flow of labour and promoting the use of retired citizens and the diaspora in regional development. Likewise, in respect of youth, the declaration simply acknowledges the role of the Caribbean Commission on Youth in "helping to chart a strategic vision and action programme for the empowerment of our youth" (CARICOM 2007). A more urgent response to youth is necessary, considering that they bear the brunt of high levels of unemployment and are highly vulnerable to poverty, crime, violence and drug abuse. Youth and their potential to contribute to development must be located at the centre of any regional development strategy. Similar considerations must be made for women, given their greater representation among the poor and unemployed. A more regional approach to human resources that extends beyond the limited initiatives in the CSME is necessary to address the problem of migration, particularly of skilled workers, that currently plagues many CARICOM countries. Expanded economic opportunities would help to increase the region's absorptive capacity, allowing for a greater use of its skilled people than is currently possible under nationally based development models. Freedom to travel without restrictions throughout the region would not only increase its attractiveness as a pole of migration, deflecting some of the outward migration, but would provide for greater popular engagement and identification with the regional project.

Under communication, the declaration includes transportation, information and communications technology, telecommunications, and public education. Ambitions in respect of transportation are to "develop and implement a regional air and maritime transportation policy designed to create affordable, reliable and safe intra-regional services" (CARICOM 2007). Regional transportation is central to fostering economic, social and political linkages crucial to a successful integration project. Transportation remains one of the weak points in the regional integration movement, hampering economic development and human interaction necessary to build a strong integration project. The policy approach to creating the above should be based on a more realistic role of the relationship between the public and private sectors in achieving this. In other words, it is unlikely that this could be achieved without government subsidy.[37] A truly regional economy could not exist in the absence of strong, safe, reliable regional air and sea transportation, but this requires deliberate government engagement. The current approach to regional air transport, which values limited (if any) government engagement and an organizational model based on competitiveness and efficiency, may well be inimical to achieving the goal of an integrated region. It is also necessary to address the adequacy of existing national infrastructure to assess their ability to service national and regional development goals. Failure to do both these things is likely to lead to increased frustration with the regional project, as Gonsalves's letter suggests (2012).

Under communications, the declaration includes telecommunications, with the aim of developing a "single domestic space for telecommunications" (CARICOM 2007). This could be expanded to include increasing access to communications technology by reducing the cost of communication software and hardware. The declaration also has a commitment to "intensifying public education with a view to further involving citizens of the region in the integration process" (CARICOM 2007). Thus, rather than viewing people as central to a successful integration process, requiring their more intimate engagement in the process, the HOG continues to treat their engagement as a matter of information, failing to acknowledge the need to fashion structures that would facilitate their engagement in policy formation and implementation. Such an approach to popular engagement would require a shift at the level of leadership away from the political bureaucratic model currently in place.

Agricultural production is an obvious area for regional action. The declaration expressed the HOG's commitment to revitalizing the agricultural sectors and stimulating entrepreneurial capacity among agricultural communities, as set out in the Jagdeo initiative (CARICOM 2007). More than this is needed to bring agriculture to the centre of economic life and integrate it with other sectors of the economy. Regional action in agriculture should be based on rationalizing food production across the region to meet food needs and raw material input into food processing enterprises. It should address the small size of national markets and low production levels to sustain processing enterprises. Currently, many large firms processing agricultural products in the region import their raw materials from outside of the CARICOM region because of instability in supply. Again, the banana model is apropos here. This would be particularly important for sustaining small farmers, particularly those of the Windward Islands.

Tourism is another obvious area for regional action, although it is not specifically mentioned in the declaration. Possibilities for integrating tourism more firmly with other economic sectors, particularly agriculture, but also industry and other services, have not been properly explored and developed at the national level. The small size of most CARICOM states justifies a regional approach to maximizing its benefits. Equally important is the need for a regional approach to identifying and supporting, by common policy, a model of tourism that is environmentally sustainable and socially inclusive, with its benefits more widely felt across all sectors of the economy/society. Such an approach is necessary to halt the stagnation in the sector and to shift it away from the mass, all-inclusive, cruise tourism models which currently prevail and are encouraged by the harmful inter-island competition that exists. The conceptualization of tourism's role in regional development should be organic to the treatment of the environment. The declaration notes the importance of coordinating the region's "response and adaptation to climate change" and disaster management, and accords a special role for the Caribbean Sea in the region's sustainable development (CARICOM 2007). Fulfilling these goals requires replacing national ad hoc, and oftentimes harmful, approaches to tourism, with a regional approach that is sensitive to environmental sustainability. A broader vision of the role of services other than tourism, such as sports and culture, in regional development is needed. A more regional approach to developing skills and skills-training facilities and their more conscious integration in regional development planning is also necessary.

Central to the viability of the regional project is the treatment of energy, which is an essential element in the production process and is currently a source of tension. The declaration pledges its support for the work of the Caribbean Regional Energy Development Programme in developing renewable energy options and in elaborating a regional energy policy. What is needed is an approach that addresses the uneven energy costs across the region, while working towards reducing the region's reliance on oil. Extending Trinidad's national subsidy to the rest of the region, even if this were feasible, would work best in a regional economic framework with integrated production. More important, though, given the desirability of moving towards renewable sources of energy, is a concerted push to explore the feasibility of a range of options. This is an obvious arena for regional action given the commonality of the problem and the high initial costs of introducing alternative technologies.

Summary and Conclusion

CARICOM is weak and in danger of collapsing, ironically, at a time when it is most needed to shore up the viability of its small member states. Challenges presented by global trade shifts and the global financial crisis and recession have exposed their vulnerability, making a regional solution even more urgent. The current response, which is an inward national focus, is already significantly weakening the movement when, paradoxically, national survival depends on a stronger, more dynamic and expansive regional project. CARICOM's collapse is not likely to expand opportunities for member states, despite its current weakness, but rather, to decrease their viability as independent states.

A failure to rethink the underlying goals of the integration process and to make improving the lives of its people the cornerstone of the movement could lead to a misdiagnosis resulting in medicine that could prove detrimental. A more limited ambition that moves it away from addressing concerns central to the project and/ or leads it in the direction of a more elitist project would do this. An example is the recommendation of Stoneman, Pollard and Inniss (2012) for a relaunch of the project on a more limited platform. With similar inimical effects would be to move in the direction of greater elitism, as suggested in their recommendation for a narrowing of the private sector's engagement to a handful of large regional and international businesses:

> A fundamental improvement in CARICOM's relations with the private sector is long overdue. . . . The private sector's views on what works and what does not and on where priorities lie would be invaluable.

> However, we currently see little value in setting up some sort of council or committee involving representatives of the private sector.

> Our proposal would be to set up a dialogue directly with leading figures in business in the region. . . . A small grouping of half-a-dozen of them could be supplemented with three or four CEOs of leading international businesses in the region; there need be no fixed membership.

We would suggest regular small and informal meetings, possibly over dinner.

> As well as providing CARICOM with invaluable insights, we believe that such meetings could lead to significant sponsorship and financing. First, the private sector could provide sponsorship to CARICOM events as long as conflicts of interest were avoided. Second, the private sector could be persuaded to pay for research, particularly in areas in which it is interested. Third, it is also likely to help with costs to defend Caribbean interests or to develop opportunities. (Stoneman, Pollard and Innis 2012, para. 32–36)

The region's survival depends on a greater shift from current limited national development strategies adopted since independence, which are increasingly less effective in improving the standard of living of its people, towards a regional platform for addressing development challenges. This cannot be based on an elitist model that privileges the larger, more "viable" private sectors, which only serves to aggravate existing divisions across the region and within countries.[38] Rather, it must seek to ground the people and their concerns for a better life and greater opportunities at its centre. This is not to say that there may not be widely divergent perspectives on the best way to do this, as hostility towards regional mobility in Barbados suggests, but mechanisms that engage people in a dialogue around these issues and mechanisms that facilitate their interaction would go a far way towards addressing and reconciling such differences.

Notes

1. This chapter, published here with permission, was previously published in Spanish as "Adonde va la integración caribeña? Refundiendo los cimientos de un nuevo proyecto de integración", in *El Caribe, sus islas y el difícil camino de independencia, identidade integración*, edited by Jacqueline Laguardia Martínez (Havana: Ciencias Sociales, Ruth CASA Editorial, 2014). It was included in this volume because it raises pertinent questions about the nature of the integration process and is one of only two chapters (the other being chapter 2) that reflects on CARICOM's functional agenda. It also explores a wider range of diverging interests among CARICOM states than the Jamaica, Trinidad and OECS schisms explored in chapter 8.

2. The draft version of the report was used here because this paragraph more succinctly expressed the authors' sentiments.

3. For a more detailed discussion of these shifts and their implications for production integration, see Girvan et al. (1993), Farrell (2005) and Lewis (2006).

4. For a discussion of the recession's effects on regional economies and the integration process, see Lewis (2010), and Lewis, Joseph and Roach (2010). For an assessment of the status of implementation of the CSME, see Arthur and Consortium (2010) and CARICOM Secretariat (2009).

5. See Deparadine (2010). The Stoneman, Pollard and Inniss (2012) report advised against the establishment of this committee, questioning its effectiveness in addressing the implementation deficit.

6. These debates are summarized in Lewis (2003).

7. The members of the OECS are Antigua and Barbuda, the Commonwealth of Dominica, Grenada, St Kitts and Nevis, St Lucia, St Vincent and the Grenadines, and Montserrat. Anguilla and the British Virgin Islands are associate members.

8. The St Ann's Declaration (*CARICOM Today*, 8 January 2019) released at the conclusion of the 18th Special Meeting of CARICOM Heads of Government expanded the categories of workers eligible to move. See chapter 8 for a discussion of the St Ann's Declaration and the report of the restructured Commission on the Economy (CARICOM Commission on the Economy, October 2020).

9. The OECS maintains diplomatic missions in Brussels, Geneva and Puerto Rico. A joint mission in Ottawa, opened in 1982, was closed in 2011.

10. The Organisation of Trade Negotiations, formerly the Regional Negotiating Mechanism, is CARICOM's trade negotiating body.

11. This fund was set up by Trinidad and Tobago in 2005.

12. This is a reference to Caribbean Airlines, which benefits from cheap oil (see discussion later in chapter). In 2009, Caribbean Airlines bought out Jamaica's airline, Air Jamaica, which was struggling from high operating costs. Since this transaction, the availability of flights between Jamaica and the OECS has contracted while the costs have sky-rocketed.

13. The source of this data is CARICOM Secretariat (2018).

14. There was no data for Suriname for 2012, but in 2009 it imported 17.5 per cent of intraregional goods. Its intraregional exports for that year were negligible.

15. See chapter 8 for a contemporary exploration of these divisions and tensions from Jamaica's perspective.

16. For an example of this argument, see Chang (2010). Chang observes that while the average cost of energy (US\$/kWh) was "Bahamas 0.23 Barbados 0.229 Jamaica 0.238 Grenada 0.266 St. Lucia 0.293", it was 0.05 for Trinidad.

17. The perceived treatment of former Air Jamaica workers by Trinidad's Caribbean Airlines, which bought out Air Jamaica, has also increased antipathy towards Trinidad, specifically, and CARICOM, more generally. The latest casualty was a remaining group of seventy-five Air Jamaica pilots who were made redundant in April 2012, although Caribbean Airlines has promised that the benefits of those re-employed would be unchanged. See *Stabroek News* (2012) and *RJR News* (2010). There is also concern over Caribbean Airlines's decision to drop the Air Jamaica brand when announcing its flights. See Mitchell (2012).

18. See chapter 12 of this volume for a discussion of the Shanique Myrie case.

19. Of particular interest to the region is the Guyana Shield Hub, which aims to connect Guyana, Suriname, French Guiana, Brazil and Venezuela. Although progress on the project has been slow with uncertain funding, a highway and bridge have already been constructed linking border towns in Guyana and Brazil.

20. See Hart (2005a, 2005b).

21. See Gonsalves (2012).

22. The Sucre is currently a virtual currency, but the aim was to move towards a physical currency over time.

23. Trinidad is the only CARICOM country which is contributing towards the construction of St Vincent's airport. Other donors include Taiwan, Mexico, Austria, Malaysia, Turkey and Iran (Caribbean Construction Magazine, n.d.).

24. Negotiations between CARICOM and Canada on a free trade agreement to replace the Caribbean–Canada Trade Agreement (CARIBCAN), which provides preferential access to the Canadian market and was set to expire in 2013, broke down in 2015. In lieu of a new agreement, the WTO waiver covering the existing arrangement was extended to 2023.

25. CARICOM suspended its consideration of the Dominican Republic's membership in 2013 following the Dominican Republic's decision to revoke the citizenship of Dominicans of Haitian descent.

26. For a more detailed discussion of the EPA's likely effects on CARICOM, see Girvan (2009).

27. See *Jamaica Gleaner* (2009). The OECS supported the proposal and responded with the establishment of a group to consider the proposal and the mechanisms by which it could be affected.

28. In his address to CARICOM's Fourteenth Inter-Sessional Meeting in 2003, Manning declared his interest in discussing "political integration" with any member state that was interested (Manning 2003).

29. Gonsalves (2012) views Jamaica engaging with these countries similarly but includes the Bahamas and Puerto Rico in this configuration.

30. Examples can be found in the sale of passports as a revenue earner by several CARICOM countries.

31. In 2005, in the wake of hurricanes Ivan (in 2004) and Emily (in 2005), Taiwan broke off diplomatic relations with Grenada after the latter accepted support from China. In retaliation, Taiwan insisted on immediate repayment of a US$30 million loan, which threatened the country with a financial crisis. Grenada eventually entered into an agreement with Taiwan in 2015 to reschedule its debt.

32. It identifies four dimensions of the Single Development Vision: economic, social, environmental and governance.

33. The report of the restructured Commission on the Economy (2020) seeks to advance initiatives that it views as people centred (see chapter 8 of this volume).

34. The Single Development Vision (Girvan 2007) identifies a cluster of goods and services – agriculture, energy, fishing, forestry, manufacturing, sustainable tourism and other export services – that would drive growth and transformation, and the measures necessary to support this.

35. Lewis (chapter 8) raises the question of whether it was feasible to treat oil as a regional good when other resources, such as bauxite, are treated as falling squarely in the domestic domain.

36. The restructured Commission on the Economy (2020) reiterated the importance of subsidiarity as a principle for delineating responsibility between the national and regional arenas but extended it to include differential time tables for implementation among at least five member states (see chapter 8).

37. It remains to be seen whether privately expanded ferry services, operating within a regional regulatory framework but without government subsidy, as advanced by the restructured commission (2020), is sufficient for the emergence of a sustainable system of sea transportation.

38. The restructured Commission on the Economy (2020), following CARICOM HOG's lead in the St Ann's Declaration (2018), took a less elitist approach than advocated here, proposing regular meetings with regional private sector and labour organizations and formalizing relevant bodies as associated members of CARICOM (see chapter 8 in this volume).

References

Arthur, Owen, and Consortium. 2010. "Revised Individual Country Analytical Reports for Phase 2 of Cisp/csme/result 1.9.1.1/ser09.10 Consultancy to Support the Full Integration of Belize and the OECS in CARICOM".

Bishop, Matthew Louis, Norman Girvan, Timothy M. Shaw, Solange Mike, Raymond Mark Kirton, Michelle Scobie, Debbie Mohammed, and Marlon Anatol. 2011a. "Caribbean Regional Integration". Draft Version – February. A report by the UWI, Institute of International Relations with the support of the UK Department for International Development.

———. 2011b. "Caribbean Regional Integration". Final Version – April. A report by the UWI, Institute of International Relations with the support of the UK Department for International Development.

Brewster, Havelock. 2001. "New Vistas for the Caribbean Community". In *The Caribbean Community: Beyond Survival*, edited by Kenneth O. Hall, 66–88. Kingston: Ian Randle Publishers.

Caribbean Construction Magazine. n.d. "Argyle International Airport, St Vincent & the Grenadines". Accessed 1 December 2012. http://www.caribbeanconstruction.com/index .php?option=com_content&view=article&id=373&Itemid=2.

CARICOM. 2007. "A Community for All: Declaration on Functional Cooperation". Issued by the Heads of Government of the Caribbean Community on the Occasion of the Twenty-Eighth Meeting of the Conference, Needham Point, Barbados, 1–4 July. https://caricom.org /media-center/communications/statements-from-caricom-meetings/a-community-for-all-declaration-on-functional-cooperation-issued-by-the-hea.

CARICOM Commission on the Economy. October 2020. Report *"Caribbean 9.58" Speeding up the Caribbean*, 10 May 2021. https://issuu.com/guyanaconsulate6/docs/att_ii_to_item_7.3_-_cce _report_-32_is_-_24-25_feb.

CARICOM Heads of Government. 2003. *The Rose Hall Declaration on Regional Governance and Integrated Development*. Adopted at the Twenty-Fourth Meeting of the Conference of the Heads of Government of CARICOM, 2–5 July. Montego Bay, Jamaica.

CARICOM Secretariat. 2009. "Report on the Appraisal of the State of Implementation of the CARICOM Single Market Arrangements Mandated by the Conference of Heads of Government of the Caribbean Community (Draft)".

———. 2011. "CARICOM Leaders Seek Greater Focus on Prosperity for the People", 22 May. Press release 192/2011. http://www.caricom.org/jsp/pressreleases/press_releases_2011 /pres192_11.jsp?null&prnf=1.

———. 2018. "Value of CARICOM's Intra-Regional and Domestic Exports". http://www .caricomstats.org/Files/Databases/Trade/eXCEL%20FILES/CC-Intraregional.htm.

CARICOM Today updated January 8, 2019, 11 May 2021. "St. Ann's Declaration on CSME". https://today.caricom.org/2018/12/04/st-anns-declaration-on-csme/.

Chang, Kevin O'Brien. 2010. "Should Jamaica Leave CARICOM?" *Jamaica Gleaner*, 11 July. http://jamaica-gleaner.com/gleaner/20100711/focus/focus6.html.

Deparadine, Lincoln. 2010. "CARICOM Agrees to Committee of Ambassadors". *Caribbean News Now*. http://www.caribbeannewsnow.com/headline-CARICOM-agrees-to-Committee -of-Ambassadors-1458.html.

Farrell, Trevor M.A. 2005. "Caribbean Economic Integration: What is Happening Now; What Needs to be Done". In *Caribbean Imperatives: Regional Governance and Integrated Development*, edited by Kenneth Hall and Denis Benn, 175–205. Kingston and Miami: Ian Randle Publishers.

Gayle, Barbara. 2012. "Myrie V Barbados Government Has First Mention in CCJ". *Jamaica Gleaner*, 17 February. http://jamaica-gleaner.com/gleaner/20120217/lead/lead6.html.

Girvan, Norman. 2007. "Towards a Single Development Vision and the Role of the Single Economy". University of the West Indies in Collaboration with the CARICOM Secretariat and the Special Task Force on the Single Economy. As approved by the Twenty-Eighth Meeting of the Conference of Heads of Government of the Caribbean Community, Needham's Point, Barbados, 1–4 July. https://www.carib-export.com/obic/documents/single_economy_girvan.pdf.

———. 2009. "Caribbean Community: The Elusive Quest for Economic Integration". In *Growth and Development Strategies for the Caribbean*, edited by A. Downes, 199–218. Barbados: Caribbean Development Bank.

Girvan, Norman, Wendel Samuel, Ian Boxill, and Jude Whitehead. 1993. "Framework, Areas and Support Measures for Production Integration in CARICOM". A study prepared for the CARICOM Secretariat by the Consortium Graduate School of Social Sciences.

Gonsalves, Ralph. 2012. "On Strategic Directions for CARICOM – CARICOM: Promise and Fulfillment". Letter from Prime Minister of St. Vincent and the Grenadines to CARICOM Secretary General, His Excellency Irwin LaRocque, 9 February.

Government of the Republic of Trinidad and Tobago, Central Statistical Office. 2012. "Trade Statistics". Accessed 2 May 2012. http://www.cso.gov.tt/statistics/statistics/-in-statistics/statistics/trade-statistics.

Hart, Robert. 2005a. "Jagdeo Raps Manning on War of Words". *Jamaica Gleaner*, 5 July. Jamaica-gleaner.com/gleaner/20050705/lead/lead7.html.

———. 2005b. "T&T's Manning Fears Venezuelan Oil Plan". *Jamaica Gleaner*, 4 July. http://jamaica-gleaner.com/gleaner/20050704/lead/lead2.html.

Heads of Government of the LAC (Latin American and Caribbean) Countries. 2010. "Latin America and the Caribbean Unity Summit Declaration". Mayan Riviera, Mexico, 23 February. http://www.europarl.europa.eu/intcoop/eurolat/key_documents/cancun_declaration_2010_en.pdf.

Hinds, David. 2006. "Domestic Non-Cooperation and Regional Integration: Problems of Caribbean Regionalism". *Social and Economic Studies* 55 (3): 32–48.

Jamaica Gleaner. 2009. "Manning Reiterates Support for Political Union with OECS", 23 June. http://mobile.jamaicagleaner.com/20090623/carib/carib1.php.

———. 2012. "Trinidad, Panama Sign Trade Agreement", 14 March. http://new.jamaica-gleaner.com/gleaner/20120314/business/business91.html.

Lanz, Rainer and Hans-Peter Werner. 2018. "Opportunities and Challenges for Small Economies in the Global Value Chain". In *Handbook of Small States: Economic Social and Environmental Issues*, edited by Lino Briguglio, 17–41. London and New York: Routledge.

Lewis, Diedron, Samantha C. Joseph, and Khellon Q. Roach. 2010. "The Implication of the Current Financial and Economic Crisis on Integration: The Caribbean Experience". *Global Development Studies* 6 (Winter-Spring): 49–98.

Lewis, Patsy. 2003. "Political Union: The Road Not Travelled by the West Indian Commission". *Global Development Studies* 3, nos. 1–2 (Winter-Spring): 1–24.

———. 2005. "The Agony of the Fifteen: The Crisis of Implementation". *Social and Economic Studies* 54 (3): 147–75.

———. 2006. "Production Integration in CARICOM: Implications for the OECS". In *Production Integration in CARICOM: From Theory to Action*, edited by Denis Benn and Kenneth Hall, 133–51. Kingston, Jamaica: Ian Randle Publishers.

———. 2010. "The Global Economic Crisis: Implications for Caribbean Integration". *Global Development Studies* 6 (Winter-Spring): 1–28.

Manning, Patrick. 2003. "Opening Address by Hon. Patrick Manning, Prime Minister of Trinidad and Tobago, at the Fourteenth Inter-Sessional Meeting of the Conference of Heads of Government of the Caribbean Community", 14–15 February. Port-of-Spain, Trinidad and Tobago.

Mitchell, Damion. 2012. "Air Jamaica Name Drop Concerns Opposition". *Jamaica Gleaner*, 20 April. http://jamaica-gleaner.com/latest/article.php?id=36698.

OECS (Organisation of Eastern Caribbean States). 2008. "Economic Union Treaty: Frequently Asked Questions". http://www.oecs.org/doc-lib/economic-union.

———. 2010. *Revised Treaty of Basseterre Establishing the OECS Economic Union.*

PMEGG (Prime Ministerial Expert Group on Governance). 2005. "Regional Integration: Carrying the Process Forward". Report on the establishment of a CARICOM Commission or other executive mechanism.

Pollard, Duke, ed. 2003. *The CARICOM System: Basic Instruments.* UWI-CARICOM Project. Kingston, Jamaica: Caribbean Law Publishing Company.

Reid, Tyrone. 2009. "Stop It, or Else? Jamaica Warns CARICOM Trading Partners". *Jamaica Gleaner*, 14 June. http://old.jamaica-gleaner.com/gleaner/20090614/lead/lead1.html.

RJR News. 2010. "JALPA Accuses New Air Jamaica Owners of Victimization", 5 May. http://rjrnewsonline.com/local/jalpa-accuses-new-air-jamaica-owners-of-victimization.

Stabroek News. 2012. "CAL Offers Jobs to Air Jamaica Pilots", 21 April. https://www.stabroeknews.com/2012/news/guyana/04/21/cal-offers-jobs-to-air-jamaica-pilots/.

Stoneman, Richard, Duke Pollard, and Hugo Inniss. 2012. "Turning around CARICOM: Proposals to Restructure the Secretariat". Landell Mills Development Consultants. Prepared for CARICOM Secretariat. https://caricom.org/documents/9400-restructuring_the _secretariat_-_landell_mills_final_report.pdf.

The West Indian Commission. 1992. *Time for Action.* Kingston, Jamaica: University of West Indies Press.

TWG (Technical Working Group). 2006. "Managing Mature Regionalism: Regional Governance in the Caribbean Community". Report of the Technical Working Group on Governance appointed by CARICOM Heads of Government. Chairperson Vaughan A. Lewis. October.

Chapter 4

Applying the Theory of Liberal Intergovernmentalism to CARICOM

The CARIFORUM-EU EPA

TAMARA ONNIS

This chapter employs the theory of liberal intergovernmentalism (LI) to analyse the Economic Partnership Agreement (EPA) between CARIFORUM countries and the European Union.[1] It examines the process of negotiation among the Caribbean Community (CARICOM)[2] members and analyses the outcome of the EPA, concentrating on the various stages of negotiations, the process of bargaining, the competencies of the relevant institutions, the interplay between the CARICOM institutions and heads of government, and member state preferences. The chapter additionally explores the following questions: What are the bargaining dynamics that shaped the EPA? What are the roles and competencies of CARICOM institutions in the process of negotiation of the EPA? How are preferences defined and negotiated? And are national choices reflected in the outcome of the EPA? It draws on LI's three-step approach and analysis, namely the formation of national preferences, negotiations and the creation of functional institutions, to answer these questions.

Examination of Liberal Intergovernmentalism

Liberal Intergovernmentalism as a Theory of International Relations

LI specifies the motivation of social actors, states and leaders, and predicts their behaviour from their interactions. Moravcsik and Schimmelfennig (2009) note that under the LI approach "a minimum of three theories, arrayed in a multi-stage model – one each of preferences, bargaining and institutions – are required to explain integration" (66–67). Moravcsik (2010) suggests that both domestic and transnational society are traditionally made up of unitary states, leading to incentives for interaction and thus integration across borders, be it economic, social or cultural. Consequently, domestic actors will either benefit or be disadvantaged by the interaction, resulting in groups pressuring government to implement policies for their benefit and therefore defining preferences.

LI advances that national preferences are the driving factors behind state actions, and without them, there would be no negotiations. Moreover, "without such social concerns that transcend state borders, states would have no rational incentive to engage in world politics at all, but would simply devote their resources to an autarkic and isolated existence" (Moravcsik 2010, 1). Hence, globalization and regional integration are a result of these preferences and interactions based on the will of subnational entities. Moravcsik (2010) further argues that in the end "what matters most is what states want, not how they get it" (1).

Assumptions of Liberal Intergovernmentalism

At its most fundamental level, LI has two basic assumptions:

1. That states are the primary actors in global politics. This implies that states enjoy political legitimacy at the international level; that they utilize national and regional institutions to serve their purpose; that they are, therefore, the real masters of any and all intergovernmental treaties, even those which are negotiated by institutions; and that preferences diverge among states, do not remain static, and are dependent on domestic policies and issues.
2. That states are rational actors in global politics. The rational actor appraises utility costs and factors for any given action and chooses the option that guarantees the most positive outcome. So long as benefits outweigh costs, then actions to cooperate, integrate and/or establish international institutions are a strategic outcome of the state's independent decision-making. Over time, the state's patterns of negotiations establish a consistent "preference function" which also assists in predicting its decisions and actions.

In addition to these two premises which define states as the dominant players at the international level, LI's main proponents assume that in interstate bargaining, states must additionally look for mutual gains and determine how these gains are divided among themselves.[3] Moreover, conflicts which arise through the negotiating process establish bargaining positions, with those gaining the least from the outcome possessing the most influence. States explicitly implement strategies such as acquiring insider information, withholding financial support and utilizing veto threats to control the direction and outcome of bargaining.

Following these assertions, this chapter employs the theory of LI to first examine the formation of preferences in CARICOM and then to investigate how these preferences are reproduced in the EPA. The chapter relies on the assumption that CARICOM states' preferences are first defined and then adjusted during the bargaining process to facilitate substantive agreements. Additionally, the national and regional institutions created after the EPA should function under the competencies of the member states, since they are merely a form of outsourcing some functions of a central government, and decentralizing government authority. That is to say, institutions act for the benefit of the states they represent and not to deepen, expand or create new competencies for themselves.[4]

Empirical Application of Liberal Intergovernmentalism to CARICOM: The CARIFORUM-EC EPA

This chapter examines the CARIFORUM-EC EPA agreement also referred to as the CARIFORUM-EU EPA, which is the most extensive trade agreement to date (2018) between any two unions. It researches the process of preference formation at the state level, scrutinizes the process of bargaining at the international level and compares EPA provisions to those of the initial preferences of the CARICOM states.

The CARIFORUM-EC EPA was the first EPA negotiated by the European Union. It essentially liberalizes trade and investment between the twenty-seven-member European Union and sixteen-member CARIFORUM. The EPA has the enforcement of an international treaty with sanctions for non-compliance. It requires all signatory states to undertake legislative amendments in areas such as customs, intellectual property, safety standards and quality assurance, consumer protection, trade and competition policies, service industries, investment and commerce, intellectual property protection, tourism, the environment, and other social and cultural issues.

Background of the Economic Partnership Agreement

In the late 1950s–1960s most of the colonies of the United Kingdom became independent and were given preferential market access to the United Kingdom. In 1973 when the United Kingdom joined the then European Economic Community (EEC), its former colonies in Africa, the Caribbean and the Pacific (ACP) were also granted preferential access to the EEC. ACP–EEC cooperation was officially made into an agreement under the Lomé Conventions, which were in place from 1975 to 2000. This agreement provided the ACP countries with preferential access to the European members' markets and aid relief, including provisions for non-reciprocal preferential access based on a quota system for agricultural exports and duty-free mineral exports from CARICOM countries to the EEC. They additionally included EEC commitments for substantial investments in CARICOM.[5] The Cotonou Partnership Agreement came into effect after their expiration in 2000. The Cotonou Partnership between the European Union and the ACP was more than an extension of the Lomé Conventions. It incorporated economic, social and political legislation, including provisions for cooperation with non-state actors, civil society groups and other local authorities regarding development commitments. It also focused on merging politics, trade and development in CARICOM, and was established on a regional institutional framework.[6]

The United States and countries in Latin America brought the Cotonou Partnership Agreement between the European Union and the ACP to the World Trade Organization (WTO) under its trade dispute settlement mechanism, citing a violation of its nondiscrimination principle as it pertains to trade in bananas.[7] A waiver with an expiry date was granted by the WTO, requiring ACP countries to renegotiate an agreement with the European Union under WTO stipulations.[8] The EPA was conceived by the European Union to replace its trade agreements with the ACP. CARICOM members like Guyana viewed the EPA as being imposed on them. For instance, Jagdeo, Guyana's president at the time (2008), suggested that the EPA was a "well thought-out ploy by Europe to dismantle the solidarity of the ACP by effectively dividing the ACP into six negotiating theatres – that is six EPAs – and playing one off against the other which they did very effectively" (*Stabroek News* 2008).[9] The theory of LI would thus define CARICOM members as being in a susceptible position in the bargaining dynamics of the EPA. They would therefore be more reactive than proactive in approaching the EPA, since they consider themselves to be in a framework initiated and created by the European Union.

The European Union included the Dominican Republic in the EPA. The imposition of the Dominican Republic in the same negotiation process as CARICOM by the European Union was also viewed by CARICOM as another move by the European Union to weaken CARICOM's bargaining stance, as this meant that CARICOM would have to first bargain internally, then with the Dominican Republic, before starting negotiations with the European Union. The CARICOM–Dominican Republic relationship was essentially constructed by the European Union and introduced new factors to the bargaining dynamics in CARICOM, including language (the working language for negotiations with the Dominican Republic is Spanish, and that in CARICOM is English), bargaining power of the Dominican Republic (the population of the Dominican Republic is over half the size of the entire CARICOM) and bargaining preferences.[10] In keeping with the theory of LI, the Dominican Republic would be expected to focus on issues affecting its economy and not those of the CARICOM members.

The Process of Negotiating the Economic Partnership Agreement

The parties negotiating the EPA were the European Union, represented by the European Commission (EC); and CARICOM and the Dominican Republic (CARIFORUM), represented by the Caribbean Regional Negotiating Machinery (CRNM).[11,12] The CRNM consisted of individuals with expertise in various subjects and trade-related disciplines, including diplomats, CARICOM dignitaries, ministers of governments, specialists and consultants employed by CARICOM, and ministry advisers of the member states.[13] LI holds that before negotiations, local government and states define preferences. In CARICOM's case, preference formation was initiated by CARICOM through consultation at the national level via interactions with individuals, interest groups and non-governmental organizations (NGOs). Consultations were consequently held at the regional level where additional input from regional entities was considered, after which Technical Working Groups refined national and regional interests into negotiating positions. These positions were then presented to regional stakeholders, the CARICOM Council for Trade and Economic Development (COTED) and CARIFORUM by a College of Negotiators comprised of NGO representatives and private individuals. COTED thereafter compiled the information and presented it to the CARICOM Heads of Government. In keeping with LI's observations of the primacy of governments in the decision-making process, notwithstanding these attempts at broadening decision-making, it was the CARICOM Heads of Governments that provided the final authorization on the bargaining position of CARICOM/CARIFORUM.

The Phases of Negotiations

EPA negotiations were organized in four phases. The first (April–September 2004), conducted between the European Union and the ACP, established priorities for negotiation, after which negotiations were conducted with individual regions. The second phase (September 2004 to September 2005) between the EC and CARIFORUM defined the nature and scope of the negotiations. The third phase (September 2005 to December 2006) focused on structuring and consolidating the negotiations.

The agreement was finalized in the fourth phase (January–December 2007), and an institutional framework was created for its implementation.

The First Two Phases of the Negotiations

During phase one of the negotiations, the CRNM posted a bulletin on its website that included "user-friendly matrices" (Office of Trade Negotiations 2008). The matrices summarized the positions of the EPA negotiations in the areas of market access in goods and services, trade facilitation, investment and a broad area called trade-related aspects (for example, innovation and competition policy). The private sector organizations in CARICOM countries were urged to include their positions and comment in specific columns provided in the matrices, after which the feedback would be included in the position briefs submitted to the ministries of commerce in each country. Additionally, the process of intra-CARICOM negotiation included harmonized strategy recommendations by the College of Negotiators that were referred to COTED and the CARIFORUM Council of Ministers for review and consideration.

Sacha Silva, the Commonwealth Secretariat/IDB market access consultant to the CRNM, notes that the CRNM found its two main tasks, building a trade and tariff database and conducting country consultations, to be the most challenging (2008). Silva (2008, 9) suggested that CARIFORUM's "biggest obstacle and greatest challenge . . . was its lack of human resources and a general funding constraint at both the national and regional level". Nevertheless, during the first two phases of the EPA, the CRNM launched a series of "Boot Camps", an education initiative primarily targeting CARICOM-based companies engaged in exporting goods and services. The CRNM characterized the Boot Camps as interactive sessions explaining market access, services and trade facilitation terms (CRNM 2006).

In 2005, the CRNM additionally initiated a series of private sector surveys. The aim was "to conduct research . . . in a manner which would sensitize the private sector to areas of data collection which would be useful for the negotiations", to reinforce "existing private sector outreach and [to] canvas current private sector opinions on and input to, the region's external negotiations" (Callender 2006, 2). In 2006, further surveys targeted member states' National Chambers of Commerce, manufacturer's associations, regional sector-specific associations and private liability companies.[14] The surveys addressed issues such as barriers to market access and competitiveness, current and future market interest, the perception of benefits to be derived from negotiations, challenges to involvement in negotiations, and what the CRNM could do to improve its outreach. The CRNM, however, admitted that the surveys revealed a lack of private sector participation. It likewise accepted that the private sector was not informed, did not utilize information made available and did not make extensive inputs in the identified matrices.

Private sector and civil society involvement in the first two stages of negotiations was initiated by CARICOM through the CRNM. Moreover, the CRNM defined matrices and set the parameters and topics to be addressed in the negotiations. No viable attempts were found from national governments to initiate private sector and civil society involvement in the first two phases of the negotiations. This is contrary to LI's prioritization of the state's role. Thus, although the process is transparent, it reveals the extensive influence of CARICOM institutions, specifically the CRNM, in defining the bargaining positions of member states.[15]

Phase Three of the Negotiations

LI predicts that the party with the least to lose has the bargaining advantage: in this case the EC member states.[16] A select committee reporting to the UK Parliament noted that "the EU is approaching the negotiations with the ACP as if they were playing a game of poker. The Commission is refusing to lay its cards on the table and to dispel the ACP's fear that it stands to lose more than it will gain. . . . The ACP is negotiating under considerable duress and the EU approach emphasizes the unequal nature of the negotiation process" (International Development Committee, House of Commons 2005, 1). This advantage affords the EC the possibility to dictate certain aspects of the EPA.

CARICOM, on the contrary, argued that the region was independent in its negotiations and that it was a vital part of defining the parameters and negotiating the contents of the EPA in phase three. CARICOM advanced that "the RNM's outreach activities are geared at engaging a broad cross-section of stakeholders, to the extent that resources allow" (CARICOM 2006). Bernal, CRNM's director general at the time (2006), adds that civil society representatives including the Barbados-based Caribbean Policy Development Centre exchanged views on the EPA with EU representatives. He noted that "this most recent consultation between the RNM and the NGO community demonstrates the RNM's commitment to regular interchange with these set of stakeholders" (CARICOM 2006). However, this reflects the informal exchange and input that regional stakeholders had in shaping the EPA. Although such exchanges are extremely valuable, they do not amount to any substantial interaction or input in defining the substance of the EPA.

There are currently very limited formal structures for local and regional civil society to participate at the regional level in CARICOM. CARICOM does not detail, nor can one find, any existing structure or formal arrangement between local government, private sector, and/or local and regional civil society and the CRNM. There are no regional political parties for aggregating political demand in CARICOM.[17] Moreover, the forum for a regional civil society is initiated and entertained by CARICOM. That is to say, CARICOM institutions initiate regional forums for civil society organizations to meet and have an input in the integration process and articulate political demand. In this case, the groups are sceptical of the tangible benefits of such an engagement.

Not only is there limited local government participation at the regional level in CARICOM, but there is also a variance in the participation at the local level across CARICOM members. That is to say, CARICOM civil society does not have the same level of functionality at the national level in all CARICOM member states.[18] Additionally, a report on a regional civil society forum commissioned by CARICOM revealed that civil society representatives were wary of the extent to which their input would impact the process of negotiating the EPA. It was made clear that participants "were vocal in their disappointment at engagement which did not offer anything more than their own national experience . . . there was dissatisfaction that the consultation was not a direct dialogue with government officials. Many consultations ended without any great expectations from participants" (CPDC 2011, 13).

Furthermore, there was no evidence of checks and balances on the implementation of civil society suggestions, nor were there any legislation or articles relating to the functionality of civil society input in CARICOM's decision-making process in the treaty for the Caribbean Court of Justice to interpret.

Although Burley (1992) suggests that states form institutions to outsource some responsibilities and that states are the sole actors in bargaining, the CRNM played a decisive role in the EPA. It defined the parameters and substance of the EPA. The parameters do not reflect a state-centric approach to the negotiations as the theory of Liberal Intergovernmentalism delineates, rather they are sector specific and address the positions of the participating groups and the CRNM.

The Final Phase of Negotiations

The final phase of negotiations consisted of fourteen rounds of negotiations between the CRNM and the EC. Girvan (2012) suggests that during the process of negotiations the EC increased its leverage against CARIFORUM members. He argues that in 2001 the EC created its "Everything But Arms" initiative, which provides free market access to the European Union for all least developed countries (LDCs) as categorized by the WTO, the effect of which "was to exert pressure on non-LDC ACP countries to conclude EPAs, so as not to be disadvantaged vis-à-vis LDCs. The pressure was substantially increased when it became apparent that the EC had maneuvered the situation so that these countries would face considerably higher tariffs on their exports to Europe from January 1, 2008, if they failed to conclude EPAs before the official deadline" (Girvan 2012, 257).

These points support LI's assertions that the party with the more influential position would use leverage in negotiating. In this case, the EC used a deadline and an indirect "threat" of higher tariffs to pressure CARIFORUM negotiators to speed up negotiations and sign the EPA. Girvan also argues that the EC put further pressure on CARIFORUM members by ruling that "the only alternative to EPAs for non-LDCs would be to access the European market under the Generalized System of Preferences (GSP) scheme or Most Favoured Nation (MFN) provisions. . . . The higher tariff payable under GSP/MFN would result in major trade disruption for ACP non-LDCs, a group that includes 14 of the 15 CARIFORUM countries" (Girvan 2012, 258). He observes that "this threat of trade disruption proved to be a potent weapon in the hands of European negotiators in the final stages of the EPA negotiations" (258).

During the negotiations for financial services, Jessop (2008) noted that the European Union attempted to have CARICOM "adopt OECD principles or developed country rules on the regulation and supervision of the financial services' sector relating to taxation, money laundering, and possible tax evasion" (1). He explained that early EU requirements included information exchange, taken as the European Union "attempting to obtain via a back door agreement on issues that would affect the competitiveness of the region's onshore and offshore financial services industry and impose a form of extra-territorial financial services supervision" (1). However, the non-disclosure stipulation in Article 104 of the EPA guarantees continued and complete banking privacy in CARICOM countries. This stipulation was of high importance for CARICOM member states who offer so-called tax havens that impose limited to no tax liabilities. For example, Dominica imposes no income, corporate or capital gains tax on income earned abroad. There are no nationality requirements to form offshore corporations, and its privacy laws protect the owners and managements of said offshore companies. Nevis provides privacy for offshore accounts that are likewise not required to pay capital gains taxes or estate taxes. Other CARICOM countries, including Anguilla, Antigua, Belize and Barbados, also provide tax exemptions, limited tax liabilities and strict privacy laws for offshore banking. This uncompromising stance of the individual CARICOM countries therefore reflects core ideas of LI, where the states would be willing to leave the bargaining table for issues that cannot be conceded. In this case, offshore banking is of higher financial importance than trade in agricultural products for these countries.[19]

During the negotiations, CARICOM member countries argued for special provisions in the EPA to take account of their small size, lack of development, and other economic and social challenges. Additionally, CARIFORUM negotiated with the EC for special treatment for some CARIFORUM members. These were entreated in Article 17, titled "Modification of Tariff Commitments". These were viewed by the CRNM as huge wins for CARICOM states given the disadvantages in size and power between the two groups. The theory of LI predicts the European Union's willingness to concede issues when they were not of high importance to its members and of higher importance for CARICOM states.

The negotiating process of the third and fourth phases moreover suggests that the CRNM did not fully address the positions of civil society and the private sector in CARICOM countries.[20] For example, in January 2008, Guyana's president asserted that the Caribbean lost in the EPA negotiations. His position, as stated in a Guyanese newspaper, is that the EPA "would cause significant shock to the regional economies since many were already running on 'bare-bone' budgets and they would incur bigger fiscal deficits and have to borrow more money, while their interest rates would go up" (*Stabroek News* 2008). He argued that "the European Union would say that they had given the region enough time to adjust, but regardless of the time-frame for adjustment, the idea of reciprocity between developed and developing states would place the region at a disadvantage" (*Stabroek News* 2008). He contended that the EPA "was a situation the region had been forced into even though the EU would claim otherwise" (*Stabroek News* 2008). Notably, during the final phase of negotiations, CARICOM heads of state could not agree on the contents and structure of the EPA. The CARICOM governments were still at loggerheads and could not agree on the final agreement. CARIFORUM countries, such as Jamaica, feared that if the agreement was not signed to replace the Cotonou Agreement, which expired 31 December 2007, then the preferences and provisions would be withdrawn by the European Unio, and the EU–CARICOM commercial relationship would revert to the Generalized System of Preferences scheme (CARICOM Heads of Government 2008). Other countries, such as Guyana, wanted to renegotiate the EPA for more preferential provisions. Critics noted that CARIFORUM countries such as Barbados and St Lucia revealed some levels of "discomfort" with the EPA (CARICOM Heads of Government 2008). Moreover,

Guyana's president Jagdeo claimed that the EPA was not a "negotiated victory" like CARICOM claims, rather "it was a capitulation to EU pressure, [and] . . . the region had little choice" (*Searchlight* 2008).

Contrary to these reservations, CARICOM argues that the EPA is "littered with examples of the asymmetrical commitments . . . where the EU's commitments are higher than those of the Caribbean" (Lodge 2008, 4). These provisions included special and differential treatment for CARICOM countries and "a modulated tariff liberalization schedule that would facilitate the reform of national tax regimes while safeguarding trade-generated fiscal revenue and domestic production" (Lodge 2008, 4). To this end, CARICOM argues that the EPA represents a compromise whereby

> nearly one in ten tariff lines was excluded from liberalisation altogether, including more than half of the tariff headings dealing with agriculture and fisheries. Nearly every significant revenue source was either placed on an exclusion list or given a phased reduction period of 15 years or longer, allowing for Caribbean states to carry out their own internally agreed tax reforms in a bid to replace potential revenue loss from the EPA. (Silva 2008, 10)

Notably, the EPA includes a provision for its review after five years and a "phase" clause which details and specifies goods from the EU market that would retain quotas and tariffs when entering the CARICOM market and would eventually be phased out over a defined period of time. The EPA also includes a list of goods requiring special protection delineated in the annex, including fisheries, which was a demand of CARICOM countries.

The aforementioned provisions give weight to LI's prediction that countries have the choice of opting in and out of certain provisions and clauses of agreements.[21] Essentially, although "the EPA appears to include a single regional liberalization schedule for CARIFORUM . . . the reality is that the schedule comprises 15 country-specific schedules" (Meyn 2008, 1). These schedules define when, and to what extent (if at all), individual CARICOM members incorporate EPA legislation in national legislation. For example, the products for commerce ranged from four hundred tariff line exceptions for Dominica to thirty-six hundred for the Bahamas (Meyn 2008). CARIFORUM liberalization commitments vary among member states: Dominica committed to liberalizing 23 per cent of items highlighted in the EPA, Antigua and Barbuda to 88 per cent, the Bahamas to more than 90 per cent, while Jamaica committed to liberalizing 11 per cent of products that face a tariff of 20 per cent (Meyn 2008).

With pressure from the European Union, the CARICOM Heads of Government reluctantly signed the EPA. Thirteen of the fifteen CARIFORUM member states signed the EPA in Barbados on 15 October 2008. Haiti and Guyana were the only exceptions. Five days after the thirteen CARICOM countries signed in Barbados, Guyana signed the EPA in Brussels, and it was agreed that the EPA would be revised every five years following the demands of CARICOM countries including Guyana. The preceding discussion revealed that during the final phase of the EPA, the member countries of CARICOM were not in unison on the provisions of the EPA. The outlined actions of Guyana also underscore key principles of the theory of LI, where member states are the actors at the international level and only sign agreements beneficial to themselves.

Contents of the Economic Partnership Agreement

The EPA is structured in six parts: Trade Partnership for Sustainable Development (Articles 1–8); Trade and Trade-Related Matters (Articles 9–201); Dispute Avoidance and Settlement (Articles 202–23); General Exceptions (Articles 224–26); Institutional Provisions (Articles 227–32); and General and Final Provisions (Articles 233–50).[22] Added to these are protocols on rules of origin, mutual administrative assistance in customs matters and cultural cooperation. Trade in goods and trade-related matters account for a considerable part of the EPA. The EPA offers market access to CARICOM goods entering the European Union. It "removes quota and tariff limitations on 98 percent of all goods from CARIFORUM countries into the EU. This provides duty-free, quota-free access for agricultural products such as beef, dairy, cereals, fruits and vegetables that previously incurred tariffs" (Thorburn et al. 2010, 6). The European Union suggests that the EPA "provides asymmetric and progressive opening of trade in goods: Asymmetric because CARIFORUM goods enter the EU duty and quota free while CARIFORUM maintains customs duties on sensitive products; Progressive because CARIFORUM tariff reduction is spread over a twenty-five-year transition period with the first reductions in 2011" (European Commission 2008, 1).

The CARICOM agricultural products given preferential access to the EC members markets under the Cotonou Agreement are addressed in the EPA. Article 42 provides conditions for CARICOM states that were similar to the previous preferential agreements. It commits the European Union to "endeavour to maintain significant preferential access within the multilateral trading system for these products originating in the CARIFORUM States for as long as is feasible and to ensure that any unavoidable reduction in preference is phased in over as long a period as possible" (*Official Journal of the European Union* 2008, 16). It essentially offers CARICOM states "preferential" access to the EC markets without any provisions for vice-versa reciprocation. Moreover, Article 16 of the EPA specifically delineates that "for a period of 10 years after the signature of this Agreement, the CARIFORUM States may continue to apply any such customs duties . . . other than those listed in Annex III to any imported product originating in the EC Party" (p. 8). This grace period affords CARICOM members a time frame to prepare for a total liberalization of their market.

Article 17 furthermore allows specific CARICOM countries to modify the level of customs duties on EU originating products, so long as these modifications comply with WTO requirements.[23] Additionally, CARICOM countries can "decide simultaneously to adjust the customs' duty commitments ... as appropriate" (p. 8). Article 23 offers CARICOM members protective measures against EU-subsidized products. It refers to anti-dumping policies and gives CARICOM states the right to take "countervailing measures in accordance with the relevant WTO agreements" to protect themselves against EU dumping (p. 10).

The services section of the EPA grants the financial institutions of both the European Union and CARIFORUM countries the same rights as local companies. These include the right to establish financial services, such as insurance, banking and money broking in each other's markets. Article 106, for example, grants financial service suppliers the right to "provide any new financial service of a type similar to those services that the

EC Party and the Signatory CARIFORUM States permit their own financial service suppliers to provide under their domestic law in like circumstances" (pp. 36–37). The schedule and annexes of the EPA also grant companies and other providers of EU and CARIFORUM member countries the "same treatment" respectively as the local competitors.

During the process of negotiations between the EC and CARIFORUM, the EC campaigned for a small section on tourism in the EPA.[24] CARIFORUM, on the other hand, wanted a much lengthier text. The chapter in the EPA on tourism covers eight articles. These include provisions for the prevention of anticompetitive practices, the protection of small- and medium-sized enterprises, mutual recognition, environmental and quality standards, development cooperation and technical assistance, and increasing the impact of tourism on sustainable development. In addition, CARIFORUM negotiated a long list of schedules which specify the area of its tourism sector that each CARIFORUM member state opens and when said state opens the area. The EPA also details strict anticompetitive practices regarding tourism, identifies development needs in the tourism industry of the CARIFORUM member countries and makes provisions for skills development of CARIFORUM members. It also specifies limitations for European agents operating and managing hotels, restaurants, travel agencies and tours.

Article 203 of the EPA defines the scope of the Dispute Avoidance and Settlement provisions as covering "any dispute concerning the interpretation and application of" the EPA (*Official Journal of the European Union* 2008, 67). The first provision is for consultations between the affected parties of the two unions. Article 205 of the EPA then offers a mediation clause where if "consultations fail to produce a mutually agreed solution, the Parties may, by agreement, seek recourse to a mediator" (p. 67). The mediators, whose opinions are non-binding, are chosen from countries that are not members of either union. If these opinions are not heeded, the matter then goes into an arbitrary procedure; the arbitrary panel is also comprised of nonmember persons.

Article 213 conjointly details that if there is non-compliance by a CARIFORUM member state to rulings from the arbitrator, then some form of compensation must be reached. Furthermore,

> if no agreement on compensation is reached within 30 days (of the arbitration ruling) then the complaining Party shall be entitled, upon notification to the other Party, to adopt appropriate measures. . . . In addition, where the EC Party has obtained the right to adopt such measures, it shall select measures which are specifically aimed at bringing into compliance the CARIFORUM State or States whose measures were found to be in breach of this Agreement. (p. 69)

Article 213 delineates that in such a situation "the other CARIFORUM States shall facilitate the adoption of measures to comply with the arbitration panel ruling by the CARIFORUM State or States found to be in breach" (p. 69). This has a direct effect on other countries that were parties to the dispute. It means that the actions of one CARIFORUM country and the ruling against one CARIFORUM country is further reflected on the other CARIFORUM countries that were not party to the dispute.

The EPA creates institutions to assist and oversee the process of implementation in the signatory member states; these include the Joint CARIFORUM–EC Council and the

CARIFORUM–EC Trade and Development Committee. Article 39 of the EPA requires that the signatory member states "commit themselves to adopting and implementing policies and institutional reforms to enable and facilitate the achievement of . . . (its) objectives" (p. 16). Under Article 227, the EPA grants the Joint CARIFORUM–EC Council the responsibility to supervise the implementation of the EPA and the mandate to "monitor the fulfilment of its objectives, . . . examine any major issue arising within the framework of this Agreement, as well as any other bilateral, multilateral or international question of common interest and affecting trade between the Parties" (p. 73). It possesses the power under Article 229 to take decisions in respect of all matters covered by the agreement; moreover, it specifies that those decisions shall be binding on both signatory parties, who are required to take all the measures necessary to implement all the EPA provisions.

The CARIFORUM–EC Trade and Development Committee supervises the implementation of the provisions of the EPA. It evaluates the results of the agreement, resolving disputes regarding the interpretation or application of the agreement, "to discuss and undertake actions that may facilitate trade, investment and business opportunities between the Parties" (p. 74). It also has the power to set up and oversee special committees and bodies relating to the EPA, in addition to making decisions and recommendations on issues relating to cases in the EPA. The national goals are set for implementing the EPA in phases, and the regional institutions oversee these goals.

Although the EPA is discussed here as being imposed on the CARICOM member countries, specific provisions in the EPA suggest that CARICOM successfully bargained for sustainable outcomes in certain areas. This underscores the ideas of the theory of LI, which supposes that both parties do achieve gains from bargaining, and, even if the general outcome is more favourable for one, there are incentives provided and concessions made to enable both parties to sign the agreement.

Discussion and Conclusion

LI is built on issues related to the competencies of the central government, member states and supranational institutions. Moravcsik (1998) argues that the "institutional structure of . . . (a union) is acceptable to national governments only insofar as it strengthens, rather than weakens, their control over domestic affairs, permitting them to attain goals otherwise unachievable" (487). Following Putnam's (1988) understanding that both international and domestic politics are entangled, the onus on LI is then to discuss where competencies are given up by governments. Under the theory of LI, unions like the European Union and CARICOM are mere platforms for states to carry out interstate bargaining efficiently. The state is the primary actor at the national and international level and would be "gatekeeper" between these levels.

International agreements are ratified by and reflect the preferences of the member states. Therefore, along the lines of rationalist state behaviour, member states first identify and define their stances on specific agendas and then negotiate and bargain along these lines or empower institutions to do so. Therefore, according to LI, outcomes of negotiations by the European Union and CARICOM, despite the central role of the CRNM, ought to reflect the will of the member states.

The application of the theory of LI to CARICOM through analysing the EPA reinforced various insights of the theory, notably that bargained agreements possess concessions and wins for both parties even in cases where there are variations in the power dynamics of the parties involved; additionally, state actions are first and foremost self-serving. This can be observed with the strict banking privacy laws negotiated in the EPA to appease the few CARICOM countries with offshore banking economies and the "phasing in" of concessions in the EPA for specific commodities and for specific member states.

At the same time, the application also revealed a contradiction of the theory of LI pertaining to the role and function of institutions in bargaining scenarios. Notably, according to LI, national governments create institutions and enter agreements to substantiate their power. These institutions are designated as extra arms of the states, which define their role and competencies. It should therefore follow that the CRNM would be an institution acting in the interest of and under the scrutiny of CARICOM members. The phases of negotiations of the EPA, however, revealed that the CRNM had one of the most important roles in the EPA process. Instead of functioning under the management of the states, the CRNM functioned independently of them. The states did not possess the expertise and knowledge of the process, and the CRNM, therefore, enjoyed little to no supervision and accountability for its actions. Moreover, the outcome of the EPA saw the creation of additional institutions, further extending the competencies of the existing institutions.

In choosing mediators and arbitrators from external member countries to address disputes, the member states that sign the EPA effectively relinquish some form of sovereignty to rule over decisions affecting commercial practices. This contradicts the theory of LI, which advances that member states are supposed to retain all sovereignty in their actions, and instead reflects institutional rule over member states. In theory, CARIFORUM member states should act and sign international agreements that reflect the character of intergovernmentalism. One of these characters is that their actions have supremacy and reflect their will. However, when an arbitrary panel consisting of other member states can make decisions that directly affect a country without its direct or indirect participation in any part of the dispute process, this directly contradicts the theory of intergovernmentalism. This could be said to reflect the presence of a soft form of supranationalism in CARICOM, where CARICOM institutions act somewhat independently of the member states due to the complexity of their mandates and the technical inability of the states to intervene. The examination also revealed that CARICOM members were dissatisfied with some aspects of the EPA, often voicing their disparagement, while CARICOM defended the EPA. Essentially, instead of being an extended arm of the states, the CRNM, for example, could be observed as possibly working "to enhance [its] own autonomy and influence" (Stone Sweet and Sandholtz 1997, 314), "thereby uncomfortably constraining governments in unexpected ways" (Moravcsik and Schimmelfennig 2009, 75). The actions of the CRNM and the outcome of the EPA, therefore, underscore the likelihood that institutional arrangements in CARICOM can expand outside of the expected range that their national governments foresaw in creating them, extending their competencies and creating soft forms of supranationalism in CARICOM.

The investigation additionally revealed that although LI was able to accurately predict the process of treaty formation, it is necessary to examine the aftermath of the treaty/agreements, including the impacts and unanticipated consequences of the process of negotiations and bargains. That is to say, it might be acceptable that governments enter grand bargains rationally, but what about the unanticipated or undesired consequences of these bargains? An additional examination of the outcomes of the bargaining process in CARICOM, especially the role, functions and competencies of institutions during and after agreements, would offer more information about CARICOM.

The preceding analysis revealed that some CARICOM Heads of Government have lamented that the EPA was being forced on them, and they were left with few options but to bargain for an EPA that would best address their needs. CARICOM's decision to enter negotiations for the EPA, therefore, can be viewed as a response to external forces and pressure. Consequently, it would be interesting to further examine the power structure and relations within CARICOM, that is to say, to see if there is a pattern in how CARICOM reacts and interacts to external situations and unions. Is there a pattern of proactive deliberation?

This study also disclosed that additional research is necessary for understanding the formation of national preferences and local government participation in "grand bargaining" situations. For example, during the round of local and national consultations in CARIFORUM, it became clear that CARICOM initiated civil society participation. The lack of mobilization and input of a regional civil society in regional matters, especially in forming national preferences, was not addressed and is important for further understanding the general process of regional integration in CARICOM. This is especially relevant since the core of the theory of LI is that nation states are the primary actors at the international level, which is based on the idea that national preferences define the scope of nation state preferences. Thus, delineating the formation of national preferences is an imperative factor to address in analysing bargaining processes. Additionally, the theory of LI assumes that national preferences are formed by domestic actors. It is therefore necessary to scrutinize the lack of engagement in regional politics at the domestic level. This is especially important since analysis revealed that such an engagement explicitly affects the overall process and outcome of bargaining. Essentially, identifying and examining the interplay of social systems in CARICOM would aid in understanding issues such as the formation of national preferences; the involvement of, or in the case of CARICOM, lack of, a regional civil society; and the institutional characteristic of CARICOM in bargaining situations.

Postscript

More than ten years after the signing of the CARIFORUM-EC EPA, exports from CARICOM to the European Union have significantly decreased.[25] In 2008, CARICOM–EU exports totalled €6,026; this decreased to under €4,500 in 2009, 2010 and 2013; to under €5,000 in 2011, 2012, 2014 and 2015; and to €3,580 in 2016 (all monetary figures are values in million). CARICOM imports from the EU, on the other hand, steadily increased, from €4,400 in 2009 to €7,410 in 2015.[26] At the third meeting of the EU–CARIFORUM Joint EPA Council Ministers, the EC's commissioner for trade, Cecilia Malmström, noted that "we must also admit that we have not met the objectives we set for this deal in 2008. The truth is that we have not seen the big increases in trade between our regions that we hoped for. In some cases, trade is even lower now than it was five years ago. And we must acknowledge this fact" (2015).[27] She pointed out that the financial crisis of 2007–08 had a negative impact on CARICOM economies, hampering their ability to use trade as a tool for development or simply to gain effective access to the EU market the EPA provided for on paper.[28] In addition to ratification delays, there were delays in implementing development projects.[29] In June 2017 the EC provided an update on its website on the CARIFORUM-EC EPA. It noted that both regions need to "continue to: work on the further implementation of the various aspects of the EPA; agree on a joint system for monitoring the EPA; [and] negotiate an agreement to protect geographical indications (GIs), valuable regional product names" (European Commission 2018, 3). The fourth EU–CARIFORUM Joint EPA Council Ministers meeting took place in Brussels in autumn 2017 and included a review of the operation of the EPA and implementation of goals set at the third EU–CARIFORUM Joint EPA Meeting, which took place in 2015 in Guyana.

Notes

1. The Dominican Republic was included in the EPA process by the European Union, and along with the CARICOM, makes up CARIFORUM.

2. CARICOM includes fifteen members: Antigua and Barbuda, Bahamas, Barbados, Belize, Dominica, Grenada, Guyana, Haiti, Jamaica, Montserrat, St Kitts and Nevis, St Lucia, St Vincent and the Grenadines, Suriname, and Trinidad and Tobago. Associate members are Anguilla, Bermuda, British Virgin Islands, Cayman Islands, and Turks and Caicos Islands.

3. See, for example, Slaughter and Alvarez (2000) and Moravcsik and Schimmelfennig (2009).

4. The theory of neofunctionalism proposes that political elite and institutions play decisive roles in interstate bargaining among unions, sometimes even acting independently of the state, resulting in them deciding on the preferences, speed and depth of negotiations between unions, even creating new institutions and defining the competencies of these institutions. It is important to note that unlike neofunctionalism, the theory of LI assumes that institutions are an extended arm of the state, act under the auspices of the states, and their competencies are granted by the state and can be taken away at any given time by the state. For more information on the theory of neofunctionalism and its application to CARICOM and the EPA, please see Onnis (2015). For an extensive discussion on the role of institutions in the theory of LI, please see Moravcsik (1998).

5. For absolute figures, please visit the European Commission's website detailing the partnership at http://ec.europa.eu/development/body/cotonou/overview_en.htm.

6. For more information on the Lomé Conventions and Cotonou Partnership, please visit the European Commission's website on development at http://ec.europa.eu/development/body/cotonou/overview_en.htm.

7. Unlike South–South agreements, according to the WTO, North–North free trade agreements must adhere to Article XXIV for goods and Article 5 under the General Agreement on Trade in Services (GATS). These delineate strict limitations where North–North and North–South trade agreements are limited to a non-reciprocal Generalized System of Preferences under the Enabling Clause or a reciprocal free trade agreement either

partially under Article XXIV, or under Article XXIV and Article 5 of the GATS. The Cotonou Agreement was challenged and upheld by the WTO as being in contradiction to these regulations.

8. For an extensive overview of the WTO dispute, labelled "banana row", please visit the WTO website at https://www.wto.org/english/tratop_e/dispu_e/cases_e/ds27_e.htm.

9. Additional concerns were raised regarding the inclusion of the Dominican Republic in the CARICOM EPA, creating the CARIFORUM. For more information, please read Girvan (2008).

10. For more information on CARICOM and Caribbean population statistics, please see the CARICOM Regional Statistics website at http://caricomstats.org/, last visited November 2017.

11. For more information on the competencies of the European Commission, please visit the European Commission's website at http://ec.europa.eu/citizens-initiative/public/competences/faq, last visited 8 February 2017.

12. The CRNM was renamed the Office of Trade Negotiations and incorporated in the CARICOM Secretariat.

13. For an exhaustive list of the college of negotiators, please visit the CRNM website at http://www.crnm.org, last visited June 2015.

14. The surveys revealed that responses were received from twenty national and sector-specific associations located in eight of the fifteen CARICOM target countries. The associations represented more than 31,512 individual enterprises, including 3,850 exporters, a large increase from 200 associations from nine countries and 4,700 individual enterprises in the prior year.

15. Although preference formation in the CARICOM member states is approached from a CARICOM perspective and not individually, there are cases where some individual member states are more active in the process than others, especially when they have particularly high interests in the matter. For example, the states whose livelihoods were dependent on offshore banking were more active in those deliberations. Additionally, the theory of LI predicts that those states with little to gain were more likely to make concessions on those issues to strengthen their bargaining power and capacity on issues that were of higher importance. For more information, see Moravcsik (1998, 38).

16. Due to the asymmetrical nature of EU–CARICOM commerce, CARICOM member states are more dependent on the EU–CARICOM trade relationship. Essentially, CARICOM countries have been historically reliant on the United Kingdom and later the European Economic Community/European Union for development and trade-related aid. For an extensive overview of the history and dynamics of the EU–CARICOM commercial relationship, please see chapter 2 of Onnis (2015).

17. For more information on the establishment of a CARICOM regional civil society, please see Onnis (2014).

18. For a general overview and analysis of the national and regional civil society in CARICOM, see Levi, Finizio and Vallinoto (2014).

19. For more information on offshore banking and the agricultural economies of CARICOM countries, please see Eldridge (2012) and Davies (2014).

20. The then head of government of Guyana made numerous speeches where he stated that the EPA was "forced" on CARICOM and not in the best interest of the member countries of CARICOM.

21. Notably, Guyana agreed to sign only a part of the agreement, and Haiti decided to opt out of the agreement altogether.

22. For an extensive review of the EPA, please refer to Onnis (2015).

23. Specifically, Antigua and Barbuda, Belize, the Commonwealth of Dominica, Grenada, the Republic of Guyana, the Republic of Haiti, St Kitts and Nevis, St Lucia, and St Vincent and the Grenadines.

24. Jessop recounts that "the first detailed textual draft was produced by the Caribbean Hotel Association, a private sector body. After a number of adjustments by trade negotiators for technical, legal and other reasons, the final text agreed contained much of the language originally proposed. This was despite strenuous resistance from the European Commission who for months argued for a minimal text on tourism" (2008).

25. All statistics are taken from the EU trade statistics database (European Commission 2006).

26. In 2008 imports were €5,747, and in 2016 they were €6,955.

27. The third EU–CARIFORUM Joint EPA Meeting was held in Georgetown, Guyana, in July 2015. More information can be found at http://caricom.org/media-center/ communications/speeches/the-way-ahead-for-the-eu-cariforum-economic-partnership -agreement.

28. For more information, please see Lawson (2009).

29. A total of 100 million euros was pledged at the meeting for the next five years for CARICOM development projects.

References

Burley, Anne-Marie. 1992. "Law among Liberal States: Liberal Internationalism and the Act of State Doctrine". *Columbia Law Review* 92 (December): 1907–96.

Callender, Lisa. 2006. "CRNM Private Sector Survey: Summary of Responses". Caribbean Regional Negotiating Machinery.

CARICOM. 2006. "Bernal: RNM Welcomes Interchange with Civil Society", 27 March. https://caricom.org/media-center/communications/press-releases/bernal-rnm-welcomes -interchange-with-civil-society.

CARICOM Heads of Government. 2008. *Fourteenth Special Meeting of the Conference of Heads of Government of the Caribbean Community*. Meeting on signing the Economic Partnership Agreement. Sherbourne Conference Centre, Bridgetown, Barbados, 10 September.

CPDC (Caribbean Policy Development Centre). 2011. "National Consultations: CARICOM Civil Society Participation and Engagement in Regional Integration Project". CPDC Draft Report.

CRNM (Caribbean Regional Negotiating Machinery). 2006. "CRNM Launches New Trade Education Initiative Bridgetown, Barbados", 2 March.

Davies, Barry, ed. 2014. *CARICOM at 40: Investing in the Future*. Georgetown, Guyana: CARICOM Secretariat.

Eldridge, Paul W. 2012. "The FATCA Challenge Facing Caribbean Banks". PricewaterhouseCoopers, Bermuda. https://www.pwc.com/jm/en/fatca/pdf /thefatcachallengefacingcaribbeanbanksv8.1.pdf.

European Commission, Directorate General for Trade. 2006. "European Union, Trade in Goods with ACP-Caribbean Countries". http://trade.ec.europa.eu/doclib/docs/2006 /september/tradoc_113476.pdf.

———. 2008. "CARIFORUM-EC EPA: Trade in Goods". http://eeas.europa.eu/archives /delegations/barbados/documents/eu_barbados/epa_trade_in_goods_en.pdf.

———. 2018. "Overview of Economic Partnership Agreements". http://trade.ec.europa.eu /doclib/docs/2009/september/tradoc_144912.pdf.

Girvan, Norman. 2012. "Caribbean Integration and Global Europe: Implications of the EPA for the CSME". In *Caribbean Integration: From Crisis to Transformation and Repositioning*, edited by Myrtle Chuck-A-Sang and Kenneth O. Hall. Guyana: Trafford Publishing.

International Development Committee, House of Commons. 2005. *Fair Trade? The European Union's Trade Agreements with African, Caribbean and Pacific Countries*. Sixth Report of Session 2004–05. London: The Stationary Office Limited.

Jessop, David. 2008. "Understanding the EPA: Tourism". *Stabroek News*, 6 April. https://www
.stabroeknews.com/2008/sunday/04/06/understanding-the-epa-tourism/.

Lawson, Tony. 2009. "The Current Economic Crisis: Its Nature and the Course of Academic
Economics". *Cambridge Journal of Economics* 33 (4): 759–77.

Levi, Lucio, Giovanni Finizio, and Nicola Vallinoto, eds. 2014. *The Democratization of
International Institutions: First International Democracy Report*. International Democracy
Watch at the Centre for Studies on Federalism. London: Routledge.

Lodge, Junior. 2008. "CARIFORUM EPA Negotiations: An Initial Reflection". *Trade
Negotiations Insights* 7 (1): 6–8.

Malmström, Cecilia. 2015. "The Way Ahead for the EU-CARIFORUM Economic
Partnership Agreement". Speech, Georgetown, Guyana, 16 July. In the third meeting of the
EU-CARIFORUM Joint EPA Council.

Meyn, Mareike. 2008. "Hearing at the European Parliament on 04 December 2008 on the
Economic Partnership Agreement EU-CARIFORUM". Statement by Mareike Meyn,
Overseas Development Institute, London, 4 December.

Moravcsik, Andrew. 1998. "Integration Theory". In *Encyclopedia of the European Union*, edited
by Desmond Dinan. Boulder: Lynne Rienner.

———. 2010. "Liberal Theories of International Relations: A Primer". Unpublished manuscript,
Princeton University.

Moravcsik, Andrew and Frank Schimmelfennig. 2009. "Liberal Intergovernmentalism". In
European Integration Theory, edited by Antje Wiener and Thomas Diez. Oxford: Oxford
University Press.

Office of Trade Negotiations, CARICOM Secretariat. 2008. "EPA Negotiation Matrices".
CARICOM. https://caricom.org/Document-Library/view-document/epa-negotiations
-matrices.

Official Journal of the European Union. 2008. "Economic Partnership Agreement between
the CARIFORUM States and the European Community and Its Member States". L 289
(October).

Onnis, Tamara. 2014. "The Caribbean Community and Common Market". In *The
Democratization of International Institutions: First International Democracy Report*, edited by
Lucio Levi, Giovanni Finizio and Nicola Vallinoto, 311–20. London: Routledge.

———. 2015. "Theorizing Regional Integration in the Caribbean: Neofunctionalism and the
Caribbean Community (CARICOM)". Doctoral dissertation, Bielefeld University.

Putnam, Robert. 1988. "Diplomacy and Domestic Politics: The Logic of Two-level Games".
International Organization 42 (3): 427–60.

Searchlight. 2008. "Caribbean Leaders at Loggerheads", 1 February https://searchlight.vc
/searchlight/editorial/2008/02/01/caribbean-leaders-at-loggerheads/.

Silva, Sacha. 2008. "Lessons Learned: The Caribbean EPA Market Access Offer". *Trade
Negotiations Insights* 7, no. 1: 2.

Slaughter, Anne-Marie and Jose E. Alvarez. 2000. "A Liberal Theory of International Law".
Proceedings of the Annual Meeting (American Society of International Law) 94 (April):
240–53.

Stabroek News. 2008. "The Caribbean Lost in the Negotiations with Europe – Jagdeo",
26 January. http://www.stabroeknews.com/2008/archives/01/06/the-caribbean-lost-in-the
-negotiations-with-europe-jagdeo/.

Stone Sweet, Alec and Wayne Sandholtz. 1997. "European Integration and Supranational
Governance". *Journal of European Public Policy* 4 (3): 297–31.

Thorburn, Diana, John Rapley, Damien King, and Collette Campbell. 2010. "The Economic
Partnership Agreement (EPA): Towards a New Era for Caribbean Trade Caribbean". The
Centre for International Governance Innovation, Caribbean Paper No. 10.

Part II

Completing the Internal Market: The Limits
of Economic Integration

Chapter 5

A Study of Economic Cycles in the CARICOM Free Trade Area

Situation, Challenges and Lessons

ALAIN MAURIN AND ROLAND CRAIGWELL

Discussing Caribbean economic integration today is certainly a much more pressing necessity than before. The countries of the region, in particular the members and associated members of the Caribbean Community (CARICOM), are experiencing economic and social crises not of their own internal making, nor do these arise from the annual episodes of natural climatic catastrophes. As with the majority of countries and regions around the world, the Caribbean must deal with the evils resulting from the coronavirus pandemic.

In recent times, few countries have not at one time or another been faced with the challenges of reconstruction following devastating shocks that have done irreparable damage to the economy. Often, the entire primary sector, the tourism industry and other sectors have taken a bad beating. In addition, social conflicts have brought entire sectors to their knees and the economy to a standstill. Even in instances when such crises have shut down economies for extended periods, countries have usually revived within a year or so, restarting their productive and commercial systems gradually and, over varying time spans, were able to regain their growth path.

By its enormity and widespread economic impact, the coronavirus crisis has positioned itself as a major event in history, of not just the Caribbean, but of humanity. In the post-war, Covid-19 world that is currently being built, Caribbean countries are expected to move into tomorrow's world with major changes in organization, production and exchange structures, and trade channels, and with new technologies and working and training methods, which will all be radically different from what had prevailed up to now.

These changes underscore the importance of economic integration processes in the geographical area concerned. It will not escape observation that even though the European Union is strong with countries at the top of the world economic hierarchy, it had to intervene to avoid economic and social collapse. Paradoxically, the countries and populations even more in need of support have largely distinguished themselves by the weakness of responses of their regional economic communities. This is particularly true in the case of the African continent, which is home to many regional economic communities (Economic Community of West African States, East African Community, and Development Community of Southern Africa, among others). But here our interest is not about questioning the beam that is in the eye of certain countries or continents, but the beam that is in the eye of the Caribbean countries. From the foregoing reflections, there is no further need to emphasize that the Caribbean needs to consolidate the implementation of its CARICOM regional integration project. The CARICOM, which is dominated by insularity and vulnerability, more than those in other geographical regions, has little choice but to reinvent itself and to rely first on its own strength to contain the impact of the shocks to come, and to anticipate in particular the new wave of globalization, induced by the profound transformation of world trade that is coming.

Let us recall the commitment of the Caribbean countries to the CARICOM project. For nearly fifty years, they have pinned their hopes on this project to improve their economic circumstances. The four signatories to the Treaty of Chaguaramas on 4 July 1973 – Barbados, Guyana, Jamaica, and Trinidad and Tobago – formalized their desire to promote a process of economic integration through the establishment of a common market and the coordination of economic policies. Originally creating a free trade area, this treaty appeared to be a solution to enable them to overcome the disadvantages posed by the narrowness of their internal markets and their limited natural resources. Through this integration process, the signatory countries aimed at three major objectives: accentuating the coordination and regulation of economic and trade relations between the members to promote accelerated and balanced development; strengthening the degree of economic integration of countries; and establishing common cooperation mechanisms for relations with third countries. In the context of building post-Covid-19 economies, reducing the strategic dependence of the Caribbean countries on the rest of the world requires a new sustainable model: economic, social and ecological. Updating the CARICOM project is now squarely on the table, with the crucial objective of increasing intra-Caribbean trade to give new impetus.

In the Caribbean, CARICOM's performance is weak, compared to economic and monetary unions in other parts of the world, including the European Union, where value is assessed according to the benefits and disadvantages of the supranational framework established. Given their complexity, the issue of assessing regional economic unions has given rise to many debates among policymakers, economists and the general public about the expected regional economic integration gains, the role of the actors in economic policy initiatives, and the arguments and decisions regarding the continuation of the integration process.

This chapter attempts to empirically verify the effects of the establishment of CARICOM on member economies by examining the problem of convergence of economic trends. Of note, while many studies on the convergence of levels of gross domestic product (GDP) per capita do exist in the literature, the evaluation of the impact of economic integration and trade liberalization calls for an analysis and verification of synchronization of cycles among partner countries. This is important since the move from one stage of economic integration to another depends heavily on the synchronization of business cycles of the countries involved. This chapter seeks to answer the following questions: What are the degrees of synchronization of business cycles in Caribbean economies? What are the determinants of these movements? What roles should institutions play in the economic regulation and coordination of growth policies in the Caribbean? The chapter essentially uses the extended version of the Bry–Boschan procedure to address the main objectives of the study (Bry and Boschan 1971).

The chapter is organized as follows: The first section addresses the challenges of identifying cycles in the Caribbean economies. It concentrates on the need for economic cycle dating and cycle synchronization. The following section dwells on data and methodological approaches. It concentrates on data, methodological approaches to business cycles and growth cycles as well as synchronization of cycles. The third section deals with the characterization of cycles. The next section analyses business cycle synchronization for the Caribbean countries, while the final section offers concluding remarks.

Challenges of Identifying Cycles in Caribbean Economies

The dating of turning points in the cycle is undoubtedly a crucial activity for the study of economic fluctuations. First, it largely determines the content of the information disseminated about the description of the characteristics of business cycles; that is, the distinction between the three types of cycles, frequency of turning points, the duration of up and down swings, the symmetric or asymmetric nature of these phases, their average length and variability, and so on. Second, the dating is also essential to properly address the comparison of profiles of cycles of different countries, especially those aimed at characterizing periods of recession and economic expansion synchronization at the international level. In a purely domestic sense, it is of great importance when classifying economic indicators based on their lagging, coinciding or leading character, compared to the reference cycle. Third, it contributes significantly to the information that must be crafted to inform policymakers in their choices: to anticipate the effects of the imminent arrival of a turning point for better understanding the consequences of situations of recession and expansion and so on.

While for many years the practice of dating was confined within a limited number of actors, since the 1990s the tendency has changed with the resurgence of research and results devoted to dating and documenting economic cycles for a given country and also for a geographic area, such as the European Union. The monopoly of the National Bureau of Economic Research (NBER) has been eroded by the introduction of a number of distinguished organizations, attached to ministries and other public bodies as well as businesses. A number of these entities have invested in the performance of the dating of the cycles. The "Conference Board", founded in 1916 in the United States, publishes information on the cycles of major industrialized countries. The Economic Cycle Research Institute, established in 1996, sells economic analysis and forecasting information as well as publishes its own diagnostics and results on the global economy and the cycles of twenty countries. The Centre for Economic Policy Research was formed in 1983 to establish the chronology of the classic cycle for the eurozone. The Reserve Bank of South Africa determines the turning points of the business cycle in South Africa and has published related studies in its quarterly newsletter since the 1970s.[1]

The painful events of the 2008 crisis highlighted the increased risks of US banks, financial markets and states' debt, and showed how the expertise provided by these different business cycle institutes are needed to better identify and reach decisions. The diagnostic usefulness of these organizations is also related to their role in spreading the feeling of confidence, which is so central to the health of the economy. This means that their announcements are expected by economic agents and influence their behaviour. Concretely, by using the media judiciously to announce the end or the beginning of a recession, these organizations are able to have significant impacts on the financial markets, households, government and the Federal Reserve. In all developed countries, such strong communication on the cycle is effective and reflects the challenges for economic policy.

These considerations are also valid for the nations of the Caribbean. For a single country or an economic community with a supranational entity, such as the European Union or the Association of Southeast Asian Nations, it is clear that the possession of a reference chronology of dates of the beginning and end of recessions is of great importance. Within the Caribbean, this process of official dating of the cycle is not yet effective in most of the countries, just as it is not for the CARICOM area as a whole where there is still a need for coordination of economic policies of member states. It goes without saying that an approach to generalize and formalize pioneer academic research in this area should be welcome.[2]

Issues of Cycle Synchronization

Much of the recent research on business cycles has focused on synchronization among countries. Synchronization generally uses a correlation measure to determine which of the sectoral industries and macroeconomic variables are procyclical or countercyclical with the business cycles. This approach was illustrated by Craigwell and Maurin (2007b) for the case of Barbados. This section discusses the similarities of various cycles among Caribbean countries before comparing the business cycles of these economies with the cyclical profiles of their key international partners.

The Economic and Monetary Union in Europe is undoubtedly the prime example that demonstrates the usefulness of cycle synchronization of different states in the process of regional integration. The lessons provided by this European experience include the difficulties faced by the control system[3] of the euro area, which in large part originate from the cyclical divergence of their member states. Lemoine (2006) observes that inclusion of information on economic cycles should help in the decision-making process. He shows that such information is crucial for regulatory bodies to conduct appropriate monetary and fiscal policies in the Economic and Monetary Union to ensure price stability and sustainable growth, as has been ordered by the treaty establishing the European Community.

It is primarily through the use of monetary policy that the European Central Bank can contribute significantly to the effective control of the economic system of the euro area. As Lemoine (2006, 219) laments, "a priori, this reaction seems simple: the ECB is expected to increase (decrease) the interest rate as GDP rises above (below) its long-term trend thus triggering inflation (disinflation)". In Europe (and the United States), the underlying model that drives this process is the Taylor[4] rule as the European Central Bank (or the Federal Reserve in the United States) determines the level of interest rates.

Fiscal policies also require information on the cycle of the aggregate area in order for governments to effectively optimize economic regulation. Indeed, the elements that define the fiscal stance of each country are more relevant when taking into account the position of each member state in its economic cycle. It is very important to differentiate between the rules of the Stability and Growth Pact in the potential and current economic situation of each country. Lemoine (2006, 22) states that "an underestimation of potential output led to wrongly identifying a period as favourable to carry out a fiscal adjustment at the incorrect time, in case of overvaluation, the coercion might cause slippage of the fiscal deficit and public debt". Reform of the pact in March 2005, described in the presidency conclusions of the European Council on 22 and 23 March 2005, explicitly refers to these notions of potential GDP as favourable (European Council 2005).

It is certain that the historical, geographical or cultural aspects of CARICOM countries are very different from those of the regions of Europe and Southeast Asia. This fact greatly explains the difficulties and the slow process of integration of Caribbean countries. Also, it may seem inappropriate to rely on the elements which have been discussed to highlight our argument about the benefits of cycle analysis in the Caribbean. But to the contrary, these practical illustrations based on the European example can highlight the need for clear steps towards greater success in regional integration.

The idea of creating a Caribbean free trade area became a reality for the first time in 1968 with the Caribbean Free Trade Association. It was followed, in 1973, by the establishment of CARICOM. The next level of integration was the Caribbean Single Market and Economy (CSME). The first phase of the CSME came into force on 1 January 2006, with Barbados, Belize, Guyana, Jamaica, Suriname, and Trinidad and Tobago. The CSME reduced trade barriers in goods, services and several categories of work. In the same year, on 3 July 2006, the CSME was consolidated with the arrival of six new members, namely Antigua and Barbuda, Dominica, Grenada, St Kitts and Nevis, St Lucia, and St Vincent and the Grenadines.

The second phase of the CSME agreed on a two-period timetable (consolidation of the single market and then the single economy) for its status as a unified free trade zone. It should be noted that the single market aspect covers, among others, the following initiatives: the harmonization of fiscal and monetary policies and the regulatory environment; implementation of common policies in the areas of agriculture, energy, transport, small and medium enterprises, sustainable tourism and agro-tourism; and the implementation of a monetary union.

The progress of the CARICOM regional integration project and, more specifically, the objectives discussed earlier highlight the need for a strong literature on economic cycles of the fifteen countries of the zone. Based on the lessons learned from economic theory and empirical applications, the link between economic cycles and monetary policy is apparent. Therefore, the projects of harmonization of fiscal and monetary policies and the implementation of a monetary union call for a greater effectiveness of monetary policy, a condition which would involve knowledge of the dates of the start and ending of recessions in the Caribbean region and the degree of synchronization.

Data and Methodological Approaches

Despite the findings of different authors during the 2000s, it is still disappointing to observe that the databases at high frequencies are still largely unavailable (see, for example, Maurin and Watson, 2002, and Watson, 2010). To corroborate, in the case of real GDP –which remains the key indicator of the system of economic accounts of all nations – there are no quarterly series of long enough spans for the majority of Caribbean countries. In the same vein, Liu and Romeu (2011, 1) state: "The lack of timely reporting of quarterly GDP in some countries presents difficulty in the assessment of current economic conditions. . . . While increasingly uncommon among emerging market economies, many countries do not report quarterly GDP growth at all – a number of these cells are found in the Caribbean – and the availability of timely indicators of economic activity is even more important for policymakers in these economies".

In fact, of the fifteen member countries of CARICOM, only one-third formally have quarterly estimates of GDP and of long enough periods to allow estimation of several complete cycles. Indeed, quarterly data exists for Barbados, Jamaica, and Trinidad and Tobago from 1970 onwards. For the other countries, the time intervals covered by the existing data are too limited to allow attempts at dating the business cycle and reviewing their characteristics.

In the case of Barbados, the quarterly output series is provided by the Central Bank of Barbados and was originally developed by Lewis (1997). It is constructed from estimates of the economic sectors, using employment. The data covers the period from the first quarter (Q1) of 1974 to the fourth quarter (Q4) of 2013, four decades of economic developments, which is more than enough to study the cycles observed in this country.

The data used for Trinidad and Tobago were developed by Watson (2003), covering the period 1971–99, and updated over the period 1999–2014. They were calculated from the original annual series of the Central Statistical Office of Trinidad and Tobago and by applying a standard temporal disaggregation procedure combined with data from the quarterly analysis of Trinidadian growth over the period after 1981.

Finally, the series for Jamaica's GDP, also used by Whyte (2008), is taken from the database of the Bank of Jamaica. Unlike Barbados, and Trinidad and Tobago, it is only available over the period 1985 Q1 to 2013 Q4.

Methodological Approach for Business Cycles

The procedure used to detect the turning points in this chapter is attributable to Bry and Boschan (1971). It selects a number of would-be turning points (peaks and troughs) and then applies a series of operations to eliminate items that do not meet the criteria characterizing the cycles. Several authors have suggested expansions. Monch and Uhlig (2005) identified the phenomenon of asymmetry of cycle phases and proposed an extension of the Bry and Boschan (1971) algorithm with an "amplitude/phase length" criterion. Specifically, they introduced the combined rule amplitude/phase length to ensure that the business cycle phases, which have both short and low amplitudes (flat), are ignored, while those short but pronounced are retained. Additionally, Everts (2006) discussed the adaptation of quarterly and monthly Bry and Boschan algorithms, pointing to the problem of determining the period attributed to quarterly cycle phases of four and five months. He concluded that the procedure was too restrictive and proposed a variant requiring the rewriting of step 2 (determination of cycles in a two-quarter moving average – extreme values replaced).

A review of the literature reveals that there are many software programs which were used to implement the algorithm of Bry and Boschan. The original Bry and Boschan's Fortran program was implemented under the GAUSS platform by Watson (1994), and at present it is carried out in econometric software programs such as RATS, MATLAB or SCILAB. These programs may give different results with the same data. In particular, it is possible to see different chronologies for GDP and industrial production, especially when these series are related to more volatile economies.

Given all of these issues associated with the methodological extension of the algorithm of Bry and Boschan and its computer implementation, a compromise decision is favoured which involves the identification of the business cycle from one set of real GDP data and the use of an expanded version of Everts' (2006) Bry–Boschan algorithm. The chronologies identified for the business cycles are shown in figures 5.1–5.3.

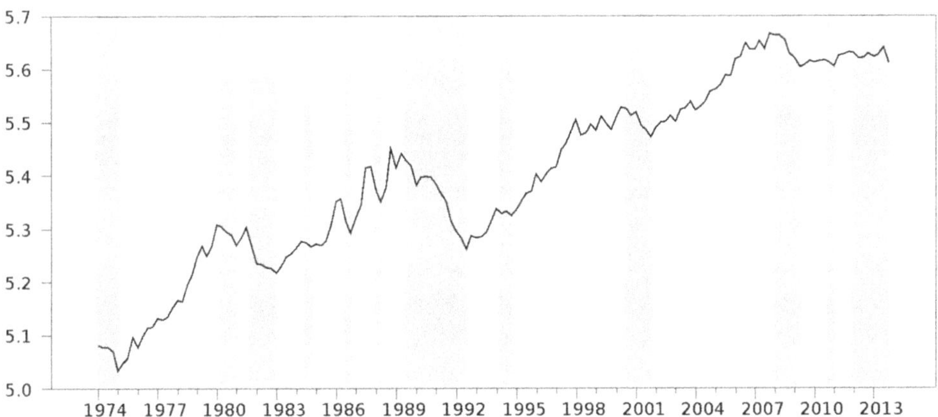

Figure 5.1. Barbados real GDP, log levels, 1974 (Q1) to 2013 (Q4) (classical business cycle contraction phases/recessions indicated by shading)

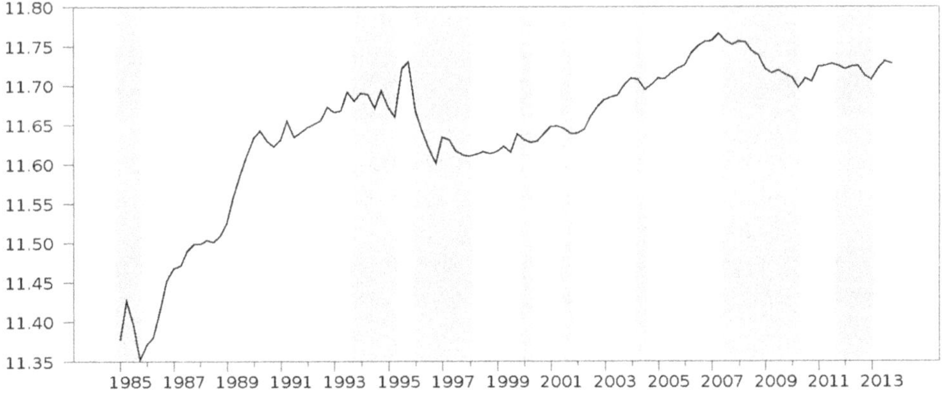

Figure 5.2. Jamaica real GDP, log levels, 1985 (Q1) to 2013 (Q4) (classical business cycle contraction phases/recessions indicated by shading)

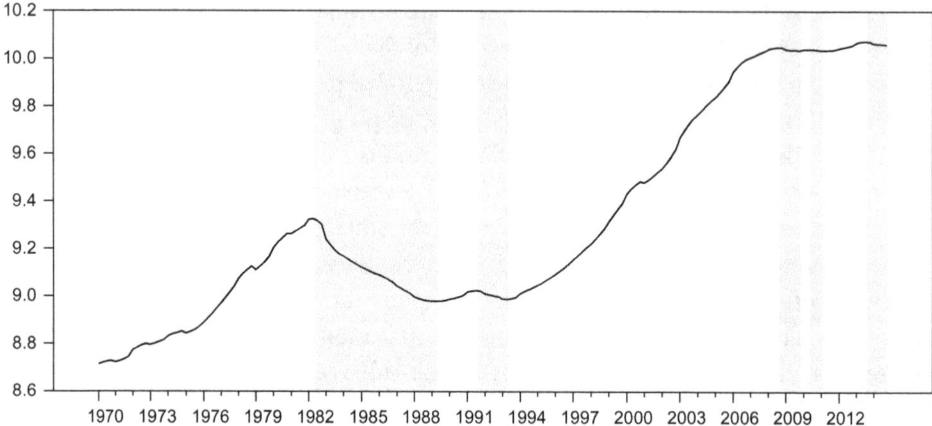

Figure 5.3. Trinidad–Tobago real GDP, log levels, 1970 (Q1) to 2014 (Q4) (classical business cycle contraction phases/recessions indicated by shading)

Methodological Approach for Growth Cycles

The identification of the turning points will, however, occur on the cyclical component of the indicator utilized to represent economic activity. It therefore requires the implementation of trend-cycle decompositions in the preliminary stage. Trend-cycle decomposition techniques grew significantly in the 1990s and 2000s. There was an accumulation of at least a dozen methods of cycle extraction. The most known are the procedures of Hodrick and Prescott (1980), the bandpass filters of Baxter and King (1995) and Christiano and Fitzgerald (1999, 2003), along with the unobserved components model of Harvey (1989). This abundance of trend-cycle decomposition methods is largely due to the increase in comparative performance empirical studies and the search for a robust technique. Bentoglio, Fayolle and Lemoine (2001), Ladiray and Soares (2001), Guay and St-Amant (2005), and Ahamada and Jolivaldt (2010) conducted research on a global scale using these different methods of extracting the trend and found that the various estimates of the cycles were near and revealed the same information about the characteristics of growth and periods of recession.

As a result of its optimal properties, ease of implementation, and use by a majority of economists and many national as well as international organizations, the method of Hodrick and Prescott (1980) is applied here. Profiles obtained from the growth cycles are shown in figures 5.7–5.10. For the sake of comparison, the cyclical components provided by the Baxter and King method have also been included on these charts. Undoubtedly, the two procedures show, for each country, strong similarities in the shape and location of the cycle peaks and troughs.

Methodology of the Measure of Cycle Synchronization
The Concordance Index of Harding and Pagan

The Concordance Index of Harding and Pagan (2002a, 2002b) is one of the most used to examine the co-movements of macroeconomic variables in the economy or match the profiles of cycles of a panel of countries that may or may not belong to the region in question. It is defined as the number of periods in which two variables are in the same phase of the cycle divided by the number of observations of the sample:

$$I_{X,Y} = \frac{1}{n}\left(\sum_{i=1}^{n} S_{X,i} S_{Y,i} + \sum_{i=1}^{n} \left(1 - S_{X,i}\right)\left(1 - S_{Y,i}\right) \right) \tag{5.1}$$

With S_X (S_Y) being a binary variable expressing the phases of the variable X, where X may be positioned in the expansion or contraction phase of the economy. In the case of the analysis of the consistency of the cycles of two countries, the index takes the value 1 (perfectly associated) if the two economies are perfectly synchronized, and if the index is 0 phase (no correlation) they are perfectly out of synchronization. Apart from these two endpoints, the index is still usable if one is able to judge its statistical significance. In this respect, Harding and Pagan (2002b) developed a procedure to test hypotheses, which has become quite popular in the literature. Using some basic calculations, equation 5.1 leads to the following relationship:

$$I_{X,Y} = 1 + 2\rho_S \sigma_{S_X} \sigma_{S_Y} + 2\mu_{S_X}\mu_{S_Y} - \mu_{S_X} - \mu_{S_Y} \tag{5.2}$$

where μ_{S_X} and μ_{S_Y} are the respective averages of the empirical series $S_{X,t}$ and $S_{Y,t}$; σ_{S_X} and σ_{S_Y} are the respective standard deviations of $S_{X,t}$ and $S_{Y,t}$; ρ_S is the empirical correlation coefficient between $S_{X,t}$ and $S_{Y,t}$. Thus, the statistics $I_{X,Y}$ and ρ_S are linked and it is up to the researcher to determine which one to use.

Regarding the significance of $I_{X,Y}$, Harding and Pagan (2002b) proposed estimating the following relationship:

$$\left(\frac{S_{Y,t}}{\sigma_{S_Y}} \right) = \alpha + \rho_S \left(\frac{S_{X,t}}{\sigma_{S_X}} \right) + \eta_t \quad \left(\frac{S_{Y,t}}{\sigma_{S_Y}} \right) = \alpha + \rho_S \left(\frac{S_{X,t}}{\sigma_{S_X}} \right) + \eta_t \tag{5.3}$$

and testing the significance of ρ_S, where η_t is white noise residuals. As it is possible for serial correlation to be transmitted from $S_{Y,t}$ to η_t under the null hypothesis of $\rho_S = 0$, the estimation procedure of equation 5.3 must be robust to residual serial correlation. In this case, the estimating method used under the null of $\rho_S = 0$ is ordinary least squares along with the Newey–West heteroskedasticity and autocorrelation consistent covariance procedure.

Cross-Correlations

The cross-correlations constitute one of the more common approaches adapted to estimating the relationships between the cycles of two economic variables. For the stationary pair (y_t, x_t), they estimate the degree to which the movements of the two variables are synchronized. In this way, they allow one to verify whether the movements of variable x_t tend to be produced at the same time as the changes of variable y_t. From the set of coefficients of cross-correlations of order k, denoted $\rho_{X,Y}(k)$, the behaviour of the X series vis-à-vis the Y series can be characterized using different approaches. The procedure described by Agenor, McDermott and Prasad (2000) and Rand and

Tarp (2002) – and then taken up by many authors – is very simple, satisfactory and robust. Among other things, given a pair of variables (X, Y), this method allows one to test the level of significance of $\rho_{X,Y}(k)$, and also for a large number of variables, it provides a typology of the degree of concordance of co-movements of expansions and recessions. Based on the approximation of the standard deviation of the sample by $\frac{1}{\sqrt{T}}$, where T is the sample size, the cross-correlation between X_t and Y_{t-k} is significant if $\left|\rho_{X,Y}(k)\right| > \frac{1}{\sqrt{T}}$. More specifically, it is significant at the 5 per cent level if $\frac{2}{\sqrt{T}} < \left|\rho_{X,Y}(k)\right| < 1$ and at the 10 per cent level if $\frac{1}{\sqrt{T}} < \left|\rho_{X,Y}(k)\right| < \frac{2}{\sqrt{T}}$. Thus, if X and Y are, respectively, cycles of countries I and j, then a significantly positive correlation is indicative of synchronization of the growth cycles of the two countries (that is, $k = 0$) or lagging (for negative k) or leading (for positive k). Conversely, a negative correlation is associated with opposing growth cycles of the two countries.

Characteristics of Cycles

Dating Caribbean Countries' Business Cycles

The dates provided by the method of Bry–Boschan (1971) for the three countries are reported in table 5.1. In the case of Barbados, the turning points identified reveal the existence of nine major peaks and ten troughs during the period 1975 Q1 to 2013 Q4. Clearly, this chronology includes most of the dates of turning points already identified in the previous work of Craigwell and Maurin (2007b) and incorporates new dates associated with the episodes of the cycle of the additional period of 2004 Q1 to 2013 Q4 (see also section "Methodological Approach for Business Cycles").

Table 5.1. Identification of the Classical Cycles

Barbados		Jamaica		Trinidad and Tobago	
Peak	Trough	Peak	Trough	Peak	Trough
	1975 Q1				
1980 Q1	1981 Q1				
1981 Q3	1983 Q1			1982 Q2	
1984 Q2	1984 Q4		1985 Q4	1991 Q3	1989 Q2
1986 Q2	1986 Q4	1993 Q3	1995 Q2	2008 Q3	1993 Q2
1987 Q4	1988 Q2	1995 Q4	1998 Q1	2010 Q2	2009 Q4
1989 Q2	1992 Q3	1999 Q4	2000 Q2	2013 Q3	2011 Q1
1994 Q1	1994 Q4	2001 Q2	2001 Q4		
2000 Q2	2001 Q4	2004 Q1	2004 Q4		
2007 Q4	2009 Q2	2007 Q2	2010 Q2		
2010 Q3	2011 Q1	2011 Q3	2013 Q1		
2011 Q4					

Source: Authors' calculations.

Table 5.2. Durations of the Phases of the Business Cycle for Barbados, 1974–2013

Classical Cycles					
Dates of Peaks and Troughs by Year and Quarter		Duration in Quarters			
Trough	Peak	Contraction Phase	Expansion Phase	Cycle	
				Trough to Trough	Peak to Peak
1975 Q1	1980 Q1		20		
1981 Q1	1981 Q3	4	2	24	6
1983 Q1	1984 Q2	6	5	8	11
1984 Q4	1986 Q2	2	6	7	8
1986 Q4	1987 Q4	2	4	8	6
1988 Q2	1989 Q2	2	4	6	6
1992 Q3	1994 Q1	13	6	17	19
1994 Q4	2000 Q2	3	22	9	25
2001 Q4	2007 Q4	6	24	28	30
2009 Q2	2010 Q3	6	5	30	11
2011 Q1	2011 Q4	2	3	7	5
Number of cycle phases/ cycles		10	11	10	10
Average duration		4.6	9.2	14.4	12.7
Median duration		3.5	5	8.5	9.5
Proportion (%)		31.3	68.7		
Standard deviation		3.26	7.97	9.05	8.44

Source: Authors' calculations.

From table 5.2, the Barbadian data show ten complete cycles of peak to peak and ten complete cycles of trough to trough. These cycles reveal various features. The average length of peak-to-peak and trough-to-trough cycles is, respectively, 12.7 and 14.4 quarters, or 3.2 years and 3.6 years. The average length of the expansion phase (trough to peak) is 9.2 quarters against a contraction phase (peak to trough) of 4.6 quarters. That is, the expansion of the economy is two times more than its contraction, and similarly, the amplitude of the cycle during the expansion phase (7.97 quarters) is more than twice that observed in the contraction phase (3.26 quarters). The 1970s and 1980s are marked by cycles of shorter durations and smaller amplitudes. The longest cycle is recorded in the 2000s, between 2000 Q2 and 2007 Q4 for the peak-to-peak phase and between 2001 Q4 and 2009 Q1 for the trough-to-trough phase. The expansion phase between 2001 Q4 and 2007 Q3 is the longest one observed. The most severe economic recession occurred between 1989 Q2 and 1992 Q3; it lasted thirteen quarters, slightly more than three years. The latest episodes of the cycle for Barbados during the 2000s show that the economy experienced a severe drop in 2001 and a long period of robust expansion, with an average annual growth rate of 3.9 per cent over the period 2002 to

2007. During this cycle, the pace of growth even accelerated at the end, reaching 4.3 per cent in the period from 2004 to 2006.

The chronology for Jamaica, over the period 1985 Q1 to 2013 Q4, shows that it has recorded five full cycles of peak to peak, and six complete cycles of trough to trough. As in the case of Barbados, the identification of the business cycle in Jamaica shows a greater number of troughs than peaks. The results here are different from Whyte (2008) for two reasons: the procedure used in this chapter allows a better identification of turning points and a different period of analysis is employed. Whyte's sample covers the period 1981–2007, while the data in this chapter involves post-2008 measures, which capture the global banking, financial and economic crisis.

The turning points for Jamaica are detailed in table 5.3. Measured from peak to peak, five complete cycles were found with an average duration of eleven quarters and a standard deviation of 3.4 quarters, and, conversely, from trough to trough, six full cycles were identified with an average of seventeen quarters and a standard deviation of 5.67 quarters. Booms have a duration which varies between two and twenty-seven quarters, for a mean duration of ten quarters and variability of 8.16 quarters. The periods 1985 Q4 to 1993 Q3 (twenty-seven quarters), 2001 Q4 to 2004 Q1 (nine quarters) and 2004 Q3 to 2007 Q2 (eleven quarters) are the longest during which the economy of Jamaica has undergone some improvement. During the period 1985–2011, the Jamaican economy

Table 5.3. Durations of the Phases of the Business Cycle for Jamaica, 1985–2013

Dates of Peaks and Troughs by Year and Quarter				Duration in Quarters			
Trough		Peak		Contraction Phase	Expansion Phase	Cycle	
						Trough to Trough	Peak to Peak
1985	Q4	1993	Q3		31		
1995	Q2	1995	Q4	5	2	36	7
1998	Q1	1999	Q4	9	7	11	16
2000	Q2	2001	Q2	2	4	9	6
2001	Q4	2004	Q1	2	9	6	11
2004	Q4	2007	Q2	3	10	22	13
2010	Q2	2011	Q3	12	5	11	17
2013	Q1			6			
Number of cycle phases/cycles				7	7	6	6
Average duration				5.6	9.7	15.8	11.7
Median duration				5	7	11	12
Proportion (%)				33.6	66.4		
Standard deviation				3.5	9.07	10.28	4.15

Source: Authors' calculations.

Table 5.4. Durations of the Phases of the Business Cycle for Trinidad and Tobago, 1970–2013

Dates of Peaks and Troughs by Year and Quarter				Duration in Quarters			
Trough		Peak		Contraction Phase	Expansion Phase	Cycle	
						Trough to Trough	Peak to Peak
		1982	Q2				
1989	Q2	1991	Q3	28	9		37
1993	Q2	2008	Q3	7	57	16	64
2009	Q4	2010	Q2	5	2	62	7
2011	Q1	2013	Q3	3	10	5	13
Number of cycle phases/cycles				4	4	3	4
Average duration				10.75	19.5	27.7	30.25
Median duration				6	9.5	16	25
Proportion (%)				33.8	66.2		
Standard deviation				10.06	21.9	24.7	22.5

Source: Authors' calculations.

experienced six recessions with three recorded between 1985 and 2000 and the other three during 2001 and 2010. Three of these recessions were short, two quarters. The two longest recessions, nine and twelve quarters, respectively, occurred between 1995 Q4 to 1998 Q1 and 2007 Q2 to 2010 Q2. Murray (2007) also identified turning points for Jamaica using a structural vector autoregression model. His results were relatively close to the description found in table 5.3.

Table 5.4 shows that the turning points identified for Trinidad and Tobago are small in numbers: 1982 Q2, 1991 Q3 and 2008 Q2 for the peaks, and 1989 Q2 and 1993 Q2 for depressions. The first peak-to-peak cycle began in the second quarter of 1982 and lasted thirty-seven quarters through to 1991 Q3. This cycle reached its minimum in the second quarter of 1989. The second peak-to-peak cycle commenced in the third quarter of 1991 and was completed in 2008 Q2, a long period of nearly seventeen years. This cycle recorded a dip in 1993 Q2. The single cycle of trough to trough covers the period from 1989 Q2 to 1993 Q2 for a period of sixteen quarters.

Dating Caribbean Countries' Growth Cycles

The investigations on dating growth cycles indicate that the economies of Barbados, Jamaica, and Trinidad and Tobago have experienced more turning points compared to business cycles over the respective periods of 1974–2013, 1985–2013 and 1970–2014 (figures 5.4–5.6). Tables 5.5–5.8 present the summary statistics of these cycles. In the case of Barbados, there are fourteen complete cycles from peak to peak and thirteen from trough to trough; the average duration and variability are almost identical. The growth cycles of Jamaica are characterized by mean durations of 10.5 and fourteen quarters,

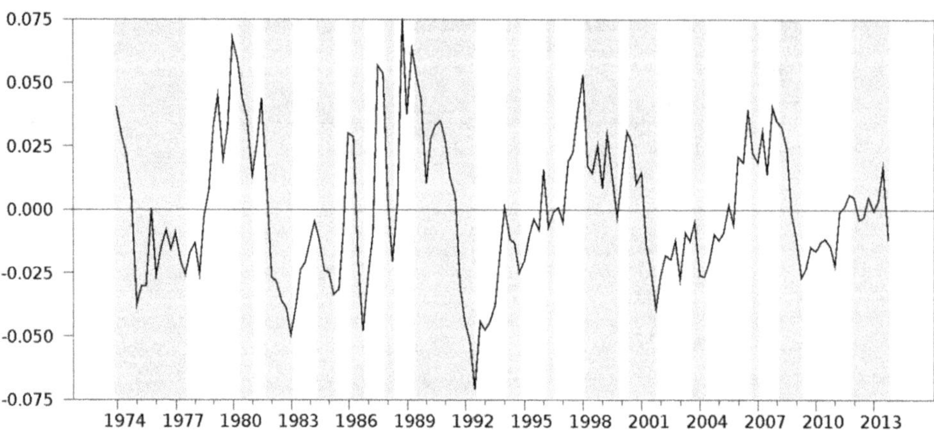

Figure 5.4. Barbados growth cycle, Hodrick–Prescott cyclical component of log levels, 1974 (Q1) to 2013 (Q4) (growth cycle downturns indicated by shading)

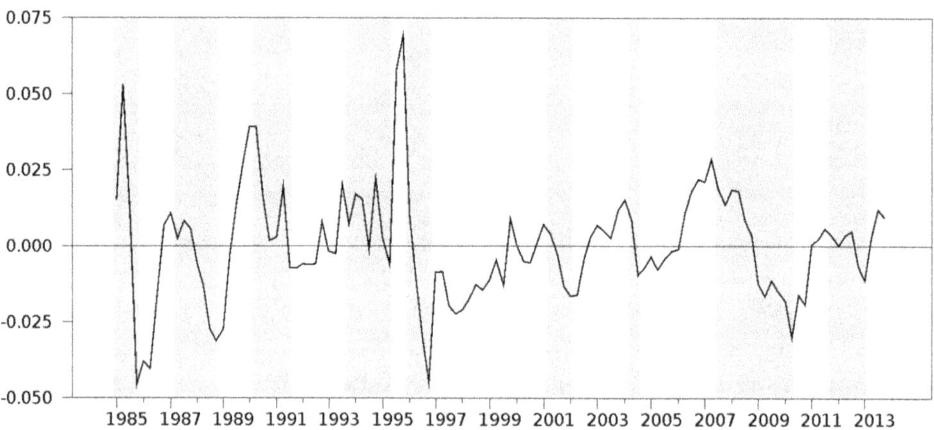

Figure 5.5. Jamaica growth cycle, Hodrick–Prescott cyclical component of log levels, 1985 (Q1) to 2013 (Q4) (growth cycle downturns indicated by shading)

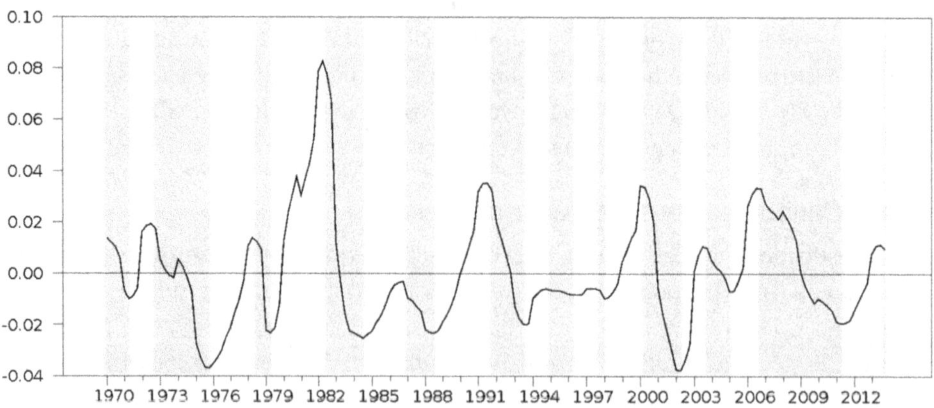

Figure 5.6. Trinidad–Tobago growth cycle, Hodrick–Prescott cyclical component of log levels, 1970 (Q1) to 2013 (Q4) (growth cycle downturns indicated by shading)

Table 5.5. Identification of Growth Cycles

Barbados		Jamaica		Trinidad and Tobago	
Peak	Trough	Peak	Trough	Peak	Trough
					1971Q2
1975 Q4				1972Q3	1975 Q4
1980 Q2	1977 Q3			1978Q2	1979Q2
1981 Q3	1981 Q1			1982Q2	1984Q3
1984 Q2	1983 Q1			1986Q4	1988Q3
1986 Q1	1985 Q2		1985 Q4	1991Q3	1993Q3
1987 Q4	1986 Q4	1987 Q1	1988 Q4	1994Q2	1996Q2
1989 Q2	1988 Q2	1990 Q1	1991 Q3	1997Q3	1998Q1
1994 Q1	1992 Q3	1993 Q3	1995 Q2	2000 Q1	2002 Q2
1996 Q1	1994 Q4	1995 Q4	1996 Q4	2003 Q3	2005 Q1
1998 Q1	1996 Q3	2001 Q1	2002 Q1	2006 Q3	2011 Q2
2000 Q2	1999 Q4	2004 Q1	2004 Q3	2013 Q4	
2003 Q3	2001 Q4	2007 Q2	2010 Q2		
2006 Q3	2004 Q2	2011 Q3	2013 Q1		
2008 Q1	2007 Q1				
2011 Q4	2009 Q2				

Source: Authors' calculations.

respectively, for observations from peak to peak and trough to trough. As in the case of Barbados, the Jamaican cycle has a strong asymmetry, with downturns much shorter than upswings. In Trinidad and Tobago, as the events of the business cycle were rare, the growth cycles are much less common. In fact, for Trinidad and Tobago, the results indicate that it is an economy with cyclical fluctuations that is particularly representative of a single growth cycle. It is worth noting here that the qualitative observations of Bourne (2008) are consistent with this sequence of phases of growth that have been identified. Indeed, his explanations are well reflected in table 5.5 in terms of dates, duration and characteristics of recessions:

> The deep recessions during the 1980s were in Guyana (25 per cent between 1982 and 1985), Trinidad and Tobago (19 per cent between 1985 and 1989) and St. Lucia (12 per cent in 1976). In 1982, world petroleum prices began to decrease, falling by mid-1986 to $8 per barrel. For Trinidad and Tobago, this was calamitous. . . . The result was an economic recession of major proportions, both in terms of magnitude and duration. . . . During the 1990s, Trinidad and Tobago experienced another deep recession of 14 per cent between 1992 and 1993, as did Barbados, whose per capita real GDP fell by 14 per cent between 1990 and 1992. (Bourne 2008, 5–6)

Furthermore, it is important to note that the dating identified for the growth cycles includes a majority of periods that are actually characterized as peaks and troughs defining growth cycles.

Table 5.6. Durations of the Phases of the Growth Cycle for Barbados, 1974–2013

Growth Cycles					
Dates of Peaks and Troughs by Year and Quarter		Duration in Quarters			
Trough	Peak	Contraction Phase	Expansion Phase	Cycle	
				Trough to Trough	Peak to Peak
	1975 Q4				
1977 Q3	1980 Q2	10	11		21
1981 Q1	1981 Q3	3	2	14	5
1983 Q1	1984 Q2	6	5	8	11
1985 Q2	1986 Q1	4	3	9	7
1986 Q4	1987 Q4	3	4	6	7
1988 Q2	1989 Q2	2	4	6	6
1992 Q3	1994 Q1	13	6	19	21
1994 Q4	1996 Q1	3	5	9	8
1996 Q3	1998 Q1	2	6	7	8
1999 Q4	2000 Q2	7	2	13	9
2001 Q4	2003 Q3	6	7	8	13
2004 Q2	2006 Q3	3	9	10	12
2007 Q1	2008 Q1	2	4	11	6
2009 Q2	2011 Q4	5	10	9	15
Number of cycle phases/cycles		14	14	13	14
Average duration		4.9	5.6	9.9	10.6
Median duration		3.5	5	9	8.5
Proportion (%)		46.9	53.1		
Standard deviation		3.15	2.72	3.49	5.06

Source: Authors' calculations.

If the focus is on a common period, that is to say, the years 1985–2011, then the chronologies of the growth cycles of the three countries also provide some lessons. The frequency of the growth cycles is variable for the three economies (about nine to ten for Barbados, six to seven for Jamaica, and five for Trinidad and Tobago). Cycle characteristics also vary. Trinidad and Tobago cycles – observed from peak to peak and trough to trough – were the longest, and also the downturns and acceleration are of the same average length. This is in contrast to Barbados, where the different phases are much shorter, almost six quarters less for cycles, and three quarters less for upswings and downswings. For Jamaica, it was found that the most pronounced asymmetry in terms of time is between phases of expansion and recession.

Table 5.7. Durations of the Phases of the Growth Cycle for Jamaica, 1985–2013

Dates of Peaks and Troughs by Year and Quarter				Duration in Quarters			
Trough		Peak		Contraction Phase	Expansion Phase	Cycle	
						Trough to Trough	Peak to Peak
1985	Q4	1987	Q1		5		
1988	Q4	1990	Q1	7	5	12	12
1991	Q3	1993	Q3	6	8	11	14
1995	Q2	1995	Q4	7	2	15	9
1996	Q4	2001	Q1	4	17	6	21
2002	Q1	2004	Q1	4	8	21	12
2004	Q3	2007	Q2	2	11	10	13
2010	Q2	2011	Q3	12	5	23	17
2013	Q1			5		10	
Number of cycle phases/cycles				8	8	8	7
Average duration				5.875	7.625	13.5	14
Median duration				5.5	6.5	11.5	13
Proportion (%)				40.52	59.48		
Standard deviation				2.80	4.36	5.45	3.62

Source: Authors' calculations.

Analyses of Business Cycle Synchronization for Caribbean Countries

We present various results on measures of synchronization between the business cycles of the three countries and also vis-à-vis countries representing external economies with which the Caribbean is most related. The availability of data allows us to conduct this analysis for the period 1985 Q1 to 2010 Q2.

Synchronization of Business Cycles

Table 5.9 reports the results from the index of Harding and Pagan for the three Caribbean countries and also those relating to the industrialized economies of the United States, Canada, the United Kingdom and Germany, which are major trading partners with the Caribbean nations. The following lessons can be learned from the findings. The Caribbean countries have the lowest synchronization index values, ranging between 0.53 and 0.58. The best synchronization for the Caribbean grouping over the review period is for Barbados, and Trinidad and Tobago. In spite of the close geographic proximity of the Caribbean territories, the synchronization profiles of these countries are quite varied relative to those of the industrialized economies which are scattered over different continents. The degree of synchronization between the cycles of the industrialized countries studied here is relatively high with correlation indices greater

Table 5.8. Durations of the Phases of the Growth Cycle for Trinidad and Tobago, 1970–2013

Dates of Peaks and Troughs by Year and Quarter				Duration in Quarters			
Trough		Peak		Contraction Phase	Expansion Phase	Cycle	
						Trough to Trough	Peak to Peak
1971	Q2	1972	Q3		5		
1975	Q4	1978	Q2	9	10	14	19
1979	Q2	1982	Q2	4	12	14	16
1984	Q3	1986	Q4	9	9	21	18
1988	Q3	1991	Q3	7	12	16	19
1993	Q3	1994	Q2	4	3	16	7
1996	Q2	1997	Q3	8	5	11	13
1998	Q1	2000	Q1	2	8	7	10
2002	Q2	2003	Q3	9	5	17	14
2005	Q1	2006	Q3	6	6	11	12
2011	Q2	2013	Q4	19	10	25	29
Number of cycle phases/cycles				10	11	10	10
Average duration				7.7	7.73	15.2	15.7
Median duration				7.5	8	15	15
Proportion (%)				43.75	56.25		
Standard deviation				4.49	2.96	4.89	5.79

Source: Authors' calculations.

Table 5.9. Degree of Bilateral Synchronization of Business Cycles between the Different Economies

	Barbados	Jamaica	Trinidad and Tobago	United States	Canada	United Kingdom	Germany
Barbados	1						
Jamaica	0.5292	1					
Trinidad and Tobago	0.5784	0.5392	1				
United States	0.7549	0.6568	0.6667	1			
Canada	0.7353	0.6176	0.6863	0.9608	1		
United Kingdom	0.7647	0.6274	0.6568	0.9708	0.9509	1	
Germany	0.6863	0.6078	0.6568	0.8333	0.8137	0.8235	1

Source: Authors' calculations.

than 0.81. Among the Caribbean countries, Barbados displays the highest degree of synchronization with the industrialized nations.

Synchronization of Growth Cycles

The use of GDP series expressed in different units calls in the first instance for their harmonization to make them comparable. A simple standardization of data resulting from classical centring and reduction operations is helpful in this regard. Figure 5.7 provides evidence aimed at comparing the profiles of the growth cycles of the three Caribbean countries. It reveals important differences among these cycles over the period prior to 2000, where it was observed that there were significant variations in the movements of their amplitudes and the gap between the actual and potential growth rates. However, the period 2000 Q4–2008 Q2 shows great similarities between the cyclical components of the domestic productions. With cross-correlations coefficients relatively insignificant or zero (regards to critical values $\dfrac{1}{\sqrt{T}}$ and $\dfrac{2}{\sqrt{T}}$ mentioned in paragraph "Methodology of the Measure of Cycle Synchronization"), it is seen that overall, the growth cycles of Barbados, Jamaica and Trinidad and Tobago are poorly synchronized (see table 5.10).

The comparison of these countries' growth cycles with those of our four developed economies also leads to results in line with those established for comparisons of business cycles. Figures 5.8–5.10 clearly point out that the growth cycles of the Caribbean countries explored show a high degree of synchronization with the

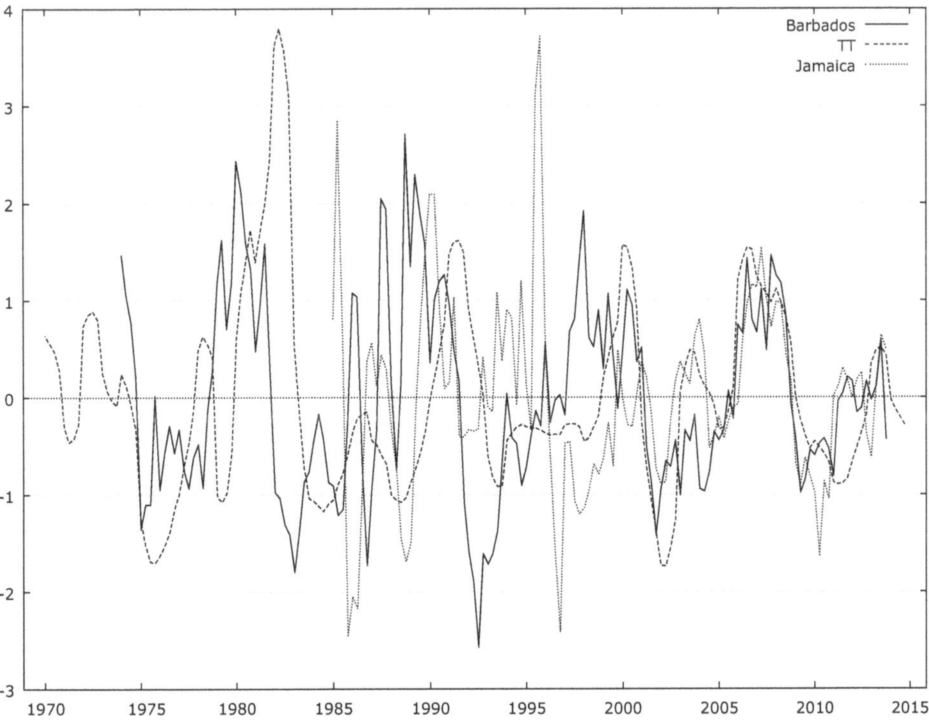

Figure 5.7. Barbados, Jamaica, and Trinidad and Tobago growth cycles

Table 5.10. Cross-Correlations between the Growth Cycles of Barbados, Jamaica, and Trinidad and Tobago in the Period 1985 (Q1) to 2010 (Q2)

Lag	−6	−5	−4	−3	−2	−1	0	1	2	3	4	5	6
Barbados–Jamaica	−0.00	−0.00	0.05	0.12	0.16	0.08	0.03	0.02	0.03	0.03	−0.03	−0.19	−0.26
Barbados–Trinidad and Tobago	0.15	0.27	0.35	0.41	0.47	0.47	0.44	0.35	0.24	0.14	0.06	−0.02	−0.08
Jamaica–Trinidad and Tobago	−0.06	0.03	0.13	0.24	0.31	0.35	0.38	0.34	0.30	0.23	0.14	0.05	−0.03

Source: Authors' calculations.

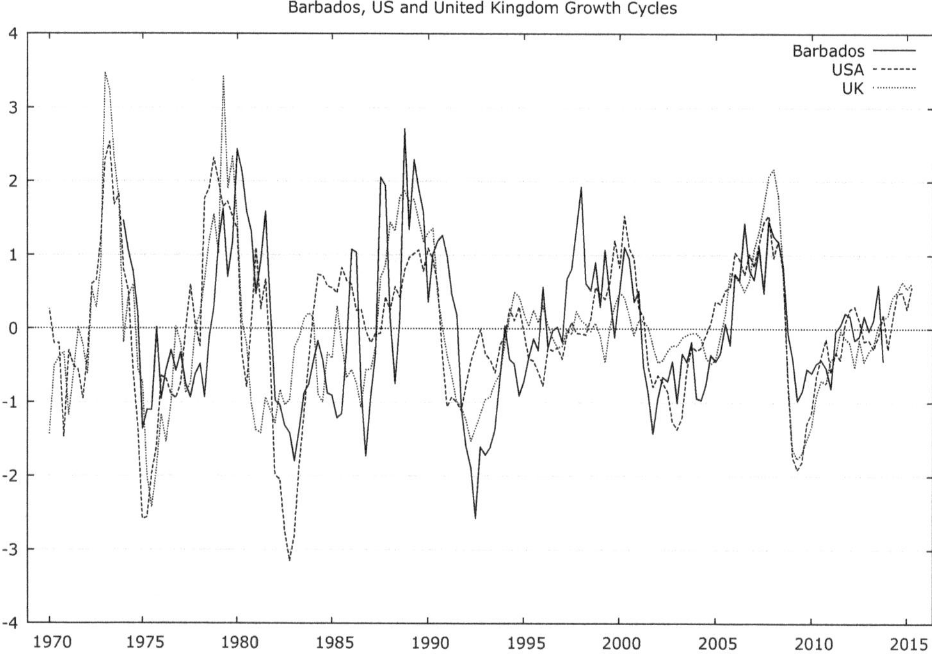

Figure 5.8. Synchronization of growth cycles between Barbados, the United States and the United Kingdom

Western powers for which trade relations are more developed, mainly the United States and England.

Interpretations and Implications of Results

It is clear that these empirical results highlight the unevenness of the degree of synchronization of real business cycles of the Caribbean countries studied. Whether we consider the concept of a business cycle or growth cycle, the different approaches of statistical tests reveal the asynchronous nature of economic cycles between these

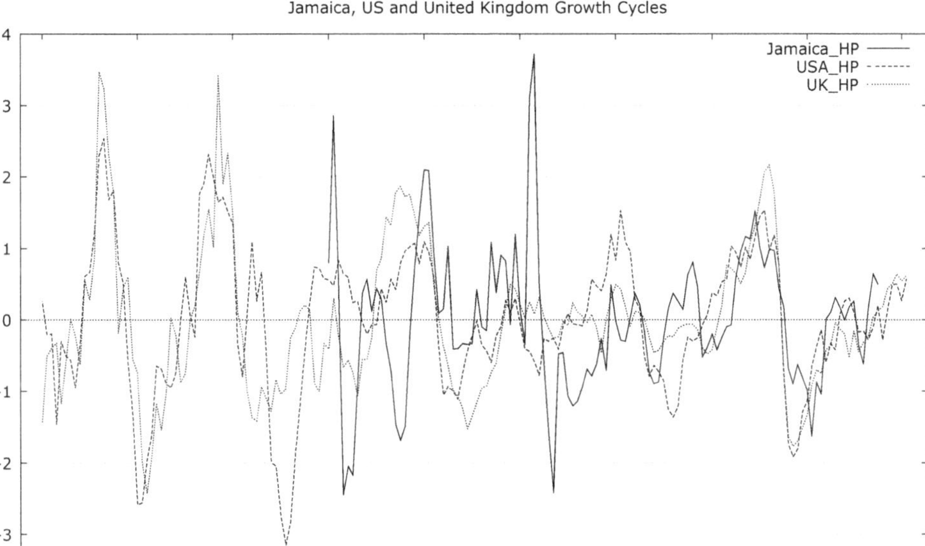

Figure 5.9. Synchronization of growth cycles between Jamaica, the United States and the United Kingdom

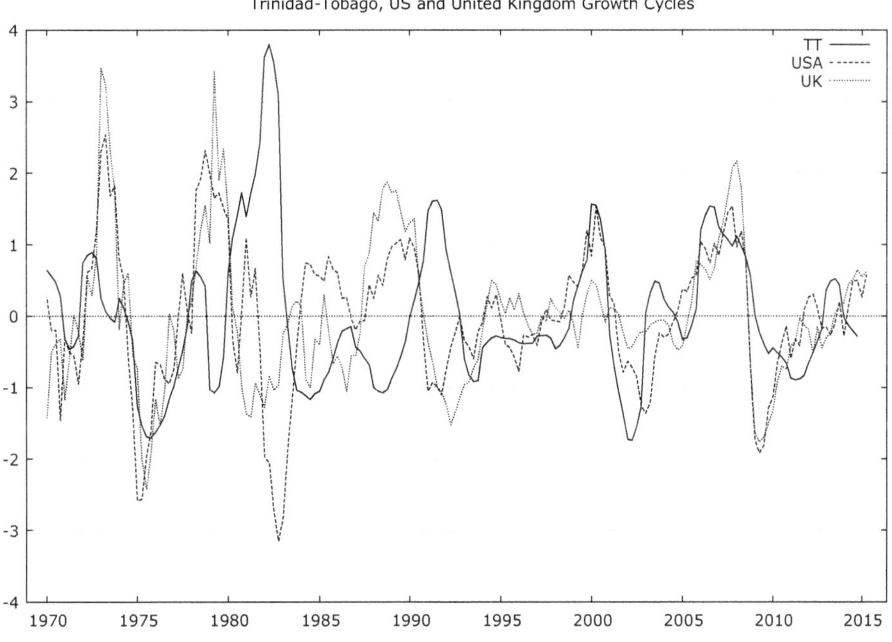

Figure 5.10. Synchronization of growth cycles between Trinidad and Tobago, the United States and the United Kingdom

Caribbean countries and, on the contrary, their highly synchronized profiles with cycles of industrialized countries with which they have close relations, business or other nature (institutional, cultural and so on).

The weak bilateral synchronization of business cycles among these Caribbean countries can be explained by the weakness of their intrazone trade flows, on the one hand, and the nature of the balance sheet of CARICOM economic integration, on the other hand. With the emergence of regional integration projects in the last decades in various parts of the world, economic theory has gradually given rise to the literature devoted to the analysis of the role of trade liberalization, and economic and monetary integration in the synchronization of business cycles.

Research dedicated to exploring determinants of the relationship between trade liberalization and convergence of economic cycles has identified the following key factors: trade intensity, structure of trade, demand shocks and exchange rate regimes. The majority of theoretical and applied studies conclude that intensification of trade integration has resulted in an increase in the homogeneity of national economic cycles.[5] Hence, it is appropriate to stress that our results – the modest correlations of business cycles of the countries of the Caribbean – can essentially be explained by the weakness of intra-Caribbean trade.

As a follow-up to the brief chronology of the integration process presented in section "Issues of Cycle Synchronization", we now consider these empirical results in the context of CARICOM. Concretely, it should be noted that they are new empirical results exploring the interactions between partner countries within this economic zone. In terms of fluctuations in the short and medium terms, these interactions are barely considered in studies dedicated to the economies of the CARICOM region. Being part of the CSME since 2006, Barbados, Jamaica, and Trinidad and Tobago are expected to register an acceleration of their trade, the coordination of their economic policies and the synchronization of economic cycles. Even today, despite institutional efforts for harmonization and consolidation of trade links within the region, the result of the dynamics of integration of countries is mixed. Not surprisingly, the econometric exercise to measure the synchronization of business cycles shows here that the integration process has not generated sufficient earnings to exert a positive impact on economic activities of CSME countries.

In this context, it should be recalled that the share of intra-Caribbean trade is still too modest. Thomas (2012, 279) specifies this point: "In CARICOM, the share of intraregional trade to total trade (imports and exports) is only 14 per cent. The share of intra regional exports to total exports is 18 per cent". The CARICOM Secretariat (2013, 9) delivers the same conclusions: "the region exports small percentages of its total production to intra-regional markets, while trade with extra-regional traditional partners – USA, Canada, the UK, and the rest of the European Union dominates by far CARICOM's total trade in goods". Thus, since most of the Caribbean trade takes place with the United States, Canada and European countries, the results of the synchronization highlighted in this work can be understood.

There are lessons to be learned from these stylized facts on the dynamics of Caribbean economies. The first is related to the transmission of the effects of shocks occurring in industrialized countries. Given the positions of industrialized countries as leaders and those of the Caribbean countries as followers, today's bilateral relations between these two regional blocks are characterized by risk, primarily for the latter. As key partners, recessions that occur in industrial cycles of the United States, Canada, the United Kingdom and Germany are transmitted to Caribbean countries and significantly affect their economies. Also, economic crises recorded in Europe and North America tend to influence the countries of the Caribbean Basin to the extent that they unquestionably lead to economic crises in the latter countries with a certain lag in transmission. The second lesson concerns weakness in transmission of cycles between Caribbean countries. As a consequence, an increase in the synchronization of economic growth could make them less sensitive to external shocks. The last lesson is that the conditions for improving the synchronization of Caribbean countries' cycles are on the agenda. Indeed, the national benefits resulting from integration agreements depend on the improvement just alluded to. Thus, for CARICOM, strengthening the union necessarily involves boosting the capacity of member states to prioritize the development of trade among the countries of the region.

Conclusion

Launched in 1973 and now comprising fifteen countries, the process of cooperation and Caribbean regional integration supported by CARICOM can be considered one of the oldest initiatives of economic union in the world. In light of the ultimate goals of a regional integration project, the tasks of describing and analysing the reality of economic fluctuations in the area are considered essential. Thus, by looking at the examples of good practices observed in the cases of the United States (dating of the American cycle by the NBER began in 1854) and Europe (from 2003 with the start of monitoring of the European cycle), as well as those of other regions of the world such as the Association of Southeast Asian Nations (Korea, Hong Kong, Indonesia, Malaysia, Philippines, Singapore, Taiwan, Thailand), it is clear that the policies of regional convergence implemented are largely dependent on insights provided by the knowledge of short-term economic states in each member state as well as that which is common to the whole area.

This chapter, written nearly fifty years after the signing of the Treaty of Chaguaramas, focuses on the evaluation of some key economic cycles and convergence issues of the CARICOM region. Essentially, it seeks to answer the following questions: What are the degrees of synchronization of business cycles in Caribbean economies? What are the determinants of these movements? What roles should institutions play in the economic regulation and coordination of growth policies in the Caribbean?

In doing so, it makes three major contributions to the literature. First, it contributes to the dating and description of the cycles for three major anglophone Caribbean countries for which infra-annual data are available (Barbados, Jamaica, and Trinidad and Tobago) and establishes the chronologies of their business and growth cycles. Second, the research sheds light on the important issue of synchronization of business cycles in these countries, examining in particular whether they show similar behaviour during the phases of contraction and expansion. The results reveal that the three countries are characterized by generally divergent economic business cycles as well as growth cycles. Third, the comparison of the Caribbean cycles with those of the major developed countries that are linked to the Caribbean indicates that the Caribbean cycles are highly synchronized with the cycles of the industrialized countries.

These findings have implications for CARICOM's regional integration policy. Despite institutional efforts to harmonize and consolidate trade ties in the region, the results of the integration process remain mixed. It has not generated enough positive benefits to have a significant impact on economic activities in partner countries and accentuate the convergence of their economic cycles. These results demonstrate that the harmonization of monetary and fiscal policies, and implementation of a monetary union may not materialize if strong initiatives for accelerating the process of integration are not launched by the governments of member states. Finally, as illustrated by the European Monetary Union, an official project dedicated to the identification of economic cycles in CARICOM needs to be established. A major challenge here will be the generation of consistent high-frequency data for the countries in the region.

Acknowledgements

Roland Craigwell died on 2 January 2014, before the chapter was fully completed. This chapter is dedicated to his memory. The authors gratefully acknowledge the very useful comments of Martin Everts and Nlandu Mamingi.

Notes

1. See Venter (2005).

2. See Whyte (2008), Craigwell and Maurin (2007a, 2007b), Cashin (2004), and Maurin and Watson (2002).

3. This is all the regulatory rules of European economic policies, scattered in various European treaties. Monetary policy is under the aegis of the European Central Bank (ECB), which is an independent institution whose main objective is to ensure price stability. Besides the ECB is the Economic and Financial Affairs Council of the Council of the European Union involving finance ministers of the member states whose mission is to formulate, after consulting the ECB, guidance on policy change towards currencies of third countries. A third important element is the Stability and Growth Pact, which monitors national budgetary policies, imposing the threshold of 3 per cent of GDP as the maximum deficit of each member state.

4. Taylor (1993) defined the rule used as a reference for central banks to calculate the level which sets the interest rate, from a weighted sum of the inflation and the cycle.

5. See, for example, Imbs (2004), Baxter and Kouparitsas (2005), and Calderon, Chong and Stein (2007) for empirical confirmation.

References

Agenor, Pierre-Richard, John C. McDermott, and Eswar S. Prasad. 2000. "Macroeconomic Fluctuations in Developing Countries: Some Stylised Facts". *The World Bank Economic Review* 14 (2): 251–85.

Ahamada, Ibrahim and Philippe Jolivaldt. 2010. "Classical vs. Wavelet-based Filters: Comparative Study and Application to Business Cycles". Sorbonne Economic Centre Working Paper 10027, University Pantheon-Sorbonne (Paris 1).

Baxter, Marianne and Robert G. King. 1995. "Measuring Business Cycles: Approximate Band-pass Filters for Economic Time Series". NBER Working Papers Series, No. 5022.

Baxter, Marianne and Michael A. Kouparitsas. 2005. "Determinants of Business Cycle Comovement: A Robust Analysis". *Journal of Monetary Economics* 52 (1): 113–57.

Bentoglio, Guilhem Jacky, Fayolle et Matthieu Lemoine. 2001. "Unité et pluralité du cycle européen". *Revue del'OFCE*, Presses de Sciences-Po 78 (3): 9–73..

Bourne, Compton. 2008. "Caribbean Economic Recessions in Historical Perspective". Nineteenth Annual Commercial Banks Conference. St Kitts and Nevis: Eastern Caribbean Central Bank, 5–7 November 2008. https://www.eccb-centralbank.org/content-manager /documents/ download/161.

Bry, Gerhard and Charlotte Boschan. 1971. *Cyclical Analysis of Time Series: Selected Procedures and Computer Programs.* New York: NBER.

Calderon, Cesar, Alberto Chong, and Ernesto Stein. 2007. "Trade Intensity and Business Cycle Synchronisation: Are Developing Countries Any Different?". *Journal of International Economics* 71 (1): 2–21.

CARICOM Secretariat. 2013. "Caribbean Community Regional Aid for Trade Strategy 2013– 2015". https://caricom.org/documents/5269-caribbean_community_aft_strategy_final.pdf.

Cashin, Paul. 2004. "Caribbean Business Cycles". IMF Working Paper No. 04/136. International Monetary Fund. https://www.imf.org/external/pubs/ft/wp/2004/wp04136.pdf.

Christiano, Lawrence J. and Terry J. Fitzgerald. 1999. "The Band Pass Filter". NBER Working Paper 7257, National Bureau of Economic Research.

———. 2003. "The Band Pass Filter". *International Economic Review* 44 (2): 435–65.

Craigwell, Roland and Alain Maurin. 2007a. "Une Analyse Comparative des Cycles Conjoncturels de la Barbade et des États-Unis". *Revue d'Economie Régionale and Urbaine* 1: 59–78.

———. 2007b. "A Sectoral Analysis of Barbados' GDP Business Cycle". *Journal of Eastern Caribbean Studies* 32 (1): 21–51.

European Council. 2005. "European Council Brussels 22 and 23 March 2005 Presidency Conclusions". http://ec.europa.eu/economy_finance/economic_governance/sgp/pdf/coc /2005-03-23_council_presidency_conclusions_en.pdf.

Everts, Martin. 2006. "Duration of Business Cycles". MPRA Paper No. 1219, University of Bern. https://mpra.ub.uni-muenchen.de/1219/1/MPRA_paper_1219.pdf.

Guay Alain and Pierre St-Amant. 2005. "Do the Hodrick-Prescott and Baxter-King Filters Provide a Good Approximation of Business Cycles?" *Annales d'Économie et de Statistique* 77: 133–55.

Harding, Don and Adrian Pagan. 2002a. "Dissecting the Cycle: A Methodological Investigation". *Journal of Monetary Economics* 49: 365–81.

———. 2002b. "Synchronization of Cycles". Working paper, Melbourne University.

Harvey, Andrew. 1989. *Forecasting, Structural Time Series Models and the Kalman Filter.* Cambridge, UK: Cambridge University Press.

Hodrick, Robert and Edward Prescott. 1980. "Post-war U.S. Business Cycles: An Empirical Investigation". Working paper No. 451, Carnegie-Mellon University.

Imbs, Jean. 2004. "Trade, Finance, Specialization, and Synchronisation". *Review of Economics and Statistics* 86: 723–34.

Ladiray Dominique and Regina Soarès. 2001. "Cycles in the Euro-zone". Working Paper 270901, EuroStat. European Commission.

Lemoine, Matthieu 2006. "Économétrie du Cycle Européen". Doctoral Thesis, Paris Institute of Political Studies. https://spire.sciencespo.fr/hdl:/2441/f4rshpf3v1umfao9lat15gci3/resources /lemoine-eco-2006.pdf.

Lewis, D. 1997. "A Quarterly Real GDP Series for Barbados, 1974–1995: A Sectoral Approach". *Central Bank of Barbados Economic Review* 24 (1): 17–56.

Liu, Philip and Rafael Romeu. 2011. "A Dynamic Factor Model of Quarterly Real Gross Domestic Product in the Caribbean: The Case of Cuba and the Bahamas". International Monetary Fund. https://ascecuba.org//c/wp-content/uploads/2014/09/v20-rromeu.pdf.

Maurin, Alain and Patrick K. Watson. 2002. "Quantitative Modelling of the Caribbean Macroeconomy for Forecasting and Policy Analysis: Problems and Solutions". *Social and Economic Studies* 51, no. 2 (June): 1–47.

Monch, Emanuel and Harald Uhlig. 2005. "Towards a Monthly Business Cycle Chronology for the Euro Area". *Journal of Business Cycle Measurement and Analysis* 2 (1): 43–69.

Murray, André. 2007. "Modelling the Jamaican Business Cycle: A Structural Vector Autoregressive Approach". Bank of America Working Paper. http://boj.org.jm/uploads/pdf/ papers_pamphlets /papers_pamphlets_Modelling_the_Jamaican_Business_Cycle__A _Structural_Vector_Autoregressive_Approach.pdf.

Rand, John and Finn Tarp. 2002. "Business Cycles in Developing Countries: Are They Different?" *World Development* 30 (12): 2071–88.

Taylor, John B. 1993. "Discretion versus Policy Rules in Practice". *Carnegie-Rochester Conference Series on Public Policy* 39: 195–214. https://web.stanford.edu/~johntayl/Onlinepapers combinedbyyear/1993/Discretion_versus_Policy_Rules_in_Practice.pdf.

Thomas, Clive. 2012. "Global Economic Crises: CARICOM Impacts and Responses". In *Regional Integration: Key to Caribbean Survival and Prosperity*, edited by Kenneth Hall and Myrtle Chuck-A-Sang, 261–307. Bloomington, IN: Trafford.

Venter, Iaan. 2005. "Reference Turning Points in the South African Business Cycle: Recent Developments". *Quarterly Bulletin*. September. Pretoria: South African Reserve Bank. https://www.resbank.co.za/Lists/News%20and%20Publications/Attachments/4376/Article %20-%20Reference%20turning%20points%20in%20the%20South%20African%20business %20 cycle%20-%20Recent%20developments.pdf.

Watson, Mark W. 1994. "Business Cycle Durations and Postwar Stabilization of the U.S. Economy". *American Economic Review* 84 (1): 24–46.

Watson, Patrick K. 2003. "Macroeconomic Dynamics in Trinidad & Tobago: Implications for Monetary Policy in a Very Small Oil-Based Economy". Department of Economics, University of the West Indies. https://ecomod.net/sites/default/files/document-conference /ecomod2003/ Watson.pdf.

———. 2010. "Data Deficiency and Caribbean Development: An Unresolved Dilemma". Sir Arthur Lewis Institute of Social and Economic Studies, University of the West Indies.

Whyte, Sashana. 2008. "An Analysis of the Jamaican Business Cycle". Bank of Jamaica Working Paper 2008/8. http://www.ccmf-uwi.org/files/publications/conference/999.pdf.

Chapter 6

Fiscal Convergence

Is It a Necessary Criterion for a Caribbean Monetary Union?

JULIA JHINKOO-RAMDASS

The primary macroeconomic policy tool available to countries on entering a monetary union is the use of fiscal policy; formally joining means the giving up of national monetary policy. Fiscal policy can be defined as government spending policies that influence macroeconomic conditions.[1] Fiscal policy is used as a tool by governments to improve the economic performance of the economy by adjusting tax rates and government spending. The main targets of fiscal policy are to improve unemployment rates, control inflation, stabilize business cycles and influence interest rates. Being a member of a monetary union limits the tools the governments have available to them to manage their economies.

A monetary union requires economic convergence for it to be successful – a goal that the Caribbean Community (CARICOM) has over the years assiduously sought to achieve by creating institutions and opportunities that will aid and promote Caribbean economic integration. The Caribbean Single Market has been its major thrust in developing economic integration, established in 2006 to establish the Caribbean Single Economy in 2015. For the region to become a single economy, there are five essential criteria that CARICOM has mandated that countries meet before joining the proposed Caribbean Monetary Union (CMU).[2] These criteria have been monitored since 1996, and over time countries have been inconsistent in meeting these criteria. However, the only criterion that the countries have been consistently failing to meet is the fiscal criterion. The fiscal criterion is one of the most evasive criteria to satisfy for proposed CMU members, as well as for members of the European Monetary Union (EMU). The question then arises, Is fiscal convergence a necessary criterion for a CMU?

The fiscal criterion adopted by the CMU is closely related to the European Union's fiscal criterion. They both require the fiscal deficit to be no more than 3 per cent of the country's gross domestic product (GDP). Two main justifications are proposed for having a fiscal convergence criterion in a monetary union. First, the convergence criteria ensure that there are no spillover effects from domestic fiscal policies, as excessive government deficits in one country may cause inflationary pressures on the common currency, which may harm the other members of the monetary union. Second, moral hazard issues such as countries borrowing unsustainable amounts of money from foreign institutions may exert pressures on the collective reserves of the monetary union in the regional central bank. They may borrow and increase their debt levels with the hope that regional central banks or other union members will bail them out to ensure the survival of the monetary union.

Studies done on the European Union by Eichengreen (1996), Chari and Kehoe (2007), and Dixit and Lambertini (2003) suggest that fiscal constraints in a monetary union may not be necessary if the monetary authority has the "power" to enforce its policies. An overview of all existing monetary unions suggests that whether fiscal commitments are implemented through self-discipline, surveillance, and persuasion or centralized enforcement, they all have a record of unsuccessful efforts to prevent excessive deficits and debt crises (Anand et al. 2011). The literature that exists on fiscal convergence for developed countries, particularly for Europe, is extensive, but there are limited studies done on the Caribbean region. Economic convergence within the Caribbean has been discussed extensively with fiscal convergence being a criterion for economic convergence, but not many studies have focused specifically on the issue of fiscal convergence.

This chapter seeks to determine if fiscal convergence is occurring in the Caribbean by examining three groups: (1) an established monetary union – the Eastern Caribbean Currency Union (ECCU), (2) CARICOM countries and (3) the CARICOM countries excluding the ECCU. The ECCU and the CARICOM economies share a similar monetary institutional background that is described in the third section, following a literature review. The trends in fiscal convergence since the introduction of the fiscal criterion are examined, as well as the data and methodology used. The chapter also focuses on the analysis and results of the three groups, followed by conclusions and recommendations.

Literature Review

Fiscal Convergence and Monetary Unions

Fiscal discipline within the context of a monetary union has been examined since the 1980s, with the main question being, What are the effects of a monetary union on fiscal discipline? That can be interpreted as asking whether the lack of fiscal discipline was an obstacle to achieving the objective of a monetary union, and what sort of fiscal constraints might be sufficient.

Buiter, Corsetti and Roubini (1993) critically examined the fiscal rules proposed in the Treaty of Maastricht of 1991 to conclude that "the fiscal convergence criteria designed to eliminate or prevent excessive deficits are badly motivated, poorly designed and apt to lead to unnecessary hardship if pursued mechanically" (87). Budd (1997) also highlights the difficulties for EU members in entering the EMU, citing the impositions of monetary and fiscal convergence as being, in fact, barriers to the broader goal of economic integration: "the fiscal criteria of the Maastricht Treaty may be 'economic nonsense' because they do not take into account the 749 ways in which the economies of the EU differ" (569). Buiter (2000) revisits his findings from Buiter, Corsetti and Roubini (1993), in which he reaffirms that the fiscal criteria of the Maastricht Treaty are arbitrary, unnecessary and insufficient for national fiscal-financial sustainability. The euro crisis[3] (2009) revealed many flaws of the Maastricht Treaty, some of which are related to fiscal policies.

The euro area was described as lacking institutional development, which restricted the ability of the European Central Bank[4] and other European institutions to make coordinated decisions and actions in response to the euro crisis, Corsetti et al. (2019). The increasing debt levels of the countries was a result of each country trying to battle the effects of the crisis on their economies. Enforcing the limits of debt and fiscal deficits of the Stability and Growth Pact was not an effective fiscal constraint measure for the EMU members. Hall (2015) described the eurozone as being built on only a minimalist set of rules that had no centralized fiscal capabilities of its own with constraints to make collective decision-making among its member governments. At the time of the financial crisis reaching Europe in 2010, there were twenty-seven different regulatory systems for banks to comply with within the EMU, all largely based on national rules and national rescue measures with minimal rules existing at the EU level. The euro area finance ministers were compelled as a result to establish a European Stability Mechanism to safeguard financial stability in the euro area (November 2010). The need for better regulation and supervision of the banking and financial sector within the European Union was met with the establishment of the European Supervisory Authorities (January 2011).[5] Also, the EMU members agreed in December 2011 to foster a stronger economic union requiring a greater level of coordination at a fiscal level for each EMU member, resulting in the signing of the Treaty on Stability, Coordination and Governance (also known as the "Fiscal Compact")[6] in March 2012. These additional measures taken by the EMU members were credited to being a little too late, because of the premature rush to establish the EMU.

> Eurozone governments systemically failed to understand the regime change implied by the adoption of a common currency. A key aspect of this was the implication of financial integration. The thinking in the 1980s and 1990s, when financial integration was introduced before the common currency, was that it would contribute to both convergence and macroeconomic stability. Instead, capital flows tended to feed non-tradable sectors in the periphery of the Eurozone. Second, financial integration did not play as a smoothing device when the crisis hit. Quite the opposite, crisis countries suffered sudden stops. In this same line is the idea that the Eurozone was as a whole a large but fairly closed economy, while Eurozone governments continued with the mind-sets of small open economies – each ignoring the impact of their actions on the situation faced by the collective. (Baldwin and Giavazzi 2015)

Studies have used fiscal indicator measures to determine whether fiscal policies are converging within the European Union. De Bandt and Mongelli (2000) conducted a study that used contemporaneous cross-correlation, dispersion and cointegration tests on key fiscal variables of government net lending and total current revenue and expenditure over the period 1970–98. It was found that the fiscal dispersion was declining at a sustained pace, and the fiscal positions of the countries were coming closer together in the euro area.

Similarly, Onorante (2006) examined whether a country should be required to meet the fiscal rule before or after entering a monetary union. The chapter uses a model of policy interactions in a monetary union focusing on wage dynamics, fiscal and monetary activism, and their consequences on inflation. It was found that a strategy of convergence in public finances before entry in a monetary union may be preferable both for the acceding country and the stability of the existing monetary union. It was also found that fiscal constraints should remain after entry in the monetary union, as they are useful in re-establishing monetary dominance.

Blot and Serranito (2006) looked at whether fiscal policies of the EMU members have converged and whether the source of the process can be identified. Their findings reveal that the convergence of fiscal policies cannot only be measured using the current fiscal balance. There is need for more fiscal indicators to be considered when examining fiscal covergence to inform policy. The structural break generally occurred before the Maastricht Treaty, indicating that the converging process results from economic and financial integration and not from institutional arrangements.

Kocenda, Kutan and Yigit (2008) examine the fiscal convergence of the new EU members concerning the EU15 using tests of convergence that allow for structural breaks. They used the Maastricht fiscal convergence of the European Union as well as other alternative measures of fiscal discipline to determine the effects of the monetary union on fiscal discipline and convergence. It was found that fiscal discipline within the union was minimal and that a monetary union may not provide fiscal discipline for its members.

Baladi (2007) and Lorde, Francis and Jackman (2009)[7] are the only two studies found that empirically examine the convergence of fiscal policy in the Caribbean in the context of establishing a monetary union, while Anthony and Hallett (2000) and Worrell (2003) extensively examined if establishing a monetary union in the Caribbean is realistic. The work of Lorde, Francis and Jackman (2009) empirically explored the disciplinary effects of a monetary union within CARICOM. They specifically investigated whether there was any systematic difference between fiscal policy in the ECCU and any other Caribbean country that retained monetary sovereignty for the period 1984–2004. The measure of fiscal policy they use is government consumption as a percentage of GDP, while they use other control variables such as real GDP per capita, international reserves, financial depth and openness. The results of their study found that within the ECCU they had less fiscal discipline compared to the rest of CARICOM, thereby suggesting that being a member of a monetary union within CARICOM may not result in greater fiscal discipline. In this situation, it was found that while the ECCU has stipulated fiscal guidelines, they are not binding and enforced by the Eastern Caribbean Central Bank, resulting in ECCU member countries pursuing less conservative fiscal policies than the non-ECCU member countries within CARICOM. Their suggestion to note in establishing a CMU was "if the actions of the ECCU members are any indication, binding fiscal rules may be necessary to avoid fiscal profligacy in a CARICOM monetary union" (Lorde, Francis and Jackman 2009, 17).

Baladi (2007) critically assessed the implications of a CMU on the monetary, fiscal and trade policies of CARICOM, and proposed that the convergence criteria of the CMU be revised and additions made. The main findings were the need to have the criteria enhanced to include limits on public sector debt and convergence of interest rates; to establish sanctions and imposing fiscal rules to discourage fiscal profligacy; to give central banks greater independence;[8] and the need for a greater level of political commitment to a union that binds them not only monetarily but fiscally as well.

Optimum Currency Area and Monetary Unions

A review of the literature on optimum currency area (OCA) reveals that there are two distinct views: the "early OCA" theory and the "endogeneity of OCA". The "early" theory of OCA, developed in the early 1960s by Mundell (1961), McKinnon (1963) and Kenen (1969), attempts to explain the conditions that are necessary for a country or region to have a common currency area with other countries or regions. They defined an OCA as the optimal geographical area for a single currency or for several countries whose exchange rates are irrevocably pegged, with high mobile factors of production and diversified production of goods and services. Countries would form a currency area in the expectation that current and future benefits exceed costs. Table 6.1 shows the existing monetary unions of the world.

Mongelli (2002) lists the characteristics of the early OCA theory that emerged in the literature: price and wage flexibility; mobility of factors of production, including labour; financial market integration; the degree of economic openness; the diversification in production and consumption; similarities of inflation rates; fiscal integration; and political integration. These prerequisites were critiqued by Robson (1987), Tavlas (1993), Emerson et al. (1992) and Mongelli (2002). The OCA framework has evolved into one that does not provide an exact model as to what exactly constitutes an OCA (Mongelli 2008). There have been attempts to operationalize the OCA theory, with a need for greater emphasis on the benefits of a currency area. This shift in emphasis resulted in a new theory called "endogeneity of OCA". This endogeneity of OCA theory was proposed by Frankel and Rose (1998), in which the authors showed that monetary integration leads to a profound increase in reciprocal trade and suggests that there is no need for the prerequisites of the early OCA theory to be met before establishing a monetary union, as the countries may turn into an OCA after the establishment of the monetary union.

Bukowski (2011), however, argues that the propositions made by the endogeneity theory of OCA to establish a monetary union without countries meeting the

Table 6.1. Existing Monetary Unions

	European Union (EU)	Eastern Caribbean Currency Union (ECCU)	CFA[*]
Number of countries	27	7	14
Population (millions)	500	0.8	255
Year of est. of single market	1992	1980	1945
Year of est. of single currency	1999	1981	1945
Name of currency	Euro	Eastern Caribbean dollar	CFA franc
Exchange rate per US$[**]	0.76	2.7	451.85

Sources: European Union (2018); ECCB (2018); Central Bank of West African States (2017).

* Communauté Financière Africaine (African Financial Community) franc zone consists of fourteen countries in sub-Saharan Africa, each affiliated with one of two monetary unions.

** The exchange was in September 2013.

prerequisites of an OCA would make the real convergence process indispensable. His work suggests that the creation of a monetary union with countries of varying levels of economic development, vulnerabilities towards inflation, and different degrees of fiscal discipline and integration with other members can be problematic. The inequalities that exist among the countries is an unwanted burden on the monetary union, as it adds increased pressure on the countries upon joining the monetary union to try to satisfy the necessary criteria. Also, it is proposed that the burden of adjustments of economic shocks within the monetary union or on individual countries will be on the market mechanism. In the Caribbean context, Anthony and Hallett (2000) argue that the Caribbean does not qualify as an optimal currency area based on traditional OCA theory, but they believed that a CMU can be established based on the new theory of the endogeneity of OCA. This was based on their findings which suggested that the establishment of a currency union will enhance the economic integration process in the Caribbean, unlike in the EU where the monetary union was formed after achieving some level of economic integration (Anthony and Hallett 2000).

The literature reviewed focused on fiscal convergence and its appropriateness for establishing a monetary union, all based on the experiences of the EMU. The common conclusion of the studies was that fiscal convergence is not necessary to join a monetary union, but having fiscal rules enforced upon joining the monetary union would be a better way to impose fiscal responsibility and control on countries.[9] The studies that were based on the Caribbean economies also found that the use of fiscal rules would be appropriate to impose on members of a monetary union,[10] and establishing a CMU without having all the convergence criteria satisfied may promote economic integration.[11]

The History of the Caribbean Monetary Union

Caribbean countries share a common history, although each country has evolved to create its own social, economic and political characteristics which define them. The Caribbean region had a common currency, the British West Indies dollar (1935), which was administered by a regional currency authority.[12] In 1950, the British Caribbean Currency Board was established as the central monetary authority for British colonies in the Caribbean[13] and introduced the Eastern Caribbean dollar (EC$). Jamaica and the Bahamas had their Board of Commissioners that issued currency and thus were not members of the British Caribbean Currency Board. The desire for political and economic independence by the British Caribbean colonies resulted in the formation of the short-lived Federation of the West Indies (1958–62), which used the British West Indian dollar as its currency. The federation dissolved when some of its members became independent states: Jamaica (1962), Trinidad and Tobago (1962), Guyana (1966), and Barbados (1966). In 1964, the British Caribbean Currency Board was dissolved and replaced with the Eastern Caribbean Currency Authority, which was established in 1965. It kept the Eastern Caribbean dollar as its currency. In 1972, Barbados left the Eastern Caribbean Currency Authority and established its central bank. In October 1983, the Eastern Caribbean Currency Authority officially became the Eastern Caribbean Central Bank.[14]

After a few years of exploring their status as independent nations, a quest for economic integration began. The Caribbean Free Trade Area was set up in 1968 and provided for the removal of tariffs on products that were produced regionally.[15] The signing of the Treaty of Chaguaramas in 1974 established CARICOM, which signalled a move towards further integration. CARICOM has, over the years, been able to foster economic integration among its member states, with one of its milestones being the proposed Caribbean Single Market and Economy (CSME). The CSME is an integrated development strategy envisioned at the tenth CARICOM Heads of Government meeting in July 1989. It was to be implemented in two phases. The first phase was implemented in 2006 with the introduction of the CARICOM Single Market (CSM).[16] The second phase was scheduled to be implemented over the period 2009–15 with the creation of the CARICOM Single Economy (CSE).[17]

The idea of having a monetary union for the region is not new; in fact, the correct statement to say would be there has been a talk to re-establish a monetary union in the Caribbean. Hilaire (1993, 56) notes: "CARICOM Heads of Government, prompted by the West Indian Commission (1992), decided to embark on the formation of a monetary union. This commitment marks the reversal to an earlier period before the advent of independent Central Banks. The British Caribbean Currency (BCCB) was established in 1950". The thrust for a CMU began in 1990. The governors of CARICOM central banks were given the mandate to conduct a feasibility study on the prospects and implementation of a CMU. In conducting their feasibility study for CMU, the experiences of regions were examined, including Europe, Germany, CFA franc zone and the United States. The region which modelled the Caribbean region the closest was the European region. Hence, most of the guidelines and implications of the CMU are based on lessons learned from the EU (Boyd and Smith 2012). In 1992, the Caribbean Central Bank governors presented the report. It outlined the process by which CARICOM member countries were to move towards establishing a monetary union. The report proposed that the monetary union be established in three stages based on two groupings: (1) the ECCU, Bahamas and Belize; and (2) Barbados, Guyana, Jamaica, Suriname, and Trinidad and Tobago.[18] These groupings were based on the fact that group one had already met the criteria for entry into the CMU in 1992; their role then was to continue to maintain its macroeconomic stability. The second group consisted of the countries that did not meet the criteria; they were required to actively pursue measures to meet the criteria.

The convergence criteria agreed to by the CARICOM are as follows:

1. The import cover criterion requires countries to have three months' import cover for the last twelve months.
2. The exchange rate stability criterion requires the exchange rate to be maintained at a fixed rate to the US dollar for thirty-six consecutive months without external debt payment arrears.
3. The debt servicing criterion requires that the country's external debt service ratio remains below 15 per cent of the value of exports of goods and non-factor services.

The first phase of the proposed CMU was to have introduced a common currency in group one, except for Belize and the Bahamas. This first phase was due to be concluded in 1996. The second phase should have begun in 1997 and ended in 2000, within which time three conditions should have been achieved: the establishment of a Caribbean Monetary Authority to oversee the regulation of a regional currency; the issuance and circulation of a common currency in the first group of countries, except for the Bahamas; and the use of the new currency in the other countries as a unit of account in settling regional transactions. There were to be continued efforts by Jamaica and Guyana to meet the criteria for entry to the union. In 2000, the third phase was to have all CARICOM countries enter the CMU.

However, in 1993 the first phase was halted due to the floating of the Trinidad and Tobago dollar. This first phase is still outstanding and yet to be completed. Since then, there have been many crises and issues affecting the implementation of the CMU. Nevertheless, there continues to be a sustained pursuit for its establishment. In 1994 the CARICOM Heads of Government realized that the timetable for the monetary union was no longer achievable. The thrust to restructure in 1997, the "Organs and Institutions of the Community", resulted in the Revised Treaty of Chaguaramas (2001). The CSME was a derivation of the Revised Treaty of Chaguaramas, which informed the need for a realignment of the proposed convergence criteria of 1992. The CARICOM Central Bank Governors' report, titled "Revised Convergence Criteria for Caribbean Monetary Union" (2002), highlighted the following issues:

1. There was a lack of convergence in the macroeconomic performances of the Caribbean economies, and thus a need for more realistic convergence criteria.
2. The relevancy of the convergence criteria agreed on in 1992 was questioned. It was argued that due to the financial liberalization occurring then, holding of foreign reserves equivalent to three months of imports were not adequate.
3. The static nature of the convergence process was questionable, as the convergence criteria are based on the country's ability to satisfy a convergent point target.

The report proposed that the existing criteria be revised and additional ones added to the list. A significant deterrent towards the CMU was the inflexibility in the convergence process. The report also suggested the convergence criteria be viewed as guideposts to assist countries in entering the monetary union rather than acting as barriers to entry. As such, the criteria have been revised accordingly:

1. The import cover criterion requires countries to have three months of import cover for the last twelve months. A certain degree of flexibility exists in this new definition because of the provision for a waiver. There is a short period that permits the violation of the target. The reason for a country not meeting the criterion should be considered, along with underlying trend inflows of foreign reserves, to appreciate performance in respect of foreign exchange holdings fully.
2. The exchange rate stability criterion requires that fluctuations in the exchange rate remain in a 1.5 per cent band for thirty-six months for the floating exchange rate regime countries and that the rate remains fixed for the fixed exchange rate economies. The amendments now allow for temporary fluctuations outside of this band to no longer constitute a violation of this criterion. Any country in violation would now be eligible for the waiver within the context of the proposed

mechanism for addressing the violation of targets, and, as an additional check, the real effective exchange rate will be monitored.

3. Debt servicing criterion: no change.

Three additional criteria that were proposed, but only two were added to the list in 2002:

- Inflation criterion: requires the country's inflation rate to be at the median inflation rate for the three countries with the lowest positive rates of inflation, plus or minus 1.5 per cent.
- Fiscal criterion: requires the country to have an overall average fiscal balance as a per cent of GDP of no more than 3 per cent.

Fiscal Convergence Criteria for the Caribbean Monetary Union

Fiscal imbalances are an inherent characteristic that most CARICOM countries have grappled with primarily because of the always increasing level of a country's expenditure as opposed to its slower increasing sources of revenues. In 2002 the fiscal criterion was introduced to the list of convergence criteria for entry into the CMU. The need for such a criterion arose based on the recommendations from the Board of Central Bank Governors that a broader range of macroeconomic variables should be monitored. A well-functioning monetary union requires all members to be aware of the spillover effects of their national policies, especially for each country's budgeting and allocation of finances and resources. The main arguments cited in the report "Revised Convergence Criteria for Caribbean Monetary Union" for the inclusion of a fiscal criterion were stated as follows:

> Theoretically, the optimum currency area theory argues that monetary union without fiscal convergence might lead to monetary and economic instability and, therefore, recommends binding fiscal values, limiting the size and financing of fiscal deficits. The Caribbean experience has shown that its macroeconomic stability is sensitive to the "quality" of economic management in the various countries; the fiscal policy has played a significant role in all the severe economic crises the region has faced. (CARICOM Committee of Central Bank Governors 2002)

The report proposed that the constraint on the fiscal deficit within the monetary union be reflective of three principles:

1. The country should avoid excessive deficits – that is, deficits that violate stated fiscal thresholds for the deficit:GDP ratio or the total debt:GDP ratio.
2. There should be a "no bail-out clause", making each member responsible for servicing its public debt, even in a crisis.
3. There should be no possibility of direct central banking financing or access to favourable financing of public deficits.

The literature and the OCA theory suggested that the ratio of the fiscal deficit to GDP is the best measure of fiscal discipline as it provides some indication of the quantum of the nation's resources which the deficit absorbs. The technical team considered several factors in setting the fiscal criterion, all of which recognized that internal and external shocks could cause short-term deviations from a planned fiscal path. A fiscal deficit greater than 3 per cent of GDP is considered as a violation of the convergence criterion.

The Fiscal Performance of the Proposed Caribbean Monetary Union Countries and the Experience of the European Union

Figure 6.1 shows the performance of the fiscal deficit-to-GDP ratio of the proposed CMU members of CARICOM over the period 1994–2012. All seven territories were not consistent in complying with the fiscal criterion of the fiscal deficit of 3 per cent of GDP. The Caribbean economies within the 1990s period experienced low and slow growth rates as well as high levels of unemployment. In 2002 when the fiscal criterion was added to the list of criteria for the establishment of the CMU, the territories of the Bahamas, Guyana, Barbados, and Trinidad and Tobago reported fiscal deficit-to-GDP ratios that fluctuated closely to and above the fiscal criterion of minus 3 per cent over the period 2002–08. However, since 2009 most of the territories were not able to maintain their fiscal balance criteria because of the external shocks of the global recession and financial crisis of 2008–09, which was exacerbated by the failure of CL Financial in 2009.[19]

Several economies responded to the crisis by loosening fiscal policy. In the Caribbean region, governments raised their expenditures considerably to curb job losses, stimulate economic activities and buffer the financial system in their country. The economies that are driven mainly by tourism (Bahamas, Barbados, and ECCU) reported more significant fiscal deficits than mineral-based economies (Guyana, and Trinidad and Tobago). Yartey et al. (2012) examined the fiscal performance of Caribbean economies over the period 1997–2011 to determine the nature of underlying fiscal problems and the

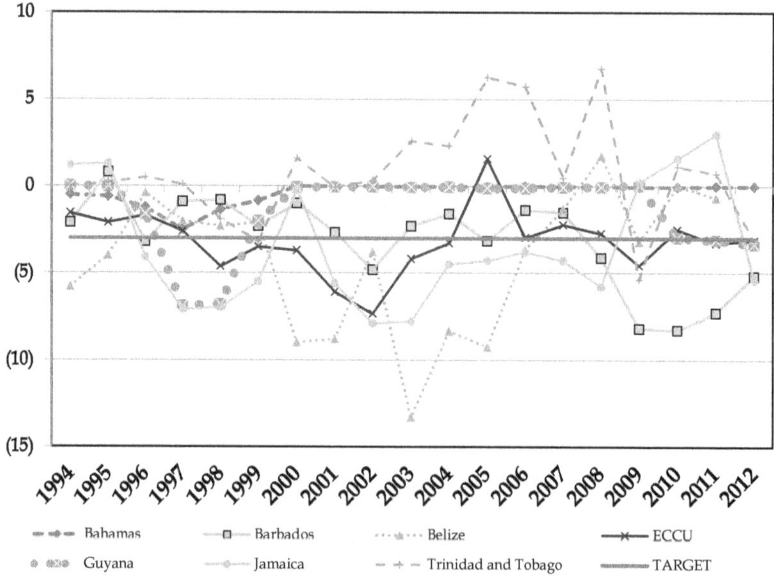

Figure 6.1. Fiscal criterion of CMU (overall fiscal balance as per cent of GDP)

extent of the impact of the global financial crisis on their fiscal outcomes. Their work found that higher total expenditure during the financial crisis (2005–07) was a result of increased spending on goods and services, and transfers. The average spending on goods and services rose from 5 to 6 per cent of GDP, while transfers climbed from 6 per cent of GDP to more than 8 per cent; capital outlays fluctuated between 3 and 5 per cent over the review period 1997–2011.

The question then arises: How appropriate is the fiscal criterion for these economies given the current state of their economies? In answering this question, the European Union's experience is taken into consideration. Before the official establishment of the European Union, the eurozone countries met the convergence criteria stated in the Maastricht Treaty of 1998.[20] However, that perceived convergence was short-lived. Demertzis et al. (2000) thought that the higher degree of convergence of the EU countries at the end of the 1990s resulted from the appropriate use of economic policy rather than from natural convergence processes. Bukowski (2011) reports that the fiscal stabilization criteria were fully satisfied by Germany, France, Finland, Austria, the Netherlands, Spain, Ireland, Luxembourg and Portugal in 1998. However, between 1998 and 2007, most EU members started to gradually not satisfy the recommended values concerning their fiscal deficit and public debt.[21] According to Bukowski (2011), the primary source of the fiscal problems for the eurozone emanated from

- the abandonment of the public finance reforms and structural changes to enhance the efficiency of markets as an adjustment mechanism;
- a high tendency towards budget deficits and public debt growth from the very beginning of the eurozone existence in Greece, Italy, Portugal and Spain;
- pro-cyclical relaxing of fiscal policy in many countries in the 2002–07 boom period;
- an increased share of fixed costs in the total budget spending and GDP;
- the economic recession of 2008–09, which caused a dramatic fall in economic growth rate and, in some countries, a decline in the absolute magnitude of GDP, which in turn resulted in lower revenues;
- the end of the boom in the markets of assets – that is, the real estate market in the United States and other developed countries;[22]
- the implementation of fiscal packages, which were to stimulate the economic climate.

The work of Bucur and Dragomirescu (2013) studied the capacity of the fiscal criteria in the EU member states to determine if it contributed to their economic development and helped in their integration in the EMU. They analysed the developments of the budget deficit and gross public debt in the European Union during 2000 and 2012 on the assumption that there were certain technical deficiencies with the fiscal criteria. Their results show that until 2007 the EU economies were able, overall, to meet the fiscal deficit criteria. However, due to the financial crisis and the prolonged slowdown in economic growth, the fiscal balance had an unfavourable evolution since 2008, accompanied by an increase and worsening of gross public debt. The sustainability of public finances was questioned, resulting in a shift for the European Union to the adoption, application and enforcement of the fiscal policy rules, which influenced the development of the Fiscal Rule Index for the period 2000–11. The importance of rules in the fiscal management of the European Union was noted.

From the European Union's experience, having only a fiscal criterion was not an effective measure to curb fiscal problems in a monetary union. The nature and structure of Caribbean economies are more fragile than those of the European Union, highlighting a need for the application and definition of the fiscal convergence criteria to be examined.

Data and Methodology

This study focuses on three critical fiscal variables that are complementary facets to fiscal policy: net lending of government,[23] current revenue and current expenditure.[24] These variables inadvertently reflect the golden rule of public finance, which states that current expenditure should be covered by current revenue and only capital expenditure can be financed by borrowing. The net lending of the government is a summary variable expressing the balance between all components of the budget.

The variables are expressed as a ratio to GDP (for 1994–2012), and their co-movement and gradual convergence are examined in the following groups:

- Group one: ECCU member countries – Anguilla, Antigua and Barbuda, Dominica, Grenada, Montserrat, St Kitts and Nevis, St Lucia, and St Vincent and the Grenadines. This group of countries was chosen because it is an existing and established monetary union in the Caribbean region.
- Group two: Although these economies have differences in their economic size and composition, monetary, and fiscal policies, this group included the CARICOM countries that have committed to joining the proposed CMU. They are Barbados, Belize, the ECCU (as a group), Guyana, Jamaica, and Trinidad and Tobago.
- Group three: CARICOM countries that have committed to joining the proposed CMU without the ECCU group. The ECCU was excluded to eliminate their bias of being a CMU from the test for fiscal convergence.

The average of each variable across the group is taken as a benchmark, and the co-movement and gradual convergence in fiscal policies – or the lack thereof – concerning countries in the groupings are examined. Similarly, to the work of DeBandt and Mongelli's (2000) study, the stylized facts of the variables and their fiscal dispersion are examined for trends and patterns of convergence. A more formal test is then employed to determine if the countries' fiscal indicators are cointegrated – that is, whether they have jointly deviated from the budgeted balance or have all returned simultaneously to equilibrium over time. The data set is based on annual data from 1994 to 2012 from the central banks of the countries in this study; the benchmark used is the weighted average of each group, minus the country being examined.[25]

For this analysis, the definition of convergence used by DeBandt and Mongelli (2000) is applied; that is, the fiscal variables are converging if the following two complementary conditions are satisfied:

$$E\left(F_t^i - F_t^j\right) = a \quad \text{and} \quad Var\left(F_t^i - bF_t^j - a\right) = \sigma^2$$

The first condition requires that the expectation of their difference tends to a constant value that is small in relative terms, but not necessarily zero, meaning that the variables need not converge ultimately to a common value. The second condition is that the variance of their relationship also tends to decline, reaching a constant value. In this section, a weighted group average indicates that the country being studied is not included in the weighted average, and the term "fiscal variable" refers to the fiscal variable in question as a per cent of GDP. Two main limitations of this study were the availability of data for net lending, and the size and frequency of the data set used for the other variables. The findings of this study should be evaluated, bearing these shortcomings in mind.

Indicators of Cross-Correlation

The correlation test is used to measure the strength of the linear association between the selected fiscal variables for each of the countries in the sample against the corresponding group weighted average. Artis and Zhang (1997) examined the synchronization of business cycles in the euro area. We use their methodology to examine the fiscal cycles in the CARICOM area and to determine if fiscal convergence is occurring. We look at two cross-correlations ratios to gauge the extent to which national fiscal policies were altered in response to the underlying fiscal trends. The first correlation ratio looks at the correlation in the first difference of the fiscal variables with respect to the weighted average of the group. This first correlation ratio is done because the fiscal variables were non-stationary and to correct for bias in the correlation. The second correlation ratio is the correlation of cyclical differences with respect to the weighted group average.

Where the cyclical differences are calculated using $C_{it} = \dfrac{\left(F_{it} - \tilde{F}_{it}\right)}{\tilde{F}_{it}}$, F_{it} is the fiscal variable of the given country i at a point in time t, and $\tilde{F}_{it}$ is the trend after smoothing with the Hodrick–Prescott filter.

Indicators of Fiscal Dispersion

The fiscal dispersion of the variables is determined by calculating the standard deviations and coefficients of variation of the fiscal variables for all the countries within their groups. Convergence or divergence of fiscal indicators over time is examined by using the average of each group as the benchmark.

Cointegration Test for Fiscal Convergence

The second condition of convergence is the equivalent to cointegration. The hypothesis being tested is whether the countries have jointly deviated from a budget balance or have all returned simultaneously to equilibrium over time – that is, whether the fiscal variables are cointegrated. The fiscal variables – that is, the fiscal variable of a specified country and the group average – are examined pairwise for cointegration.

Analysis and Results

Indicators of Cross-Correlation

The limited data set requires the correlation results to be taken as simple indicators of fiscal change. To appropriately assess the fiscal convergence of the Caribbean economies for the proposed CMU over time, four sample periods are examined.

Current Revenue

In group one, the correlation across indicators of current revenue in the first difference and cycles for the period 1994–2012 both reported low values of correlation, suggesting divergence of fiscal policy. The correlation values for current revenue for the ECCU ranged from –0.35 (St Lucia) to 0.68 (Montserrat) for the first difference correlations, while for the cyclical difference correlations the range was –0.17 (Montserrat) to 0.65 (Grenada). Over time, there are positive correlations within the ECCU for 1999–2003 and 2004–08 for both the first difference and cyclical differences correlation values, which are notably low in countries like Antigua and Barbuda, and Anguilla. For the last period of 2009–12, there is a significant decline in the correlation values, with most of the member countries having negative values. The only country to display any sort of fiscal convergence tendency over time with current revenue is Montserrat.

The correlations reported for group two for current revenue for both first differences and cyclical differences were considerably low for all countries and negative in some cases for the period 1994–2012. The first difference correlations ranged from –0.23 (Barbados) to 0.53 (Belize), while cyclical difference correlations ranged from –0.25 (Guyana) to 3.5 (Belize). The initial findings of the correlations suggest that there is no fiscal convergence tendency with this grouping of countries. The correlation ratios over the various time frames examined exhibited mostly negative values. The only period that had significant results that hinted towards fiscal convergence for both difference and cyclical correlations was 2004–08.

Low correlations values were reported for group three for the fiscal indicator of current revenue. The overall time frame of 1994–2012 ranged from –0.25 (Barbados) to 0.533 (Belize) for the correlations in first differences, while for the correlations in cyclical differences ranged from –0.244 (Guyana) to 0.34 (Guyana). All countries, except for Belize, had notable improvements in both their correlation values over time. However, within the period 2009–12, they reported a significant decline in their correlations. Belize is the only country that reported consistent correlation values over all periods for the current revenue variable.

Current Expenditure

The correlation ratios in the first difference for current expenditure for the period 1994–2012 was considerably low for group one, ranging from –0.14 (Anguilla) to 0.38 (St Lucia). In contrast, the correlation indicators in cyclical differences had positive but low values that ranged from 0.09 (St Kitts and Nevis) to 0.58 (Dominica and Grenada).

The sub-periods 1999–2003 and 2004–08 both reported high positive correlations in both the first difference and cyclical difference, suggesting that there was a converging trend for that period.

In group two, the correlations were low for both first and cyclical differences, ranging from –0.07 (Belize) to –0.16 (Jamaica) and –0.008 (Guyana) to 0.19 (Belize), respectively. Over time, although the correlation indicators across the current expenditure values were negative and low, there were improvements in their values. Three countries out of the six in group two – Barbados (0.66), Jamaica (0.79), and Trinidad and Tobago (0.76) – reported significant and positive correlation values for the period 2004–08 with respect to first difference and, to a lesser extent, cyclical differences.[26] In the last period 2009–12, the correlation indicators were considerably low and negative for the countries that were reporting converging trends in earlier periods. Guyana is the only country to have a high correlation indicator of 0.75 in cyclical differences for the period 2009–12.

Current expenditure correlations indicators in group three for the review period of 1994–2012 were low, ranging from –0.18 (Jamaica) to 0.06 (Belize) for the first differences. The correlations indicators in cyclical differences for the same period were also low, ranging from –0.01 (Guyana) to 0.21 (Trinidad and Tobago). The correlation indicators for both types were considerably low and negative in 1994–98, with moderate improvements, although still negative in most cases over the period 1999–2003. Guyana was the only country to report a high correlation value of 0.84 for the correlation of cyclical differences in the period 1999–2003. However, in 2004–08 three countries appeared to display convergence tendencies, having correlation indicators in first differences that were positive and high: Barbados (0.67), Jamaica (0.81), and Trinidad and Tobago (0.75). However, the correlations indicators went downward, hinting at divergent tendencies for the last period of 2009–12, with Guyana being the only country having improved correlation indicators.

In summary, both fiscal variables' current revenue and current expenditure seem to display convergence tendency in all three groups for the period 1994–2008. The cross-correlation values for both fiscal variables improved consistently over time from 1994 to 2003, with the period 2004–09 displaying the most significant convergence tendencies. However, for the period 2009–12, the cross-correlation indicators worsened signalling a divergence of the fiscal indicators.

Indicators of Fiscal Dispersion

The analysis of the results assumes that convergence is occurring if the difference of the variables for each country and the benchmark of the group tends to a constant value that is small in relative terms, however, not necessarily zero, or the variance of their relationship also tends to decline, reaching a constant value.

Montserrat was the only outlier in group one, which consists of the ECCU member countries. This was for the current expenditure:GDP ratio. The standard deviation and covariance of the fiscal indicators used for this study show that for the ECCU, although the ranges appear to be broad, they are not significantly wide. For example, the standard deviations of member countries within the ECCU for the year 2000 ranged from 0.008 (St Kitts and Nevis) to 0.21 (Montserrat). The range of the standard deviations increased over time moving to a range of 0.022 (St Kitts and Nevis) to 0.21 (Montserrat) for 2012. This increase in range over time, however, is minimal; there is no change in the range at 0.07 (Grenada in 2000, and Antigua and Barbuda in 2012) when Monserrat is excluded. Based on the definition of convergence being used, it can be concluded that fiscal convergence has been occurring within the ECCU over the period 1994–2012 at a prolonged rate, as the deviations and variances associated with its fiscal indicators are tending towards zero.

The ratios of the fiscal indicators to their benchmark for this group show that two countries have ratios that are out of range: Guyana and, to a lesser extent, Barbados. The standard deviation of the current expenditure:GDP ratio in 2000 ranged from 0.11 (Guyana) to 0.91 (Barbados).[27] Moreover, the current revenue:GDP ratio similarly ranged from 0.14 (Trinidad and Tobago) to 1.05 (Barbados).[28] In 2012 the range reported for the standard deviation was from 0.12 (Jamaica) to 1.64 (Barbados) for the current expenditure:GDP ratio.[29] Moreover, there was a range of 0.36 (Jamaica) to 4.55 (Barbados) for the current revenue:GDP ratio.[30] The covariances of the fiscal variables behaved similarly over the period examined. Although the range of the deviations and variances were considered minimal, over time they have been increasing and not tending towards zero. Fiscal convergence within this group of countries appears to be occurring at a minimal rate.

The third grouping of countries examined was those countries that do not have any common monetary policies. Contrary to what was expected, the measures of fiscal dispersion for group three were remarkably close to those of group two, implying that common monetary policies do not enhance fiscal convergence. The only significant difference in the values reported for the standard deviations and covariances was the range, which was wider. The range of the standard deviations and covariances increased over time. For example, the range of the standard deviation of the current expenditure-to-GDP ratio for 2000 was 0.159 (Guyana) to 0.908 (Barbados). It increased to 0.208 (Jamaica) to 1.621 (Barbados) in 2012. Since 2000, both fiscal variables have been displaying diverging tendencies. Their deviations and variances are considerably high in some cases. Fiscal convergence is almost non-existent within this group, as the fiscal variables based on the fiscal dispersion measures show no real signs of convergence.

Cointegration Test for Fiscal Convergence

The fiscal variables, current revenue and current expenditure displayed non-stationary properties based on the augmented Dickey–Fuller (ADF) and Phillips–Perron (PP) tests. Most of the countries had a unit root, while the others were stationary. Guyana and Trinidad and Tobago reported $I(2)$ when the ADF test was used, but using the PP test they were $I(1)$. Bearing in mind that the sample size was considerably small with only nineteen annual observations per variable and that countries may have changed governments and uncontrolled global events have occurred which impacted on the fiscal policies of certain countries, the Johansen cointegration test is used.[31]

The hypothesis tested was whether the countries have converged over time to a similar equilibrium, that is, whether the fiscal indicators cointegrated. The pairwise cointegration of the fiscal variable for a specific country and the average of the other countries for the same variable in the group is used as this measure.

Johansen (1991) suggests that when testing for cointegration, a sequential process be used; that is, one should start testing with the strictest assumptions for its null hypothesis and then move to looser assumptions.[32] The pairwise cointegration was done for the five assumptions because of the limited data on the Caribbean countries, which restricts any sort of analysis on the trends in the fiscal indicators to make an accurate assessment of which assumption is valid for the region. The results reveal that within the groups, there is no consistent convergence for the assumptions. Only in group one and group three did certain countries have convergence for all assumptions used, but only for the current expenditure variable.[33] The Appendix (table 6.A1) reports the results for the Johansen cointegration test for the first and fifth assumptions used for simplicity, and an asterisk (*) is used to indicate that there is evidence of cointegration at the 5 per cent level. St Lucia and Grenada are the only countries to display evidence of convergence for all five assumptions of the Johansen test for the current expenditure variable within group one; similarly, in group two for the same variable, Jamaica was the only country, while the current revenue variable revealed no consistent results for any country.

Conclusion

This work examined whether common monetary policies can facilitate fiscal convergence in the Caribbean by testing for fiscal convergence within three groupings of countries in the Caribbean: one grouping, the ECCU, which is an established monetary union; and two other groupings of countries including countries within the Caribbean. Evidence of fiscal convergence was found to be convincing within group one using measures of fiscal dispersion. This result was reflective of the established CMU for the ECCU, with its stipulated criterion for each member country to satisfy. The nature and size of the non-ECCU member countries chosen in group two and group three would have influenced the fiscal policy of their economies but based on the endogeneity theory for OCA, they were examined. It was found that in group two, the level of fiscal convergence was minimal, but in group three, there was no fiscal convergence. The more formal test of fiscal convergence, the Johansen cointegration test, revealed that none of the groups had any significant fiscal convergence occurring.

Is fiscal convergence a necessary criterion for a CMU? No, it is not a necessary criterion for a CMU. The Caribbean's performance to date in fulfilling the existing fiscal criterion has highlighted the need to redefine how fiscal convergence is measured and monitored in the Caribbean region.[34] Both internal and external factors influence the fiscal behaviour of these Caribbean economies: internal factors, such as changes over time in their economic conditions, governments,[35] institutional arrangements and businesses; and external factors, such as world output and oil prices. The 2008 global financial crisis profoundly slowed the pace of the fiscal convergence process within CARICOM economies over this review period. The new definition for the fiscal convergence criterion should be linked and reflective of the countries' debt burden as well. Baladi (2007) stated that the fiscal convergence criteria for Caribbean economies should be amended to include limits on public sector debt. Similarly, for the European

Union, and Ayala and Blazsek (2012) have found that the fiscal deficit criterion of the Maastricht Treaty is irrelevant, and they suggested that a limit to debt accumulation may be a more suitable measure. The imposition of fiscal rules on members of a CMU may be more effective than a fiscal criterion as was seen for the European Union in the work of Bucur and Dragomirescu (2013).

Fiscal convergence is an elusive criterion for Caribbean economies that are linked to economic convergence. Seerattan (1997, 1) states "economic convergence is critical to the viability of a monetary union". Hilaire (1993) suggests CARICOM countries will have a more extended transition period to the CMU; the further apart their economic performances are, the longer their path to a CMU will be. Some countries may need to adjust faster and deeper, as governments in member countries may need to adhere to stringent fiscal policies and subscribe to fiscal rules if they committed to a CMU. Therefore, achieving fiscal convergence hinges on the economic convergence of CARICOM economies. The reality of CARICOM economies attaining economic convergence continues to be intangible and plagued with problems that are inherent to small open economies. These problems include their vulnerabilities to global shocks, the economic conditions of major countries, international financial market conditions, and their economic limitations, such as limited financial resources and high debt. The CARICOM's push towards a CMU was motivated by the benefits that Caribbean economies would have, such as improved economic stability with higher growth rates and improvements in intraregional trade, lower unemployment rates that will lead to improved labour markets, and improved capital flows. In the early 1990s, Caribbean economies were hyped to revitalize their integration process towards a CMU. However, the financial crisis of 2007 hindered the Caribbean economies' stride not only towards fiscal convergence but also economic convergence and the CMU. Most governments have since then been struggling to contain their fiscal balances and have been further strained by natural disasters and lower commodity prices. A CMU being established in the near future is bleak given the current economic state and the focus of most Caribbean economies' governments on other country-specific issues. A considerable amount of resources, effort and work remain to be done for the establishment of the CMU. As the decade ends, the support and effort needed by regional institutions from governments to implement and monitor the mechanisms and policies needed to establish a monetary union are currently not available. Caribbean economies, although still committed to a CMU, simply do not currently have the financial resources to commit to it, as many of them are trying their best to maintain their economic stability.

Postscript

CARICOM's initiatives towards the CMU from 2012 to date (August 2020) have been significantly stalled. Many of the CARICOM member economies continue to grapple with external shocks and a depressed economic and financial environment. Major external shocks that have hindered the thrust of Caribbean economies towards the CMU are the global financial crisis (2007), natural disasters (2007–17), de-risking (2016) and the Covid-19 pandemic (2020).

The financial crisis of 2007 hindered the Caribbean economies' strides towards economic convergence significantly and indirectly. CARICOM was at a 64 per cent implementation level of the CSME in 2007 (CARICOM Secretariat 2014).[36] However, the economic performance and the concerted focus of the macroeconomic policy of governments became diverted following the financial crisis, and the thrust towards regional integration became a low-level priority for them. Governments have since then been primarily focused on maintaining economic and financial stability. Most CARICOM economies have been in an economic recession since then, with fiscal deficits, increasingly high levels of debt and high unemployment rates (table 6.2).

Natural disasters have adversely affected CARICOM economies; many of them have experienced a worsening of their fiscal deficits and increased debt levels.[37] Natural disasters can undo all the developments of a country in only one instance; for instance, the destruction of Hurricane Irma to Antigua and Barbuda, and St Martin in 2017. An estimated cost of US$200 million was needed for the recovery of Antigua and Barbuda, while for St Martin the cost was an estimated US$41.4 billion. The financial burden of countries affected by natural disasters is enormous and their impact severe, not just on their overall economic performance but on human and social indicators.

At the CARICOM Heads of Government meeting in July 2016, de-risking was identified as a threat to Caribbean economies' economic and financial stability (Caribbean Centre for Money and Finance 2016). This loss of correspondent banking relationships from 2015 to 2017 has had a varying impact across Caribbean countries depending on the size of the affected banks and the level of foreign presence in the affected countries' banking systems.[38] The full extent of the impact and cost is yet to be quantified, but the unmeasured effect has been a loss in business confidence and a lower number of some basic transactions. A survey conducted by the Caribbean Association of Banks (2016) found that banks in twelve countries in the region have experienced the loss of correspondent banking, including the Bahamas, Belize, Guyana, Jamaica, Suriname, Trinidad and Tobago, and several countries in the ECCU.

The combined adverse effects of the global financial crisis, natural disasters, and de-risking over the period 2012–19 have significantly worsened the overall fiscal balance and debt levels of the CARICOM economies. In 2020, the external shock of the Covid-19[39] pandemic significantly exacerbated the fiscal strain on Caribbean economies, forcing many governments to source funds to provide relief and assistance for their citizens and businesses. Reported figures as of May 2020 (figure 6.2) showed that Caribbean economies have spent between 1 per cent and 4 per cent of GDP to mitigate the immediate effects of Covid-19 on their economies (Bárcena 2020). The economic impact of the Covid-19 pandemic on economies has far exceeded that of the global financial crisis. Severely affected were economies that are tourism-dependent, due to a decline in travel, and oil exporters as commodity prices plummeted. As the pandemic continues, many economies are experiencing high-debt levels and have limited flexibility for undertaking additional discretionary fiscal policy. The longer the Covid-19 pandemic lasts, the higher the cost and more intense the economic contraction will be for Caribbean economies and the world.

Re-examining the performance of the fiscal balance-to-GDP ratio of the proposed CMU members of CARICOM, figure 6.3 shows that all the seven territories continued

Table 6.2. Snapshot View of Caribbean Economies

Country	Real Economic Growth Rates (%)				Overall Fiscal Balance (% of GDP)				Total Debt (% of GDP)				Unemployment Rate (%)			
	2007	2012	2017	2019	2007	2012	2017	2019	2007	2012	2017	2019	2007	2012	2017	2019
Bahamas	1.5	3.1	1.3	1.8	−2.7	−6.8	−5.8	−1.8	31.7	41.0	64.9	66.8	7.9	14.7	10.1	10.7
Barbados	1.8	0.3	1.0	−0.1	−1.6	−5.6	−3.5	3.7	69.3	104.9	133.5	120.2	7.4	11.5	10.3	10.1
Belize	1.2	3.7	1.2	0.3	−1.2	−0.8	−3.0	−3.4	87.8	76.8	94.9	99.3	8.5	14.4	9.7	7.7
ECCU	4.8	0.3	1.8	3.3	−2.7	−2.1	0.15	−2.3	76.1	84.1	70.0	65.1	n.a.	n.a.	n.a.	n.a.
Guyana	7.2	5.3	2.9	4.7	−4.1	−4.7	−7.2	−4.7	60.9	63.5	46.1	40.9	11.0	12.5	12.0	n.a.
Jamaica	1.5	−0.5	0.5	0.9	0.5	−5.49	−0.3	1.4	113.9	129.7	108.9	93.8	9.7	13.9	10.4	7.2
Trinidad and Tobago	4.8	1.3	−2.3	0.0	0.5	−3.2	−6.9	−2.4	13.9	23.39	44.3	46.86	5.6	5.0	4.90	5.0

Sources: National Central Banks of the various countries and the IMF World Economic Outlook 2017, 2018a, 2018b, 2020).

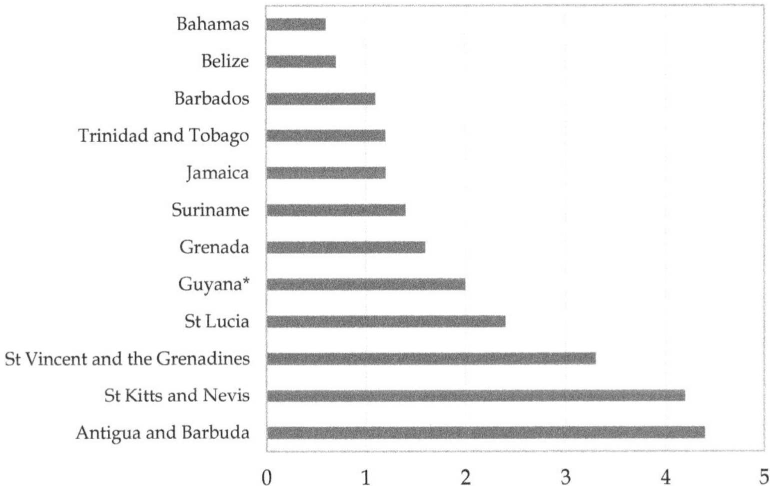

Figure 6.2. Caribbean economies initial fiscal response to Covid-19 (per cent of GDP)
*Guyana figure is an estimated value

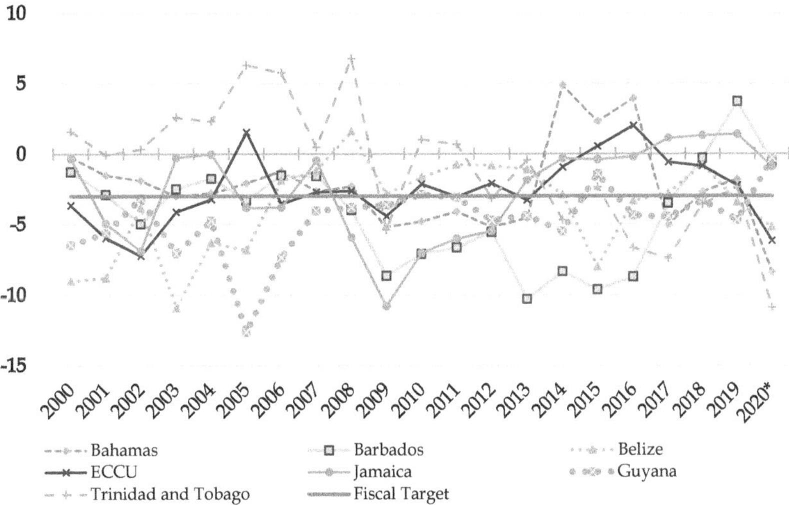

Figure 6.3. Fiscal criterion (overall fiscal balance as per cent of GDP)
*Represents projections data for 2020 from the IMF World Economic Outlook, April 2020

to struggle to meet the fiscal criterion of the negative 3 per cent of GDP. The trend of the countries over the period 1991–2020 (figure 6.4) shows that CARICOM economies' fiscal balances have been deteriorating over the years. The ECCU and Jamaica's fiscal balances, although still negative, have been improving over time, as their trend lines show. This improvement is linked to enforced conditionalities on government expenditure from their International Monetary Fund Stand-by Arrangements and Extended Credit Facility. CARICOM members are faced with the challenge of trying to lower their fiscal deficits in order to achieve growth, while at the same time stabilizing their high-debt levels. The current state of CARICOM economies is not compliant with the requirements of the proposed CMU.

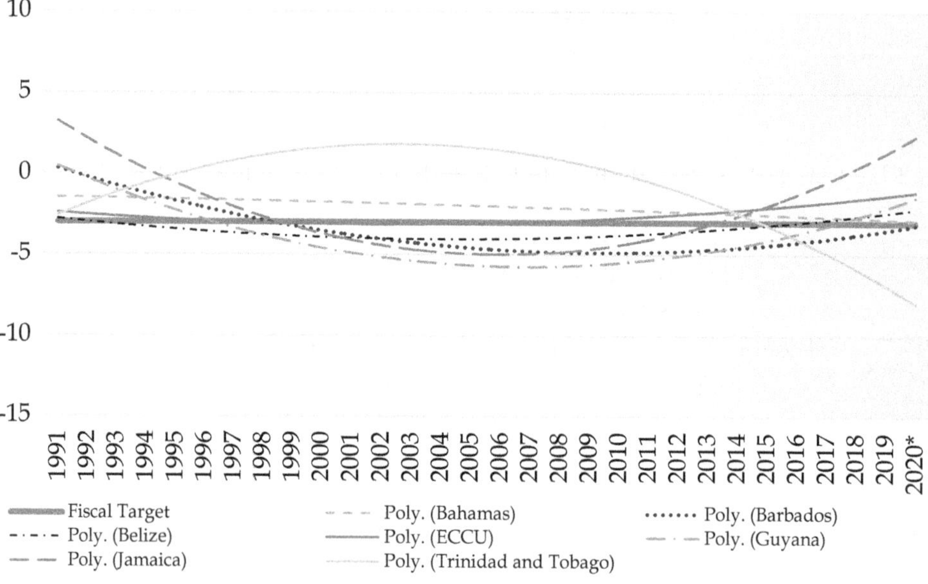

Figure 6.4. Trend lines for overall fiscal balance as per cent of GDP
*Represents projections data for 2020 from the IMF World Economic Outlook, April 2020

Wright et al. (2017) stated that the Caribbean's fiscal performance over the past twenty years has highlighted a need for them to strengthen fiscal discipline, promote credibility and entrench countercyclical fiscal policy through mechanisms such as fiscal rules. They propose an indicative framework for the design and implementation of fiscal rules, based on specific country nuances. Their work also found that the attainment of crucial economic targets depends on governments' ability to design and manage binding rules to guide a useful fiscal framework. They propose that an independent authority continuously monitor the required assessment of the country's major fiscal challenges and institutional frameworks.

CARICOM's efforts to foster increased cooperation with Caribbean economies to achieve greater economic convergence, increased intraregional trade and cooperation has been strained since 2007. The changing global environment has challenges of its own that have harmed CARICOM – significant shifts in geopolitical and economic dominance; technological changes with implications for finance, trade and production processes; an increasing need for a global consensus on climate change and environmental protection, and increasing advocacy for social issues such as gender equality, education and health. These pressures of a changing global environment have provided CARICOM with an opportunity to reposition itself, making the organization more relevant and capable of assisting its members to deal with these new emerging global challenges.

In 2014, CARICOM outlined a new way forward in its publication "Strategic Plan for the Caribbean Community 2015–2019: Repositioning CARICOM" (CARICOM Secretariat 2014).[40] The desired outcomes of this plan are robust economic growth and reduction in poverty and unemployment, improved quality of life, reduced environmental vulnerability, and an integrated community with equity for all. To achieve these desired outcomes, CARICOM has meticulously developed a resilience model that is based on a set of integrated strategic priorities to guide CARICOM and its members in their planning period from 2015 to 2019. Expanding on the strategic priority of building economic resilience, CARICOM states that it intends to create an enabling environment for the stabilization and transitioning of growth of its member economies by several factors one of which is to accelerate the implementation and use of the CSME. Currently, in 2020, CARICOM's strategic plan and move to complete the CSME is still to be realized, and global and current events have dwindled its prospects of becoming a reality. A consideration for CARICOM would be the inclusion of the fiscal rules for Caribbean economies proposed by Wright et al. (2017) to replace the fiscal convergence criterion in the 1992 CARICOM Central Bank Governors' Report. CARICOM can be the independent authority that they suggest should continuously monitor the required assessment of the country's major fiscal challenges and institutional frameworks.

CARICOM's proposed strategic plan is still being discussed within many regional forums, signalling that the interest and desire for the CSME still exists, but it continues to be hindered from being implemented because of the inconsistent alignment between the regional agenda and the priorities of the national agenda, the failure or inability of CARICOM members to commit to regional decisions, and the slow rate of execution of the regional integration arrangement. The reality of a CSME is also compounded by the persistent need for governments to devote their resources and efforts towards the external shocks and economic challenges their countries encounter. The evolving international and regional environment motivated CARICOM to redefine its way forward in 2014 towards achieving greater regional integration. This way forward, however, appears to be halted once more and may always need continuous adjustment based on the duration of time it takes for the CSME to be a reality.

Acknowledgements

This chapter was originally a paper presented at the forty-second Annual Monetary Studies Conference (2009) and CARICOM-SALISES: Rethinking Regionalism Conference (2013). Thank you to attendees for the comments received at both conferences.

Appendix

Table 6.A1.Johansen Cointegration Results

Country	Hypothesis	Current Revenue			Current Expenditure		
		Trace	Max		Trace	Max	
		$r = 0$	$r = 0$	$r = 1$	$r = 0$	$r = 0$	$r = 1$
Antigua and Barbuda	#1	4.33	3.11	1.23	6.00	4.70	1.30
		No Cointegration			No Cointegration		
	#5	15.55	8.17	7.38	15.84	11.47	4.37
		No Cointegration			Cointegration*		
Anguilla	#1	9.32	7.68	1.63	7.05	4.92	2.13
		No Cointegration			No Cointegration		
	#5	7.42	7.04	0.38	16.75	12.20	4.55
		No Cointegration			Cointegration*		
Dominica	#1	14.53*	12.69*	1.85	3.55	3.38	0.17
		No Cointegration			No Cointegration		
	#5	16.05	11.72	4.33	15.74	10.85	4.89
		Cointegration*			No Cointegration		
Grenada	#1	3.69	3.36	0.33	12.35	12.05	0.30
		No Cointegration			Cointegration		
	#5	11.01	6.01	4.99	34.25	25.48	8.77
		No Cointegration			Cointegration*		
Monserrat	#1	4.02	3.01	1.02	17.63	15.72	1.91
		No Cointegration			Cointegration		
	#5	33.58*	28.09*	5.49*	15.47	13.08	2.39
		No Cointegration			Cointegration*		
St Kitts and Nevis	#1	5.76	3.78	1.98	12.03	10.96	1.07
		No Cointegration			No Cointegration		
	#5	16.46	10.25	6.21	17.05	9.58	7.47
		No Cointegration			Cointegration		
St Lucia	#1	13.33*	9.62	3.72	29.68	28.68	1.00
		No Cointegration			Cointegration		
	#5	20.68*	12.00*	8.68*	33.82	29.62	4.21
		No Cointegration			Cointegration		
St Vincent and the Grenadines	#1	5.96	4.83	1.13	7.14	6.43	0.72
		No Cointegration			No Cointegration		
	#5	19.69*	14.80	4.89*	18.25	15.76	2.49
		Cointegration*			No Cointegration		
5% Critical Value	#1	**12.32**	**11.22**	**4.13**	**12.32**	**11.22**	**4.13**
	#5	**18.40**	**17.15**	**3.84**	**18.40**	**17.15**	**3.84**

(Continued)

Table 6.A1: (Continued)

		Johansen Cointegration – Group 2					
		Current Revenue			Current Expenditure		
Country	Hypothesis	Trace	Max		Trace	Max	
		$r = 0$	$r = 0$	$r = 1$	$r = 0$	$r = 0$	$r = 1$
Barbados	#1	24.60	20.96	3.64	8.81	7.42	1.39
		No Cointegration			No Cointegration		
	#5	5.57	3.64	1.92	4.97	3.98	0.99
		No Cointegration			No Cointegration		
Belize	#1	11.94	11.89	0.05	10.53	6.53	4.00
		No Cointegration			No Cointegration		
	#5	22.55	13.09	9.45	20.49	19.55	0.94
		No Cointegration			No Cointegration		
ECCU	#1	8.60	5.86	2.74	4.49	3.81	0.68
		No Cointegration			No Cointegration		
	#5	18.79	13.25	5.54	12.82	12.62	0.20
		No Cointegration			Cointegration*		
Guyana	#1	13.87	13.33	0.54	14.33	10.82	3.51
		No Cointegration			No Cointegration		
	#5	20.15	18.53	1.61	21.75	18.44	3.31
		Cointegration*			No Cointegration		
Jamaica	#1	5.27	4.96	0.31	17.68	16.23	1.45
		No Cointegration			No Cointegration		
	#5	4.27	3.68	0.59	26.98	19.18	7.80
		Cointegration*			No Cointegration		
Trinidad and Tobago	#1	2.21	1.47	0.74	10.13	6.24	3.89
		No Cointegration			No Cointegration		
	#5	14.25	10.34	3.90	16.50	16.49	0.01
		No Cointegration			Cointegration*		
5% Critical Value	**#1**	**12.32**	**11.22**	**4.13**	**12.32**	**11.22**	**4.13**
	#5	**18.40**	**17.15**	**3.84**	**18.40**	**17.15**	**3.84**

		Johansen Cointegration – Group 3					
		Current Revenue			Current Expenditure		
Country	Hypothesis	Trace	Max		Trace	Max	
		$r = 0$	$r = 0$	$r = 1$	$r = 0$	$r = 0$	$r = 1$
Barbados	#1	24.18	20.74	3.44	7.23	5.99	1.23
		No Cointegration			No Cointegration		
	#5	5.82	3.94	1.88	4.65	3.99	0.66
		No Cointegration			No Cointegration		

(*Continued*)

Table 6.A1: (Continued)

Belize	#1	11.66	11.59	0.07	9.34	5.69	3.66
			No Cointegration			No Cointegration	
	#5	22.38	12.95	9.43	18.77	17.89	0.88
			No Cointegration			No Cointegration	
Guyana	#1	14.01	13.03	0.99	14.25	11.06	3.19
			No Cointegration			No Cointegration	
	#5	18.45	16.67	1.78	20.79	18.13	2.66
			Cointegration*			No Cointegration	
Jamaica	#1	5.74	5.74	0.00	9.35	6.05	3.31
			No Cointegration			Cointegration	
	#5	4.42	4.01	0.41	12.79	12.43	0.36
			Cointegration*			Cointegration*	
Trinidad and Tobago	#1	3.24	2.26	0.98	11.18	7.11	4.07
			Cointegration			No Cointegration	
	#5	13.44	9.42	4.02	20.81	20.73	0.08
			Cointegration*			Cointegration*	
5% Critical Value	#1	**12.32**	**11.22**	**4.13**	**12.32**	**11.22**	**4.13**
	#5	**18.40**	**17.15**	**3.84**	**18.40**	**17.15**	**3.84**

Source: Authors' calculations.
* Evidence of cointegration at the 5 per cent level.

Notes

1. It is based mainly on the ideas of British economist John Maynard Keynes (1883–1946).

2. In the case of the European Union, they feared that the Economic Monetary Union (EMU) without economic convergence might be fragile and a source of tension. European Commission governments agreed that four criteria would be necessary for admission to the EMU (Buiter, Corsetti and Roubini 1993).

3. The euro crisis was a period when several European countries experienced the collapse of financial institutions, high government debt and rapidly rising bond yield spreads in government securities. Some of the contributing causes included the financial crisis of 2007–2008, the Great Recession of 2008 to 2012, the real estate market crisis and property bubbles in several countries. The fiscal policies of their member countries regarding government expenses and revenues also contributed.

4. At the time of its establishment, the European Central Bank was tasked with maintaining financial stability but forbidden from purchasing sovereign debt.

5. Creating a stronger financial framework, the European Union established in January 2011 three European Supervisory Authorities. Established to create a supervisory architecture for the European Union, the European Supervisory Authorities are (1) the European Banking Authority, (2) the European Securities and Markets Authority, and (3) the European Insurance and Occupational Pensions Authority.

6. The Treaty on Stability, Coordination and Governance in the Economic and Monetary Union – better known as the "Fiscal Compact" – came into force on 1 January 2013 after

ratification by twelve member states of the euro area. https://www.consilium.europa.eu/uedocs
/cms_data/docs/pressdata/en/ecofin/134543.pdf

7. This chapter is an updated version of the work done by Troy Lorde, Sunday Osaretin
Iyare and Brian M. Francis, 2005, "Monetary Union and Fiscal Discipline Evidence from the
Caribbean", presented at the Caribbean Centre for Money and Finance 37th Annual Monetary
Studies Conference, Nassau, Bahamas, 3–5 November.

8. An independent central bank is needed to compel national governments to make the
necessary adjustments towards an externally executed monetary policy by an independent
authority.

9. Buiter, Corsetti and Roubini (1993); Budd (1997); Buiter (2000); De Bandt and Mongelli
(2000); Onorante (2006); and Kocenda, Kutan and Yigit (2008).

10. Baladi (2007), and Lorde, Francis and Jackman (2009).

11. Frankel and Rose (1998), and Anthony and Hallett (2000).

12. Between 1935 and 1965, the British West Indies dollar had been the currency used in
the British dominions of the Eastern Caribbean (as well as in British Guiana). In 1949, the
British government formalized the system of dollars in the accounts of all these territories
by introducing this monetary unit at the existing conversion rate of 4.80 dollars per pound
sterling.

13. This currency board governed Barbados, Guyana, Trinidad and Tobago, and the ECCU
countries.

14. For more details, see Farrell and Worrell (1994).

15. For products to satisfy the origin criteria, 50 per cent of the value-added had to be
created in the more developed countries, while only 40 per cent of the value-added had to be
created in the less developed countries (Central Bank Task Force January 1995).

16. The CARICOM Single Market is an arrangement that allows CARICOM goods, services,
people and capital to move throughout the Caribbean without tariffs and without restrictions,
which would assist in achieving a single, sizeable economic space, and provide a common
economic and trade policy.

17. The CARICOM Single Economy is an arrangement that further harmonizes economic,
monetary, and fiscal policies and measures across all member states of CARICOM to
strengthen and support the sustainable development of the region. This includes the
coordination of foreign exchange and interest rate policies, the harmonization of tax regimes
and laws, the convergence of economic performance, and common policies on agriculture and
the energy sectors. To date, some strides have been made towards the creation of this single
economic space, but it is still a long way off from being fully achieved. For more information,
see CARICOM's overview webpage on the CSME: https://caricom.org/work-areas/overview
/caricom-single-marke-and-economy.

18. Suriname joined CARICOM in 1995.

19. The failure of CL Financial on 30 January 2009 resulted in many Caribbean governments
having to provide financial support for the group's financial services companies in their
jurisdictions. The cost incurred for saving their financial system was very burdensome since
most Caribbean economies were already in deficits. "Governments chose to intervene despite
their fiscal constraints because the consequences of not intervening would have been more
detrimental to the affected economies, with one key reason being to maintain the confidence in
the financial sector" (Caribbean Centre for Money and Finance 2013).

20. The initial group of countries which formed the European Union in 1999 did not satisfy
the criteria for the OCA nor the endogeneity criteria for the OCA (Bukowski 2011).

21. Note that from the very beginning, Greece never met the fiscal stabilization criteria.

22. This resulted in the financial crisis and had a significantly negative effect on countries
where the share of the construction industry in the economy was high. The crisis entailed costs

of financial assistance for financial institutions, especially in countries with a weak banking system and inadequate banking supervision (e.g. Ireland).

23. The net lending:GDP ratio and its benchmark were too close to zero to infer any reasonable conclusions.

24. The methodology used is similar to that of De Bandt and Mongelli (2000).

25. For example, the relations examined for Antigua and Barbuda for current expenditure is the current expenditure of Antigua and Barbuda and the weighted average of the ECCU excluding Antigua and Barbuda.

26. The correlation values for the cyclical differences for 2004–08 were Barbados (0.68), Jamaica (0.23), and Trinidad and Tobago (0.96).

27. Removing the outlier of Barbados, the range would end at 0.226 (Belize).

28. Removing the outlier of Barbados, the range would end at 0.29 (Jamaica).

29. Removing the outlier of Barbados, the range would end at 0.399 (ECCU).

30. Removing the outlier of Barbados, the range would end at 0.349 (Guyana).

31. This test is used in the literature on convergence for studies done on the European Union for varying periods and country groupings. It measures the speed of adjustment of the short run to the long run.

32. The assumptions were as follows for the vector autoregression model (VAR):

> Assumption 1: No intercept or trend in the cointegrating equation or associated VAR – assumes there is no deterministic trend in data. This is the most restrictive of the five assumptions.
>
> Assumption 2: Intercept and no trend in the cointegrating equation, and no intercept and trend in the associated VAR – assumes no deterministic trend in data.
>
> Assumption 3: Intercept and no trend in the cointegrating equation or associated VAR – allows for the linear deterministic trend in data.
>
> Assumption 4: Intercept and trend in the cointegrating equation and no intercept in the associated VAR – allows for the linear deterministic trend in data.
>
> Assumption 5: Intercept and trend in the cointegrating equation and intercept in the VAR – allows for a deterministic quadratic trend in data.

33. For the variable current expenditure:GDP ratio, the countries were Grenada, Montserrat and St Lucia in group one, and Jamaica in group three.

34. The findings of this chapter are based on an analysis that was constrained by limited data availability.

35. Most Caribbean economies have general government elections every five years.

36. As aforementioned, the CSME is an integrated development strategy envisioned at the tenth meeting of the CARICOM Heads of Government in July 1989. It was to be implemented in two phases. The first phase was implemented in 2006 with the introduction of the CSM. The second phase was to be implemented over the period 2009–15 with the creation of the CSE. To date, this is not a reality.

37. These natural disasters included Hurricane Dean (2007), Hurricane Thomas (2010), Hurricanes Irene and Sandy (2012), Hurricane Joaquin (2015), Hurricane Matthew (2016), and Hurricanes Irma and Maria (2017).

38. Large correspondent banks, domiciled in the United States, Europe and Canada, provide Caribbean states with vital access to the international financial system by offering services to smaller, domestic banks and financial institutions to complete international payments and settlements. Due to the mandatory compliance of the Foreign Account Tax Compliance Act in 2015, many of these international banks which provide correspondent banking services have been seeking to manage their risks by severing ties with institutions in the Caribbean region.

39. Covid-19 is the infectious disease caused by coronavirus. The first known case was in Wuhan, China, in December 2019. Covid-19 is now a pandemic affecting many countries

globally. According to the World Health Organization, as of 20 August 2020, global statistics on the Covid-19 pandemic were 22,536,278 confirmed cases; 789,197 deaths; and 216 countries, areas or territories with cases.

40. The Strategic Implementation Framework details the process of collaborative work planning across CARICOM entities and partners as a critical tool for CARICOM's ongoing strategic management. It will assist in the selection among initiatives/key measures that will be undertaken each year over the plan period 2015–19.

References

Anand, Shriya, John Anderson, Rochelle Guttmann, Ruiwen Lee, Matthew Mandelberg, Samuel Maurer, Kristy Mayer, Shawn Powers, Caitlin Sanford, and Mary Yang. 2011. Moving toward a Monetary Union and Forecast-Based Monetary Policy in East Africa. Princeton University: Woodrow Wilson School of Public and International Affairs..

Anthony, Myrvin L. and Andrew Hughes Hallett. 2000. "Is the Case for Economic and Monetary Union in the Caribbean Realistic?" *The World Economy* 23 (1): 119–44.

Artis, Michael J. and Wenda Zhang. 1997. "International Business Cycles and the ERM: Is There a European Business Cycle?" *International Journal of Finance & Economics* 2 (1): 1–16.

Ayala, Astrid and Szabolcs Blazsek. 2012. "How Has the Financial Crisis Affected the Fiscal Convergence of Central and Eastern Europe to the Eurozone?" *Applied Economics Letters* 19 (5): 471–76.

Baladi, Andre. 2007. "Realising a Caribbean Monetary Union". *Journal of Business, Finance, and Economics in Emerging Economies* 2 (1): 1–30.

Baldwin, B. and F. Giavazzi. 2015. "The Eurozone Crisis: A Consensus View of the Causes and a Few Possible Solutions". VoxEU.org. 7 September 2015.

Bárcena, Alicia. 2020. "Regional Dialogue to Share Experiences on Fiscal Responses to the Crisis Generated by the COVID-19 Pandemic: The Caribbean Perspective". Presentation in the virtual meeting of Ministers of Finance to discuss the economic impact of the COVID-19 pandemic in the Caribbean. https://www.cepal.org/en/presentations/regional-dialogue-share-experiences-fiscal-responses-crisis-generated-covid-19.

Blot, Christophe and Francisco Serranito. 2006. "Convergence of Fiscal Policies in EMU: A Unit-Root Tests Analysis with Structural Break". *Applied Economics Letters* 13 (4): 211–16.

Boyd, Derick and Ron Smith. 2012. *Monetary Policy, Central Banking and Economic Performance in the Caribbean*. Kingston, Jamaica: University of the West Indies Press.

Bucur, Iulia A. and Simona E. Dragominrescu. 2013. "An Analysis of the Fiscal Convergence Criteria on the European Union in Terms of Sustainability". *Studies and Scientific Researches. Economics Edition*, no. 18: 137–49. https://ideas.repec.org/a/bac/fsecub/13-18-17.html.

Budd, Leslie. 1997. "Regional Integration and Convergence and the Problems of Fiscal and Monetary Systems: Some Lessons for Eastern Europe". *Regional Studies* 31 (6): 559–70.

Buiter, Willem. 2000. "Optimal Currency Areas: Why Does the Exchange Rate Matter?" Centre for Economic Policy Research. CEPR Working Paper No. 2366.

Buiter, Willem, Giancarlo Corsetti, and Nouriel Roubini. 1993. "Excessive Deficits: Sense and Nonsense in the Treaty of Maastricht". *Economic Policy* 8 (16): 57–100.

Bukowski, Sławomir I. 2011. "Economic and Monetary Union – Current Fiscal Disturbances and the Future". *International Advances in Economic Research* 17 (3): 274.

Caribbean Association of Banks. 2016. "Summary of Findings: Correspondent Banking Survey". October Revised Report. http://cab-inc.com/files/documents/Correspondent_banking_survey_Report _Revised_Latest.compressed.pdf.

Caribbean Centre for Money and Finance. 2013. "The CL Financial Debacle – Four Years Later". *CCMF Newsletter* 6, no. 1 (January). http://www.ccmf-uwi.org/files/publications/newsletter/Vol6No01.pdf.

———. 2016. "CARICOM's Response to the Threats to Correspondent Banking and Brexit". *CCMP Newsletter* 9, no. 7 (July). http://www.ccmf-uwi.org/files/publications/newsletter /Vol9No07.pdf.

CARICOM Committee of Central Bank Governors. 2002. "Revised Convergence Criteria for Caribbean Monetary Union". Draft report of the technical team on the Caribbean Monetary Union to the Committee of Central Bank Governors, August.

CARICOM Secretariat. 2014. "Strategic Plan for the Caribbean Community 2015–2019: Re-positioning CARICOM". Volume 2 of the Strategic Plan. Accessed 6 January 2018. https://caricom.org/documents/11853-the_strategic_plan_vol2-final.pdf.

Central Bank of West African States. 2017. "History of the CFA Franc". https://www.bceao.int /en/content/history-cfa-franc.

Central Bank Task Force. January 1995. "Report on Monetary Union and Currency Convertibility in the CARICOM countries" (Mimeo).

Chari, Varadarajan V. and Patrick J. Kehoe. 2007. "On the Need for Fiscal Constraints in a Monetary Union". *Journal of Monetary Economics* 54 (8): 2399–408.

Corsetti, G., Barry Eichengreen, Galina Hale, and Eric Tallman. 2019. "The Euro Crisis in the Mirror of the European Monetary System". VoxEU.org, 15 February 2019.

De Bandt, Olivier and Francesco Mongelli. 2000. "Convergence of Fiscal Policies in the Euro Area". European Central Bank. ECB Working Paper No. 20. https://papers.ssrn.com/sol3 /papers.cfm?abstract_id=355580.

Demertzis, Maria, Andrew Hughes Hallett, and Ole Rummel. 2000. "Is the European Union a Natural Currency Area, or Is It Held Together by Policymakers?" *Review of World Economics* 136 (4): 657–79.

Dixit, Avinash and Luisa Lambertini. 2003. "Symbiosis of Monetary and Fiscal Policies in a Monetary Union". *Journal of International Economics* 60 (2): 235–47.

ECCB (Eastern Caribbean Central Bank). 2018. "About the ECCB". https://www.eccb -centralbank.org/p/about-the-eccb.

Eichengreen, Barry. 1996. "Institutions and Economic Growth: Europe after World War II". In *Economic Growth in Europe since 1945*, 38–72. Centre for Economic Policy Research (London). Cambridge: Cambridge University Press.

Emerson, Michael, Daniel Gros, and Alexander Italianer. 1992. *One Market, One Money: An Evaluation of the Potential Benefits and Costs of Forming an Economic and Monetary Union.* Oxford: Oxford University Press.

European Union. 2018. "The Euro". https://europa.eu/european-union/about-eu/money /euro_en.

Farrell, T. and D. Worrell. 1994. "Caribbean Monetary Integration". Port-of-Spain: Caribbean Information Systems and Services.

Frankel, Jeffrey A. and Andrew K. Rose. 1998. "The Endogeneity of the Optimum Currency Area Criteria". *The Economic Journal* 108 (449): 1009–25.

Hall, Peter A. 2015. "The Euro Crisis and the Future of European Integration". In *The Search for Europe, Contrasting Approaches*, edited by Alberto Alesina, Christopher J. Bickerton, and Daron Acemoglu, 46–67. Madrid: BRVA. https://www.bbvaopenmind.com/en/articles/the -euro-crisis-and-the-future-of-european-integration/.

Hilaire, A. 1993. "A Prospective Caribbean Monetary Union: Convergence Issues". Presented at the 30th Meeting of Technicians of the Central Banks of the American Continent, Montevideo, Uruguay, 15–19 November.

IMF (International Monetary Fund). 2017. "Guyana: 2017 Article IV Consultation-Press Release and Staff Report". The International Monetary Fund. http://www.imf.org/en/Publications /CR/Issues/2017/06/28/Guyana-2017-Article-IV-Consultation-Press-Release-Staff-Report -and-Statement-by-the-45010.

———. 2018a. "Jamaica: 2018 Article IV Consultation, Third Review under the Stand-by Arrangement and Request for Modification of Performance Criteria-Press Release and Staff Report". The International Monetary Fund. http://www.imf.org/en/Publications/CR /Issues/2018/04/16/Jamaica-2018-Article-IV-Consultation-Third-Review-Under-the-Stand -By-Arrangement-and-Request-45801.

———. 2018b. "The Bahamas: 2018 Article IV Consultation-Press Release and Staff Report". Western Hemisphere Department. http://www.imf.org/en/Publications/CR /Issues/2018/05/14/The-Bahamas-2018-Article-IV-Consultation-Press-Release-and-Staff -Report-45874.

———. 2020. "World Economic Outlook, April 2020: The Great Lockdown". The International Monetary Fund. https://www.imf.org/en/Publications/WEO/Issues/2020/04/14/weo-april-2020.

Johansen, Soren. 1991 "Estimation and Hypothesis Testing of Cointegration Vectors in Gaussian Vector Autoregressive Models". *Econometrica: Journal of the Econometric Society*, no. 6: 1551–80.

Kenen, Peter. 1969. "The Theory of Optimum Currency Areas: An Eclectic View". *Monetary Problems of the International Economy* 45(3): 41–60.

Kocenda, E., A.M. Kutan, and T.M. Yigit. 2008. "Fiscal Convergence and Discipline in MU: Evidence from the European Union". International Policy Center, University of Michigan. IPC Working Paper No. 61. https://deepblue.lib.umich.edu/bitstream/handle/2027.42/57763 /Paper%20No.%2061.pdf?sequence=1&isAllowed=y.

Lorde, Troy, Brian Francis, and Mahalia Jackman. 2009. "Monetary Union and Fiscal Discipline: Evidence from CARICOM". *Ekonomia* 12 (2): 109–26. https://www.researchgate .net/publication/227428390_Monetary_Union_and_Fiscal_Discipline_Evidence_from _CARICOM.

McKinnon, Ronald. 1963. "Optimum Currency Areas". *The American Economic Review* 53 (4): 717–25.

Mongelli, Francesco. 2002. "'New' Views on the Optimum Currency Area Theory: What is EMU Telling Us?" Frankfurt, Germany: European Central Bank. ECB Working Paper No. 138. https://www.ecb.europa.eu/pub/pdf/scpwps/ecbwp138.pdf.

———. 2008. "European Economic and Monetary Integration, and the Optimum Currency Area Theory". No. 302. Directorate General Economic and Financial Affairs (DG ECFIN), European Commission. http://ec.europa.eu/economy_finance/publications/pages /publication12081_en.pdf.

Mundell, Robert A. 1961. "A Theory of Optimum Currency Areas". *The American Economic Review* 51 (4): 657–65.

Onorante, Luca. 2006. "Fiscal Convergence before Entering the EMU". Frankfurt, Germany: European Central Bank. ECB Working Paper No. 664 (July). https://www.ecb.europa.eu /pub/pdf/scpwps/ecbwp664.pdf?7dae5aaae773259e3848fccf43996347.

Robson, Peter. 1987. *The Economics of International Integration*. London: Allen & Unwin.

Seerattan, Dave. 1997. "Economic Convergence and Monetary Union: The Experience since 1991 and Prospects for the Future". Presented at the Annual Monetary Studies Conference, Bridgetown, Barbados, 27–31 October. http://www.ccmf-uwi.org/files/publications /conference/659.pdf.

Tavlas, George S. 1993. "The 'New' Theory of Optimum Currency Areas". *The World Economy* 16 (6): 663–85.

Worrell, DeLisle. 2003. "A Currency Union for the Caribbean". Washington, DC: International Monetary Fund. IMF Working Paper No. 3/35. https://www.imf.org/en/Publications/WP /Issues/2016/12/30/A-Currency-Union-for-the-Caribbean-16217.

Wright, Allan, Kari Grenade, and Ankie Scott-Joseph. 2017. "Fiscal Rules: Towards a New Paradigm for Fiscal Sustainability in Small States". No. IDB-WP-780. IDB Working

Paper Series. https://publications.iadb.org/en/fiscal-rules-towards-new-paradigm-fiscal-sustainability-small-states?eloutlink=imf2adb.

Yartey, Charles Amo, Machiko Narita, Garth Peron Nicholls, and Joel Chiedu Okwuokei. 2012. "The Challenges of Fiscal Consolidation and Debt Reduction in the Caribbean". Washington, DC: International Monetary Fund. IMF Working Paper No. 12/276. https://www.imf.org/en/Publications/WP/Issues/2016/12/31/The-Challenges-of-Fiscal-Consolidation-and-Debt-Reduction-in-the-Caribbean-40110.

Chapter 7

CARICOM Policy Formulation Process: Review and Reconfiguration

RONALD M. GORDON AND JOHN J. VANSICKLE

Background

The evolution of the Caribbean Community (CARICOM) was driven by political and economic considerations. It evolved from the short-lived West Indies Federation, transitioned through the Caribbean Free Trade Association and culminated with the Treaty of Chaguaramas that established CARICOM in 1973. Its membership comprised entities with similar cultural and historic backgrounds promoting ideas of political and economic cooperation and a common destiny.

Initially there was a strong trade cooperation focus, with members envisaging the creation of a customs union to ultimately foster their economic growth and development. Foreign policy coordination, intraregional trade regimes and various cooperation programmes in sectors such as agriculture, industry, health, education and tourism were anticipated. States were the main players, crafting agreements on various intraregional strategies and programmes in trade as well as the agricultural and industry sectors. As a consequence, intra-country deliberations on policy issues at the key decision-making bodies involved almost exclusively representatives of the states. The involvement of representatives from the business sector was minimal or non-existent (CARICOM Secretariat 2006c, 2006d, 2006e).

Policy Formulation Process

Initial policy considerations for economic integration were shaped in the absence of much empirical analysis and focused mainly on the concept of regional industrial programming, a top-down strategy of governments agreeing among themselves on the country allocation of specific industrial activities (Brewster and Thomas 1967). Production integration in the industrial and agricultural sectors was also advocated, as outlined in the Treaty of Chaguaramas establishing the Caribbean Community (CARICOM Secretariat 1973). The Conference of Heads of Government and the Common Market Council were the two organs of the CARICOM with policy formulation and oversight authority, with the council reporting to the Conference of Heads of Government. In accord with the provisions of the treaty, the overriding philosophy was that governments were the "drivers" in the economies. Hence, initially, there was minimal effort to invite input from the private sector in policy deliberations. In the mid-1980s some segments of the private sector were encouraged to submit comments and recommendations to the council through representatives of their associations that met just prior to the meetings of the council. In most instances these private sector representatives were not entrepreneurs themselves but managers of the associations of business people (Stoneman, Pollard and Inniss 2012). In essence they served as proxies for the entrepreneurs. They were also allowed to sit in on council meetings as observers. However, some states encouraged a stronger input from their business sector with the inclusion of private sector representatives on the national delegations to the council meetings. This allowed the private sector's voice to have the weight of that of the state.

The Conference of Heads of Government, at a meeting in Grand Anse, Grenada, in 1989, decided to establish the CARICOM Single Market and Economy (CSME) as a means of enhancing the region's economic growth and combating the global economic challenges buffeting the region. In a follow-up to this seminal decision, the treaty was revised and agreed to in 2001 (CARICOM Secretariat 2001). The Revised Treaty of Chaguaramas established a suite of organs of the community, each with various designated policy formulation roles. The Council for Trade and Economic Development (COTED) was assigned a policy oversight role for a range of sectors including agriculture, industry, services, trade and economic development. The revised treaty acknowledges the need for "sustained public and private sector collaboration" related to market-led economic activities (CARICOM Secretariat 2001, 31). Similar collaboration was envisaged for "the prospects of the industry for successful production integration" (CARICOM Secretariat 2001, 32). Yet, the revised treaty neglects addressing any modus operandi for the views of the business sector to be incorporated into the policy formulation process. Implicitly, the policy formulation process as outlined in the revised treaty suggests a procedure that is dominated by inputs from governments with little or no regard to the views of or factors influencing the business environment.

At a 1989 conference of the Association of Caribbean Economists, Girvan (1990) posited that the integration process should be more inclusive and interactive in all its dimensions. More recently, a World Bank research team that investigated the issue of Caribbean development advocated, inter alia, that greater dialogue among all relevant stakeholders was needed to achieve growth and competitiveness (World Bank 2005). Given the aforementioned context, this chapter argues the need for a review and reformulation of the CARICOM policy formulation process, with a focus on establishing an environment for growth of the business sector of the CARICOM countries. Deliberate input from the sector into the policy formulation process is envisaged. The next section discusses policy formulation modelling drawing from perspectives of a successful Caribbean entrepreneur, the experience of key global business enterprises, insights from a World Bank survey of the global business environment and the writings of a Caribbean economist. The third section presents the results and analysis of a survey of the CARICOM business environment represented by five CARICOM countries. The next section examines issues and outlines proposals specific to the policy reconfiguration processes. Some concluding comments then follow.

Policy Formulation Modelling to Stimulate the Business Environment

Economic Considerations

Generally, in the context of a market-led philosophy, it is accepted that the economic output of firms is what stimulates economic growth. The more robust the output, the greater the observed growth in the economy. Specifically, small and medium enterprises (SMEs) are thought to be key contributors to growth in the economies of both developed and developing countries (Mohamad and Said 2012). In Fiji, small businesses play an important role in employment creation and income generation despite facing constraints such as security, access to capital and a less than robust human capital base (Reddy 2007). The role of SMEs in some economies is further emphasized by examining the circumstances of Malaysia. In that country SMEs, comprising 97 per cent of the business sector in 2010, were responsible for absorbing 52.7 per cent of employment and contributed 28.5 per cent of the total output in 2010 (Department of Statistics Malaysia 2011). In the Caribbean context, the late Peter D'Aguiar expressed a vivid analogy when, in an address to the Chamber of Commerce of Trinidad and Tobago in the late 1970s, he stated as his theme that "Caribbean Governments should clear the runway to enable the private sector to take off".[1]

Global Insights

Germany's Mittelstand

The Mittelstand sector of the German economy, generally consisting of small- and medium-sized family firms, has been the backbone of the German economy for the majority of the last century (Berghoff 2006). In his review of the Mittelstand over the period 1949–2000, Berghoff (2006) indicated that the sector was the dominant segment of the economy up to 1970. The firms in the Mittelstand vary in characteristics such as size, number of employees, scope of operations and annual sales volume. However, they display a unique management system with sociocultural qualities. They exhibit similar features such as family ownership, focused long-term strategies, a patriarchal culture and informality. In 1999, close to 99 per cent of German businesses were SMEs, meeting the stated qualifying criteria of fewer than 500 employees and an annual sales volume of 100 million DM. Collectively, these firms accounted for about 70 per cent of employment, 45 per cent of sales, 46 per cent of gross investment and 57 per cent of total value added (Berghoff 2006). In addition, they accounted for 30 per cent of direct exports in 1998. They also fulfilled a critical role within the German economy, that of strengthening human capital through the training of interns (Berghoff 2006). Berghoff observed that elements of the Mittelstand existed even in large German corporations and suggested that the success of the Mittelstand model in Germany might be due, inter alia, to transaction cost efficiencies and a resilience in the structural arrangements that contributed to the adaptability of the Mittelstand firms when faced with challenges in the business environment.

Schuman and Himmelreich (2011) in their discussion of the importance of the Mittelstand to the German economy, noted that the German power tool manufacturer

STIHL Inc., a Mittelstand firm, became one of the world's leading exporters in that market by its attention to the technological improvements and quality of its products. They observed that the managers of Mittelstand firms as well as policymakers were creative in addressing cyclical downturns in the economy, so as to maintain a competitive edge for businesses. Berghoff (2006) suggests that the Mittelstand model is of economic importance. The question then arises as to what lessons are there from the Mittelstand model for CARICOM? In the German context, the SMEs that constitute the Mittelstand make an important contribution to factors in the economy such as absorption of labour, gross investment, total value added, direct exports and human capital building. While the SME characteristics of the Mittelstand are not directly comparable with the SME characteristics of the CARICOM business environment, we advocate that the profile of CARICOM SMEs suggests that they are poised to make a similar contribution to the economies of CARICOM countries within an appropriate policy environment.

The Global and Caribbean Business Environment: A Macro Perspective

Working with the assumption that the investment of firms and entrepreneurs was a precursor to successful development, the World Bank conducted a survey of the investment climate and business environment in 80 countries, using a uniform core questionnaire to which more than 10,000 firms responded (Batra, Kaufmann and Stone 2003). This World Business Environment Survey was an extremely useful tool for analysing the global business environment.[2] Respondents were invited to comment on issues such as taxes and regulations, finance, policy instability, inflation, corruption and governance, and the quality of public services. As would be expected, the constraints to enterprises varied across countries, regions, and between developed and developing countries. However, the analysis of the responses indicated that the interaction of firm size and the business environment is complex, with SMEs perceiving themselves as more constrained than larger firms, and within the SME group, smaller firms self-identified as more constrained than medium-sized firms (Batra, Kaufmann and Stone 2003). Analysis of the World Business Environment Survey demonstrated that such surveys are an invaluable tool for evaluating a country's business climate and that there is value to be derived from monitoring business environment indicators over time (Batra, Kaufmann and Stone 2003).

In presenting a Caribbean perspective on the management of national economies as this pertains to economic development, Blackman (2006) stressed, inter alia, that CARICOM governments should pursue economic and political strategies to facilitate effective responses to the complex global environment. He also emphasized that business leaders must be sensitive to changes in the environment, respond promptly and make effective use of the new information technologies. While we accept the gist of Blackman's argument, we assert that, as suggested by the World Business Environment Survey and illustrated by experience of the Mittelstand model in Germany, the design of potentially successful policy measures is contingent upon an understanding of the profile of economic indicators of a targeted business environment.

CARICOM's Business Environment: Another View

Characterization

The CARICOM business environment was evaluated through a structured survey of firms and interviews with firms' representatives across five countries: Dominica, Guyana, Jamaica, St Lucia, and Trinidad and Tobago.[3] Firms' representatives were sourced primarily from the membership of the national associations of chambers of commerce or business/industry associations. This was based on the knowledge that the representatives from the umbrella association of these groups participated in the deliberations of the COTED where they were accorded an observer status allowing voice but no vote. In-person interviews conducted with representatives of forty-seven firms revealed that 53 per cent of these indicated that the CARICOM arrangements did strengthen their business environment by, inter alia, providing access to a larger market and improvements in the rules facilitating trade. However, some respondents identified non-tariff barriers as major constraints to investment and growth (Gordon 2007).

A structured two-part survey was administered to 1,104 firms across the five countries. The valid responses received totalled 153 for part A of the survey and 112 for part B, making the response rate 13.8 and 9.8 per cent, respectively. In addition to eliciting information on firms' characteristics and operations, the survey sought firms' perception of the importance of eleven key variables with regard to their business and investment environment. Firms were also invited to indicate their perception of the impact of national policies versus CARICOM policies on their business and investment environments.

The business environment was revealed to be heterogeneous and multifaceted with important differences pertaining to firm size, area of operation and geographical scope of operation. The size profile of the respondent firms indicates that micro firms constitute the largest group followed by large firms, small firms and then medium firms (see figure 7.1).[4] At 46 per cent, the proportion of micro firms with an annual sales volume (ASV) of less than US$1 million exceeded twice that of large firms, with an ASV in excess of US$6.5 million (21 per cent). At 17 per cent, the proportion of small firms with an ASV between US$1 million and US$2.5 million is similar to that of medium

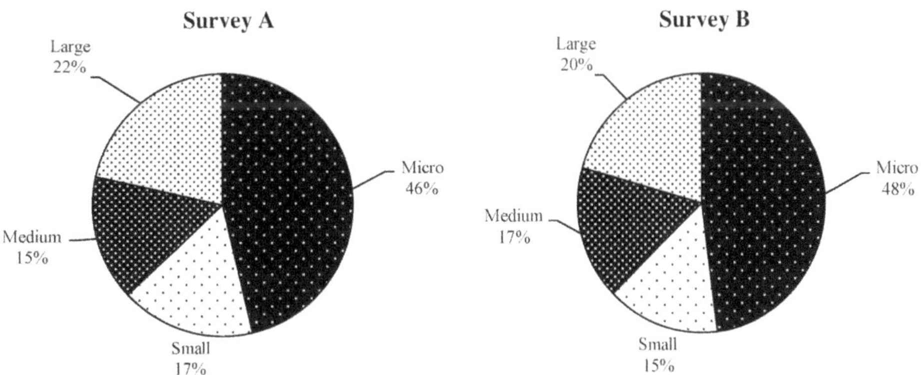

Figure 7.1. Profile of size of firms (Gordon 2007)

firms with an ASV between US$2.5 million and US$6.5 million (15 per cent). Some firms operated only in one sector. Others, across the firm-size groups, reported multisectoral operations with combinations such as agriculture and manufacturing; agriculture, manufacturing and services; manufacturing with trade and commerce; and agriculture and professional services (Gordon 2007). In comparison, the scope of operations of the membership of the Trinidad and Tobago Chamber of Commerce spans twenty-eight areas, with the size profile of these businesses being similarly skewed towards smaller firms (Ferreira 2007).

Twenty per cent of those surveyed operated in another country. Of these, the geographical scope of operations also transcended the firm-size groups, with micro and large firms among those indicating global operations. Global locations included Brazil, Canada, China, Colombia, Costa Rica, Honduras, Kenya, Nigeria, Sri Lanka, the United Kingdom, the United States and Venezuela. Most respondents viewed CARICOM positively, but only 53 per cent thought CARICOM arrangements strengthened their business environment (Gordon 2007).

The respondents were invited to evaluate their business by rating the impact of the eleven factors identified as critical to the conduct and profitability of businesses and investments, using a specified ranking scale. These factors were (1) cost of capital, (2) exchange rate, (3) exchange rate management, (4) inflation, (5) cost of unskilled labour, (6) cost of skilled labour, (7) cost of local inputs, (8) cost of foreign inputs, (9) availability of technology, (10) access to markets and (11) institutional arrangements or rules for doing business. They were also invited to rank their perception of the impact of their respective national government policies and a suite of CARICOM policies on these critical business factors, using the same ranking scale. The summary of responses presented in figure 7.2 indicates the perception of a definite negative impact of governments' policies on all factors, albeit less pronounced for technology and access to markets. For the ranking of CARICOM policies on these business factors, the summary of the responses presented in figure 7.3 shows a neutral view for about six

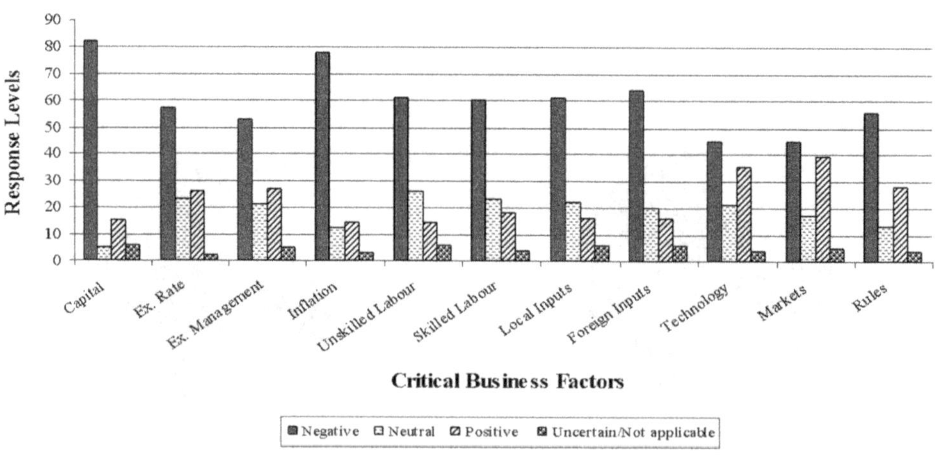

Figure 7.2. Perception of the influence of national government policies on critical business factors (Gordon 2007)

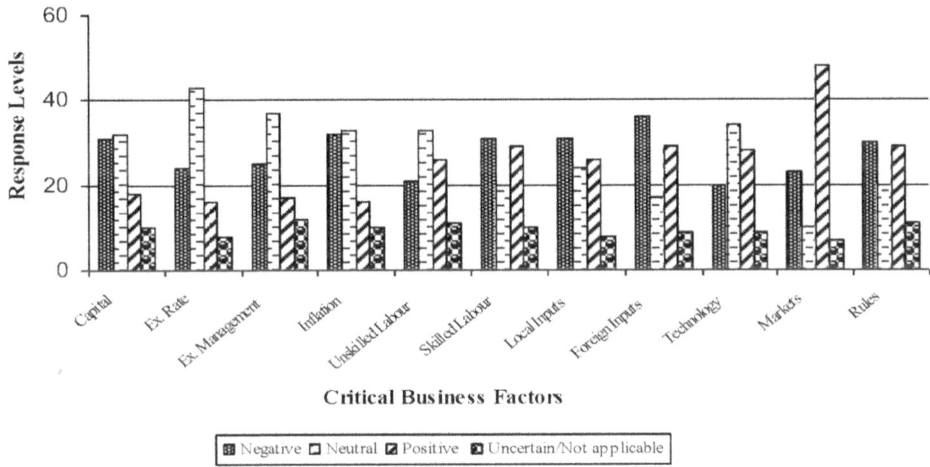

Figure 7.3. Perception of the influence of CARICOM policies on critical business factors (Gordon 2007)

of the eleven critical factors, namely cost of capital, exchange rate and its management, inflation, cost of unskilled labour, and the availability of technology. There was a definite positive perception with respect to access to regional markets and a negative perception in relation to three factors: cost of skilled labour, cost of local inputs and cost of foreign inputs. Respondents were ambivalent on the impact of CARICOM policies on institutional arrangements or rules.

Survey respondents were also invited to compare the importance of their national government's policies versus CARICOM policies with respect to critical business factors important to the viability of their enterprise. Among those respondents most optimistic about the impact of the two groups of policies, there is a perception of greater national policy influence on ten of the eleven critical factors. In the instance of the other factor, market access, there appears to be a perception of greater CARICOM policy influence. When invited to indicate their perception of the CARICOM integration arrangements to the economic gains of their country, a relatively conservative response was offered, with the majority (67 per cent) indicating that the contribution was either "minimal" or "somewhat". A minority (15 per cent) thought the contribution was "considerable" and fewer still (7 per cent) thought there was no impact (Gordon 2007).

Gordon (2007) also undertook econometric analyses of the survey responses for four critical business variables (cost of capital, exchange rate, availability of technology and access to markets) for both the current business environment and the investment environment. The dependent variable was the firms' core ranking of the respective critical business variable, and the explanatory variables were the associated rankings for national policy impact and CARICOM policy impact. The results indicated that in all instances the perception of influence of national policy was statistically significant at either the 1 per cent level or the 5 per cent level, as detailed in tables 7.1–7.4. In contrast, except for the availability of technology, in no instance is CARICOM policy perceived to be influential at least at the 10 per cent statistically significant level. CARICOM policy pertaining to the availability of technology was perceived of influence at the

Table 7.1. Ordered Probit Regression Results for Policy Influences on the Business Environment of Selected CARICOM Countries for the Variable Cost of Capital

Parameter	Estimate	t-Statistic
$C_{\text{intercept (Dominica and large firms)}}$	0.596817 (0.705251)	0.846249
Firms $_{\text{(agriculture and manufacturing)}}$	−0.295191 (0.296789)	−0.994613
Service $_{\text{(T\&H)}}$	−0.681041 (0.395286)	−1.72291*
Service $_{\text{(P)}}$	0.217115 (0.348411)	0.623156
Guyana $_{\text{(dummy)}}$	0.217115 (0.527332)	0.520273
Jamaica $_{\text{(dummy)}}$	−0.408762 (0.465246)	−0.878595
St Lucia $_{\text{(dummy)}}$	−0.223651 (0.484597)	−0.461519
Trinidad and Tobago $_{\text{(dummy)}}$	−0.216052 (0.457826)	−0.471909
Micro	−0.708196 (0.386005)	−1.83468
Small	0.179104 (0.489512)	0.365883
Medium	−0.279393 (0.471834)	−0.592143
NCAP	0.544069 (0.111066)	4.89859***
CCAP	−0.174482 (0.114419)	−1.52494
μ_3	0.703040 (0.169925)	4.13734***
μ_4	1.71047 (0.265101)	6.45217***
μ_5	2.19527 (0.303112)	7.24242***
μ_6	2.37244 (0.316612)	7.49321***
μ_7	2.57258 (0.332685)	7.73280***

Source: Gordon (2007).

Notes: Dependent variable is core ranking of importance of cost of capital. $N = 75$. Scaled R squared = 0.524386. ***, **, * denotes significance level at 0.01, 0.05 and 0.10, respectively. Standard errors in parentheses.

Table 7.2. Ordered Probit Regression Results for Policy Influences on the Business Environment of Selected CARICOM Countries for the Variable Availability of Technology

Parameter	Estimate	t-Statistic
$C_{\text{intercept (Dominica and large firms)}}$	−0.746558 (0.725754)	−1.02867
Firms $_{\text{(agriculture and manufacturing)}}$	−0.070142 (0.352279)	−0.199110
Service $_{\text{(T\&H)}}$	0.547801 (0.392013)	1.39740
Service $_{\text{(P)}}$	0.506781 (0.384705)	1.31732
Guyana $_{\text{(dummy)}}$	−0.080390 (0.540775)	−0.148657
Jamaica $_{\text{(dummy)}}$	0.185136 (0.500900)	0.369606
St Lucia $_{\text{(dummy)}}$	−0.753882 (0.555641)	−1.35678
Trinidad and Tobago $_{\text{(dummy)}}$	−0.231357 (0.485555)	−0.476479
Micro	0.539543 (0.364551)	1.48002
Small	0.762221 (0.493740)	1.54377
Medium	0.102644 (0.508133)	0.202002
NEXRT	0.563498 (0.105339)	5.34937***
CEXRT	−0.059609 (0.125680)	−0.474295
μ_3	0.858810 (0.221234)	3.88191***
μ_4	1.75312 (0.278494)	6.29498***
μ_5	2.41966 (0.317858)	7.61240***
μ_6	2.57526 (0.327338)	7.86728***
μ_7	3.04978 (0.363676)	8.38597***

Source: Gordon (2007).

Notes: Dependent variable is core ranking of importance of exchange rate. $N = 62$. Scaled R squared = 0.498633. ***, **, * denote significance levels at 0.01, 0.05 and 0.10, respectively. Standard errors in parentheses.

Table 7.3. Ordered Probit Regression Results for Policy Influences on the Business Environment of Selected CARICOM Countries for the Variable Availability of Technology

Parameter	Estimate	t-Statistic
$C_{\text{intercept (Dominica and large firms)}}$	−1.42361 (0.684461)	−2.07989**
Firms $_{\text{(agriculture and manufacturing)}}$	0.353236 (0.289969)	1.21818
Service $_{\text{(T\&H)}}$	−0.267493 (0.324045)	−0.825479
Service $_{\text{(P)}}$	0.267222 (0.326487)	0.818479
Guyana $_{\text{(dummy)}}$	0.931110 (0.485652)	1.91724*
Jamaica $_{\text{(dummy)}}$	0.391376 (0.431663)	0.906671
St Lucia $_{\text{(dummy)}}$	0.819300 (0.496024)	1.65174*
Trinidad and Tobago $_{\text{(dummy)}}$	0.973246 (0.444860)	2.18776**
Micro	−0.083061 (0.339953)	−0.244330
Small	0.088108 (0.463426)	0.190124
Medium	−0.178706 (0.427427)	−0.418097
NTEC	0.418988 (0.099729)	4.20159***
CTEC	0.242890 (0.114187)	2.12711**
μ_3	1.00608 (0.262023)	3.83967***
μ_4	1.46343 (0.285950)	5.11779***
μ_5	2.17187 (0.311869)	6.96406***
μ_6	2.4170 (0.320080)	7.53466***
μ_7	3.48621 (0.374566)	9.30733***

Table 7.4. Ordered Probit Regression Results for Policy Influences on the Business Environment of Selected CARICOM Countries for the Variable Access to Markets

Parameter	Estimate	t-Statistic
$C_{\text{intercept (Dominica and large firms)}}$	0.240375 (0.692345)	0.347189
Firms $_{\text{(agriculture and manufacturing)}}$	−0.242927 (0.353529)	−0.687148
Service $_{\text{(T\&H)}}$	−0.316875 (0.387242)	−0.818286
Service $_{\text{(P)}}$	−0.202524 (0.384891)	−0.526185
Guyana $_{\text{(dummy)}}$	0.207232 (0.547138)	0.378757
Jamaica $_{\text{(dummy)}}$	−0.303915 (0.530881)	−0.572474
St Lucia $_{\text{(dummy)}}$	−0.018211 (0.580341)	−0.031379
Trinidad and Tobago $_{\text{(dummy)}}$	0.085329 (0.505150)	0.168918
Micro	−0.353037 (0.364672)	−0.968096
Small	0.102944 (0.478983)	0.214922
Medium	−0.565589 (0.486231)	−1.16321
NMKT	0.371784 (0.119276)	3.11701**
CMKT	0.00273 (0.117931)	0.023163
μ_3	0.447132 (0.157719)	2.83143**
μ_4	0.897005 (0.204245)	4.39181***
μ_5	1.46502 (0.244510)	5.99167***
μ_6	1.97354 (0.270837)	7.28682***
μ_7	2.45110 (0.298674)	8.20660***

Source: Gordon (2007).

Notes: Dependent variable is core ranking of importance of access to markets. $N = 61$. Scaled R squared = 0.345316. ***, **, * denote significance levels at 0.01, 0.05 and 0.10, respectively. Standard errors in parentheses.

5 per cent statistically significant level (Gordon 2007). These results imply an almost non-existent impact of CARICOM level policies on the critical business environment factors that influence the investment decisions of firms. They suggest that a more in-depth assessment and understanding of the economic profiles of the constituents of the business environment of the respective CARICOM countries is a prerequisite to the design of policies intended to stimulate economic growth in the countries. And, further, that there may be need for a targeted and differentiated policy framework across the CARICOM countries.

Relevant Insights from the Jamaican Business Environment

Arising from a study of the competitiveness of small enterprises in Jamaica, Williams (2007) concluded that their success in the export market was threatened by the use of unsophisticated strategies. As a result, their long-term survival was in jeopardy with a likely negative impact on the Jamaican economy. In related research on female entrepreneurs, Williams and K'nIfe (2012) observed that important gender and entrepreneurship differences exist in small Jamaican firms. This study specifically examined the interaction of gender and credit behaviour in small firms in Jamaica and concluded that gender does play an important role in influencing the financing prospects available to small firms. Female owners are more challenged in securing financing than male owners. One critical conclusion is that policies designed to promote the growth and success of these firms must be targeted to the circumstances of their principals (Williams and K'nIfe 2012).

Taken together, the results of the aforementioned research suggest the need for changes in the policy formulation process intended to promote economic activities within the CARICOM. We advocate that initially a dynamic database of firms be developed, segmented by an appropriate size parameter, comprising critical economic business factors such as capital requirements, skilled and unskilled labour needs, input needs, technological requirements and target markets. This may be best accomplished in collaboration with the national business/industry/commerce associations. Policymakers can then seek to develop policies and strategies that encourage the firms to pursue investment options that induce the firms to optimize their investments. Using such a database, policymakers will have options for designing targeted policies that cater to the differences among the categories of the firms. Monitoring and evaluation of the policy impacts will also be facilitated, thereby more easily facilitating policy adjustments as may be required.

Robustness of Survey Significance

Gordon (2007) concluded that coverage and sampling errors were considerably reduced, measurement errors minimal and non-response bias acceptable in comparison to other studies. The results of the survey can therefore provide useful insights into the CARICOM business environment, providing an empirical basis for policy formulation. Consequently, despite it being dated, the survey illustrates the diversity of the CARICOM business environment and conveys the importance of expressly recognizing these differences in the regional policy formulation process. It is acknowledged, however, that an exercise like this should be updated periodically in order to accommodate the dynamism within the economies of the countries.

Characterization and Implications of Countries' Business and Economic Environments

Business Environment

The results of the survey pointed to considerable heterogeneity among firms in the countries studied, with important differences highlighted pertaining to firm size, geographical scope of operations and areas of operations. It is also noteworthy that firms perceived national policies to be more influential on the eleven factors identified as critical to the conduct and profitability of business and investments even though this policy influence was viewed negatively. This suggests that firms' business and investment decisions are affected more by national policies than regional ones.

Economic Environment

The economic environment in CARICOM countries is as diverse as the business environment. At US$23,808.1 million (2018), the gross domestic product (GDP) of Trinidad and Tobago is 1.5 times that of the next largest national output, that of Jamaica, which stands at US$15,713.9 million. Dominica has the smallest output with a GDP of US$550.9 million, with that of the other countries varying between Trinidad and Tobago and Dominica (see table 7.5). All the countries except Trinidad and Tobago

Table 7.5. Selected Economic Indicators of Selected CARICOM Countries

Selected CARICOM Countries	Economic Indicators					
	GDP (Constant 2010 US$ million)	GDP (Current US$ million)	GDP Growth (Annual %)	FDI, Net Inflows (% of GDP)	Inflation, GDP Deflator (Annual %)	Current Exchange Rate[a] (Local currenty units (LCU) per US$)
Antigua and Barbuda	1,457.3	1,610.6	7.4	8.4	2.1	2.7
Bahamas	1,051.3	12,424.5	1.6	4.0	0.7	1.0
Barbados	4,625.5	5,086.5	0.6	3.8	2.8	2.0
Belize	1,615.6	1,871.2	2.1	6.4	−0.2	2.0
Dominica	479.5	550.9	2.3	2.4	3.6	2.7
Grenada	1,013.3	1,168.7	4.1	13.2	−0.3	2.7
Guyana	3,109.9	3,878.7	4.1	30.4	5.4	210.97
Haiti	8,123.2	9,658.7	1.5	1.1	12.8	111.92
Jamaica	14,249.5	15,713.9	1.9	4.9	4.8	141.3
St Kitts and Nevis	888.5	1,010.8	2.9	9.3	−1.5	2.7
St Lucia	1,680.2	2,065.9	8.9	1.9	0.7	2.7
St Vincent and Grenadines	755.2	811.3	2.2	13.6	0.2	2.7
Suriname	4,667.6	3,458.1	2.6	3.8	4.6	7.396
Trinidad andTobago	21,071.7	23,808.1	−0.2	−2.9	6.1	6.808

Source: World Bank (2018).
[a] Exchange rate sourced from the internet on 3 August 2020.

experienced positive GDP growth, with St Lucia, Grenada and Guyana leading at 8.9 per cent, 4.1 per cent and 4.1 per cent, respectively. The countries experienced a wide variation in the rate of foreign direct investment inflows measured as a percentage of GDP with Guyana leading at 30.4 per cent followed by St Vincent and the Grenadines at 13.6 per cent and Grenada at 13.2 per cent. At the bottom end of this metric are Haiti at 1.1 per cent and Trinidad and Tobago at −2.9 per cent. The rate of price change in the economy as a whole, indicated by the GDP deflator, ranges from −1.5 per cent in St Kitts and Nevis to 12.8 per cent in Haiti. The countries also have different exchange rates with the US dollar. For nine of the countries, the exchange rate is fixed, albeit at different rates: Bahamas at 1:1, Barbados and Belize at 2:1, and the seven OECS states at 2.7:1. For the other countries, the exchange rate is market determined, ranging from 6.8:1 in Trinidad and Tobago to approximately 211:1 in Guyana.

These economic indicators illustrate the stark differences in the economic environments of the CARICOM countries. Enterprises do not face the same costs of capital and simultaneously experience different price changes in the economy as a whole, as indicated by the GDP deflator. Dissimilarities in the rate of growth of the economies and the exchange rates with the US dollar are also important factors that will influence business and investment decisions. As a consequence, we argue that differential economic policy proposals and strategies are required to catalyse growth and investment in the respective business environments of the CARICOM countries.

CARICOM's Policy Formulation Process: Some Reconfiguration Issues

Policy Design

We submit that for the successful achievement of economic growth objectives within CARICOM, the policy design process must deliberately take cognizance of the diversity within the business and investment environments of the countries. Provision must also be made for the key differences in the national economic environment as pertains to the factors influencing business activities. As a consequence, the seeming one-size-fits-all policy formulation process should be discontinued in favour of a targeted process directed to the needs of the various segments of the business environment. The policy formulation process should also embody specific consideration of the characteristics of the national economic environment within which the respective firms function. This implies the establishment of closer collaboration between the national policy design process and that obtained at the regional level on policy specifics. It will also be important for the policy design process to establish and maintain effective arrangements for continuous inputs from the diverse segments of the business environment, across all countries. Success in this regard will likely require innovative and effective use of the internet and electronic media. If a strategy to incorporate comprehensive input from the business environment into the policy process is adopted, it is inconceivable that the current process of periodic physical meetings can be efficiently maintained.

Institutional Arrangements

In its 2003 World Development Report, the World Bank conducted a comprehensive review of the role of institutions in promoting and supporting growth and sustainable action in a wide cross section of sectors, inclusive of productive, social and environmental (World Bank 2003). In relation to the coordination of human behaviour, institutions were defined as

> the rules, organisations and social norms that facilitate coordination of human action. On the informal end, they go from trust and other forms of social capital (including deeply rooted norms governing social behaviour) to informal mechanisms and networks for coordination. On the formal end, they include a country's codified rules and laws, and the procedures and organisation for making, modifying, interpreting and enforcing rules and laws (from the legislature to the central bank). (World Bank 2003, 38)

Among other things, the World Bank's treatise on institutions for development noted that institutions provide the basis for, among other things, urbanization, economic growth, sustainable use of natural resources and the promotion of intercountry linkages. It argues that institutions should be stable yet capable of changing and adapting to emerging circumstances. Also, they ought to be supportive of the private sector while simultaneously protecting public interests. It made the important observation that the private sector's preparedness to invest was contingent upon the safeguards offered by the prevailing institutional arrangements (World Bank 2003). Another World Bank report that focused specifically on the development of institutions to support the functioning of markets argued that, in the context of markets, institutions serve three main purposes – channelling information about market exchanges, providing a framework for the enforcement of property rights and contracts, and the promotion of competition – collectively resulting in enhanced productivity and economic growth (World Bank 2002). However, the report cautions about the complexity associated with the design and building of institutions in support of markets, and notes that effective policymaking is necessary to complement the role and impact of the institutional structure within the economy (World Bank 2002).

In order to stimulate economic activity within the community, the Conference of Heads of Government agreed to the establishment of the CSME. The CARICOM Single Market (CSM), the first component of the CSME, is generally perceived, within the community and among CARICOM officials, to have become operational in January 2006, following the signing of the Revised Treaty of Chaguaramas in 2001 (LaRocque 2013). The treaty revision enabled the establishment of a suite of institutional arrangements deemed necessary to facilitate economic activity envisaged within the CSM. As indicated earlier, the vast majority of the required institutional arrangements were seen to have been established by the countries by January 2006. Stoneman, Pollard and Inniss (2012) observed that there was a prevailing view, among countries and officials of the CARICOM Secretariat, that the enactment of legislation signalled the achievement of the implementation of the CSM. However, they noted that, in 2012, there were no effective institutional arrangements regarding regional governance pertaining to the establishment of the CSME (131). Some acknowledged deficiencies with respect to the CSM include the weak integration of national markets and associated cross-border activities, the need for a greater mobilization of resources to enhance the supply of skills and increase exports, and the importance of a greater involvement of labour and the private sector in the policy formulation process (Carrington 2010). Despite the expressed assertions about the economic growth potential of the CSM and the established supportive institutional framework, tangible output was extremely weak, prompting the heads of government to call for a reprioritization of the activities being pursued to promote economic development within the community (CARICOM Secretariat 2011).

We argue, however, that the core issue is a more fundamental one, namely the absence of a policy environment designed to stimulate private sector investment that will result in the desired economic output. In this regard it is important to heed the World Bank's caution that institution building does not diminish the critical importance of appropriate policies (World Bank 2002).

The strong push for the design and establishment of an appropriate set of institutions to support the entrepreneurial activity and investment within the CSM is certainly commendable, including initiatives such as the Free Movement of People and Skills, the Double Taxation Agreement, the CARICOM Competition Commission, the Caribbean Court of Justice, the Right of Establishment, and the CARICOM Regional Organisation for Standards and Quality. In light of the findings of the World Bank (2002) report "Building Institutions for Markets", it is unlikely that the economic goals envisaged for the CSM is attainable without the network of these institutions.

Participants at a 2010 regional conference involving representatives from governments, the business sector, labour and civil society agreed on the need for additional work (on promoting the CSM), particularly involving labour and the private sector. While acknowledging success with the implementation of the CSM's institutional arrangements, the participants recognized that some member states were constrained in being able to effectively participate in the CSM (Carrington 2010).[5]

These circumstances suggest that, while the network of institutions as established is necessary to support the economic activity envisaged within the CSM, the experience of weak economic activity to date within the CSM is an indication that the network of institutions is not sufficient to promote the envisaged economic pursuits.

Enhanced National-Level and Regional-Level Collaboration

The diverse and heterogeneous characteristics of the business environment suggest the need for closer collaboration between and among national-level policymakers and those who function at the regional level in the policy design process. Such a strategy will facilitate more efficient targeting of policy measures to specific segments of the business environment as may be desired. It is envisaged that this strategy will also allow firms to more easily contribute to the policy design process and may lead to differentiated foci of policies across countries. Differentiated policy foci, however, should not preclude possible policy harmonization in some areas, such as agricultural health, industrial and health standards, and tourism promotion. Increased collaboration as advocated will also facilitate improved monitoring of the impact of the respective policies.

Monitoring, Evaluation and Reporting

The ongoing monitoring and evaluation of policy impacts is crucial to determining the effectiveness of the respective policies and for informing policy adjustments to more effectively promote goal achievement. This will require determination of suitable performance indicators, agreement on their appropriateness among all relevant stakeholders, and the collection and analysis of data to evaluate the impact of the policies. Periodic objective reports on the policy impacts should be provided to all those that have a stake and interest in the economic output of the business environment. The time frame established for the evaluation of the policies' impacts should be sufficiently adequate to facilitate an objective measure of the economic output of firms in response to the respective policies.

The diversity and operational scope of the business environment should also be monitored periodically. A regional business environment census may be the best way of achieving this, but resources for such an activity may be unavailable. One alternative is to conduct periodic surveys of the business environment using structured instruments administered electronically via the internet, augmented with mail surveys for those areas/sectors that lack access to the internet.

Regional Policy Formulation Fora

COTED is the CARICOM organ charged with policymaking authority pertaining to the CSM/CSME. Since its establishment by virtue of the Revised Treaty of Chaguaramas, COTED meets at least once annually. Occasionally, COTED meets more than once in a given year. The efficacy of such a meeting schedule is questionable since the same issues are sometimes discussed at many of these meetings, as alluded to by former CARICOM secretary general Irwin LaRocque in chapter 2 of this volume. A more pragmatic meeting schedule for COTED would be one in which the intervening time between meetings is sufficient for an objective evaluation of the impacts of respective policy decisions. This will greatly facilitate any policy adjustment that may be required for goal achievement. In addition, it will foster a more efficient utilization of the human and budgetary resources of the agencies involved in COTED meetings.

Another important issue pertaining to the policy deliberations of COTED is the non-existence of the arrangements for inputs into the policy design process from the voices of firms in the diverse and heterogeneous business environment across the community. Initially, providing for such an input may seem exceedingly problematic, especially if the current meeting model is maintained, with the convening of physical gatherings. However, we suggest that innovative utilization of the internet and the adaptation of available information technology software can easily resolve this seemingly overwhelming challenge.

In like manner, it may be useful for the CARICOM organs charged with policy formulation authority in areas such as finance, foreign affairs, and human and social development to re-evaluate and adjust their meeting schedules to permit a more efficient utilization of time and other resources, as well as allow for the objective evaluation of the policy decisions of the respective organs.

Concluding Comments

Acknowledging that the economic output of firms is the main contributor to a country's economic output and ultimately its economic growth, it follows that the diversity and heterogeneity of the CARICOM business environment should not be ignored in the regional policy formulation process, if success in achieving the goals and objectives of the CSM and ultimately the CSME is desired. Consequently, the regional policy formulation process should be deliberately designed to specifically seek input from the various groups of firms that constitute the business environment. The fact that micro firms constitute the largest segment of firms in the business environment (46 per cent), twice that of the segment of large firms (21 per cent), and approximately three times that of medium firms (15 per cent) and small firms (16 per cent) indicates that policies should be targeted to catalyse the growth of, and greater output from, the respective groups of firms. This may result in differentiated policy foci across countries, given the diversity in the business environment and in national economic circumstances. A one-size-fits-all approach seems suboptimal if the overall policy objective is to seek greater output from the economic agents that collectively constitute the region's business environment.

A comprehensive suite of rules for conducting business, namely institutional arrangements, are required for efficient business operations as well as to catalyse investment and greater business activity. However, institutional arrangements in themselves are not sufficient to encourage increased economic output, as evidenced by the less than sterling output from the CSM since its inception in 2006. An appropriate policy framework is essential to complement the established institutional arrangements. Towards this end, an innovative approach will be required in reformulating the regional policy formulation process in order to secure comprehensive inputs from the business environment and effect a closer collaboration with national policy formulation processes.

The results of the survey discussed in this chapter suggest that the CARICOM business environment is comprised of approximately 77 per cent of SMEs. Rather than ignoring these firms in the policy formulation process, perhaps there are some valuable lessons to be gleaned from examining the SME experience of the global business environment in general, and that of Germany's Mittelstand in particular. In this regard, we suggest that the implementation of a suite of targeted policies designed to simulate investment and growth of CARICOM SMEs will ultimately enhance the economies of CARICOM countries.

Notes

1. D'Aguiar's comments were reported in the daily newspapers of Trinidad and Tobago at that time, but, regrettably, a precise reference is unavailable.

2. This is a unique survey, providing a comprehensive picture of the diverse global business environment, that has not been repeated to date. It demonstrates the complexity of the business environment across countries and illustrates the importance of assessing the profile of economic indicators of a targeted business environment that is the focus of a suite of policies designed to stimulate its economic growth.

3. This survey is also unique since there have been no published reports of a similar exercise conducted within CARICOM to date (August 2020).

4. Firm size is defined by annual sales volume. Micro: less than US$1.0 million; small: US$1.0 million to 2.5 million; medium: US$2.5 million to 6.5 million; large: greater than US$6.5 million. Concerning SMEs in the Caribbean versus SMEs in Germany, the relative profile will be similar, but the absolute sizes will differ with the German firms being considerably larger.

5. Carrington (2010) listed the following: (1) challenges of the extant global economic downturn; (2) enhancement of the (CARICOM) market integration process and stimulation of cross-border activity; (3) promotion of investment in infrastructure, production and job creation; (4) accessing labour and other inputs to promote export expansion; and (5) overall challenges to establish a single economic space.

References

Batra, Geeta, Daniel Kaufmann, and Andrew H.W. Stone. 2003. *Investment Climate around the World*. Washington, DC: The World Bank.

Berghoff, Hartmut. 2006. "The End of Family Business? The Mittelstand and German Capitalism in Transition, 1949–2000". *Business History Review* 80 (2): 32.

Blackman, Courtney N. 2006. *The Practice of Economic Management: A Caribbean Perspective*. Kingston, Jamaica: Ian Randle Publisher.

Brewster, Havelock and Clive Yolande Thomas. 1967. *The Dynamics of West Indian Economic Integration*. Kingston, Jamaica: Institute of Social and Economic Research, University of the West Indies.

CARICOM Secretariat. 1973. "Treaty Establishing the Caribbean Community". Georgetown Guyana: CARICOM Secretariat.

———. 2001. "Revised Treaty of Chaguaramas Establishing the Caribbean Community Including The CARICOM Single Market and Economy". Georgetown Guyana: CARICOM Secretariat.

———. 2006a. "The Caribbean Free Trade Association (CARIFTA)". CARICOM.

———. 2006b. "The Original Treaty". CARICOM.

———. 2006c. "Programme 9: External Economic and Trade Relations. Work Programme 2004". CARICOM.

———. 2006d. "Programme 10: Foreign Policy and Community Relations. Work Programme 2004". CARICOM.

———. 2006e. "Programme 11: Mobilisation of Resources from External Agencies and Caribbean Community Technical Section". CARICOM.

———. 2006f. "The West Indies Federation". CARICOM.

———. 2011. "Press release 192/2011. CARICOM Leaders Seek Greater Focus on Prosperity for the People". Georgetown, Guyana: CARICOM.

Carrington, Edwin W. 2010. "Annual Report of the Secretary General 2008–2009". CARICOM Secretariat. https://caricom.org/documents/9399-annual_report_08_09.pdf.

Coderre, Francois, Anne Mathieu, and Natalie St-Laurent. 2004. "Comparison of the Quality of Qualitative Data Obtained through Telephone, Postal and Email Surveys". *International Journal of Market Research* 46 (3): 347(11).

Couper, Mick P. 2000. "Web Surveys". *Public Opinion Quarterly* 64 (4): 464–94.

Department of Statistics Malaysia. 2011. "Economic Census 2011: Profile of Small and Medium Enterprises". Malaysia.

Ferreira, Joan. 2007. "Trinidad and Tobago Chamber of Industry and Commerce: Membership Size Categories". CEO of the Trinidad and Tobago Chamber of Industry of Commerce.

Fricker, Scott, Mirta Galesic, Roger Tourangeau, and Yan Ting. 2005. "An Experimental Comparison of Web and Telephone Surveys". *Public Opinion Quarterly* 69 (3): 370–92.

Girvan, Norman P. 1990. "Reflections on Regional Integration and Disintegration". In *Integration and Participatory Development*, edited by Judith Wedderburn. Kingston, Jamaica: Friedrich Ebert Stiftung & Association of Caribbean Economists.

Gordon, Ronald M. 2007. "Impact of CARICOM Economic Integration Arrangements on the Economic Gains of Selected CARICOM Countries". Thesis in partial fulfilment of the PhD in Food and Resource Economics, *Food and Resource Economics Department*. Gainesville: University of Florida.

LaRoque, Irwin. 2013. "The Status and Future of CARICOM". Key note presentation at conference to mark CARICOM's fiftieth anniversary, "Rethinking Regionalism: Beyond the CARICOM Integration Project" Mona, Jamaica: SALISES, published in this volume (chapter 2).

Mohamad, Nordin Haji and Fatimah Said. 2012. "Decomposing Total Factor Productivity Growth in Small and Medium Enterprises". *Indian Journal of Science and Technology* 5 (5): 12.

Reddy, Mahendra. 2007. "Small Businesses in Small Economies: Constraints and Opportunities for Growth". *Social and Economic Studies* 56 (1&2): 17.

Schuman, Michael and Claudia Himmelreich. 2011. "How Germany Became the China of Europe". *Time* 177 (9): 3.

Stoneman, Richard, Duke Pollard, and Hugo Inniss. 2012. "Turning around CARICOM: Proposals to Restructure the Secretariat". Georgetown, Guyana: Landell Mills Ltd.

Williams, Densil A. 2007. "Competitiveness of Small Enterprises: Insights from a Developing Economy". *The Round Table: The Commonwealth Journal of International Affairs* 96 (390): 16.

Williams, Densil A. and Kadamawe A.K. K'nIfe. 2012. "Correlates of Gender and Credit Behavior in Small Firms: Evidence from a Small Developing Economy". *Entrepreneurial Executive* 17.

World Bank. 2002. "World Development Report 2002: Building Institutions for Markets". New York: The World Bank.

———. 2003. "World Development Report 2003: Sustainable Development in a Dynamic World: Transforming Institutions, Growth and Quality of Life". New York: World Bank.

———. 2005. "A Time to Choose: Caribbean Development in the 21st Century". Washington, DC: World Bank.

———. 2018. World Development Indicators: Online. Accessed 3 August 2020. https://databank.worldbank.org/source/world-development-indicators.

Chapter 8

CARICOM beyond the Single Market and Economy

PATSY LEWIS

This reflection on the Caribbean Community (CARICOM) was written at a time when the European Union, the most advanced regional integration scheme and the progenitor of Caribbean integration, appeared in crisis, or at any rate less stable than at any time in its history. Before Britain's decision to leave the group following the 2016 referendum for what was commonly referred to as Brexit, financial crisis and global recession had highlighted clear schisms in key elements of the arrangement, among them issues concerning the common currency; Germany's economic and political dominance; the economic and structural imbalance between richer and poorer members, despite regional transfers over the years; antipathy towards freedom of movement; and friction in the transfer of power from national to regional institutions, especially in law making and norm setting. Elements of these were evident in the arguments used by pro-Brexiters in making a case for Britain to leave the European Union (Lee 2018). Tensions over monetary union and Germany's dominance of macroeconomic governance were an earlier response to the crisis, primarily in Greece, but also in Italy and Portugal.[1] Further, a new right-wing nationalism, expressed in opposition to the European project, was in evidence across Europe, reflected in the strong showing of far-right parties in elections in Poland, Italy, Hungary and France, among others (BBC 2018).

Although amplified in the European Union, some of these tensions were already manifest in CARICOM. The latest challenge to its coherence was evident even before Britain's decision to leave the European Union, when the Jamaica Labour Party (JLP), under the leadership of Andrew Holness, won the 2016 general elections. After the JLP's victory, election promises to review Jamaica's membership in CARICOM were made good, and the Holness government set up the Commission to Review Jamaica's Relations within the CARICOM and CARIFORUM Frameworks. The JLP's antipathy towards CARICOM was evident in the criticisms described in chapter 3 of this volume and represented a formalization of these. Brexit appeared to have further animated those voices most critical of CARICOM, with some urging Jamaica to follow Britain's lead to initiate its own JAMEXIT (Brown 2016; Thompson 2017). The commission, chaired by former prime minister Bruce Golding, returned after months of deliberation with the recommendation that if CARICOM did not fully implement the single market and economy (CSME) within five years, Jamaica should leave the arrangement, retaining its membership only in CARICOM's functional arrangements, along the lines of the Bahamas model (Government of Jamaica 2017). The slim likelihood of achieving, within five years, the feat of full market integration that had eluded CARICOM governments for eleven years, suggested the likely outcome of Jamaica leaving CARICOM. However, the Jamaican government, despite endorsing the recommendations of the committee in its report (herein referred to as the Golding report–GR), rejected the specific recommendation to withdraw from the CSME if CARICOM failed to meet the five-year deadline.

Nevertheless, the GR's recommendations, despite the government's decision to remain in CARICOM, raised questions about the viability of integration projects such as CARICOM, which have used the EU experience as model and guide. The CARICOM approach mirrors the European Union in its commitment to a customs union, freedom of movement, macroeconomic convergence, a single currency, a regional court and harmonization of policy across a wide range of activities, including foreign and trade policy. While CARICOM has made significant strides in functional cooperation (see LaRocque, chapter 2, and Lewis, chapter 3, in this volume), it has struggled to achieve much progress in most other areas of the CSME. It has successfully brought the Caribbean Court of Justice (CCJ) into being, albeit primarily in its original jurisdiction to interpret the treaty, but not entirely in its full function as final court of appeal to replace the Privy Council.[2] It has established a number of institutions to support implementation, such as the Council for Finance and Planning and the Community Council, but, as the Golding and Landell-Mills reports note, these were not necessarily functioning (Government of Jamaica 2017, 25; Stoneman, Pollard and Inniss 2012, 21–23).[3] Arguably, the GR illustrates not just Jamaica's frustration with CARICOM but also the quite distinct and differing perceptions of the movement and the potential for exacerbating existing differences, particularly with the smaller CARICOM states, grouped in the Organisation of Eastern Caribbean States (OECS).[4]

This chapter engages with the GR to assess the present moment of uncertainty in which CARICOM is situated. This includes challenges in implementing the necessary measures to give effect to the CSME and the fissures in CARICOM revealed in the GR, which would likely deepen if some of the report's recommendations were accepted. It offers a critique of the report, including that of Ralph Gonsalves, prime minister of St Vincent and the Grenadines and current chair of the OECS. It explores competing visions of the regional integration process represented by the GR, the Landell-Mills report (Stoneman et al. 2012) and CARICOM's Strategic Plan for the Caribbean Community 2015–19 (CARICOM Secretariat 2014a, 2014b). It argues for a more expanded agenda for CARICOM beyond achieving the CSME and suggests that it has a crucial role in preventing the alienation of nationals from economic processes. The GR is important as it reflects tensions within the movement, discussed in this volume by Lewis (chapter 3), and implicitly raises questions about the viability of the CSME model of regional integration (Lewis 2003). Its broad acceptance by the Jamaican government would indicate that it reflects its views of CARICOM and the changes it would wish to see. It concludes with a discussion of CARICOM's response to the report, namely the St Ann's Declaration (December 2018) and the report of the restructured Commission on the Economy (October 2020).

One of the challenges in reflecting on the regional integration movement is that it is constantly unfolding, with new agreements and pronouncements emerging from each Heads of Government (HOG) summit, which provide fertile ground for commentary, even if they are not ultimately implemented. In addition, changes in government can also bring uncertainty or push the process in new directions, as with the Barbadian electorates' rejection of Freundel Stuart's Democratic Labour Party in the May 2018 elections in favour of Mia Mottley's Barbados Labour Party. These, nevertheless, provide their own insights into the challenges of multicountry consensus that is at the heart of the CARICOM process. The GR is thus a good place to inspire further discussions on CARICOM.

Report of the Commission to Review Jamaica's Relations within the CARICOM and CARIFORUM Frameworks

The commission's remit was to review CARICOM's performance along the following lines:

- The extent to which Jamaica benefited from the following main areas of CARICOM activity:
  - Economic integration: whether it fostered "economic growth and development" especially in "trade in goods and services, investment, international competitiveness and employment";
  - Foreign policy: benefits from CARICOM's coordination of foreign policy and its value to Jamaica in influencing "critical international fora and with third state trade and development partners";
  - Functional arrangements: the extent to which Jamaica benefits "through functional cooperation within CARICOM Institutions and its framework";
  - Dispute resolution: the utility of the CCJ to Jamaica as providing "realistic options for settlement of disputes for Jamaica". Considerations around implementing the CCJ as Jamaica's final court of appeal were excluded from the commission's remit.
- CARICOM's performance against the goals set in the Revised Treaty of Chaguaramas.
- Jamaica's relationship with other countries in the wider Caribbean: its engagement with the Dominican Republic, Cuba and "other Caribbean territories"; enlargement of CARICOM membership (Government of Jamaica 2017, v).

The GR concluded that CARICOM has not shown "demonstrable success or improvement in the quality of lives" of its people, as was evident in its decreasing share of world trade, "anemic" output, and "too many of its people remain[ing] poor, jobless and hopeless" (Government of Jamaica 2017, xi). It attributes CARICOM's failings to the inability to complete the single market and economy. Thus, in the fashion of so many reports that have preceded it (see, for example, West Indian Commission 1992; CARICOM Secretariat 1981), the GR places the blame on CARICOM's "implementation deficit" (Government of Jamaica 2017, xi, 22) – its inability to put into practice the decisions taken by regional heads of government. It argues – somewhat surprisingly, given the trenchant critiques of CARICOM which launched this investigation – that

CARICOM was "as relevant and useful and, perhaps, even more urgent than it was at its inception and can provide us a more secure passage to a brighter future than can each of us trying to row his boat alone" (Government of Jamaica 2017, xii). The report then proceeds to present recommendations for completing the CSME which, if not achieved within five years, should lead to Jamaica's withdrawal from the CSME, athough it would remain in CARICOM. These can be divided into four broad categories: (1) those required to and already agreed as necessary to implement the CSME; (2) those that seek to address the implementation deficit; (3) those that address the divide between more developed countries (MDCs) and less developed countries (LDCs) built into the original treaty and carried over into the revised treaty; and (4) the Landell-Mills recommendations, some of which are geared towards strengthening the CARICOM Secretariat. This chapter cannot reasonably engage with a critique of all these measures but will focus on some of the key ones. These include Jamaica's relationship with CARICOM, some aspects of the CSME and the MDC/LDC divide.

Jamaica's Relationship with CARICOM

The report noted Jamaica's negative trade balance with CARICOM. Over the period 2012–14, 5.1 per cent of Jamaica's exports were to CARICOM, while 15.9 per cent of its imports were from CARICOM, of which Trinidad and Tobago accounted for 75 per cent (Government of Jamaica 2017, 14). It observed, though, that this was more a reflection of Jamaica's competitiveness than CARICOM policy, nor could the blame be laid completely at the feet of Jamaica's manufacturing sector. It argued that policies pursued by the Jamaican government, "especially fiscal, monetary and regulatory policies, the level of crime and the high cost of security . . . inefficient and costly electricity generation, the educational level of the workforce and the quality of infrastructure" were all to blame (Government of Jamaica 2017, 14). Notwithstanding, the GR focused on the pricing of energy from Trinidad and Tobago as an important factor in Jamaica's uncompetitiveness.[5] Its main argument was that Trinidad and Tobago provided an energy subsidy to domestic producers and consumers which was not extended to Jamaica, while Jamaica also had to pay the common external tariff on energy supplies originating from outside of CARICOM, which increased energy costs. Not only did this reduce Jamaica's ability to compete within CARICOM but undermined its competitiveness in other markets as well (Government of Jamaica 2017). The GR's assertion was that Trinidad's pricing of oil should be based on national treatment provisions under the revised treaty and that the matter should be sent to the CCJ for a ruling (Government of Jamaica 2017).[6] In respect of services, it could not determine CARICOM's effects on Jamaica's services trade, as there was not much data to assess this, nor could it ascertain its effect on employment. While Jamaica's Ministry of Foreign Affairs and Foreign Trade estimated between 30,000 and 40,000 Jamaicans living and working within the region in 2013 (primarily in Antigua and Barbuda, Barbados, and Trinidad and Tobago) and that 16,000 CARICOM skills certificates had been approved for Jamaicans, it was not clear how many of them were actually working (Government of Jamaica 2017). The effect that CARICOM's mobility regime had on the employment levels of Jamaicans in the region was thus not clear. A similar assessment was made with regard to CARICOM's impact on investment, as the bulk of foreign direct investment from the region was from Trinidad and Tobago – most of which resulted from the acquisition of existing enterprises and did not rely on the provisions of the CARICOM treaty (Government of Jamaica 2017).

CARICOM's Performance against the Goals Set in the Revised Treaty

The GR concluded that the anticipated economic development and growth expected from the Revised Treaty of Chaguaramas had not materialized, but placed the blame squarely on the failure to implement its provisions. As the GR put it: "Something cannot be said to have failed until it has been tried and the reality is that the CSME as an integrated economic arrangement is yet to be functionally established" (Government of Jamaica 2017, 20). It identified ten areas of prioritization of the CSME: (1) macroeconomic convergence, including "an agreed fiscal responsibility framework", debt strategy, "alignment of monetary policies [and] abolition of exchange control and full convertibility of currencies"; (2) "integrated capital market"; (3) "free movement of people"; (4) "removal of all non-tariff barriers"; (5) "harmonization of laws and regulations governing the registration of businesses"; (6) creating the conditions for a services market by removing restrictions to services provision and introduction of a protocol to recognize professional accreditation; (7) removal of all restrictions to the rights of establishment; (8) ensuring "fair competition and consumer protection"; (9) implementing a regional government procurement regime that would allow providers from member countries to qualify for government contracts in other member states; and (10) harmonization of intellectual property and establishment of a regional intellectual property office (Government of Jamaica 2017, 22–24).

Macroeconomic Convergence

The GR argued that the CSME could not operate "with a variety of different fiscal, monetary, foreign exchange and debt management regimes" among its member states (Government of Jamaica 2017, 25). Among the measures the GR identified as necessary to complete the CSME were "macroeconomic convergence including a Fiscal Responsibility Framework, Debt Management Strategy, abolition of exchange controls and full currency convertibility" (as well as "alignment of monetary policies") (Government of Jamaica 2017, xiv, 22). The GR eschewed a common currency as necessary to complete the CSME, arguing that "what is required is exchange rate stability and the confidence that exchange rate fluctuations will be minimal" (Government of Jamaica 2017, 22). It expressed dissatisfaction with the progress of CARICOM's strategic plan (CARICOM 2014a) to put these measures into place (Government of Jamaica 2017).

Free Movement of People

The GR was impatient with both the degree of compliance with agreed measures on freedom of movement within the CSME as well as the slow approach to liberalizing movement. Only three countries–Grenada, Jamaica and Guyana–recognized the ten categories of workers allowed to work without work permits (Government of Jamaica 2017, 22). Impediments to free movement include requirements for police permits for those seeking skills certificates; failure to adopt a protocol on contingent rights to allow the dependents of nationals allowed to work in another country to access security benefits available in that country; and in demeaning treatment of a small minority of Jamaicans, which fuelled a perception that Jamaicans were not welcome in the rest of the region (Government of Jamaica 2017, 27). The latter was evident in the call for the removal of "all restrictions on the free movement of people except for security and public health reasons" within five years (Government of Jamaica 2017, 27). This would move the agenda beyond the provisions of the Revised Treaty of Chaguaramas, which provides for eventual free movement, but left this to the discretion of individual governments (Article 45). The GR argued that this was important to "rekindl[e] public interest and support for the integration process" (Government of Jamaica 2017, 27). It is not clear if this extends to removing all work permit requirements. The GR specifically sought the removal of restrictions on the right of Haitians, who faced visa restrictions in many CARICOM countries, to travel freely within the region (Government of Jamaica 2017, 27–28).[78] CARICOM's thirty-ninth HOG meeting agreed in principle to revisit the matter, but Grenada's prime minister Keith Mitchell's cautious response would suggest that the matter may not be easily resolved (*Haiti Libre* 2018).

CARICOM's Governance

Improving Governance

In keeping with its characterization of the problem as one of implementation, the GR also made a number of recommendations geared at strengthening CARICOM's ability to implement decisions. These include making HOG decisions the basis for community law to be given effect in the domestic law of each member state and relaxing the unanimity rule to allow for majority voting on specific issues. The GR suggested a six-month timeline for implementation, which would be strengthened by the inclusion of sanctions for non-compliance. These include suspending obligations to states not in compliance and barring the offending state from accessing loans from the Caribbean Development Bank, and introducing a wider range of retaliatory action. Finally, the GR called for the implementation of the Landell-Mills report (Stoneman, Pollard and Inniss 2012), in particular its recommendations for strengthening the "powers and capacity of the CARICOM Secretariat – to provide technical support to help implement decisions; to monitor the effectiveness of CARICOM institutions and agencies and conduct surveillance of Member States' compliance and conformity with Treaty obligations and CARICOM decisions" (Government of Jamaica 2017, xvi). It also made its own suggestions around rationalizing CARICOM bodies (Government of Jamaica 2017).

Fuelling the Divide between More Developed Countries and Less Developed Countries

The GR explicitly called for elimination of "the differentiation between More Developed Countries (MDCs) and Less Developed Countries (LDCs)" which was in the original Treaty of Chaguaramas and was included in the revised treaty. It argued that this division was included in the CSME with no "stated rationale other than an 'acknowledgement' in the preamble that '*some Member States, particularly the Less Developed Countries are entering the CSME at a disadvantage by reason of the size, structure and vulnerability of their economies*'" (italics in original; Government of Jamaica 2017, 41). As far as the GR was concerned, there was no longer any justification for this, as the countries classified as LDCs (OECS and Belize) were outperforming the so-called MDCs, as represented in higher per capita gross domestic product (GDP)[9] and lower debt-to-GDP ratio for many LDCs (Government of Jamaica 2017, 41–42). Its authors argued that the provisions in the revised treaty for special treatment of disadvantaged countries, regions or sectors should be maintained. Notably, these provisions would benefit Jamaica.

In addition, the GR made a number of recommendations that ignored the differential capabilities among the group. Among these were recommendations to fully implement the free circulation of goods. These included "harmonization of customs laws and procedures"; agreement on a "protocol on Sanitary and Phytosanitary standards, procedures and certification", "the application of Rules of Origin to goods produced within Free Zones in Member States" and the "free circulation of goods imported from outside the CSME once the appropriate import charges have been paid at the port of first entry"; and removal of restrictions on government procurement in respect of goods and services (Government of Jamaica 2017, 23–24).

CARICOM's External Relations and Relations with the Wider Caribbean

The GR acknowledged CARICOM's role in foreign policy, especially in negotiating trade agreements and recommended strengthening the Office of Trade Negotiations (formerly the Regional Negotiating Machinery) to increase its capacity in the then upcoming negotiations with Britain (post-Brexit), Canada (on a replacement for CARIBCAN) and the European Union (on a post-Cotonou arrangement) (Government of Jamaica 2017, 49). It noted, however, the failure to achieve common positions on foreign relations with Taiwan and China and on Venezuela. It also urged for a CARICOM response to citizenship by investment (CBI) programmes, disparagingly referred to as "citizenship for sale", offered by most of the countries of the OECS.[10] The GR's concern was that these programmes threatened the security of the entire region, as they gave these new citizens rights within CARICOM.

The GR was also critical of CARICOM's hesitance to engage more fully with the northern Caribbean, in particular the Dominican Republic, Cuba and Haiti,[11] arguing that while CARICOM was the best mechanism for engaging with these countries, Jamaica would pursue bilateral relations if CARICOM did not make headway (Government of Jamaica 2017, 64).

Response to the Golding Report

Completing the Single Market and Economy

When the HOG decided to move the regional process towards creating a single market and economy, the main aim was to put firms operating in the region on a more competitive basis by easing restrictions on the factors of production. The removal of national restrictions on the establishment of goods and the provision of services and the movement of capital (chapter three of the revised treaty) were meant to facilitate the emergence and consolidation of more competitive firms, which would be more likely to be competitive regionally and internationally. In 1992 when the decision was taken, global shifts towards a more liberal, rather than protectionist, approach to trade was already evident in the European Union's decision to create a single market; the United States' negotiation of the US–Canada Free Trade Agreement; the beginning of talks to create the North American Free Trade Area; and negotiations towards the formation of the World Trade Organization with the aim of further liberalizing global trade. It was already clear by then that the trading arrangements which granted CARICOM countries one-way preferential access to major markets would likely be reconfigured in the direction of greater reciprocity. The CSME was thus perceived as providing the basis for the cultivation of firms that were more likely to survive in this increasingly competitive environment. The GR's frustration that the CSME had still not been completed some twenty-five years later is understandable. The GR placed the onus for the failure to complete the CSME on CARICOM's "implementation failure", which usually infers a failure of political will to implement decisions taken as well as weak institutional structures. The GR's recommendations for implementation reflect this perspective. This chapter does not engage with an analysis of the implementation deficit,[12] nor does it address all of the GR's recommendations, but draws attention to some of the challenges inherent in pursuing the model on which the CSME is based. Specifically, it speaks to issues with macroeconomic convergence and the MDC/LDC "divide", and suggests a more expansive role for CARICOM in addressing the region's development challenges.

Macroeconomic Convergence

The GR identified macroeconomic convergence as an area of priority for CARICOM action. Macroeconomic convergence is viewed as important to regional integration, in particular the move towards a monetary union and single currency. The main aim of macroeconomic convergence is to bring economies in line with one another, especially in terms of per capita GDP, thus reducing differences between economically stronger and weaker states. Zhang (2012, 8) sums up its importance as follows: "inflationary pressures generated by unsustainable fiscal deficits and monetary expansion can cause untenable current account deficits that can eventually undercut trade liberalization and stifle economic growth. Moreover, macroeconomic instability, reflected in unsound financial sector and external debt difficulties, limit the ability to address structural difficulties and promote growth". Thus, the GR's call for CARICOM countries to have common policies on debt, fiscal responsibility and monetary policies is not unreasonable given the goals of the CSME and member states' agreement to bring these into effect. Yet the reluctance of some countries to move forward reflects some of the underlying challenges the regional integration process faces.

CARICOM HOG gave up on a monetary union years ago, deciding that the conditions set for achieving macroeconomic convergence were not feasible when key member states were unable to meet the requirement for stabilizing exchange rates.[13] Instead, the Committee of Central Bank Governors charged the Caribbean Centre for Monetary Studies to monitor the indicators for convergence in regional economies (Kendall 2000). In 2011, in the wake of the global recession and following years of stagnation in completing the CSME, the HOG decided to put the completion of the

CSME on pause. It was restarted in 2015 with the adoption of CARICOM's Strategic Plan for the Caribbean Community 2015–19, which prioritized implementing the CSME, "macroeconomic stabilization" and "ensuring an enabling business environment for growth" (CARICOM Secretariat 2014a, 7). The progress report on the plan shows little movement on achieving macroeconomic stabilization, largely because CARICOM's Council for Finance and Planning had "not met since February 2014 to advance the programme" (Government of Jamaica 2017, 23). This failure to meet suggests a deeper problem than weak institutional mechanisms for implementation and more likely reflects ambivalence around these goals.

The Caribbean Development Bank (CDB) 2018 report by Ram et al. on the Caribbean eight years after the recession was thought to have ended illustrates the challenges that CARICOM faces in achieving macroeconomic convergence, especially currency stability. The authors outlined the main challenges with achieving macroeconomic convergence within CARICOM as, "low growth and high indebtedness", "low savings and declining reserves", "output volatility and trade concentration", "poor sovereign debt ratings", and "financial sector vulnerabilities and stability risks" (p. 23). The region experienced sluggish growth since the recession, averaging 0.8 per cent between 2009 and 2017 (p. 13).[14] In 2017, growth averaged 0.5 per cent, well below the global economy (3.7 per cent) and "comparable small island developing states" (4.3 per cent) (p. 13). The averages masked differences in performance, with Dominica at the lower end experiencing a 6.9 per cent decline in growth and Grenada at the upper end with an increase of 3.7 per cent (Ram et al. 2018, 15). It also masked differences in fortune between the service-based economies and those driven by commodity exports, with the latter (Trinidad and Tobago, Belize and Suriname) exhibiting higher levels of volatility (Ram et al. 2018, 15). Ram et al. also noted that Caribbean economies had closer synchronization of growth with the United States and the European Union, rather than with one another, reflecting the low levels of intraregional trade vis-à-vis external trade. Maurin and Craigwell (chapter 5 in this volume) make a similar observation in respect of growth and business cycles. Ram et al. recommended strengthening intraregional trade, but did not suggest how this could be done. Maurin and Craigwell also argued that greater synchronization of business cycles of CARICOM countries depended on increasing intraregional trade. CARICOM's strategic plan also speaks to increasing trade among member states, based in part on economies of scale within the CSME (CARICOM 2014a, 5). It also spoke of measures to rebalance intraregional trade, which one could read as a response to Jamaica's vocally expressed dissatisfaction with its trade imbalance in respect of CARICOM countries. Unlike Ram et al.'s failure to speak to the impediments to increasing intraregional trade, the strategic plan identifies removing these as one of its goals (CARICOM 2014a, 15).

The region remains one of the most indebted in the world, even after efforts to reduce individual national debt. Although the median debt was 64.6 per cent of GDP, debt ranged from a low of 6.1 per cent for Montserrat[15] to 157.1 per cent for Barbados (Ram et al. 2018, 16). The high levels of debt were related to low savings rate (an average of 13 per cent of GDP); heavy reliance on foreign direct investment, which had not reached the levels they were before the financial crisis; borrowing for budgetary support; and poor financial ratings from international rating companies (Ram et al.

2018). Ram et al. (2018) see a clear relationship between the fiscal policies governments pursued and the debt they incurred. Fiscal imbalances were not solely the result of poor government policy, but included external shocks such as reduced preferences, debt-financing obligations, financial crisis and recession, weak growth, and natural disasters (Ram et al. 2018). There were also wide differences in inflation rates with Jamaica at a historic low of 1.7 per cent and Suriname at a high of more than 60 per cent[16] in 2016 (Ram et al. 2018). There were also differences in import cover. While Trinidad and Tobago maintained reserve coverage for nine months of imports, Barbados and the Bahamas fell below three months (Ram et al. 2018). While the GR called for CARICOM to implement debt management and a framework for fiscal control, it is difficult to see how CARICOM can effectively intervene in the absence of ample financial resources to facilitate their transfer to individual countries confronting crises that are typically not of their making and in the absence of enforcement mechanisms to compel countries to comply with fiscal policy guidelines.[17]

Interestingly, Ram et al.'s (2018) recommendations for the region to reverse this decline and build resilience were for adjustments at the national level, with no suggestion of a regional approach despite the commonality of these problems. These included removing subsidies or targeting them more carefully to the poor, divesting state enterprises, inter alia; reducing debt to 50 per cent, allowing for an adjustment to 60 per cent in the event of hurricanes; and maintaining compulsory savings from government revenues of 10 per cent to be placed in a "sovereign wealth fund or stabilization fund" and "prioritize borrowing for productive enterprise" (Ram et al. 2018, 23–26). It should be noted that, recommendations for achieving a "resilient financial sector" would undercut any effort at exchange rate stability. This includes introducing "a more flexible real exchange rate regime that allows the currency to depreciate in line with the difference between the domestic inflation rate and the inflation rate of the country's main trading partners" (Ram et al. 2018, 27), which would make aligning monetary policies, as the GR called for, difficult. Ram et al. also stressed the importance of an independent central bank. These recommendations could not be adopted by states that are part of the Eastern Caribbean Currency Union (ECCU) and already have a common currency fixed to the US dollar, and who have given control of monetary policy to the Eastern Caribbean Central Bank (ECCB),[18] without undermining the stability of their economies and plunging the OECS into crisis. In the past, non-ECCB countries, most notoriously Jamaica, have used sovereignty over monetary policy to devalue their dollar in attempts to increase competitiveness of their exports and reduce the value of domestic debt. Though the results have been overwhelmingly negative for Jamaica, the government is unlikely to cede its autonomy over monetary policy, irrespective of the GR's recommendations.

The GR's perspectives on CARICOM's role in Caribbean economies are contradictory. Even as the GR laid the blame for the failings of regional economies, especially their ability to address unemployment and poverty, on failure to implement the CSME, as mentioned earlier, it acknowledges that Jamaica's competitiveness can be laid at the door of policies Jamaican governments have pursued, as well as its high crime rate. Moreover, the assessment ignores the international climate within which governments are pursuing national policy and attempting to complete the CSME. Most CARICOM countries have been subjected to International Monetary Fund programmes of various kinds in the years following the financial crisis, including debt management programs. CARICOM's strategic plan noted governments' responses to these challenges with "home-grown or multilateral supported stabilization and structural adjustment programmes", observing that these failed to achieve "sustained growth" in countries "experiencing significant macroeconomic imbalances" (CARICOM Secretariat 2014a, 4). Others have experienced currency fluctuations. For example, between 2004 and 2018 the Jamaican dollar fell in value from $59.80 to the US dollar to $131.72 (as of 27 July 2018) (Trading Economics 2018). Given CARICOM's inability to offer financing to member states, it has little influence in driving national economic policy, despite agreement on paper to put in place common macroeconomic policies.[19]

In rejecting the GR's insistence on achieving macroeconomic stability, St Vincent's prime minister Ralph Gonsalves spoke to the challenges in reconciling these wide divergences in economic challenges and performance, arguing:

> It is difficult for me to envisage, in practical terms, an effective fiscal responsibility framework, an efficacious debt management strategy, and full currency convertibility in the absence of a central authoritative monetary mechanism and in a context of individual Central Banks, economies at various levels of development and possessed of varied structural features, currencies with wildly different real effective exchange rates to the US dollar, and individual monetary policies which are hugely divergent.[20] (Gonsalves 2018, 8)

Central to his rejection of the GR recommendations is the perception that these policies were inimical to the OECS's own subregional integration project. This raises a larger issue of whether OECS countries viewed the completion of key elements of the CSME as being in their interests. This can be inferred from Gonsalves's suspicion that measures to effect macroeconomic convergence would undermine the ECCB's "prudent banking practices":

> I am open to be educated as to how this would work practically in the context of CARICOM, but I remain not only "agnostic" but "atheistic" on it. I simply cannot see effective macroeconomic convergence between the economies of the ECCU and Barbados on one hand and those of Jamaica, Guyana, Suriname, Belize, and Haiti, on the other. I cannot see, too, such an effective macroeconomic convergence between Trinidad and Tobago, on the one hand, and the latter five-named economies, on the other hand. I can envisage, though, the possibility of such a convergence between the economies of Trinidad and Tobago, Barbados, and the ECCU. Undoubtedly, it is possible to draw up a list of guiding principles on macroeconomic convergence within a CSME but they are most unlikely to go beyond declaratory good intentions, with absolutely no sanctions possible. In any event it is the market and the real world of trade and production which determine full currency convertibility. (Gonsalves 2018, 9–10)

The European Union's experience in the wake of the recession suggests some of the challenges in maintaining convergence even after common monetary and fiscal policies, including monetary union, had been achieved. Holinski, Kool and Muysken (2012, 2) and Weber (2011, 238) observed that economies in the eurozone were showing greater economic divergence, especially after the recession, and reflected on growing macroeconomic imbalances in respect of the northern and southern euro area countries

– or the "core and periphery" as Axel Weber, former president of Deutsche Bundesbank, referred to them. Holinski, Kool and Muysken argue that while these imbalances have been aggravated by the financial crisis of 2008, "the divergence process" began when the common currency was introduced in 1999 (2012, 2). Weber noted that monetary policy did not avert the sovereign debt crisis, which he characterized as "the major challenge for economic and monetary union" (2011, 238). In addition to bailing out Greece, this required the European Union to "agree to establish a permanent stabilization mechanism" to "prevent the recurrence of fiscal crises in the future" (Weber 2011, 240). The EU experience would suggest that strong monetary and fiscal policy, even with a monetary union in place, does not necessarily lead to macroeconomic convergence, especially in the face of financial crisis.[21]

Factor Mobility: Land and Labour

Central to the completion of the CSME is the removal of restrictions on the factors of production – labour, capital and land. While most restrictions on capital flows within the region had been removed, two of these remain contentious: restrictions on access to land in the OECS and the movement of people. Despite the smaller OECS countries agreeing to remove restrictions on impediments to establishing businesses, including land, this has been more challenging to put into practice. In some countries, restrictions are in place on non-nationals buying land, considered essential in tiny countries where land is a scarce commodity, and the alienation of land can quickly lead to skyrocketing prices and its unavailability to locals. St Vincent registered its reservation about lifting alien landholding requirements in respect of CARICOM nationals when it signed the Revised Treaty of Chaguaramas. The GR's call for the removal of all such restrictions, while legitimate in the context of commitments undertaken under the revised treaty, reflects a lack of understanding of the real differences in land availability within CARICOM. It is not clear that the commission reflected on the difference between the availability of land in St Kitts, with 269 square kilometres, and Jamaica, with 10,991 square kilometres. These differences should have been taken into account in the revised treaty, with some guidelines developed as to how this obligation could be met while minimizing the challenge of nationals of smaller OECS territories being marginalized from owning land. This remains an area that is fertile for CARICOM guidelines, not least because, despite alien landholding acts which limit foreign ownership of land, OECS states have been selling land, particularly for extensive tourism projects. This is already driving up land prices in the OECS, raising the cost of land to nationals and reducing prospects for owning a piece of their own country. It is difficult to justify the sale of land to non-CARICOM nationals while retaining restrictions on accessing land by CARICOM nationals. Barbados's experience with the sale of land, in particular coastal land, and the effect it has had on the price of land and potential access to beaches, would suggest that this highly sensitive matter requires a regional response. The promotion of all-inclusive and high-end tourism risks undermining historical access to beaches, despite legal protections. This is evident, for example, in the Jamaica-owned Sandals resort in Grenada, which has built jetties into the sea, restricting beach access from land and, in effect, creating an exclusive beach for its hotel. Countries are also selling offshore islands for tourism "development" without legal protections for traditional access to these islands. A case in point is Grenada's Calivigny Island, which now hosts an exclusive resort, advertised as a "private island destination"[22] (Calivigny Island 2018). This model is likely to intensify without a regional approach to protecting rights of access to beaches for nationals and measures to ensure that land prices are not inflated out of the reach of nationals, inter alia. This is a clear area for regional intervention in recognizing that land is a scarce commodity for most CARICOM states, and issues of protecting the rights of citizens to affordable land and access to the sea demand a regional approach.[23]

Closely associated with tourism growth, but equally relevant to the preservation of the natural environment, is the need for more stringent regulations to ensure the integrity of mangroves, endangered species and the quality of beaches. Of course, the issue of environmental cooperation extends beyond the tourism industry to the impact of other economic sectors such as mining and agriculture. There is also the broader issue of addressing the negative effects of global warming such as coral bleaching, sea-level rise and stronger hurricanes. CARICOM's strategic plan seeks to address some of these concerns, as one of its strategic priorities includes legislative reform around land use and management as well as the control of pollution and waste, inter alia (CARICOM Secretariat 2014a, 28).

While the CSME provides for hassle-free travel and stay for up to six months in member states, this has not been without controversy (see chapters in this volume by Lewis, chapter 3; Dietrich Jones, chapter 11; and Saunders, chapter 12). Moreover, the Revised Treaty of Chaguaramas has taken an incremental approach to movement by identifying a limited number of categories of those who are allowed to move to seek jobs in the region, while leaving the further lifting of restriction at the discretion of individual countries. As noted, the GR is impatient of this approach, calling for unrestricted movement, including for Haitians. Sensitivity around the issue of freedom of movement was evident in the June 2018 general elections in Barbados in the campaign of outgoing prime minister Freundel Stuart and his party. Stuart sought to exclude CARICOM nationals from voting in the elections, despite provisions in law (the Representation of the People's Act) to allow Commonwealth citizens residing in Barbados for three years before an election to vote (CCJ 2018). After a successful challenge to this position under the CCJ, Stuart threatened to pull Barbados out of the CCJ were he to be returned to power. The close relationship between the vagaries of national politics and the regional project was evident in the action of his successor, Mia Mottley, and her Barbados Labour Party government, which moved in the opposite direction by supporting greater relaxation of movement. Regional governments also further embraced the GR by agreeing at the July 2018 HOG Summit in Montego Bay, Jamaica, to a protocol on contingent rights, which made it easier for those working in other CARICOM states to travel with family. By the following year, all twelve of the countries participating in the CSME (Bahamas and Montserrat are not signatories, and Haiti was yet to apply the CSME) had signed on to the protocol, with nine agreeing to provisionally apply it (CARICOM Secretariat, Single Market and Economy News, 1 March 2019).

These developments do not signal that sensitivities around full rights to move and work in the region have abated. The GR, in arguing for a more expansive approach to freedom of movement, was at pains to point out that unrestricted movement was a good thing for member states, arguing that based on the EU experience, the countries that had opened their economies to free movement immediately after the admission of an additional eight countries (the United Kingdom, Ireland and Sweden) were among the European Union's fastest growing economies (Government of Jamaica 2017, 28). Gonsalves's response suggests the challenges that remain. In his response to the GR, Gonsalves rejected this as unrealistic, given high levels of unemployment across the region (two hundred thousand in Jamaica alone); higher levels of per capita GDP in the OECS, Trinidad and Tobago, and Barbados than Jamaica; and the implication that this would hold for the much smaller countries of the OECS, as well as for Barbados and Trinidad and Tobago. One could surmise from this a fear that unemployed Jamaicans would swamp these countries. Regardless of whether this presents an accurate picture of the likely effect of full movement, it is clear that it is a politically charged issue which, if pursued without finding a way to address these concerns, could widen the fissures that already exist. It is worth noting that the role of immigration, both from within and outside the European Union, was critical in Britain's decision to leave the European Union and in fuelling the growth of right-wing parties in Europe. Nevertheless, the willingness of CARICOM states to move further in the direction of making it easier for nationals to move within the community suggests that, despite reservations, they are committed to advancing the process. As the GR and Mottley have noted, facilitating the movement of people within the community, something that would strengthen their investment in the regional process, goes beyond the relaxation of regulations and requires an approach to regional transportation that would reduce costs and increase availability (CARICOM Secretariat 2018b). Accepting the GR's recommendation for removing individual national taxes, which have made intraregional travel exorbitant, would be a move in the right direction.

The Divide between More Developed Countries and Less Developed Countries, and the Golding Report

The discussion so far suggests some of the real differences that exist in CARICOM between the smaller OECS countries and other member states. Thus, while most of the GR's recommendations appear uncontroversial and are necessary to effect a genuine economic union, there are areas of differential capability among members of the community. These include, for example, uneven access to technical/scientific expertise to address sanitary and phytosanitary standards, and absence of competition commissions in most states, among others – areas ripe for the development of regional institutions. The GR noted the need for harmonized regional intellectual property legislation and a regional intellectual property office. Unfortunately, CARICOM's ability to expand the number of regional institutions is stymied by its inability to adequately fund existing institutions, as the GR notes.

One of the GR's recommendations for completing the customs union that is potentially polarizing is for the collection of import duties at the first port to entry. The GR does not suggest how these funds should be allocated among member states, thus ignoring the challenges that are likely to arise. There are two issues worth exploring here. First, countries currently maintain many exceptions to the common external tariff, in recognition of the importance of certain sectors to their economies (IDB 2005, 9). Duties collected at the first point of entry would then be allowed to circulate freely within the community, avoiding further duties, thus undermining the existence of these exceptions, unless this applies only to goods that are not subject to exceptions. Even if such exceptions were abolished, as the GR demands, there remains the question of the fair allocation of duties among member states, as goods entering the community would not necessarily remain in the first point of entry. Without such an accounting mechanism, countries with closer proximity to major markets or with more efficient transportation links to major markets would benefit at the expense of countries with weaker connections. Given the importance of duties in national revenue, especially in small countries with high unemployment and a narrow tax base, this approach is likely to be explosive. Jamaica, with its relatively close proximity to North America, stands to be one of the winners in this scenario, at the expense of some of the LDCs. Further, the GR does not consider a regional stake in the apportioning of customs revenue, especially given the paucity of monies to fund CARICOM and the CARICOM Development Fund (CDF).[24]

The GR's dismissal of differences in size of population, geography and economy suggests a lack of understanding of the wide differences that exist among countries considered "small" that could constrain their ability to benefit from the CSME. Although Jamaica is included in the World Bank/Commonwealth Secretariat's classification of small states based on a population of 1.5 million (which it exceeds by almost the same number), there are real differences in physical size that affect not only competitiveness and efficiency, but the ability of smaller CARICOM states to provide many health, education and social services. Most LDCs do not have access to sophisticated laboratory testing and specialist services, such as oncology and radiology, and are forced to access such services from neighbouring countries (often Barbados, Trinidad and Martinique) or the United States. Most residents simply cannot afford these expensive trips, hospitals and treatment regimes, so they remain without access to these options.

By focusing on per capita GDP, the GR ignores other performance indices such as unemployment, poverty and inequality, which, in most OECS countries, are higher than in Jamaica (see Ram et al. 2018, 45–46). Size of economy, although not the only factor, is nevertheless important to a country's ability to make effective use of access to a single economy. Nearly 70 per cent of CARICOM's GDP is accounted for by four out of fifteen countries: Trinidad (28 per cent), Jamaica (18 per cent), Bahamas (13 per cent) and Haiti (10 per cent) (CDB 2018, 16). The region as a whole has also been experiencing low rates of growth, as shown earlier. Most CARICOM countries have been struggling with high debt and have been undergoing debt restructuring programs. For example, in 2012, debt in St Kitts and Nevis and Grenada was on par with Jamaica's, at 144.9 per cent, 112.6 per cent and 143.3 per cent, respectively (Robinson 2014, 38). While Grenada and St Kitts and Nevis have managed to lower their debt below 100 per cent, to 66.3 per cent and 64.6 per cent, respectively, Jamaica has struggled to reduce its debt, which remained at 111.9 per cent.[25] However, this is way below Barbados's debt, which rose to 157.1 per cent in 2018 (CDB Annual Report 2018, 18), giving it the dubious distinction of having the third-highest debt in the world (*Caribbean360* 2018b).

The GR also ignores the disproportionate effects of hurricanes and other weather events on smaller territories, even as Jamaica itself is vulnerable to hurricanes. Gonsalves sums up these differences in his response to the GR's recommendations:

> Undoubtedly, in the OECS member states of CARICOM, the small size of their domestic markets, the underdeveloped manufacturing sector, the absence of oil and mineral resources, the relatively weak condition of the financial sector, and the paucity of certain vital skill sets, place them at a marked disadvantage compared to the traditionally more developed countries in CARICOM (Barbados, Guyana, Jamaica, and Trinidad and Tobago) – the recognised MDCs in the CSME. Further, in this era of debilitating climate change, the vulnerability and lack of resilience to natural disasters of the Member Countries of the OECS place them in an even more disadvantaged or precarious state than the other CARICOM Member States. For us in the OECS there is an undoubted case for a designation which accommodates the notion of "Small Island Exceptionalism" on account of their structural weaknesses or deficiencies in their economies and the unfamiliarity, unprecedentedness and urgency of the on-rushing natural disasters. To be sure, the larger CARICOM countries are also subject to climate change and debilitating natural disasters, but the consequential damage and destruction has not been to the same extent as in the OECS Member States. The veritable "wipe-out" of Grenada in 2004 and Dominica in 2017 attests to this fact. (Gonsalves 2018, 5)

His point was underscored by the catastrophic effects of the eruption of the La Soufrière volcano in his country (St Vincent) in 2021, leading to the dislocation of thousands of Vincentians and causing substantial damage to the agricultural sector.

CARICOM's decision to designate some countries as LDCs, with special measures to ensure that their small firms/producers are able to access the CARICOM market, was in keeping with a recognition of the real danger of polarization in integration schemes with differences in size of economies and natural endowments. The Revised Treaty of Chaguaramas also recognized that polarization was a danger, not only among countries but within countries as well, hence the inclusion of disadvantaged regions for access to CDF funding. As noted earlier, despite compensatory funding from the European Union to its weaker economies, they were still disproportionately affected by the recession.

The GR's recommendation here also undermines CARICOM's claims for special and differential treatment in the World Trade Organization, the Economic Partnership Agreement, and in negotiations with Canada and the United Kingdom and future negotiations with the United States. CARICOM's claims for special and differential treatment have taken the form of insisting on the inclusion of "development chapters" to address some of their challenges and differences in size of economies and in institutions with developed country counterparts.[26] Further, Jamaica's stance here can undermine its own claim for redress from Trinidad and Tobago, because if Jamaica cannot outperform Trinidad and Tobago, then it is even less likely that the LDCs will be able to become competitive within the CSME. It raises the question of why Jamaica's claims for redress to address its competitiveness issues should be taken any more seriously than LDCs claims for special consideration.

It is worth noting that Dominica, an LDC, has one of the highest costs per unit of electricity in the world.

Gonsalves, the most outspoken head of government in the OECS, all of whose countries are categorized as LDCs, has argued that "from the standpoint of the OECS, including St. Vincent and the Grenadines, a Single Economy is a non-starter unless there is a special carve-out for the OECS Member States within CARICOM. Thus far, at least three larger CARICOM Member States are opposed to such a carve-out" (Gonsalves 2018, n.p.). Gonsalves did not detail the specific measures requested by the OECS, but it may well be that the OECS has a vested interest in not seeing the CSME completed because of fear of polarization and concern that the Revised Treaty of Chaguaramas, including the CDF, does not properly address these concerns. To push for the full implementation of the CSME within a relatively short time frame given the challenges to date, in the wake of a recession which sees countries still struggling to recover, and without considering the insecurities of some states, might further imperil CARICOM's survival. The GR acknowledged that the CDF was underfunded, with the Jamaican government being one of those negligent in meeting its commitments, having made no contributions to the CDF's second funding cycle from 2015 to 2020 (Government of Jamaica 2017, 33). The GR's recommendation here is ambiguous and appears contingent on the removal of the MDC/LDC distinction as this quote suggests: "Given the proposal we make in Chapter 5 for the removal of the differentiation between MDCs and LDCs and the certainty that there are vulnerable sectors in Jamaica that should qualify for CDF assistance, we recommend that Jamaica make an appropriate commitment to the CDF's Second Funding Cycle" (Government of Jamaica 2017, 33).

The reduction of disparities among participants in regional integration schemes, both among countries and within countries, is a concern for such schemes. As Brexit and Jamaica's dissatisfaction with CARICOM show, countries that perceive little benefit from such schemes could decide to leave, undermining their integrity. Hence, measures to cushion negative economic and social fallouts are important. The EU experience shows that despite a commitment to achieve cohesion across the region, with mechanisms in place for resource transfers to reduce disparities, the recession had a more negative effect on the poorer southern countries. Farole, Rodríguez-Pose and Storper (2011, 1090) note that the largest share of the EU budget went to support its cohesion policy. Yet, it did not end economic divergences once and for all. The problem of maximizing winners and minimizing losers from the implementation of the CSME is likely to be even more challenging given CARICOM's weak capacity to direct economic policy, its general inability to fund its regional bodies, its even more limited ability to finance meaningful compensatory measures among and within countries, and the absence of strong sanctions or incentives to drive implementation of its policies. In its discussion of CARICOM's failings, the GR ignored the EU experience and the differential effects of the recession on EU economies despite strong programmes, including control over financing and fiscal and monetary policy, to facilitate economic convergence between the more prosperous north and countries in the south. It similarly failed to acknowledge how the recession might have dampened countries' enthusiasm for meeting their obligations to give effect to the CSME.

Strengthened Governance Framework

The thirty-ninth regular meeting of CARICOM HOG concluded with a commitment to accelerate the implementation of the CSME, which can be read as a direct response to the GR. It emphasized establishing "an Investment Policy and Investment Code, and Incentives Regime, an Integrated Capital Market and . . . model Securities Legislation" (CARICOM Secretariat 2018a, n.p.). While not embracing new structures for implementation, the HOG set a new timeline mandating the Council for Finance and Planning to put these in place by July 2019 and set quarterly meetings, beginning in September 2018, for the Prime Ministerial Sub-Committee on the CSME to meet to "guide and invigorate the implementation process" (CARICOM Secretariat 2018a, n.p.). It also agreed to a "Special Meeting of the Conference in November 2018" to take account of the GR (CARICOM Secretariat 2018a, n.p.) and appeared to be moving in the direction of embracing sanctions in respect of dispute settlement via the CCJ (CARICOM Secretariat 2014a, 40), although not as far as the GR wanted. On the specific recommendation of barring offending countries from access to the CDB, Gonsalves (2018) noted the impracticability of this, arguing that CARICOM did not control the CDB.[27] Even if it did, a "sizeable" amount of CDB funds in 2017 went to disaster recovery (CDB Annual Report 2018, 9). The broader question here is whether non-compliance, especially in the wake of a prolonged recession, should be viewed only as intransigence rather than as a reflection of broader challenges of development that member states face. The GR also recommended relaxing the unanimity rule to allow for majority voting on specific issues. The OECS has already revised its treaty to allow for this without doing any damage to its cohesiveness, so this recommendation is not controversial in its own right, although it is not clear that this would not become a contentious element in CARICOM given current interstate relations and countries' (most notably, Jamaica's) proclivity to concede as little sovereignty as possible.

The Limits of the CARICOM Single Market and Economy

Challenges in completing the CSME raise the more fundamental question of the relevance of the model of integration it represents. Palankai, reflecting on Hungary's participation in the European Union, reminds us of the conditions that were considered necessary for countries to benefit from regional integration schemes:

> The advantages to be gained from a customs union depend on the *economic structures* of the participating countries. According to the classical theories, the more competitive the "rival" structures of the countries forming the union are with each other, the greater the benefit. From the point of view of gains, the ideal situation is if before the union the maximum range of products was produced in every country, and if the maximum differences existed in the production costs of the various products, that is, the number of overlapping protected goods or sectors was as big as possible. (italics in original; Palankai 2003, 150)

These conditions were never present in CARICOM, where countries inherited production structures that were geared at raw material for export. This fundamental feature of Caribbean economies has not changed and is also largely true of the tourism-based services sector. Regional trade has long been stagnant, and it is not clear how freeing up the factors of production on its own can stimulate countries to produce for the regional market or whether, even if they were to do so, they would be any more competitive than producers from outside the region, even with the common external tariff in place. The GR's observation that Jamaica was uncompetitive in all of its export markets would suggest that the problem goes beyond this.

Integration schemes among developing countries, especially Caribbean small states which did not meet the conditions for a successful customs union, were expected to benefit from the dynamic effects of economies of scale, increased competition and efficiency (Palankai 2003; Lewis 2002). The rationale for completing the CSME was made explicit in CARICOM's strategic plan as "to achieve sustained economic development based on international competitiveness and coordinated economic policies and enhanced trade and economic relations with third states. The CSME is intended to, inter alia, provide larger market opportunities; take advantage of greater economies of scale; stimulate increased competitiveness; and increase opportunities for investment" (CARICOM Secretariat 2014a, 14). There are more fundamental questions for CARICOM, though, around the impediments to production at the national and regional levels. This has been a starker issue for CARICOM's LDCs, with significantly smaller populations and physical size, reflected in firm size, with competitiveness at the national level an elusive goal. Nor would freeing up the factors of production necessarily benefit them, as investment and labour could be attracted to countries with the potential for greater efficiencies (see Myrdal 1957; Eckenstein 1969; Kitamura 1966). The inherent vulnerabilities of small Caribbean states, in particular those of the OECS, to trade liberalization were the basis for CARICOM's insistence on the inclusion of development chapters in its negotiations with the European Union and Canada. It would be a glaring omission for CARICOM to fail to consider their development concerns within the CSME.

One way to address this is to consider how goods are produced and the possibilities for integrating production structures across the region. The Revised Treaty of Chaguaramas did speak to the possibility of integrating production across the region (Article 52), but its energies were clearly focused on increasing trade. CARICOM's strategic plan moves the discussion beyond trade to specifically address production[28] as a key element in increasing the production capacity of regional firms. The CARICOM Commission on the Economy, in its preliminary 2014 report, identified as a medium-term goal "defining a production integration model for the Community with supportive frameworks for trade facilitation and finance" (cited in CARICOM Secretariat 2014a, 16). The strategic plan also speaks to promoting economic growth by "leveraging the regional integration arrangements to develop resource-based (natural resource and value added) products and promote production integration" (CARICOM Secretariat 2014a, 17). It thus presents a more considered approach to the problem, in contrast to the GR's explicit focus on trade. It is interesting that the commission did not speak to possibilities for production integration and how Jamaica could insert itself more centrally in this process.

The GR's discussion around the cheaper supply of oil from Trinidad to reduce the cost of producing goods and services, even though not intended, moves the conversation in the direction of treating national resources as regional goods, although it was narrowly focused on Jamaica's needs. The strategic plan speaks to greater use of energy inputs to reduce production costs, increase efficiency and drive diversification by way of "optimizing existing assets, reducing the high cost of energy inputs (particularly in production) through enhanced functional cooperation, and development of alternative energy to meet CARICOM's target of 20% by 2017[29] for the contribution of renewable energy to the total electricity supply mix" (CARICOM Secretariat 2014a, 18). Though it is not clear how this will be achieved, it does reflect a more thoughtful approach to tackling the region's productivity challenges and points the integration process in a new direction.

Such an approach of bringing regional resources under the "functional" umbrella, could be justified only within the framework of a broader vision that employs national endowments to create new production structures, not simply to produce goods more efficiently, but to change the orientation of national economies from raw material production. This also involves shifting perceptions of the region as resource poor to an awareness that the region is rich in resources, but that their exploitation has followed the usual pattern of ownership and control by foreign companies with different objectives than strengthening economies and improving the lives of the region's people. It is increasingly evident that the region is rich in oil resources, as oil finds in Guyana in 2015 would suggest. Grenada has also had interest in exploration of its waters for oil. As traditional sources of oil dry up, one can expect oil extraction companies to seek to open up Caribbean sources of oil. CARICOM has a crucial role to play in ensuring that this resource does not go the way of foreign ownership and control with little benefit to the national or regional economy. Guyana, rich in minerals and gold, but one of the poorest and formerly most indebted countries in the region, is a stark example of this problem. A priority must be to develop model contracts that govern the exploitation of oil to change this pattern and supervisory guidelines that reduce the scope for corruption.[30] Efforts should go beyond this to consider how this resource can be best used to benefit the country and the region and to avoid the resource curse of crowding out other economic activities. An important consideration for the region is how to exploit its oil resources while avoiding the danger of investing in dying technologies at the expense of the environment and investing in renewable sources of energy.

The CARICOM strategic plan also sees a role for ocean management as part of a broader effort to manage the environment and natural resources. This would focus on controlling invasive species, marine litter and "biodiversity beyond national jurisdiction" (CARICOM Secretariat 2014a, 28). The plan also envisions the agricultural and fisheries sector as "one economic space" for achieving growth and food security (CARICOM Secretariat 2014a, 17). There is also scope for a more expansive treatment of fisheries resources than management of stocks. Most of the focus of the CSME has been on land resources, with little progress on the use of the sea, particularly for CARICOM fishermen. The strategic plan speaks to this by envisioning the "positioning [of] the regional agricultural and fisheries sector as one economic space for growth and export development and enable food and nutrition security taking in account existing strategies to remove key binding constraints and to deliver on the Common Agriculture Policy, the Regional Food and Nutrition Policy, the Common Fisheries Policy" (CARICOM Secretariat 2014a, 17). The challenge here is to reduce restrictions over territorial waters without creating new imbalances within and among countries. Put differently, the challenges of marginalizing traditional fishermen must be recognized and addressed.

The strategic plan ignores another potential source of wealth, which is member states' extensive exclusive economic zone and all that lies beneath it. Exploration of the seabed by foreign companies has already begun. By early 2020 the International Seabed authority had already granted eighteen contracts to twenty-one contractors to explore the deep seabed, in the Clarion-Clipperton Zone, the Indian Ocean, Mid-Atlantic Ridge, South Atlantic Ocean and the Pacific Ocean for polymetallic nodules, polymetallic sulphides and cobalt-rich ferromanganese crusts (ISA, n.d.). The contracts were dominated by a small group of countries – China, France, Germany, India, Japan, Russia, South Korea – and a small group of companies from the United States, the United Kingdom, Canada and Belgium (Deep Sea Conservation Coalition, n.d.). A number of Pacific islands were involved in sponsoring some of these companies to explore the Clarion-Clipperton Zone, which extends from Kiribati to Mexico, with the Cook Islands issuing a licence to explore its national waters (Alberts 2020). It is imperative that CARICOM countries adopt a regional approach to the exploitation and use of the resources of their seabed that prioritizes regional development, while being mindful of potential negative consequences to the environment. Jamaica has already joined the fray, sponsoring the company Blue Minerals Jamaica Ltd,[31,32] (the first in the region apart from Cuba,[33] which is part of the Interoceanmetal Joint Organization) to explore the Clarion-Clipperton Zone.

An approach to the region's resources which also recognizes a regional claim to support the work of the CARICOM bureaucracy and drive the integration process requires developing a model that accepts national interests in resources but also takes account of regional interests. These regional interests include channelling resources to fund regional structures and to strengthen CARICOM's capacity to respond to challenges of marginalization within and among countries and to provide protection against natural hazards and man-made disasters. Such funds should also be used to augment the CDF or create other funding mechanisms with clear guidelines on how these should be disbursed to reduce the region's dependence on foreign aid and to address social issues. Frustration with seemingly destructive national policies, as evident in the GR's critique of policies such as CBI programmes operating in the OECS, and failure to coordinate foreign policy reflect the drive of individual countries to find sponsors for their "development" projects, in particular infrastructure, in an international climate that is less than sympathetic to their problems. Harnessing the region's wealth as suggested would provide the basis for financing hugely expensive social and economic projects that individual countries cannot afford. These include infrastructure for which funding is challenging to find (such as roads, airports, schools, hospitals), social security (including unemployment support), pensions, health care, education, and the development of efficient and affordable regional air and sea transport. CARICOM's strategic plan acknowledged the importance of developing a regional air and maritime transportation system that is safe, facilitates the movement of people and goods within the region, and contributes to the "global" competitiveness of producers (CARICOM 2014a, 18).

A more expansive role for CARICOM in the identification, management and exploitation of national resources, with some stake in the earnings from these, would also require a significant revamping of not only CARICOM's structure, but, more importantly, its relationships to governments, opposition parties and the citizenry. These issues should be part of a broader conversation on CARICOM's role, along the lines addressed here. As I have argued elsewhere, this would also contribute to addressing implementation challenges (Lewis 2005). CARICOM's role cannot be limited to liberalizing trade, though important, but should be more directed at addressing the structural challenges which lead to potentially destructive practices/industries such as offshore finance and CBI programs. A greater role for the region would reduce the incoherence in foreign policy, most recently reflected by their divided stances in the Organization of American States on whether to suspend Venezuela from the organization and voting in the United Nations on the recognition of Jerusalem as the capital of Israel (*Jamaica Observer* 2017).[34,35] At the heart of these votes were differential national interests based on the need for resources to fund development. The OECS countries that voted against Venezuela's expulsion were members of the Bolivarian Alliance (formerly Alternative) of the Americas, which has been an important source of financial and general developmental support for them. Countries' votes in the United Nations were also influenced by perception of threat of retaliation made by the United States.[36] The failure to agree on diplomatic relations with either Taiwan or China was also influenced by national perceptions of benefit. Coherence in foreign policy will remain challenging as long as countries are forced to look outside the region for their economic salvation. A fortified CARICOM would also obviate the untenable situation of another country devising a "development plan" for a member state, at that state's request, as happened in China's proposed development plan for Grenada which envisaged Grenada as a tax haven (GCR 2017) and as a source of investment for Chinese companies, accompanied by the introduction of strong laws to protect investors (*Barnacle* 2018).

CARICOM, with the support of other regional organizations such as the CDB and the ECCB, should also play a more active role in the financial policies adopted by countries, in order to reduce the region's exposure to negative fallout. The GR identified the CBIs of OECS countries and the region's role in seeking to address the challenges facing financial institutions from the de-risking[37] issues countries now face as appropriate areas for CARICOM intervention.[38] Security is another obvious area, particularly given the region's exposure through a significant number of Trinidad's citizens fighting with the Islamic State (ISIS) in Syria and Iraq. The GR noted, with dismay, that for four years, Jamaica had not participated in the meetings of the Council for National Security and Law Enforcement, which provides policy direction for the Implementation Agency for Crime and Security, the regional organization coordinating security cooperation (Government of Jamaica 2017, 34). The offshore financial and information technology sectors are obvious areas for intelligence sharing and expert advice. This is particularly important given the charges that Cambridge Analytica was active in elections in seven CARICOM countries – Trinidad and Tobago, Grenada, St Vincent and the Grenadines,

St Lucia, St Kitts and Nevis, Antigua and Barbuda, and Guyana – and the important role that bitcoin has played as a means of financing Russian interference in the US elections (*Quartz* 2018; Glaser 2018). Bitcoin is already functioning in the region, as evidenced by the installation of an ATM machine dealing in the currency in St Kitts and Nevis in 2018. The ECCB posted a warning on its website that a regulatory framework to govern the operation of cryptocurrencies such as bitcoin had not yet been developed for the ECCU area and advised that potential consumers were offered no protection under the law (ECCB 2018). This is an example of the kind of intervention that one would hope for. The development of such a regulatory framework should be a matter of urgency not just for the ECCU region but the entire CARICOM. This is particularly important as cryptocurrencies are already being proposed as a way of addressing the de-risking challenge, which could expose the region to greater economic and political instability (Williams 2016).[39]

What Vision of Regional Integration?

This approach, of treating the region as having a call on national resources, raises the question of compatibility with the regional trade-centred vision that the CSME represents. It suggests considering a model of development that seeks to establish control over the exploitation, use and allocation of natural resources within a regional framework to address intractable issues of underdevelopment. Central to a shift to this broader role for regional integration is how the region is perceived, or in other words, its raison d'être. This question of the role of the regional integration process was raised by the GR, which saw a conflict with some visions of the process and what it thought the vision ought to be. It is worth quoting from the GR:

> This Commission feels that while CARICOM has been the victim of an over-reliance on the shared history of its members, the value of regional integration, notwithstanding the current wave of economic nationalism in various parts of the world, is as relevant and useful and, perhaps, even more urgent today than it was at its inception and can provide us a more secure passage to a brighter future than can each of us trying to row his boat alone. But set sail we must, whether separately or together as a crew. (Government of Jamaica 2017, xii)

There are two broad contending visions of CARICOM inherent in this comment: one that sees the rationale for regional integration as going beyond the economic self-interest of member states to a shared concern for the well-being of the region's people, connected by intangible bonds arising from a shared history of slavery, colonial and post-colonial exploitation, which the GR rejects, and the other that views the nation state as primary. The latter perspective is in sharp contrast to Gonsalves's (1998) argument for a Caribbean civilization which centres the common historical (and postcolonial) experiences of its people. The strategic plan presents a different vision of CARICOM from the GR's, as reflected in its goal to strengthen the "CARICOM Identity and spirit of Community" (CARICOM Secretariat 2014a, 31). This vision included "engender[ing] a sense of belonging and commitment to the region" and "refining and promoting the CARICOM Identity and Civilization" in an effort to "[engender] a sustained sense of belonging" (CARICOM Secretariat 2014a, 31).

The irony of the GR's nationalist approach is that even as it eschews these less than economic grounds for regional integration, it evokes a regional interest in the pursuit of foreign affairs, admonishing that "the exercise by Member States of the right to independently pursue diplomatic engagement without regard for their implications for the region as a whole is not in keeping with the spirit of the CARICOM Treaty and will only lead to our being divided and manipulated" (Government of Jamaica 2017, 30). The implicit perspective here is that a country acting in its perceived national interest may be acting against the regional interest. This is a contradiction if the goal of the regional movement is to advance national interests. If, however, there is a deeper basis on which CARICOM countries seek to integrate, where countries recognize a common regional goal that takes precedence over national goals, then it is possible to have the kind of regional approach to resources I have proposed. This can happen only if the regional integration mechanisms are viewed as more effective vehicles for advancing national interests or if countries are committed to the well-being of one another so as to refrain from adopting policies that may be inimical to the well-being of others. To put it in more material terms, why would Trinidad and Tobago want to supply its oil at a cheaper rate to its CARICOM neighbours if not doing so gives them a competitive edge?

The GR's perspective on the centrality of Jamaica's interests in assessing the value of the CSME was expressed in the sentiment that "the CSME must become a stepping stone, not a stumbling block or nuisance, to Jamaica's advancement and Jamaica must be prepared to explore other economic relations if it turns out that the CSME is stillborn" (Government of Jamaica 2017, 63). It is also evident in its endorsement of David Jessop's perspective on the way forward for CARICOM, which suggests that "if full integration is not achievable . . . [the Caribbean should pursue] a much wider range of market-led complementary economic relationships" which would see deeper integration among the OECS and the French overseas territories and with Jamaica and the "northern Caribbean and Cayman" (Jessop, cited in Government of Jamaica 2017, 63).

CARICOM's Response to the Golding Report

CARICOM HOG responded to both the GR and the OECS's response to it with a special session in December 2018, which ended with the "St Ann's Declaration on CSME" (*CARICOM Today* 8 January 2019). In addition to outlining a number of measures to be taken to address some of these concerns, the declaration also established a restructured Commission on the Economy "to advise Member States on a Growth Agenda for the Community". The commission, headed by Avinash Persaud,[40] a special adviser to the Barbados government on the economy, released its report in October 2020. The St Ann's Declaration contained a number of measures directed at engaging more closely with the private sector and labour, widening the ambit for movement throughout the region and strengthening compliance. It agreed to amend the Revised Treaty of Chaguaramas to include representative bodies of labour and the private sector as associate institutions and to put in place a "formalised, structured mechanism to facilitate dialogue between the Councils of the Community and the private sector and labour" (para. 3).[41] Additional measures to strengthen the private sector's involvement in the CSME included a commitment to finalize the regime on public procurement by 2019[42] and to "take all necessary steps to allow for the mutual recognition of companies incorporated in a CARICOM Member State" (para. 16). It also included measures to strengthen and broaden the freedom of movement regime that added four new categories of workers eligible to work in the community ("agricultural workers, beauty service practitioners, barbers and security guards") (para. 12); moving to ensure that all "legislative and other arrangements" necessary to facilitate freedom of movement for approved categories of workers were put in place; working towards reintroducing a "single domestic space for passengers in the region" (para. 9) and "a single security check for direct transit passengers on multi-stop intra-Community flights" (para. 10). The declaration also included a number of suggestions for strengthening implementation that included applying the principle of "accelerated implementation" already provided for in Article 50 of the RTOC (para. 5) and allowing states "so willing . . . (to) move towards full free movement within the next three (3) years" (para. 6).

The Report of the Restructured Commission on the Economy

The measures proposed by the restructured Commission on the Economy were largely in line with those in the St Ann's Declaration, although they went further to cover an expanded number of initiatives. Characterizing CARICOM's problem as one of implementation, the report advanced measures that its authors argued should cost government little; focused on few, clearly defined and easily implemented initiatives; would not need strong political will to implement; and called, more generally, for CARICOM to follow principles of subsidiarity[43] as a way of overcoming its implementation failures. The key recommendation for pushing implementation along was to allow for a group of at least five countries ("a coalition of the willing") to advance different elements of the CSME among themselves, provided they opened up to others who wished to join (CARICOM Commission on the Economy 2020, 18, 19). Two recommendations were specifically pitched at involving people centrally in the integration process by addressing shortcomings in regional transportation and lowering education barriers to freedom of movement. Key barriers to movement across the region were the high cost of air transport and the general absence of alternative sea transport, with the exception of the recently introduced ferry services operating among a small number of territories in the Eastern Caribbean. This service, while regulated by governments and CARICOM, would be based on a fleet of private providers, at little cost to governments. Relatedly, the report advocated reducing education requirements for employment across the region from university certificates to passing grades in two subjects of the regional school–leaving exam, the Caribbean Secondary Education Certificate, which represents a more expansive approach, with a more dynamic impact than the limited approach of the declaration. The report also addressed the need to advance "environmental resilience". It suggested that this could be targeted at the individual level with new housing being required to meet certain standards in respect of hurricane resilience, alternative energy, water collection systems and communication, by those who could afford, with low-cost loans provided to those who could not. This would address resilience at the household level, reducing the scope of devastation after a hurricane and the associated personal and national costs.

As a way of addressing challenges with de-risking, it proposed the establishment of a regional financial conduct authority to establish and oversee financial conduct rules and provide certification (13).

In advancing a focus on a few initiatives that would have a significant impact on popular engagement in the process and on easing the implementation roadblock, the report of the Commission on the Economy observed that global changes had already rendered some of the CSME's goals irrelevant, a perspective that resonates with Lewis's (chapter 3) perspective (CARICOM Commission on the Economy 2020). Beyond singling out the goal of financial integration (18), which was undermined by the recession, the report does not explore this in any detail. Nor does it address the question of what was most worthwhile to be implemented, especially given its recognition that some of the original CSME goals might well be redundant. It also does not consider how or to what extent differential implementation and among which group of countries might affect the integrity of the organization. CARICOM already has an example of differential integration among the full member states of the OECS. This includes unrestricted movement of OECS nationals in member states, an arrangement that is not open to CARICOM members not part of the grouping. It is not clear that such arrangements among a different configuration of countries might not have a more marked (potentially negative) impact. Gonsalves's response to the GR raises the question of whether the OECS integration process is compatible with the completion of the CSME.

Conclusion

The question that both the St Ann Declaration and the report of the restructured Commission on the Economy raise is whether their proposals are sufficient to overcome the deep-seated divisions within the community explored in this chapter. The commission departed from the GR's insistence that all elements of the CSME should be implemented by suggesting that not all elements of the CSME remained relevant. In this it aligns more closely with the OECS's (as presented by Gonsalves) observation that not all elements of the CSME were feasible and that implementation of some aspects would undermine the OECS's own integration scheme. And while the expanded freedom of movement in both documents aligns with the GR's demands, these measures are likely to remain contentious, as even when governments support such measures (as Barbados under the leadership of Mia Mottley), there is likely to remain strong sentiments in the population against this. Within months of the St Ann's Declaration, Antigua and St Kitts and Nevis requested and were granted a five-year deferral on their commitment to implement freedom of movement of the enlarged agreed category of workers, based on concerns related to their small size (CARICOM Community News – CARICOM Single Market & Economy 4 March 2019). Of note is that only eight of fifteen heads of government attended the special meeting of HOG called to discuss the GR report, which raises the question of whether there exists strong commitment to completing the CSME or the political will to implement it. In this environment, it is not at all evident that the use of sanctions to force compliance would strengthen the organization; it may well weaken it. Moreover, CARICOM LDCs continue to invoke Article 164 of the

Revised Treaty of Chaguaramas to protect infant industries (IDB 2020, 68) against their non-LDC counterparts, going against the GR's insistence that they should be treated no differently from the MDCs.

The strength of the commission's report is that it seeks to connect with the desire among a significant section of the people of the CARICOM to move more freely within the region and to have a greater sense of belonging, which is in sharp contrast to the Landell Mills's more elitist approach (discussed in chapter 3) and more in keeping with the strategic vision. As with all previous efforts at moving Caribbean economic integration along, it requires the commitment of governments to take the initiative to make this happen. By identifying measures that are regulatory and do not affect the economic balance in the region, or those that cost governments little or nothing to implement, the commission has increased the chances of some of its recommendations being implemented. For example, its attempt to shift the focus of attention from the more challenging aspects of the CSME to the creation of a "digital and delivery" economy is both an indication of how economic activities have shifted beyond the physical trade in goods and an attempt to find ways around governments' reluctance to remove barriers to trade and physical movement of people, among others. Ultimately, though, the region has to confront whether the differences and interests of its members are compatible or irreconcilable, and whether the CSME itself should not be subjected to more rigorous analysis to determine which elements remain relevant and are likely to advance the interests of most of its members. Allied with this, and to underscore the commission's recommendation that the integration process should be governed by the principle of subsidiarity, with clear distinctions made between what is best pursued at the regional and national levels, regional institutions have a larger role to play in creating the regulatory environment that would strengthen the region's engagement with external economic and political players and protect the rights of its citizens.

In conclusion, any real advancement in the CARICOM integration project requires a broader agenda than completing the CSME along the lines of the EU model. The region's problems are substantially different from those of Europe. They go beyond efforts at making it cheaper and more efficient to produce goods, even if substantial gains were to be made in these small markets. There is a real danger that were the CSME to be completed without adequate measures to ensure that OECS nationals and their firms are not marginalized or that nationals in MDCs do not remain marooned in poverty, the regional project could well collapse. A more viable future for Caribbean integration is to look to a more ambitious project that would seek to transform the region's production structures – as limited as these opportunities might be – to harness its resources and to replace the region's constant search for external saviours while gifting away its resources. This requires a rethink of the role of the state in leading this approach and creating the conditions for it to happen.

While implementing agreed measures to bring the CSME into effect is no doubt important, it cannot be the main basis on which CARICOM's value is assessed. I argue that even if the CSME is achieved, it is unlikely to address key features of the economies of small Caribbean states: Who owns resources and in whose interests are they employed? How are goods produced and who does production benefit? What model of integration is best suited to raise the quality of life of the region's people?

These go beyond improving economic growth and well-being to consider whether regional "development" contributes to the empowerment or marginalization of the region's people. I argue that CARICOM has an important role in ensuring that its citizens are not marginalized from the economic processes adopted. By focusing on whether Jamaicans benefit from CARICOM, the GR is encouraging us to reflect on the much more important question: What is the purpose of CARICOM?

Notes

1. For an analysis of Germany's role in addressing the eurozone crisis, see Currie and Teague (2017).

2. Barbados, Guyana, Belize and Dominica are the only countries that have embraced the CCJ as their appellate court.

3. The Landell-Mills report is cited as Stoneman, Pollard and Innis (2012). In this chapter, it is referred to as the Landell-Mills report to coincide with the usage in the Golding report.

4. The members of the OECS are Antigua and Barbuda, Dominica, Grenada, St Kitts and Nevis, St Lucia, St Vincent and the Grenadines, and Montserrat. Associate members are Anguilla, British Virgin Islands and Martinique.

5. The IDB (2020, 37) reported that in 2017, "the cost of energy for industrial purposes, was about 9 US cents per kWh, for Trinidad" and close to 20 US cents per kWh in Jamaica.

6. This was based on an advisory opinion on the matter by Winston Anderson, who went on to become a judge on the CCJ. Trinidad's position, as described in the GR, was that national treatment applied only within the Trinidad domestic market (Government of Jamaica 2017).

7. The only CARICOM countries without visa restrictions on Haitians were Belize, Grenada, Guyana, Montserrat, St Vincent and the Grenadines, and Suriname (IDB, 2020, 49, citing IOM 2019). Note that Jamaica was not included in this list.

8. Haiti was to have begun implementing the CSME in 2020, but continued political unrest has relegated this to the back burner.

9. GDP per capita estimates for 2018 showed Jamaica as having one of the lowest GDP per capita ratios in the region (US$5,353) behind Guyana at the time (US$4,901), Belize (US$4,885) and Haiti (US$835); in contrast to the LDCs, whose GDP per capita ranged from a low of US$7,361 for St Vincent and the Grenadines to a high of US$19,275 for St Kitts and Nevis (IDB 2020, 23, table 3.1.1).

10. CBI programmes were introduced in the 1980s, then revived in the 2000s. Despite more stringent security measures introduced, including more careful requirements for background checks of applicants, they continue to be controversial. They have already led to Canada imposing visa requirements on holders of Grenadian and Antiguan passports. Nevertheless, these programmes have been targeted as the main source of support for the social sector (Citizen Lane 2017; Government of Canada 2014).

11. Haiti is a member of CARICOM, so it is not clear what the GR is expecting CARICOM to do here.

12. See Lewis (2003) for a discussion of the implementation deficit.

13. Member states were expected to maintain the following: "foreign reserves equivalent to three months of import cover for a period of 12 months", amended in 1996 to allow for an alternative measure of 80 per cent of central bank liabilities; "a fixed rate to the US dollar for 36 consecutive months without external debt payment arrears", amended in 1996 to allow for a floating rate of 1.5 per cent for countries with floating exchange rates "and . . . debt service ratio . . . within 15% of the export of goods and services" (Kendall 2000, 3–4).

14. The CDB's borrowing countries are all CARICOM countries, not just those in the single market and economy. It also includes the British non-independent states that, with the exception of Montserrat, which is a full member, hold observer status within CARICOM: Anguilla, British Virgin Islands, Cayman Islands, and Turks and Caicos.

15. Montserrat's low debt is partly explained by the control Britain exercises over its overseas territories' ability to borrow.

16. The authors attributed this to adjustments in the exchange rate.

17. St Ann's Declaration proposed addressing this by "mandating the Community Council to develop appropriate recommendations . . . for the introduction of a regime of sanctions for the consideration of the Conference" (para. 17).

18. The member countries of the ECCB are Anguilla, Antigua and Barbuda, Dominica, Grenada, Montserrat, St Kitts/Nevis, St Lucia, and St Vincent and the Grenadines.

19. Although the CDF was established to offset negative effects arising from the implementation of the CSME, its modest funding does not allow it to address large infrastructure needs of member states. For example, at the end of 2016, the CDF's capital fund was valued at US$94.53 million (CDF Annual Report 2016), far below the cost of St Vincent's international airport, which was US$259 million and was constructed with support from a large group of countries that included Venezuela, Cuba, Trinidad and Tobago, Austria, Mexico, Turkey, Libya, Georgia and Iran (Chance 2017; Myers 2017). The CDF's contribution to the construction of the airport was US$7.47 million (CDF 2017).

20. See note 14. Monetary union was to be achieved in phases, with the ultimate goal of a common currency. This was abandoned after 1993 when Trinidad and Tobago moved from a fixed to a floating exchange rate (Kendall 2000).

21. See Constantine (2018) for a more detailed discussion of the lessons that the EU experience holds for the CSME.

22. Melinda Gates reportedly rented the entire island in March 2021 for US$132,000 per night to avoid scrutiny over the announcement of her divorce from her husband Bill Gates (TMZ 6 May 2021).

23. Access should also be extended to controlling visual barriers to sea views. For example, the luxurious Silver Sands hotel which opened in 2018 at Grenada's Grand Anse beach has erected a wall that bars the beautiful views of the sea along the main Grand Anse road that is a crucial aspect of Grenadian life. Grenadians protested against the construction of luxury apartments along a section of St George's Harbor, which had also planned to erect a wall to protect the privacy of potential residents, while depriving Grenadians of their traditional views of the sea.

24. See Andriamananjara (2011) for a discussion of different mechanisms for allocating customs union funds.

25. This could be in part a result of the high levels of domestic borrowing in Jamaica's debt, for which debt relief is not available. In the mid-2000s domestic debt accounted for over 50 per cent of debt in Jamaica, Barbados, St Kitts and Nevis, and Antigua and Barbuda. See Robinson (2014, 40–42).

26. This has been a major sticking point contributing to the collapse of trade talks with Canada.

27. In addition to CARICOM countries categorized as "borrowing members" of the CDB, its membership also includes the following "non-borrowing" members: Brazil, Canada, China, Columbia, Germany, Italy, Mexico, the United Kingdom and Venezuela.

28. See Lewis, chapter 3, for a brief discussion of some of the challenges of achieving production integration and references to more detailed considerations of these.

29. Under the CARICOM Energy Policy signed in 2013, governments committed themselves to increasing the contribution of alternative energy to 20 per cent by 2017,

28 per cent by 2022 and 47 per cent by 2027. The IDB (2020, 67, table 4.4) suggested that based on CARICOM's work plans for 2018 and 2019, it appeared to have "achieved much re its mandate".

30. Mardenberg and Andreoni (2018), commenting on oil finds in Guyana, note the potential for corruption and for aggravating existing conflicts.

31. Government of Jamaica, Ministry of Foreign Affairs and Foreign Trade, 5 March 2019 "Blue Minerals Ltd to Lead Jamaica's Pursuits in Deep Seabed Mining", https://mfaft.gov.jm/jm /blue-minerals-ltd-to-lead-jamaicas-pursuits-in-deep-seabed-mining/.

32. The ISA approved the company's application in December 2020. ISA, n.d., "ISA Council Approves Blue Minerals Jamaica Limited's Plan of Work for Exploration of Polymetallic Nodules in the CCZ", https://www.isa.org.jm/news/isa-council-approves-blue-minerals-jamaica-limiteds-plan-work-exploration-polymetallic-nodules.

33. The Interoceanmetal Joint Organization includes in its membership Bulgaria, Cuba, Czech Republic, Poland, Russia and Slovakia. https://iom.gov.pl/. 14 May 2021.

34. The June vote in the Organization of American States on whether to suspend Venezuela from the organization showed significant differences among CARICOM states, with four supporting the resolution to suspend (Barbados, Bahamas, Guyana and Jamaica), two voting against it (Dominica and St Vincent) and the rest abstaining. See *Caribbean360* (2018a).

35. No CARICOM country supported the United States, but four abstained (Antigua and Barbuda, Bahamas, Jamaica, and Trinidad and Tobago), while two (St Lucia and Haiti) did not register a vote.

36. CARICOM's solidarity on Venezuela was further undermined by the Trump administration's preference for engaging with Jamaica and a few other amenable governments rather than with CARICOM.

37. De-risking refers to banks removing clients, such as other banks or individuals, from accessing their services. In the Caribbean, some local financial institutions have lost access to correspondent services provided by international banks that allow them to conduct international trade or send money across borders.

38. See Zhang (2016) for regional responses to de-risking.

39. Also see the curriculum vitae of Gabriel Abed, who spoke at CDB's "Caribbean Leadership and Transformation Forum", 18 September 2017, and which appears on the CDB website (http://www.caribank.org/cltf/speakers/gabriel-abed).

40. The other members of the commission were Chester Humphrey (trade union leader, Grenada), Damien King (department of government, University of the West Indies, Mona, Jamaica), Gregory McGuire (senior manager, Office of Strategy Management, National Gas Company, Trinidad and Tobago), Roger McLean (Health Economics Unit, University of the West Indies, St Augustine, Trinidad and Tobago), Wendell Samuel (Caribbean Regional Technical Assistance Centre, St Vincent and the Grenadines), P.B. Scott (chairman, Musson Group, Jamaica), Therese Turner-Jones (Inter-American Development Bank and the Bahamas), Ngozi Okonjo-Iweaka (co-chair of the Global Commission for the Economy and Climate and former finance minister of Nigeria), and Pascal Lamy (former EU commissioner for trade and director general of the World Trade Organization and president of the Paris Peace Forum).

41. CARICOM HOG agreed at their thirtieth intersessional meeting in February 2019 to meet with "representatives of national Business and Labour Advisory Committees (BLAC) twice a year" (CARICOM Secretariat, Single Market and Economy News, 1 March 2019).

42. CARICOM reached agreement on a protocol for public procurement, which was opened for signature in February 2019 and was to be provisionally applied once seven

members had signed a declaration on intent (CARICOM Single Market and Economy News, 1 March 2019).

43. As defined by the commission, subsidiarity requires "that decisions are taken as closely to the citizen as possible, and should only be done at the higher level, such as at CARICOM versus the national level, if doing it at the CARICOM level would be more effective and efficient than doing it at the national level" (p. 19).

References

Alberts, Elizabeth Claire. 16 June 2020. "Deep-sea Mining: An Environmental Solution or Impending Catastrophe?" *Mangabay*, 12 April 2021. https://news.mongabay.com/2020/06/deep-sea-mining-an-environmental-solution-or-impending-catastrophe/.

Andriamananjara, Soamiely. 2011. "Customs Unions". In *Preferential Trade Agreement Policies for Development: A Handbook*, edited by Jean-Pierre Chauffour and Jean-Christophe Maur, 111–20. Washington, DC: World Bank.

Barnacle. 2018. "PM Mitchell: China's National Development Plan for Grenada was in Response to Request for Help", 6 February. https://www.thebarnaclenews.com/pm-mitchell-chinas-national-development-plan-grenada-response-request-help/.

BBC News. 2018. "Europe and Nationalism: A Country-by-country Guide", 5 June. https://www.bbc.com/news/world-europe-36130006.

Brown, Roger. 2016. "The EU and Brexit: Blueprint for CARICOM". *Jamaica Observer*, 7 July. http://www.jamaicaobserver.com/business/The-EU-and-Brexit--Blueprint-for-Caricom_66439.

Calivigny Island. 2018. "The Island". http://www.calivigny-island.com/theIsland.php.

Caribbean360. 2018a. "CARICOM Countries Divided in OAS Vote on Suspending Venezuela", 6 July. http://www.caribbean360.com/news/caricom-countries-divided-in-oas-vote-on-suspending-venezuela.

———. 2018b. "New Barbados Government Uncovers Massive Debt and 11th Hour Contracts Signed by Previous Administration", 1 June. http://www.caribbean360.com/news/new-barbados-government-uncovers-massive-debt-and-11th-hour-contracts-signed-by-previous-administration.

CARICOM Commission on the Economy. October 2020. Report *"Caribbean 9.58" Speeding up the Caribbean*. https://issuu.com/guyanaconsulate6/docs/att_ii_to_item_7.3_-_cce_report_-32_is_-_24-25_feb.

CARICOM Secretariat. 1981. *The Caribbean Community in the 1980s: Report by a Group of Caribbean Experts*. Guyana: CARICOM Secretariat.

———. 2014a. *Strategic Plan for the Caribbean Community 2015–2019: Repositioning CARICOM*. Volume 1. The Executive Plan. https://caricom.org/documents/11265-executive_plan_vol_1_-_final.pdf.

———. 2014b. *Strategic Plan for the Caribbean Community 2015–2019: Repositioning CARICOM*. Volume 2. The Strategic Plan. https://caricom.org/documents/11853-the_strategic_plan_vol2-final.pdf.

———. 2018a. "Communiqué Issued at the Conclusion of the Thirty-Ninth Regular Meeting of the Conference of Heads of Government of the Caribbean Community", 7 July. https://caricom.org/media-center/communications/communiques/communiqu-issued-at-the-conclusion-of-the-thirty-ninth-regular-meeting-of-the-conference-of-heads-of-government-of-the-caribbean-community.

———. 2018b. "Start with the Single Domestic Space for Hassle Free Travel – PM Mottley", 4 July. https://caricom.org/media-center/communications/news-from-the-community/caricom-leaders-charged-not-to-forget-our-purpose-and-passion.

CARICOM Secretariat, Single Market and Economy News. 01 March 2019. "Member States in CSME Sign On to Contingent Rights Protocol", csme.caricom.org/press-releases/content /news.

———. 04 March 2019. "CARICOM Grants Deferral to Two Member Countries on Freedom of Movement", csme.caricom.org/press-releases/content/news.

CCJ (Caribbean Court of Justice). 2018. "Appeal from the Court of Appeal of Barbados – CCJ Appeal No. BBCV2018/002 between Eddy David Ventose and the Chief Electoral Officer". Judgement Summary. http://www.ccj.org/wp-content/uploads/2018/06/2018-CCJ-13-AJ1.pdf.

CDB (Caribbean Development Bank). 2018. *Annual Report 2017*. Barbados. http://www .caribank.org/publications/featured-publications/2017-annual-report.

CDF (CARICOM Development Fund). 2017. "CDF Annual Report 2016". http://caricom developmentfund.org/downloads/cdf-annual-report-2016/.

Chance, Kenton X. 2017. "St. Vincent and the Grenadines Opens New Multi-million Dollar International Airport". *Montserrat Reporter*, 16 February. https://www.themontserrat reporter .com/st-vincent-and-the-grenadines-opens-new-multi-million-dollar -international-airport/.

Citizen Lane. 2017. "What Do Canada's New Visa Requirements Mean for Caribbean Citizens?" 1 July. http://citizenlane.ch/canadas-new-visa-requirements-mean-caribbean-citizens/.

Constantine, Colin Mervin. 2018. "Whither CSME? A Reply to the Golding Report". *Social and Economic Studies* 69 (3&4): 27–54

Currie, Denise and Paul Teague. 2017. "The Eurozone Crisis, German Hegemony and Labor Market Reform in the GISP Countries". *Industrial Relations Journal* 48 (2): 154–73.

Deep Sea Conservation Coalition. n.d. "Deep-Seabed Mining: The Main Players". 14 May 2021. http://www.savethehighseas.org/deep-sea-mining/the-main-players/.

ECCB (Eastern Caribbean Central Bank). 2018. "Bitcoin ATM Not Authorized by Regulators in ECCU", 4 July. https://www.eccb-centralbank.org/news/view/bitcoin-atm-not-authorised-by -regulators-in-eccu.

Eckenstein, C. 1969. "Regional Integration among Unequally Developed Countries". In *Regionalism and the Commonwealth Caribbean: Special Lecture Series No. 2*, edited by Roy Preiswerk, 51–55. St. Augustine, Trinidad: Institute of International Relations.

Farole, Thomas, Andrés Rodríguez-Pose, and Michael Storper. 2011. "Cohesion Policy in the European Union: Growth, Geography, Institutions". *Journal of Common Market Studies* 49 (5): 1089–111.

GCR (Global Construction Review). 2017. "China Submits Comprehensive Development Plan for Granada" (sic). Website of the Chartered Institute of Building. 20 December. http://www .globalconstructionreview.com/news/china-submits-comprehensive-development-plan -grana/.

Glaser, April. 2018. "How Shady Was Cambridge Analytica? Considering the Work Its Parent Company did Trying to Win Caribbean Elections . . . Potentially Pretty Shady". *The Industry*, 29 March. https://slate.com/technology/2018/03/cambridge-analyticas-work-in-the -caribbean-was-pretty-shady.html.

Gonsalves, Ralph E. 1998. "Our Caribbean Civilisation: Retrospect and Prospect". *Caribbean Quarterly* 44 (3/4): 131–50.

———. 2018. "Some Salient Issues for Resolution in CARICOM". Address delivered on 22 February, Ministry of Foreign Affairs, Kingstown, St. Vincent. https://www.iwnsvg.com /2018/02/28/some-salient-issues-for-resolution-in-caricom/.

Government of Canada. 2014. "St. Kitts and Nevis Citizens Now Need a Visa to Travel to Canada", 22 November. https://www.canada.ca/en/immigration-refugees-citizenship/news /notices/notice-kitts-nevis-citizens-need-visa-travel-canada.html.

Government of Jamaica. 2017. *Report of the Commission to Review Jamaica's Relations within the CARICOM and CARIFORUM Frameworks*. Kingston, Jamaica: CARICOM/CARIFORUM Review Commission Secretariat, Ministry of Foreign Affairs and Foreign Trade.

Haiti Libre. 2018. "Haiti - Flash: CARICOM Examines the Free Movement of Haitians", 5 July. http://www.haitilibre.com/en/news-24859-haiti-flash-caricom-examines-the-free-movement -of-haitians.html.

Holinski, Nils, Clemens Kool, and Joan Muysken. 2012. "Persistent Macroeconomic Imbalances in the Euro Area: Causes and Consequences". *Federal Reserve Bank of St. Louis Review* 94 (1): 1–20.

IDB. 2005. *CARICOM Report No. 2*. by Anneke Jessen and Christopher Vignoles, August 2018. https://publications.iadb.org/publications/english/document/CARICOM-Report-No -2-(2005).pdf.

———. 2020. "CARICOM Report: Progress and Challenges of the Integration Agenda", by Samuel Braithwaite, 14 May 2021. https://publications.iadb.org/publications/english /document/CARICOM-Report-Progress-and-Challenges-of-The-Integration-Agenda.pdf.

ISA (International Seabed Authority). n.d. 14 May 2021. https://www.isa.org.jm/minerals /exploration-areas.

Jamaica Observer. 2017. "Update: C'bean Divided on Recognition of Jerusalem as Capital of Israel", 21 December. http://www.jamaicaobserver.com/latestnews/UPDATE:_Cbean _divided_on_recogniti on_of_Jerusalem_as_capital_of_Israel?profile=1228.

Kendall, Patrick. 2000. "Exchange Rate Convergence in CARICOM". Caribbean Development Bank. http://www.caribank.org/uploads/publications-reports/staff-papers/EXCHANGE %20RATE%20CONVERGENCE%20IN%20CARICOM.pdf.

Kitamura, Hiroshi. 1966. "Economic Theory and the Economic Integration of Underdeveloped Regions". In *Latin American Economic Integration: Experience and Prospects*, edited by Miguel Wionczek, 42–63. New York: Praeger.

Lee, Timothy B. 2018. "Brexit: The 7 Most Important Arguments for Britain to Leave the EU", 25 June. *Vox*. https://www.vox.com/2016/6/22/11992106/brexit-arguments.

Lewis, Patsy. 2002. *Surviving Small Size: Regional Integration in Caribbean Ministates*. Kingston, Jamaica: University of the West Indies Press.

———. 2003. "Is the Goal of Regional Integration Still Relevant among Small States? The Case of the OECS and CARICOM". In *Living at the Borderlines: Issues in Caribbean Sovereignty and Development*, edited by Cynthia Barrow-Giles and Don Marshall, 325–52. Kingston, Jamaica: Ian Randle Press.

———. 2005. "The Agony of the Fifteen: The Crisis of Implementation". *Social and Economic Studies* 54 (3): 145–75.

Mardenberg, Micah and Manuela Andreoni. 2018. "The Country That Wasn't Ready to Win the Lottery: Guyana Discovered It Owns Enough Oil to Solve All Its Problems and Cause Even Bigger Ones". *Foreign Policy*, 19 June. http://foreignpolicy.com/2018/06/19/the-country-that -wasnt-ready-to-win-the-lottery-guyana-oil/.

Myers, Gay Nagle. 2017. "New Airport Opens on St. Vincent". *Travel Weekly*, 14 February. https://www.travelweekly.com/Travel-News/Airline-News/New-airport-opens-on-St -Vincent.

Myrdal, Gunnar. 1957. *Economic Theory and Underdeveloped Regions*. London: Gerald Duckworth.

Palankai, Tibor, ed. 2003. *Economics of European Integration*. Budapest: Akademiai Kiado.

Quartz. 2018. "Mapped: The Breathtaking Global Reach of Cambridge Analytica's Parent Company", 28 March. https://qz.com/1239762/cambridge-analytica-scandal-all-the-countries -where-scl-elections-claims-to-have-worked/.

Ram, Justin, Raquel Frederick, Dindial Ramrattan, Kevin Hope, and Wayne Elliott. 2018. "A Policy Blueprint for Caribbean Economies". Caribbean Development Bank, CDB Working

Paper No. 1. http://www.caribank.org/publications/featured-publications/a-policy-blueprint
-for-caribbean-economies.

Robinson, Michele. 2014. "The Debt Experience of SIDS in the Caribbean". In *Debt and
Development in Small Island Developing States*, edited by Damien King and David Tennant,
329–69. New York: Palgrave Macmillan.

Stoneman, Richard, Duke Pollard, and Hugo Inniss. 2012. "Turning Around CARICOM:
Proposals to Restructure the Secretariat". Landell-Mills Development Consultants. Prepared
for CARICOM Secretariat. https://caricom.org/documents/9400-restructuring_the
secretariat-_landell_mills_final_report.pdf.

Thompson, Davin-Kyle. 2017. "Time for JamExit from Caricom". *Jamaica Observer*, 16 May.
http://www.jamaicaobserver.com/opinion/time-for-jamexit-from-caricom_97465?profile
=1096.

TMZ. 6 April 2021. "Bill Gates Family Furious at Him during Secret Trip Ahead of Divorce".
Accessed 6 April 2021. https://www.tmz.com/2021/05/06/bill-melinda-gates-divorce-island
-angry.

Trading Economics. 2018. "Jamaican Dollar 2004-2018". Accessed 30 July 2018. https://
tradingeconomics.com/jamaica/currency.

Weber, Axel A. 2011. "Challenges for Monetary Policy in the European Monetary Union".
Federal Reserve Bank of St. Louis Review 93 (4): 235–42.

West Indian Commission. 1992. *Time for Action*. Kingston, Jamaica: University of West Indies
Press.

Williams, Morvin G. 2016. "De-risking/De-banking: 'The Reality Facing Caribbean Financial
Institutions'". Paper presented at Annual Monetary Conference, Caribbean Centre for
Money and Finance, 9–11 November, Nassau, Bahamas. http://www.ccmf-uwi.org/files
/publications/conference/2016/2_1-Williams-p.pdf.

Zhang, Jian. 2012. "Supporting Macroeconomic Convergence in African RECs". African
Development Bank. Regional Integration Policy Papers, no. 1 (December). https://www.afdb
.org/fileadmin/uploads/afdb/Documents/Publications/Regional_Integration_Policy_Papers
_Supporting_Macroeconomic_Convergence_in_African_RECs.PDF.

Zhang, Tao. 2016. "The Caribbean Response to the Withdrawal of Correspondent Banking".
Conference on the Withdrawal of Correspondent Banking Relationships, 28 October. IMF.
https://www.imf.org/en/News/Articles/2016/10/28/SP102816-The-Caribbean-Response-to
-the-Withdrawal-of-Correspondent-Banking/.

Part III

Bringing the People In

Chapter 9

Is CARICOM Politically Sustainable? Assessing the (Youth) Participation Deficit

TERRI-ANN GILBERT-ROBERTS

Almost a decade ago, a team of development management consultants commissioned to review the regional governance structure of the Caribbean Community (CARICOM) concluded that the framework could collapse by 2017 (Stoneman, Pollard and Inniss 2012).[1] That frank prognosis reflected a long-standing frustration among many stakeholders with the slow progress of integration and raised further concerns about waning commitment among member governments and growing indifference among Caribbean citizens.

Within eighteen months of that prediction, popular criticism of CARICOM leadership, particularly from young leaders, emerged in contrast to the fortieth-anniversary celebrations of the signing of the Treaty of Chaguaramas and echoed concerns about the impact of protracted implementation and democratic deficits on the sustainability of the regional integration movement. The lament of a Jamaican youth participant during CARICOM's 2013 "Change Facilitation" consultations reflected the concerns and distrust many young people held about the governance of the community: "Our leaders are not protecting us. Personal interests are clouding the interests of the people" (Gutzmer 2013, 8).[2]

Even after the expiry of the first five-year CARICOM strategic plan (2015–19) towards economic, social, environmental and technological resilience; the initiation of a second plan; and the appointment of a new secretary general in 2020, questions remain about the relevance of the current model of regional governance. In the last five years, the government of Jamaica created a commission to review that country's role in the integration movement, while Grenadians rejected constitutional amendments that would have paved the way for the adoption of the Caribbean Court of Justice as the final court of appeal. It is in that context – and against the background of global trends of regional fragmentation – that the issue of CARICOM's political sustainability is raised as an important area for analysis.[3]

The perspective offered here is conceptually framed at the intersection of the politics of integration and of youth development to propose that CARICOM's sustainability depends on two main factors. First, it relies on the extent to which the movement has formulated a comprehensive construct of regional citizenship within its governance framework. Second, CARICOM's sustainability hinges on the extent to which that governance framework facilitates the identification and participation of an incoming generation of leaders and considers their views on the preferred direction of the regionalist movement. In summary, I argue that political sustainability depends on a citizenship framework which reinforces rights to participation in decision-making and includes young people as important actors in governance.[4] In the context of this discussion, sustainability is defined, simply, as the continued maintenance of institutions and implementation of strategies which meet the evolving development aspirations of Caribbean citizens. Regional institutional sustainability does not preclude transformation or abandonment of specific institutional forms. Citizenship refers to the rights and responsibilities of belonging to a community; participation means sharing in decisions which affect one's life and community.

This chapter demonstrates that while, rhetorically, CARICOM has signalled a shift towards greater citizen participation, the existing spaces for youth participation in governance are inadequate, create frustrations among young people and pose a significant challenge to the sustainability of CARICOM in its current institutional form. This argument is advanced in four main sections. First, I offer an overview of critical perspectives on CARICOM's crises of implementation and democratic participation. Second, I briefly examine the evolution of policy frameworks for broad citizen participation in the regional governance structure. In the third section, I offer an assessment of youth-specific participation in regional governance by juxtaposing changes in the youth development policies with the story of three main programmes that have provided spaces for direct youth participation. I conclude with a discussion of the implications of youth experiences and views for CARICOM's longevity.

The Politics of CARICOM Integration

The democratization of regional governance has not been a priority for CARICOM, despite increasing and varied interest in politics and democracy promotion in (Latin) American regionalism (Krickovic 2015; Acharya 2014; Riggirozzi and Tussie 2012; Dabène 2009). In fact, given the apolitical integration legacy of the collapsed West Indies Federation and, more significantly, the 1989 decision to focus on a CARICOM Single Market and Economy (CSME), the internal politics of integration have, arguably, been subordinated to the pursuit of an open economic regionalism (Lewis 2007). In addition, despite the evolution of analytical diversity in the post-1990s "New Regionalism" grappling with multilevel interactions involving both state and non-state actors, in Caribbean literature and practice, the role of non-state actors and individual citizens has received limited attention (Caballero Santos 2015; Dabène 2009; Nesadurai 2009; Fawcett 2008; Phillips 2003). That is, the dominant analytical focus on state agency within International Relations and in traditional theories of regional integration reflects the reality of the politics of CARICOM integration (Byron 2016; Gilbert-Roberts 2013; Payne 2008; Lewis 2002). Lewis (2002, 28) argued that traditional schools of regional integration "suffer from a low democratic content, failing to move beyond bureaucratic and grand nationalist projects of development to find both a popular interest and operating space for groups not directly involved in this process".

Two assumptions are inherent to the practical application of CARICOM governance to date. The first is that domestic democratic traditions are strong and legitimate. Therefore, the positions of state representatives on regional matters are assumed to be reflective of the will of the people. The second assumption, contingent on the first, is that direct citizen participation in governance at the regional level is unnecessary. The consequence of these assumptions has been misguided attention to CARICOM's crisis of implementation without reference to the associated democratic deficit.

CARICOM's Protracted Crises

Although CARICOM has been lauded for its successes in areas of functional cooperation, particularly in relation to joint education administration, sports and culture cooperation, and the financing of regional development, a prominent critique has focused on a long-standing implementation deficit reminiscent of Clive Y. Thomas's (1977) description of CARICOM as "a big paper tiger".[55] The observed gap between the objectives set out in the 1973 Treaty of Chaguaramas and the 2001 Revised Treaty of Chaguaramas and their full attainment has been made worse by recent global economic and financial crises and increasing existential threats to CARICOM's small member states (Girvan 2010; Lewis 2010). Today, the process of economic integration remains incomplete as various elements of the CARICOM Single Market regime have routinely malfunctioned and the Heads of Government decided in 2011 to defer the pursuit of a single economy (Girvan 2007, 2012). Foreign policy coordination has been inconsistent (Byron 2014). Proposals to address the executive capacity of the community have not been implemented (Clement 2015; Girvan 2007; Prime Ministerial Expert Group on Governance 2005; Ramphal 2005; West Indian Commission 1992).[6]

However, another area of critique argues that a partial source of the implementation deficit is the inadequacy of civic and political engagement in regional governance. Rarely is CARICOM a part of national political dialogue and rarely are consultative mechanisms for regional governance inclusive (Lewis 2005; Girvan 2011a, 2011b; Hinds Harrison 2013). The mechanism for parliamentary representation – the Assembly of Caribbean Community Parliamentarians – has failed, having only held three sittings since its 1994 establishment and excluded participation by opposition parliamentarians and civil society representatives. Lewis (2005) explained that the exclusion contributed to the implementation deficit by hindering consensus-building at the national level. In addition, popular participation has been limited to framed consultation with "recognised social partners" – that is, the Caribbean Congress of Labour, the Caribbean Association of Industry and Commerce, and the Caribbean Policy Development Centre. Annual meetings of these representatives with Heads of Government have ceased and, notwithstanding the resurrection of the Civil Society Project in 2010, there is limited deliberative interaction between governing and non-governing elites. The lack of parliamentary and public debate and limited public information in some member states have meant that the governance gap is also filled with a legitimacy deficit and a sustainability crisis (Girvan 2007).

These aforementioned executive and participatory weaknesses describe an overarching political crisis associated with governing elites' preoccupation with the threat of popular participation to personalized conceptions of sovereignty (Gilbert-Roberts 2013). While these dimensions of the crisis are significant to the continued evolution of CARICOM, attention should also be paid to a third dimension – that of inadequate reconceptualization of Caribbean regionalism. That is, the future popular construction of regionalism is also critical to CARICOM's survival. The sustainability of a sense of Caribbean community does not preclude the reform and reconstruction of CARICOM institutions or even their abandonment in favour of popularly constructed alternatives. Such alternatives could emerge from the younger generation of citizens if they are enabled to develop and experiment with new ideas about regionalism.

The limited documentation and analysis of the views of young people on Caribbean regionalism is a serious indictment on the leadership of the movement. Elsewhere, the British referendum on European Union membership is instructive of the way in which decision-making that ignores intergenerational divisions in political orientation can breed frustrations that may destabilize the political environment. With an estimated 64 per cent youth turnout, 75 per cent of eighteen- to twenty-four-year-old Britons voted to remain, against the total 48 per cent remain average (Helm 2016).[7] The European Union's strategy of placing young people at the forefront of efforts to forge a construct of regional identity and citizenship likely influenced these results (European Commission 2014). Interviews with sampled youth "remainers" reveal the way in which their thwarted political choice on retaining EU membership was intimately tied to their acceptance and association of EU institutions with perceived progressive European values of integration, tolerance, inclusivity and compassion (Cresci 2016). The post-referendum youth protests, albeit peaceful, may be early signs of potential future instability in response to negative outcomes of Brexit.

In contrast, the exclusion of youth from CARICOM governance is partly due to the shortcomings in broader civil society engagement. However, it is also due to the dominance of deficit orientations in youth development practices, which ignore the political role of young people. Despite the fact that inspiration for regionalist ideologies has long emerged from student and youth activist dialogue, once in power, former young integrationists fail to consult today's youth on the future of the region.[8]

Youth sentiments on the progress of the movement are significant to an assessment of sustainability. In examining the evolution of the Caribbean integration movement, excluding the Eastern Caribbean experience, we observe a relatively quick succession of institutional modes of regionalism in the early years. The recovery from the failed Federation in 1962 was quickly overcome by a renewal of regionalism in the first Conference of Commonwealth Heads of Government in 1963, the signing of the Dickenson Bay Agreement on free trade in 1965 and the full Caribbean Free Trade Association agreement in 1968. The decision to pursue the CARICOM in 1972 was followed by the signing of the Treaty of Chaguaramas a year later.

However, the decision to pursue the CSME in 1989 resulted in a seventeen-year wait until the first elements of the single market were brought to fruition in 2006. Notwithstanding the recommitment to the CSME occasioned by the 2018 St Ann's Declaration of the Heads of Government and the subsequent recommendations from the Second CARICOM Commission on the Economy, the pursuit of a single economy has in fact been deferred, as the political (sovereign) implications of deeper integration have proved a stumbling block for leaders. There is no doubt that the implementation deficit has resulted in broad-based scepticism about economic regionalism in the Caribbean. At the same time, the failure to achieve a functioning CSME in a timely fashion has also affected the relevance of integration to youth aspirations. The protracted inertia has disappointed those coming of age at the key focal points of promise of a single market and economy – 1989 and 2006. Plausibly, young people under thirty years old today represent the generation which would have come of age in an era in which they had reasonable expectations of reaping the benefits of a regional economy. For example, a young woman leaving secondary school when the single market was established in 2006 might have held high hopes of pursuing further education in order to access unfettered freedom of movement, goods, services, capital and rights to establishment. However, the limited and uneven administrative progress on real freedom of movement since then means that young people like her will now have been disabused of the view that the CSME can be considered a viable means to meeting their dreams and aspirations.

The subsequent sections of this chapter contextualize a prospective lens on regionalist politics by analysing critical junctures in CARICOM decision-making at which efforts have been made to address CARICOM's crises, particularly in relation to the youth participation deficit.

Evolution of Regional Policy Spaces for Citizen Participation

Readings of the decisions and declarations issued by the Conference of Heads of Government from 1973 to present, which are treated as CARICOM policy, suggest that people are initially treated merely as instruments or technologies of national economic development. Although the 1973 treaty outlined a people-centred objective – "to fulfil the hopes and aspirations of peoples for full employment and improved standards of work and living" – the benefits of regionalism were really intended to accrue to member states on behalf of the people (CARICOM Conference of Heads of Government 1973, 2). The people were not, at that time, intrinsically seen as political actors per se. They had no individual agency in the decision-making around meeting their aspirations. After 1989, however, there was greater emphasis in the decisions and declarations of the Conference of Heads of Government on the role of the people in pursuing international economic competitiveness through the CSME. Unfortunately, in the context of the implementation deficit, many of those commitments have not been realized. This creates a duality of, on the one hand, theoretical openness to participation and, on the other hand, a practical non-enforcement of decisions, which facilitates marginalization and exclusion of people from regional governance.

This section summarizes six main critical junctures which demonstrate attempts towards greater citizen inclusion and which have also laid a foundation for greater youth participation.[9] A gradual shift in the political culture of regionalism towards participatory modes of governance began at Grande Anse, Grenada, in 1989, when the decision was taken to establish the CSME. Although the language of the Grande Anse Declaration maintained an instrumentalist view of the Caribbean people as technologies of economic production, it also established the West Indian Commission (WIC), which, after three years of public consultation, would completely reorganize the view of the Caribbean person in regionalism.

However, before the WIC's report was presented, Heads of Government met in 1990 to discuss recent security threats to democracy, adopting the Kingston Declaration on Democracy and Popular Participation, which recognizes the rights and responsibilities of people – treating them, in some way, as citizens, though citizenship is still regarded as a national construct. The Heads declared their intentions towards "the full involvement of all . . . citizens in the governance of their affairs, in particular, the deepening of our integration effort toward the achievement of a truly authentic Caribbean personality" (CARICOM Conference of Heads of Government 1990, n.p.). This innovative inclusive policy is as important in its declaration of citizen participation as it is in its underlying connotations. The meeting had been called in response to an attempted coup in Trinidad and Tobago. It is, in some way, the threat of dangerous, radicalized youth that acts as impetus for this people-centred language and is instructive of the prominent role that young people play (unacknowledged and indirectly) in the evolution of the participatory framework.

The WIC's 1992 report *Time for Action* is the third critical juncture which made some important recommendations about regional governance, including citizen inclusion. The commission proposed a Charter of Civil Society, which was eventually signed in 1997, acknowledging the need for popular consultation and, importantly, documenting the rights to participation, including for children. Unfortunately, the charter itself, as the fourth key agreement, limited the definition of politically enfranchised groups to the three recognized social partners – the Caribbean Congress of Labour, the Caribbean Association of Industry and Commerce, and the Caribbean Policy Development Centre – and not to "the people" directly. The WIC also proposed a regional parliamentary system, which, as previously noted, has since failed.

However, for the purposes of this discussion, the WIC's comments on youth are particularly important. The section of the report on the "Concerns of Youth" documented a broad sense of political powerlessness of young people and called for a firm commitment to meeting the aspirations of distressed young West Indians in the agenda for the 1990s and giving them a "say in the decision-making process" (West Indian Commission 1992, 379). The commission also reprimanded older adults for their hypocrisy in denying youth rights to political participation but seeking to claim youth contributions in social, economic and cultural arenas. It went on to recommend the strengthening of National Youth Councils as a way of enhancing youth participation in decision-making.

The recommendations of the commission were far-reaching in changing the policy and institutional framework towards participatory governance, even though the proposals were not perfectly or fully implemented. In fact, it was in the post-WIC era of emerging citizen participation that the first documented engagement of Heads of Government with youth representatives was held at their 1999 retreat in Saramacca, Suriname. During that retreat – the fifth critical juncture – youth representatives shared their vision for the region, which had been partially developed at a Youth Assembly of Caribbean Community Parliamentarians in the Bahamas in 1998.[10] The "Vision for the Caribbean in the 21st Century" (see figure 9.1) suggested high expectations of that generation of young leaders for political citizenship rights, including participation in decision-making, to be applied at national, regional and international levels. Interestingly, they also desired a society committed to regional political (and not just economic) integration, at a time when the broad regionalist discourse among politicians had shifted towards economic integration and away from political union.

> **"Different Countries; Different Cultures; One Region; One Understanding among all segments of our Community; One Voice."**
>
> - A society which values genuine **democracy**, freedom, mutual respect and equal fundamental **rights**, which understands and believes in the ability of citizens to shape and change society in progressive ways; which affords **citizens** opportunities to make a meaningful contribution to development.
> - A society in which institutional infrastructure along with legal and administrative frameworks permit **citizens** access to resources, employment, education and training and making them fully aware of their rights and responsibility with **a forum to promote their issues and concerns at the highest policymaking levels**.
> - A society free from discrimination because of age, class, race, religion, educational attainment, sexual orientation, gender, physical disabilities or other factors.
> - A society in which the **citizens participate fully in the rejuvenation and maintenance of its cultural heritage** and in which culture is a resource for everyday living.
> - A society which is **committed to achieving the goal of regional integration at the <u>political</u>, economic, cultural and social level** as a means of promoting equitable development and the well-being of all Caribbean people.
> - A society which recognizes the interdependent relationship between human beings and the environment and is committed to the proper management of its resources.
> - A society which promotes healthy lifestyles and ensures that its citizens have easy access to the essential health information, services and facilities.
> - A society in pursuit of excellence striving to achieve freedom from all social ills.

Figure 9.1. Visions for the Caribbean in the twenty-first century
Source: CARICOM Secretariat (1998).
Note: Emphasis added.

Youth political aspirations also extended to the "rejuvenation and maintenance of a cultural heritage", which was presumably the basis for their version of a sustainable community (CARICOM Secretariat 1998).

By the time that the Revised Treaty of Chaguaramas was signed in 2001, the rhetoric of governance had become much more inclusive. Explicit objectives were set for restructuring decision-making frameworks to enhance popular participation, though the general focus was still placed on the recognized social partners (CARICOM Conference of Heads of Government 2001). Still, the Revised Treaty identified women and youth as special groups for which the Council on Human and Social Development (COHSOD) should encourage participation. The ring-fencing of their roles within social development (and not other areas of integration) is noticeable. The subsequent Liliendaal Statement (which followed a 2002 "Forward Together" encounter between government and civil society), as well as the adoption of the 2003 Rose Hall Declaration on Regional Governance and Integrated Development and the 2007 Single Development Vision, also signalled intentions to strengthen democratic governance.

To be clear, none of the policy decisions – the Grande Anse Declaration, the Kingston Declaration, the Charter of Civil Society or the Revised Treaty – legally created regional CARICOM citizens. Formal rights of citizenship remain bound to the nation state. However, there has been a process of "citizenization" of regional governance which involves the onset of recognition for the rights to participate in decision-making at the regional as well as national levels and consideration of the creation of institutional spaces for CARICOM nationals to participate.

Ironically, there has been greater progress on engaging youth than any other group in the process of citizenization of regional governance. The 2010 Declaration of Paramaribo on the Future of Youth in the Community, which is the point of departure for an assessment of the youthscape of governance and participation, is one of the most advanced instruments of citizenization. The subsequent section describes the policy space specific to youth participation in CARICOM governance and reviews youth experiences in three initiatives that institutionalized youth participation.

The Youthscape of Participatory Regional Governance in CARICOM

Against the background of vacillating progress on broader civil society participation, the Heads of Government at the Special Summit on Youth Development in January 2010 declared an intention to "explicitly recognise and clearly articulate the role of youth in Caribbean development in the amended Revised Treaty of Chaguaramas; and to ensure that this role is enshrined in national and regional development strategies, together with provisions for youth mainstreaming, youth-adult partnership and youth participation across all sectors" (CARICOM Conference of Heads of Government 2010, 3).

This rhetoric is qualitatively more advanced than the broader civil society participation language of the Charter of Civil Society and Revised Treaty. In its expectation of youth contribution to regional development, the Declaration of Paramaribo accords partnership and participation rights to young people. In effect, the Paramaribo Declaration indicates an intention to treat youth as regional citizens of the community. The position is paradoxical since the conceptualization of citizenship in CARICOM has respected the traditional boundaries of the nation state. Notwithstanding, elsewhere, there have been examples of the European Union and the African Union placing young people at the forefront of efforts to create constructs of regional citizenship, in the case of the former, or of pan-regional identity, in the latter (Gilbert-Roberts 2014). In the Caribbean context, there is no full or comprehensive citizenship framework. However, there is, arguably, an emerging construct of the regional youth citizen. The evolution of this "Paramaribo construct" is documented in the next section.

Evolution of Pro-citizen Youth Development Agenda and Policies

Paramaribo signalled an intention to pursue youth development strategies towards promoting citizenship and Caribbean identity; youth health protection and well-being; new and younger leadership in governance and increased participation; as well as social and economic empowerment, productivity and competitiveness (CARICOM Conference of Heads of Government 2010). Put in context, the road to Paramaribo was paved by small advances in youth development internationally, against the background of tensions between asset-/rights-based orientations and deficit orientations to youth development.

Youth participation rights gained increasing support after the first UN International Youth Year in 1985, the adoption of the Convention on the Rights of the Child in 1989, and Roger Hart's (1992) seminal essay on models and hierarchies of youth participation. At the same time, this new "rights-based" agenda was overshadowed by a "deficit" orientation in youth development practice, which focused on neutralizing the threats to society posed by dangerous, vulnerable and incapable youth (Carter 2008; Charles and Jameson-Charles 2014). We recall that the 1990 Kingston Declaration was, effectively, a deficit response to the threat of radicalized youth to democracy. Similarly, the inclusion of participatory rights for children in the Charter of Civil Society, perhaps in tribute to the Convention on the Rights of the Child, was disappointingly limited to consultation and representation in specific spheres of child welfare (CARICOM Conference of Heads of Government 1997). In sum, initially, young people were not considered to be full political actors in relation to formal decision-making. Their roles were limited to the areas in which they excelled and posed no threat to established political orders: sports, music, culture and community development. Their involvement at local, national and regional governance levels was limited.

However, in 1996, CARICOM began to pursue the idea of formulating the first regional youth policy. Discussions with international development partners eventually led to the formulation of a Regional Strategy for Youth Development as a mechanism for harmonizing youth development approaches and coordinating national activities. The 2001 strategy offered a useful treatment of the main concerns of and about youth, and outlined important objectives towards the participation and strengthening of the Caribbean Federation of Youth and its member National Youth Councils (Directors of Youth of the Caribbean Community 2001). Yet it was primarily used as an instrument for the mobilization of development financing from international development partners for an under-resourced youth division in the CARICOM Secretariat, fondly referred to as the "Youth Desk". The resource mobilization agenda likely caused CARICOM to emphasize the weaknesses of youth, in keeping with a deficit model. By 2003, youth were characterized by the secretariat as 60 per cent of the population who are "alienated and marginalized, excluded from participation in key social institutions and increasingly vulnerable to a range of social, economic and public health ills such as unemployment, substance abuse, HIV/AIDS, violence and crime" (CARICOM Secretariat 2003, 16).

That strategy, which was updated and revised on several occasions, received limited attention from young people and national governments. Against the background of a lack of popular and governmental ownership of the strategy, coupled with the changing context for youth development occasioned by periods of global economic crisis, the community decided to update its approach and revise the strategy. This led to a series of new forms of engagement with young people, which will be discussed in the penultimate section of this chapter.

Those new forms of engagement included the formation of a CARICOM Commission on Youth Development (CCYD), which is the direct conceptual source of the principles of the Paramaribo Declaration. As a result of the work of the CCYD, a new strategy emerged – the Draft CARICOM Youth Development Action Plan (CYDAP) for 2012–17 – which outlined a citizenship approach to youth development. Alongside objectives for strengthening youth leadership and participation in governance, the plan identifies "Culture, Identity and Citizenship" as one of six goal areas of the CARICOM Youth Development Goals (CARICOM Secretariat 2012, 14). The CYDAP's specific citizenship language is intriguing. It is important to acknowledge that the plan does not explicitly speak to a notion of a regional citizenship and perhaps defers to a position of reinforcing citizenship rights at the national level. However, by associating the citizenship component with objectives for the creation of a regional identity and strengthened participation in governance, it signals, at the very least, an interest in developing a cadre of Caribbean citizens, separate and apart from monitoring the protection of rights at the national level.[11]

Similarly, the CARICOM's first overall strategic plan highlighted a special role for youth in strengthening governance towards the achievement of resilience in different areas. The strategic plan reprised many of the recommendations of the WIC on reviving the Assembly of Caribbean Community Parliamentarians and having a permanent forum for civil society discussion. However, in that document, youth are identified as separate stakeholders to civil society, which suggests that the youth agenda has successfully achieved prominence, though perhaps regrettably, at the expense of more strategic mainstreaming and connection to broader civil society movements. Certainly, the increasing prominence of the CARICOM youth programme, including its identification as a specific area of functional cooperation in CARICOM's public education materials, speaks to the theoretical influence that the youth agenda has over the future of community governance.

Cases of Participation: CARICOM Youth Ambassador Programme, CARICOM Commission on Youth Development and Social Media Interaction

The evolving policy environment has encouraged the emergence of practical efforts to include young people in governance. This section analyses three cases of youth participation in regional governance: the CARICOM Youth Ambassador Programme (CYAP) (2000–14); the CCYD (2007–10); and the online interaction of the CARICOM secretary general with young people, paying closest attention to the fortieth-anniversary Twitter relay in 2013.

The CARICOM Youth Ambassador Programme

The CYAP has evolved from its 1993 origins as a loosely structured peer education and public relations initiative intended to raise awareness among primary and secondary school students about other member states. Today, it represents the community's formal instrument for youth leadership and participation in regional integration. The modern programme, launched in 2001, parallel to the formulation of the first Regional Strategy for Youth Development, expects CARICOM Youth Ambassadors (CYAs) to act as the communication bridge between national and regional levels of governance. CYAs help bring national issues to the attention of regional decision-makers and support the translation of regional priorities into initiatives for youth at the national level. The programme is coordinated at the regional level by the CARICOM Secretariat, which is expected to provide the CYAs with the necessary information, skills and resources to play their roles and enable them to participate in decision-making. At the same time, the CYAP was designed to be facilitated at the national level by Departments of Youth Affairs, which nominate the ambassadors.[12]

Three main strengths of the programme are apparent. First, its emphasis on youth leadership training and regionalist education is an important strategy to overcome information deficit among Caribbean people. Having spent two to three years in leadership training and awareness sessions about the CSME, former ambassadors surveyed demonstrate high levels of knowledge about CARICOM and its objectives, and cite the training and sensitization sessions as the most useful experiences in their personal development.[13]

In addition, the programme moves beyond raising awareness among young leaders to encouraging their adoption of regionalist values based on a strong sense of regional identity among members of the Ambassador Corps. In some ways, former CYAs demonstrate the effects of strong indoctrination in "CARICOM-ness". Ninety per cent of former ambassadors surveyed maintained their residence in the CARICOM region – 83 per cent in their home countries and 7 per cent in another CARICOM country.[14] Further, a clear majority of survey respondents (80 per cent) considered themselves to be firm advocates of regional integration despite only 20 per cent of them having held that view prior to their participation in the programme.

The third strength of the CYAP is depicted by the secretariat's championing of the rights for young people to participate in decision-making. CYAs are afforded access to meetings of decision-making organs and bodies. CYAs have been present in meetings of the COHSOD, COTED on information and communication technologies, CCYD, and Technical Working Groups on Youth; fourteen of them have held internships within the secretariat or associated institutions. Ambassadors have also been active in the design and implementation of successful projects for youth on HIV/AIDS awareness and on promotion of the CSME. The increased visibility of young people in CARICOM meetings and programmes has, in the view of former administrators and ambassadors, made a small contribution to changing perceptions of youth capabilities in governance. In general, former CYAs surveyed felt that they and their views were "taken seriously" by CARICOM officials and by young people at the local level, though less so by their national governments and the society in general.

Notwithstanding these strengths, the CYAP has four significant weaknesses in relation to addressing the youth participation deficit. The profile of the CYA is of a well-educated, productive citizen who is well connected to local political and/ or development networks. However, they are not necessarily representative of the young people in their countries. There are concerns about the susceptibility of the national nomination process to partisan political manipulation and nepotism in some countries (Mangal and Alexis 2009). In addition, CARICOM has reinforced the elitism of its Ambassador Corps to the detriment of the external legitimacy of other regional youth organizations, including elected youth councils. There has been an exclusive focus on CYAs as torchbearers of the community, raising concerns about the inclusivity, representativeness and effectiveness of youth participation in regional governance (Gilbert-Roberts 2009; CARICOM Commission on Youth Development 2010). Admittedly, having recognized the limited reach of the CYAP, the March 2016 COHSOD on youth and culture attempted to address the youth representation challenge by endorsing the proposal for a youth-led alliance between the CYAP; the Caribbean Regional Youth Council; and the University of West Indies Students Today, Alumni Tomorrow Ambassador Programme to expand the scope of youth representation in regional governance.

The second weakness is that the level of formal access CYAs have to regional decision-making is not matched by their actual experiences of participation. The unevenness of opportunities to participate in regional governance among CYAs has challenged the successful cases of youth engagement in decision-making. Only approximately 31 per cent of those surveyed had the opportunity to participate in community meetings. These privileged young leaders were either members of the Bureau or Executive Committee of the Ambassador Corps or had progressive governments who included them in national delegations. In the role of decision-maker, the CYA's presence is notably absent from most organs and bodies of the community, except in the COHSOD (2 per cent of former CYAs participated), meetings with the secretary general (10 per cent participated), and in meetings of Directors of Youth and other institutions. Otherwise, CYAs are usually observers or silent participants in regional governance meetings. This suggests a minimalist understanding of the role of youth in governance – one that has been limited to perceived socio-economic "youth issues" rather than to overall regional development. Although the majority of former CYA's surveyed felt that their views were taken seriously by CARICOM and by young people, less than half of respondents (48 per cent) felt that their contributions were influential in the decision-making process.

The third challenge faced by the CYAP is its tokenistic status in CARICOM, having not received any dedicated financing to support its activities or those of the wider youth programme of the secretariat. There has been no progress on advancing the CARICOM Youth Development fund, initially capitalized by Suriname with US$50,000 (CARICOM Secretariat 2014). In addition, the reasons cited by the single CYA, who indicated he remained sceptical of regional integration after participating in the programme, centred on the lack of both political and financial support by national governments and the regional political collective. That participant noted:

> We were left on our own to do everything, from raising our own funds to implementing programs. Then, Ministers just show up, give these generic "the future is bright with these youth" speeches, take a few pictures and don't look back until it's time to give another speech. That's why I left the program, I thought my role was a facade designed to make the heads look like they care but they didn't. (Unpublished findings from survey by Gilbert-Roberts 2015)

Finally, the programme is challenged by its limited time horizon. Youth ambassadors are highly skilled and active young professionals including, at the time of survey, two former ambassadors serving as elected political representatives. Significant proportions of the survey respondents were working in government and public service (20 per cent), education and youth work (19 and 15 per cent, respectively), international development (7 per cent) and legal services (7 per cent). However, after completion of their term as ambassadors, these young people were rarely engaged further, notwithstanding their positive orientation to regional integration and CARICOM in particular. Although 91 per cent of respondents remain highly interested in CARICOM governance, only 22 per cent had ever been asked by CARICOM to, as alumni, share their skills or expertise on regional governance issues. Only 46 per cent had been asked to share the same with their home governments. The level of engagement in the non-governmental sector (whether in schools, community organizations or the workplace) was much higher, with 71 per cent being asked to share their expertise and knowledge on regional integration in those settings. Of the fifty-nine survey respondents, only four were in possession of a CARICOM Skills Certificate to ready themselves to take advantage of the free movement of skills in the CSME. Only 22 per cent of them indicated that they had been engaged in the consultations for the Change Facilitation process which started in 2013. In interviews with regional civil servants who have engaged with CYAs on CSME public education programmes, an erroneous conceptualization of youth contributes to the lack of inclusion. One interviewee suggested: "I see the term CYA as a misnomer because we see youth as children, not realizing that they are qualified people who may have MBAs and be experienced business people" (interview by Gilbert-Roberts, 2015). Given the profile of former CYAs, CARICOM has an untapped resource of regional integration advocates who should be engaged on an ongoing basis in technical consultation and popular discussion on the future of the movement.

To date the CYAP, notwithstanding its privileged status in the CARICOM framework, has not yet achieved full partnership status based on political and financial inclusion. The secretariat has been engaged in discussions with ministers and directors of youth since the 2016 COHSOD meeting, to reposition the CYAP in line with the principles of Paramaribo to raise the profile and scope of the programme in regional governance. Indeed, another initiative for youth participation, which led to the Paramaribo Declaration, envisioned a radically different setting for youth involvement in regional governance. The high-level CCYD employed two significant approaches to its work, which contributed to moderately reducing the participation deficit, while also recommending strategies for greater inclusiveness thereafter.

The CARICOM Commission on Youth Development

First, the CCYD advanced, in its practice, a novel model of youth–adult partnership. The CCYD appointed eight young leaders as commissioners alongside seven older technocrats. The commission was co-chaired by one "youth" and one "adult" commissioner.[15] In addition, it engaged young people, including CYAs, in the research process. Young people were involved in designing instruments, administering questionnaires, facilitating focus groups, analysing data and making inputs into the final report. This model of youth–adult partnership, which the commission intended to be replicated in youth work across the region, signalled a conceptual shift from perspectives of youth as helpless and vulnerable problems towards a perspective of them as partners in development. Of course, the operationalization of the partnership was a learning process for all involved, but it set a standard for the role youth were expected to play in the community going forward.[16] Yet, to date, a similar inclusive composition has not been achieved in subsequent commissions, for example on the economy.

A second useful approach by the CCYD was to document in its report, alongside calculations of the opportunity costs of the lack of investment in youth development, the voices of youth who would not normally have access to Heads of Government. Following surveys, focus groups, workshops and town hall discussions with young people, the commission decided to reproduce quotes from young people, including those which were critical of the leadership of members states and the entire CSME enterprise. This was useful since it offered a picture of youth engagement with regionalism, which differed greatly from that of the privileged CYAs. The survey revealed widespread ignorance of the CSME; irrelevance of existing youth governance structures; emigration from the region as a valid option for meeting youth dreams and aspirations; dissatisfaction with national, regional and international governance; and a sense of "voicelessness" among ordinary youth (CARICOM Commission on Youth Development 2010). Caribbean youth offered these comments to the commission:

"We know too little of the Caribbean to consider ourselves citizens";

"I know very little about CARICOM and the Caribbean . . . because of my own [lack of] interest or because you don't get the information. I just feel like a world citizen"; and

"I know that I am a pure Caribbean citizen because I know my history". (CARICOM Commission on Youth Development 2010, 26–27)

These comments suggested youth alienation from the CARICOM project and, therefore, likely abandonment of it should they be given the choice to leave or remain,[17] that is, unless they are socialized to appreciate and value the shared history, cultures and development interests of Caribbean states. The comments also remind us that the pursuit of international opportunities feature prominently in youth aspirations – at least prior to more recent anti-immigration movements and policies in North America and Europe. Other young leaders who commented on the commission's report suggested that "'intergovernmentalism' is defective and has stymied efforts to achieve the stated goals of economic integration" (Abiola DaSilva 2010, 17), and that "political union and the unavoidable ceding of sovereignty . . . to some degree may be an idea whose time has eventually and perhaps inevitably come, if the integration movement is to be saved from an implosion" (Johnson 2009, 4).

One of the interesting contributions of the CCYD report was the updating of the 1998 vision of Caribbean youth, based on new visioning exercises with young people between fifteen and twenty-nine years old in twelve countries. The youth construction of community in the 2010 vision (see figure 9.2) is broadly integrationist but challenges the CARICOM institutional model in three main ways.

First, young people at that time continued to express interest in the political union of the region, devoid of the concerns with sovereignty often expressed by heads of

A productive, knowledge-based and diverse society that
- is **united**, strong, stable, recognized and respected by First World countries;
- is **sensitive to the problems of other countries in the Caribbean**, assists each other, is conscious that what concerns one concerns all;
- exploits a unique niche, is self-sufficient, fair, open-minded, friendly, caring;
- is safe, secure and free from discrimination, corruption, drugs and HIV and AIDS;
- provides all nationals a good quality of life and reasonable cost of living; **affordable inter-island travel** with no restrictions; quality education and decent employment for all;
- protects the interests of smaller states and affords all the same rights, privileges and benefits;
- recognizes, appreciates and keeps the power of culture alive;
- empowers youth to be politically aware and involved in development;
- puts in place foundations for **economic, political and social unity**.

Figure 9.2. Abridged regional youth vision of the ideal Caribbean community
Source: CARICOM Commission on Youth Development (2010, 26).
Note: Emphasis added.

government. Second, the vision does not place limits on the geographical scope of community, making specific reference to cooperation with "other" countries in the region. Third, the vision highlights the failure of the CSME, making specific reference to desires for "affordable inter-island travel" and "decent employment".

The period following the commission's work (post-2010) was a turning point for regional youth development and the citizenization of regional governance. The new youth agenda that emerged holds great potential for rights to participation.[18] However, the two participatory initiatives revealed mass youth ignorance of CARICOM and the CSME (based on the CCYD findings) alongside elite faithfulness to the CARICOM ideal coupled with growing frustration with its exclusive democratic governance culture (based on survey findings on CYAP indoctrination and experiences). Shortly after the work of the CCYD, CARICOM embarked on another mode of youth engagement through social media.

Social Media Interactions with the CARICOM Secretary General

Beginning in 2013, former CARICOM secretary general Irwin LaRocque, in partnership with the CYAP, created a digital space for youth participation via an annual "exchange of views" between the secretary general and young people on various social media platforms. This section focuses on the eight-hour exchange – dubbed a Twitter relay – convened on 30 June 2013 under the theme "CARICOM@40: Relaying Issues, Creating Awareness". In reporting to the Heads of Government, the secretary general celebrated a viewership of 74,000 people and engagement of some 8,613 persons (CARICOM Secretariat 2013b; National Centre for Youth Development 2013).

The primary strength of this new form of engagement lay in its innovativeness. Unlike the prior attempts at bringing youth into the existing formal and traditional frameworks of regional governance, the Twitter relay required the leadership of the secretariat to reach out to young people in their online world. The challenge, however, is that social media is often, erroneously, treated as a panacea for addressing youth participation deficits. In fact, political engagement via social media tends to reproduce patterns of participation present in face-to-face forums. While, most young people engage in online participation, pockets of marginalization and exclusion emerge from varied internet penetration rates across the Caribbean region and marked urban–rural digital divides. In addition, by choosing to engage youth via Twitter – at that time not a broadly popular platform among Caribbean young people vis-à-vis Facebook and other platforms – the 2013 Twitter relay ring-fenced the participation forum. Furthermore, the public anonymity afforded to participants, notwithstanding its role in also encouraging frank critique of CARICOM, created a challenge of certainty in understanding which youth (or older persons) were participating in the discussion.

Using the assigned relay hashtags [#CARICOM; #caricom], this author curated a list of 331 interventions made in the discussion which were posted by only forty-one individual participants (including six organizational or institutional profiles) from nine countries. Based on the profiles of male and female participants, most were either current or former CYAs or had a close working relationship with the CYA network or regionally engaged youth organizations. Youth engaged in less prominent youth clubs and associations or disconnected from organized youth groups did not seem to be present in the discussion. In addition, more than half of the curated responses came from a single participant who was a member of the CYAP executive that organized the relay.

Nonetheless, the discussion was useful in its reinforcement of youth perspectives on the challenges of regionalism which had also been identified by the CCYD. The discussion suggested that some engaged young leaders shared the concerns of other young people. While a broad level of optimism about the continued relevance and potential of regionalism was present – with participants expressing their "belief in CARICOM" (indoctrination of CYAs)[19] – the discussion also allowed for public sharing of youth visions for the community and concerns about its status. The online discussion creates additional value, despite the relatively low numbers of active participants, since it remains accessible to a wide range of stakeholders, even after the fact.

When asked to tweet one word to describe the CARICOM they wished to live in, the most frequently cited responses included "productive", "peaceful", "progressive", "prosperous", "enabling", "cohesive" and "united". The discussion featured a dominant socio-economic discourse, as participants also envisioned a community with higher wages, free trade and "tangible" development results. The young people spoke about various goal areas of the CARICOM Youth Development Goals. Other parts of the discussion raised young leaders' dissatisfaction with the direction and leadership of CARICOM.

Concerns were raised about the lack of transparency in governance – framed as a communications challenge. The participants were concerned about the lack of information on the activities of the secretariat and the CARICOM institutions in the traditional media and formal education systems. Prunella Mungroo (@ PrunellaMungroo) (2013a) noted on Twitter, "Ppl [sic] have lost confidence in CARICOM & many others are ill-advised as to its purpose". Participants also raised concerns about the ineffectiveness of the CYAP in its peer education and representation mandates, even as the secretary general affirmed the secretariat's ongoing reliance on the challenged programme, and young people more broadly, to lead the "communications revolution". The secretary general's account (@caricomsec) tweeted: "What can Youth do to rebuild that hope. Need to build a sense of 'regional nationalism'. . . . We are trying to do more to reach out to the people of CARICOM. Efforts like this with the CYA is significant" (2013a, 2013b).

The other concerns raised about regional leadership speak directly to the issue of sustainability. The young leaders shared their frustrations and scepticism about the political interests of leaders meeting their own interests. One participant (@suraze) claimed that "integration will be an illusive dream as long as our leaders/countries continue to think insular" (Smith 2013). Others raised concerns about their leaders' lack of vision and preoccupation with partisan political interests:

@TamiBe: "Leadership and governance are important because we have had too many stops and starts with changes in govt" (Browne 2013b) . . . "Leadership & governance are important because I believe where there is NO vision ppl [sic] bound to PERISH!" (Browne 2013c)

@PrunellaMungroo: "Do our HoGs [Heads of Government] have vision? R [sic] individual visions lining up with regional goals? . . . one can have vision but no idea how to implement it eh. so vision alone honestly doesn't [sic] impress me."[20] (Mungroo 2013b)

@PrunellaMungroo: "strategic planning and succession planning is a serious issue." (Mungroo 2013c)

@BelizeYouth: "The youth have a right to be heard and be involved in decisions. They have a right to choices and to voice their opinions." (Belize Youth Support 2013)

@kestontnt: "Unfortunately, I have lost most hope in #CARICOM as an institution. Time for a youth-led equivalent." (Perry 2013)

Interestingly, the latter participant had, two years earlier, launched a regional civil society movement for accountability in regional governance which had, by this time, been abandoned (Perry 2011). Unfortunately, the nature of a Twitter discussion, involving simultaneous tweets corresponding to multiple points of reference, limits the time and space for follow-up on some of the comments and proposals offered by young people. For example, it would have been useful to explore the proposals made for succession planning and a youth-led integration alternative.

Subsequent social media interactions with the secretary general have become more sophisticated, including live-streamed town-hall-style gatherings complemented by text submissions on a wider variety of social media platforms including Facebook, WhatsApp, Blackberry messenger, Instagram and email. The length of time of these sessions has generally been limited to two hours of dedicated time with the secretary general in the evenings.[21] The concerns raised in these forums are corroborated by the online and offline comments made by young people in a small regional survey and the Jamaican pre-consultations conducted as a part of the Change Facilitation process (Gutzmer 2013; Gutzmer and CARICOM Youth Ambassador Programme 2013).[22] The anonymous comments document, by virtue of the capital letters to express some sentiments, a palpable frustration among those who have been engaged in discussion on the future of the movement:

"Our leaders are not protecting us. Personal interests are clouding the interests of the people."

"Maybe what is needed is not a REFORM PROCESS but a REVOLUTION."

"Impose stricter penalties for countries that don't adhere to the rules of the community."

"Enough TALK TALK TALK and PROMISES PROMISES PROMISES we must move to a phase where we IMPLEMENT IMPLEMENT IMPLEMENT!"

The secretariat's strategic plan addresses some of the socio-economic concerns raised by the young people in these consultations, although young leaders criticized it for inadequate mainstreaming of the concerns of youth across strategies for building regional resilience (Gutzmer et al. 2014). From young people's experiences participating in regional governance, we can draw some preliminary conclusions about the state of youth participation and the extent of popular support for the maintenance of CARICOM institutions, the continued implementation of its current strategies, and confidence in the potential for the movement to meet citizen aspirations for development. In the concluding section, we reflect on each of these three dimensions of sustainability.

Conclusion: Is CARICOM Sustainable?

The preceding review suggests that the emerging construct of regional citizenship, supported by policy changes at the regional level, is not yet comprehensive enough to secure CARICOM's future. Advances in the recognition of democratic rights to participation in decision-making, particularly in the explicit Paramaribo partnership rights for youth, have not been fully operationalized as legally binding regional citizenship rights.

Even so, the varied efforts at engaging young people, notwithstanding deficit and tokenistic undertones, are encouraging signs towards regional citizenization. Qualitatively, there have been some important steps towards inclusion, representation and documentation of youth voices in decision-making through the CYAP, CCYD, social media interactions and the strategic planning process. In addition, the CYAP and social media interactions show modes of leadership development which reinforce regionalist values among young people on the verge of assuming broader (non-youth) leadership roles in society.

At the same time, quantitatively, there remains a significant popular participation deficit as young leaders are engaged and the youth masses remain excluded by information deficit. The youth experience mirrors the elitism of broader civil society participation. While elite young leaders "believe" in CARICOM, a broad-based popular CARICOM identity is not secure. Not having been cultivated by exposure, CARICOM is a meaningless construct to the majority of young people. However, both the mass exclusion of youth and the minimal inclusion of young elites is building frustration among the entire Caribbean youth cohort who still believe that regional integration as a process of unity and solidarity remains relevant to meeting their aspirations.

There are two significant youth challenges to the current institutional framework and the strategic direction of CARICOM. The first is that the documented youth discourse suggests a strong interest in experimenting with political union. Their frustrations with the lack of implementation of the CSME have suggested to them the need for restructuring the model of integration to embrace closer political association of member states.

The second is that the youth discourse also reflects pan-Caribbean regionalist affiliations. In that context, an ongoing participation deficit could potentially lead young people to abandon the CARICOM framework and seek to revolutionize integration by building new political alliances and institutional frameworks. The proposal for the formation of a Caribbean Youth Regional Alliance among members of the CYAP; Caribbean Regional Youth Council; and the University of West Indies Students Today, Alumni Tomorrow Ambassador Programme represents an opportunity to connect the CARICOM framework to the pan-Caribbean youth vision. The leadership of the Caribbean Regional Youth Council in this alliance could be particularly important, given the participation of non-CARICOM states as well as non-independent territories in their annual youth leaders' summit. This alliance could influence the geographical scope of future youth advocacy around Caribbean unity and integration. However, Caribbean youth networks still lack the requisite financial and social capital to influence the political classes and institutions. Many regionalist youth movements, including the Federation of Youth and the Caribbean Movement for Civic Empowerment/Caribbean Civil Society Network, have dissolved. The potential for a "Caribbean Spring" against the regional implementation deficit is uncertain, given the governance weaknesses of youth organizations and the international aspirations of youth.

So, what will CARICOM have to do to gain support of youth for its strategies? Interestingly, young leaders have not disagreed explicitly with the broad technical strategies advanced for the CYDAP or the CARICOM strategic plan. However, transparency and accountability are youth priorities. The secretariat was vilified by youth for the presentation to COHSOD of the monitoring and evaluation plan for the first CYDAP less than a year before it was scheduled to expire. This, for youth, was among many signals of ineffectiveness in strategic management. The leadership and communication modes of the secretariat and institutions must be updated and extended to meet youth requirements for their political support. In addition, the temporal and location criteria for participation in the CYAP may need to be extended to offer a broader base for youth representation within CARICOM decision-making organs and bodies. I propose that youth be engaged not only on a geographical basis via national nomination but also via an open call based on technical expertise in the areas of competence of each organ and body. The Caribbean is not short on talented young scientists, teachers, politicians, economists, and so forth, including alumni of the CYAP who can offer sound contributions to implementation. Rights of access to decision-making should be accorded to a diversity of medium-term (nationally appointed), short-term (technical selections from open thematic calls) and alumni youth ambassadors, and should be complemented by responsibilities to coordinate their activities with strengthened, elected, and representative national and local youth councils. Furthermore, their participation should not be siloed into "special mechanisms". Rather, the new programme should model the Paramaribo principle of youth–adult partnership to connect youth leaders with broader civil society groups, so as to promote a united effort towards claiming regional citizenship rights and so as to build the capacity and capital of youth agency in regional governance.

Finally, will CARICOM be able to meet the development aspirations of young people? The ongoing challenges of making the CSME work pose a significant threat to the economic aspirations of Caribbean youth, who face high levels of unemployment. Against the background of Jamaica's review of its participation in CARICOM, these failings could eventually lead to rejection of the CSME model of integration. Coupled with dissatisfaction with leadership and governance, CARICOM could be abandoned. That process could begin with a sharp and decisive rejection of the whole framework because of greater generational divides between older and younger leaders in respect of their conceptions of regionalism. Alternatively, it could begin with gradual rejection of individual institutions, as in the case of Grenada's rejection of the Caribbean Court of Justice. As intimated earlier, based on the youth discourse analysed, it is possible that young people could pursue new forms of deeper political union or reject the entire Anglo-based regionalist enterprise in favour of creating a new pragmatic development institution, stripped of the traditions of formal CARICOM regionalism and imbued with "make-do" opportunism and pan-Caribbean non-governmental unity. The elaboration of the alternative institutional arrangements must be left in the hands of young people, with partnership from the rest of the society. The time for rethinking is opportune as CARICOM approaches its fiftieth anniversary.

Notes

1. The Caribbean Community is composed of fifteen member states and five associate member states pursuing shared objectives of economic integration, foreign policy coordination and functional cooperation on matters of socio-economic and cultural development, including security cooperation.

2. A process of Change Facilitation, involving public consultations in each member state, was initiated in 2013 on the recommendation of the consultants in their 2012 review report. Prior to the visit of the Change Facilitation team, national stakeholders often held pre-consultations with interest groups in order to better represent their perspectives to the team. The feedback from consultations fed into the secretariat's first strategic plan.

3. In Europe, the relevance and effectiveness of regionalism has been tested by the EU monetary crisis; the United Kingdom's exit from the European Union (Brexit); and the increasing popularity of right-wing groups which campaign against closer integration in Italy, France, Germany and Austria. In 2017 in Africa, a "Coalition of the Willing" began exploring alternative paths to economic development outside of the framework of the East African Community.

4. In the context of the research for this chapter, and in line with CARICOM's current framework for youth development, "young people" are defined loosely as those persons under thirty years of age who currently represent approximately 60 per cent of the regional population. "Youth" and "young people" are used interchangeably.

5. The relative successes of the Caribbean Examinations Council, the University of the West Indies, the West Indies Cricket Board, the Caribbean Festival of Arts and the Caribbean Development Bank are widely cited as preferred modes of intergovernmental cooperation and governance.

6. One of the more recent institutional reforms was the formation of the CARICOM Committee of Ambassadors in March 2015 to implement the CARICOM strategic plan, which is still seen as an inadequate mechanism for addressing the troublesome disconnect between national administrations and the regional governance framework.

7. The youth turnout rate was just eight percentage points below estimates of the national average turnout rate. International definitions of "youth" tend to cluster around a fifteen to twenty-four policy-focused age range. Although Scottish youth can vote at sixteen in Scottish elections, they were excluded from the British Referendum of June 2016.

8. See, for example, Patsy Lewis's (2002) discussion on youth exclusion from consultations on the Organisation of Eastern Caribbean States Union.

9. For a comprehensive review, see Gilbert-Roberts (2014).

10. There were a series of youth meetings in that year which also engaged in visioning exercises. It is plausible that the visions developed by young people in those discussions will have influenced the vision presented to Heads.

11. There was a hiatus between the expiry of the action plan in 2017 and its renewal with the same goals and objectives, with limited communication from the secretariat's youth division with stakeholders about the successor arrangements.

12. National nomination processes varied widely from country to country. Some ignore CARICOM's recommended guidelines that nominations emerge from elected National Youth Councils or other representative national youth organizations.

13. An online survey conducted by this author in 2015 targeted 171 ambassadors who served in the programme between 2002 and 2014, receiving a 35 per cent response rate (90 per cent confidence rate, ±9 per cent margin of error).

14. Those who were outside the region at the time of survey were either studying overseas or working with international organizations.

15. These designations were used only loosely by the commission and the secretariat, since youth commissioners were, in fact, young adults.

16. Members of the Commission reported, in the early stages of the study, suspicion of the motives on either side of the youth–adult divide, with great underestimation of the capabilities of young people by some of the adult commissioners.

17. Interestingly, a SALISES study in Jamaica six years earlier found, similarly, that young people called for the features of integration, though they had limited confidence and affiliation or identification with CARICOM as an institution (Duncan et al. 2004).

18. It is interesting that it is in this post-2010 period a twenty-two-year-old Jamaican woman decided to protest her denial of entry into Barbados and ill-treatment involving verbal and physical sexual abuse, as a denial of her fundamental rights under the Revised Treaty of Chaguaramas. Although the court did not address the issue of her assault, it upheld her claim of a breach of her rights to freedom of movement, awarding her financial damages in 2013.

19. For example, participant @TamiBe asserted, "we must never doubt that our quest is: the importance and permanence of the Caribbean Community" (Browne 2013d).

20. This question was intended for the secretary general, who was not online at that point in the discussion.

21. These include sessions on July 2016 on "Quality Education: Focused on Tech Advances and Problem Solving"; 27 February 2016 session on "Reduction of Youth on Youth Violence"; 29 June 2015 on "Entrepreneurship: CARICOM''s Economic Life Jacket"; January 2014 on "Work of the CARICOM Secretariat and the CYDAP"; and a follow-up discussion to the Twitter relay in 2013 on "The CARICOM We Want". The issue of non-implementation and concerns about leaders' commitments to the integration project also abound in some of the Facebook posts from those discussions.

22. The online survey received seventy-eight responses from thirteen member states and two associate member states. Of those indicating nationality, the largest proportions were Jamaicans, Trinidadians, Guyanese and Vincentians.

References

Abiola DaSilva, Dianna. 2010. "Are the Benefits of the CARICOM Single Market and Economy Real or Imagined?" *Integration Quarterly* 2: 14–17.

Acharya, Amitav. 2014. "Global International Relations and Regional Worlds". *International Studies Quarterly* 58 (4): 647–59.

Belize Youth Support (@BelizeYouth). 2013. "@cyapinfo Agreed! The Youth have a Right to be Heard and be Involved in Decisions. They have a Right to Choices and to Voice their Opinions". Twitter, 30 June, 6:01pm. https://twitter.com/BelizeYouth/status/351460385112604672.

Browne, Tami (@TamiBe). 2013a. "@cyapinfo ...We must never Doubt that Our Quest Is: The Importance and Permanence of the Caribbean Community. #caricom #784". Twitter, 30 June, 11:52am. https://twitter.com/TamiBe/status/351367597008232449.

———. 2013b. "@cyapinfo Leadership and Governance Are Important because We have had too many Stops and Starts with Changes in govt #CARICOM #784". Twitter, 30 June, 5:59pm. https://twitter.com/TamiBe/status/351460087900012546.

———. 2013c. "@cyapinfo Leadership & Governance Are Important because I Believer where there Is NO Vision ppl Bound to PERISH! #CARICOM #784". Twitter, 30 June, 6:00pm. https://twitter.com/TamiBe/status/351460332394393601.

———. 2013d. Twitter post. 30 June 2013, 10.52 a.m. https://twitter.com/TamiBe.

Byron, Jessica. 2014. "CARICOM Foreign Policy since 2009: A Search for Coherence in National and Regional Agendas". In *La CELAC en el Escenario Contemporáneo de América Latina y el Caribe*, edited by Adrian Bonilla and Grace Jaramillo, 79–100. San Jose, Costa Rica: FLACSO/CAF.

———. 2016. "Summitry in the Caribbean Community: A Fundamental Feature of Regional Governance". In *Summits and Regional Governance: The Americas in Comparative Perspective*, edited by Gordon Mace, Jean-Phillippe Therien, Diana Tussie, and Olivier Dabene, 88–105. Abingdon, UK: Routledge.

Caballero Santos, Sergio. 2015. "Identity in Mercosur: Regionalism and Nationalism". *Global Governance* 21 (1): 43–59.

CARICOM Commission on Youth Development. 2010. *Eye on the Future: Investing in Youth Now for Tomorrow's Community. Report of the CARICOM Commission on Youth Development (CCYD)*. Georgetown: CARICOM Secretariat. Accessed 5 January 2018. http://caricom.org/images/publications/9498/eye_on_the_future_ccyd_report.pdf.

CARICOM Conference of Heads of Government. 1973. *Treaty of Chaguaramas Establishing the Caribbean Community*. Georgetown: CARICOM Secretariat. Accessed 4 January 2018. https://caricom.org/documents/4905-original_treaty-text.pdf.

———. 1990. *The Kingston Declaration*. Georgetown: CARICOM Secretariat. Accessed 4 January 2018. http://caricom.org/communications/view/the-kingston-declaration.

———. 1997. *Charter of Civil Society for the Caribbean Community*. Georgetown: CARICOM Secretariat. Accessed 4 January 2018. https://caricom.org/documents/12060-charter_of _civil_society.pdf.

———. 2001. *Revised Treaty of Chaguaramas Establishing the Caribbean Community Including the CARICOM Single Market and Economy*. Georgetown: CARICOM Secretariat. Accessed 4 January 2018. https://caricom.org/documents/4906-revised_treaty-text.pdf.

———. 2010. *Declaration of Paramaribo on the Future of Youth in the Community: Special Summit of Heads of Government of the Caribbean Community on Youth*. Georgetown: CARICOM Secretariat. Accessed 5 January 2018. http://caricom.org/communications/view /declaration-of-paramaribo-on-the-future-of-youth-in-the-caribbean-community.

CARICOM Secretariat. 1998. "Caribbean Youth Come Up with Vision for 21st Century. Press Release 85/1998". CARICOM Secretariat, Last Modified 16 October. http://caricom.org /media-center/communications/press-releases/caribbean-youth-come-up-with-vision-for -21st-century.

———. 2003. "Integrating Youth in Regional Development". *CARICOM View*, January: 16–22.

———. 2012. *Draft CARICOM Youth Development Action Plan (CYDAP). Prepared by Technical Working Group on a CARICOM Youth Agenda*. Georgetown: CARICOM Secretariat. Accessed 5 January 2018. http://caricom.org/documents/13930-cydap_2012-2017 _rev.pdf.

———. 2013a. *CARICOM Youth Development Action Plan (CYDAP) 2012–2017, Revised*. Georgetown: CARICOM Secretariat (unpublished document, October 2013).

———. 2013b. *Remarks by the Secretary-General of the Caribbean Community (CARICOM) Ambassador Irwin LaRocque at the Opening of the Thirty-Fourth Meeting of the Conference of Heads of Government of the Caribbean Community, Port-of-Spain, Trinidad and Tobago.*

CARICOM Secretariat, 3 July. Accessed 10 December 2016. https://caricom.org/media
-center/communications/speeches/remarks-by-the-secretary-general-of-the-caribbean
-community-caricom-am.

———. 2014. *Communique Issued at the Conclusion of the Twenty-Fifth Inter-Sessional Meeting
of the Conference of Heads of Government of the Caribbean Community, 10–11 March,
Buccament, St. Vincent and the Grenadines*. CARICOM Secretariat, 12 March 2014. Accessed
23 December 2017. http://caricom.org/media-center/communications/communiques
/communique-issued-at-the-conclusion-of-the-twenty-fifth-inter-sessional-mee.

CARICOM Secretary-General (@caricomsec). "@Lavz_ @cyapinfo We are trying to do more to
reach out to the people of #CARICOM. Efforts like this with the CYA is significant". Twitter,
30 June, 3:45pm. https://twitter.com/caricomsec/status/351426404354768896.

———. "@PrunellaMungroo @TamiBe @cyapinfo What can Youth do to rebuild that hope.
Need to build a sense of 'regional nationalism'. SG #CARICOM". Twitter, 30 June, 3:27pm.
https://twitter.com/caricomsec/status/351421768159866880.

Carter, Richard. 2008. "Caribbean Youth: An Integrated Literature Review". Report prepared
for the CARICOM Commission on Youth Development (unpublished).

Charles, Henry and Madgerie Jameson-Charles. 2014. "Youth Development Policy and Practice
in the Commonwealth Caribbean: A Historical Evolution". *Social and Economic Studies* 63
(3 and 4): 23–57.

Clement, Paul C. 2015. "Implementation Deficit: Why Member States Do Not Comply with
CARICOM Directives". St. Augustine, Trinidad: Caribbean Future Forum. Accessed
10 December 2016. http://caribbeanfutureforum.com/.

Cresci, Elena. 2016. "Meet the 75%: The Young People Who Voted to Remain in the EU". *The
Guardian*, 24 June. Accessed 24 June 2016. https://www.theguardian.com/politics/2016
/jun/24/meet-the-75-young-people-who-voted-to-remain-in-eu.

Dabène, Olivier. 2009. *The Politics of Regional Integration in Latin America: Theoretical and
Comparative Explorations*. Edited by Christian Lequesne, Series in International Relations
and Political Economy. New York: Palgrave Macmillan.

Directors of Youth of the Caribbean Community. 2001. "Communique on the Second Meeting
of Directors of Youth of the Caribbean Community, 7–9 May, Trinidad and Tobago".
Georgetown: CARICOM Secretariat. Accessed 15 November 2016. https://caricom.org
/communications/view/communique-on-second-meeting-of-directors-of-youth-of-the
-caribbean-community-7-9-may-2001-trinidad-and-tobago.

Duncan, Neville, Kristin Fox, Aldrie Henry-Lee, Patsy Lewis, and Jimmy Tindigarukayo. 2004.
"Jamaican Perspectives of Regional Integration. SALISES Paper". Mona, Jamaica: University
of the West Indies (unpublished, December 2004).

European Commission. 2014. "EU Youth Strategy" [webpage]. European Commission.
Accessed 4 September 2014. http://ec.europa.eu/youth/policy/youth_strategy/index
_en.htm.

Fawcett, Louise. 2008. "Regionalism in World Politics: Past and Present". In *Elements of
Regional Integration: A Multidimensional Approach*, edited by Ariane Kösler and Martin
Zimmek, 15–28. Baden-Baden: Nomos.

Gilbert-Roberts, Terri-Ann. 2009. "Youth Governance Structures in CARICOM: Regional
Review of Organizational Relevance. Report to the CARICOM Commission on Youth
Development" (unpublished, November 2009).

———. 2013. *The Politics of Integration: Caribbean Sovereignty Revisited*. Kingston: Ian Randle
Publisher.

———. 2014. "CARICOM Governance of Youth Development: Prospects for Regional
Citizenship". *Social and Economic Studies* 63 (3 and 4): 59–106.

———. 2015. Online Survey of CARICOM Youth Ambassadors (unpublished).

Girvan, Norman. 2007. "Towards a Single Development Vision and the Role of the Single Economy". In *Report Approved by the Twenty-Eighth Meeting of the Conference of Heads of Government of the Caribbean Community (CARICOM), 1–4 July, 2007, Needham's Point, Barbados*. Georgetown: Special Task Force on the Single Economy, CARICOM Secretariat.

———. 2010. "Are Caribbean Countries Facing Existential Threats?" *Caribbean360*. 2 November 2010. Accessed 3 June 2018. http://www.caribbean360.com/opinion/are _caribbean_countries_facing_existential_threats.

———. 2011a. "CARICOM'S 'Original Sin'". Presentation to CARICOM Regional Civil Society Consultation, Port of Spain, Trinidad and Tobago, 10–11 February. *América Latina en Movimiento Online*. Accessed 3 June 2018. https://www.alainet.org/images/caricoms -original-sin.pdf.

———. 2011b. "Existential Threats in the Caribbean: Democratising Politics, Regionalising Governance". Presented at the CLR James Memorial Lecture, Valsayn, Trinidad and Tobago, 12 May. *Caribbean Review*. Accessed 3 June 2018. http://www.caribbeanreview.org/2017/08 /existential-threats-in-the-caribbean/.

———. 2012. "50 Years of In-Dependence in Jamaica: Reflections". Presentation to SALISES 50–50 Conference, *Critical Reflections in a Time of Uncertainty*. *América Latina en Movimiento Online*. Accessed 23 August 2012. http://www.alainet.org/images/girvan -jamaica-in-dependence.pdf.

Gutzmer, Dwayne. 2013. "CARICOM Reform Process: Notes from Jamaican Youth Pre-Consultations. Report Presented to CARICOM Change Facilitation Team". Kingston, Jamaica: CARICOM Youth Ambassador Programme (unpublished report).

Gutzmer, Dwayne and CARICOM Youth Ambassador Programme. 2013. "Reform Process in CARICOM: Youth Online Survey Raw Data Analysis", compiled by Dwayne Gutzmer. Kingston, Jamaica: CARICOM Youth Ambassador Programme (unpublished dataset, November 2013).

Gutzmer, Dwayne, Terri-Ann Gilbert-Roberts, Alecia Maragh, Dane Campbell, Mario Rose, Marlon Gregory, Simone Green, Terisa Thompson, Tijani Christian, and Theon Scott. 2014. "Review of CARICOM Strategic Plan 2015–2019 in Relation to Youth Mainstreaming". Kingston, Jamaica (unpublished).

Hart, Roger A. 1992. "Children's Participation: From Tokenism to Citizenship". In Innocenti Essays *Series (no 4)*. Florence: United Nations Children's Fund.

Helm, Toby. 2016. "EU Referendum: Youth Turnout Almost Twice as High as First Thought". *The Guardian*, 10 July. Accessed 10 July 2016. https://www.theguardian.com/politics/2016 /jul/09/young-people-referendum-turnout-brexit-twice-as-high.

Hinds Harrison, Kristina. 2013. "Civil Society Consultation in the Caribbean Community (CARICOM): Why Conceptual Clarity Matters". *Journal of Eastern Caribbean Studies* 38 (1/2): 1–34.

Johnson, Ruel. 2009. "Is the Caribbean Region on the Verge of Shipwreck?" *Integration Quarterly* 1: 4–5.

Krickovic, Andrej. 2015. "'All Politics Is Regional': Emerging Powers and the Regionalization of Global Governance". *Global Governance: A Review of Multilateralism and International Organizations* 21 (4): 557–77.

Lewis, Patsy. 2002. *Surviving Small Size. Regional Integration in Caribbean Ministates*. Kingston: University of the West Indies Press.

———. 2005. "The Agony of the Fifteen: The Crisis of Implementation". *Social and Economic Studies* 54 (3): 145–75.

———. 2010. "Implications of the Global Economic Crisis for Caribbean Regional Integration". *Global Development Studies* 6 (1–2): 1–27.

Lewis, Vaughan. 2007. "What Purposes for CARICOM Integration Today?". Third Distinguished Lecture in a series in honour of Sir Arthur Lewis, the English-speaking Caribbean's first Nobel Laureate, 15 April. https://sta.uwi.edu/nlc/2008/documents/Lewis _Lecture_full.pdf.

Mangal, Henry and Armstrong Alexis. 2009. "Final Integrated Report on CARICOM Youth Ambassador's Evaluation and Planning Workshop, Held in the Bahamas, December 2007". Turkeyen, Guyana: CARICOM Secretariat (unpublished report).

Mungroo, Prunella. 2013a. Twitter post. 30 June 2013, 2.23 p.m. https://twitter.com /PrunellaMungroo/.

Mungroo, Prunella. 2013b. Twitter post. 30 June 2013, 5.08 p.m. https://twitter.com /PrunellaMungroo/.

Mungroo, Prunella. 2013c. Twitter post. 30 June 2013, 5.04 p.m. https://twitter.com /PrunellaMungroo/.

National Centre for Youth Development. 2013. "CARICOM Youth Tweet for Regional Integration". National Centre for Youth Development, Jamaica. Last Modified 1 July 2013. Accessed 31 October. http://www.youthjamaica.com/content/caricom-youth-tweet-regional -integration.

Nesadurai, H.E. 2009. "ASEAN and Regional Governance after the Cold War: From Regional Order to Regional Community". *The Pacific Review* 22 (1): 91–118.

Payne, Anthony. 2008. *The Political History of CARICOM*. Kingston: Ian Randle.

Perry, Keston. 2011. "Call to Action". *Caribbean Movement for Civil Empowerment* (blog), 22 April. Accessed 3 June 2018. http://caribmove.blogspot.com/2011/04/call-to-action.html.

———. (@kestontnt). 2013. "Unfortunately I have Lost Most Hope in #CARICOM as an Institution. Time for a Youth-led Equivalent". Twitter, 30 June, 2:59pm. https://twitter.com /kestontnt/status/351414772627030016.

Phillips, Nicola. 2003. "The Rise and Fall of Open Regionalism? Comparative Reflections on Regional Governance in the Southern Cone of Latin America". *Third World Quarterly* 24 (2): 217–34.

Prime Ministerial Expert Group on Governance. 2005. "Report of the Expert Group of Heads of Government on the Establishment of a CARICOM Commission or Other Executive Mechanism, Automatic Resource Transfers and the Assembly of Caribbean Community Parliamentarians", edited by Ralph Gonsalves. Georgetown: CARICOM Secretariat, 12 February.

Ramphal, Shridath. 2005. "The CARICOM Commission: Towards a Mature Regionalism". In *Caribbean Imperatives: Regional Governance and Integrated Development*, edited by Kenneth Hall and Denis Benn, 71–77. Kingston: Ian Randle.

Riggirozzi, Pia and Diana Tussie, eds. 2012. *The Rise of Post-Hegemonic Regionalism: The Case of Latin America*. New York: Springer.

Smith, Lorenzo. (@suraze). 2013. "@cyapinfo @TamiBe #CARICOM #876 Integration will be an Illusive Dream as Long as Our Leaders/Countries Continue to Think Insular". Twitter, 30 June, 11:29am. https://twitter.com/suraze/status/351361967002357760.

Stoneman, Richard, Duke Pollard, and Hugo Inniss. 2012. "Turning Around CARICOM: Proposals to Restructure the Secretariat. Report of Landell Mills Development Consultants". Georgetown: CARICOM Secretariat. Accessed 4 January 2018. http://caricom.org /documents/9400-restructuring_the_secretariat_-_landell_mills_final_report.pdf.

Thomas, Clive Y. 1977. "The Community Is a Big Paper Tiger". In *The Caribbean Community: Beyond Survival*, edited by Kenneth O. Hall. Kingston: Ian Randle Publisher. Edition, 2001.

West Indian Commission. 1992. *Time for Action: Report of the West Indian Commission*. Blackrock: The West Indian Commission.

Chapter 10

CARICOM Model Legislation on Domestic Violence

Negotiating Love, Intimacy and Abuse in Caribbean Law

HALIMAH A.F. DESHONG

The emergence of the Caribbean Community (CARICOM) Model Legislation on Issues Affecting Women between 1989 and 1991 can be situated within a long history of women's rights and feminist activism, the global women's movement, the findings of the Women in the Caribbean Project (WICP), the promotion and production of functional cooperation within the regional integration movement, and what Tracy Robinson (2007) has defined as legal regionalism. This confluence of national, regional and global forces, events, and movements – in particular the engagement of activists in national and regional law and policymaking; the United Nations' proclamation of, first, the International Year of Women in 1975, and later the Decade for Women 1975–85; Caribbean women's involvement in the UN Commission on the Status of Women; the research findings of the WICP; and the establishment of regional and national women's desks and later gender machineries – is the collective context out of which model legislation to promote gender equality among member states emerged.

The adoption, reach and limitations of domestic violence legislation within member states, as part of the CARICOM Secretariat's creation of Model Legislation on Issues Affecting Women, is the central focus of this chapter. The chapter begins with a discussion of CARICOM Model Legislation on Domestic Violence as interpolated within CARICOM's broader mandate to address gender inequality, articulated first in the Treaty of Chaguaramas, and later in its Model Legislation on Issues Affecting Women. The legal naming and framing of "domestic violence" in these regional and national documents are interrogated for how they inhere notions of love, intimacy, family and violence. The vagaries of enacting, revising and implementing domestic violence legislation within member states is also read against the actual socio-legal response to violence in the context of intimacy. Based on seventeen interviews conducted with police officers, family court counsellors, activists, prosecutors and defence attorneys in St Vincent and the Grenadines, I assess the efficacy of domestic violence legislation as a key pillar of state and regional response to intimate partner violence, in particular. The possibilities and tensions inherent in implementing regional legislation on domestic violence are assessed through a focus on its operation in St Vincent and the Grenadines as a case study.[1]

The space where regional/national lawmaking meets the social is my point of departure in this chapter. Gendered[2] violence is profoundly political and results from structural relationships of power, domination and privilege between and among men, women, girls, boys and persons who do not conform to normative expressions of gender and sexuality. It is violence that occurs as a consequence of the gendered organization of society. Women, girls and persons who self-define or are socially defined as disrupting gender and sexual normativity are the most frequent targets of those who perpetrate gendered violence. While gendered violence manifests as various forms of physical, sexual and non-physical acts of control, coercion and a range of other harms at the interpersonal level, it is maintained within broader arrangements of power and domination. An appreciation of the structural arrangements of power which produce this violence is necessary when examining state and regional responses.

Caribbean governments have prioritized the creation and application of legislation, as well as legislative reform, as their main response to addressing gendered violence (Pargass and Clarke 2003). Here, I examine what this focus on legislation means for responding to intimate partner violence, in particular. While a comprehensive legislative framework should form part of the state's attempt to prevent and mitigate gendered violence, the reach and possibilities of law are often misunderstood. To illustrate, the possibility of preventing and mitigating violence in the context of domestic violence legislation is read against the experience of responding to this violence in the Vincentian criminal justice system.

Emergence of the CARICOM Model Legislation on Domestic Violence

The recommendation of the 1980 CARICOM meeting of technical officials of Women's Bureau in the region to introduce the Model Legislation on Issues Affecting Women must be understood in a context of a growing regional and global feminist movement; regionalism; and the obvious tensions between what Tracy Robinson (2007) refers to as notions of a "Caribbean Common Law" and the history of colonial legislatures making their own laws. Based on research commissioned by the CARICOM Secretariat, it was agreed that model legislation would be enacted to redress the institutionalized gender inequality within the legal system across member states (CARICOM Secretariat 1997). In this regard, model legislation was created on:

- Citizenship
- Domestic violence
- Equality for women in employment
- Equal pay
- Inheritance
- Maintenance and maintenance orders
- Sexual harassment
- Sexual offences

A committee was established that included representatives from the CARICOM Women's Desk – its legal unit – as well as legal experts from the Organisation of Eastern Caribbean States (OECS) subregion, the wider community and the Commonwealth Secretariat. Also central to the process was engagement with government agencies and

Caribbean women's networks, in particular, the Caribbean Association of Feminist Research and Action (CAFRA) and the Caribbean Women's Association (CARIWA) – key organizations within the regional feminist movement.

The focus for this chapter is the context out of which Model Legislation on Domestic Violence was established by the CARICOM Secretariat and implemented within member states, as well as the possible reach and efficacy of said legislation. In assessing the role of the secretariat, Tracy Robinson's (2007, 119) observation that "laws across the region may look similar, but law-making and most judicial decision-making in the Caribbean is markedly local and national, not regional" requires consideration for its relevance to the possibility of a CARICOM-driven response to gendered violence, as part of a larger regional process to address gender inequality. Indeed, much of the impetus to prioritize legislation in this CARICOM-driven process came from an active women's/feminist movement in the region, even as the regional body (with the prompting of member states) was also responding to its various international obligations to improve/establish laws to address gender inequality. Notwithstanding the specificities in lawmaking and judicial decision-making in the Caribbean, law remains a site for the production and contestation of "Caribbeanness", according to Robinson (2007). In other words, she points to legal regionalism, in spite of the imprecision in the lawmaking and judicial decision-making processes across member states. In this regard, the language of what was eventually implemented among member states as "The Domestic Violence Summary Proceeding Acts" and "The Revised Domestic Violence Acts" bears great similarities across member states.

While the CARICOM model legislation functions as a key exemplar of legal regionalism in lawmaking and a regional response to address gender inequalities, there remains inconsistency in court rites, judicial decision-making and the enactment/ engagement with domestic violence legislation at the national level. One such example of inconsistencies within judicial decision-making, as it relates to court rites in cases involving gendered violence, is the issuance of the corroboration warning in cases of sexual offences. A sexist retention in the English legal practice, the corroboration warning requires judges in sexual offence cases to instruct juries that it is harmful to convict an accused on the "uncorroborated" evidence of women and children. The warning, read out to juries, defines a woman or child as having a tendency to fabricate events and/or distort reality, a "fact" that should be taken into account in their deliberations. Trial judges are no longer mandated to read the warning since the Privy Council decided, in *R v Gilbert* (2002) 61 WIR 174, that the decision should be left to the discretion of the specific judge (UN Women Caribbean, n.d.). In the OECS subregion, trial judges differ in how they regard the corroboration warning. Some judges admit that they do not read the warning, as it embeds asymmetrical relations of gender, while others argue for the need to read the warning to ensure that accused persons are not unfairly convicted.[3] Both defence attorneys and prosecutors interviewed in St Vincent and the Grenadines confirmed that trial judges no longer read the warning, with one citing *R v Gilbert* as the basis upon which the warning is no longer issued. It is precisely these tensions between regional lawmaking on domestic violence and the enactment of said legislation at the local and national levels that I wish to interrogate in this chapter.

Caribbean Feminist Organizing and Regional Lawmaking on Domestic Violence

Rhoda Reddock (1998, 2008) historicizes the emergence of women's organizing in the region around a specific feminist consciousness in the 1970s, which she locates within a broader global women's movement. Stalwarts of traditional women's organizations (such as women's arms of political parties from the 1950s onwards) were among the first to be networked within and influenced by the global movement for gender justice. In this regard, Peggy Antrobus (2013) is careful to outline the formative role of Caribbean feminist activists in shaping this global agenda as part of a transnational feminist network that would emerge to centre gender justice. Viola Burnham of the People's National Congress in Guyana called together her colleague activists across the region and they established CARIWA in 1970, with a mandate to create a regional network of national women's councils and their affiliated organizations. In this same year, the Women's Revolutionary Socialist Movement of the People's National Congress and the Women's Auxiliary of the People's National Party in Jamaica worked to create national women's affairs machinery. According to Reddock (1998), the establishment, in Jamaica, of one of the first Women's Bureau to emerge in the world was due, in large part, to the work of feminist-oriented women in the People's National Party such as Lucille Mathurin Mair and Mavis Gilmore.

A regional position on the UN Decade for Women emerged after members of CARIWA; the then director of the Jamaican Women's Bureau, Peggy Antrobus; and the affiliate women's organizations of the Caribbean Conference of Churches organized a meeting in Jamaica in 1977, which included twelve representatives from Caribbean governments, the University of the West Indies, CARIWA, international and regional development agencies, and other representatives from other Jamaican government and non-governmental organizations (Reddock 1998).

In addition, the formation of CAFRA in April 1985 by a regional network of feminist activists and organizations was followed by the establishment of a series of CAFRA committees that functioned nationally while networking into the regional body. CAFRA collaborated with the Inter-American Legal Services Association in 1987 and conducted a survey on legal services throughout the Caribbean in which violence against women and the legal framework for addressing such violence was prioritized in research. In 1989, CAFRA also conducted the Women and the Law project in ten countries to investigate the effects of the law on women's daily lives. In this research, domestic violence emerged as an issue to be prioritized within the law. Following the completion of this research, CAFRA hosted conferences on domestic violence in 1990, 1991, 1995 and 1996, and in 1996 embarked on a regional project funded by the UN Development Fund for Women on violence against women and the non-state responses in the Caribbean.

At the regional level, CAFRA was designated as the focal point for the UN Development Fund for Women/UN Development Programme inter-agency campaign on violence against women and girls with the theme "A Life Free from Violence: It's Our Right". At the national level, local CAFRA committees had their own programmes. For example, the Guyana membership provided counselling services for women affected by intimate partner violence; and the Suriname group hosted a national workshop for police officers and social workers, and the success of the programme prompted the regional CAFRA committee to host the Regional Domestic Violence Intervention Training Programme for Police Officers and Social Workers in 2000.[4] CAFRA's research, advocacy and action provided significant impetus for the emergence of domestic violence legislation and response among member states. Both CAFRA and CARIWA were central to the work produced by the secretariat in the emergence of its Model Legislation on Domestic Violence.

In short, a network of women's and feminist organizations in the region provided much of the impetus, expertise and labour for the emergence and development of regional model legislation and, by extension, state laws, policies and actions to address gendered violence. Addressing the underlying assumptions, systems and actions which produced this violence became part of a larger thrust toward securing gender justice. Regarded as one of the most heinous manifestations of gendered inequality, it is no surprise that gendered violence became and remains the most significant issue around which regional and national women's and feminist organizations mobilize. While this emphasis by these organizations (in collaboration with development agencies and regional governments) on the extent to which national and regional lawmaking has transformed gender relations requires attention, such a discussion falls outside of the scope of this chapter.

The 1980s onwards saw Caribbean governments becoming signatory to a number of conventions and treaties which set a global mandate for ending violence against women. Most member states are signatory to the Convention on Elimination of All Forms of Discrimination Against Women (CEDAW) and the Beijing Platform for Action (BPfA) in which governments commit to ratifying and implementing the Convention, particularly the recommendations which speak to ending gendered violence. Between 1995 and 1996, a number of member states also signed the Inter-American Convention on the Prevention, Punishment and Eradication of Violence Against Women, the Convention of Belém do Pará. In short, a combination of global, regional and national feminist and women's rights organizing, as well as national commitments to global treaties and conventions, created the conditions for the emergence of a CARICOM-wide initiative to address gendered violence and, by extension, gender inequalities.

Domestic Violence Legislation within Member States

In her ethnographic work in Trinidad and Tobago, Mindie Lazarus-Black (2007) refers to the moment in which domestic violence legislation was introduced in 1991 as an act of "regendering the state". Regendering the state, according to Lazarus-Black, is a process by which categories and activities that silenced, denied rights to, constituted harm to or limited women's capacity to engage in actions available to men were formally named in law. In this regard, both domestic violence and sexual offence legislation addressed gendered experiences of rape, other forms of sexual violence and intimate partner violence.

In 1991, the CARICOM Women's Desk spearheaded the introduction of Model Legislation on Domestic Violence, and in that same year this legislation was introduced in Trinidad and Tobago, and Barbados. Belize, and St Vincent and the Grenadines would follow with the introduction of similar legislation in 1993 and 1994, respectively. An activist in St Vincent and the Grenadines, referred to here as Lois, who was employed in the state gender machinery at the time of the introduction of the CARICOM Model Legislation on Domestic Violence, recalls the process by which a regional network of state agents and activists were brought together to secure institutionalization at the national level.[5] She says:

> Trinidad was I think, the first in the region that had some piece of legislation. But then you had harmonisation of the legislation across the Caribbean region because you had the CARICOM draft legislation and so a lot of the individual Caribbean countries adopted the legislation, based on what was going on in their individual countries, based on their culture and so on; and, at that particular time we had the Attorney General, PR Campbell, you also had the engendering of a number of pieces of legislation across the Caribbean region.

Tracing the history of the adoption of domestic violence legislation by member states as simultaneously regional and national, Lois describes a situation in which a range of state and non-state expertise was mobilized by the secretariat (catalysed by the regional women's movement) to secure regional lawmaking on an issue that had been prioritized by activists in the Caribbean for over a decade and a half.

In the following, she describes how both legal and policy expertise were deployed in the implementation of the legislation at the national level:

> We had our AG [attorney general] at the time, and he was very, very supportive, so when you travelled across the region you had Women's bureaus and Attorneys General travelling and discussing. And then you went into groups where you looked at your individual scenarios and your culture, what was going on in the individual countries – So the AG must be congratulated, not only for participating but for getting things done in St Vincent and the Grenadines. . . . And we had people like . . . our only legal drafter at the time in St. Vincent and the Grenadines. And we had people . . ., who are now judges, . . . part of the entire process. Those people we could have depended on from the level of the Bureau. So you were in constant dialogue with them to ensure that when anything was drafted we were consulted to see whether or not this is what we would have liked the legislation to depict and to say.

The exercise of political will on the part of the attorney general is highlighted here as a necessary requirement for the successful implementation of domestic violence legislation at the national level. However, Lois is careful to note that not only did St Vincent and the Grenadines mobilize its limited legal expertise in ensuring the timely adoption of the model legislation, but that it was done with close consultation with the state gender machinery, as it was here that the expertise on domestic violence resided. Notwithstanding this assertion, the first set of domestic violence legislation to emerge among member states (in Trinidad and Tobago, Barbados, the Bahamas, Jamaica, St Vincent and the Grenadines, and Belize) were limited in their scope in how they defined the intimate relationship. For example, cohabitation was embedded as a requirement for persons seeking protections under the first set of domestic violence acts. The reality of some Caribbean families being spread across different households and the ambiguous legal status of "visiting relationships" (Robinson 2013), notwithstanding their sociological significance in the Caribbean, failed to be reckoned with in the first round of domestic violence acts in the region. However, according to Lois:

> The cross-Caribbean network existed, and in a very powerful manner, very powerful. Because, not only did we meet from the level of the bureaus but from the Attorneys General as well, and [we] not only met in isolation, but we were part and parcel of the discussion as they met, because they had legal brains, but we are the ones who sit in the seat, and we are the ones who meet with the women and deal with the women on a daily basis.

Catalysed by regional and transnational feminist networks and activism, as well as Caribbean governments' policy commitments to redress violence against women, having ratified several UN and Organization of American States treaties and conventions, CARICOM's attempt to redefine the role of the state in relation to gender, family and violence must be noted. In the post-Beijing Platform period (post-1995), Jamaica, the British Virgin Islands, Antigua and Barbuda, St Kitts and Nevis, Grenada and Dominica all implemented domestic violence legislation.

It is important to note, however, that in Trinidad and Tobago the passage of the Domestic Violence Act in 1991 was due, in large part, to the activism of a small group of women who petitioned lawmakers, wrote in the newspapers, spoke in public forums, and dressed in black and staged protests outside of Parliament (Reddock 2008). The role of the women's movement in securing legal protection from violence in the home is well documented in the scholarly literature. It is within this context that the emergence of CARICOM Model Legislation on Domestic Violence must also be understood.

It should also be noted that, often in the region, women's rights and feminist activists may work within, outside and/or across state and non-state entities, as was the case with Peggy Antrobus at the Jamaican Women's Bureau and the participant referred to here as Lois at the state gender machinery in St Vincent and the Grenadines. This may indeed be a feature of small states which was significant in how countries in the region confronted the process of the implementation of domestic violence legislation. In addition, state gender machineries in the Caribbean have historically engaged women's and feminist organizations as partners in the implementation of actions, policies and laws, all in support of meeting their commitment to address gender inequalities. In research on state, activist and media responses to intimate partner violence in the Caribbean, one activist noted that the national response to intimate partner violence is largely led by non-governmental organizations, notwithstanding existing state policies, and her organization's collaboration with the existing state gender machinery (DeShong and Haynes 2016). It is also in this context that we must understand the process by which regional legislation on domestic violence emerges and is implemented by CARICOM member states.

The original CARICOM Model Legislation on Domestic Violence, adopted by member states, is regarded as a socio-legal response and is, in the first instance, non-criminal. Emphasis is placed on ending violence through the granting of court orders – protection and occupation orders. It is only if a respondent breaches the order that a crime (against the court) is deemed to have been committed. Prior to (and even with the implementation of) legislation within member states, cases involving domestic violence were/are prosecuted under the criminal codes without necessarily being recorded as cases involving intimate partners. In other words, the CARICOM model focuses on a civil remedy as opposed to punishment (Pargass and Clarke 2003). In its original instantiation, those for whom protection could be sought were married, formerly married, or otherwise cohabiting or formerly cohabiting partners. The insistence on either marriage and/or shared residence in both the CARICOM model and the early national domestic violence legislation is regarded as a key failure of the original acts to account for the heterogeneity of both Caribbean socio-sexual unions and Caribbean family forms, as previously indicated. In fact, this failure can be situated within a long history of distorting, maligning and misrepresenting how we make family in the region. In short, non-residential intimate unions (or visiting relationships, as they are often regarded in the sociological literature) were invisibilized in state law on domestic violence.

In 2007, a draft Domestic Violence Bill was created by the OECS to redress a set of shortcomings identified during a review of the national domestic violence acts that were at the time based on the CARICOM model legislation. The OECS Domestic Violence Bill sought to increase the protection of children under the act by instituting a system of mandatory reporting of violence against children. It provided frontline workers (such as police officers, social workers, teachers and medical professionals) the ability to intervene and apply for protections on behalf of children and gave police officers the right to apply for protection on behalf of survivors of intimate partner violence. It included non-cohabiting intimate partners among those who could seek protections under the act and expanded the definition of domestic violence "to include 'physical, sexual, emotional or psychological or financial abuse' and a pattern of behaviour of any kind, the purpose of which is to undermine the emotional and mental wellbeing of a person" (OECS 2007, 2). It also introduced family courts in countries where they did not previously exist. The move to strengthen domestic violence legislation within some countries of the OECS subregion, and to introduce it for the first time in others, with the creation of the OECS Domestic Violence Bill, should be understood as emerging out of what Patsy Lewis (2002) refers to as a history which forced countries within the subregion to recognize common economic, social, political and legal challenges.

Given the centrality of lawmaking in state response to intimate partner violence in the form of domestic violence legislation, the materiality and enactment of law and court rites, as well as the ability of those affected by this violence to access protections, require examination. It is here that I wish to turn my attention to how agents of the state negotiate and navigate within the criminal justice system in ways that simultaneously adhere to and disregard the protections imagined in the creation of regional and national domestic violence legislation.

Intimacy, Love and Law

It is worth acknowledging the complications that arise when explanations of gendered violence, often replete with popular discourses on love, intimacy and family, influence how agents of the state understand their role in addressing intimate partner violence. Popular explanations of gendered violence are saturated with love narratives, the materiality of which animates criminal justice response, media representations, service provision and the actions of those directly involved in violent relationships (DeShong 2014; DeShong and Haynes 2016). In other words, perfect and enduring love narratives (Gavey 2013; Jackson 2001; Towns and Adams 2000) regulate the responses of not only those directly involved in intimate partner violence situations, but also frontline agents of the state charged with enacting and challenging the protections under the domestic violence acts. Such narratives exist as part of the dangers and turbulence of tangible acts of violence, the force of which exists beyond the reach of law but are also refracted by law.

Scholarship on intimate partner violence in the Caribbean points to the inconsistent response of law enforcement in their attempts at policing gendered violence, especially when compared to other forms of violence listed as part of the criminal codes (Danns and Parsad 1989; DeShong and Haynes 2016; Hayes et al. 2018; Robinson 2004). This inconsistent response to intimate partner violence exists in the context of a regional and national legal framework, which simultaneously outlines and limits official state attempts at remediation. Interviews with nineteen female survivors of intimate partner violence (in my previous research) confirm a lack of consistency in police response (DeShong 2018). While the police officers interviewed as part of the research for this chapter all agree that intimate partner violence requires serious attention, they admit to responding in ways that are more conciliatory toward the accused, when compared to other violent crimes. In explaining why he does not agree with arresting someone for the first report of intimate partner violence, one police officer, named here as Keith, explains:

> Domestic violence, I mean it don't really happen all of a sudden just like that. Domestic violence is like something that's been building, building, building. . . . So I think it's somewhat different compared to the [other crimes]. Cause I don't think, it's just like at the spur of the moment. Something has to be happening in the home that would cause one of the party to reach to that point, because it's love you know, and for you to move from love to hate, it has to be, it definitely has to be something that has been building, building over that period of time.

Love, intimacy and family dynamics function to qualify intimate partner violence as less than ordinary violence. Framing violence as an accumulation of actions and emotions that will eventually explode is a move that also allows for the externalization of responsibility. These explanations figure prominently not only in how meaning is attached to violence, but they also have material effects in how the police respond. The endorsement of violence as build-up – a build-up animated by love – influences societal response to violence in general. Police officers were asked about their knowledge of the mandatory arrest clause in the amendments to the Domestic Violence Act in St Vincent and the Grenadines, based on the adoption of the OECS Domestic Violence Bill, and they all expressed knowledge of this new requirement by the police. Notwithstanding the existence of protection orders in the CARICOM-driven process and the subsequent amendments to the legislation created under the OECS bill, a combination of affective, personal, social and institutional arrangements often militate against initiating such protections.

Furthermore, Tracy Robinson (2004, 12) observes:

> Some police officers who see victims routinely suggest they get protection orders under the new legislation, ignoring their responsibilities to put the criminal justice process in motion.

Ironically, the legislation has in some instances meant that domestic violence is pigeonholed as a family law matter, effectively sidestepping its criminal dimensions. This can have deadly consequences, as seen with the number of women, in Trinidad especially, who have been murdered while they had valid protection orders against the murderers.

Robinson (2018), in a recent presentation, argues that "loving law" often masks the more complex relations of power out of which law is created. In other words, the high esteem within which law is held militates against an understanding of intimate partner/ domestic violence as enmeshed within complex relations of power, and how such relations are often reproduced in law, as well as by mechanisms of and agents operating within the criminal justice system.

Addressing Silences in the Domestic Violence Act through the Caribbean Common Law Tradition

Countries formerly colonized by Britain inherited a legal system in which precedence in law, or what Robinson (2007, 120) calls a system of judge-made or non-statutory law, also emerged in contrast to "a judicial interpretation of legal text such as a statute or constitution". This principle of legal precedence can be observed in how judges rule in intimate partner/domestic violence cases in ways that advance the legal framework, sometimes exposing the narrow conceptualization of violence outlined in the regional domestic violence legislative framework. The failure of legislation to define violence in intimate relationships as repeated, structurally produced and maintained, and involving a constellation of abusive and often non-physical acts, can affect the ability of presiding judges and magistrates to mitigate harms in such cases. However, in some instances, judgments reflect a consciousness among presiding judges and magistrates well beyond the narrowly defined understandings of domestic violence included in early versions of the model legislation. In my interview with a public prosecutor, referred to here as Ramon, he made the following observation:

> I think different persons have different views in relation to different offences. Even judges, you know, judges might have their own views, their own personal views in relation to domestic violence. I know Justice A treats it as something very seriously. When you read her judgements you would see that one of the things she had in mind was to send a message to society, you know, you'll see it in the judgement. I know Justice B. He had a very serious view. He took a very serious view of domestic violence as well. In fact, there were several cases where women were before the court charged with murder, murdering their common law spouses. And in those cases they pleaded guilty to the lesser account of manslaughter, and when the facts were read out in court and they indicated that, you know, there was a relationship and the deceased partner was an abuser, was aggressive and so on, he would send that person, he would send that female home. If you had done two years on remand, he would say that is the sentence, you know, sentence the person to two years or three years, and that would be the time they already spent on remand so that is time served. But he would say that any person who dies in those circumstances where they were abusing a woman, they are the art of their own demise; that was his position.

In defining domestic violence, both the original acts informed by the model legislation and the revisions to the acts under the OECS Domestic Violence Bill do not account for this form of violence as repeated, over the course of the relationship and often unreported through the official channels of the state. The effort by the court, through presiding judges, to take repeated violence into account in cases of homicide (which is treated under the criminal code) is an effect of the consciousness-raising and public education on intimate partner/domestic violence led by feminist and women's rights activists in the region. However, the inconsistencies in how such judgments are made should also be noted.

The examples Ramon provided were corroborated in my analysis of case files of violent crimes involving intimate partners. Of the seven case files reviewed, two women were charged with a homicide offence. The original charge of murder was later commuted to manslaughter, based on overwhelming evidence of reported violence by their deceased partners. Two defence attorneys interviewed also pointed to the use of provocation as a legal defence in cases where women who killed their partners experienced repeated violence over the course of the relationship. Provocation, as a defence in law, was also cited by the lawyers interviewed in cases where men killed their female partners and defined their violence as "crimes of passion", a point I shall return to in the following section. Ramon highlighted specific rulings by two High Court judges that were consistent with an understanding of intimate partner violence as repeated. However, he implies that all presiding judges do not necessarily share this understanding of violence in the context of intimacy.

Crimes of Passion: "Man Can't Tek Butt"

Infidelity as a rationalization for violence appears in scripts produced in media and interviews with women and men affected, as well as those conducted with agents of the state (DeShong and Haynes 2016; DeShong 2018). Research on men who kill their intimate partner reveals that, although these men have a history of violence against their victims, they are often situated as existing outside of the category of an "ordinary killer" (Dobash et al. 2004). Again, where domestic violence legislation is silent on the context within which intimate partner violence and intimate partner homicide occurs, agents within the criminal justice system produce understandings informed by socially available explanatory frameworks, as well as so-called mitigating factors as defined in the criminal codes. A defence attorney, referred to here as Geoffrey, explains in the following:

> Well first of all, if you kill a person in a domestic situation, by an act of domestic violence, it is a mitigating factor. It doesn't aggravate the offence. You get a lesser sentence for a crime of passion. . . . Because the law is, you know, a person wouldn't normally behave in a violent way, and especially where there is some trigger like for instance, infidelity, you know, a man just lose it and kill their partner for that. That is almost, that would almost automatically break it down to manslaughter because it's an issue of provocation, and the law is still kind of old fashioned in that way that a man, that *man can't really tek butt* like what Touch say. . . . And that they would lose, a normal person would lose their self-control if something like that is to happen. And they probably right you know, because emotionally if you come and meet your husband and a fella thing, you know if a man come and meet he wife and a man in a position you would expect that they would be some passion evoked in them, yeah, you know, so, that is a mitigating circumstance immediately. Almost all the murder cases in those circumstances I would immediately advise the client to take the manslaughter once it's on the table.

Attorneys consistently used the term "a crime of passion" and described it as a "mitigating factor" in cases of intimate partner homicide involving presumed infidelity. In these moments, domestic violence legislation fell out of the conversation and seemed to have no bearing on how they understood the legal response to violence. This was the case for both prosecutors and defence attorneys. There is serious investment in understandings and articulations of gender, and masculinity in particular, as contingent on women's fidelity. This is a consistent finding in interviews with women and men about intimate partner violence (DeShong 2015, 2018; Sukhu 2012), in media analysis of cases of intimate partner violence (DeShong and Haynes 2016; Haynes and DeShong 2017) and in how attorneys frame their explanations of what obtains in cases of intimate partner homicide. Antonio de Moya (2004) demonstrates the operation of gender, intimacy, love and violence in the "emasculating carnival", "La Fiesta de Cuernos" or the "Cuckholding Festival", which was outlawed in the Dominican Republic in 2000. During this event, a "cuckhold" of the year was chosen and greeted with a crown of horns to signal that he was the man whose partner had humiliated him most by her infidelity. The violence which ensued as part of this practice led to it being officially outlawed.

Geoffrey's reference to the 1990s Vincentian Road March by the band Touch, "Man Can't Tek Butt", titled after a popular Vincentian idiomatic expression, resonates across the society in ways that provide a readily available rationalization for men's violence in intimate relationships. In fact, women's infidelity as the ultimate act of emasculation is one of the most widely expressed themes in Calypso music across the region (Rohlehr 2004). The ease with which the attorney mobilized presumed/actual infidelity as a rationalization for men's violence in the context of heterosexual relationships, as well as its wider acceptance as a mitigating factor, makes visible the enactment of legal practice as embedded within broader social and structural dynamics of gendered power and intimacy. In other words, the enactment of law, whether in the form of domestic violence legislation, legal precedence or what Robinson (2013) refers to as judge-made law, cannot be understood outside of the historical, social and political forces in operation within a given society.

Conclusion

Outside of the interview with the former agent at the state gender machinery, Lois, who is also an activist, interviews with police officers, attorneys, counsellors and social workers revealed a lack of consciousness of the legal framework for domestic violence legislation as embedded in a wider set of social, political, local, regional and global processes. However, among police officers, prosecutors, defence attorneys, counsellors and persons working within state gender machinery in St Vincent and the Grenadines, there is a clear consciousness of the existence, content and operation of the domestic violence legislation.

The operation of legal regionalism at both the CARICOM and OECS subregional levels is evidenced in how most member states enacted legislation aimed at mitigating the effects of gendered violence in the 1990s. This was made possible, in large part, due to the activism and organizing of regional and national feminist and women's rights activists, regional research on women, and the involvement of Caribbean governments and organizations in broader global networks for gender justice. This work notwithstanding, there remains great dissonance between the intent and spirit of the law, and the operation of gender, intimacy and love in attempts at remediating violence at the national level, within the criminal justice system. Furthermore, widely held assumptions about arrangements of love and violence by agents of the state in their capacity as members of law enforcement and as lawyers, inter alia, function to limit intended protections under revised versions of the legislation. Tracy Robinson (2004) has argued that the rule-making capacity of courts provides a space in which to strengthen the administration of justice in cases involving gendered violence. This is particularly important given the complexities of intimacy and love, so difficult to name in law. Enacting both the CARICOM Model Legislation on Domestic Violence and the revision to the legislation at national and regional levels has shown that, in spite of the existence of strong legislation, the role of human agents in effectively implementing said legislation is paramount. In other words, the court's capacity to appropriately enforce legislation and adjudicate in cases of intimate partner violence is dependent on the class, race and gender consciousness, investments and politics of its agents.

Notes

1. Assessing the implementation of regional legislation in St Vincent and the Grenadines is not intended to be read as representative of how lawmaking on domestic violence unfolds in other countries in the Caribbean. Instead, the intention is to trace how the process of developing domestic violence legislation regionally, manifests at the national level, in other words, a focus on the complications of regional and national lawmaking.

2. What gender means and its use as a tool of analysis for explaining gendered violence should not be taken for granted. Eudine Barriteau's (1998 and 2001) theorizing of Caribbean gender systems as inhering ideological and material dimensions in ways that are often masked in their presentation as normal and natural is applicable for exposing the operation of gender, broadly speaking. However, in societies with histories of European colonialization, gender never operates away from race, and a range of other social relations of power and difference. In much of anti-/decolonial feminist writings, gender is regarded as a colonial/modern institution (see works by Maria Lugones, 2010 and 2016; Xhercis Mendez, 2015; and Sylvia Tamale, 2020), and, as such, gender analysis in the Caribbean requires an ant-icolonial reckoning with the term "gender" itself.

3. On 18 November 2011, I attended a workshop for judges, organized by the Eastern Caribbean Supreme Court's Judicial Education Institute and the United Nations Entity for Gender Equality and Women's Empowerment (UN Women), as a presenter. At the event, there was a robust debate about whether the corroboration warning should be read out in sexual offences cases. It became clear that individual judges made the decision to issue or omit the warning before juries deliberated on the outcome of these cases.

4. See Reddock (1998, 2008) and Deare (1995) for a fuller discussion of the role of CAFRA in regional and national feminist organizing.

5. The data analysed in this chapter is drawn from interviews with seventeen police officers, counsellors, prosecutors, defence attorneys, representatives from non-state organizations and government officials in St Vincent and the Grenadines on state responses to intimate

partner violence that were conducted between 2015 and 2016. The discussion is also informed by previous research with survivors and perpetrators of intimate partner violence for over a decade, as well as my observations of the operation of state responses to gendered violence. All interviews were transcribed and analysed as part of a larger project on scripting violence in intimate relationships, which also includes a focus on media and popular culture. For the purposes of this chapter, however, I focus specifically on selected interviews with state and non-state actors to capture the fraught process of what Folade Mutota in an interview with Deborah McFee (2017) has named as the state's attempt at "legislating love".

References

Antrobus, Peggy. 2013. *The Global Women's Movement: Origins, Issues and Strategies*. London: Zed Books.

Barriteau, Eudine. 1998. "Theorizing Gender Systems and the Project of Modernity in the Twentieth-Century Caribbean". *Feminist Review* 59 (1): 186–210.

———. 2001. *The Political Economy of Gender in the Twenty-First Century Caribbean*. Houndmills: Palgrave.

CARICOM Secretariat. 1997. *Model Legislation on Issues Affecting Women*. Accessed 15 December 2017. https://caricom.org/model-legislation-on-isues-affecting-women/.

Danns, George K. and Basmat Shiw Parsad. 1989. "Domestic Violence in the Caribbean: A Guyana Case Study". Georgetown: Women's Studies Unit, University of Guyana.

Deare, Fredericka M. 1995. "Feminist Research and Action Methodology: The Experiences of the Caribbean Association for Feminist Research and Action". *Caribbean Studies* 28 (1): 30–60.

de Moya, Antonio. 2004. "Power Games and Totalitarian Masculinity in the Dominican Republic". In *Interrogating Caribbean Masculinities: Theoretical and Empirical Analysis*, edited by R. Reddock, 68–102. Kingston: University of the West Indies Press.

DeShong, Halimah A.F. 2014. "Gendered Discourses of Romantic Love/ing and Violence". In *Doing Gender, Doing Love: Interdisciplinary Voices*, edited by S. Petrella, 103–22. Oxford: Inter-Disciplinary Press.

———. 2015. "Policing Femininity, Affirming Masculinity: Relationship Violence, Control and Spatial Limitation". *Journal of Gender Studies* 24 (1): 85–103.

———. 2018. "The Language of Partner Violence in the Caribbean: A Decolonial Feminist Analysis". In *Caribbean Crime and Criminal Justice: Impacts of Post-Colonialisms and Gender*, edited by K.J. Joonsen and C. Bailey, 123–38. London: Routledge.

DeShong, Halimah A.F. and Tonya Haynes. 2016. "Intimate Partner Violence in the Caribbean: State, Activist and Media Responses". *Global Public Health* 11 (1–2): 82–94.

Dobash, Rebecca E., Russell P. Dobash, Kate Cavanagh, and Ruth Lewis. 2004. "Not an Ordinary Killer—Just an Ordinary Guy: When Men Murder an Intimate Woman Partner". *Violence Against Women* 10 (6): 577–605.

Gavey, Nicola. 2013. *Just Sex?: The Cultural Scaffolding of Rape*. London: Routledge.

Hayes, Rebecca, Christina DeJong, Souyenne Dathorne, and Velika Lawrence. 2018. "Participatory Action Research: Identifying and Addressing Sexual Violence in St. Lucia". In *Caribbean Crime and Criminal Justice: Impacts of Post-Colonialisms and Gender*, edited by K. J. Joonsen and C. Bailey, 139–56. London: Routledge.

Haynes, Tonya and Halimah A.F. DeShong. 2017. "Queering Feminist Approaches to Gender-Based Violence in the Anglophone Caribbean". *Social and Economic Studies* 66 (1/2): 105–284.

Jackson, Sue. 2001. "Happily Never After: Young Women's Stories of Abuse in Heterosexual Love Relationships". *Feminism and Psychology* 11: 305–21.

Lazarus-Black, Mindie. 2007. *Everyday Harm: Domestic Violence, Court Rites, and Cultures of Reconciliation*. Chicago: University of Illinois Press.

Lewis, Patsy. 2002. *Surviving Small Size: Regional Integration in Caribbean Ministates*. Kingston: University of West Indies Press.

Lugones, Maria. 2010. "Toward a Decolonial Feminism". *Hypatia* 24 (4): 742–59.

———. 2016. "The Coloniality of Gender". In *The Palgrave Handbook of Gender and Development*, edited by W. Harcourt, 13–33. Houndsmill: Palgrave Macmillan.

McFee, Deborah. 2017. "Caribbean Feminist Disruptions of International Public Policy, Human Security and the ATT: An Interview with Folade Mutota". *Caribbean Review of Gender Studies* 11: 269–322.

Mendez, Xhercis. 2015. "Notes toward a Decolonial Feminist Methodology: Revisiting the Race/Gender Matrix". *Transcripts* 5: 41–59.

OECS (Organisation for Eastern Caribbean States). 2007. "Draft Domestic Violence Bill". Prepared by P. Sealy-Browne. https://www.law.cornell.edu/sites/www.law.cornell.edu/files /women-and-justice/OECS-Draft-Domestic-Violence-Bill.pdf.

Pargass, Gaietry and Roberta Clarke. 2003. "Violence against Women: A Human Rights Issue Post Beijing Five Year Review". In *Gender Equality in the Caribbean: Illusion or Reality*, edited by G. Tang Nain and B. Bailey, 39–72. Kingston: Ian Randle Publishers.

Reddock, Rhoda. 1998. "Women's Organizations and Movements in the Commonwealth Caribbean: The Response to Global Economic Crisis in the 1980s". *Feminist Review* 59 (1): 57–73.

———. 2008. "Global Feminist Networks on Domestic Violence". In *Women, Crime and Social Harm: Towards a Criminology of the Global Age*, edited by M. Cain and A. Howe, 179–200. Oxford: Hart Publishing.

Robinson, Tracy. 2004. "An Analysis of Legal Change: Law and Gender-Based Violence in the Caribbean". Presented at the Caribbean Judicial Colloquium on the Application of International Human Rights Law at the Domestic Level. 17–21 May, Nassau, Bahamas.

———. 2007. "A Caribbean Common Law". *Race and Class* 49 (2): 118–24.

———. 2013. "The Properties of Citizens: A Caribbean Grammar of Conjugal Categories". *Du Bois Review: Social Science Research on Race* 10 (2): 425–46.

———. 2018. "What Do We Mean by Politics? Feminist Political Engagement: A Case Study". Presentation at Politics for Social and Environmental Justice in the Caribbean: A Regional Meeting. 24–25 March, Barbados.

Rohlehr, Gordon. 2004. "I Lawa: The Construction of Masculinity in Trinidad and Tobago Calypso". In *Interrogating Caribbean Masculinities: Theoretical and Empirical Analysis*, edited by R. Reddock, 326–403. Kingston: University of the West Indies Press.

Sukhu, Raquel, L. 2012. "Masculinity and Men's Violence against Known Women in Trinidad— Whose Responsibility?" *Men and Masculinities* 16 (1): 71–92.

Tamale, Sylvia. 2020. *Decolonization and Afro-Feminism*. Ottawa: Daraja Press.

Towns, Alison. and Peter. Adams. 2000. "If I Really Loved Him Enough, He Would Be Okay: Women's Accounts of Male Partner Violence". *Violence against Women* 6: 558–85.

UN Women (United Nations Entity for Gender Equality and Women's Empowerment) Caribbean. n.d. "GBV Developments in the Law". caribbean.unwomen.org/en/caribbean -gender-portal/caribbean-gbv-law-portal/gbv-developments-in-the-law.

Chapter 11

A Failure to Comply? Explaining Dissonance between Regional and National Migration Policy in CARICOM Using the Case of Barbados

NATALIE DIETRICH JONES

The Revised Treaty of Chaguaramas (RTC), which established the Caribbean Community (CARICOM) Single Market and Economy (CSME), envisages freedom of movement for CARICOM nationals, with mobility arrangements included in three of the five core regimes of the RTC (Prendergast 2011).[1] Yet, the CSME mobility framework operates in parallel with national policy instruments that also regulate migration. This chapter reflects on the experience of Barbados and, in particular, the events leading to a shift to a restrictionist immigration policy regime after January 2008. It juxtaposes this with an evolving framework governing intraregional mobility within the CSME. Using the case of Barbados, the chapter illustrates how national imperatives continue to shape member states' interpretation and observance of their regional commitments to freedom of movement. I argue that these and other internal (and external) factors place constraints on states, at times resulting in the sacrifice of the mobility component of the integration project.

This chapter is based on field research undertaken between October 2010 and March 2011 as part of the requirements for completion of a doctoral thesis, which had examined the lived experiences of undocumented CARICOM migrants residing in Barbados (Dietrich Jones 2014). It merges two distinct sections of the thesis, each discussing a historical analysis of the regulation of migration within the context of the CARICOM integration movement and a contemporary example reflecting on Barbados's approach to the management of undocumented intraregional migration. Through this analysis, this chapter advances scholarship on contemporary Caribbean migration and, in particular, national responses to the increase in undocumented migration in the region (IOM 2005; IOM 2008). It contributes to an emerging body of literature which aims to explore intraregional migration within CARICOM and the CSME from a range of disciplinary, theoretical and methodological perspectives (Robinson 2020; J. Haynes 2016; Dietrich Jones 2014; Brathwaite 2014).[2]

Barbados presents an interesting case to analyse non-complementary national and regional migration policies. As indicated earlier, it provides a contemporary setting for the examination of restrictive migration policy measures, which mirror past actions undertaken by CARICOM member states. During the period under examination, other Eastern Caribbean islands faced similar constraints with managing undocumented intraregional migration. For example, Antigua and Barbuda, like Barbados, was also accused of ill treatment of Guyanese (and Jamaican) nationals and in 2010 considered introducing an amnesty (BBC 2009a, 2009b; *Gleaner* 2010). In this respect, therefore, Barbados is not unique. What does distinguish Barbados is that unlike the smaller Eastern Caribbean nations confronted with concerns of high inward migration, it was a founding member of the CSME, which is premised on the free movement of labour as a factor of production. In addition, within the context of CARICOM's internal management of policy issues, the Quasi Cabinet, Barbados has exercised leadership of the CSME (CARICOM 2020). Its adoption of a policy approach which contravened the tenets of the free movement regime thus provides a quite vivid illustration of the tensions between national and regional aspirations for development facilitated by free movement of peoples.

After this introduction, the chapter is divided into six sections. The first provides an overview of the earliest attempt at integration in the region – the West Indies Federation – and links the demise of the union to the contention surrounding freedom of movement. The second section discusses the evolution of the mobility regime within the framework of CARICOM, outlining the provisions governing freedom of movement in the RTC and other CARICOM arrangements. It highlights the fact that, prior to the CSME, integration mechanisms did not include provisions for free movement, which is significant given the existence of a deeply entrenched migration culture, discussed in the third section. I indicate that this culture, and the attendant patterns of migration, predates integration projects within the CARICOM context. This is significant as it shows that the RTC only provides partial treatment of freedom of movement, which has resulted in the exclusion of particular segments of migratory patterns in the region. As discussed in the fourth section, this can be problematic for CSME member states, like Barbados, which resort to the use of national policy to manage migration. This section thus argues that notwithstanding the existence of a regional mobility framework, national priorities at times supersede regional aspirations. I conclude by suggesting the need for greater convergence between national and regional imperatives.

A postscript has also been included to provide an overview of the operation of the CARICOM mobility regime since 2013, when this chapter was first conceptualized.[3] The arguments articulated remain relevant in light of the polemic which surrounds freedom of movement in the region, as well as concerns regarding the future of CARICOM. While Brexit encourages further scrutiny of the Caribbean integration project, the actions of member states in the sphere of migration policy, which predate Brexit, underscore the need for re-examination of the governance of migration within the CARICOM integration model.

Federation, Integration and Freedom of Movement

Regional integration in the Caribbean has its roots in the West Indies Federation (WIF) of 1958, a failed attempt by the British government to facilitate a transition to collective administration of its colonial territories. The tenuous life of the federation movement was shaped by a number of tense negotiations among its potential members. Sir Grantley Adams (former premier of Barbados) had predicted that "if it [WIF] broke up, the major causes would be differences of opinion about freedom of movement and the federal government's power to tax" (Wallace 1977, 191). These two principal issues reflected power dynamics between the larger players of the WIF – Jamaica and Trinidad – but also between Trinidad and lesser developed nations of the Windward Islands, which benefited tremendously from intraregional migration (Mordecai 1968; Wallace 1962). Prompted by the withdrawal of Jamaica following a national referendum, the WIF imploded without the further support of Trinidad (Wallace 1962).[4]

This highlights that the earliest attempt at regional integration within the (Anglophone) Caribbean was shaped, among other issues, by regional governments' reluctance to sacrifice national interests for a regional commitment to free movement of community nationals. A popular destination at the time, Trinidad did not wish to include provisions facilitating the free movement of WIF nationals in the WIF constitution (Wallace 1962). But Trinidad was not alone; similar reservations in British Honduras and British Guiana had led them to opt to remain outside of the union (Burns 1955). In addition, migration was an issue of contention even among the smaller states, with Barbados, the Leeward Islands and the Windward Islands utilizing barriers to curb migration between them (Wallace 1962). The WIF did not include provisions for the free movement of labour (Wallace 1962; Maingot 1982; Springer 1962, cited in CADRES 2004), despite a 1955 conference where Trinidad had agreed to ease restrictions on fifty-three categories of migrant workers (Burns 1955; Rohlehr 2001). Migration thus remained a contentious issue throughout WIF negotiations and the short life of the WIF.

Subsequent integration projects, such as the Caribbean Free Trade Area and CARICOM, also excluded provisions relating to migration. It is noteworthy that the Treaty of Chaguaramas, which established the CARICOM, placed no obligation on contracting parties to allow freedom of movement and implied the right of member states to restrict free entry of CARICOM nationals. Specifically, Article 38 reads, "Nothing in this Treaty shall be construed as requiring, or imposing any obligation on, a Member state to grant freedom of movement to persons into its territory whether or not such persons are nationals of other Member States of the Common Market" (The Treaty of Chaguaramas 1973). The RTC, however, contains express provisions which govern the freedom of movement of CARICOM nationals within the community, marking a departure from the previous approach to the management of migration within the region.

Towards a Mobility Regime

The absence of provisions concerning freedom of movement, prior to the RTC, reflects the Caribbean Free Trade Area and CARICOM agreements' focus on trade, as well as the extent of integration/harmonization among member states. The introduction of a mobility regime within the RTC is therefore an expression of deepening integration.

In 1989, with the Grande Anse Declaration, free movement of peoples became a fundamental part of the integration process. The Grande Anse Declaration called for the establishment of an intergovernmental committee tasked with the revision of the original treaty. The committee's work resulted in nine protocols which together comprise the RTC (CARICOM Secretariat 2011). The revised treaty, which established the CSME, makes explicit reference to free movement of community nationals in Articles 32–37 and 45–46, which relate to rights of establishment and free movement of persons, respectively (The Revised Treaty of Chaguaramas 2001).[5] Rights of establishment enable non-wage earners the right to move within the region, for the purposes of creating and managing business enterprises and providing services. The arrangements for the free movement of nationals enable ten categories of skilled nationals, including university graduates, media personnel, sportspersons, artists, musicians, teachers, nurses, artisans, persons with associate degrees and domestics, the right to live and work in another CSME territory without the need for a permit (Prendergast 2011).[6]

In addition, the RTC freedom of movement provisions are complemented by the decision taken by the CARICOM Heads of Government (HoG) in 2007 regarding hassle-free travel for CARICOM nationals. In light of this decision, all CARICOM nationals ought to be afforded ease of movement between CSME member states and the right to stay for up to six months (definite entry). Table 11.1 summarizes the fundamental differences between the various elements of the national and regional mobility frameworks.

The CSME's current mobility regime is thus characterized by conditional freedom of movement. Hassle-free travel is proscribed to six months definite entry. Similarly, free movement of labour is contained to specific categories of qualified nationals and certified non-wage earners, who are issued with relevant certification by local accreditation councils. Community nationals moving for the purposes of work must therefore fall within the ten designated categories or seek the benefits of rights of establishment; otherwise they are governed by the discretionary migration policies of destination countries (MacAndrew 2005). Under these local systems of migration management, migrants must obtain a work permit to reside and work in the host country. In this way, CARICOM nationals are treated no differently from third-party nationals.

Table 11.1. Regional versus National Mobility Frameworks in CARICOM

	Regional (CSME)		National
Type of regime	Freedom of movement	Hassle-free travel	Discretionary migration
Conditions for mobility	Skills/service provider certification	CARICOM/CSME member state national passport	Work permit required for non-certified CARICOM nationals and all third-party nationals
			Visa for non-exempt countries (specific to member states)
Duration of stay	Indefinite stay	Definite entry	Tied to duration of work permit

Sources: Author's elaboration based on Mac Andrew (2005), Prendergast (2011) and CARICOM Secretariat (2008).

A Migratory Culture

The provisions regarding freedom of movement underscore the importance of the movement of labour as a factor of production within the CSME. The West Indian Commission, which was also established by the Grand Anse Declaration to review the way forward for CARICOM in the wake of accelerated globalization, recognized this when it drafted its findings. Freedom of movement was one of the key areas of foci of the commission, which made recommendations regarding hassle-free travel for all CARICOM nationals and freedom of movement of skilled nationals. Undergirding these recommendations was what the commission referred to as a "history of movement", in particular among the Eastern Caribbean states (the West Indian Commission 1992, 140).

Migration is a well-established element of Caribbean consciousness and culture. As Marshall observes, "people have been moving out of their islands, almost continuously, for 150 years" (1982, 6). With the abolition of slavery in the 1830s, the process of (voluntary) intraregional migration increased significantly when migrants travelled among the island and mainland territories to work on sugar plantations (Ferguson 2003; Brown 2005). The period 1885–1920 was a high-point for regional mobility, with significant intra-Caribbean migration from the Anglophone Caribbean to the Latin and Dutch Caribbean (Marshall 1982; Thomas-Hope 2001).

The Caribbean's migratory culture thus predates, considerably, attempts within the region to integrate; moreover, it exceeds the geographical scope of the integration project within the insular Caribbean, as migrants have moved to other destinations within the Caribbean Basin. Thus, within the context of CARICOM, most intraregional migration has taken place outside of a formal regime governing intraregional mobility.

Yet, the selectivity of the categories of persons who can benefit under the provisions related to the free movement of skilled professionals and self-employed individuals results in a framework that is at odds with the deeply embedded culture of intraregional migration, especially as contemporary intraregional migration is typically constituted by labour migration (IOM 2008). The migratory culture, as well as unfamiliarity with the rules governing freedom of movement within the CSME, has thus produced a cohort of undocumented migrants who travel within the framework of CSME but ultimately end up in breach of local policy. This is so, as they overstay the period of definite entry (afforded through hassle-free travel) and reside and work without a permit, contrary to the requirements of discretionary national regimes. The following blurb from the CSME website highlights how migrants may (mis)interpret freedom of movement:

> Free movement of skills is not a right to permanent residency or citizenship!
>
> There are currently no rights regarding free movement solely for purposes of residency or permanent naturalisation or citizenship. If a person wishes to migrate from one CARICOM state to live in another, he/she must still apply for residency or citizenship, in accordance with the laws of the host country.
>
> The persons who are eligible for free movement of skills/labour must be engaged in some kind of legitimate economic activity in the CSME as either a wage earner or a non-wage earner. (CARICOM Secretariat CSME Unit 2013)

It should be noted that undocumented migration is not new to the region.[7] However, migrants' perception of an inherent right to mobility (based on an entrenched migratory culture), as well as an "open" intraregional border, results in migration that falls outside of the three CSME regimes. High unemployment levels in sending countries, as well as high levels of growth in the productive sector in receiving countries (and attendant improvements in social equality), continue to fuel migration movements within the region (Pizarro and Villa 2006; Addy 2003).

The region's experience demonstrates that governments have engaged flexible policy regimes, which accommodate migrants during times of need. During times of crisis, which can take the form of global economic downturn, high inward migration, and/or growing concerns over the extent of inward migration, there is a shift to a restrictionist agenda. For example, between 1920 and 1940, as a result of global economic downturns, a number of countries – Venezuela, Cuba and the Dominican Republic – enacted restrictive immigration legislation which discriminated against Afro-Caribbean migrants (Conway 2009). Similarly, during the 1950s and 1960s (the federation era) the absence of free movement provisions under the framework of the federation did not curtail migration to Trinidad (Maingot 1982). Maingot notes that "the expectations of an open door into the island were widespread and had created pressures which were 'formidable and intolerable'" (1982, 16). The government had thus decided that the solution was managed (planned) migration. The question thus arises, with the implementation of the CSME, how have member countries sought to manage migration? Barbados presents an interesting case study, as it demonstrates how internal and external dynamics shape the evolution of national immigration policy, and how constraints lead countries to sacrifice the mobility component of the integration project to manage migration.

The Case of Barbados

After years of a pro-integrationist agenda, Barbados changed course when a new political administration came to power. The following sections seek to explain the rationale behind attempts to manage migration in the island of Barbados after the Democratic Labour Party (DLP) assumed leadership of the government in 2008.

The Migration Transition

In the post-emancipation era, the decision to restrict the external mobility of enslaved labour was quickly reversed when the decline of the sugar industry made it increasingly difficult to contract labour and meet the demands of an increasing ex-enslaved population. External migration was encouraged in the later nineteenth to early twentieth century to ease population growth on the island (Roberts 1955, cited in Potter and Dann 1987). This emigration of "surplus" labour continued well into the post-independence era, when the government encouraged the migration of semi-skilled workers to the United Kingdom, the United States and other parts of the Caribbean (Tinker Salas 2011; ECLAC 2001).

The active encouragement of migration to ease the constraints of high fertility rates, high unemployment and small size transformed Barbados into a labour-exporting country. This soon began to have an impact on the sugar industry, the main foreign exchange generator up until the 1970s (ECLAC 2001), with the result that labour was

Table 11.2. CARICOM Nationals Residing in Barbados, by Country of Birth

Country	1990	2000	2010	% Change, 1990–2000	% Change, 2000–10
Bahamas	54	53	47	−2	−12
Dominica	446	410	321	−8	−27
Grenada	559	504	371	−10	−35
Guyana	2,529	4,349	6,277	58	69
Jamaica	615	844	947	27	21
St Lucia	3,279	2,805	2,073	−16	−35
St Vincent and the Grenadines	3,635	3,791	2,964	4	−27
Trinidad and Tobago	1,829	1,730	1,419	−5	−21
Other CARICOM countries	641	605	387	−6	−56
Total CARICOM countries	13,488	15,190	14,610	12	−3

Sources: Barbados Statistical Service (1990, 2002, 2013).

contracted from other islands in the Eastern Caribbean, such as St Vincent, to meet local labour demands (Marshall 1984). However, the subsequent diversification of the Barbadian economy into tourism and light manufacturing, as well as economic decline in neighbouring countries, have resulted in higher levels of inward migration in contemporary times. In 2005, inward migration was equivalent to about 10 per cent of the population (ECLAC 2006). This "transition" of Barbados to a labour-importing country has supported the industrial and service-based development of the Barbadian economy.

Barbados has therefore become a popular destination for migrants from neighbouring countries (table 11.2). Historically, Barbados attracted intraregional migrants from other Eastern Caribbean countries, in particular St Lucia and St Vincent and the Grenadines. However, post-1999, intraregional migrants to Barbados were increasingly Guyanese nationals (Barbados Statistical Service 1990, 2002). Guyanese migrants in particular are thought to play an invaluable role in the labour market. Former Barbadian prime minister Owen Arthur noted: "If it were not for Guyanese labourers in this country doing work that Barbadians no longer seem to want to do, agriculture would have collapsed" (Niles 2006). Formal recruitment of migrant labour has continued in the contemporary era for the agricultural sector (Barbados Ministry of Labour and Immigration 2009). However, in other sectors, such as tourism, construction and care work, no similar programmes exist.[8]

The Management of Migration in Barbados

The implementation of the CSME in Barbados in 2006 created a dual migration policy regime, which consisted of the regional legislative framework governing freedom of movement and subsequently hassle-free travel as described earlier, and the national (discretionary) framework (see table 11.3). The latter entailed two components: the formal regime covered by the Immigration Act Cap. 190 and an informal amnesty regime.

Table 11.3. Barbados Immigration Regime

	Framework	Beneficiaries
Regional	Revised Treaty of Chaguaramas	CSNs and non-wage earners
National	Immigration Act	All immigrants
	Amnesty system	Undocumented CARICOM nationals

CSN: CARICOM Skilled Nationals.

It is useful to recall the earlier discussion that CARICOM skilled nationals and non-wage earners would have qualified to reside and work in Barbados, once they had received the required certification. Therefore, non-CARICOM skilled nationals and third-party nationals had to obtain a permit to work and reside in Barbados as under the act; it is illegal to work without a permit and to hire persons without a permit (Barbados Immigration Act 1979).

Notwithstanding this, the Barbados private sector relied heavily on undocumented CARICOM migrants as a source of cheap and reliable labour (Walcott 2010, personal communication). As discussed earlier, Barbados has been typified by high rates of outward migration. In addition, high levels of educational attainment among the local resident population had resulted in high demand for low-skilled workers in the agricultural and service industries (including care work, tourism, construction). Thus, a tight labour market, as well as the culture of circular migration, encouraged migration to Barbados. The employment of undocumented workers became an embedded element of the Barbadian labour market, creating a shadow economy (Walcott 2010, personal communication). The informal migration policy framework no doubt contributed to inward migration, since migrants were also motivated by the possibility of a more permanent status.[9] This de facto amnesty policy enabled Caribbean nationals who had resided continuously without papers for a period of five years to regularize their status, once they were gainfully employed and had not run afoul of the law (Comissiong 2009).

Despite the contribution of CARICOM migrants to the Barbadian economy, there was significant resistance among Barbadians to perceived high levels of inward migration, in particular of Guyanese nationals. The populace shared its concerns on local radio airwaves (Niles 2006), as well as online blogs (such as the Barbados Underground and Barbados Free Press). A national poll conducted in 2006 found 59 per cent and 49 per cent of respondents were unsupportive of the then prime minister Owen Arthur's "tolerance of illegal migration" and "attitude towards the influx of Guyanese migrants", respectively (CADRES 2006). The opposition party, the DLP, had issued calls for a managed migration regime in the same year (Niles 2006). This intolerance was harnessed by the DLP during its election campaigning, and in the period following its electoral victory.

The Turn Inward

The Barbados Labour Party's defeat at national polls in 2008 resulted in a transition not merely of administrations but of political agenda and ideology, occasioning a shift to a managed migration regime. The new DLP administration established a Cabinet Sub-Committee on Immigration in June, six months after entering office (Thompson 2009).

From its deliberations, the subcommittee agreed that current levels of undocumented migration were "unacceptably high, increasingly difficult to control and pose potentially negative socio-economic challenges for the country" (Thompson 2009, 1). It should be noted that there were no official estimates available for the number of undocumented migrants residing in Barbados. In formulating the new policy, the government thus drew on extant views concerning immigration to Barbados.

The DLP's actions came at a critical period in Barbados's history as the onset of the global recession and a change in migratory patterns had fuelled greater social anxiety surrounding the levels of undocumented migration to the island (BBC 2009a; Ramjeet 2008).[10] The turn inward by the DLP, as evidenced by the introduction of reforms to the national migration policy framework encapsulated in a green paper, the end of the de facto amnesty arrangement and the introduction of an extraordinary amnesty, as well as the conduct of raids and deportations (Ferguson, 2009a, 2009b), made rights to mobility a contentious issue in intra-CARICOM relations during that period (*Antillean* 2009).[11,12] It yielded intense debate among regional scholars and political commentators about the status of freedom of movement in the CSME.[13]

Evaluating the Approach

The restrictive policy turn was complemented by other steps taken to police immigration at the border – the Sir Grantley Adams International Airport – in the form of heightened surveillance techniques and the "sifting" of undesirable migrants.[14] In 2005, the year before implementation of the CSME, 572 CARICOM nationals were refused entry into Barbados. However, in 2008, after the DLP administration assumed office, 1,165 CARICOM nationals were denied entry into the island (Ferguson 2009a). What is significant about these figures is not only the increase in turnarounds but also that they occurred in the wake of a well-publicized (and politicized) shift to managed migration. The actions of immigration officials can be viewed as part of the overall strategy of the Barbadian state to manage migration by detecting and deterring unwanted intraregional migrants.

It is important to highlight that in its entirety the DLP approach was not compliant with the provisions of the RTC. The amnesty, for example, focused on the regularization of CARICOM nationals; however, the majority of this migrant cohort had travelled to Barbados well in advance of the introduction of the CSME (Comissiong 2009). The allegations of discrimination against CARICOM nationals, in particular, Guyanese nationals, were vehemently refuted by the DLP. In response to criticisms about the new migration regime, the government had emphasized the national imperative to manage migration and, while acting on this imperative, to still meet its commitments to various international treaties and initiatives, including the CSME (*Caribbean360* 2010). The reactionary component of the policy – the introduction of an amnesty and the drafting of a more restrictive policy framework (the green paper) – thus filled a gap in the RTC, which does not currently include a governance mechanism for the management of undocumented migration within the region. It is noteworthy that Thompson was able to justify the actions of the DLP by indicating that the Barbadian government had undertaken interim action to regularize undocumented migrants (via the amnesty) in light of the absence of a consensus in CARICOM on *full* freedom of movement, as well as the absence of a community policy on managed migration (Ferguson 2009a, emphasis mine). Political elites across the region, in particular prime ministers Gonsalves of St Vincent and the Grenadines and Jagdeo of Guyana, nevertheless labelled the policies as contradictory to the "spirit of CARICOM" (BBC 2009a; Ferguson 2009b; Singh 2009).

However, pre-emptive manoeuvres to deter undocumented migration, as reflected in the ill treatment and summary repatriation of CARICOM nationals at the Grantley Adams airport, represent a failure to comply with the principle of hassle-free travel. The 2013 Caribbean Court of Justice ruling on the Shanique Myrie case underscores the significance of the 2007 HoG decision, and the corresponding responsibility of CSME member states to grant definite entry to non-nationals.[15] It is this recognition of a breach of the principles of the RTC which drew the ire of sister governments in the region following the actions of the Barbadian government. The actions of the DLP administration were seen to be especially problematic given the contribution of intraregional migrants to the development of the Barbadian economy (Davis 2009).

Conclusion: The Need for Convergence

This chapter has made three main arguments in respect of the management of migration within the CARICOM context. First, it highlighted that notwithstanding the provisions for freedom of movement within the RTC, the CSME has merely been grafted unto existing systems to manage migration at the national level. National attempts to manage inward migration therefore may on face value appear to be non-compliant with CSME provisions, despite the absence of relevant provisions within the regional framework governing freedom of movement. The response of CSME member states to actions undertaken by the Barbadian government suggest that there is dissonance regarding how nations should approach the management of migration, which does not fall under the purview of the RTC.

Second, it showed that the RTC is not comprehensive enough to address the varying types of migratory patterns which have arisen as a consequence of the embedded migration culture. While the introduction of the CSME has served to regularize particular streams of skilled labour migration, it has also resulted in the politicization of others – low-skilled and, usually, undocumented migration. That the categories covered within the RTC have been expanded suggests recognition on the part of policymakers that the RTC is incomplete. But there is much more that needs to be done to get to the point of full freedom of movement within the region.

Third, the chapter also demonstrated that there are varying levels of complicity with the intraregional mobility framework. This is most evident with the provision related to hassle-free travel. Officials acting on behalf of the state at times fail to comply with these provisions. This suggests that by and large, immigration matters remain the purview of individual states (and officials acting on their behalf), and that countries exercise their sovereignty during moments of perceived threat to economic and social stability.

The aforementioned indicates the need for convergence between national approaches to the management of migration and regional aspirations regarding freedom of movement. This is not to suggest a blanket commitment to freedom of movement irrespective of internal/external constraints. Rather, it purports a more concerted effort at the CARICOM level to address the diversity of migration patterns not dealt with within the RTC. This approach would prioritize not only the interests of those countries served by intraregional migration but also the interest of CARICOM peoples. Such a policy would therefore need to take into account the encouragement of a regional identity. It is not merely that migration is seen as a "problem" during times of decline, but also that responses are increasingly xenophobic, especially as CARICOM citizens continue to be referred to as "foreigners'" in other CSME member states (BBC 2009).

Before concluding, it is worthwhile to point to two key observations regarding the European experience and relate this to broader questions regarding mobility in intraregional contexts. The first is that the history of the European Union (and other regional integration mechanisms) shows that the harmonization of regional and national agendas on migration is a progressive exercise, which evolves in response to the deepening of the integration project (cf. Jurge and Lavenex 2015). Dissonance in national and regional migration agendas could therefore be explained by the stage of maturity of integration efforts, especially as shifts to freer movement are often accompanied by transitional periods in member states. Second, even full freedom of movement may not be the answer to this question of divergence of national and regional agendas. Notwithstanding a strong legislative and juridical framework, which enshrines full freedom of movement as a foundational element of the EU community, member states still exert control over immigration, implementing at their discretion policies which thwart (citizens') free movement and access to rights tied to free movement. Thus, recognition of free movement (and its related benefits) in national jurisdictions is *conditional* on vagaries of populist sentiment and economic performance (Trimikliniotis 2009; Heindlmaier and Blauberger 2017; Schmidt, Bluaberger and Sindberg Martinsen 2018). The "openness and closure", which characterizes the European Union, may very well be a hallmark of regional integration projects which incorporate single market economies supported by free movement of peoples.

Postscript

Events which have taken place since this chapter was first conceptualized provide further support to the thesis that there is inconsistency between the regional policy framework governing freedom of movement and its application at the national level, in specific jurisdictions. Within the context of hassle-free travel, for example, immigration officials have denied Jamaican nationals definite entry in countries such as Barbados and Trinidad and Tobago (*Gleaner* 2013; Johnson 2016a, 2016b). Officials from the Ministry of Foreign Affairs and Foreign Trade in Jamaica have also noted lengthy processing periods for the verification of CARICOM skills certificates in Barbados (Reckord 2017).[16] Reports on turnarounds in the media have elicited calls for a boycott of Trinidadian products from members of the Jamaican private sector and required engagement at the ministerial level (K. Haynes 2016; *RJR News* 2016). To improve travellers' awareness of their rights under the CSME framework and of the official avenues to address alleged breaches, the Ministry of Foreign Affairs and Foreign Trade in Jamaica has prepared an advisory for travellers moving between CSME member states, and sensitization sessions have been held with key populations (Reckord 2017).[17]

In 2016, the Jamaican government called for a commission, chaired by former prime minister of Jamaica Bruce Golding, to review Jamaica's relationship with CARICOM and the Caribbean Forum (CARIFORUM). The request was prompted in part by the treatment of Jamaican nationals at the ports of entry of CSME member states (Holness 2016; Johnson 2017). The commission, in its report submitted to the Jamaican Parliament in 2017, recommended implementation of full freedom of movement, with the sole exceptions for public health and security reasons (CARICOM/CARIFORUM Review Commission 2017). Although the review had sparked concerns regarding a "JExit" from CARICOM (Nationwide News Network 2016), the move was endorsed by other CARICOM HoG who believed the exercise a stimulus for renewal of the integration initiative (Johnson 2017).

In addition to the application of restrictive national policies, which are in breach of the regional framework, it is evident that there are gaps in implementation related to facilitation of travel across the region. In 2016, a CARICOM report revealed that, with the exception of Guyana, CSME participating states were yet to amend immigration legislation to guarantee definite entry to service providers (Richards 2017). At the thirty-seventh CARICOM HoG meeting held in Guyana, member governments outlined key recommendations to ensure member states' compliance with the CARICOM mobility framework, including effecting in full the free movement regimes, as well as regular reporting of statistics on refusal of entry and the operation of the free movement regimes. These recommendations were issued despite consensus among HoG that CARICOM nationals were moving throughout the region without "hindrance" (CARICOM Secretariat 2016). Similarly, at the Twenty-Eighth Intersessional Meeting, HoG prioritized completion of the protocol on procedures relating to the facilitation of travel (CARICOM Secretariat 2017). The latter points to a deficit of implementation at the regional level and underscores the earlier point that a more comprehensive regional framework for the governance of migration should be developed to complement the regimes for free movement.

Mobility is central to the sustainability of the CSME. However, more than a decade since its implementation, national immigration policies and practices are at times dissonant with the regional policy framework, as was demonstrated with the case of Barbados. While dissonance is not the ideal, it may in fact preserve the CSME. It enables states to take steps to manage migration, where necessary, while maintaining a measure of commitment to the free movement regimes as evidenced by member states' continued participation in, and not their withdrawal from, the CSME.

However, Brexit signals caution to CARICOM heads of state (Grenade 2016) on the impact of anti-immigration discourse – which in turn fuels nationalist migration policy approaches – on key decisions regarding regional integration (Walker 2016; Johnston 2017). In addition, as explained earlier, the region's story demonstrates that migration can be a deciding factor for or against regionalism. An encouraging sign is the 2018 St Ann's Declaration. Following the 18th Special Meeting of the Conference of Heads of Government of CARICOM in Port of Spain, Trinidad and Tobago, the declaration indicated regional governments' commitment to the implementation of full freedom of movement in the next three years (CARICOM Secretariat 2018). The caveat "member states so willing", however, could facilitate maintenance of the status quo, leading to divergent national and regional imperatives in respective member states.

Notes

1. Implementation of the CSME began in 2006. To date, the goal of a single market and economy has only partially been realized with the formal implementation of the single market (CARICOM Secretariat 2011). Harmonization at the macroeconomic level has been stalled. The three regimes are rights of establishment, freedom of movement and free movement of services.

2. Brathwaite (2014) also examines the case of Barbados, discussing the ways free movement has been securitized by diverse actors in the Barbadian state.

3. The paper "Locating Regionalism within National Agendas and Contexts: An Examination of the CARICOM Mobility Framework Using the Case of Barbados", which formed the basis for this chapter, was presented in October 2013 at the SALISES Regional Integration Conference "Rethinking Regionalism: Beyond the CARICOM Integration Project". See Dietrich Jones (2013b).

4. See Mordecai (1968) and Springer (1962) for discussion of the federation movement.

5. It should be noted that not all CARICOM members have joined the CSME with one – the Bahamas – remaining outside of the CSME precisely because of concerns surrounding the potentially negative impact of migration on the economy. After some consideration by the Bahamian government, the opposition of Bahamian nationals to the free movement of peoples resulted in the Bahamas refusing to sign onto the CSME (Joseph 2005). Haiti and Montserrat also do not currently participate in the CSME.

6. The RTC originally allowed for the movement of five categories of CARICOM skilled nationals (CSNs) – university graduates, media personnel, sports persons, artists and musicians. The list of CSNs has since been expanded to these ten categories in keeping with Article 46(4)a. At the time of the research in 2010, domestics had not yet been added to the list of CSNs. In 2018, HoGs agreed to add agricultural workers, beauty service practitioners, barbers and security guards to the list (CARICOM Secretariat 2020). There is flexibility in application of the rules, with permission for exemptions of certain skilled categories in a few jurisdictions. For example, Antigua was granted a five-year exemption on the free movement of domestic workers, which was expanded for a further three years in 2015. It also had exemptions for the free movement of teachers and nurses (Butler 2015; *Jamaica Observer* 2015).

7. See, for example, Marshall (1979) with respect to undocumented Haitian migration to the Bahamas and Olwig (1998) on Nevisians in the United States Virgin Islands.

8. Introducing guest worker programmes was one of the recommendations of the green paper on immigration reform (Barbados Ministry of Labour and Immigration, 2009).

9. The informal amnesty regime is generally associated with the Barbados Labour Party, which governed Barbados between 1995 and 2008 (Comissiong 2009). While Comissiong (2009) dates the origin of this policy to 1995, Symmonds (2008) indicates that it emerged during the 1970s.

10. Between 2003 and 2005, the economy grew on average 3.6 per cent. However, there was a severe contraction in the economy of –0.2 per cent and –5.7 per cent in 2008 and 2009, respectively (Worrell 2010).

11. The implementation of the reforms seemed to have stalled following the death of Prime Minister Thompson.

12. The extraordinary amnesty effectively changed common practice placing more extraneous requirements on migrants with respect to the duration of their residence, that is, from five years (under the de facto policy) to eleven years. The time frame thus excluded

individuals who would have resided for a significant period of time but would not qualify for regularized status because they had been resident in Barbados for less than eleven years (Comissiong 2009).

13. See Davis (2009), Brathwaite (2009a, 2009b) and Girvan (2009).

14. "Sifting" refers to bio-social profiling based on race, nationality and gender. See Dietrich Jones (2013a, 2014) for a discussion on migrants' experiences prior to the introduction of the amnesty.

15. Myrie had alleged violation of her rights to free movement under CARICOM when she attempted to travel to Barbados in 2011 (*RJR News* 2013). The Caribbean Court of Justice had also ruled that where member states seek to limit the free movement of a national due to undesirability, the burden of proof rests with that member state (*Jamaica Observer* 2013).

16. In Barbados, CSME Skills Certificates issued by ministries/departments in other jurisdictions are verified by the local accreditation council.

17. The advisory can be found on the Ministry of Foreign Affairs and Foreign Trade website at http://mfaft.gov.jm/wp/caricom-travel-advisory/.

References

Addy, David Nii 2003. "Trends in Labour Migration and Its Implications for the Caribbean". In *Living at the Borderlines: Issues in Caribbean Sovereignty and Development*, edited by C. Barrow-Giles and D. Marshall, 376–93. Kingston, Jamaica: Ian Randle Publishers.

Antillean. 2009. "David Thompson to Fellow CARICOM PMs: Butt Out". 18 June. Accessed 25 May 2012. http://www.antillean.org/2009/06/18/thompson-to-caricom-pms-butt-out/.

Barbados Immigration Act, Cap. 190. 1979. Bridgetown, Barbados: Parliament of Barbados.

Barbados Ministry of Labour and Immigration. 2009. "Comprehensive Review of Immigration Policy and Proposals for Legislative Reform". Bridgetown, Barbados: Barbados Ministry of Labour and Immigration.

Barbados Statistical Service. 1990. *Population and Housing Census*. Bridgetown, Barbados: Barbados Statistical Service.

———. 2002. *Population and Housing Census*. Bridgetown, Barbados: Barbados Statistical Service.

———. 2013. *Population and Housing Census*. Bridgetown, Barbados: Barbados Statistical Service.

BBC (British Broadcasting Corporation). 2009a. "Migration Headache for CARICOM Talks", 30 June. http://www.bbc.co.uk/caribbean/news/story/2009/06/090630_caricom.shtml.

———. 2009b. "Caricom Talks Trade and Travel", 03 July. Accessed 6 August 2020. http://www.bbc.co.uk/caribbean/news/story/2009/07/printable/090703_caricomfriday.shtml.

Brathwaite, George. 2014. "CARICOM and the Politics of Migration: Securitisation and the Free Movement of Community Nationals in Barbados". Phd Thesis. Newcastle University.

———. 2009a. "Intra-regional Migration in the Caribbean" [podcast]. *Nationwide*, 12 June. Accessed 1 March 2010. http://creole-chant.blogspot.com/2009/06/nationwide-radio-postcast.html.

———. 2009b. *CARICOM and the Politics of Migration: Securitisation and the Free Movement of Community Nationals in Barbados*. Unpublished thesis (PhD), Newcastle University.

Brown, Laurence. 2005. "Experiments in Indenture: Barbados and the Segmentation of Migrant Labor in the Caribbean 1863–1865". *New West Indian Guide/Nieuwe West-Indische Gids* 79: 31–54.

Burns, Alan S. 1955. "Towards a Caribbean Federation". *Foreign Affairs* 34: 128–40.

Butler, Rory. 2015. "A&B Gets Three-Year Exemptions of Free Movement of Domestic Workers". *Antigua Observer*, 4 July. https://antiguaobserver.com/ab-gets-three-year-exemption-on-free-movement-of-domestic-workers/.

CADRES (Caribbean Development Research Services). 2004. *Freedom of Movement: The Cornerstone of the Caribbean Single Market and Economy*. Bridgetown, Barbados: Caribbean Development Research Services.

———. 2006. *Final Quarter Poll Report Part II*. Bridgetown, Barbados: Caribbean Development Research Services.

Caribbean360. 2010. "Illegal Migrants Stressing Barbados Resources", 29 March. Accessed 16 May 2010. http://www.caribbean360.com/news/illegal_migrants_stressing_barbados _resources.html.

CARICOM Secretariat. 2008. *Single Market and Economy Free Movement – Travel and Work*. Georgetown, Guyana: CARICOM Secretariat.

———. 2011. "The Caribbean Community". Georgetown, Guyana: CARICOM Secretariat. http://www.caricom.org/jsp/community/community_index.jsp?menu=community.

———. 2016. *Communiqué Issued at the Conclusion of the 37th Regular Meeting of the Conference of Heads of Government of the Caribbean Community (CARICOM), 4–6 July, Georgetown Guyana*. Georgetown, Guyana: CARICOM Secretariat.

———. 2017. *Communiqué – 28th Intersessional Meeting of CARICOM Heads of Government, 16–17 February, Georgetown Guyana*. Georgetown, Guyana: CARICOM Secretariat.

———. 2018. *St. Ann's Declaration on the CSME – 18th Special Meeting of the Conference of Heads of Government of CARICOM, 3–4 December, Port-of-Spain, Trinidad and Tobago*. Georgetown, Guyana: CARICOM Secretariat.

———. 2020. "Quasi Cabinet – Portfolio Allocation". Georgetown, Guyana: CARICOM Secretariat. https://caricom.org/our-community/who-we-are/quasi-cabinet-portfolio -allocation/.

CARICOM Secretariat CSME Unit. 2013. "Skilled Labour: What It's Not!". Bridgetown, Barbados: CARICOM CSME Unit. Accessed 14 February 2012. http://www.csmeonline.org /en/skilled-labour/item/91-what-its-not.

Comissiong, David. 2009. "Open Letter to the Prime Ministers of CARICOM", 17 May. *Norman Girvan Blog*. Accessed 4 February 2010. http://www.normangirvan.info/open-letter-to -caricom-prime-ministers-on-the-immigration-crisis/.

Conway, Dennis. 2009. "The Caribbean Diaspora". In *Understanding the Contemporary Caribbean*. 2nd edition, edited by R. Hillman and T. D'Agostino, 367–90. Boulder, CO: Lynne Rienner Publishers.

Davis, Annalee. 2009. "Thoughts on Prime Minister Thompson's New 'Amnesty'". *Stabroek News*, 25 May. https://www.stabroeknews.com/2009/features/05/25/thoughts-on-prime -minister-thompson%E2%80%99s-new-%E2%80%9Camnesty%E2%80%9D/.

Dietrich Jones, Natalie. 2013a. "In Defence of Barbados?" *The Gleaner*, 13 October. http:// jamaica-gleaner.com/gleaner/20131013/focus/focus1.html.

———. 2013b. "Locating Regionalism within National Agendas and Contexts: An Examination of the CARICOM Mobility Framework Using the Case of Barbados". Presented at the SALISES Regional Integration Conference, Rethinking Regionalism: Beyond the CARICOM Integration Project, University of the West Indies, Jamaica, 9 October.

———. 2014. *The Ma(r)king of Complex Border Geographies and Their Negotiation by Undocumented Migrants: The Case of Barbados*. Unpublished thesis (PhD), The University of Manchester.

ECLAC (Economic Commission for Latin America and the Caribbean). 2001. *An Analysis of Economic and Social Development in Barbados: A Model for Small Island Developing States*. Port-of-Spain, Trinidad: ECLAC.

———. 2006. *Migración Internacional/International Migration*. Santiago, Chile: América Latina y el Caribe Observatorio Demagráfico/Latin America and the Caribbean Demographic Observatory.

Ferguson, Heppilena. 2009a. "Barbados Open to 'Structured' Readmission of Overstays". *Stabroek News*, 2 July. http://www.stabroeknews.com/2009/archives/07/02/barbados-open -to-%E2%80%98structured%E2%80%99-readmission-of-overstays/.

———. 2009b. "Fewer Guyanese Deported Recently from Barbados – Reports". *Stabroek News*, 21 July. http://www.stabroeknews.com/2009/archives/07/21/fewer-guyanese-deported -recently-from-barbados-reports/.

Ferguson, James. 2003. *Migration in the Caribbean: Haiti, the Dominican Republic and Beyond.* London: Minority Rights Group International.

Girvan, Norman. 2009. "Intra-regional Migration in the Caribbean" [podcast]. *Nationwide*, 10 June. Accessed 1 March 2010. http://creole-chant.blogspot.com/2009/06/nationwide -radio-postcast.html.

Gleaner. 2010. "Committee Recommends Antigua Immigrant Amnesty", 12 February. http:// jamaica-gleaner.com/power/16855.

———. 2013. "Jamaicans, Guyanese Top List of CARICOM Nationals Denied Entry to Barbados", 8 March. http://jamaica-gleaner.com/gleaner/20130308/news/news5.html.

Grenade, Wendy. 2016. "Paradoxes of Regionalism and Democracy. Brexit's Lessons for the Commonwealth". *The Round Table* 105 (5): 509–18.

Haynes, Jason. 2016. "The Right to Free Movement of Persons in Caribbean Community (CARICOM) Law: Towards 'Juridification'?" *Journal of Human Rights in the Commonwealth* 2 (2): 57–66.

Haynes, Kejan. 2016. "PM Avoids Jamaica Boycott . . . Calms Angry Jamaican Businessmen". *Trinidad Express*, 20 July. Accessed 24 July 2017. http://www.trinidadexpress.com/20160720 /news/pm-avoids-jamaica-boycott.

Heindlmaier, Anita. and Michael Blauberger. 2017. "Enter at Your Own Risk: Free Movement of European Citizens in Practice". *West European Politics* 40 (6): 1198–217.

Holness, Andrew. 2016. "Launch of CARICOM Review Commission" [speech]. 28 June. Office of the Prime Minister, Kingston, Jamaica. 28 June. http://opm.gov.jm/speech/7616-2/.

IOM (International Organization for Migration). 2005. *Exploratory Assessment of Trafficking in Persons in the Caribbean Region.* Washington, DC: International Organization for Migration.

———. 2008. *World Migration Report 2008: Managing Labour Mobility in the Evolving Global Economy.* Washington, DC: International Organization for Migration.

Jamaica Observer. 2013. "Executive Summary of the Judgement in the Shanique Myrie Case", 4 October. http://www.jamaicaobserver.com/news/Executive-Summary-of-the-judgement -in-Shanique-Myre-case.

———. 2015. "Antigua Wants Another Stay on Free Movement of Domestic Workers", 28 April. http://www.jamaicaobserver.com/news/Antigua-wants-another-stay-on-free-movement-of -domestic-workers.

Johnson, Jovan. 2016a. "CARICOM Report Condemns Member States for Free Movement Breaches". *The Gleaner*, 6 July. http://jamaica-gleaner.com/article/lead-stories/20160706 /caricom-report-condemns-member-states-free-movement-breaches.

———. 2016b. "Trinidad Denied 320 Jamaicans Entry Last Year". *The Gleaner*, 16 July. http:// jamaica-gleaner.com/article/lead-stories/20160716/trinidad-denied-320-jamaicans-entry -last-year.

———. 2017. "Golding Commission Submits CARICOM Review Report to PM". *The Gleaner*, 1 April. http://jamaica-gleaner.com/article/lead-stories/20170401/golding-commission -submits-caricom-review-report-pm.

Johnston, Ian. 2017. "Brexit: Anti-immigration Prejudice Major Factor in Deciding Vote, Study Finds". *The Independent*, 21 June. Accessed 24 July 2017 http://www.independent .co.uk/news/uk/politics/brexit-racism-immigrant-prejudice-major-factor-leave-vote-win -study-a7801676.html.

Joseph, Anita. 2011. "The Bahamas Rejects the Creation of CSME, Thus Compromising CARICOM's Integration Bid". *Council on Hemispheric Affairs*, 11 July. http://www.coha.org /the-bahamas-rejects-the-creation-of-csme-thus-compromising-caricom%E2%80%99s -integration-bid/.

Jurge, Flavia and Sandra Lavenex. 2015. *ASEAN Economic Community: What Model for Labour Mobility?* NCCR Trade Working Paper No. 2015/02/January.

Mac Andrew, Stephen. 2005. "Migration in the CARICOM Single Market and Economy Caribbean". Presented at the Caribbean Expert Group Meeting on Migration, Human Rights and Development. 14–15 September, Port of Spain, Trinidad.

Maingot, Anthony. 1982. "Caribbean Migration as a Structural Reality". Kimberley Green Latin American and Caribbean Center (LACC). LACC Occasional Paper Series, Paper 49.

Marshall, Dawn. 1979. *"The Haitian Problem": Illegal Migration to the Bahamas*. Kingston, Jamaica: Institute of Social and Economic Research, University of the West Indies (Mona).

———. 1982. "The History of Caribbean Migrations". *Caribbean Review* XI: 6–9 and 52–53.

———. 1984. "Vincentian Contract Labour Migration to Barbados: The Satisfaction of Mutual Needs?" *Social and Economic Studies* 33 (3): 63–92.

Mordecai, John. 1968. *The West Indies: The Federal Negotiations*. London: Allen and Unwin.

Nationwide News Network. 2016. "Holness Not Contemplating a CARICOM 'JExit'", 28 June. Accessed 6 August 2020. https://nationwideradiojm.com/holness-not-contemplating-a -caricom-jexit/.

Niles, Bertram. 2006. "Are Guyanese Welcome in Barbados?" *BBC Caribbean*, 6 September. http://www.bbc.co.uk/caribbean/news/story/2006/09/060906_guyaneseinbdos.shtml.

Olwig, Karen Fog. 1998. "Constructing Lives: Migration Narratives and Life Stories among Nevisians". In *Caribbean Migration: Globalised Identities*, edited by M. Chamberlain, 63–80. London: Routledge.

Pizarro, Jorge and Miguel Villa. 2006. "International Migration in Latin America and the Caribbean: A Summary View of Trends and Patterns". Presented at the *Caribbean Expert Group Meeting on Migration, Human Rights and Development in the Caribbean*, 14–15 September, Port of Spain, Trinidad.

Potter, Robert and Graham Dann. 1987. *Barbados*. Oxford, UK and Santa Barbara, CA: Clio Press.

Prendergast, David. 2011. "Labour Migration in the Context of the CARICOM Single Market and Economy". Presentation at the Global Forum on Migration and Development, 7–8 September, Kingston, Jamaica.

Ramjeet, Oscar. 2008. "Immigrants a Headache for Barbados Says Ambassador to CARICOM". *CaribbeanNetNews*, 6 November. http://www.caribbeannewsnow.com/caribnet/barbados /barbados.php?news_id=12013&start=520&category_id=26.

Reckord, Hartman. 2017. "Foreign Ministry Irons Out Kinks in CSME". *Jamaica Information Service*, 13 June. http://jis.gov.jm/foreign-ministry-ironing-kinks-gsat/.

Richards, Ken. 2017. "CSME's Struggling Status Up for Discussion at CARICOM Summit in Grenada". *CaribbeanNewsNow*, 5 July. Accessed 24 July 2017. http://mail.caribbeannewsnow .com/headline-CSME%27s-struggling-status-up-for-discussion-at-CARICOM-summit-in -Grenada-34945.html.

RJR News. 2013. "CCJ Reserves Judgement in Shanique Myrie Case", 10 April. Accessed 30 April 2013. http://rjrnewsonline.com/local/ccj-reserves-judgment-in-shanique-myrie-case.

———. 2016. "JCC Disagrees with Proposal to Boycott T&T Products", 4 April. Accessed 24 July 2017. http://rjrnewsonline.com/local/jcc-disagrees-with-proposal-to-boycott -tt-products.

Robinson, Oral. 2020. *Migration, Social Identities and Regionalism within the Caribbean Community Voices of Caribbean People*. London: Palgrave MacMillan.

Rohlehr, Gordon. 2001. "A Scuffling of Islands: A Dream of Reality of Caribbean Unity in Poetry and Song". In *New Caribbean Thought: A Reader*, edited by B. Meeks and L. Folke, 265–309. Kingston: University of the West Indies Press.

Schmidt, Susanne, Michael Blauberger, and Dorte Sindberg Martinsen. 2018. "Free Movement and Equal Treatment in an Unequal Union". *Journal of European Public Policy* 25 (10): 1391–402.

Singh, Ricky. 2009. "CARICOM's Migrant Problem". *Trinidad Express*, 3 June. Accessed 7 September 2017. http://www.trinidadexpress.com/commentaries/Caricom_s_migrant _problem-115411194.html.

Springer, Hugh. 1962. *Reflections on the Failure of the First West Indian Federation*. Cambridge, MA: Centre for International Affairs, Harvard University.

Symmonds, Andrea. 2008. "Towards a Regional Policy on Migration". *Sir Arthur Lewis Memorial Conference 2008*, 25–27 September, St. Augustine University of the West Indies (St. Augustine).

The Revised Treaty of Chaguaramas. 2001. Georgetown, Guyana: CARICOM Secretariat.

The Treaty of Chaguaramas. 1973. Georgetown, Guyana: CARICOM Secretariat.

The West Indian Commission. 1992. *Time for Action: Report of the West Indian Commission*. Black Rock, Barbados: West Indian Commission.

Thomas-Hope, Elizabeth. 2001. "Trends and Patterns of Migration to and from the Caribbean Countries". *Revista Notas de Poblacion*, Special Issue.

Thompson, David. 2009. "Ministerial Statement on a New Comprehensive Immigration Policy for Barbados" [speech], 5 May. Parliament of Barbados, Bridgetown, Barbados.

Tinker Salas, Keith. 2011. *The Migration of Peoples from the Caribbean to the Bahamas*. Gainesville: University of Florida Press.

Trimikliniotis, Nicos. 2009. "Exceptions, Soft Borders and Free Movement of Workers". In *Rethinking the Free Movement of Workers: The European Challenges Ahead*, edited by P. Minderhoud and N. Trimikliniotis, 135–54. Nijmegen: Wolf Legal Publishers.

Walcott, Tony. 2010. *Conversation with Natalie Dietrich Jones*, 24 November.

Walker, Peter. 2016. "Poorer Voters' Worries on Immigration Fuelled Brexit Vote, Study Finds". *The Guardian*, 15 December. Accessed 24 July 2017. https://www.theguardian.com /politics/2016/dec/15/poorer-voters-worries-immigration-fuelled-brexit-vote-study-finds.

Wallace, Elisabeth. 1962. "The West Indies Federation: Decline and Fall". *International Journal* 17 (3): 269–88.

———. 1977. *The British Caribbean from the Decline of Colonialism to the End of Federation*. Toronto: University of Toronto.

Worrell, DeLisle. 2010. "The Barbados Economy in 2009 and Prospects for 2010". Statement at the Central Bank of Barbados, Bridgetown, Barbados, 13 January.

Chapter 12

New Hope for Caribbean Integration

The Revised Treaty of Chaguaramas and the Jurisdiction of the Caribbean Court of Justice

ADRIAN D. SAUNDERS

The Revised Treaty of Chaguaramas (RTC) established the Caribbean Community (CARICOM) including the CARICOM Single Market and Economy (CSME). The treaty is one of CARICOM's responses to the challenges posed by the forces of globalization and liberalization. The RTC is premised on the commitment of the CARICOM states[1] to deepen regional economic integration in order to achieve sustained economic development based on international competitiveness, coordinated economic and foreign policies, functional cooperation and enhanced trade and economic relations with third states.[2] It represents a critical milestone in the path taken by these states "to avoid the looming threat of marginalization".[3]

The centrepiece of the RTC, the feature that most fundamentally distinguishes it from its predecessor Treaty of Chaguaramas,[4] is the enshrinement of a court of law to hear and determine disputes.[5] As the preamble to the RTC notes, "the Caribbean Court of Justice is essential for the successful operation of the CSME". Although the Caribbean Court of Justice (CCJ) is pivotal to the operation of the CARICOM, the court is not established as an organ of the CARICOM, a measure no doubt taken to strengthen the court's independence.[6]

A distinctive feature of the CCJ is that it is not only the principal dispute resolution forum for the CARICOM, but it is also a final appellate court in civil and criminal cases for those CARICOM states that opt to use it as such in replacement of the Judicial Committee of the Privy Council.[7] So as to distinguish it from the court's appellate jurisdiction, the court's RTC jurisdiction is therefore referred to as the original jurisdiction of the court as court hearings are simultaneously both original and the decisions on them final. Evidence is led before the judges of the court, legal submissions are made and there is no appeal against the court's decision.

In its original jurisdiction, the CCJ is mandated both to interpret the RTC as well as to apply its provisions. The court is invested with "compulsory and exclusive jurisdiction to hear and determine disputes concerning the interpretation and application of the Treaty".[8] Unlike the case in the domestic courts of almost all CARICOM states, the court does not apply the common law.[9] The court applies such rules of international law as may be applicable.[10] In order to guarantee, at the local level, consistency and uniformity, national courts must refer to the CCJ for its determination any question arising before them that concerns the interpretation or application of the treaty.[11]

Further, Article 212 of the RTC confers on the court the authority to deliver advisory opinions concerning the interpretation and application of the treaty at the request of member state parties to a dispute or the community. The legal architecture therefore provides the court with significant scope to ensure that CARICOM states conform to the obligations they have voluntarily undertaken in the RTC.

The statutory framework that supports the court's original jurisdiction includes the RTC itself (in particular Articles 211–222); the Agreement Establishing the Court (CCJ Agreement); Agreements, Resolutions and Decisions of the Conference of CARICOM Heads of Government and other Organs of CARICOM; and the Original Jurisdiction Rules of the court.[12]

The CCJ Agreement has been enacted into domestic law by CARICOM member states.[13] Invariably the enactment statute has given the Original Jurisdiction Rules the force of law.[14] The CCJ delivers a single judgment in its original jurisdiction. No dissenting opinions are permitted, a rule the judges have imposed upon themselves.[15] Judgments of the court constitute legally binding precedents for parties in proceedings before the court unless such judgments have been revised in keeping with the provisions of the treaty.[16] CARICOM states recognize the jurisdiction of the CCJ as compulsory, ipso facto and without special agreement.[17] In the event of a dispute as to whether the CCJ has jurisdiction, the matter is to be determined by decision of the court itself.[18]

Article 211 of the RTC establishes the parameters of the court's original jurisdiction in contentious proceedings. The court is entitled to hear:

(a) disputes between member state parties to the agreement;
(b) disputes between the member state parties to the agreement and the community;
(c) referrals from national courts of the member state parties to the agreement; and
(d) applications by persons in accordance with Article 222

concerning the interpretation and application of the treaty.

To date, all the contentious matters brought before the court have fallen within the aforementioned fourth category (d).[19] This is not entirely surprising. With respect to (a) and (b), the RTC contains a raft of alternative measures that can be utilized to produce a non-litigious settlement of any such dispute. These measures include good offices, mediation, entering into consultations, conciliation, arbitration and third-party intervention.[20] While there is no obligation on states first to exhaust these modes of settlement for resolution of their disputes, one may well believe that this will normally be the case in practice.[21]

On 6 March 2020, the CARICOM formally made a request of the court for an advisory opinion. This was the first occasion any such request was made. The request sought the court's advice on two questions pertaining to Article 46 of the treaty (which references the movement of skilled community nationals) and Article 27(4) (which makes provision for a member state to opt out of obligations arising from a decision of a competent organ of CARICOM). The request came in the wake of decisions by the conference to permit the states of Antigua and Barbuda and St Kitts and Nevis temporarily to opt out of a conference decision to widen the net of skilled nationals entitled to move and work freely throughout the community. Could a member state lawfully opt out of such a decision? Does the principle of non-reciprocity enable nationals of those member states which opt out of a decision under Article 27(4) nevertheless to derive the benefits of the decision? In response to the first question, the court advised that in all the circumstances it was lawful for the states in question to request and for the conference to grant the opt-outs in question. In response to the second question, the court advised that the principle of non-reciprocity applies to enlargement decisions, so that nationals of the opting out states were entitled to enjoy the benefits of the enlargement decision during the period their respective states were permitted to opt out of the obligations.[22]

Somewhat surprisingly, there has been to date no referral to the CCJ from a national court or tribunal. It is unclear whether this is the result of courts and counsel alike not being sufficiently alert to the possibility, and indeed the necessity, for referring appropriate questions to the CCJ. Whatever the reason, the court has been engaged in efforts to address this issue. The primary thrust has been in developing a manual for referral proceedings which will provide to judges and officials of courts and tribunals relevant information about the substantive and procedural aspects in relation to referrals to the CCJ and also serve as a training guide.

Private Entities and the Revised Treaty of Chaguaramas

CARICOM often refers to itself as "an Association of sovereign states", and the CCJ has had to confront the assertion that such sovereignty implied that states, entitled to act in accordance with their best interests within their own borders, could not be sued by individuals before the CCJ.[23] In *TCL v The Community*, the court responded robustly to any such assertion.[24] The court ruled that by signing and ratifying the RTC, the states had transformed the erstwhile voluntary arrangements in CARICOM into a rule-based system, thus creating and accepting a regional system under the rule of law. A challenge by a private party, whether to decisions of the CARICOM or of a state, was therefore not only permissible, but itself a manifestation of such a system. Neither the functioning of the CARICOM nor the exercise of state sovereignty is unduly constrained by any such challenge.[25] Indeed, stated the court, it is by the exercise of state sovereignty that each state has opted voluntarily to become a member of the CSME and thus participate in a regime that guarantees to the state rights that are more extensive than were hitherto enjoyed. States, and their nationals, have the right to call to account before the CCJ any member state for breaches of the RTC. This is a right which carries with it a reciprocal obligation on the part of all states to abide by the treaty. At para. 52 of the judgment[26] the court noted that

if binding regional decisions can be invalidated at the Community level by the failure on the part of a particular State to incorporate those decisions locally the efficacy of the entire CARICOM regime is jeopardized and effectively the States would not have progressed beyond the pre 2001 voluntary system that was in force. The original jurisdiction of the Court has been established to ensure observance by the Member States of obligations voluntarily undertaken by them at the Community level.... It is the obligation of each State, having *consented to the creation of the Community obligation,* to ensure that its domestic law, at least in its application, reflects and supports Community law.

The court ensures that the CARICOM is accountable, operates within the rule of law and respects any legitimate expectations engendered in the individual. Conduct of a state that has negative consequences on the CARICOM plane cannot be excused or justified because it has been sanctioned by the local parliament.[27]

As states are usually reluctant to institute proceedings against other states, much of the court's jurisprudence has focused on the role, status and rights of private entities under the RTC and interpretation of the difficultly worded Article 222. That article, headed *Locus Standi of Private Entities*, states:

> Persons, natural or juridical, of a Contracting Party may, with the special leave of the Court, be allowed to appear as parties in proceedings before the Court where:
>
> (a) the Court has determined in any particular case that this Treaty intended that a right or benefit conferred by or under this Treaty on a Contracting Party shall enure to the benefit of such persons directly; and
>
> (b) the persons concerned have established that such persons have been prejudiced in respect of the enjoyment of the right or benefit mentioned in paragraph (a) of this Article; and
>
> (c) the Contracting Party entitled to espouse the claim in proceedings before the Court has:
>   (i) omitted or declined to espouse the claim, or
>   (ii) expressly agreed that the persons concerned may espouse the claim instead of the Contracting Party so entitled; and
>
> (d) the Court has found that the interest of justice requires that the persons be allowed to espouse the claim.

The court has stated that, in light of the prominence accorded to private economic entities in achieving the objectives of the CSME, CARICOM states clearly intended that such entities should be key actors in the regime created by the treaty and as such should be encouraged to play that role.[28] As a result of the jurisprudence of the court, we now know that the phrase "persons, natural or juridical, of a CARICOM state" is not synonymous with nationals of a contracting state as the term "national" is narrowly defined in Article 32 of the RTC.[29] A private entity seeking to institute an action is not therefore required first to meet the tests of citizenship and belonging that are to be found in Article 32 which is housed in a chapter of the treaty that grants rights peculiarly to be enjoyed by CARICOM citizens. Instead, for a company to be within the meaning of the phrase "persons, natural or juridical, of a CARICOM state", it is sufficient for it to be incorporated or registered in a CARICOM state. Individuals who are not nationals of a CARICOM state but who have a sufficient connection with such a state, as well as companies owned by CARICOM non-nationals but registered or incorporated in a CARICOM state, will have the same qualified right of access to the CCJ to complain of a breach of the treaty as do CARICOM nationals and companies controlled by such nationals. Where an entitlement to a treaty right or benefit is being asserted by virtue of any such connection, conclusive evidence in support of that connection must be readily produced. So, for example, the court determined that it was insufficient for a Grenadian citizen who attempted to enter Trinidad and Tobago on a passport issued by the United States to furnish a Grenadian driver's licence and a Grenadian voter identification card to establish conclusively his entitlement to the right to freedom of movement within CARICOM.[30]

In keeping with the ethos of promoting the role of private entities, the CCJ's decision in *TCL & TGI v Guyana*[31] demonstrates a desire to remove potential barriers that could stand in the way of access to the court by private entities. In that case the court determined that – notwithstanding the provisions of Article 222(c), which require a private entity to obtain specific or constructive permission from their own state in order to institute proceedings – it was yet possible for a private entity to bring proceedings against its own state. The court held that a literal interpretation of the provision would have placed an unduly restrictive limitation on the category of persons entitled to complain about the conduct of a CARICOM state. The CCJ cited three important reasons justifying this conclusion.[32] First, any such prohibition would frustrate the achievement of the goals of the RTC[33] because a national of a state in breach would be powerless to render that state accountable before the court for a perceived breach. Second, the treaty did not envisage that it was impermissible for a private entity to be on the opposing side of its own state in litigation because nothing in the CCJ Agreement precluded a private entity that had a substantial interest capable of being affected by a decision of the court from applying to intervene in a matter in which its own state was the defendant.[34] Third, the literal interpretation collided with Article 7 of the RTC, which proscribed discrimination on grounds of nationality only. The court reasoned that the fundamental objective of the requirement to obtain permission in order to institute proceedings was to avoid a duplication of suits; that the provision was a procedural device to avoid a state allegedly in violation being twice vexed, once by an injured private entity and again by the CARICOM state of that private entity.

The RTC rarely explicitly confers rights on private economic actors. Article 222 nevertheless speaks to the enjoyment of and prejudice to such rights as a prerequisite for accessing the court's original jurisdiction. The court addressed this seeming paradox in its early years by extracting rights from correlative obligations imposed by the treaty upon CARICOM states. Unless specifically otherwise indicated, each obligation imposed on member states (or a class of member states) collectively yields a correlative right that enures directly to the benefit of private entities throughout the entire CARICOM.[35] This principle was applied in the cases that dealt with the common external tariff. Article 82 of the RTC requires CARICOM states to establish and maintain such a tariff in respect of all goods which do not qualify for community treatment in accordance with plans and schedules set out by the CARICOM Council for Trade and Economic Development. Guyana's wrongful failure to impose the tariff on cement[36] as did Suriname's to impose it on flour[37] gave a correlative right to regional cement and flour producers to complain about the violation of the treaty by these states. In each case, the court declared the breach and ordered the state in breach immediately to impose the tariff.

Private entities must first approach the court to obtain special leave to be able to put forward the substance of their complaint. As the RTC imposes obligations only on states and the CARICOM, suits may be brought only against states or the CARICOM.[38] The court cannot entertain a suit filed against a mere institution of CARICOM, at least certainly not in circumstances where there is nothing to suggest that the institution is at the material time acting as an agent of the CARICOM.[39] A clear distinction is drawn between the organs and bodies[40] of the CARICOM on the one hand and the institutions and associate institutions of the CARICOM on the other.[41] The CARICOM implements its policies and carries out its work principally through its organs and bodies. These bodies are agents that reflect the will of the CARICOM. Although recognized as entities working within the CARICOM system, however, the acts and omissions of the institutions are not necessarily attributable to the CARICOM as are the acts and omissions of the organs and bodies. If a complaint is to be lodged against an organ or body, such complaint must really be made not against that organ or body but against the CARICOM.

At the special leave stage, in keeping with Article 222, the court is concerned to see whether the threshold for standing has been met. The article performs a gatekeeping function.[42] Its import has been examined in a line of cases.[43] The main burden on a private entity is to establish at the special leave stage that there is an arguable case that the litigant enjoys a right or benefit directly conferred under the RTC and that he, she or it has been prejudiced in the enjoyment of the same. The court will not grant leave unless the right has been directly conferred by the RTC. So, where a Dominican private entrepreneur sustained loss as a result of the possibly unlawful action by that state in denying Jamaican musical artistes entry into Dominica, the court held that the entrepreneur had no standing. The treaty right allegedly breached was one conferred directly not on the entrepreneur but on the artistes and they themselves had not sued.[44]

Only after special leave is granted will the court proceed, at a separate hearing, to entertain the substance of the complaint. At that substantive hearing, the court does not revisit the question of whether special leave should in fact have been given but instead concerns itself with discovering whether the claimant has made out its case.[45]

The Case of Shanique Myrie

Perhaps the most significant case the CCJ has tried has been the case of Shanique Myrie, a young Jamaican woman who attempted to visit Barbados for a short vacation. When she arrived at the Grantley Adams International Airport, she was denied entry, detained overnight in a cell at the airport and deported to Jamaica the following day. She alleged that, in the process, she was made to undergo a body cavity search and that her detention cell was insanitary. She claimed a right to free movement based on the combined effect of Article 45 of the RTC and a decision of the Conference of Heads of Government of the CARICOM taken at their twenty-eighth meeting ("the 2007 conference decision"). Barbados denied the humiliating conduct attributed to it but justified the other treatment on the premise that Myrie was untruthful about the identity of her Barbadian host. Barbados further submitted that the 2007 conference decision did not create any legally binding rights.

After hearing several witnesses in Jamaica and in Barbados, the court was satisfied that the facts alleged by Myrie were proved. The question was, what rights, if any, do CARICOM citizens have as a result of the 2007 conference decision? This was a decision arrived at by CARICOM Heads of Government that, on its face, committed each state to permit CARICOM citizens an automatic stay in each other's state for six months subject only to the visitor not being an undesirable person or someone who was likely to become a charge on public resources. The 2007 conference decision was always treated as valid and binding by the CARICOM Secretariat and various organs of the CARICOM.

Barbados argued that Myrie's detention and deportation could not be impugned because they were in keeping with the domestic law of Barbados, and Article 240 of the RTC is to be interpreted as suggesting that decisions such as the conference decision must be domestically enacted before they become binding on the CARICOM plane.[46] The court rejected this argument. The court held that Article 240 is not concerned with the creation of rights and obligations at the CARICOM level but speaks to giving effect to such rights and obligations in domestic law. If binding regional decisions can be invalidated at the CARICOM level by the failure on the part of a particular state to incorporate those decisions locally, then the efficacy of the entire CARICOM regime would be jeopardized. Domestic incorporation could not be a condition precedent to the creation of community rights, as it would then be open to states to incorporate or not incorporate as they pleased. This would destroy the certainty, predictability and uniformity of CARICOM law.

The court situated the 2007 conference decision within the broader concept of free movement of CARICOM nationals within the CARICOM, a goal to which each CARICOM state had expressly committed itself in Article 45 of the RTC. The court clarified practical aspects of the right. Where a community national is refused entry into a member state on a legitimate ground, that national should be given the opportunity to consult an attorney or a consular official of his or her country or to contact a family member. The refusing state must give, promptly and in writing, reasons for refusing entry and inform the refused community national of his or her right to challenge the decision. States are also obliged to interpret and apply their domestic laws liberally so as to harmonize them with CARICOM law or, if this is not possible, to alter them. Since refusal is an exception to a right, the scope of the right to refuse (i.e. undesirability or the risk of becoming a public charge) must be construed narrowly, and the burden of proof rests on the member state that seeks to invoke either ground. Undesirability must be concerned with the protection of public morals, the maintenance of public order and safety and the protection of life and health, and the visiting national must present a genuine, present and sufficiently serious threat affecting one of these fundamental interests of society. Moreover, the threat posed should, at the very least, be one to do with something prohibited by national law. But if national law in this regard is inconsistent with CARICOM law, the latter must prevail.

The *Myrie* decision was welcomed by many in the region. This was the first occasion on which an individual, as distinct from a corporation, had obtained leave to institute proceedings, and so the case allowed ordinary people of the region to draw the link between the CSME and their daily lives in a vivid way. The case clarified several aspects of the contradiction between domestic and CARICOM law. *Myrie* provides a solid platform upon which regional governments can consolidate their commitment to freedom of movement, and once again it demonstrated the absolutely indispensable role of the CCJ in closing the implementation deficit that has plagued and threatened to destroy CARICOM. The court's judgment, according to St Vincent and the Grenadines prime minister Ralph Gonsalves, "has bolstered the faith of the regional public in the possibilities of CARICOM" and "accelerated the pace of the regional integration process in respect of freedom of movement of community nationals".[47] Since *Myrie*, two other cases, filed respectively in 2018[48] and 2019,[49] have been brought by individuals alleging a breach of their right to freedom of movement guaranteed under the RTC and the 2007 conference decision.

The notion that, subject to specific exceptions, CARICOM nationals enjoy a right of "hassle-free" entry into all CARICOM member states was restated in the consolidated cases of *Tomlinson v Belize* and *Tomlinson v Trinidad and Tobago*.[50] Tomlinson, a Jamaican homosexual, had complained that the two states in question had prejudiced his enjoyment of this CARICOM right of entry by maintaining an express prohibition on the entry of homosexuals in their Immigration Acts. Unlike Myrie's case, Tomlinson was never actually refused entry or otherwise wrongfully treated by either state. His complaint was that the mere existence of these laws was sufficient to prejudice the enjoyment of his CARICOM rights.

The court confirmed that all CARICOM nationals (including of course homosexuals) have a right to freedom of movement. Tomlinson's matter was dismissed because, in the case of Belize, the court noted that a proper interpretation of the relevant Act of Parliament revealed that it did not in fact exclude entry to homosexuals. In Trinidad and Tobago, despite the provisions of the Immigration Act,[51] there was no evidence to suggest that there was any practice of excluding homosexuals. Mere retention of the pre-RTC immigration legislation did not, in and of itself, amount to a breach of Trinidad and Tobago's international obligations, especially when subsequent legislation in that state promoted the goals of the RTC and eschewed discrimination on the basis of sexual orientation. The factual evidence suggested that, in practice, Trinidad and Tobago consistently ignored the impugned provision of its Immigration Act and properly conformed to its treaty obligations. The court noted that violation of CARICOM law is not so much caused by the existence of domestic laws that seemingly contradict it, but by whether and how these laws are applied in practice.

Remedies and Their Enforcement

The RTC does not contain any specific provisions prescribing the remedies available to a litigant or the sanctions that may be imposed for breach of the treaty. It has been left to the CCJ to fill this gap. In one of the cases,[52] the court brushed aside the notion that it is entitled only to make declaratory awards. The court affirmed that its competence to review the legality of acts of states and/or the CARICOM includes competence to award appropriate relief to private entities that have suffered and established loss as a result of an illegality.[53] The court has extended this reasoning to include the making of coercive orders. So it was that the States of Guyana and Suriname were ordered to impose the common external tariff on cement and flour, respectively,[54] and Guyana was ordered to remove an illegal tax on goods being imported from Suriname.[55]

The CCJ has also made it clear that the remedy of compensatory damages is available to individuals and private entities whose rights under the treaty are infringed by member states. Such damages would, however, not automatically be awarded simply because a litigant has suffered loss. The losses must be incurred in circumstances that rendered them sufficiently proximate to the precise breach in question.[56] An aggrieved party would first have to demonstrate that the provision alleged to be breached was intended to benefit that person, that the breach was serious, that there is substantial loss and that there is a causal link between the breach by the delinquent state and the loss or damage to that person.[57] Shanique Myrie, for example, was awarded damages amounting to BB$75,000 (approximately US$37,500).

The RTC mandates prompt compliance with the court's judgments.[58] In Barbados, Dominica, Grenada, Jamaica, and St Vincent and the Grenadines express provision is made in domestic law for the enforcement of the judgments in the same manner as judgments of the local supreme court are enforced in keeping with the provisions of the Caribbean Court of Justice (Original Jurisdiction) Act 2004 and Caribbean Court of Justice (Agreement) Act 2003. But even where no such provision has been made, the experience of the court so far has demonstrated that regional governments can be relied upon to comply even with those judgments of the CCJ with which they may disagree. Every judgment issued by the court has been satisfied within a reasonable time. The court has, however, gone out of its way to adopt measures to monitor and oversee compliance with its judgments. In *Rudisa*,[59] in which Guyana was ordered to cease collecting an environmental tax and to return to a Surinamese company over US$6,047,244.47 in wrongfully levied taxes, the court stated:

> Member States and others to whom a judgment of the Court applies have an obligation under Article 215 RTC to comply promptly with the judgment and orders made by this Court. In order to ensure the protection of the Community rights of CARICOM nationals, compliance with and implementation of the Court's orders are essential. Such compliance and implementation are also required by fundamental principles of Community law, in particular the principles of access to justice, effectiveness of Community law and the rule of law itself. Community rights under the RTC would be illusory if the orders of the Court are not executed. The Court therefore has a responsibility to monitor compliance with its orders. This responsibility is reflected in Rules 29.3(3) and 29.3(4) of the Court's Rules and also in the Court's practice so far as it has allowed parties to apply to the Court in respect of matters arising out of its judgment and orders. (CCJ 2014, 17–18).

The court then proceeded to outline suitable monitoring mechanisms.

Conclusion

The existence of the CCJ, the jurisdiction accorded to it and the jurisprudence it has handed down have fundamentally altered the CARICOM landscape. The erstwhile voluntary system of treaty implementation has now been replaced with a framework governed by the rule of law with scope for ordinary individuals to hold regional states to account for breaches of the promises made by CARICOM. The people of the region can now regard seriously agreements made by the Heads and other Organs of CARICOM. Those decisions have the force of CARICOM law and on the CARICOM plane local legislation must yield to CARICOM law. These developments can only have a beneficial effect on CARICOM and provide a firm foundation for the advancement of the regional integration movement. It is a pity that too few persons recognize that, similarly, subscribing to the appellate jurisdiction of the court can also provide a catalyst for the enhancement of domestic justice systems in the region. Indeed, while the decisions of the court in its appellate jurisdiction are outside the purview of this chapter, it must be mentioned that in that sphere of its operations, the court has already made a profound contribution to maintenance and enhancement of the rule of law in the region.[60]

Notes

1. Antigua and Barbuda, Bahamas, Barbados, Belize, Dominica, Grenada, Guyana, Haiti, Jamaica, Montserrat, St Kitts and Nevis, St Lucia, St Vincent and the Grenadines, Suriname, and Trinidad and Tobago.

2. See the first recital of the Preamble to the Revised Treaty.

3. Hall (2003, x).

4. Treaty Establishing the Caribbean Community '13489' 946 United Nations Treaty Series 17.

5. See Article 211 of the RTC. The Bahamas, Haiti and Montserrat have not ratified the agreement establishing the CCJ, but the Bahamas has voluntarily contributed to the expenses of the court.

6. The organs of the Caribbean Community are set out in Article 10 of the revised treaty. The absence of the court on the list is to be compared, for example, with Article 7(1) of the Common Market for Eastern and Southern Africa Treaty where the court of justice there is declared to be an organ of the common market and Article 6(1) of the Economic Community of West African States Treaty where the community court of justice is declared to be an institution of the community.

7. At the time of writing, Barbados, Belize, Dominica and Guyana use the CCJ as their final appellate court. By not taking the requisite constitutional steps to subscribe to the appellate jurisdiction, the states of Jamaica, St Kitts and Nevis, St Lucia, St Vincent and the Grenadines, and Trinidad and Tobago are in breach of the treaty commitment they undertook to this end.

8. See Article 211(1) of the RTC. See also Article XII (1) of the Agreement Establishing the Caribbean Court of Justice. The term "exclusive" has to be viewed in context. The RTC also provides for a range of dispute settlement modes between states. See Carnegie (2009), "Dispute Settlement under the Revised Treaty of Chaguaramas and the Private Sector: A Consideration of Recent Developments" (unpublished), presented at the Faculty Workshop Series of the Faculty of Law of the University of the West Indies on 25 November 2009.

9. The domestic courts of Suriname apply the civil law.

10. Article 217 of the RTC.

11. Article 214 states: "Where a national court or tribunal of a Member State is seised of an issue whose resolution involves a question concerning the interpretation or application of this Treaty, the court or tribunal concerned shall, if it considers that a decision on the question is necessary to enable it to deliver judgment, refer the question to the court for determination before delivering judgment" (CARICOM Secretariat 2001, 110). Article XIV is worded in identical manner.

12. The Caribbean Court of Justice (Original Jurisdiction) Rules 2019.

13. See the Caribbean Court of Justice Act No. 10 of 2004, Antigua and Barbuda; Caribbean Court of Justice Act, Cap. 117, Barbados; Caribbean Court of Justice (Original Jurisdiction) Act No. 16 of 2004, Belize; Act No. 23 of 2005, Commonwealth of Dominica; Act No. 3 of 2005, Grenada; Act No. 16 of 2004, Guyana; Act No. 17 of 2005, Jamaica; Act No. 7 of 2004, St Christopher and Nevis; Act No. 34 of 2003, Saint Lucia; Act No. 32 of 2004, St Vincent and the

Grenadines; Act of 10 March 2003 containing the approval of the Agreement with regard to the Establishment of the Caribbean Court of Justice, Act No. 22 of 2003, Suriname; Act No. 8 of 2005, Republic of Trinidad and Tobago.

14. See section 3 of the respective CCJ acts.

15. See Part 3.4(4) of the Original Jurisdiction Rules.

16. See Article 221 of the RTC.

17. Article 216(1) of the RTC.

18. See Article 216(2) of the RTC.

19. The state of Jamaica did seek and obtain permission, however, to intervene in *Shanique Myrie v Barbados*. See *Myrie v Barbados* [2012] CCJ 3 (OJ), (2012) 81 WIR 232 (26 October 2012).

20. See Articles 191–210.

21. Article 188(4) specifically states that the use of any of these voluntary modes of dispute settlement is "without prejudice to the exclusive and compulsory jurisdiction of the court in the interpretation and application of the treaty".

22. See [2020] CCJ 1(OJ)(AO).

23. Havelock Brewster, *Mature Regionalism: The Rose Hall Declaration States*. See also Hall and Chuck-A-Sang (2007, 120).

24. *Trinidad Cement Limited v The Caribbean Community* [2009] CCJ 2 (OJ), (2009) 74 WIR 319 (5 February 2009).

25. See paragraph 32.

26. *Myrie v State of Barbados* [2013] CCJ 3 (OJ).

27. See *Rudisa Beverages & Juices N V and Caribbean International Distributors Inc v The Cooperative Republic of Guyana* [2014] CCJ 1 (OJ), (2014) 84 WIR 217.

28. See *Trinidad Cement Limited and TCL Guyana Incorporated v The Co-operative Republic of Guyana* [2009] CCJ 1 (OJ) [18], (2009) 74 WIR 302.

29. Article 32 in very general terms stipulates that a person shall be regarded as a national of a member state if such person (i) is a citizen of that state; (ii) has a connection with that state which entitles him to the benefits of citizenship; or is a company or other legal entity constituted in the member state and which that state considers as belonging to it provided that the company is substantially owned (i.e. in excess of 50 per cent of the equity interest therein) and controlled by persons described in (i) and (ii). See also *TCL v Cooperative Republic of Guyana* [2009] CCJ 1 (OJ).

30. *Bain v The State of Trinidad and Tobago* [2019] CCJ 3 (OJ).

31. *TCL* (n25).

32. *TCL* (n25) [40].

33. For a discussion on the goals and objectives embraced by the RTC, see, for example, the Advisory Opinion issued by the court on 18 March 2020 at the request of the Caribbean Community, [2020] CCJ 1 (OJ).

34. See Article XVIII(1) of the CCJ Agreement.

35. *TCL* (n25) [32].

36. *Trinidad Cement Limited and TCL Guyana Incorporated v The Co-operative Republic of Guyana* [2009] CCJ 5 (OJ), 75 WIR 327.

37. *Hummingbird Rice Mills v Suriname and The Caribbean Community* [2012] CCJ 1 (OJ), (2012) 79 WIR 448.

38. Article 175(12) permits a party aggrieved by a determination of the Competition Commission to apply to the court for a review, and Article 180 entitles the Competition Commission to apply to the court to review a decision of its own that was induced by deceit.

39. See *Johnson v CARICAD* [2009] CCJ 3 (OJ), (2009) 74 WIR 57.

40. Articles 10 and 18, respectively, of the RTC lists the organs and bodies of the Caribbean Community.

41. There are several bodies established by or under the auspices of the Caribbean Community that are referred to in the RTC as "institutions". The Caribbean Agricultural Research and Development Institute, the Caribbean Disaster Emergency Response, and the Caribbean Centre for Development Administration are examples. The University of the West Indies is an associate institution. Articles 21 and 22, respectively, list the institutions and associate institutions of the Caribbean Community.

42. *Rudisa* (n24) at [3].

43. *Myrie* (n18), *Trinidad Cement Limited v The Competition Commission* [2012] CCJ 4, 81 WIR 247 at [8], *Hummingbird Rice Mills* (n32) at [12], *Trinidad Cement Limited v The Caribbean Community* 75 WIR 194 at [16]–[18] (CCJ 2009b), *TCL* (n25) at [33].

44. See *Douglas v Commonwealth of Dominica* [2017] CCJ 1 (OJ), (2017) 70 WIR 251, [2018] 1 LRC 36.

45. *Myrie* (n18).

46. Article 240 states: "Decisions of competent Organs taken under this Treaty shall be subject to the relevant constitutional procedures of the Member States before creating legally binding rights and obligations for nationals of such States" (CARICOM Secretariat 2001a, 117).

47. "The Caribbean Community, the Caribbean Court of Justice, Shanique Myrie and Community Law", distinguished lecture sponsored by the Norman Manley Law School on 17 April 2014, at Kingston, Jamaica, http://www2.sta.uwi.edu/uwiToday/pdfs/FREE %20MOVEMENT%20OF%20COMMUNITY%20NATIONALS.pdf (accessed August 2018).

48. *Tamika Gilbert and others v The State of Barbados* [2019] CCJ 2 (OJ).

49. *Marsha-Lee Cooke v The State of Barbados*, CCJ Application No JAOJ2019/001.

50. [2016] CCJ 1(OJ), (2016) 88 WIR 273, [2017] 1 LRC 40.

51. Immigration Act Chap. 18:01 (Trinidad and Tobago).

52. *TCL* (n31) at [27],

53. *TCL v The Caribbean Community* [2009] CCJ 4, (2009)75 WIR 194 at [42]–[43].

54. See footnotes 36 and 37.

55. *Rudisa* (n24).

56. *TCL* (n31) at [33].

57. *TCL* (n31) at [27].

58. Article 215.

59. [2014] CCJ 1 (OJ), (2014) 84 WIR 217 at [38].

60. See, for example, the cases of *The Attorney General and others v Joseph and Boyce* [2006] CCJ 3 (AJ), (2006) 69 WIR 104; *Gibson v Attorney General of Barbados* [2010] CCJ 3 (AJ), (2010) 76 WIR 137; *Maya Leaders Alliance and others v Attorney General of Belize* [2015] CCJ 15 (AJ), (2015) 87 WIR 178; *Ventose v Chief Electoral Officer* [2018] CCJ 13 (AJ), (2018) 92 WIR 118; *The Attorney General of Guyana v Cedric Richardson* [2018] CCJ 17 (AJ), (2018) 92 WIR 416; *Nervais v The Queen, Severin v The Queen* [2018] CCJ 19 (AJ), (2018) 92 WIR 178; *Ram v Attorney General, Jagdeo v Attorney General, Persaud v Reid* [2019] CCJ 14 (AJ); *McEwan and others v Attorney General of Guyana* [2018 CCJ 30 (AJ), (2019) 94 WIR 332; and *Ali v David and others* [2020] CCJ 10 (AJ) (GY).

References

Agreement Establishing the Caribbean Court of Justice (CARICOM Secretariat, 2001). http://www.caribbeancourtofjustice.org/wp-content/uploads/2011/09/ccj_agreement.pdf.

Antigua and Barbuda. 2004. The Caribbean Court of Justice Act No. 10. http://laws.gov.ag/acts/2004/a2004-10.pdf.

Caribbean Court of Justice – Cabral Douglas v. The Commonwealth of Dominica. [2017] CCJ 1 (OJ). Accessed August 2018. http://www.caribbeancourtofjustice.org/wp-content/uploads/2017/02/2017-CCJ-1-OJ-2.pdf.

[2009] CCJ 5 (OJ). http://www.caribbeancourtofjustice.org/wp-content/uploads/2012/12/2009-CCJ-5-OJ.pdf.

Caribbean Court of Justice – CCJ. 2010. Trinidad Cement Limited (TCL) and TCL Guyana Incorporated (TGI) v. The State of the Co-operative Republic of Guyana.

Caribbean Court of Justice – Doreen Johnson v. Caribbean Centre for Development Administration. [2009] CCJ 3 (OJ). http://www.caribbeancourtofjustice.org/wp-content/uploads/2012/02/ar2_2008.pdf.

Caribbean Court of Justice – Hummingbird Rice Mills Ltd v. Suriname and the Caribbean Community. [2012] CCJ 1 (OJ). Accessed August 2018. http://www.caribbeancourtofjustice.org/wp-content/uploads/2012/12/2012-CCJ-1-OJ.pdf.

Caribbean Court of Justice – Maurice Tomlinson v. Belize and Maurice Tomlinson v. Trinidad and Tobago. [2016] CCJ 1 (OJ) and [2016] CCJ 2 (OJ). Accessed August 2018. http://www.caribbeancourtofjustice.org/wp-content/uploads/2016/06/2016-CCJ-1-OJ.pdf.

Caribbean Court of Justice – Rudisa Beverages & Juices N.V. and Caribbean International Distributors INC v. The State of Guyana. [2014] CCJ 1 (OJ). Accessed August 2018. http://www.caribbeancourtofjustice.org/wp-content/uploads/2014/05/OA-003-of-2013-RUDISA-JUDGMENT-REVISED-6-7May14-2.pdf.

Caribbean Court of Justice – Shanique Myrie v. The State of Barbados. [2012] CCJ 3 (OJ). Accessed August 2018. http://www.caribbeancourtofjustice.org/wp-content/uploads/2013/10/2013-CCJ-3-OJ.pdf.

Caribbean Court of Justice – Trinidad Cement Limited (TCL) v. The Caribbean Community: Judgment. [2009] CCJ 2 (OJ). http://www.caribbeancourtofjustice.org/judgments/ar3_2008/ar32008.pdf.

Caribbean Court of Justice – Trinidad Cement Limited v. The Competition Commission. [2013] CCJ 2 (OJ). Accessed August 2018. http://www.caribbeancourtofjustice.org/wp-content/uploads/2013/06/2013-CCJ-2-OJ.pdf.

Caribbean Court of Justice Original Jurisdiction Rules. 2017. Accessed August 2018. http://www.caribbeancourtofjustice.org/wp-content/uploads/2011/06/OJR-2017-1.pdf.

CARICOM Heads of Government. 2003. *The Rose Hall Declaration On 'Regional Governance And Integrated Development'*. 24th Meeting of the Conference of Heads of Government of CARICOM. Montego Bay, Jamaica, 2–5 July 2003.

Carnegie, A. Ralph. 2009. "Dispute Settlement under the Revised Treaty of Chaguaramas and the Private Sector: A Consideration of Recent Developments" (unpublished), presented at the Faculty Workshop Series of the Faculty of Law of the University of the West Indies on 25 November 2009.

Commonwealth of Dominica. 2005. "Caribbean Court of Justice (Original Jurisdiction) Act 2005–23". https://www.ilo.org/dyn/natlex/docs/ELECTRONIC/73703/87784/F363799499/DMA73703.pdf.

Gonsalves, Ralph. 2018. "The Caribbean Community, the Caribbean Court of Justice, Shanique Myrie and community law". Distinguished lecture sponsored by the Norman Manley Law School on April 17, 2014, Kingston, Jamaica. Accessed 31 August 2018. http://www2.sta.uwi.edu/uwiToday/pdfs/FREE%20MOVEMENT%20OF%20COMMUNITY%20NATIONALS.pdf.

Gonsalves, Ralph Everard. 2014. "Bridge over Troubled Waters: The Caribbean Community, The Caribbean Court of Justice, Shanique Myrie and Community Law", 17 April 2014. Kingston, Jamaica.

Government of Barbados. 2002. "The Constitution of Barbados". http://www.oas.org/dil/the_constitution_of_barbados.pdf.

———. 2003. "Caribbean Court of Justice Act. Cap. 117". https://www.legal-tools.org /doc/6f51a6/pdf/.

Government of Grenada. 2016. "Constitution of Grenada (Caribbean Court of Justice and Other Justice-Related Matters) Amendment". http://grenadabar.com/wp-content /uploads/2016/09/CONSTITUTION-OF-GRENADA-CARIBBEAN-COURT-OF-JUSTICE -AND-OTHER-JUSTICE-RELATED-MATTERS-AMENDMENT.pdf.

Guyana. 2004. "Caribbean Court of Justice Act 2004. Act No. 16 of 2004". http://parliament .gov.gy/documents/acts/4644-act_no._16_of_2004.pdf.

Hall, Kenneth, ed. 2003. *Reinventing CARICOM: The Road to a New Integration*, 2nd edition. Kingston: Ian Randle Publisher.

Hall, Kenneth and Myrtle Chuck-A-Sang, eds. 2007. *CARICOM Single Market and Economy Challenges, Benefits, Prospects*. Kingston: Ian Randle Publisher.

Jamaican Parliament. 2005. "Caribbean Court of Justice Act 2005–17". http://www.japarliament .gov.jm/attachments/article/339/The%20Caribbean%20Court%20of%20Justice%20Act,%20 2015-hp.pdf.

Republic of Trinidad and Tobago. 2005. "Act No. 8 of 2005". http://laws.gov.tt/ttdll-web /revision/download/73693?type=amendment.

The Revised Treaty of Chaguaramas Establishing the Caribbean Community including The CARICOM Single Market and Economy (CARICOM Secretariat, 2001a). Accessed August 2018. https://caricom.org/documents/4906-revised_treaty-text.pdf.

Chapter 13

Weighed and Found Wanting

Global, Regional and Local Scales in a Caribbean Environmental Discourse

APRIL KAREN BAPTISTE AND HUBERT DEVONISH

Introduction

Within the Commonwealth Caribbean, the promotion of certain large industrial projects has taken place within the framework of regional economic integration. The view is that small countries with weak economies stand to benefit by pooling resources. Key efforts at regional integration include the West Indies Federation 1958–62 (O'Brien 2011) and the Caribbean Community and Common Market (CARICOM) established in 1973 (Revauger 2008; Newstead 2009; O'Brien 2011; Carrillo Roa and Santana 2012).

Regional integration and industrialization are linked very closely to each other in the Caribbean public imaginary. Each is seen as contributing to the other and ultimately to the economic development of marginalized small island states. A specific version of this, the regional aluminium smelter, owes its origins, as Barclay (2012, 53) points out, to academic proposals made by Brewster and Thomas (1977). In 1973, this becomes formal policy with the signing of an agreement for the setting up of an aluminium smelter using the petroleum and natural gas resources of Trinidad and Tobago, along with the bauxite of Guyana and Jamaica. The proposed smelter, due to begin operations in 1977, would be jointly owned by the three governments. The deal quickly collapsed, however, when Jamaica concluded a parallel agreement with extraregional partners (Barclay 2012, 53). Ever since, the idea of putting together a similar project has been a dream of many regional integrationists.

The idea of an aluminium smelter combining the natural resources of the three Caribbean countries was resurrected in 2004. This took the form of two aluminium smelter project proposals for Trinidad and Tobago involving bauxite from the same two regional source countries (*Engineering and Mining Journal* 2006; *Engineering and Mining Journal* 2004). One of the smelters, Alutrint, was slated for the southwest peninsula of Trinidad on a new industrial estate (figure 13.1). The project involved a US$400 million loan from China and a joint partnership between the Trinidad government and Sural, a Venezuelan regional company. Further, Jamaica and Guyana were to supply the necessary bauxite ore. The smelter was part of a larger project, which included a port and a power plant as additional components. This project was to be located on a site surrounded by five local communities (*Engineering and Mining Journal* 2006; Weik 2009; Wilkinson 2004). Site preparation began in 2006, but the

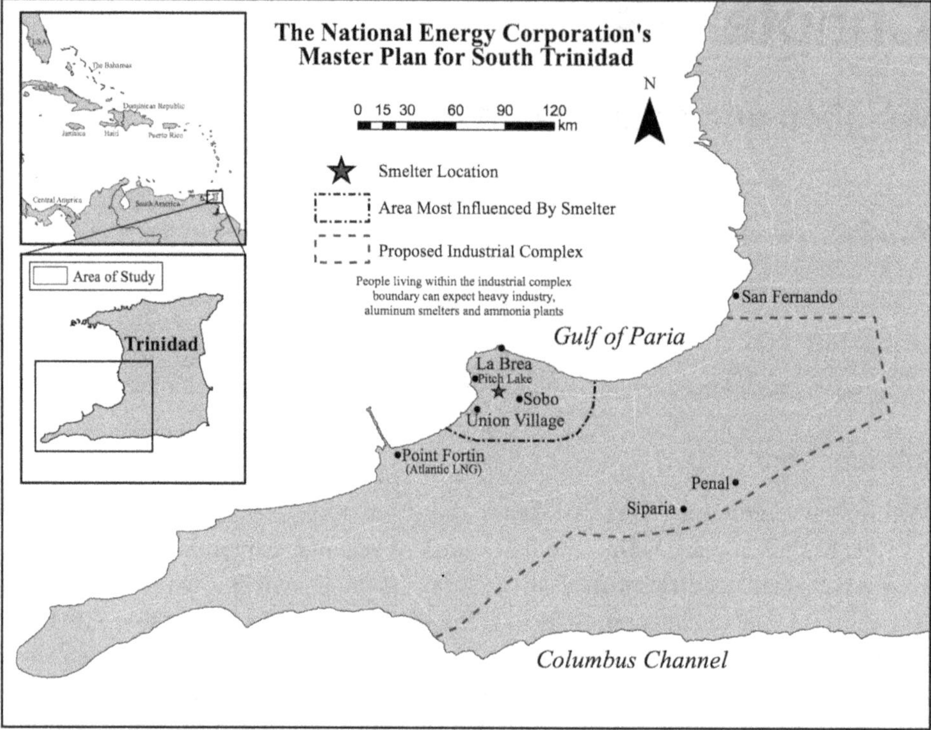

Figure 13.1. Location of proposed industrial complex, proposed Alutrint smelter and some of the surrounding communities to the smelter project (created by Josh Rosen, former research assistant and Colgate University student, 2011)

entire project came to a halt in 2010. One factor leading to the abandonment of the smelter project was public discontent.

Public Discourse and the Local Scale

Active and very vocal public discourse on industrial projects is a new complicating factor in the implementation of industrial projects, particularly those in the Caribbean. New considerations beyond the traditional intraregional political rivalry, economic viability and efficiency, now play an important role in the process of implementing such projects. These considerations involve greater awareness of and concern for environmental factors as expressed through public opinion formed and amplified by the communication media.

The way that people view industrial projects has changed since the 1970s. Industrial projects are now viewed as almost inevitably negatively affecting human and environmental health. This comes into conflict with the "developmental" view that for "underdeveloped" states industrialization promotes the productive capacity of economies and improves quality of life for citizens (Lewis 2009; Newstead 2009). It is within the context of this changed view of industrialization that the physical location of such projects is now often a matter of great public contention. Intense arguments occur about the benefits of the industrial project and who receives these benefits.

Large-scale regional industrial projects operate simultaneously at different geographical scales – the international, the regional, the national and the local. Typically, public discourse focuses on issues at the local scale, and specifically the perceived positive and negative local consequences associated with the project. This study examines the mismatch between meanings of particular bodies of discourse when these are interpreted by individuals who are operating at different geographic scales.

Scaled Considerations in Caribbean Industrial Projects

As previously identified, the scales which are the subject of this study are the international, regional, national and local. At the international scale, a project is considered from the perspective of whether it is beneficial or otherwise to the global economy. The next scale down is that of the Caribbean region. Here, the project is evaluated for the benefit it provides to the productive capacities of the economies of the region. This is against the background that regional economic integration is generally viewed as providing a benefit to small underdeveloped economies. Such projects, in addition, are viewed as having moral value, coming as they do with the aura of contributing to Caribbean regional identity.

The next level down is the national level. At this level, the project is considered based on the benefit it confers on to the economy of the country within which it is located.

There is then the local scale. This is the scale where the physical presence of the industrial operation is most manifest. The industrial operation is constructed and located in some specific local geographical space. Its construction and operation will be perceived to have either a positive or negative effect on the lives and livelihoods of the people who live in its vicinity. It is the impact of industrial activities at this very local scale that transfixes public opinion and public discourse. The chapter's ultimate goal is to understand the role of local public opinion typically oriented towards localized concerns and the way it interprets discourse emanating from other scales. Our interest is in the way that discourse, focused on the concerns at the local scale, serve as a complicating factor in the development of industrial projects with a significant regional collaborative component.

For regional industrial projects to succeed, public discourse with its orientation towards the perspective of the local scale has to be taken into account. The fact is that discourse on any such project will take place and be interpreted at all the scales, including the often-ignored local scale. Significantly, in the case of the particular Caribbean regional industrial project under discussion in the present study, it was the protesting discourse at the local scale that eventually brought it to a halt.

Chapter Outline

The analysis of the public discourse surrounding the Alutrint smelter project employs a politics of scale approach, grounded in environmental justice. First to be examined is the concept of scale and its application to understanding industrial projects. Next is a summary of events associated with the smelter project.

The data is drawn from the public discourse as reported in the main national newspaper, the *Trinidad Express* (hereafter the *Express*). The analysis focuses on the themes, sub-themes and issues addressed or otherwise at each scale. The analysis seeks to provide an understanding of the nature of the public discourse that took place and the extent to which it permitted efficient communication between stakeholders at all scales. The chapter concludes by discussing the implications of scale for understanding public discourse around large industrial projects with a significant regional cooperation component.

Scale: Application to Industrial Projects

Scale may be understood as socially constructed (Bickerstaff and Agyeman 2009; Chapple and Goetz 2011; Darby 2012; Kurtz 2003; Middleton 2012). Alternatively, it can be defined as physical space involving, as examples, the global, regional, national and local (Haughton 1998; Middleton 2012; Muradian, Martinez-Alier and Correa 2003; Walker 2009; Wolford 2008).

Whatever the approach to scale, the concept has been invoked in several studies on the implementation of industrial projects. Darby (2012) and Middleton (2012) have discussed the complexity of working across scales in these situations. For example, in a work that studies scales within a single country, Darby (2012) deals with a smelter development in El Paso, Texas. She demonstrates that the scale at which regulation was taking place, the national/federal level, did not match the scale at which the contamination was taking place, the town level, and incidentally, transnationally across the border into Mexico.

The case study of an electricity generation project involving Thailand, Myanmar and Laos as partners focuses specifically on the issue of scale across the national boundaries of neighbouring countries. According to Middleton (2012), the project led to injustices at the level of specific countries within the region. The poorer countries of Myanmar and Laos suffered the negative environmental consequences of the generation and export of electricity to the more prosperous Thailand (Middleton 2012).

Within the literature, scale is used to examine how a problem is perceived, the way in which it is addressed and the manner in which the problem is responded to (Bickerstaff and Agyeman 2009; Chapple and Goetz 2011; Darby 2012; Middleton 2012; Kurtz 2003; Muradian, Martinez-Alier and Correa 2003; Towers 2000; Wolford 2008). There is often a disjuncture between the scales at which the decisions are made to implement industrial projects and the effects that arise as a result of such decisions (Bickerstaff and Agyeman 2009; Chapple and Goetz 2011; Darby 2012; Kurtz 2003; Middleton 2012; Muradian, Martinez-Alier and Correa 2003; Towers 2000). This body of literature points to the importance of understanding the interaction of stakeholders in the decision-making processes across multiple scales (Bickerstaff and Agyeman 2009; Walker 2009). One component of this interaction among stakeholders is effective communication. A key feature of communication in these circumstances is public communication, more specifically, the kind of public discourse that appears in sections of the mass media. One question which arises from an examination of the case studies is that of the kind of discourse that can take place between stakeholders across different scales. How can such discourse be conducted to ensure efficient communication and, as an outcome, effective decision-making?

The Alutrint smelter project in Trinidad involved multiple stakeholders at various scales. It included the citizen as taxpayer and voter, as well as government ministers as policy implementers at the national scale. It also included the company, Alutrint, which had an identity at both the international and national scales. Also engaged in this discourse were activists operating at the national and local scales. The communication between these stakeholders at the public level manifested itself as public discourse within the mass media, notably the national newspapers. It is within this context that meaning became socially constructed as a result of communication within and across scales. This chapter explores the particular manifestation of public discourse on the Alutrint project.

Method

Alutrint Case

The Alutrint smelter project was located in La Brea, south Trinidad, and had the potential to affect the villages of Sobo, Union Village, New Deal, Vessigny and La Brea (figure 13.1). The smelter was part of a new industrial complex of about 1,000 acres proposed for the southwestern peninsula of Trinidad (*Engineering and Mining Journal* 2006; Wilkinson 2004). Alutrint was expected to produce 125,000 metric tons/year of alumina with the capacity to increase to 450,000 metric tons/year. The goal of the smelter project was to create aluminium downstream industries (Rapid Environmental Assessments Ltd 2009; Weik 2009). The smelter project had regional implications as the plan was to source bauxite from Jamaica and Guyana (Wilkinson 2004). The energy for the project, however, was to be provided in country using Trinidad's vast oil and gas reserves (*Engineering and Mining Journal* 2006).

Data Source

Articles from the *Express* addressing the Alutrint project were used as a source of data. The data took the form of quotes from the various stakeholders in the smelter project debate, as reported in the *Express*. The *Express* was used as it was the most widely circulated of the three national daily newspapers in Trinidad and Tobago, with 53 per cent of all newspaper readers (Richards 2012). The *Express* was formed by a group of journalists who lost their jobs in the early 1960s as a result of a merger between two British owned newspapers, the *Daily Mirror* and the *Guardian*. The *Express* became the first locally owned daily newspaper and was funded by small business people (Advameg, Inc. 2013; One Caribbean Media Limited 2013). Over the decades, the *Express* has sought to maintain its profile as the "alternative" newspaper, giving coverage to dissenting movements such as the Black Power Movement of 1970, which was much more extensive than that given by its competitor, the *Guardian* (Meghoo 2003).

The *Express* is now part of One Caribbean Media, a Caribbean-wide media conglomerate owning newspapers in several other Caribbean countries. The owner of the *Guardian*, the *Express*'s main competitor, is the ANSA McAL group of companies, a Trinidad-based industrial conglomerate (Cruickshank 2005). We thus have a regional media conglomerate, represented by the *Express*, versus a local industrial conglomerate, which has a newspaper, the *Guardian*, as one element of its portfolio.

The key characteristics of the *Express* are that it represents the interests of the nontraditional, smaller owners of capital in Trinidad and Tobago and has a regional focus. Both of these characteristics are relevant to the coverage of the Alutrint case. The *Express* has an orientation and history which makes it more open to anti-establishment protest, albeit in the interest of the less well-established sections of the capitalist class. There is, as well, its regional focus as represented by its regional investment in the mass media (Cruickshank 2005; Meghoo 2003).

This populist position of the *Express* is reinforced by an examination of its editorials on the smelter project. Though few in number, they presented a faintly populist stand aligned with the newspaper's own history and its appeal to a mass readership. In terms of other coverage of the issue, the newspaper sided strongly with the eco and community groups opposed to the project. This coverage is likely to have skewed our sample of the public discourse, creating a bias in favour of local views and voices. Though a recognized bias, and perhaps because of this, the *Express* had more articles on the smelter project controversy than any of the other daily newspapers.

The actual source of the data is the online version of the *Express*. During June to August 2012, the *Express* website was used to gather the articles on the smelter project (*Trinidad Express* 2012). A general keyword search was done for "Alutrint smelter", "Alutrint", and "smelter". Using the advanced search option, the years were narrowed to "2006-2010", generating 546 articles. One of the limitations of using the online version of the paper was the apparent delay between the time the article appeared in the printed newspaper and the time of posting online. Since the articles carried the date of posting rather than the date on which it appeared in print, the researchers have had no choice but to use the online date as the reference date for these articles.

Each of the 546 articles was examined for direct quotes made by different stakeholders relevant to the smelter project. Of the 546 articles, 250 were not usable, either because they did not directly address the Alutrint smelter project or they did not have direct quotes from stakeholders. Thus, 296 articles became part of the sample.

A structured content analysis and thematic coding process (figure 13.2) were used to assess the arguments about the smelter project from direct quotes of the stakeholders reported in the sample articles. The quotes were classified as belonging to international, regional, national and local scales based on the content. They were then assessed to determine the main themes for each scale. These broad themes were then divided into sub-themes, and then further categorized into issues. The themes were then compared across the scales.

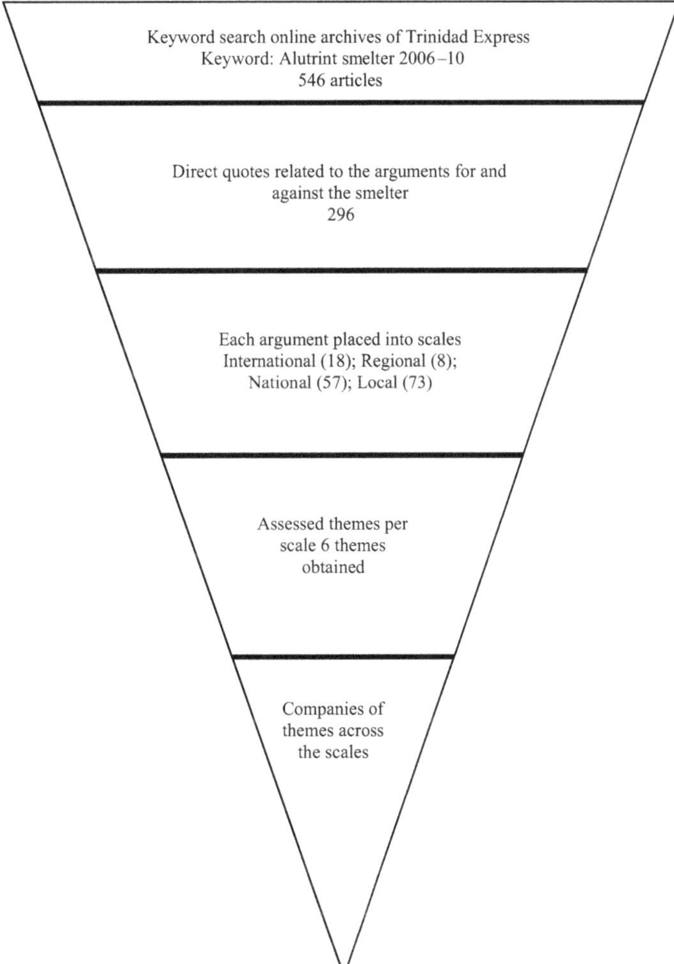

Figure 13.2. Schematic of the content analysis and thematic coding process used to analyse the data

Thematic Analysis

The four themes identified are presented in the following sections. Also presented are the sub-themes and issues within each theme, as well as the scale at which each is raised (table 13.1).

Rights

The rights theme had three sub-themes in the data (table 13.1). The first was the sub-theme of right to information, dealt with at the national and local scales only. This sub-theme included the issue of information on economic costs and revenues to the government as stated by a national activist, Wayne Kublalsingh: "We just want to see what the State has spent on Alutrint, what it will spend, and what it will gain. This much I think the citizens of this country have a right to know" (Kublalsingh in the *Express* 4 February 2011).

Table 13.1. Summary of Themes, Sub-Themes and Issues at the International, Regional, National and Local Scales Concerning the Smelter Project in Trinidad

| Theme | Component Issues | | | |
Sub-Theme	International Scale	Regional Scale	National Scale	Local Scale
Rights *Right to information*			Right to information on revenues earned and financial costs Right to information on management of oil and gas sector	How should information be requested Is community entitled to requested information
Rights *Right to land*				Negotiation about and finalization of compensation before physical preparation of site begins Rights of ownership of land rights questioned
Rights *Right to compensation*	Repatriation for Chinese workers Compensation for Chinese workers		Compensation provided according to constitutional guidelines	Compensation provided according to constitutional guidelines Terms for relocation of local families not acceptable
Economic effects *Economic costs*	Financial liability to foreign countries Reduction in foreign investments and investor confidence		Use of public money to fund project	
Economic effects *Economic benefits*		Improved trade between countries	Economic diversification Increased industrialization and development Provision of jobs	Provision of jobs (who will be employed, skills required for employment)

Ecological consequences *Climate change*		Climate change will endanger lives of people	
Ecological consequences *Sustainable development framework*		Industrialization taken against the backdrop of sustainable development principles	
Ecological consequences *Harmful construction effects*			Physical environment damaged with loss of forest and excessive dust
Ecological consequences *Cumulative operation effects*			Smelter operations compounded effects with other nearby industrial developments
Health and safety concerns *Operation of smelter*	International standards used for assurances about health and safety	Need for review of national standards dealing with risks associated with industrial plants	Effect of smelter operations on safety of surrounding communities
Health and safety concerns *Physical health*		The health of nation put at risk by smelter project	Fears of developing cancer community medical monitoring

Since the quote refers to what the state spent and would gain, along with what the rights of the citizens of the country were as a whole, the scale being dealt with here was the national one. The national scale was also present in the following quote by the minister of energy,[1] Conrad Enill. This dealt with the issue of the management of the oil industry and the responsibility of the government to provide the public with information on these matters. The suggestion was that the public did not have a right to this information. "The matter of the economic viability of the project and all of those are commercial arrangements the Government does not provide [information on] as it relates to the petrochemical sector, as it relates to the oil and gas sector, as it relates to all of those" (Enill in the *Express*, 4 February 2011).

The local scale paralleled the national one by addressing the same theme of the right to information. However, the focus here was on the local recipients of information, be they the communities, local groups or individuals. Two issues related to local right to information came up: how this information should be requested and whether the community was entitled to the requested information. There was, as well, the matter of the process to be followed by communities to access this information.

As the minister of energy indicated in response to community and national protesters who had gathered in front of the ministry in order to press for information on the project: "so what if they [the community] are waiting . . . if they requested for this information appropriately, the Government will respond, if they should" (Enill in the *Express* 4 February 2011). He went on further to state: "It was agreed that the group would submit their concerns to the Minister in writing and a further meeting will be held" (Enill in the *Express* 4 February 2011).

In the first quote, the minister suggested that a proper procedure existed for requesting information from the government, but that the local community did not follow this. This, he suggests, in a somewhat scolding tone, could be the reason the community did not receive the information. He made it clear in the second quote that concerns should be submitted by letter. He would then respond by holding a meeting with those groups seeking information. The minister, consistent with the position he took at the national scale, indicated that information at the local scale would only be provided if the government considered such provision appropriate. Neither the nation, nor the affected local communities, in his view, had any automatic right to information.

The second sub-theme involved individual right to land (table 13.1). Interestingly, this sub-theme was prominent at the local scale but was not addressed at any other scale. The issue at this scale was that national players should negotiate for land purchase with individual landowners prior to the completion of the preparation and compensation phases with community members. Local activists from the community used the following quote from the Certificate of Environmental Clearance to highlight this problem: "All final negotiations for the acquisition of all properties and compensation shall be completed before the commencement of all works" (Certificate of Environmental Clearance in the *Express* 6 February 2011).

Here community leaders suggested that the smelter project was proceeding even though the agreements between property owners and decision-makers on the terms of compensation had not been finalized. This violated the accepted procedure set out by the governing principles laid out in the Certificate of Environmental Clearance.

The next issue at the local scale under the right to land was that actual ownership rights were being brought into question. This issue was raised by EG, a local community activist, in the following quote dealing with squatters' landownership rights or lack thereof, and the status they may or may not have in any process of negotiation over land: "The Minister told the people that they are squatters and the Government could move them out, because they have no rights . . . [but] there are some of them who, although they don't have a deed they have been living on those spots for 25 plus years and there are those with deed of comfort" (EG in the *Express* 5 February 2011).

The role of landowners' rights in the discourse at the local scale was contrasted with that of the rights of squatters. In addition, the squatters were split into two: those who had a deed of comfort and those who did not. The view, at the level of the community activists, was that this separation into categories of legal entitlement would inevitably have led to the fragmentation of the community when dealing with the proposers of the project. The following statement made by a local community resident illustrates this issue: "They are asking that we cooperate and meet with them individually because there is always problems when they meet with us as a community. But I totally disagree with that approach because we are a community and they should deal with us as a community" (WJ in the *Express* 3 February 2011).

That community fragmentation was a shared concern can be seen by the following quote, from another La Brea community resident: "Those who had businesses and close family in the La Brea area would have suffered. We want the country to know that our community is not one of squatters with no future. Most of us live in good houses and have jobs and small businesses. Most of us did not want this smelter" (SD in the *Express* 6 February 2011).

The speaker, a community member, identified himself and people like him, as people with "businesses and close family" who "live in good houses, have jobs, and small businesses". He sought to put distance between his group and "squatters with no future". The speaker seemed to imply that only the former had any role in the discourse about land rights related to the smelter project.

A third sub-theme under rights was the right to compensation (table 13.1). This sub-theme was more developed at the local scale than at the international or national scales. It was not mentioned at the regional scale. When compensation was discussed at the international scale, the issue arose in relation to the foreign workers who lost job opportunities with the halting of the smelter project, as presented by Norris Deonarine, the CEO of the National Food Crop Farmers Association in the following quote: "Also, the Chinese workers connected to Alutrint should be dealt with in a humane way. They should be adequately compensated and repatriated" (Deonarine in the *Express* 6 February 2011).

Deonarine proposed that compensation was required for groups who had a vested interest in the smelter project but who were unable to realize any benefits once a decision was taken to cancel the project. From the international perspective given that Chinese workers were brought into Trinidad specifically to work on the construction of the smelter, Deonarine argued that there should have been adequate compensation for the loss incurred. One form of compensation was repatriation, returning workers to their countries of origin at no cost to themselves.

At the national scale, specific compensation terms were not highlighted in the arguments. Rather the issue involved standards by which compensation would have been provided in keeping with the constitution of Trinidad and Tobago. The minister of local government, Chandresh Sharma, stated: "The Partnership government is going to deliver the goods and services to the people as is provided for in the Constitution of the country" (Sharma in the *Express* 19 February 2010).

Though not explicit in the preceding quote, the minister was most likely referring to the specific concessions demanded by the local community, the most obvious being relocation, an argument made with reference to the local scale.

At the local scale, the focus of the argument centred on the specific type of compensation – relocation – that was sought by the community. The issue dealing with expectations of relocation covered the question of whether relocation was the best form of compensation and the reasons for the resistance to relocation. These issues were exemplified in the following local scale quotes from community residents:

> The move would have seriously affected us. Those who had businesses and close family in the La Brea area would have suffered. We want the country to know that our community is not one of squatters with no future. Most of us live in good houses and have jobs and small businesses. Most of us did not want this smelter. (SD in the *Express* 6 February 2011)

> We agreed that we don't want those houses. The front of the house is at the same level with the road. When it rains the whole gallery is going to flood out and there are also several other defects on the houses. (CR in the *Express* 6 February 2011)

SD stated that relocation was inappropriate for the community as it led to its fragmentation. Additionally, SD raised the issue of the rights of the majority who were legal owners of land against the backdrop of a relocation based on an assumption that squatters predominated within the community. SD was arguing that relocation designed for squatters might deny some of the property rights of legal owners. CR, who indicated that the new homes that were provided to the relocated families were substandard, reinforced the point. The houses did not meet standards of decent living conditions, nor did they match the quality of the housing that the community enjoyed. The community, therefore, did not consider relocation an appropriate official response in the situation.

Economic Effects

The theme of economic effects was addressed at all scales. Two sub-themes of economic costs and economic benefits were prominent. Three issues emerged under the sub-theme of economic costs – two at the international scale and one at the national scale.

Financial liability to foreign countries and investment/investor confidence were raised at the international scale. These issues arose in the context of arguments against the smelter project being abandoned. Pro-smelter views were presented by EV, a local community activist, and by John Donaldson, the vice chairman of the People's National Movement, a national political party, in the following quotes.

> What we are not being told is how much penalties we will have to pay to the Chinese and the Brazilians for rescinding on the contracts that we have with them. (EV in the *Express* 6 October 2010)

Concerns were raised about the other states, China, Brazil, Venezuela that participated in this very important project, that our international affairs will be impacted. Not to mention, of course, investor confidence and if they choose to invest in Trinidad and Tobago there is always, in the back of their minds, perhaps that [at] some point in time things can happen which should not happen. (Donaldson in the *Express* 12 September 2010)

EV was indicating in her statement above that "we" – the country of Trinidad and Tobago – would be liable to pay financial penalties to international partners if the project was abandoned. She named the Chinese and Brazilians as ones who would have to be paid. Donaldson also expressed concern for the economic effects of abandoning the project, claiming investor confidence would be damaged and foreign investment discouraged. It can be argued that these international scale concerns also simultaneously existed at the national scale, since the question was one of how the country, Trinidad and Tobago, would be affected by the behaviour of international players. Given the specific non-local nature of these concerns, it was perhaps expected that they would not manifest themselves at the local scale.

The third issue under the sub-theme of economic costs raised at the national scale concerned the use of public money to fund the smelter project as stated by Keith Rowley, an opposition member of Parliament, and Wayne Kublalsingh, a national activist:

And I want to also ask them what contracts will be affected by your decision to stop it and what will it cost the people of Trinidad and Tobago? (Rowley in the *Express* 23 July 2010)

This is a State enterprise that if allowed to build the smelter will be using millions of the people's tax dollars to do so. They can't treat us like this. (Kublalsingh in the *Express* 4 February 2011)

The references to the "people of Trinidad and Tobago" made by Rowley and to "the people's tax dollars" made by Kublalsingh both indicated that the general public had a stake in the smelter project and should be provided with the cost associated with the project.

While the first sub-theme dealt with the economic costs associated with the smelter project in either its implemented or non-implemented form, the second sub-theme focused on the economic benefits. Several issues fell under this sub-theme at the regional, national and local scales.

At the regional scale, the issue of trade between the countries of the region was raised. The prime minister of Trinidad and Tobago, Patrick Manning, indicated this in the following quote: "At the same time Mr Speaker, we confidently anticipate that as we construct our aluminium smelter here, we can enter into a guaranteed arrangement with Jamaica for the supply of alumina to that smelter, ensuring that Jamaica is now able to earn substantial foreign exchange and reduce the imbalance in trade between Jamaica and Trinidad and Tobago. This was the dream of Eric Williams and Michael Manley among others" (Manning in the *Express* 6 February 2011).

The prime minister indicated two regional economic benefits. First, he was explicit that Jamaica would earn foreign exchange from selling alumina to Trinidad and Tobago. This benefit, though claimed for Jamaica, can also be applied to Guyana, another potential supplier of raw materials to the smelter project. Second, the prime minister indicated that the smelter project would improve the balance of trade between Jamaica and Trinidad and Tobago, given the projected increase in imports from that country, as a counterbalance to the existing huge volume of exports from Trinidad and Tobago to Jamaica. In both quotes, we see optimism that regional trade would be boosted with the implementation of the smelter project.

Specific to the national scale were two issues: the benefit of economic diversification as well as increased industrialization. The minister of energy, Conrad Enill, and Prime Minister Manning illustrated these issues in the following quotes:

> [The smelter] will be one of this country's major economic ventures. (Enill in the *Express* 6 February 2011)

> You are going to be home to the first aluminium smelter in Trinidad and Tobago. And those who are against it will tell you that it is not that they are opposed to the smelter, but to the whole concept of industrialisation on the whole. (Manning in the *Express* 5 February 2011)

The minister of energy stated that the smelter project would expand the country's economic activity. The prime minister made a similar point by indicating that the smelter would contribute to further economic development through industrial activity. A developed national economy would then lead to improvements in the quality of life for the citizens of the country.

The final issue of job provision was presented as an economic benefit, raised at the national and local scales. At the national scale, the former prime minister of Trinidad and Tobago, Basdeo Panday, and the member of Parliament for the area, Fitzgerald Jeffrey, indicated that the smelter project had the potential to provide jobs for the general population. They stated in the following quotes:

> Trinidad and Tobago's 30-year quest to establish a local smelter is finally within our grasp. . . . This project would provide sustainable jobs and further economic development. (Panday in the *Express* 5 February 2011)

> In the case of Alutrint, 775 permanent high paying jobs would have been created. (Jeffrey in the *Express* 26 September 2010)

At the national scale, the actors were emphasizing that job provision was important, as the wider Trinidad public would benefit from the jobs associated with the smelter project. These jobs were seen as sustainable, permanent and high paying.

At the local scale, however, the focus was on the provision of jobs for members of the local communities. The issues raised by the community included the employment situation within the community, hope for younger community people who would be employed, and the skills required for community members to receive employment. BD, a resident of La Brea stated that "the people of the area are being left out" (BD in the *Express* 6 February 2011). This quote by BD expressed wider concerns about the lack of community employment coming from the preparation of the smelter site. This quote demonstrated a perception that the jobs were not being provided to the community. Outsiders were being given preference. Linked to this issue was the view that community members did not have the necessary skills to be employed in the smelter. As KS, a resident of La Brea, indicated: "But I also have reservations about this because you have to possess certain qualifications and I think Alutrint needs to ensure that the people they select are qualified" (KS in the *Express* 8 February 2011).

KS was expressing his concern about the kind of qualifications required for employment at the smelter. He was also placing the onus on Alutrint to provide training for the selected persons.

Ecological Consequences

Ecological consequences of the smelter project emerged at the national and local scales. At the national scale, the first sub-theme covered climate change, by way of its potential impact on Trinidad and Tobago: "And why does the Government pay lip service to climate change and global warming when they plan to construct smelters, which will endanger the lives of our people?" (Panday in the *Express* 4 February 2011).

The former prime minister of Trinidad and Tobago, Basdeo Panday, indicated in the preceding quote that the government, given its decision to implement the smelter project, did not take the matter of climate change seriously. Here he was arguing that the smelter project would contribute to climate change. He was probably alluding to the greenhouse gas emissions, which would affect the lives of the general public.

A second sub-theme raised at the national scale was the concern about the need for a sustainable development framework within which to pursue the smelter project. "We believe in the environment but we also believe in the substantial development of the country so that it does not prejudice future generations from enjoying what Trinidad and Tobago has to offer" (Manning in the *Express* 5 February 2011). By making the statement that we do "not prejudice future generations from enjoying what Trinidad and Tobago has to offer", Prime Minister Manning claimed a sustainable development approach, which promoted development while reducing harm to future generations. Hence, at the national scale, the ecological consequences were linked to the use of the environment, masked by the terminology of sustainable development.

In contrast, at the local scale, the ecological consequences fell under two sub-themes that were different to that of the national scale. The first sub-theme dealt with the harmful effects to the physical environment of the construction of the smelter. The second addressed the cumulative impacts of the operations of the smelter on the community and physical environment. These sub-themes were illustrated in the following quotes:

> We have been affected by this, the construction of the smelter plant, from day one. When they cleared out acres of virgin forests leaving us in a dust bowl and now that the construction has started, we are being affected by dust and noise. (FF, Vessigny resident, in the *Express* 6 February 2011)

> They are going about this development in a piecemeal fashion and the overall consequences are therefore hard to predict. Nobody can say what the eventual effect of that port will be. (Julian Kenny, national environmentalist, in the *Express* 6 February 2011)

> [The process is] procedurally irregular, irrational and made without regard to . . . consideration of the cumulative impact of the three related projects. . . . the power plant, the aluminium complex [and] the port facility. (Mira Dean-Armorer, High Court judge, in the *Express* 6 February 2011)

FF in the first quote gave a list of the physical ecological consequences that had been experienced by the villagers. He was here referring to the damage being done to the physical environment. Kenny and Dean-Armorer both mentioned that the implementers of the project were not considering the cumulative impacts, as the "overall consequences" were "hard to predict". With the new port and a power plant being constructed alongside the smelter, at the local scale, a perception existed among members of the community that they were not receiving adequate information about how the two developments might potentially affect them.

Health and Safety Concerns

Concerns about health and safety relating to the smelter project were raised at three of the four scales: the international, national and local. The first sub-theme covered the operation of the smelter. At the international scale, the issue was treated as one of international comparators. These comparator countries were used as a basis for justifying the location of the smelter in close proximity to communities. Based on the experience from these countries, smelter operation did not threaten the surrounding communities. Member of Parliament for the area Fitzgerald Jeffrey and Prime Minister Patrick Manning respectively are quoted as stating:

> Bahrain has had a smelter since 1971 and their death rate is lower than Trinidad, their birth rate is better than Trinidad and their infant mortality rate is low. So that smelter can't be all that bad. . . . It is the same thing with Norway, which has seven smelters in the midst of communities. (Jeffrey in the *Express* 21 September 2010)

> It is possible and it is being done right now where aluminium smelters are operating, and operating in a manner that poses no threat to the health and well-being of animal, plant or human life in the countries in which they operate. There are some people who are just not prepared to accept that. (Manning in the *Express* 4 February 2011)

In the first quote, international birth and death rates of countries with aluminium smelters were used to compare with those of Trinidad. The comparison was used as an indication that health effects should not be a significant concern in the case of Trinidad. In the second quote, international comparators were also invoked, this time by Prime Minister Patrick Manning, to reduce the safety concerns and justify the location of the smelter close to communities.

At the national scale, the issue of the operation of the smelter was dealt with specifically in relation to national standards and how they might be used to measure the risks associated with industrial development. EV, a local community activist, stated: "Since we know there are risks associated with the smelter and other types of industrial development, maybe we need to raise the bar on safety measures and practices" (EV in the *Express* 12 October 2010). EV seemed to be suggesting that the national operating standards for industrial safety were not rigorous. She suggested that a revision of these standards would be needed if the smelter project were to be safely implemented.

Finally, at the local scale, the issue of the safe operation of the smelter in relation to surrounding communities was also raised, as seen in the following quote by KS of La Brea: "I was one of the people who had reservations about what would happen when a smelter plant is built near our homes. And my first impression of China was that it was a clean place. There were communities next to the smelter plants. This was interesting to me because the smelter plant would be in my backyard" (KS in the *Express* 8 February 2011).

This resident indicated that he had had concerns about living close to a functioning smelter plant. However, these concerns were dispelled once he visited China and observed communities living close to smelters.

The second sub-theme addressed the physical health of individuals at the national and local scales only. At the national scale, the physical health of the population was raised as a concern as indicated by the following quote: "In my view, the instant case falls into a category of its own, where errors on the part of the defendant can have far reaching consequences for the health and national safety of the national population" (Mira Dean-Armorer, High Court judge, in the *Express* 6 February 2011). In her quote, Justice Dean-Armorer indicated that the decision-makers of Alutrint made errors during the preparatory phases of the smelter project, which would have led to health consequences for the public.

At the local scale, the physical health sub-theme was specific to the local communities and involved two underlying issues. The first was the fear of developing cancer, and the second was concern about the continuous medical monitoring proposed for the community. These issues were illustrated in the followings quotes:

> We have been affected by this, the construction of the smelter plant, from day one . . . we are being affected by dust and noise. . . . And now learning that we are going to have to be tested for cancer. (FF, Vessigny resident, in the *Express* 6 February 2011)

> We are presently in discussions with a consultant regarding the implementation of the Medical Monitoring Plan, which must be undertaken with the full engagement of the Ministry of Health, as it involves public health issues. (Josieann Richards, Alutrint communications manager, in the *Express* 6 February 2011)

> Monitoring includes personal and family history for allergies, asthma, liver conditions, skin conditions, and cardiovascular issues, clinical chemical analysis, pulmonary function tests, urine for fluoride, vital signs and history of bronchitis. (Emily Gaynor Dick-Forde, minister of housing and the environment, in the *Express* 6 February 2011)

Resident FF expressed some of the health concerns that the community members believed they had suffered, notably the dust and noise experienced from the time the land began to be prepared for the construction of the smelter. He also listed testing for cancer as a community concern. As indicated by Richards, the communications manager for Alutrint, in the second quote, the medical monitoring plan was essential since the implementation of the smelter project created a "public health concern". The medical monitoring plan was designed to monitor the local community for a variety of ailments, in addition to cancer, as indicated by Minister Emily Gaynor Dick-Forde in the third quote.

Characterizing the Alutrint Public Discourse

The analysis identified three important features of the debate as manifested on the different scales. The first of these features involved the presence or absence of themes, sub-themes and issues at each scale. In several cases, individual themes, sub-themes and issues were not discussed at every scale. Given the special importance of the national and local scales in relation to shaping a public discourse on the project, the absence of a theme, sub-theme or issue at one of these two scales was of particular interest.

The sub-theme right to land, under the theme of rights, only appeared at the local scale (table 13.1). It took two forms: that of the rights of persons who had legal title to land and those who were informal occupiers of land and had no such rights. The local treatment of this sub-theme was perhaps to be expected given that the only land in question was land at the locality where the smelter project construction would take place. Land rights could have, of course, been discussed at other levels since landownership rights were governed by national law as well as, potentially, regional and international treaties and rules. The fact was, however, that land rights were not discussed at those scales.

Under the theme of ecological consequences, four different sub-themes were spread across two scales – the national and local (table 13.1). The two which appeared at the national scale were climate change and use of the sustainable development framework for industrialization. The sub-theme of the effects on the environment of constructing the smelter and the cumulative effects of operations of the smelter, port and power plant appeared at the local scale. We note that even though the same theme was dealt with at the two scales, the sub-themes were different at each scale. Also worthy of attention is that all these sub-themes were absent from the regional and international scales.

The second characteristic of the debate on the Alutrint smelter project was the mismatch of issues across scales. Here, although the same themes and sub-themes appeared across scales, they took the form of different issues. Under the rights theme, the sub-theme right to information appeared at the national and local scales. At the national scale, the issue was one of concern about rights to information, specifically information related to the economics of the project. This was understandable since the question here was one of how much the taxpayer was going to be required to contribute and the projected economic national benefit from this investment. At the local scale, the specific economic element in the information being sought was not covered. Rather, the issue under the information sub-theme was that of what actions community members should take, and what the state could do to ensure that these individuals were granted the right to information about the project (table 13.1).

Other mismatches occurred under the rights theme. The sub-theme of right to compensation was manifested in the form of three specific issues (table 13.1). At the international and local scales, the issues concerned groups of people who were to receive the compensation. At the international scale the relevant group was the Chinese workers, the main employees of the smelter project, while at the local scale it was the individual families being relocated under agreed terms and conditions. The issue at the national scale was one of the principles to be used to guide the compensation process. These principles were to be derived from Trinidad and Tobago's constitution. This produced an overlap with the local scale issue already discussed, where the relocation was also to be guided by the constitution.

For the sub-theme of economic costs, the international scale, as might be expected, covered intercountry relations. The issues were those of the penalties that Trinidad would pay to other countries for withdrawing from the contract and the negative effects on foreign investment and investor confidence. The national scale involved concerns for the use of tax dollars to develop a smelter project perceived as having limited overall benefit for the country or the local community (table 13.1).

Under the economic benefits sub-theme, at the regional scale, intercountry relations also featured. Here the issue was the trade relationship between Trinidad and Tobago and Jamaica. At the national scale, the issue was that of the benefits to the nation as a whole through economic diversification, increased industrialization and even job creation. At the local scale, the issue of economic benefit involved the creation of jobs, specifically jobs for local people (table 13.1).

The sub-theme of the health and safety effects of the smelter project operation was addressed across three of the scales (table 13.1). At the international scale, the health and safety issue was presented in relation to international standards established using other countries as comparators. At the national scale, the issue was national standards, which would apply to the smelter and its operations. At the local scale, though, the issue of standards did not appear. Instead, the health and safety sub-theme manifested itself in the shape of an issue about the safety of the community with a smelter project located nearby. A final sub-theme, under the theme of health and safety, emerged. This sub-theme, at the national scale, dealt with the health of the inhabitants of the country as a whole. At this scale, the issue took the form of a general reference to health. At the local scale, the issue was one of the health of the communities surrounding the smelter project (table 13.1).

The third characteristic of the debate involved issues which appeared to be the same across scales but which turned out to have different meanings. Only one example of this characteristic was seen in the data. It involved the issue of jobs. At the national scale, jobs referred to permanent, sustainable and high-paying jobs for people of the nation. At the local scale, the issue of jobs was parochial. It involved jobs for the members of the local community, particularly the youth. It also had an additional element consisting of the hope for training to equip local labour for employment in the project.

Findings and Conclusion

The observed patterns in the analysis were quite instructive. They sometimes presented themes with each of their respective sub-themes being addressed at a different scale. At other times, themes and sub-themes were addressed at one scale only. Finally, where issues were addressed across scales, they had a different meaning at each scale.

In the review of the case studies of large-scale industrial projects discussed earlier, we see projects being aborted because of differences in how the project was viewed across scales. We seek to extend this insight to cover public debate on such projects. We have posited that a requirement for an efficient public discourse is that everybody is talking about the same thing. Given the analysis in this chapter, this requirement can be expressed in very specific terms. Communication among stakeholders, as manifested in the public discourse, should address the same themes and sub-themes across all relevant scales. It is worth noting that, in relation to the data discussed in the chapter, all scales were relevant. In addition, issues, which manifest specific themes and sub-themes, should mean the same thing across the different scales. From what was seen in the data presented in this chapter, the requirement for matching themes, sub-themes and issues at each scale frequently was not met. We conclude that, across scales, a breakdown in communication had occurred among the parties.

From our analysis of the public discourse around the Alutrint project, we conclude that an efficient public communication in relation to large industrial-type developments is one of the necessary conditions for successful implementation of such projects. Though the politics of scale literature has not explicitly addressed the role of the nature of public discourse, this is frequently implied. One example is Muradian, Martinez-Alier and Correa (2003), in which the authors concluded that when different stakeholders – in their case, experts, local populations and industry – disagree, there is difficulty in getting projects, such as the Tambo Grande mine in Peru, approved. Opposition to the project reflected the views of local communities and activist groups, which focused on themes of rights, risk, trust and equity. By contrast, support for the project, typically expressed at the level of the national government and the mining industry, focused on themes of economic growth, progress and modernization.

Darby's (2012) case study on the El Paso smelter also implied a breakdown in communication across scales. The scale at which the local community perceived the contamination, which was based on the biophysical extent and degree of the contamination, was different from the scale of the national borders of the United States, within which laws, regulations and clean up would apply. Thus, regulatory and clean-up responses functioned on the national scale. By contrast, the geographical range of the contamination that the local community wanted addressed extended beyond the national borders and into Mexico (Darby 2012).

As it relates to the current case presented in this chapter, both aforementioned case studies illustrate the breakdown in communication that this chapter emphasizes. Darby's (2012) case was an example of stakeholders at different scales talking about the same things, which had different meanings. The study by Muradian, Martinez-Alier and Correa (2003) involved different concerns being focused on at two different scales. In both cases, the authors suggest that a mismatch in issues, whether in terms of content or meaning, have resulted in undesirable outcomes.

The lesson from the Alutrint case is that when there is a breakdown in communication within public discourse, the stakeholders with the greatest power prevail. In the Trinidad case, the most powerful party turned out to be the local community, with its concerns about the fate of the local land and local neighbourhoods where the project was going to be implemented. Their public protest brought the project to a halt.

Actors at the local scale led the movement to stop the project. However, this was a complex project involving interconnections at multiple scales. In addition to the stakeholders at the local level, there were international stakeholders such as China's Exim Bank, in addition to regional stakeholders such as Venezuela's Sural, Brazil's Votorantim, and bauxite suppliers from Jamaica and potentially Guyana. There was, as well, involvement at the national scale in the form of the majority interest of the project by the Trinidad and Tobago government in the smelter plant. The breakdown in public discourse documented here can be explained by the already established recognition of the importance of relationships between and across all scales in promoting large industrial projects such as Alutrint (Darby 2012; Kurtz 2003; Muradian, Martinez-Alier and Correa 2003). The lesson of the Alutrint public discourse is that relationships across scales should be integrated into the conduct of the public discourse surrounding the implementation of such projects.

Against this general background, one can address the specifics of the Alutrint case. This project originated in a dream of Caribbean regional economic integration extending back at least five decades previously (Lewis 2009; Newstead 2009). Yet, as we have seen, the regional scale concerned itself with the economic benefits of the project for regional trade and remained silent on all local scale matters. The specific lesson here is that, for the economic and trade benefits to be realized, the regional scale, along with the international and national scales, had to address the issues which concerned the local community. The issues relevant to the local scale should properly have been addressed at the other scales. These would have included

- the right to information and the community's actual ability to access that information;
- land rights, both formal and informal;
- rights to relocation and compensation;
- the creation of jobs for members of the local community;
- damage to the natural environment in and around the communities where the smelter would be located; and
- potential health and safety effects on members of the local communities.

The smelter project was shelved with the promise that Guyana would be its future location (Richards 2010). Since a regional and/or international industrial project has to be implemented in a physical locality, the rights of citizens in the new locality (somewhere in Guyana) will be affected. With the change in government in Trinidad and Tobago in 2015, there was an indication that the smelter project will not be pursued (Sant and Julien 2016). This put an end to an almost ten-year controversy over the development of an aluminium smelter in Trinidad. However, according to reporting by the *Trinidad Guardian* newspaper, the government has reconvened talks to start up downstream aluminium industries. These products include "pressed aluminium, coils, aluminium sheets for the vehicle industry and wheel rims. Aluminium ingots will be imported to make cast aluminium products" (*Trinidad Guardian* 2017, para. 2). While there is no indication as to where these discussions will lead, so far there has been no national-level resistance from citizens against this effort.

Citizens are gaining an increasingly powerful voice globally in defence of their rights (Davis and Jha 2011; Middleton 2012; Muradian, Martinez-Alier and Correa 2003). This makes even more critical the need for an efficient public discourse that addresses at all other scales the issues of concern to local communities. The failure of public discourse on Alutrint to consider the weight of concerns at the local scale caused the discourse, once weighed, to be found wanting.

Acknowledgements

The authors would like to thank the reviewers for their comments on the earlier drafts of this chapter. Additionally, we would like to thank all the Colgate students who served as research assistants on this project, with special thanks to Josh Rosen for creating images for the chapter. Finally, we would like to say thank you to the voices of those community members who are represented in this chapter.

Note

1. The designations of public officials are representative of their status during the time of the controversy 2006–10.

References

Advameg, Inc. 2013. "Press Reference: Trinidad and Tobago". Accessed 23 October 2013. http://www.pressreference.com/Sw-Ur/Trinidad-and-Tobago.html.

Barclay, Lou Anne. 2012. "The Anatomy of a Failed Industrial Policy: Developing an Aluminium Industry in Trinidad and Tobago". *Transnational Corporations* 21 (2): 47–76. https://unctad.org/en/PublicationChapters/diaeia2013d1a3_en.pdf.

Bickerstaff, Karen and Julian Agyeman. 2009. "Assembling Justice Spaces: The Scalar Politics of Environmental Justice in North-east England". *Antipode* 41 (4): 781–806.

Carrillo Roa, Alejandro and José Paranaguá de Santana. 2012. "Regional Integration and South-South Cooperation in Health in Latin America and the Caribbean". *Revista Panamericana de Salud Publica* 32 (5): 368–75.

Chapple, Karen and Edward G. Goetz. 2011. "Spatial Justice through Regionalism? The Inside Game, the Outside Game, and the Quest for the Spatial Fix in the Unit". *Community Development: Journal of the Community Development Society* 42 (4): 458–75.

Cruickshank, Cassandra D. 2005. "Trying to Go It Alone and Failing in an Authoritarian Developing State: A Case Study of the Independent Trinidad". Unpublished thesis. University of Florida.

Darby, Kate. 2012. "Lead Astray: Scale, Environmental Justice and the El Paso Smelter". *Local Environment* 17 (8): 797–814.

Davis, Coray and Manoj K. Jha. 2011. "A Dynamic Modeling Approach to Investigate Impacts to Protected and Low-income Populations in Highway Planning". *Transportation Research Part A* 45 (7): 598–610.

Engineering and Mining Journal. 2006. "Alcoa Eyes Trinidad Smelter Project". *Engineering and Mining Journal* 207 (3): 12.

———. 2004. "Around the World: The Caribbean". *Engineering and Mining Journal* 205 (7): 16.

Haughton, G. 1998. "Geographical Equity and Regional Resource Management: Water Management in Southern California". *Environment and Planning B: Planning and Design* 25 (2): 279–98.

Kurtz, Hilda E. 2003. "Scale Frames and Counter-Scale Frames: Constructing the Problem of Environmental Injustice". *Political Geography* 22 (8): 887–916.

Lewis, Vaughan A. 2009. "What Purposes for CARICOM Integration Today?: A Public Lecture". *Journal of Eastern Caribbean Studies* 34 (4): 123–55.

Meghoo, Kirk. 2003. *Politics in a 'Half Made Society': Trinidad and Tobago, 1925–2001.* Kingston, Jamaica: Ian Randle Publisher.

Middleton, Carl. 2012. "Transborder Environmental Justice in Regional Energy Trade in Mainland South-East Asia". *Austrian Journal of South-East Asian Studies* 5 (2): 292–315.

Muradian, Roldan, Joan Martinez-Alier, and Humberto Correa. 2003. "International Capital versus Local Population: The Environmental Conflict of Tambogrande Mining Project, Peru". *Society and Natural Resources: An International Journal* 16 (9): 775–92.

Newstead, Clare. 2009. "Regional Governmentality: Neoliberalization and the Caribbean Community Single Market and Economy". *Singapore Journal of Tropical Geography* 30 (2): 158–73.

O'Brien, Derek. 2011. "CARICOM: Regional Integration in a Post-colonial World". *European Law Journal* 17 (5): 630–48.

One Caribbean Media Limited. 2013. "Trinidad Express Newspapers". One Caribbean Media Limited. https://www.onecaribbeanmedia.net/media-group/newspapers/trinidad-express/.

Rapid Environmental Assessments Limited. 2009. *Noise and Particulate Monitoring at Union Industrial Estate La Brea: CEC 1033/2005 – Compliance Monitoring Report for Period June 2008 – December 2008*. Port of Spain, Trinidad: Rapid Environmental Assessments Limited.

Revauger, Jean-Paul. 2008. "Regional Integration in the Commonwealth Caribbean and the Impact of the European Union". *The Round Table* 97 (399): 857–69.

Richards, F. 2012. "'Express' Tops All in Readership". *Trinidad Express*, 29 May. Accessed 27 June 2013. http://www.trinidadexpress.com/news/_Express__tops_all_in_readership-155553825.html.

Richards, Peter. 2010. "Trinidad Scraps Controversial Smelter". *Inter Press Service News Agency*, 24 September. http://www.ipsnews.net/2010/09/trinidad-scraps-controversial-smelter/.

Sant, Rosemarie and Joel Julien. 2016. "Govt Agrees to Restart Alutech". *Trinidad Guardian*, 19 June. Accessed 22 December 2017. http://www.guardan.co.tt/news/2016-06-18/govt-agrees-restart-alutech.

Towers, George. 2000. "Applying the Political Geography of Scale: Grassroots Strategies and Environmental Justice". *Professional Geographer* 52 (1): 23–36.

Trinidad Express. 2012. "Daily Express". One Caribbean Media Limited. https://www.trinidadexpress.com.

Trinidad Guardian. 2017. "Government Still Pursuing Aluminium Downstream Options". *Trinidad Guardian*, 29 March. http://www.guardian.co.tt/business/2017-03-29/government-still-pursuing-aluminium-downstream-options.

Walker, Gordon. 2009. "Beyond Distribution and Proximity: Exploring the Multiple Spatialities of Environmental Justice". *Antipode* 41 (4): 614–36.

Weik, Juan. 2009. "Votorantim Will Build Alutrint Smelter in Trinidad". *Metal Bulletin Daily Alerts* (4 December): 1–2.

Wilkinson, Bert. 2004. "Bauxite Smelter Could Spur Caribbean Manufacturing". *The New York Amsterdam News* 95 (22): 14.

Wolford, Wendy. 2008. "Environmental Justice and the Construction of Scale in Brazilian Agriculture". *Society and Natural Resources: An International Journal* 21 (7): 641–55.

Part IV

Emerging Priorities for CARICOM

Chapter 14

Climate Change and the Integration Project

JAY R. MANDLE

The Caribbean integration project is mired in an immobilizing equilibrium. It has not come fully to fruition, but neither has it entirely disappeared. There are important forces propelling integration. Cultural affinities – a sense that there really is a Caribbean community – is foremost in that regard. But for regional integration to deepen, a way must be found to strengthen that sense of community. Failure to do so risks not simply arresting the integration project. It might trigger as well a process of fragmentation that would splinter the region into competing blocs. It is in this perspective that Rudolph A. Collins's argument for the importance of functional cooperation should be understood. This is a sphere by which common bonds can be strengthened.

Collins argues that "any reasonable analysis will show that what has served to keep the Community together, enabling it to pursue its economic integration agenda over the years, has been the historical sense of common identity which still persists, despite the many failed federal experiments and other regional integration initiatives" (2012, 501). Joint regional efforts in such fields as disaster preparedness, health, education and security – described in official statements and in the academic literature as functional cooperation – have been important in maintaining and building that sense of community. Indeed, Collins advocates such regional efforts precisely because they do so. He writes that functional cooperation "is a cross cutting issue that must permeate all the actions and activities of the Community and must do so for a very specific purpose", namely "to ensure the creation of a Community for all" (Collins 2012, 506). In this regard, a recent International Monetary Fund Working Paper agrees, arguing "functional policy cooperation in areas where the region faces significant common challenges could provide low-hanging fruit . . . building momentum toward full integration" (International Monetary Fund 2019, 45).

Though these promotive forces ensure that the idea of integration persists, they have not been strong enough to overcome political indifference to regionalism. That indifference exists because no powerful interest group is present promoting and financing a politics of shared regional governance. As Havelock Brewster points out, "a transnational constituency, and thus a source of pressure for the CSME [Caribbean Single Market and Economy] whether of business or civil interests, is almost wholly absent" (2003, 47). The upshot is, as Lloyd Best once put it, that there is no "regional politics": "There [is] no regional political party or political movement" (Girvan 2011, 30). Without such pressure, deep integration remains an unobtainable objective. Even a strong sense of community is not sufficient to ensure its achievement. Cultural bonds may be a necessary condition for successful integration, but they are not sufficient.

Those bonds must be institutionalized with legislation for the project to be realized. It is in the political process that integration's fate resides.

It is possible that a recent Caribbean Court of Justice (2013) decision concerning the right to hassle-free travel in the region might prompt such a constituency from among members of the legal profession. But that awaits future developments. For now, few if any candidates run for office advocating even a limited ceding of authority to a regional body such as the Caribbean Community (CARICOM).

Climate Change and Tourism

Such a politics might, however, be possible if the Caribbean were to be confronted with a shock whose negative repercussions exceed the coping capacities of even the best financially endowed West Indian nation. An exogenous shock could alter perceptions of the potential benefits of regionalization. If that occurred, it is possible that the current political leadership might be galvanized to support a shared response. Such a change of circumstances might also mobilize public opinion in ways that could propel an insurgent cadre of pro-integrationist politicians to electoral success. What is highly unlikely, however, is that any of this will occur without a triggering mechanism.

The effects of global climate change could produce such a shock. Already, the region has started to experience the consequences of the warming of the earth's atmosphere. Three leading climate scientists have recently reported that "the effects of climate change in the Caribbean are not events in some distant future. The tourism sector and the economies and livelihoods in the region are already being affected by sea level rise and erosion and also by extreme impacts such as coral bleaching, flooding and drought" (Simpson, Scott and Trotz 2011, 5). It is at least reasonable to speculate that the damage associated with these events could serve to strengthen the attractiveness of regionalist politics, since the need to respond adequately when they occur will be beyond the capacity of any of the individual CARICOM nations.

Without dramatic mitigation efforts on the part of the countries that are the principle sources of greenhouse gas emissions – a response that today seems more unlikely than ever in light of the failure of international agreements to substantially limit global warming – the negative impact in the Caribbean of climate change will become substantial in the not too distant future. A recent estimate of the cost to the region of increased hurricane destruction, loss of tourism revenue and infrastructure damage comes to US$10.7 billion by 2025 and US$22 billion by 2050. These estimates represent 5 per cent and 10 per cent, respectively, of the region's 2004 gross domestic product (CCCCC 2012). Adding the costs associated with hurricane-induced wind damage, coastal and inland floods resulting from storm surges caused by hurricanes and non-tropical weather systems would add another 1–3 per cent of the gross domestic product by 2030. If anything, the report of the Caribbean Community Climate Change Centre (CCCCC) understates the resulting problems when it indicates that "the net effect of costs on this scale is equivalent to causing a perpetual economic recession in each of the CARICOM Member States" (CCCCC 2012, 199).

More important than these aggregate estimates is the fact that the region's tourist industry will be more adversely affected by climate change than other sectors. The CCCCC's "mid-range" estimate is that as early as 2050, sea-level rise will add US$3.6 million to the industry's annual costs, far exceeding the additional burden that will be borne either by the region's agricultural or industrial sectors. If, as seems increasingly likely, the sea-level rise will more closely approximate the CCCCC's high estimate, that figure could balloon to US$5.6 million (Simpson et al. 2010).

The problem is that, with the exception of Trinidad and Tobago and the mainland countries of Belize, Guyana and Suriname, all CARICOM nations depend heavily on the tourism sector for their economic well-being. The World Travel and Tourism Council ranks the Caribbean, as a whole, as the region in the world most dependent on that industry. In its estimates, Antigua and Barbuda possesses virtually a one-industry economy; the Bahamas, Barbados and St Lucia see more than half of their total output dependent upon the tourist sector; and elsewhere tourism is responsible for about a quarter of the gross domestic product (World Travel and Tourism Council 2011).

The threat emanating from climate change is that in the future the industry will not be able to play the role of leading economic sector that it has in the past. Tourism is a sector that more than most is dependent on a complementarity between specific natural factor endowments, physical capital and infrastructure. It is that combination that will be upset by rising sea levels and intensified storms. It is true that other tourist destinations may be confronted with similar competitive difficulties. But it is also likely that under the new climate regime, additional locations will emerge to attract tourists. Caribbean tourism is certain to struggle as it confronts the costs of global climate change and the pressures created by competing tourist destinations.

In short, the consequences of global climate change are almost certainly going to impose a profound shock to the people of the member nations of CARICOM. Tourism, the industry upon which the region's relative prosperity has been based, is faced with the likelihood of contraction. Whether global climate change and the damage done to tourism results in a strengthening of integrationist politics remains, however, uncertain. Success depends on whether its advocates are persuasive in arguing that an integrated Caribbean will be better positioned to offset the damage caused by global climate change than each nation could individually.

Addressing Climate Change

To date, global climate change has not been a salient political issue in the Caribbean. Nevertheless, at the governmental level, the importance of the issue has been acknowledged. The first response to the threat of global warming occurred in 1997 when a project called Caribbean Planning for Adaptation to Climate Change came into existence, overseen by a committee chaired by CARICOM. From that emerged a proposal to create a regional Climate Change Centre, which became operational in 2004 with headquarters at the University of Belize (CCCCC n.d.). But it was not until 2009 that regionalism with regard to the climate was made explicit. In that year, the CARICOM Heads of Governments issued the Liliendaal Declaration on Climate

Change and Development, which affirmed "the importance of a common Regional approach to address the threats and challenges of climate change" (CARICOM Heads of Government 2009, n.p.). To that end, those leaders affirmed their support for the CCCCC and, later in the same year, approved a document prepared by the CCCCC titled "A Regional Framework for Achieving Development Resilient to Change" (CCCCC 2009). The CARICOM Heads of Government mandated that the CCCCC prepare an implementation plan, a document that appeared under the title "Delivering Transformational Change 2011–21" and was approved by the CARICOM Heads of Government at its meeting in Suriname in March 2012 (CCCCC 2011).

The first of these documents indicates that its authors intended "to systematically address the development challenges posed by climate change for the Caribbean" (CCCCC 2009, 14). But, in fact, its content falls short of that objective. It does not deal with future economic growth in the region nor the consequences of climate change for that growth. The objectives that are made explicit are to (1) reduce greenhouse gas emissions in the region; (2) reduce the region's vulnerability to greenhouse gas emissions by, for example, constructing flood defences and changing land use patterns; (3) build citizen awareness with educational programmes; (4) augment CCCCC's organizational capacity; and (5) disseminate information concerning successful adaptation experiences. There is, however, no discussion of how to respond to damage inflicted on tourism, despite the fact that the regional framework itself explicitly points out that "the productive sectors, especially agriculture and tourism, are likely to be adversely affected by climate change" (CCCCC 2009, 12).

The second report concerning implementation broke little new ground. It does recommend what it calls a "Three-Ones" principle of organization, in which the region agrees to one plan, creates one coordinating mechanism and utilizes one monitoring and evaluation system (CCCCC 2011, 21). But the objectives contained in the first document largely remained intact in the second, as did its omission of the need to find new industries to pick up the slack left by tourism's decline. It too seeks to reduce greenhouse gas emissions in the region; mainstream and promote adaptation measures with regard to water supply, health, and coastal and marine ecosystems; and reduce tourism's vulnerabilities. A major thrust of this document is to identify sources of funding for these activities. The intention is to facilitate "the ongoing involvement of the international community to efficiently strengthen the capacity of the CARICOM countries to adapt to a changing climate" (CCCCC 2011, 46).

Yet no obligatory responsibilities were placed on CARICOM members. The document cautions that its recommendations should not be considered prescriptive. As it puts it, "each member country and each regional organization has different challenges, organizational processes and governance. The process developed by each government and regional organisations to mobilise resources should reflect this and work within and build upon the effective governance and institutional arrangements that already exist" (CCCCC 2011, 20). With such a voluntarist approach, little impetus towards integration was provided.

It remains the case, therefore, that integration's immobilizing equilibrium persists. Despite the alarming assessments made by the CCCCC concerning the regional consequences of rising sea levels and increasingly damaging weather systems, little regional cooperation in response exists or is foreseen. And consideration of what the region's economy should look like with tourism damaged is a subject that has not been seriously considered.

Ideas about Integration

Because of sea-level rise and increased storm intensity, tourism will not be able to continue to act as the region's leading sector, responsible for most of its economic growth. The industry will survive, but it will not be possible for it to retain its status as the principle prop upon which the well-being of the Caribbean people relies. The very real threat that faces CARICOM countries is that the damage done to tourism will cause unemployment to rise, poverty to increase, and political instability and unrest to make an appearance. The region faces a profound crisis.

But crisis brings with it not only reduced incomes and protest; it also creates an opportunity to advance fresh ideas. In the new context, advocates of integration will be presented with an enhanced opportunity to influence the region's political agenda. The Caribbean people will be looking for an alternative to economic decline. For integrationists to be successful, they will have to persuade what is likely to remain a sceptical population that regional cooperation is the best way to respond to changed circumstances. They will have to possess a clear, understandable economic strategy. But they also will have to respect the fact that national allegiances will remain strong. What is needed is a proposal that strikes a careful balance between persisting parochial loyalty on the one hand, and the promise of gains to be secured if at least some economic decision-making is ceded to a regional body. Integration proposals will have to fall short of nation-building or even a single unified economy. Both are too ambitious. An attenuated version of integration will have to be offered; one that, despite its limitations, speaks effectively to the need for new sectors of economic activity to provide an alternative to tourism.

The strategy that is adopted will have to provide a path to overcoming the region's technological weaknesses. This is because the new industries needed to compensate for tourism's relative decline will have to be able to successfully compete in global markets. In the words of a document produced by the World Bank's Global Forum Action Plan, "experience suggests that building appropriate science and engineering capacity tailored to achieving . . . priority social and economic development objectives is the best and surest way to generate sustainable progress" (Watkins and Mandell 2010, 3). The problem is that, at the moment, the region possesses very little ability to engage in either the product or process innovation that is required. According to the World Economic Forum survey, the mean ranking for Barbados, Guyana, Jamaica, and Trinidad and Tobago (the only regional countries included in the study) is 84th of 144 countries with regard to firms' capacity for innovation, and 81st with regard to company spending on research and development (Schwab 2012). The region's technological weakness means that its need to restructure will confront formidable obstacles.

A report to CARICOM by the late Norman Girvan in 2007 suggested an approach to deal with those obstacles. Girvan wrote that "CARICOM will require both a regional policy on research and development (R&D) to encourage the development, adaptation, and diffusion of technology in production and a regional institutional mechanism to drive the process" (2007, 42). To that end, Girvan advocated the creation of a Caribbean Research and Competitiveness Funding Agency. He argued that "by allowing critical mass to be attained in the development of new technologies, avoiding costly duplication of effort and promoting technology sharing" through such a fund, the region could progress in ways that individual nations would not be able to do (43). He advocated the creation of "product clusters" and suggested that "the regional universities and local research institutions should be encouraged to work closely with industry science and technology" (42). The agency would relate to external donor agencies that would be "asked to support the regional policy by providing direct subventions to approved R&D by regional and national R&D institutes and/or by supporting the establishment and operation of the proposed Agency if this option is pursued" (43–44). In short, a cross-Caribbean agency would be tasked with mobilizing the resources necessary to advance the technological capacity of the region and allocating those resources to achieve that growth.

Important as the idea of a technology-funding agency is, Girvan understated what will be required to advance technological modernization in the Caribbean. Building an enhanced technological capability is a multidimensional activity. This involves curricular changes at all levels of schooling, mobilizing scientists and engineers in appropriately supportive institutions, providing the funding they require, creating mechanisms to facilitate the movement of laboratory innovations to the market and ensuring that intellectual property rights are protected. In the circumstances of the Caribbean, it probably also means tapping into the human capital that is present in the region's diaspora. It will also be necessary to establish mechanisms to ensure that the fruits of these efforts are fairly distributed over the entire region. In short, more than just a funding agency is required.

Such an effort will require policy harmonization across the region. It is just not possible for the smaller countries in the Windward and Leeward Island chains, or for Barbados, Guyana or Belize to mount such efforts separately. The scale of what is required is beyond their financial and human resources. And while the problem of scale may not be as acute in Jamaica or Trinidad and Tobago, the relatively poor record of each regarding technological change, in conjunction with the very high emigration rates of tertiary-educated individuals (especially from the former) suggests that they too would benefit from cross-regional collaboration. Sharing competencies that are in scarce supply in each country is the most efficient way to deploy the high-level human resources that remain in the Caribbean (Mandle 2011).

Though Girvan's suggestion is limited and does not go far in the direction of shared policies, its implementation would be a valuable first step. Its modesty means it does not represent an overreach. It challenges no country's sovereignty. Further, it does not require the extensive realignment in the marketing of the region's products away from the United States, Canada and the European Union, to Central and Latin America and Asia, that the Economic Commission for Latin America and the Caribbean calls for (ECLAC 2014, 22). But a technology agency such as that proposed by Girvan would be attractive in two dimensions. If implemented, it could begin the process of advancing technology in the region. At the same time, its success in that regard could provide enhanced credibility to the integration project. Seen in this light, such an agency would not be an end in and of itself, but part of a long-term strategy to bolster CARICOM's ability to construct a post-tourist dominated economy.

One question that arises is whether it is realistic to expect that CARICOM as an institution could become the vehicle by which to achieve technological modernization. The content of a 2012 consultant's report commissioned by CARICOM titled "Turning around CARICOM" casts doubt on its ability to do so. The authors believe that the organization suffers from deep structural problems that are not amenable to quick solutions. They conclude that underfinancing, internal inefficiencies and a failure to prioritize its objectives have brought CARICOM to a crisis point in which its very survival is questionable. To stave off collapse, they argue that CARICOM will have to target "the delivery of a narrow range of specific, practical and achievable benefits over a reasonably short time horizon" (Stoneman, Pollard and Innis 2012, 30).

The systematic identification and implementation of the priorities that would promote technological change has not occurred. CARICOM is not up to that task. When and if the member states move to enable it to provide an offset to the problems caused by climate change, they will first have to correct what the Report of the West Indian Commission in 1992 called CARICOM's "Achilles Heel": the "virtual absence of effective machinery for implementing regional decisions" (WIC 1992, 462). Though the Caribbean Court of Justice may have broken new ground in this regard concerning the right of CARICOM nationals to travel without harassment in the region, it nonetheless remains the case that, all too frequently, decisions taken by the CARICOM Heads of Government are left, as the commission puts it, "to gather dust in the files of the CARICOM Secretariat" (WIC 1992, 462). What CARICOM needs, the commission argues, is "a central authority, freed of national domestic responsibilities and allegiances and appropriately empowered to implement CARICOM's decisions" (WIC 1992, 476). Unless and until such a central authority is agreed to, there is little likelihood that the level of cooperation and harmonization that regional technological advancement requires can be achieved.

For CARICOM to be strengthened, the people of the region will have to be convinced that it can be effective. Demonstrable achievements will have to be available to be pointed to. Girvan's funding agency could fill that function. Its success, in combination with the escalating damage to tourism caused by climate change, could prompt a radical change in public attitudes. The possibility exists that, as people in the region come to appreciate the calamity that awaits a technologically impoverished Caribbean and observe that a Caribbean Research and Competitiveness Funding Agency produces positive results, the immobilizing equilibrium with regard to integration will be disrupted. If that occurs, CARICOM would become an effective vehicle of technological modernization.

Conclusion

The damage that global climate change will inflict on the Caribbean is an unambiguous injustice. The region has contributed only negligible amounts to the build-up of greenhouse gas emissions responsible for global warming; nevertheless, it is one of the principal victims of that phenomenon. Further, there is little likelihood that the nations that have been the main polluters will offer adequate compensation for the damage they have inflicted. The burden of adaptation will fall on the people and governments in the region. This is not an adjustment process that will be easily implemented. New sectors of economic activity will be required. The use of modern technology in production and the ability to be innovative will be critical. The region's economy will have to become modern.

The Caribbean has not previously made a concerted effort to be technologically progressive. Successful tourism did not require it to be so. But the conditions that did not penalize that neglect will soon be gone. In response, the region will have to address its scientific and engineering weaknesses. That requires a carefully crafted integrationist politics that could result in a strengthening of CARICOM. To accomplish those ends, a strategy is needed that respects prevailing localist attitudes, but at the same time is designed to reduce their salience. Climate change makes a technology-promoting integrationist strategy a necessity.

References

Brewster, Havelock. 2003. "Review of the Rose Hall Declaration: Provisions on Regional Governance". In *CARICOM Single Market and Economy: Genesis and Prognosis*, edited by Kenneth O. Hall and Myrtle Chuck-A-Sang, 46–60. Kingston, Jamaica: Ian Randle Press.

Caribbean Court of Justice. 2013. "Media Release: CCJ Delivers Judgment in Matter of Shanique Myrie v The State of Barbados". Available at https://ccj.org/wp-content/uploads/2021/02/MEDIA-RELEASE-Shanique-Myrie.pdf.

CARICOM Heads of Government. 2009. "Liliendaal Declaration on Climate Change and Development". Georgetown, Guyana: Conference of Heads of Government of CARICOM. 6 July 2009. https://caricom.org/media-center/communications/statements-from-caricom-meetings/liliendaal-declaration-on-climate-change-and-development-issued-by-the-thir.

CCCCC (Caribbean Community Climate Change Centre). 2009. "Climate Change and the Caribbean: A Regional Framework for Achieving Development Resilient to Change". http://www.widecast.org/Resources/Docs/CCCCC_2009_Climate_Change_and_the_Caribbean_2009-2015.pdf.

———. 2011. "Delivering Transformational Change 2011-21". https://cdkn.org/wp-content/uploads/2010/12/IP_version-verificar-si-final.pdf.

———. 2012. "The Implementation Plan for the CARICOM 'Regional Framework for Achieving Development Resilient to Climate Change'". https://www.cdema.org/cris/ews_toolkit/Implementation_plan_CARICOM _regional_framework.pdf.

Collins, Rudolph A. 2012. "Strengthening the Caribbean Community: A Comment on the Role of Functional Cooperation". In *Regional Integration: Key to Caribbean Survival and Prosperity*, edited by Kenneth Hall and Myrtle Chuck-A-Sang, 497–509. Bloomington, IN: Trafford.

ECLAC. 2014. "Regional Integration in the Caribbean: The Role of Trade Agreements and Structural Transformation". Sheldon McLean, Machel Pantin, Nyashsa Sketette, Series: Studies and Perspectives, no. 37.

Girvan, Norman. 2007. "Toward a Single Development Vision and the Role of the Single Economy". Barbados: Heads of Government of CARICOM.

———. 2011. "From Independence to Globalised Colonialism". *The Caribbean Review*, 5 June 2011. http://www.caribbeanreview.org/2011/06/from-independence-to-globalised-colonialism/.

International Monetary Fund, Abdullah Al Hassan, Mary Burfisher, Julian T.S. Chow, Ding Ding, Fabio Di Vittorio, Dmitriy Kovtun, Arnold McIntyre, Inci Otker, Marika Santoro, Lulu Shui, and Karim Youssef. 2019. "Is the Whole Greater than the Sum of Its Parts? Strengthening Caribbean Regional Integration". IMF Working Paper WP/2018.

Mandle, Jay R. 2011. "The Role of Migration in Caribbean Integration and Development". *Social and Economic Studies* 60 (3/4): 3–19.

Schwab, Klaus. 2012. "The Global Competitiveness Report 2012–2013". Geneva: World Economic Forum. http://www3.weforum.org/docs/WEF_GlobalCompetitiveness Report_2012-13.pdf.

Simpson, M.C., Daniel Scott, M. Harrison, E. O'Keefe, Ruth Sim, S. Harrison, Michael A. Taylor, G. Lizcano, M. Rutty, H. Stager, J. Oldham, M. Wilson, Mark George New, J. Clarke, Owen Day, Nicholas Fields, Jeanal Georges, Roxanne Waithe, and P. McSharry. 2010. "Quantification and Magnitude of Losses and Damages Resulting from the Impacts of Climate Change: Modelling the Transformational Impacts and Costs of Sea-Level Rise in the Caribbean". Barbados: United Nations Development Programme (UNDP).

Simpson, Murray, Daniel Scott, and Ulric Trotz. 2011. "Climate Change's Impact on the Caribbean's Ability to Sustain Tourism, National Assets, and Livelihoods". Inter-American Development Bank. https://issuu.com/idb_publications/docs/_en_35758.

Stoneman, Richard, Duke Pollard, and Hugo Inniss. 2012. "Turning around CARICOM: Proposals to Restructure the Secretariat". Trowbirdge, UK: Landell Mills Limited.

Watkins, Alfred and Joshua Mandell. 2010. "Science, Technology and Innovation: Capacity Building Partnerships for Sustainable Development". World Bank Global Forum Action Plan. http://siteresources.worldbank.org/INTSTIGLOFOR/Resources /STI_ GlobalForum_ActionPlan.pdf.

WIC (West Indian Commission). 1992. *Time for Action*: *Report of the West Indian Commission*. Kingston, Jamaica: University of the West Indies Press.

World Travel and Tourism Council. 2011. "World Travel and Tourism Economic Impact". http://www.foresightfordevelopment.org/sobipro/55/840-world-travel-and-tourism-economic-impact-2011.

Chapter 15

Second-Generation Reform

Political Party and Election Financing in the Organisation of Eastern Caribbean States

CYNTHIA BARROW-GILES

All Commonwealth Caribbean states have signed and ratified the 1996 Inter-American Convention against Corruption, committing them to

- promote and strengthen the development by each of the States parties of the mechanisms needed to prevent, detect, punish and eradicate corruption; and
- promote, facilitate, and regulate cooperation among the States to ensure the effectiveness of measures and actions to prevent, detect, punish and eradicate corruption in the performance of public functions (Organization of American States 1996, 2).

While the convention does not directly address political party and elections financing, a link has long been established between such financing and corruption. Indeed, Article 7 of the United Nations Convention against Corruption requires countries to adopt appropriate legislative reform aimed at the promotion of greater transparency in electoral funding (United Nations 2004). In 2001, the issue of political financing was incorporated in the agenda of the Third Summit of the Americas (held in Quebec), which itself was included in the Inter-American Charter of Democracy as a key concern.

Money is a critical component for the functioning of democratic politics. It is generally accepted that without necessary political financing for electioneering, politicians cannot articulate their ideas and visions to the public, and, consequently, citizens cannot make informed choices during elections. In that vein, Daniel Zovatto has argued that while "democracy does not have a price, it certainly has an operational cost" (2013, 3). It is this need that creates serious danger for parties and by extension democracies. In his view, it is precisely because of the potential for money in politics (given its operational cost) to negatively impact political parties, and therefore the quality of democracy, that there is a need for clear guidelines to control the relationship between the two. Given its corrupting influences, political finance is also increasingly seen as a bane to democratic consolidation.

Moreover, it is increasingly argued that electioneering and the cost of politics generally are rising as a direct result of not only the expectations of the voter but also the cost of undertaking politics in a modern democracy (new politics). This has placed increasing emphasis on such things as advertising in the mass media, in particular television and newspaper ads, opinion polls, professional image making (buying of public relations expertise), and billboards (democracy by photographs). Increasing costs thus inevitably lead to a race among political parties and candidates for political money.[1]

The post-1951 period in the Caribbean has been associated with increased political party spending, as mass-based parties attempted to win the loyalty of the newly enfranchised citizens. Indeed Barbados prime minister Freundel Stuart (2013) argued that in this era, as distinct to the former where the wealthy had a decided advantage, "candidates still had to make provisions for what the political analysts referred to as 'corned beef and biscuits' in Barbados and 'rum, roti and sardines' in other countries". Ultimately, this perceived "arms race" in political spending is seen as a primary cause of corruption in political financing and consequently scandals related to party financing are widespread. This is not unique to the Commonwealth Caribbean. Table 15.1 provides a summary of some of the major corruption scandals related to party financing in some Caribbean jurisdictions.

In May 2013, the Organization of American States (OAS) held a two-day forum on political party and elections campaign financing in Barbados. There, Prime Minister

Table 15.1. Examples of Scandals Associated with Political Party and Election Spending in Selective Commonwealth Caribbean Countries

Country	Year	Scandal
Bahamas	2004	• Alleged contribution of US$10 million by Irish businessman (and permanent resident of the Bahamas) Mohammed Harajchi to the PLP (CountryWatch 2018) • Alleged US$5 million contribution of Finnish–Canadian billionaire fashion designer Peter Nygard to the PLP's 2012 election campaign (Rolle 2017)
Barbados	2007	• BLP claims of Taiwanese contributions to the opposition DLP (Ischyrion 2008)
Grenada	2007–12	• NNP provided with EC$100,000 by a failed offshore bank, First International Bank of Grenada (AirBourne 2007) • Opposition allegations of Saudi Arabian contribution to the NDC (RJR News 2012)
Jamaica	2006	• $31 million campaign contribution by the Dutch oil company Trafigura Beheer to the then governing People's National Party (Office of the Contractor-General 2010)
St Lucia	2006–11	• Taiwanese US$1–2 million to every UWP parliamentarian (Government of St Lucia 2013)
St Vincent and the Grenadines	2009–10	• Allegation of EC$1 million donation to the ruling ULP by foreign donors • Alleged EC$5 million for election purposes by SCL and Behavioural Dynamics Institute (foreign sources) to the opposition NDP (*Searchlight* 2010)
Trinidad and Tobago	2007	• Alleged $5 million cheque made out to the People's National Movement by former CL Financial giant Lawrence Duprey (*Trinidad and Tobago Guardian* 2012)

Stuart expressed the view that, in order for the Caribbean to successfully consolidate itself as a democracy, the region needs to overcome the excesses that occur in the electoral environment. In that regard, he noted the lavish spending and vote-buying as major concerns for Caribbean democracies. Yet Stuart also maintained that care must be taken in order to ensure that constitutional and human rights are not infringed in the process of controlling political party and election spending. In his view, "If the journey towards the realization of our Caribbean civilization . . . is to be successfully completed, then we must take responsibility for curbing these excesses without, however, denying genuine funders, political leaders and voters their human and constitutional rights to finance projects of their choice, and to do so with a degree of confidentiality" (Stuart 2013).

There are of course several uses to which such monies are directed. These include but are not limited to spending on banned actions such as vote-buying, advertising in media and lavish entertainment. The practice of vote-buying often takes the form of financial payments; short-term jobs; public contracts; scholarships; trips; access to public services and programmes; infrastructure; and gifts such as food, clothing, medicine, construction materials or other goods (Dekel, Jackson and Wolinsky 2004).

Locating the Commonwealth Caribbean in Global Financing Systems

An assessment of global regimes of political party and elections campaign financing systems would reveal that the Caribbean, particularly the Commonwealth Caribbean, remains one of two areas in the world where effective legislation for the regulation of political parties and elections campaign financing is virtually absent. A review of the Caribbean would also reveal that, whereas in parts of the wider Caribbean Community (CARICOM) area there is a perceptible attempt to engage in a reform of the system, this is clearly lacking in the subregion of the Organisation of Eastern Caribbean States (OECS).[2]

An example of CARICOM member nations' efforts is Jamaica's revised Representation of the People Act of 2016, which introduced a fairly robust legislative framework for the regulation of political party and election spending.[3] One of the flagship provisions of the Act is the establishment of a National Election Campaign Fund, whose major responsibility is to receive contributions from individuals, Jamaican diasporic groups, companies and other entities (Government of Jamaica, 2016). The Act also addresses issues of contribution limits, impermissible donors, disclosure, accounting requirements, registration of political parties and sanctions for violations of the provisions of the Act (Government of Jamaica, 2016). Accordingly, under Section 52AT(3) of the Act, any candidate or registered political party who knowingly accepts monies from an impermissible donor is liable after summary conviction to a fine not exceeding J$3 million or a prison term not exceeding twelve months (Government of Jamaica, 2016).[4] While the monetary sanctions for violations are not excessively punitive (approximately US$15,000), the prison term of up to one year is fairly prohibitive and, if effectively policed and enforced, should be dissuasive. The Jamaican provisions are further reaching in scope and more punitive than existing laws elsewhere in the Commonwealth Caribbean.

Without negating the importance of enhanced political institutions, increased avenues for greater participation in the political arena and the need to remove all remaining democratic deficits regionally, this continued absence in the OECS remains one of the main dangers to the full realization of substantive democracy. As Hayden Phillips observed in his review of the funding of political parties in the United Kingdom, the debate about financing political parties is intrinsically linked to the debate about the health of democracy (Phillips 2007).

Given the inadequacy of the legislative agenda in the subregion and the difficulty of monitoring the flow of money in politics, it is difficult to make clear and decisive statements on both the quantity of money entering the political system and the impact on the policymaking process. However, what is clear is that throughout the Caribbean, democracy is vulnerable and its sustainability endangered given potential erosion of the public trust in the institutions of governance. Indeed, a link has been made between the openness of the regime of political party and elections financing, and the incidence of political corruption.

For example, the Organization for Economic Cooperation and Development argues that money is vital to the democratic process facilitating competition and enabling representation (Terracino and Hamada 2014). Further, the organization makes it clear that, notwithstanding the importance of money for the democratic process, democracy itself can become corrupted by risks associated with political money. In that regard, it is important to note that governments will be more vulnerable and responsive to the parties and candidates who, once in office, will be more responsive to the interests of their donors rather than to the public interest (Terracino and Hamada 2014). This is confirmed by the Open Society, which sees the potential for corruption in three broad categories: "quid pro quo donations where parties or candidates receive resources in exchange for favorable treatment, misuse of state resources by candidates or parties for electoral purposes, and bribery of voters and election officials" (2005, 14).

Corrupt political finance can thus be regarded as any activity that revolves around the improper or unlawful conduct of financial operations whether by a candidate or a party for the profit of an individual candidate, political party or interest group (Walecki, n.d.). Robert Williams concurs, stating:

> Corruption and party finance are inextricably linked. It is obvious that whatever the origins, structure, character and ideology of a political party and irrespective of the prevailing party system, political parties solicit funds over and above those received from their members or, where available, from state subsidies. The sources, scale, forms and distribution of party finance all have profound political implications. Political parties form linkages and conduits between executive, legislative and administrative institutions and between such institutions and the wider political, economic and social environment. In short, they provide a bridge between state and society. They offer the prospect of durable forms of political organization and a means of controlling and directing the power of the state. It is the prospect of the party capturing state power which attracts the attention of financial backers who require some benefit, favour or concession from government. (Williams 2000, 8)

The frequency of scandals associated with political party and elections campaign financing as indicated in table 15.1 makes it apparent that very clear rules and transparent accounts by parties and candidates are warranted. This would serve, not only to bolster the democratic character of the governance systems, but would contribute to the restoration and preservation of the trust of citizens in both politicians and political parties.

Unfortunately, notwithstanding the perception of widespread corruption in the Commonwealth Caribbean and indeed the OECS and the challenges posed to democratic fulfilment, there is no major regional regulatory initiative or regional guidelines to prevent corruption nor to protect and enhance democratic governance. This can be compared to Western European countries where the process of Europeanization is viewed as an important pressure point for the enactment of legislation to govern political party and election campaigns.

Europeanization has been a critical driver for political parties and the electoral environment primarily because of the impact that the European Community's rules, directives and norms have at the domestic level leading to substantial institutional and policy changes in the member states of the European Union. These largely take the form of European Union-wide anti-corruption policies, fuelled largely by numerous scandals in Western European countries.[5]

As early as 1997, the Committee of Ministers of the Council of Europe adopted Resolution (97) 24 on the 20 Guiding Principles for the Fight against Corruption. Principle 15 specifically indicated that states should promote rules for the financing of political parties and election campaigns which deter corruption (Committee of Ministers 1997). Further developments occurred in 1998 at the 3rd European Conference of Specialised Services in the Fight against Corruption on the subject of Trading in Influence and Illegal Financing of Political Parties.[6] In its guidelines, the committee acknowledged the importance of political parties as a fundamental element of democratic systems of states and an essential tool of expression of the political will of citizens. The Council of Europe took the view that political parties and electoral campaigns funding in all states should be subject to standards in order to prevent and fight against corruption (Council of Europe 2011).

In 2001, the European Union intensified its efforts with the adoption of Recommendation 1516 on the financing of political parties.[7] The European Union's goal was not to impose a specific model throughout the community but anticipated that the guidelines would lead to the adoption of common standards for the setting up of transparent systems for the funding of political parties in an effort to prevent corruption (Council of Europe 2001). The guidelines thus fell short of prescribing a specific or ideal type regime for the financing of the system.

In furtherance of that agenda, in 2004 the European Union published its guidelines on financing political parties and election campaigns (Committee of Ministers 2003). These guidelines were based on the 2003 set of procedures and strategies which were defined by the Committee of Ministers Recommendation 2003(4) on common rules against corruption in the funding of political parties and electoral campaigns (Council of Europe 2011). By far the most important recommendation to emerge from the 2004 guidelines was that member states adopt in their national legal systems rules against corruption in the funding of political parties and electoral campaigns based on a common set of rules specified by the 2004 document. The Council of Europe considered these critical contributions to the "defense of pluralist democracy and the transparency of the electoral process" (Committee of Ministers, 2003, 1). In addition the 2004 European Union Guidelines provided for the Group of States against Corruption to monitor the implementation of this particular recommendation.[8]

The guidelines identified eight priority areas for legislative action throughout the European Community. Directed at political parties and candidates, their main focus was to ensure transparency and regulate electoral financing contributions:

- Under Article 1, the guidelines provided for both public and private support to political parties but noted that state support should not undermine the independence of the political parties. Such support should be of a financial nature only. Additionally, Article 1 specifically states that such contribution should be a "reasonable contribution" with "objective, fair and reasonable criteria" applied with respect to the distribution of its support (Committee of Ministers 2003, 3).
- Articles 2 and 3 focus on donation to a political party which the guidelines defined as "any deliberate act to bestow advantage, economic or otherwise, on a political party" (Committee of Ministers 2003, 3). The main concerns were to ensure that states enact legislation that was transparent and avoided conflict of interests and secret donations, establish limits to donations and disclose donations that exceed these, and ensure the independence of political parties.
- Article 5 recommends that "States should take measures aimed at limiting, prohibiting or otherwise strictly regulating donations from legal entities which provide goods or services for any public administration". It further recommends that "States should prohibit legal entities under the control of the State or of other public authorities from making donations to political parties" (Committee of Ministers 2003, 4).
- Article 7 recommends that states regulate donations from foreign donors by limiting or prohibiting these.
- Article 9 requires states to adopt "measures to prevent excessive funding requirements of political parties, such as, establishing limits on expenditure on electoral campaigns" (Committee of Ministers 2003, 5).
- Articles 10–13 require all political parties and candidates to maintain a record of "all expenditure, direct and indirect, on electoral campaigns" which should be checked by a relevant political party and elections body (Committee of Ministers 2003, 5).
- The guidelines provide for the establishment of an independent monitoring body to scrutinize the accounts of political parties in respect of the funding of these organizations and electoral campaigns (Committee of Ministers 2003).
- Article 16 requires that states should ensure that "the infringement of rules concerning the funding of political parties and electoral campaigns to be subject to effective, proportionate and dissuasive sanctions" (Committee of Ministers 2003, 6).

In contrast to this organized and region-wide approach to this issue, neither CARICOM nor the OECS have been proactive in inducing change in the area of political party and elections campaign financing. Further, national parliamentary debate and various constitutional reform forums have failed to give concrete expression to this issue. In the absence of such centripetal forces, it is important to assess the impact if any that agents and structures external to the state, such as hemispheric bodies, may have on inducing reform. Regionally where such external pressure has been applied it has originated from the OAS.

The State of Affairs in the Organisation of Eastern Caribbean States

Available data on the OECS exposes the weaknesses of the regulatory model in place. A review of election laws shows that none of the countries within the subregion has implemented legislation to govern financing of political parties and election campaigns. In several countries, the regime of party and election financing is subsumed under the Representation of the People Acts, which often merely stipulate the maximum amounts which can be spent by each candidate. Second, the general tendency of existing legislation is to impose limited expectations on political parties. Yet it is parties that play a central role in organizing their members and mobilizing for elections. It is precisely for this reason that legislation which attempts to cover candidates only is deemed inadequate.

The general attitude towards party and election financing in the OECS is captured by Cecilia Babb in her work on the Commonwealth of Dominica. Noting the lack of any such regulation in the country, Babb posits that "beyond a limited concern about the leftist connections of the party leader who came into office in the year 2000, and recognition that private sector support of political campaigns implies preferential contracts, concessions and other special benefits, sources of campaign financing have not been sufficiently an issue to merit the attention of legislators, political parties and the media" (2003, 4).

Though the OAS observer mission to Dominica for the 2009 elections voiced concerns, not much progress has taken place since the 2000 elections, although media houses are now more inclined to report on scandals associated with party and election spending (Dominica News Online 2009). Following the 2014 general elections, the observer mission expressed concerns related to instances of alleged and apparent abuses of the election law which often took the form of treating and bribery. In its recommendations to the Elections Commission, the report strongly recommended that the commission undertake a revision of the elections law in line with international best practice. Among a number of election-related reforms, the report recommended strengthening and enforcing the law prohibiting bribery and treating, as well as prohibiting financial support by foreign companies to parties for electoral purposes and from persons who are not citizens of Dominica (Commonwealth Secretariat 2014).

Notwithstanding these strong recommendations, in early 2017, the Roosevelt Skerrit administration introduced a bill which the media regarded as being designed to "legalise bribery and treating" in the electoral environment (Dominica News Online 2009). Barrow-Giles (2017), in her examination of the proposed legislation, argued that it is not in conformity with international norms and best practices, thus representing a retrograde step that could have dire consequences for the consolidation of democracy in Dominica.

The proposed legislation would reinforce the pervasiveness of patron–client relations and ensuing political culture of vote-buying that exists in the country. There is widespread criticism regarding the increasingly expensive provision of entertainment and other forms of electoral patronage, and the transportation of voters from overseas to cast their ballots in elections. Legislation prohibiting or strictly regulating vote-buying is a necessary (though not sufficient) condition to guarantee equity and probity of the electoral environment. As such, various observer missions to Dominica anticipated the enactment of anti-vote-buying legislation that would include, among other things, enabling detection provisions and adequate punishment for violation of the rules. Instead, Section 57B of the proposed 2017 amendment to the House of Assembly (Elections) Act states: "For the avoidance of doubt, the transportation of electors or the facilitation of the transportation of electors to or within Dominica for the purpose of an election does not constitute an offence unless the transportation is provided or facilitated with the intention to corruptly induce an elector to vote for a particular candidate or party" (*The Sun* 2017).

While the government has denied that legislation such as that cited here constitutes attempts to legalize corrupt practices, parties and individuals opposed called for protests on the grounds that the proposal would legitimize the electoral offence of bribery (Dominica News Online 2017).

As shown in table 15.2, none of the OECS countries have imposed limits on the spending of political parties and candidates. However, laws governing the regime of political party and elections spending in Antigua and Barbuda differ in two key aspects to those that define the regime elsewhere in the subregion. Under Section 83 of the representation of the People (Amendment) Act 2001, both candidates and parties are required to disclose contributions. The Act also requires that political parties keep accounts of all electoral contributions, and the names and addresses of individuals with contributions exceeding a value of EC$25,000 (Parliament of Antigua and Barbuda

Table 15.2. Status of Regulatory Regime in the OECS up to 2013

Country	Disclosure	By Party	By Candidate	Contribution Limit	Spending Limit
Antigua and Barbuda	Yes	Yes	Yes	No	No
St Kitts and Nevis	No	No	No	No	No
Dominica	No	No	No	No	No
Grenada	No	No	No	No	No
St Lucia	No	No	No	No	No
St Vincent and the Grenadines	No	No	No	No	No

Sources: Compiled from review of existing legislation (Government of Antigua and Barbuda 2011; Government of the Commonwealth of Dominica 1995; Government of St Kitts and Nevis 2009; Government of St Lucia 2012; Government of St Vincent and the Grenadines 1998).

2001).[9] Under this Act, the Independent Elections Commission is empowered to impose penalties on offending parties who fail to have their accounts audited within six months of a general election (Barrow-Giles and Joseph 2006).

These changes followed a 1999 Commonwealth elections observer mission, which criticized the existing electoral law and aspects of the electoral environment. In its report, the observer mission noted that major concerns were raised about the nature of the funding and spending system. The report also noted that the ruling Antigua Labour Party's tendency to repair roads prior to the calling of a general election, provide land at low prices to supporters, supply jobs for current and potential supporters, and waive import duties on cars and other equipment was not coincidental. Further, the elections observer mission stated: "We understand that there are no . . . methods for ensuring the transparency or probity of political donations. We heard many allegations that the governing party had at its disposal considerable resources due to the active support of the foreign investors. We observed lavish spending by both political parties on sophisticated campaign materials and events, which made the disparities in the resources available to the candidates all the more marked" (Commonwealth Secretariat 1999, 15).

Unfortunately, the language of the legislation does not require that political parties record contributions received before elections nor does it adequately address whether individuals, groups or companies can make several contributions not exceeding EC$5,000. Sir Fred Phillips, writing for the OAS Unit for the Promotion of Democracy, noted that the tendency for individuals and entities to possess multiple bank accounts across jurisdictions poses serious difficulties for electoral overseeing bodies (1998). While these limitations are a fundamental weakness, the Antiguan legislation is nonetheless an important development within the OECS in the context of the general inadequacy of the existing legal environment.

Apart from the fact that the existing legislation fails to cover political parties and creates opportunities for legal requirements to be circumvented by channelling funds through them, there is also no serious attempt to regulate the nature, extent and quantity of funds entering the system from private donors. Table 15.3 depicts the prevalence of this unregulated environment in the OECS, which is striking given the importance of private donorship for political parties and candidates.

Further, the current stock of legislation makes no attempt to manage the possibility of foreign governments influencing the political system. In this sense, the nature of the evolving relationship between the Caribbean and foreign governments, in particular Taiwan, is most revealing. For instance, the relationship between Taiwan and the United Workers Party (UWP) governance of St Lucia between 2006 and 2011 depicts the glaring influence of foreign money on the formulation of public policy.

In May 2013, the government of St Lucia released a document exposing the extent of Taiwanese financial contribution to the UWP (Government of St Lucia, 2013). The 190-page audit report was submitted to Parliament and publicly released, revealing the magnitude of the financial wrongdoings associated with the injection of Taiwanese monies into St Lucia (see table 15.4). The report calls attention to the urgent need to be proactive with respect to the regulation of both political party and elections campaign financing (Government of St Lucia, 2013).

Table 15.3. Controls (Bans) on Private Financing for Political Parties and Candidates

Country	Foreign Private Donation to Parties and Candidates	Corporate Donations to Parties and Candidates	Anonymous Donations to Political Parties and Candidates
Antigua and Barbuda	No	No	Yes
St Kitts and Nevis	No	No	No
Dominica	No	No	No
Grenada	No	No	No
St Lucia	No	No	No
St Vincent and the Grenadines	No	No	No

Sources: Compiled from a review of existing election laws (Government of Antigua and Barbuda 2011; Government of St Kitts and Nevis 2009; Government of the Commonwealth of Dominica 1995; Government of Grenada 1993; Government of St Lucia 2012; Government of St Vincent and the Grenadines 1998).

Table 15.4. Total Monies Received by Village Councils: Taiwanese Funds

Village Councils	Funds Received (EC$)	Percentage of Total Funds
Babonneau District Council	2,933,329.98	73.61
Soufriere Town Council	2,357,546.44	73.14
Dennery Village Council	4,788,389.88	83.04
Micoud Village Council	2,020,478.84	70.89
Micoud South District Council	2,919,077.00	87.52
Vieux-Fort North District Council	980,202.24	69.56
Vieux-Fort Town Council	675,202.87	59.31
Choiseul Village Council	1,999,999.99	50.82
Total	18,674227.24	

Source: Cynthia Barrow-Giles, "Political Financing in the Caribbean: Time to Dismantle the Fence", paper presented at the VI Inter-American Electoral Training Seminar. Organizers: GS/OAS, Mexican Federal Electoral Institute (IFE), International Institute for Democracy and Electoral Assistance (International IDEA).

The audit report showed that a total EC$18,674,227.24 (US$ 6,909,854) was granted by the Taiwanese government to eight village councils.[10] This was a fraction of Taiwanese contributions, as a number of councils failed to report any such financing (Government of St Lucia 2013). The report further revealed that funds received by councils were not treated as public monies and were in violation of Section 30(1) of the Local Authorities Ordinance, and Chapter 239 of the Revised Laws of St Lucia, 1957 (repealed), which stipulated that "all monies due to a local authority shall be paid to the Treasurer and shall form a fund to be called the Urban, Village or Rural District Fund which shall be kept distinct in the Treasurer's books from all other accounts" (Government of St Lucia 2013, 15). The report also stated that

> during the period January 2008-December 2011, Councils received and deposited monies into bank and credit union accounts from a variety of sources including Central Government and the Taiwanese Government. These monies were not treated and classified as "Public Monies". They were never paid to the Treasurer and was [sic] not deposited into the Urban, Village or Rural District Fund as required by Section (30) (1) of the Local Authorities Ordinance. (Government of St Lucia 2013, 15)

Although these monies were supposed to be invested in community development projects and organized by local councils, "90% of project-proposals submitted to the Taiwanese Government under the so-called 'community grass roots programmes' did not originate from Town, Village and Rural Councils. In the constituencies of Choiseul, Micoud South, Micoud North, Dennery South, Dennery North, Anse La Raye/ Canaries, Babonneau and Gros Islet project-proposals originated from the Offices of Parliamentary Representative and not Town, Village or Rural Councils" (Government of St Lucia 2013, 32).

The report thus concluded that "Town, Village, and Rural Councils acted as 'rubber stamp' and were used as conduits for channeling of both Taiwanese and Central Government funds to selected parliamentary representatives for their own whims and fancies" (Government of St Lucia 2013, 32).

In many instances, the legally statutory controls were not enforced by the councils. Consequently, contracts for goods or services in excess of EC$50,000 (US$18,500) were not acquired through competitive bidding as required under the Procurement and Stores Regulations, nor were alternative proposals or quotations obtained before contracts were issued. Accordingly, the report noted that

> in the constituencies of Choiseul, Micoud South, Dennery South and Babonneau, it was the Office of the Parliamentary Representative that identified and selected works projects to be implemented. In fact, the practice was so adept in Choiseul that [the] Office of Parliamentary Representative had a specifically designed form for the purpose of issuing "works orders". In the case of Soufriere, these tasks were handled by the Office of the UWP Candidate for Soufriere in the 2011 General Elections, Senator Allen Chastanet.[11] (Government of St Lucia 2013, 24)

It is clear that these monies were used by parliamentarians for the purpose of conducting clientelistic activities which usually took the form of procurement and issuing of contracts. Ultimately such monies provided the ruling political party with a clear advantage over the opposing parties and severely compromised fair governance in the country.

Two other important features of the regulatory regime in the OECS deserve attention. These are state funding and access to the media. None of the OECS countries provide state funding to political parties and candidates. In St Lucia, the government provides a subsidy to parliamentarians to assist in the operation of their constituency offices. Yet such funds are held by the speaker of the House of Assembly, to whom parliamentarians must submit funding requests. State financing is thus not directly provided to political parties in the subregion. This can be compared to the general tendency in more developed countries, where state funding constitutes between 2 and 68 per cent of parties' total expenditure.[12]

With regard to state media, it is often alleged by opposition groups that the ruling political party has disproportionate access which grants them an unfair advantage. As shown in table 15.5, only St Lucia provides political parties with free access to the state media. The overall conclusion that emerges is that the current legal frameworks governing the regime of political party and elections campaign financing are woefully inadequate. Equally important are the attitudes of the political elites, which point to the absence of political will. But it remains clear that further regulation is required.

This situation can be compared to the broader CARICOM region, where restrictions on candidates are mandated in three countries. In Jamaica, existing laws stipulate how much individual candidates can spend. Prior to the amendment to the Representation of People Act in Jamaica, an upper limit of US$50,000 was imposed on election candidates. The revised act of 2016 makes provision for an upper limit on candidates of J$15 million (US$120,000) during the reporting period. Given that the amendments require political parties to be registered, the act also stipulates spending limits for political parties. Accordingly, an upper spending limit of J$630 million (US$5 million) is established during the reporting periods for election-related expenses (Government of Jamaica, 2016).[13]

In Trinidad and Tobago, candidates are legally allowed to spend only TT$50,000 (US$7,420), and in Barbados, candidates can spend up to BD$10 (US$5) per constituent. The 2000 amendment to the Representation of the Peoples Ordinance (RPO) further allows candidates or their agents to receive electoral gifts and other contributions up to a statutory limit of TT$5,000 (US$742) per general election. Candidates are also allowed personal expenses, not exceeding TT$5,000 (US$742), incurred in connection with the elections. The ordinance prohibits promotion and advertisement expenditures by persons other than the candidate, the election agent and persons authorized by the election agent (Government of Barbados 2007).

Table 15.5. Access to State Television and State Funding

Country	Free TV Time to Parties or Candidates	Direct Public Funding
Antigua and Barbuda	No	No
Dominica	No	No
Grenada	No	No
St Kitts and Nevis	No	No
St Lucia	Yes	No
St Vincent and the Grenadines	No	No

Sources: Compiled from interviews conducted from 2003 to 2008 and election laws (Barrow-Giles 2002a, 2002b, 2002c, 2002d, 2002e, n.d.; Government of Antigua and Barbuda 2011; Government of the Commonwealth of Dominica 1995; Government of St Kitts and Nevis 2009; Government of St Lucia 2012; Government of St Vincent and the Grenadines 1998).

The Organization of American States Draft Model Legislation

The OAS has played a pivotal role in CARICOM's democratic progress. The organization has been involved in training electoral officials and in the process of ensuring the credibility of elections and legitimacy of elected officials. Since 2006, the OAS has directed over two dozen electoral observation missions in the region. A review of its reports shows that, in the majority of cases, missions have commented on the absence of an effective finance regulatory framework. They conclude this has the potential to affect the equity and transparency of the electoral process. Reports suggest that the absence of such financial regulations could lead to the possibility of the more endowed candidates and parties having an unfair advantage in getting their messages across to the electorate, and to the real possibility of unlawful financing entering the political system (OAS 2007, 2011, 2015).

Given its commitment to enhancing the democratic process throughout Latin America and the Caribbean, in September 2010 the OAS held a stakeholders meeting in Jamaica at which it presented a comprehensive draft model law on the Registration and Regulation of Political Parties. All the OECS ruling and main opposition political parties were represented at that meeting.

One of the key provisions of the draft legislation is the establishment of an autonomous Political Party Commission as the main regulatory agency for the supervision of political parties and their finances. The legislation therefore calls for the establishment of an independent Political Parties Commission as a separate commission to the Elections and Boundaries Commissions which have been given general oversight of the conduct of elections and to which some rudimentary provisions on elections financing have been attached. To ensure that the rules are not only implemented but enforced, the Political Parties Commission would be given an appropriate level of autonomy from political parties and the political directorate. This would be secured through the method of appointment and membership and a level of financial independence. The proposal for the establishment of an independent oversight agency is therefore designed to avoid the risks of partisan bodies which may consequently lack the political will to undertake their task in an impartial manner.

Not only are existing Elections and Boundaries Commissions throughout the OECS overly influenced by political parties, but they are also generally inadequately staffed. Currently, these bodies have no legal authority to authenticate the reports that are sometimes submitted to them. The proposed legislation therefore would move the OECS specifically in a similar direction to countries that are at an advanced stage of development with respect to regulating money and politics. Indeed the recommended establishment of an independent Political Parties Commission in conjunction with the requirement that declarations be made to such an agency would provide the opportunity to observe the nexus between donations and influence peddling, which, in the current environment, electoral officials are unable to monitor and expose.

The legislation requires that the commission establishes and maintains a register of political parties along with all the requisite particulars, such as the leader and officers. The intent of the draft legislation is to ensure that the parties should in turn register their candidates who would be "certified" by those parties regardless of whether these persons are subsequently elected. The draft legislation also makes provision for the right of the commission to refuse to register political parties on the grounds of falsification of information, where the party appears to support or incite hatred or violence, or where there is confusion regarding the ownership of party symbols or where more than one entity submits similar symbols.

On the sensitive issue of spending disclosures, the OAS draft model legislation is premised on a hybrid model that combines public and private funding, and contains a number of positive provisions regarding the need for disclosure of donors' identities. First, the legislation acknowledges that both candidates and political parties must be accountable and, as such, includes the obligation for each political party to account for its campaign revenue and expenses to the Political Parties Commission. Further, under the draft legislation, electoral donations are restricted to citizens and what the act describes as permissible donors (OAS 2013). A permissible donor is defined as a firm, enterprise or business that is at least 75 per cent owned by a citizen of that state. The proposal thus bans all donations to political parties from non-citizens, foreign governments, foreign organizations or parties, international institutions, or other non-local entities or persons. Certain categories of anonymous donors are also ineligible (OAS 2013).

However, given the historical importance of donations to the political parties by foreign governments and entities, the proposed legislation makes allowance for the maintenance of such donations but in a highly controlled manner. Under the proposed legislation, such donation is permissible only in the context of a donation to the commission, which would be used to benefit all political parties. It is anticipated that this would enforce the issue of equity and transparency in the regime of party financing. Moreover, it will also obviate the tendency towards influence peddling. Clearly, if this was accepted by the OECS governments, developments such as those that occurred under the 2006–11 UWP administration of St Lucia would be avoided.

Overall, as the proposed legislation makes no attempt to impose a specified limit for donations, it is anticipated that in the context of a relatively small-sized population with large percentages suffering from the debilitating effects of poverty, the recommended limit would be sufficient to permit small donations by the less financially fortunate without the danger of exposing their political affiliation. This is critical, given the perception that in a political environment of entrenched two "partyism" and increasingly highly "tribalistic" political communities which are engendered by adversarial Westminster politics, public declaration of contributions may be associated with victimization. Second, the proposed ceiling for an automatic declaration to the relevant agency will undoubtedly provide a counterbalance to the very real possible mischief of individuals or groups exercising considerable influence in the political arena given the size of their financial contributions (Barrow-Giles 2010a). Moreover such declarations would enable the electorate to make better-informed decisions with respect to their vote as greater transparency will be the ultimate effect of the proposal. A third major consideration is the impact that such a recommendation would have on unearthing and limiting the financial contributions from illicit sources, as such donations carry with them the real possibility of criminal elements hijacking the policymaking process.

The proposed legislation also addresses state financing, which in several democracies, old and new, is seen as critical to the survival of political parties and to ensuring equity in the political process. The draft legal framework envisions a role for public or state financing as a means of supplementing, but not replacing or dominating, private party and candidate funding. Given the regional tendency towards third-party marginalization and extended periods of single-party dominion, incautiously designed state financing could serve to reinforce existing obstacles for less supported parties to penetrate and acquire relevancy within the system. The draft legislation supports the creation of a Political Party Fund to be directed by the Political Parties Commission, and suggests two models of fund redistribution:

1. Allocation of funds using the principle of proportionality, taking into account the party's ratio of representatives in the National Assembly.
2. Redistribution on the basis of the principle of equity, using a fixed threshold for minimum allocation of funds to each party represented in the National Assembly (OAS 2013).

The proposal thus seeks to prevent dominant political parties from benefiting excessively from the fund and to ensure that minor political parties are not discriminated against.

Unfortunately, general election results in the OECS reveal that a single political party has dominated the electoral environment to the point of virtually excluding second parties, not to speak of newer and minor parties. For instance, the 1997 and 2001 elections in St Lucia resulted in 16–1 and 14–3 outcomes. In St Vincent and the Grenadines in 1989 and in Grenada in 1999 and 2013, one political party won all of the parliamentary seats. The net effect of a provision that seeks to provide monies on the basis of membership in the national assembly would be to continue the pattern of discrimination against all but the dominant political party and does not in itself facilitate equity, which is critical to good democratic practice. Far more preferable is the allocation of funding on the basis of achievement of a minimum threshold for qualification, which can incorporate both membership in the national assembly and actual votes gained in the previous elections. This may in fact give support to minor and third political parties.

While there is no documented proof of state resource abuse by governing parties, rumours and reports abound throughout the region. Consequently, the use of state resources is extremely sensitive, and opposition political parties routinely claim that ruling parties hold an unfair advantage over them.

The draft legislation establishes prohibitions related to the use of state resources for electoral purposes. It also promotes the use of government buildings for official purposes. In the event that a government building is used to host a political function by or on behalf of a political party or candidate, every other registered political party or candidate under the legislation shall be entitled to the use of that government building. While this would go some way to eliminating this bias and discriminatory practice, nonetheless it is difficult to envisage the ability of an oversight commission to adequately regulate or supervise the use of government buildings for party purposes.

The mass media currently plays a critical role in politics generally and electoral competition specifically. Consequently, a heavy financial burden is placed on political parties that many of them cannot sustain without considerable financial support. The amount of coverage any political party receives in the private media is dependent on the finances of the parties. Where private media is unavailable, access to state media is critical. Yet in the OECS as well as the rest of the Commonwealth Caribbean, we are confronted with allegations of the abuse of state media by the ruling political party, which it is argued is often used as a propaganda tool. Several opposition political parties have complained about the privileged status of the ruling political parties with regard to broadcast time and stress the essential inequity between parties.

Additionally, the nature of reportage, the language used, and the framing of the headlines and story content in several newspapers across the region as well as the ownership of the media houses make it clear that the print media, in particular, have very strong political leanings. In many instances journalists are outwardly biased. Many of their editorials tend to be biased towards specific political parties. This ultimately produces a tremendous level of imbalance or adverse publicity for parties that are not supported by the owners of the media houses. The unequal environment becomes particularly acute during the campaign period.

On the issue of the state media, the legislation attempts to provide for fair opportunity to all political parties to present their programmes to the public by ensuring equal access. Specifically, the legislation provides for the right of access of all political parties to the state media, whether print or electronic, on similar terms and conditions. It also enjoins the state media to be balanced and impartial in their reporting. However, private media – which dominates regionally – is more difficult to regulate.

At this juncture, an effective strategy should avoid utopian ideals generated from review of international best practices. Instead, relevant legislation in the OECS should be tailored for small island states and defined by limited, practical objectives aiming to provide the following achievable ends: a regulated regime, banning of foreign government financing, limits on contributions, some form of disclosure and enforcement. These limited objectives, especially in relation to disclosure, will no doubt provide the system with much-needed transparency that can only serve to bolster the democratic content of governance throughout the OECS.

Ring Fencing: Size and Stability Should Not Inhibit Second-Generation Reforms

Like many other CARICOM states, OECS countries, with few exceptions, have done remarkably well with regards to democratic expansion over the last twenty years. This is despite recent developments, such as the 2012 proroguing of the Parliament in Grenada, the continued refusal of Prime Minister Denzil Douglas of St Kitts and Nevis to debate a 2012 no confidence motion, the frequent realignment of electoral boundaries and acts of representatives crossing the floor (RJR News 2012; Caribbean News Now 2017; Nation News 2018; Jamaica Observer 2015; St. Lucia Times 2018). Yet democracy across the Caribbean needs further strengthening in order to ensure that democratic progress (for which the Caribbean is understandably proud) is not reversed or further compromised.[14]

Several ruling political and opposition political parties in the OECS view the tightening of the regime of party and elections campaign in a negative light arguing that such legislation in the context of small states would invariably lead to victimization and threaten the ability of the parties to raise vital funds for election purposes. However, Eleston "Namba" Adams, a member of Parliament in Antigua and Barbuda, stated in a recent parliamentary debate: "In small countries like Antigua, where in some constituencies it could be less than 2,000, one man could easily buy out an election. . . . If you are on the campaign, trail and somebody is prepared to take maybe $20, or $100 or $500, you pay their light bill or give them a turkey, this sort of thing, one person can easily buy out an election" (cited in Observer Media 2013).

The problem, however, is not limited to the capacity of an individual to buy an election. Even more problematic is the real possibility of the small OECS states being infiltrated and decision-making hijacked by criminal elements, both domestic and international. Writing on the small island states within the Commonwealth Caribbean, Michael Pinto-Duschinsky argued: "While there is a strong argument for simplicity, economy and for few laws and subsidies for parties and political campaigns in small states, these very countries are especially vulnerable to foreign pressures and to corruption. When it comes to safe havens for money obtained by international organised crime syndicates or safe storage points for drug traffickers, microstates are tempting targets" (2002, 24).

Further, as Douglas Payne (1999) noted in his work on the 1999 general elections in Antigua and Barbuda, even in a context where political parties routinely understate the actual amounts spent on elections, political parties in the region spent more per capita on elections than the more developed economies, for example the United States.[15] Given the repeated failure to regulate the regime of political money regionally, these small island states, lacking in economic resources and in a context of the escalating cost of election campaigns remain vulnerable to the corrosive influence of not only money in politics but to the possibility of penetration of the political system by criminal elements.

Balancing Non-Interference in the Domestic Affairs of States and the Charter of Civil Society: From Sovereignty Respect to Democratic Assistance

On 19 February 1997, the brainchild of the West Indian Commission, the non-binding Charter of Civil Society, was formally adopted by Heads of Government of the CARICOM. Its adoption was preceded five years earlier by positive comments made by community leaders in the Protocol of Port of Spain, which described the charter as an "important element of the Community's structure of unity to deal with matters such as free press; a fair and open democratic process; the effective functioning of the parliamentary system; morality in public affairs; respect for fundamental civil, political, economic, social and cultural rights; the rights of women and children; respect for religious diversity; and greater accountability and transparency in government" (1997, 5).

Among other things, the stated goals of the charter are to enhance public confidence in governance and to ensure continuing respect for internationally recognized civil, political, economic, social and cultural rights. Article VI(1) specially calls for member states of the Caribbean Community to "ensure the existence of a fair and open democratic system through the holding of free elections at reasonable intervals, by secret ballot, underpinned by an electoral system in which all can have confidence and which will ensure the free expression of the will of the people in the choice of their representatives".[16]

It is clear from the earlier discussion on the nature of political party and election campaign finance regimes in the subregion that the material conditions for greater regulation of political money exist throughout the CARICOM space and by extension the member states of the OECS. Yet, all available evidence suggests that there is reluctance to engage in what can clearly be democratic enhancing mechanisms in keeping with the Charter for Civil Society.

Every election observation mission to the Eastern Caribbean, whether organized by the OAS or the Commonwealth Secretariat, while acknowledging that elections are generally credible, tends to give credence to the view that much more needs to be done in relation to the promotion of democracy regionally. Most reports signal the lack of an appropriate regime for political money and the need for states to undertake action in relation to this gap in the democratic development of the region.

Unfortunately, governments throughout the subregion as indeed for all member countries of the CARICOM, apart from Jamaica, have been obstinate in relation to undertaking even the most basic of reforms in the current system of political party and election campaign financing.

Despite its stated aim of seeking an improvement in the governance of individual Caribbean states and unlike regional organizations such as the European Union, CARICOM's reluctance to intervene in matters such as these is consistent with the policy decision of non-interference in the domestic affairs of states and helps to explain the seeming reticence of the community to issuing harsh or condemnatory pronouncements on internal developments, especially with respect to the conduct of elections. In that regard, Guyana stands out as easily the most notable recent example of exceptionalism adopted by the CARICOM. Such exceptionalism is associated with the disputed 2 March 2020 general elections in the country following allegations by the international community and the opposition political parties that there was a clear intent to defraud the people of Guyana through the falsification of the election data in Region 4, a geographic and electoral district that has traditionally been the stronghold of the then governing coalition APNU+AFC. In the aftermath of the international outrage caused by the sabotage of the election, the president of Guyana and the leadership of the opposition People's Progressive Party/Civic agreed to a CARICOM high-level team to scrutinize the recount of the votes for all ten regions.[17] Though the efforts of CARICOM were in fact frustrated, an observation team for the recount of the March 2020 general and regional elections was dispatched to Guyana in May 2020 and submitted its report in June 2020 signalling that the elections had indeed resulted in the defeat of the governing coalition.[18] Though the recount was completed, it was not until 2 August 2020 that the Elections Commission (GECOM) was finally able to declare a winner of the elections.[19] In the interim, the then chair of the CARICOM, the prime minister of Barbados, Mia Mottley, was subjected to intense criticism with one labour leader, Lincoln Lewis, accusing the prime minister in June 2020 of engaging in "political interference, diplomatic bullyism and (interfering in) our right to resolve our conflicts judicially".[20]

Contrary to the view that the various regional bodies are silent conspirators to democratic wrongs, CARICOM and the OECS have indeed responded to some democratic infractions. Both organizations have occasionally taken verbal or physical action when democracy was perceived to be under threat in one of its member states other than in Guyana. Noteworthy are comments from Trinidad and Tobago following the 2015 general election in St Kitts and Nevis and the delayed declaration of the results. The prime minister of Trinidad and Tobago, Kamla Persad-Bissessar, publicly voiced concerns noting:

> We respect the independence of all lawful institutions in St. Kitts and Nevis, but at the same time we feel that the failure of the Supervisor of Elections to declare the results in a timely manner might create the impression that there is interference in the democratic process, which we in the Caribbean Community cherish.
>
> I am also concerned that the region's reputation for free and fair elections will be under threat as long as this issue in St. Kitts and Nevis remains unresolved.[21]

But given the apparent priority that non-interference/intervention often plays[22] in the decisions of CARICOM governments' interactions with one another, opposition political parties have often accused the CARICOM specifically and individual member states of condoning electoral fraud and or tacitly supporting governments' attempts to facilitate election-related bribery and sabotage. As recently as the 2015 elections in St Kitts and Nevis and in Dominica, and the 2019 elections in Dominica for example, the official opposition political parties decried the seeming paralysis of the CARICOM in the face of perceived election-related issues.

Few would disagree that democratic governance and minimally integrity-based elections including fairness in competition are critical benchmarks by which governmental legitimacy is measured. The CARICOM's Charter for Civil Society contains the basis for regional organizations to undertake action aimed at improving democratic governance. CARICOM, for instance, has been in the forefront of election observation across the Caribbean and has established itself as one of the most legitimate voices on the conduct of elections across the Caribbean. Based on its history of observations, the principles established under the Charter for Civil Society with respect to democratic governance, CARICOM is well placed to advance the conditions for the furtherance of reform of the electoral environment inclusive of a regulatory framework for political party and elections campaign regulations.

Conclusion: Democracy and Political Party and Election Campaign Financing in the Organisation of Eastern Caribbean States

The prevailing model for funding political parties and election campaigns in the subregion remains one which is primarily and predominantly rooted in private funding.

It is therefore a regime that does not easily lend itself to transparency and control. It is evident that the small size of the states within the OECS, large pockets of both urban and rural poverty, and the development and increasing consolidation of a system of patronage have proven to be difficult to overcome. The evidence also suggests that it is the dominance of money in politics and the source of that money that lead to the persistence of the perception that democracy and public policy formulation have been hijacked by money interests and foreign governments.

While recent controversies and other political developments in the region have served to highlight the myriad problems associated with money politics and have therefore energized the public debate in some quarters, the regime remains intact. This state of affairs continues unabated. For the most part, existing legislation covers little and therefore provides for a very liberal environment which lacks the minimum requirements of transparency, and as such is open to abuse. Increasingly the narrative on party and election financing has embraced the notion of greater monitoring of both candidate and political party spending as well as some element of public support for the parties. However, given the historical and contemporary reliance on patronage and the growing expectations of the electorate for even more services from elected and aspiring parliamentarians, the narrative on reform may fail to find fertile soil to germinate into a sustained public call for reform in line with newer and older democracies.

Indeed, it appears that the current imperative for reform stems not from domestic, subregional or even regional circumstances, but rather from hemispheric interest and action. While Jamaica has addressed concerns raised by domestic, regional and international stakeholders, national governments within the OECS have failed to grasp the opportunity provided by the draft OAS model legislation. It is sufficient to note that while the European Union took decisive steps to advance the region's efforts in combating not only the disequilibrium in the regime of political finance but also the potential for influence peddling, the same cannot be said of the regional political climate. At both the level of CARICOM and the OECS, there remains a deafening silence. Neither institution has identified political party and election financing as an agenda issue to be pursued. It therefore remains clear that what will drive the developments in the subregion, as in CARICOM, is interest on the part of the political elite, inclusive of opposition forces. Unfortunately, at this present juncture, there is little evidence to suggest that this will be forthcoming.

Notes

1. The cost of conducting "old politics", with its emphasis on door-to-door campaigning, vote-buying and gift-giving – what Prime Minister Freundel Stuart of Barbados describes as "corn beef politics" – as well as rallies and other labour-intensive techniques of reaching individual electors, tends to be expensive given costs associated with such things as vehicles and public address systems.

2. The Organisation of Eastern Caribbean States was created in 1981 and comprises all independent countries within the Eastern Caribbean except for Montserrat, which remains a British overseas territory, and Barbados, which is not a member of the group. Associate members include the British Virgin Islands and Anguilla (British overseas territories), and Martinique and Guadeloupe (overseas departments of France).

3. For example, after years of public agitation by the National Integrity Action and other civil society groups, and leadership provided by the Electoral Commission of Jamaica and international and regional groups, in early 2016 the government of Jamaica finally passed into law the Representation of People (Amendment) Act (Government of Jamaica 2016).

4. Under the Act, impermissible donors are identified as commonwealth governments or agents of commonwealth governments, a public body, any entity whose activities are illegal, an undisclosed contributor, persons or entities making contributions through an intermediary, or a person or entity using a false identity when making a contribution.

5. The influence of "Europeanization" on party funding regulations has been particularly important in the cases of Latvia, Poland, Slovakia, Bulgaria and Romania, as well as Turkey and the Balkan in the enlargement process.

6. The conference was held in Madrid from 28 to 30 October 1998.

7. Adopted on 22 May 2001 by the Council of Europe's Parliamentary Assembly. See the ACE Electoral Knowledge Network (Jouan 2018).

8. The function of the Group of States against Corruption is to monitor compliance with the Council of Europe's anti-corruption standards, serving as a platform for both the exchange of best practices and peer pressure. There are two aspects to the group's monitoring procedure. These are an evaluation round and a compliance procedure. During the evaluation rounds, all members are evaluated based on both written replies to questionnaires and information received from public officials and members of civil society during country visits. An evaluation may be followed by either recommendations or observations. Members are required to provide follow-up reporting on recommendations within eighteen months after the evaluation report.

9. The Act also prohibits political parties from accepting anonymous contributions exceeding EC$5,000 and establishes sanctions for non-compliance.

10. All conversion rates presented in this chapter are approximate and accurate as of May 2018.

11. On 6 June 2017, Allen Chastanet was swept into office when the United Workers Party under his leadership defeated the Kenny Anthony-led Saint Lucia Labour Party with eleven of the seventeen parliamentary seats.

12. It is estimated that between 2000 and 2010, public funding accounted for 2 per cent of the British Labour Party's income, 15 per cent for the Conservative party and 51 per cent for the Democratic Unionist Party. In the Netherlands, state financing for political parties accounted for 26 per cent of total parties' income in 2000, to 42 per cent in 2005–06. This can be compared to the heavy dependency on the state by political parties in Spain, Portugal, Belgium and Italy, where public funding amounts to an estimated 80 per cent of the parties' income.

13. https://ecj.com.jm/resources/campaign-financing/

14. See also Barrow-Giles (2010b).

15. Payne cites Lester Bird's finding that for the 1999 general elections the Antigua Labour Party spent $2 million. He concluded that, based on the population of Antigua and Barbuda, the party spent $30 per capita compared to the 1996 presidential campaign in the United States, where the parties spent approximately $4 per capita (1999).

16. CARICOM Community (1997, 2).

17. See Barrow-Giles and Yearwood (2020).

18. CARICOM Secretariat 2020.

19. See the following for information on the official end to the disputed elections and the swearing in of the new president of Guyana:

http://amsterdamnews.com/news/2020/aug/06/guyana-finally-gets-elections-winner-5
-months-afte/

https://www.looptt.com/content/ali-declared-president-guyana-5

https://www.bbc.com/news/world-latin-america-53637085

https://caricom.org/guyana-gets-new-president/

https://demerarawaves.com/2020/08/02/granger-says-elections-petition-is-next-move-after
-gecom-declares-winner/

https://www.reuters.com/article/us-guyana-election-idUSKBN24Y0PJ

20. See Brown (2020).

21. See News.Govt.tt (2015).

22. CARICOM did in fact intervene in Haiti following the overthrow of Jean Bertrand
Aristide in 1991 and the establishment of a brutal military government. Not only did the
community express its concerns over the human rights abuses in the country, but the
organization sent troops as part of the peacekeeping mission of 1994. CARICOM was
also involved in the second administration of Aristide and in January 2004 negotiated the
Kingston Accord.

References

AirBourne. 2007. "Ruling Political Party in Grenada Admits to Getting Money, but Stops Short
of Smearing Keith Mitchell". *Bajan Reporter*, 07 September 2007. http://www.bajanreporter
.com/2007/09/ruling-political-party-in-grenada-admits-to-getting-money-but-stops-short
-of-smearing-keith-mtchell.

Babb, Cecilia. 2003. "Political Party and Campaign Financing in Dominica". OAS Unit for the
Promotion of Democracy and the IDEA.

Barrow-Giles, Cynthia. 2002a. Interview with the Supervisor of Elections. Basseterre,
St Kitts-Nevis.

———. 2002b. Interview with the Supervisor of Elections. Roseau, Dominica.

———. 2002c. Interview with the Supervisor of Elections. St Georges, Grenada.

———. 2002d. Interview with Prime Minister Kenny D. Anthony. Castries, St Lucia.

———. 2002e. Interview with Prime Minister Lester Bird. St John, Antigua.

———. 2010a. "Regional Consultation on Political Parties and Campaign Financing in the
Caribbean". Prepared for the OAS.

———. 2010b. "Regional Trends in Constitutional Developments in the Commonwealth
Caribbean". Prepared for the Conflict Prevention and Peace Forum. http://www.cpahq.org
/cpahq/cpadocs/Cynthia%20Barrow.pdf.

———. 2017. *Governance and the National Integrity Systems in the Commonwealth Caribbean*.
Bridgetown: Carib Research and Publications.

———. n.d. Interview with the Acting Supervisor of Elections. Kingstown, St Vincent and the
Grenadines.

Barrow-Giles, Cynthia and Tennyson S.D. Joseph. 2006. *General Elections and Voting in the
English-Speaking Caribbean 1992–2005*. Kingston: Ian Randle Publisher.

Barrow-Giles, Cynthia and Ronnie Yearwood. 2020. "CARICOM and the 2020 Unsettled
Elections in Guyana: A Failed Political (Legal) Solution?" *The Round Table* 109, issue 5
(September): 506–25. DOI: 10.1080/00358533.2020.1819621.

Brown, Calvin G. 2020. "Guyanese Lambasts Mia Mottley for Comments on March 02
Elections". Wired Jamaica Online News. https://www.wiredja.com/index.php/news/politics
/guyana-votes-guyanese-lambast-mia-mottley-for-comments-on-march-2-elections.

Caribbean News Now. 2017. "High Court Rules in Favour of Claimants in Motion of No
Confidence Case in St Kitts-Nevis", 9 November 2017. https://wp.caribbeannewsnow
.com/2017/11/09 /high-court-rules-favour-claimants-motion-no-confidence-case-st-kitts-nevis/.

CARICOM. 1997. https://caricom.org/communique-of-the-special-meeting-of-the-conference-
of-heads-of-government-of-the-caribbean-community-28-31-october-1992-port-of-spain-
trinidad-tobago/.

CARICOM Community. 1997. Charter of Civil Society for the Caribbean Community. https://caricom.org/documents/12060-charter_of_civil_society.pdf.

CARICOM Secretariat. 2020. "Report of CARICOM Observer Team for the Recount of the Guyana March 02, 2020 Elections". https://guyaneseonline.files.wordpress.com/2020/06/report-of-the-caricom-observer-team-on-gy-elections.pdf.

Committee of Ministers. 1997. "Resolution (97)24 on the Twenty Guiding Principles for the Fight against Corruption". Council of Europe. https://rm.coe.int/16806cc17c.

Committee of Ministers. 2003. "Financing of Political Parties: Recommendation 1516 (2001)". Doc. 9774, Council of Europe. http://www.ifes.org/sites/default/files/recommendations _for _financing_political_parties_0.pdf.

Commonwealth Secretariat. 2014. "Report of the Commonwealth Observer Mission: Commonwealth of Dominica General Elections", 8 December 2014.

Commonwealth Secretariat Election Observer Group. 1999. "The General Election in Antigua and Barbuda", 9 March 1999. London: Commonwealth Secretariat. https://read .thecommonwealth-ilibrary.org/commonwealth/governance/the-general-election-in-antigua-and-barbuda-9-march-1999_9781848596979-en#page21.

Council of Europe. 2001. *International Co-operation in the Fight against Corruption and Offshore Financial Centers: Obstacles and Solutions*. Programme of action against corruption, 4th European Conference of Services Specialized in the Fight against Corruption (Limassol, Cyprus, October 1999). Strasbourg: Council of Europe Publishing.

———. 2011. "Opinion on the Need for a Code of Good Practice in the Field of Funding of Electoral Campaigns". European Commission for Democracy through Law (Venice Commission). http://www.eods.eu/library/VC.Opinion%20on%20Code%20of%20Good%20 Practice%20on%20Campaign%20Finance.pdf.

CountryWatch. 2018. "Bahamas: 2018 Country Review". http://www.countrywatch.com /Content/pdfs/reviews/B344968Z.01c.pdf.

Dekel, Eddie, Mathew O. Jackson, and Asher Wolinksy. 2004. "Vote Buying". Kellogg School of Management, Northwestern University. http://www.kellogg.northwestern.edu/research /math/papers/1386.pdf.

Dominica News Online. 2009. "Officials Ponder Campaign Financing", 22 December 2009. http://dominicanewsonline.com/news/homepage/news/politics/officials-ponder-campaign -financing-legislation/.

———. 2017. "Amendment to the House of Assembly (Election) Act Causes Controversy", 19 May 2017. http://dominicanewsonline.com/news/homepage/news/politics/ammendment -to-the-house-of-assembly-election-act-causes-controversy/.

Government of Antigua and Barbuda. 2011. "The Representation of People Act, Antigua and Barbuda (Amendment 2011)". https://www.oas.org/es/sap/deco/moe/antiguabarbuda2014 /docs/Representation%20of%20the%20People%20Act,%202011%20.pdf.

Government of Barbados. 2007. "Chapter 12: Representation of the People". Laws of Barbados. http://aceproject.org/ero-en/regions/americas/BB/barbados-representation-of-the-people -act-2007.

Government of the Commonwealth of Dominica. 1995. "House of Assembly (Elections) Act Chapter 2:01". http://www.dominica.gov.dm/laws/chapters/chap2-01.pdf.

Government of Grenada. 1993. "Representation of the People Act". http://www.peogrenada.org /Documents/CAP%20286A%20Representation%20of%20the%20People%20Act.pdf.

Government of Jamaica. 2016. "An Act to Amend the Representation of the People Act. No 10-2016". http://www.japarliament.gov.jm/attachments/article/341/The%20Representation%20 of%20the%20People%20(Amendment)%20Act,%202016%20No.%2010.pdf.

Government of St. Kitts-Nevis. 2009. "The National Assembly Elections Act Cap. 162". http:// www.parliament.gov.kn/wp-content/uploads/2017/06/National-Assembly-Elections-Act -Chap-2.01-R-Camera-Rea.pdf.

Government of St Lucia. 2012. "The Representation of Peoples Act St. Lucia".

———. 2013. "Review of Financial Operations of Town, Village and Rural Councils: Gros Islet, Babonneau, Dennery North, Anse La Raye, Canaries, Soufriere, Dennery, Micoud, Micoud South, Vieux Fort North, Vieux Fort, Laborie, Choiseul". http://gosl-uat.images.inkositech.com/www/resources/publications/ReviewFinancial OperationsCouncils.pdf.

Government of St Vincent and the Grenadines. 1998. "The Representation of Peoples Act (Amendment) 1998".

Ischyrion, Peter. 2008. "Barbados: Another Incumbent Bites the Dust". *Inter Press Service News Agency*, 16 January 2008. http://www.ipsnews.net/2008/01/barbados-another-caribbean-incumbent-bites-the-dust/.

Jamaica Observer. 2015. "Is Crossing the Floor a Betrayal of Party?", 14 June 2015. http://www.jamaicaobserver.com/editorial/Is-crossing-the-floor-a-betrayal-of-party_19133913.

Jouan, Barbara. 2018. "Campaign Finance". ACE Electoral Knowledge Network. http://aceproject.org/ace-en/focus/campaign-finance/onePage.

Nation News. 2018. "Atherley Sworn in as Opposition Leader", 1 June 2018. http://www.nationnews.com/nationnews/news/163035/atherley-sworn-opposition-leader.

News.Govt.tt. 2015. "PM Persad-Bissessar Concerned about Delay in Releasing St Kitts and Nevis Election Results". http://news.gov.tt/content/pm-persad-bissessar-concerned-about-delay-releasing-st-kitts-and-nevis-election-results#.X9aKKNhKhPY.

OAS (Organization of American States). 1996. "Inter-American Convention against Corruption". http://www.oas.org/en/sla/dil/docs/inter_american_treaties_B-58_against_Corruption.pdf.

———. 2007. "Report to the Permanent Council". Electoral Observation Mission in St Lucia. http://scm.oas.org/pdfs/2007/CP17869s.pdf.

———. 2011. "Electoral Observation Mission Final Report: General and Regional Elections in Guyana". Secretariat for Political Affairs. http://caribbeanelections.com/eDocs/election_reports/gy/GY_OAS_2011.pdf.

———. 2013. "Draft Model Law on the Registration and Regulation of Political Parties". Unpublished.

———. 2015. "Report to the Permanent Council". Electoral Observation Mission, General and Regional Elections in the Cooperative Republic of Guyana. http://caribbeanelections.com/eDocs/election_reports/gy/GY_OAS_2015 _verbal.pdf.

Observer Media. 2013. "Namba Wants Controls on Campaign Financing". *The Daily Observer*, 25 October 2013. http://www.antiguaobserver.com/namba-wants-controls-on-campaign-financing/.

Office of the Contractor-General. 2010. "Special Report of Investigation Conducted into the Oil Lifting Contracts between the Petroleum Corporation of Jamaica (PCJ) and Trafigura Beheer". Jamaican Ministry of Energy and Mining. http://www.japarliament.gov.jm/attachments/496_OCG%20Investigation%20Report%20-%20Trafigura%20Beheer%20Part%201.pdf.

Open Society. 2005. "Election Campaign Finance: A Handbook for NGOs". Justice in Action Series. https://www.opensocietyfoundations.org/sites/default/files/Handbook_in_full.pdf.

Parliament of Antigua and Barbuda. 2001. "An Act to Amend the Representation of the People Act Cap. 379". http://laws.gov.ag/acts/2001/a2001-17.pdf.

Payne, Douglas. 1999. "The Failings of Governance in Antigua and Barbuda: The Elections of 1999". *Centre for Strategic and International Studies* 10 (4). https://www.csis.org/analysis/policy-papers-americas-failings-governance-antigua-and-barbuda-elections-1999-volume-x-1999.

Phillips, Fred. 1998. "Political Party and Campaign Finance in Antigua and Barbuda". OAS Unit for the Promotion of Democracy and the IDEA. https://archivos.juridicas.unam.mx/www/bjv/libros/4/1593/42.pdf.

Phillips, Hayden. 2007. *Strengthening Democracy: Fair and Sustainable Funding for Political Parties: The Review of the Funding of Political Parties*. United Kingdom: House of Commons Library. http://image.guardian.co.uk/sys-files/Politics/documents/2007/03/15/partyfunding.pdf.

Pinto-Duschinsky, Michael. 2002. "Political Financing in the Commonwealth". The Commonwealth Secretariat.

RJR News. 2012. "Grenada's PM Refutes Allegations Made by Opposition Leader". Multimedia Jamaica Ltd, 1 June 2012. http://rjrnewsonline.com/regional/grenadas-pm-refutes -allegations-made-by-opposition-leader.

Rolle, Rashad. 2017. "Nygard Gave Gibson $94,000: $5,000 A Month Paid to Minister's US Bank Account". *Tribune 242*, 24 April 2017. http://www.tribune242.com/news/2017/apr/24 /nygard-gave-gibson-94000-5000-month-paid-ministers/.

Searchlight. 2010. "Gonsalves to NDP: What's the Source of Your $5 Million", 7 September 2010. http://testwp05.tecnavia.com/searchlight/news/news/2010/09/07/gonsalves-to-ndp-whats -the-source-of-your-5-million/.

St. Lucia Times. 2018. "Braff Says: Accept Neville Cenac and Move On!", 11 January 2018. https://stluciatimes.com/2018/01/11/braff-says-accept-neville-cenac-and-move-on/.

Stuart, Freundel. 2013. Address to Participants at the Regional Forum: "Strengthening Political Parties and Campaign Finance in the Caribbean". Bridgetown, Barbados, 8–9 May 2013.

Terracino, Julio Bacio and Yukihiko Yamada. 2014. "Financing Democracy". OECD. https:// www.unodc.org/documents/treaties/UNCAC/WorkingGroups/workinggroup4/2014 -September-8-10/Responses_NV/OECD_EN.pdf.

The Sun. 2017. "A Little Clause with Big Controversy – The UWP Finds It Intolerable", 15 August 2017. http://sundominica.com/articles/a-little-clause-with-big-controversy-4427/.

United Nations. 2004. "United Nations Convention against Corruption". New York: United Nations Office on Drugs and Crime. https://www.unodc.org/documents/brussels/ UN _Convention_Against_Corruption.pdf.

Walecki, Marcin. n.d. "Political Money and Corruption". IFES Political Finance White Paper Series, September 2014. http://www.legislationline.org/download/action/download /id/2821/file/Walecki%20IFES%20White%20Paper%20on%20Political%20Money%20 and%20Corruption.pdf.

Williams, Robert. 2000. "Aspects of Party Finance and Political Corruption". In *Party Finance and Political Corruption*, edited by Robert Williams, 1–13. London: Macmillan Press.

Zovatto, Daniel. 2013. Inaugural Speech at the Regional Forum: "Strengthening Political Parties and Campaign Finance in the Caribbean". Bridgetown, Barbados, 8–9 May 2013. https:// www.idea.int/sites/default/files/speeches/Strengthening-political-parties-and-campaign -finance-in-the-Caribbean-Inaugural-speech-by-Dr-Daniel-Zovatto-PDF.pdf.

Chapter 16

The Reparatory Justice Movement in the Caribbean

The Role of CARICOM since 2013

VERENE A. SHEPHERD

Introduction

In July 2013, at its thirty-fourth meeting held in Trinidad and Tobago, the Heads of Government of the Caribbean Community (CARICOM) aligned themselves publicly with the reparation movement that had intensified its activities under Rastafari leadership since the 1960s, and even before. Why did CARICOM decide to pursue this en bloc after having paid little attention to the matter for decades, with only a few individual politicians showing any interest in the matter? One clear and immediate reason could be the influence on the heads of the persuasive arguments mounted by historian Hilary Beckles in his book *Britain's Black Debt* (Beckles, 2013). When it did become involved, what was CARICOM's conceptualization of, and structures for, promoting a reparations agenda, and what were the challenges faced in pursuing it? These are some of the questions that this chapter aims to address. The chapter also tracks the actions and decisions of Heads of Government and the CARICOM Reparations Commission since 2013, and assesses their impacts and implications.

The perspective presented here is that of an "insider", having been asked to serve as one of the vice chairs of the CARICOM Reparations Commission since its inception. But I think my participation in this anthology is still legitimate, and I leave it to others to use the "outsider" approach to add to the discussion. Of course, in my reading of the developments since 2013, I am conscious of the questions raised around the timing and purpose of CARICOM's intervention, with some speculating that it was fuelled by the failure to get any traction internationally (especially in organizations such as the World Trade Organization), as well as the region's peculiar challenges as small states. Some dismiss CARICOM as a trade grouping with no political authority to lead the reparation struggle, even doubting the ability of this one issue to bring the region closer together; others say that CARICOM has captured the movement from the people and has established a top-down approach that marginalizes the grassroots and Rastafari. Still others view it as CARICOM finally understanding that a unified approach, a collective voice and state leadership are vital if this movement is to succeed where other unifying efforts failed. Slavery was a state-sanctioned enterprise, and governments and political allies are critical to negotiate on behalf of the Caribbean people. Whatever is the reasoning behind CARICOM's involvement, the reality is that such intervention has given long-time advocates much-needed support and reignited the reparation movement in other parts of the world. Whether the movement will succeed any time soon and result in reparation as demanded by CARICOM cannot be predicted with certainty, although the responses of universities (Georgetown, Glasgow, Brown, Harvard), and in wake of the murder of George Floyd and the intensification of the Black Lives Matter Campaign, as well as the responses of business enterprises (e.g., Green King Pub chain), insurance companies (e.g., Lloyds of London) and financial institutions in the United States and the United Kingdom (most notably the Bank of England) have reduced the scepticism. Doubters are now thinking that reparation seems possible as some of these institutions have committed to some form of reparative justice.

Genealogy of the Movement

I must acknowledge from the outset, though, that the policy and practice of reparatory justice predates CARICOM's participation. Before delving into that genealogy, I will discuss its definition and objectives. In its simplest definition, *reparation* means redressing a wrong which has been done and the attempt to remove the long-term effects of the crime upon the victims and their descendants. In recent years the term has come to be used specifically in the context of the wrongs done to people of African descent in the period of the maangamizi, or African Holocaust, and the system of African enslavement in the Americas. The concept of reparation is a part of a theory of justice known as restorative justice. This concept of justice emphasizes repairing the harm caused or revealed by criminal action. A part of identifying and taking steps to repair harm is to unequivocally acknowledge that wrong was done and to make amends not only through monetary compensation but also through infrastructural development and acknowledging and making a statement of unreserved apology to the victims or their descendants who continue to bear the legacy.

In the Caribbean, the call for redress for native genocide, trafficking and enslavement of Africans by Europeans, deceptive Asian indentureship, and post-slavery and post-colonial injustices has been a feature of Caribbean history and negotiations with Europeans for over two centuries. The pioneers of the reparation movement were enslaved Africans all over the Caribbean, who used resistance strategies to demonstrate their firm conviction that slavery was a violation of their human rights and inalienable claim to freedom. In the immediate post-slavery period, the newly emancipated took up the struggle, enforcing ideas of moral economy in their efforts to secure the resources to make a living (e.g. land on which to develop peasant agriculture). The eighteenth- and nineteenth-century enslaved-led wars all over the Caribbean, freed people's struggles for justice in the mid- to late nineteenth century, and the 1930s labour protests across the region all continued this search for reparatory justice in the face of attempts to maintain the vestiges of slavery. The Rastafari continued the movement for reparation, framed within the context of repatriation to Africa, until joined by civil society, academics, individual politicians and, since 2013, the governments of CARICOM.

Even before CARICOM, as a bloc, lent support to the movement, individual politicians in the region had aligned themselves with the movement, notably the late Jamaican ambassador Dudley Thompson. Thompson was a key figure at the 1993 Abuja Conference in Nigeria, attended also by Nigerian politician and reparation advocate Moshood Abiola and UK peer Anthony Gifford; long-standing Jamaican member of Parliament Lester Michael (Mike) Henry; and St Vincent and the Grenadines prime minister Ralph Gonsalves. But this action by CARICOM made them the latest advocates, as a collective, to articulate the view that European governments have a reparatory justice case to answer for African enslavement, colonialism and continuing post-colonial harm.

Immediate Impetus

A combination of factors eventually pushed the CARICOM Heads of Government to join civil society in the call for reparatory justice, but we can dismiss mass lobbying from Caribbean citizens as one of them. None seemed pushed by their citizens and constituents to lobby Europeans for reparation, and the matter never became an election issue. In other words, no political careers seemed in danger because citizens of the region gave their leaders an ultimatum. Indeed, there was (and still is) no groundswell of grassroots support, and the majority of Caribbean people are at best aloof from the movement or at worst totally opposed to it, regarding it either as a pipedream or undignified begging. What is clear is that those who were at the 2001 World Conference against Racism held in Durban, South Africa, returned to the region utterly offended by the attempts, especially by Europeans and the United States, to keep reparation off the agenda. Attendees like journalist and author Barbara Makeda Blake-Hannah of Jamaica, Pan-African attorney David Commissiong of Barbados, and leading reparation historian and scholar-activist Hilary Beckles (now vice chancellor of the University of the West Indies) stepped up the activism in the Caribbean upon their return. They had willing supporters among some politicians like Mike Henry and Prime Minister Ralph Gonsalves.

Developments in the period 2002–13 cannot be ignored as having given impetus to CARICOM's decision. Just after the World Conference against Racism, the United Nations established the Working Group of Experts on People of African Descent (WGEPAD) (which I later chaired, 2012–14); the Jamaica Reparation Movement, led by Blake-Hannah, was formed; and the Durban Declaration and Programme of Action was given wide publicity within and outside of the United Nations. In 2007, Britain and some Caribbean states marked the bicentenary of the passing of the British Slave Trade Abolition Act. And in the same year that Jamaica made history by establishing a National Reparations Commission (led by the late sociologist Barry Chevannes), the UN General Assembly, on 18 December 2009, proclaimed the year beginning on 1 January 2011 the International Year for People of African Descent.[1] The realization that a year was insufficient to bring new attention to the issues faced by African people led to lobbying by some Latin American and Caribbean States and non-governmental organizations for an International Decade for People of African Descent (2015–24). The process involved in getting support for the decade was not an easy one, but the Working Group under my leadership and then the leadership of Mireille Fanon Mendes France persisted and managed to build alliances that led those who eventually took over the process to finalize the programme of activities and secure the endorsement of the UN General Assembly, which launched the International Decade for People of African Descent on December 2014. The importance of all these activities and developments was that reparation was very much central to the agendas and programmes of action, and Caribbean states placed themselves firmly behind them. Consequently, when Hilary Beckles made his pitch to the Heads of Government of CARICOM at its meeting on July 2013, impressing upon it the necessity to support the movement and establish processes and structures to do so, the groundwork had already been laid. A convincing aspect of that presentation, however, was the link made between the region's underdevelopment, continuing post-colonial harm and vulnerabilities to global financial instabilities as a result of the stifling strictures of World Bank, International Monetary Fund and other international agencies, and the burden of debt repayment, on the one hand, and the failure of former colonial powers to leave a region they had exploited for centuries in a position to achieve sustainable development, on the other. Reparation framed within the discourse of development, rather than a one-time financial settlement, was appealing. Admittedly, there are those who believe reparation should come in the form of a financial settlement and that such a settlement should be divided among the descendants of victims. But most movements are now showing a preference for a community development plan, rather than a one-time payment to the descendants of the victims. A Ten Point Plan for Reparatory Justice (after which the National African-American Reparations Commission has patterned its ten point plan), outlined the strategy to be pursued.

Concrete Structures, Directives and Strategy

In terms of the organizational structure, the July 2013 Conference of Heads of Government agreed to set up the CARICOM Reparations Commission (CRC), led by the Core Committee (consisting of a chair and three vice chairs) and a representative of the University of the West Indies. The CRC was expected to "establish the moral, ethical and legal case for the payment of reparations by the governments of all the former colonial powers and the relevant institutions of those countries, to the nations and people of the Caribbean Community, for the Crimes against Humanity of Native Genocide", the transatlantic trafficking of Africans, a racialized system of chattel enslavement, and an unjust colonial and neocolonial system which continued to harm the region (CARICOM Reparations Commission 2018, n.p.).[2] The Heads of Government further agreed that there should be national committees on reparation in each CARICOM state, following Jamaica, which had first established a National Commission on Reparation in 2009. The CRC chair, Core Committee and the chairs of national committees (who were also members of the CRC) would report directly to the Prime Ministerial Sub-Committee on Reparations, comprising the heads of government of Barbados (Freundel Stuart at the time, now Mia Amor Mottley), St Vincent and the Grenadines, Haiti, Guyana, and Suriname, who would provide political oversight. The Heads of Government also requested that the University of the West Indies establish a Centre for Reparation Research to support the CRC, which was duly established in 2017.

An event in St Vincent and the Grenadines's Victoria Park on 15 September 2013, followed by the first regional reparation conference on that island, publicly launched the regional movement and cemented the structure and the organizational dimension of the work. Indeed, the CRC was officially established at that conference, and the first meeting of the CRC was held in the following days on 17 September. Hilary Beckles was appointed chair of the CRC and three vice chairs were selected to oversee specific portfolios: Verene Shepherd (research and public education), Jomo Thomas (regional political engagement) and Armand Zunder (coordination of national committees). Since then Dorbrene O'Marde has taken over Thomas's role, leaving him free to chair a legal Working Group to consider the route to a legal challenge; and Eric Phillips of Guyana has replaced Armand Zunder. Hilary Brown of the CARICOM Secretariat in Georgetown, Guyana, was assigned to the CRC to provide administrative support.

By January 2014, national committees had been established in eight member states, namely Antigua and Barbuda, Barbados, Belize, Guyana, Jamaica, St Lucia, St Vincent and the Grenadines, and Suriname. Dominica, Trinidad and Tobago, and the Bahamas later followed. Change of governments since 2013 has affected the re-establishment and funding of some national committees. At the same time, new committees have been established. The countries in which national committees have been formed are Antigua and Barbuda, The Bahamas, Barbados, Dominica, Grenada, Guyana, Jamaica, St. Kitts and Nevis, Saint Lucia, St. Vincent and the Grenadines, Suriname and Trinidad and Tobago. Members in these national groupings are drawn from a wide cross section of Caribbean society, including Rastafari, academics, legal practitioners, grassroots organizations, church leaders and artistes. They have established links with reparation activists and networks in the non-independent Caribbean countries of Guadeloupe, Martinique, the UK and US Virgin Islands, and the Dutch-colonized Caribbean. They have also established links with reparation committees and organizations in Africa, Asia, Canada, the European Union, Latin America, the United Kingdom and the United States. In other words, what CARICOM has joined is a global African reparation movement.

The CARICOM Reparations Commission and National Committees

This section will outline the Terms of Reference of the CRC and the national committees, which were agreed on at the first meeting of the commission in September 2013. According to the Terms of Reference, the CRC has ten aims and objectives, as follows:

CRC Aims and Objectives (CARICOM Secretariat 2013b, n.p.)

1. Establish the moral, ethical and legal case for the payment of Reparations by the Governments of all the former colonial powers and the relevant institutions of those countries, to the nations and people of the Caribbean Community for the Crimes against Humanity of Native Genocide, the Trans-Atlantic Slave Trade and a racialised system of chattel slavery;
2. Advise and make recommendations for coordinated CARICOM action by the Prime Ministerial Sub-Committee on Reparations;

3. Coordinate and support the work of National Reparations Commissions and Task Forces and encourage the development of Commissions in those countries that have not yet established national bodies;

4. Receive reports from National Reparations Commissions;

5. Develop and implement a regional strategy to pursue Reparations, including the following actions:

    a. Coordinate and/or undertake relevant historical research at the national, regional and international levels;

    b. Coordinate and/or undertake legal research to inform case preparation and litigation strategies;

    c. Coordinate national and regional public education campaigns;

    d. Coordinate and/or conduct national and regional public consultations on Reparations;

    e. Develop and recommend diplomatic strategies to advance the case for Reparations in multilateral institutions such as the United Nations, African Union, CELAC [Community of Latin American and Caribbean States] and with other supportive governments;

    f. Identify and recommend the appointment of eminent spokespersons and champions for the cause of Reparations among artists, attorneys, scholars, Indigenous Peoples, Rastafarians, youth, women and politicians;

    g. Engage and partner with national and regional civil society organizations involved in the Reparations Movement, especially the Rastafarian and Pan-Africanist formations of the Caribbean;

6. Develop and recommend decisive political action at the national and regional levels through Parliamentary debates and resolutions and national, regional and international popular mobilization;

7. Conduct consultations to develop proposals on appropriate forms of redress through reparative programmes and projects;

8. Coordinate and/or undertake the preparation of a detailed brief on the cost of the damages and current manifestations of such damage on indigenous people and their descendants and on enslaved Africans and their descendants, in the following and other relevant areas:

    a. Economic (including land deprivation)

    b. Social, Cultural and Psychological

    c. Spiritual and Religious

    d. Demographic

    e. Medical

    f. Educational

    g. Separation from homeland (repatriation)

9. Assume the responsibility for the preparation and presentation of the legal case for Reparations and highlight the special case of Reparations for Haiti;

10. Serve as a quick response mechanism to address negative publicity on Reparations that may arise in regional or international media, and develop a pro-active media campaign to raise public awareness and canvas support.

It was agreed that the Regional Commission would review the Terms of Reference from time to time and amend the activities as deemed appropriate. However, so far, these Terms of Reference have remained in place.

While each national committee would draft its own Terms of Reference, each was broadly expected to operate along the lines set out for the CRC, but with a national focus. So each was mandated to develop and implement a national strategy to pursue reparations, including coordinating national public education campaigns; conducting national public consultations; identifying and recommending the appointment of eminent spokespersons and champions for the cause of reparations among artistes, attorneys, scholars, Indigenous Peoples, Rastafarians, youth, women and politicians; and engaging and partnering with national and regional civil society organizations involved in the reparation movement, especially the Rastafarian and Pan-Africanist formations of the Caribbean.

CARICOM'S Strategy

The rest of this chapter will discuss CARICOM's strategy for demanding reparatory justice for native genocide, African enslavement, deceptive Asian indentureship and the legacies of colonialism, and highlight the challenges faced in doing so. Once the organizational structure was established and the Terms of Reference laid down, the full strategy was articulated. The strategy involved establishing the CRC and the Centre for Reparation Research to drive needed content building; to secure a budget through contributions from each member state to finance the administrative activities, public education and stakeholder building exercises; to engage in diplomatic negotiations with the intention of a settlement outside of a legal case; to secure a legal opinion and work out the legal strategy should a negotiated settlement fail to materialize; and to secure political and diplomatic support from the United Nations, the African Union, the Community of Latin American and Caribbean States, and other governments. A public education strategy was also worked out (to be activated by the CRC as well as national committees), consisting of:

- Town hall meetings and national consultations
- Traditional media: broadcast media, newspapers, brochures, quick facts, press conferences
- New media: social media
- Eminent spokespersons and champions
- Youth engagement
- Civil society engagement
- Engagement with Rastafari and Pan-African movements
- Caribbean public and European public engagement

The next step was to agree on an action plan, now known as the Ten Point Action Plan for Reparatory Justice, which was crafted at a meeting of the Core Committee of the CRC in Jamaica on 9 December 2013. The action plan was accepted by the Heads of Government and launched at a press conference at the regional headquarters of the University of the West Indies on 10 December 2013, co-chaired by Hilary Beckles and the then minister with portfolio responsibility for reparation in Jamaica, Lisa Hanna.

The Ten Point Plan

The Ten Point Plan (TPP) begins with a restatement of the rationale for the reparation movement in the region, asserting that the region's indigenous and African descendant communities who are the victims of crimes against humanity in the forms of genocide, enslavement, human trafficking and racial apartheid have a legal right to reparatory justice, and that those who committed these crimes, and who have been enriched by the proceeds of these crimes, have a reparatory case to answer (CARICOM Secretariat 2013a). The plan recognizes the special role and status of European governments in this regard, being the legal bodies that instituted the framework for developing and sustaining these crimes, the primary agencies through which slavery-based enrichment took place, and national custodians of criminally accumulated wealth.

The plan then sets out the charges against the transgressors, asserting that European governments:

- invaded and captured the lands of the region that were occupied by Caribbean civilizations;
- instructed genocidal actions upon indigenous communities; and as the Indigenous Peoples declined drastically in numbers, missionaries used racist justification to protect native peoples from enslavement and Europeans opposed white systems of labour, started the capturing and forced relocation of Africans to the Caribbean, and became owners and traders of enslaved Africans;
- defined and enforced African enslavement and native genocide as in their national interests;
- created the legal, financial and fiscal policies necessary for the enslavement of Africans;
- imposed a system of terror on Africans through the plantation system;
- opposed for decades the efforts to end the African Holocaust and punished severely Africans who resisted;
- refused compensation to the enslaved with the ending of their enslavement;
- compensated enslavers at emancipation for the loss of legal property rights in enslaved Africans;
- attempted to recreate the slavery relations of production in the post-slavery period;
- imposed policies designed to perpetuate suffering upon the emancipated and survivors of genocide and those imported and indentured to add to the freed African labour force and keep the plantation going; and
- refused to date to acknowledge such crimes or to compensate victims and their descendants who continue to suffer harm and the legacies of colonialism. Indeed, Africans and their descendants living in the United Kingdom contributed through their taxes to the repayment of the planter compensation loan, a loan paid off only in 2015.

The specifics of the plan follow (CARICOM Secretariat 2013a):

1. *Full formal and explicit apology* (not a statement of regret) on the basis that the healing process for victims and the descendants of the enslaved and enslavers requires, as a precondition, the offer of a sincere formal apology by the governments of Europe. An apology represents an admission of wrongdoing, takes responsibility for such wrongdoing, commits to reasonable reparatory actions (which can take various forms) and commits to non-repetition.

2. *Indigenous people's development programme* on the basis that the Indigenous Peoples of the Caribbean were subjected to the violence and brutality of European conquest and colonization that resulted in genocide and the destruction of their communities, the result of which was the movement of Indigenous Peoples within countries and throughout the region. Reparatory justice in this instance means rebuilding these communities that were destroyed. Developing CARICOM member states are unable to carry out the reconstruction of these communities without the assistance of those who were instrumental in their destruction.

3. *Funding for repatriation to Africa*, as the resettlement of displaced Africans throughout the CARICOM who wish to return to their homeland, is an instrumental part of the process of correcting the atrocities of European colonialism and enslavement. CARICOM, in an effort to facilitate repatriation, has been in contact with certain African states who are welcoming of the return of their stolen people. The strain of resettlement, however, cannot be shouldered by the victims of this crime. A fully funded repatriation programme that undertakes citizenship and reintegration must be established.

4. *The establishment of cultural institutions/return of cultural heritage* is essential to reparatory justice. Under European colonization and enslavement, the cultural heritage (inclusive of the history and language of Indigenous Peoples, enslaved Africans and indentured labourers) were systematically destroyed. With the limited resources that are available, CARICOM member states have not been able to allocate funds for the establishment of these cultural institutions. Looted cultural heritage must also be returned.

5. *Addressing and remedying the public health crisis* within the CARICOM has been a difficult process for heads of government who are committed to ensuring proper health care services for their citizens. Several of the diseases faced by Caribbean nationals are a direct result of European invasion and slavery, and necessitate advanced technology, capital and science to effectively manage them. It is therefore the responsibility of former colonial powers to participate in the remedying and restoration of good health through the provision of hospitals and health care.

6. *Education programmes*: CARICOM member states were left with the legacy of a flawed educational system. Though significant efforts and progress have been made to rectify this, they still struggle with high levels of functional illiteracy, dilapidated schools and a system based on discrimination, which has dwarfed the economic and social development of these nations. European countries involved

in the colonization of these states have an obligation to build educational capacity and provide scholarships to address the inequitable education system.

7. *The enhancement of historical and cultural knowledge exchanges*: An important part of reparatory justice is for European nations to be involved in the restoration of pride through programmes that will facilitate the learning and an understanding of indigenous and African history. It is a fact that CARICOM states have spent the better part of their independence attempting to rebuild and reconnect their citizens to their history.

8. *Psychological rehabilitation as a result of the intergenerational transmission of trauma*: The legacy of slavery and colonialism by certain European states has deeply affected the psychological well-being of indigenous and African descended peoples from centuries of trauma. It is, therefore, the responsibility of European nations involved in the carrying out of the evil act of slavery to provide rehabilitative services and programmes to begin the process of repairing and healing the trauma of enslavement and discrimination.

9. *Technology transfer*, which can be located within the right to development framework. Clause 158 of the Durban Declaration and Programme of Action recognizes that "historical injustices have undeniably contributed to the poverty, underdevelopment, marginalization, social exclusion, economic disparities, instability and insecurity that affect many people in different parts of the world, in particular in developing countries; and recognizes the need to develop programmes for the social and economic development of these societies and the Diaspora, within the framework of a new partnership based on the spirit of solidarity and mutual respect" (United Nations 2001, 49).

Rohan Kariyawasam (2012) endorses technological transfer as an alternative strategy to remedying past transgressions citing the 1982 declaration on the right to development. Kariyawasam posits that perpetrators of historical violence have an obligation to "invest in the affected countries in technical skills, technology, research and development, education, health and services" (Shepherd 2015, 5). He concludes that the right to development should be a legally enforceable right and that transgressors should uphold this right to development and be held accountable through the United Nations' Universal Periodic Review.

Calls for development that incorporate inputs from former colonial powers continue (Shepherd 2015). This is especially the case as leaders of the 1960s, while pressing for a "golden handshake" to be able to actualize the financial requirements of independence, only got meagre sums from Britain. Consequently, the new nations, founded with much hope, faced daunting economic challenges. Seely quotes Ahmad and Wilkie (1979) who noted: "These nations soon began to realize that political freedom could not be construed as an end in itself and that achieving it did not automatically ensure the social and economic well-being of their people" (Seely 2003, 11, quoting Ahmad & Wilkie 1979).

As the Caribbean world prepares its citizens to be advocates and beneficiaries of social advancement and economic development in the "long twenty-first century", the still unsettled relationship between historical injustices, persistent poverty and diminishing opportunities looms larger than ever before as a primary obstacle to development.

10. *Debt cancellation*: Finally, the Caribbean Reparatory Justice Programme includes debt cancellation on the basis that the Caribbean governments that emerged from slavery and colonialism have inherited the massive crisis of community poverty and institutional unpreparedness for development. The pressure of development has driven governments to carry the burden of public employment and social policies designed to confront colonial legacies. As Amartya Sen argued in his 1999 book *Development as Freedom,* overcoming these socio-economic problems is a central part of the exercise of development and of the process of ensuring that freedom that will otherwise fall at the feet of underdevelopment. Support for the payment of domestic debt and cancellation of international debt are necessary reparatory actions. Poverty is a consequence of colonialism and has always been tied to its discriminatory practices and legacies (Sen 2000).

The Second Regional Reparation Conference

In order to publicize the TPP and build content around each point, the action plan was the focus of the awareness-raising and public education campaign at the reparation conference held in Antigua and Barbuda in 2015, and has subsequently been discussed and embraced at reparation fora all over the world, recently in Berlin, Germany, where from September to December 2017, Ballhaus Naunynstraße hosted Republik Repair under the theme "Ten Points, Ten Demands, One Festival", curated by Karina Griffith. Over the two days of the Antigua conference, academics and practitioners, including barristers from the legal firm Leigh Day that won compensation from the British on behalf of the Mau Mau of Kenya for those that were still alive, debated the TPP and provided content that would be vital for understanding the reparation cause as well as content for approaches to the former colonizing nations and any legal team that might take the case to an international court, should negotiations break down. The legal firm had been invited by St Vincent and the Grenadines prime minister Ralph Gonsalves to give an opinion on the most effective strategy the Caribbean could utilize to claim reparatory justice. The firm was never hired by CARICOM, despite rumours to that effect, but its legal opinion was that an advisory opinion could be requested from the International Court of Justice on the recommendation of either the UN Committee on the Elimination of Racial Discrimination or the General Assembly of the UN.

As a first step, a decision was taken that the chair of the Prime Ministerial Sub-Committee on Reparation (PMSC) should write to the heads of the former enslaving nations setting out the basis of the reparation movement and the evidentiary basis of a reparation claim. From the perspective of the Caribbean, the evidentiary basis of the claim rests on the following justifications, as laid out by Beckles (2013, 14–15):

- A defendant (or perpetrator) exists: There is incontrovertible evidence that European countries were heavily involved in human trafficking, and in the deaths of millions of enslaved Africans, which subsequently led to the criminal enrichment of their societies. Plantation slavery provided the scaffold for Britain's industrial advancement, so the evidence shows the considerable value of enslaved people's labour to British/European economic development.

- The injustice is well documented: Scholars worldwide have presented evidence of the brutal nature of the African Holocaust and the demographic disaster that was plantation slavery. For example, a total of about 5.5 million Africans were trafficked to the British-colonized Caribbean over 2 centuries; yet in 1834, just 800,000 remained.
- The victims are identifiable as a distinct group: The indigenous Caribbean people who survived the harsh policies of European countries and the descendants of enslaved Africans constitute identifiable communities. Should they decide to do so, descendants of indentured labourers, some of whom experienced forced relocation and violations of contractual obligations, also have a claim.
- The descendants of victimized groups continue to suffer harm: The discriminatory system of enslavement during the colonial era, based on race and ethnicity, continues to have a debilitating impact on the descendants of enslaved Africans and Indigenous Peoples in modern-day Caribbean society.

Action of the PMSC

Since that second conference, there have been several developments, the most important and historic being that in 2016 when the chair of the CARICOM PMSC, Freundel Stuart of Barbados, acting on behalf of the other members of the PMSC and heads of CARICOM, and ultimately the people of the Caribbean, dispatched a historic letter relating to reparatory justice for indigenous genocide and African enslavement in the Caribbean to six heads of European governments: Denmark, France, Portugal, Spain, the Netherlands and the United Kingdom. The letter, which to date has not been made public by CARICOM, although summaries have been revealed, set out, in a generic way, the basis for the Caribbean reparatory justice movement and the reasons such countries were singled out for claims of redress.

CARICOM has chosen, as a first step, to resolve the matter in a diplomatic approach – a meeting request with European heads to discuss, in a non-confrontational way, the issues raised in that letter. To date, only Portugal has not responded to the letter. From what has been gleaned from CARICOM, the responses, which also have not been made public, have not directly addressed the issues raised in that first letter, and the request for a meeting has not been granted. David Cameron, in his April 2016 reply to CARICOM's letter, reiterated the United Kingdom's long-standing position that reparations are not the answer (Shepherd 2017). Spain, in turn, indicated it has taken sufficient steps by contributing to the permanent memorial to honour victims of slavery at the United Nations in New York and that, through the Spanish Development Cooperation, has developed educational programmes for schools that focus on the good and bad aspects of the Spanish presence in America (Shepherd 2017). President Hollande of France claimed that that "history cannot be erased. We do not erase it. It cannot be the subject of transactions at the end of an accounting exercise which would be, at all points, impossible to establish" (cited in Shepherd 2017).[3]

This is ironic because emancipation was made an accounting exercise when the British compensated the 46,000 enslavers to the tune of £20 million-plus, as Beckles has noted, another £27 million earned through the scamming called the apprenticeship system – as settlement for the loss of their "property". Incidentally, some calculate that the £20 million in today's value, multiplying by the objective factor of 839, amounts to £16.78 billion (Beckles 2013; Manning 2013). This was an enormous sum of public money. It represented 40 per cent of British national expenditure for that year, which would be £200 billion today. Economists in and out of Parliament justified this action on the basis that reparation payments would constitute an impactful national financial stimulus package. They were correct. Some 85 per cent of the public funds assigned to private owners were reinvested in the country. Reparation payment to enslavers represented the greatest mobilization of public/private capital in nineteenth-century Britain and was responsible for propelling the sagging economy out of the doldrums. It promoted industrial modernization and assured sustained economic growth for another fifty years; and the loan borrowed to finance the payment was not finally dispensed with until February 2015, making nonsense of the claim that slavery belongs in the past with no contemporary meaning.[4]

Meanwhile, the enslaved people of the Caribbean received no compensation for the centuries of criminally enforced labour and legal denial of their human identity, all crimes against humanity. In addition, the Indigenous Peoples of the region, especially those in the Windward Islands who were forcefully removed from their lands and deported in order to make room for plantations, were not considered worthy of reparation. They had experienced genocide as an imperial policy. Today, these communities of Kalinagos and Garifunas are struggling to rebuild numbers in the islands and are still at risk of slipping into extinction.

Despite the rightness of the claim, western European powers have refused to engage in any meaningful dialogue on the issue of reparation. As a reminder, between 1825 and 1922, the Haitian government paid the French enslaving community over 90 million francs (US$21 billion, at 2004 value) in reparations for the loss of 400,000 enslaved persons and other forms of property when freedom for all and national independence were secured in 1804. Europeans have always opposed the legitimacy of the movement on what they raise as legal grounds. At the 2001 anti-racism conference in Durban, they refused to deem the maangamizi a crime against humanity. Beckles (2013, 193–94) identifies and responds to a number of arguments raised by Europeans at this conference:

- Chattel slavery and trading in enslaved people were legal at the time because the British state had legalized the system and so no crime was committed.

    However, international law provides that in respect of crimes against humanity, national law is no cover and refuge. The German state argued at Nuremberg that the mass murder of Jews was governed by national laws passed by the Third Reich. The court determined otherwise.
- If the British government were to admit to criminal misconduct, the crimes are now far too distant and cannot be the subject of legal or political reconciliation.

    The remoteness principle also states that living memory is an acceptable response. There are thousands of persons in the region who can attest to knowing their enslaved (great-)grandparents and who can link successfully their suffering to their plight.

- The crime of slavery, if admitted, is too large to contemplate legal recuperation and political dialogue.

   Justice, however, has always advanced on the basis that law, and the creativity of jurists, are sufficiently elastic to accommodate new and innovative solutions to challenges of an unprecedented nature.

- Some African governments were collaborators.

   This also has no legal bearing on Caribbean enslavement from the perspective of Caribbean citizens. Furthermore, the following are true:

   (i)   All major international crimes require local collaboration. This relationship makes the crime more, rather than less, heinous on the part of those who forced others to collaborate.

   (ii) The hundreds of military forts and other war facilities built along the West African coast to create and sustain the capture and sale of Africans were monuments to terror that served to subvert and destroy governments and leaders who opposed the trade. African leaders were assassinated and states were destroyed for getting in the way of the biggest and most lucrative commerce in the European-dominated world economy. This, of course, did not prevent Queens, Kings and other Africans from protesting and finding ways to destabilize the maangamizi from capture, sale, storage in barracoons, shipment across the Middle Passage and on Caribbean plantations.

   (iii) Slavery in Africa was not chattel slavery (an argument they use as justification).

   (iv) Africa was enriched (but economic historians like Joseph Inikori claim the net profit to the continent was 0 per cent, even if a few leaders got wealth from it).

Clearly, jurists, theologians and philosophers all differ from the European states in their thinking on the matter. While there exists no specific policy on reparation within international human rights frameworks, the agreement that states must be held accountable for their human rights violations is enshrined in several international, legal documents, for example, the International Covenant on Civil and Political Rights (1966); the International Convention on Elimination of All Forms of Discrimination (1966); and the Convention against Torture and Other Cruel, Inhuman and Degrading Treatment (1984). Article 8 of the Universal Declaration of Human Rights of 1948, the legal document on which international human rights is based, states the following: "Everyone has the right to an effective remedy by the competent national tribunals for acts violating the fundamental rights granted him by the constitutions or by law" (United Nations General Assembly 1948, 3).

According to Queen's Counsel Anthony Gifford (2007) the following arguments provide the legal foundation for reparation:

- *Enslavement [and the trade in Africans were and are] crimes against humanity.* Defined as certain acts of violence, such as enslavement and murder, perpetrated against a distinguishable segment of a population or any ill-treatment based on race, religion or political belief that brings about disruption to global peace.

European governments have claimed that slavery was legal during that time, therefore no crime was committed and they cannot be held accountable. However, citing international reparation scholar Nora Wittmann (2013), Gifford demonstrates that there exists statutes and common law that point to the illegality of enslavement and the transatlantic trafficking of Africans during the period of enslavement.

- *No statute or common law principle gave precedent to any legality of transatlantic slavery;* it is not maintained by any authority to be a natural right. It was not until the creation and establishment of the Company of Royal Adventurers Trading to Africa in 1663, which later became the Royal African Company in 1672, that regulations were passed dealing with transatlantic slavery.
- *There is no legal barrier to prevent those who still suffer the consequences of enslavement from claiming reparation even though the crimes were committed against their ancestors.*
- *International law provides the means for descendants to receive recompense on behalf of their ancestors.*
- *Legal responsibility is not affected by any collaboration [with Africans].* There is no principle of law which permits the organizers of a criminal enterprise to escape responsibility because others collaborated in carrying out the enterprise (National Commission on Reparation 2013, 33–36).

There are those who believe that the British state, despite the public pronouncements to the contrary, is aware that it has a case to answer. Beckles (2013) argues that British officials, despite formal reticence, have hinted at this understanding. Britain is also aware that the Caribbean has a legally strong and morally just claim. The government of India has also reopened the files on the Amritsar massacre of 1919 in which hundreds of citizens were gunned down by British imperial troops. An official reparatory process has started.

Centre for Reparation Research

The final aspect of CARICOM's strategic plan was implemented in 2017 with the establishment and launch (on 10 October) of the Centre for Reparation Research (CRR) at the University of the West Indies. The objective of the CRR is to provide support to the CARICOM Reparatory Justice Movement, engage in awareness raising around the issue of reparation and conduct research that forms the basis for the reparation claim to Europe. As far as can be ascertained, this is the only research centre of its kind in the academy, even though universities and cities with a history of slavery are increasingly establishing institutes/centres to research slavery and its legacies. The University of Amsterdam does have a War Reparations Centre, but it does not cover the anti-slavery and post-slavery wars of liberation in the African diaspora.

In addition to supporting the pursuit and implementation of CARICOM's Reparatory Justice Programme, the CRR is primarily motivated by two other interlocking objectives: to broadly foster awareness around the lasting and adverse consequences of colonialism in the Caribbean, and to offer practical solutions to halting and reversing them. Both of these objectives grow out of an understanding that many of the injustices and adverse effects of colonialism in the Caribbean did not end with formal independence and still need to be addressed and repaired. The overarching strategy for public engagement and research is the TPP crafted by the members of the CARICOM Reparation Commission. Among the early tasks of the CRR are to review and revise the TPP based on feedback from national, regional and international stakeholders and to draft a second round of letters to each European country based on their unsatisfactory responses to the first letter sent to them by Freundel Stuart. The initial letter to Portugal will be resent. The second-round letters have been written to Denmark, France, Spain, the Netherlands, the United Kingdom, Germany, Norway, Sweden and Switzerland, setting out in greater detail the justification for the reparation claim against them. As of this writing, the letters had not been sent.

The CRR has also been active in public education through the hosting of several seminars; participation in international, regional and local outreach activities; and the project of youth education and motivation through a "Run for Reparation" baton relay, partnering with the CRC and Jamaica's National Council on Reparation. The baton, expertly fashioned in Guyana, has since passed through Antigua and Barbuda, Barbados, Guyana, Jamaica, and Suriname, and will move to the Bahamas next.

Challenges of Implementation

In addition to the attitude of the former enslaving nations, the other big challenge reparation advocates in the region face is that too many people in the Caribbean and its diaspora are not on board. One indication is the population's support for the Monarchy, despite some of its members historical involvement in the trade in Africans and enrichment from the whole slavery enterprise. In a 2011 Bill Johnson poll on the matter of maintaining Queen Elizabeth II as Jamaica's Head of State, 60 per cent of the people polled said the island would have been better off under British rule, with only 17 per cent saying the island would have been worse off. (*Gleaner* June 28, 2011). Influential voices in letters to newspaper editors in the region and in opinion pieces reveal both ignorance and opposition to the idea of reparation. A 2017 Gleaner-commissioned Bill Johnson poll found that 49 per cent of Jamaicans believed the country would be better off if it had remained a colony of Great Britain, with only 27 per cent of respondents disagreeing (Gleaner August 3, 2017). There has been movement, however. More recently (Observer, August 10, 2020) more than half of respondents in the latest Bill Johnson poll (55 per cent) said Jamaica should not continue to have the Queen as head of State. The November 30, 2021, transition of Barbados to a Republic has re-ignited the issue in Jamaica, and only time will tell if the Diamond Jubillee in 2022 will see the island following the example of Barbados and other Republics in the Region.

A recent delegation of the Jamaica National Council on Reparation to the United Kingdom revealed support from many jurists, but there is deep division among grassroots organizations, and even hostility towards the CARICOM reparation initiative, on the basis that civil society, not governments, should lead the movement. There is some merit to this view, especially within the context of mixed messages coming from some heads of governments in the region. They reiterate their commitment at regional meetings but are not always vocal on the international stage, in particular in the General Assembly at the United Nations, where they were vocal in 2013 and 2014, but have been mostly silent on the issue in recent years. There is high expectation, however, of the new chair of the PMSC, Barbados prime minister Mia Mottley, who has not only been publicly supporting reparation but has also appointed a member of her government to be the focal point person on reparation. Nevertheless, the scepticism of civil society persists. They opine that regional heads appear to be intimidated by the prospect of economic pressure from such countries who provide aid and grants if they articulate a reparation message. There is also the view that former colonial powers will "ride out the storm", hoping that the regional political leadership will not follow post-colonial cohorts in other parts of the world and press claims for reparatory justice for its citizens, that the issue will diminish in importance in the region, and that diplomatic pressure on small states will be effective.

Conclusion

In the end, it is impossible to predict the outcome of the movement, especially in the face of the obstinate stance of former colonial powers and the lack of unity around the issue by Caribbean people of all classes and backgrounds. According to chair of the CRC, Hilary Beckles:

> Growing in academic importance on the outside is the argument that the Caribbean is solely responsible for its development failures and challenges. Emerging from this perspective is that the region's post-independence political leadership has produced a growing number of "failed states", and has run out of indigenous energy to drive progress. These arguments reject any historical perspective and locate development shortfalls and frustrations squarely at the feet of the regions' political and corporate leadership. The purpose of this conceptual approach is to deny the importance of a legacy of colonial wealth extraction, ethnic and racial oppression, debilitating imperial governance, and crude infrastructural capacity, as factors still shaping the region's destiny. (Cited in National Commission on Reparation 2013, 63–64)

But the struggle will continue. Ellis Clarke, the Trinidadian government's UN representative to a sub-committee of the Committee on Colonialism (now called the Special Committee on Decolonisation) made this point in a 1964 address:

> An administering power . . . is not entitled to extract for centuries all that can be got out of a colony and when that has been done to relieve itself of its obligations by the conferment of a formal but meaningless – meaningless because it cannot possibly be supported – political independence. Justice requires that reparation be made to the country that has suffered the ravages of colonialism before that country is expected to face up to the problems and difficulties that will inevitably beset it upon independence. (Cited in Lewis 2004, 410)

Ta-Nehisi Coates holds that "reparations . . . is the indispensable tool against white supremacy" (2015, n.p.). But at the same time, white supremacy is the obstacle to reparation, and moral suasion will not cause it to yield. History has not shown many instances of action on the part of colonizers and oppressors because of moral suasion rather than when white economic interests are threatened (Coates 2014, 2015). According to Coates, history shows us too many examples of heroic people whose struggles were not successful in their own time or at all. On the contrary, to the extent that they were successful, black politics was a necessary precondition but never enough to foment change.

Coates admits that not even emancipation should be viewed as a triumph of black activism or the moral force of the actions of the just over the unjust. He holds that

> it became impossible, for instance, to think about emancipation without the threat presented by disunion, to talk about the civil-rights movement without the ghost of Nazism or the Cold War. It began to seem to me that black politics was the wind at the American window. At rare moments the window opened and black people pushed through. The window seemed to open for one reason and one reason alone – some threat to white interests becoming intolerable. (Coates 2015, n.p.)

In this formulation, it is not enough to be hopeful that good will triumph over evil because "'hope' [might be] an overrated force in human history – unlike fear" (Coates 2015, n.p.).

The question is what will be the wind at the American and Caribbean window that will open up, creating fear among former colonizers to enable the cause of reparatory justice to push through, especially in the face of the tenacity of white supremacy and injustice. Only time will tell.

Notes

1. See the webpage of the International Year for the People of African Descent on the United Nations Human Rights Office of the High Commissioner site at http://www.ohchr.org /EN/NewsEvents/Pages/IntlYearPeopleAfricanDescent.aspx.

2. This 2009 National Commission on Reparation ended its term in 2011 and was reappointed, mostly with new members and only a few of the 2009 members continuing, in 2012. The current National Council on Reparation (there was a name change) was appointed in 2016.

3. The quotes referenced here were extracted from responses by European heads of government to the letter sent by CARICOM.

4. A tweet made by Her Majesty's Treasury on 8 February 2018, which was subsequently deleted, stated that taxpayers were instrumental in the compensation of enslavers. See Olusoga (2018).

References

Ahmad, A. and A.S. Wilkie. 1979. "Technology Transfer in the New International Economic Order: Options, Obstacles, and Dilemmas". In *The Political Economy of International Technology Transfer*, edited by J. McIntyre and D.S. Papp, 77–94. New York: Quorum.

Beckles, Hilary. 2013. *Britain's Black Debt: Reparation for Caribbean Slavery and Native Genocide*. Kingston, Jamaica: University of the West Indies Press.

CARICOM Reparations Commission. 2018. "About Us". http://caricomreparations.org /about-us/.

CARICOM Secretariat. 2013a. "CARICOM Ten Point Action Plan for Reparatory Justice". https://www.caricom.org/caricom-ten-point-plan-for-reparatory-justice/.

———. 2013b. "Terms of Reference for the CARICOM Reparations Commission (CRC)". http://ncr.org.tt/about-us/terms-reference-caricom-reparations-commission-crc.

Coates, Ta-Nehisi. 2014. "The Case for Reparations". *The Atlantic*, June. https://www.theatlantic
.com/magazine/archive/2014/06/the-case-for-reparations/361631/.

———. 2015. "Hope and the Historian". *The Atlantic*, 10 December. https://www.theatlantic
.com/politics/archive/2015/12/hope-and-the-historian/419961/.

Gifford, Anthony. 2007. *The Passionate Advocate*. London: Wildy, Simmonds and Hill
Publishing.

Gleaner. 2017. "Independence Error! - Only 27% of Jamaicans Think the Country Would Be in
a Worse Position If It Had Remained a British Colony", 6 August. http://jamaica-gleaner.com
/article/lead-stories/20170806/independence-error-only-27-jamaicans-think-country
-would-be-worse.

Kariyawasam, Rohan. 2012. "Reparations: The Universal Periodic Review and the Right to
Development". In *Colonialism, Slavery, Reparations and Trade: Remedying the Past?*, edited
by Fernne Brennan and John Packer, 56–74. Abingdon, UK: Routledge.

Lewis, Gordon K. 2004. *The Growth of the Modern West Indies*. Kingston, Jamaica: Ian Randle
Publishers.

Manning, Sanchez. 2013. "Britain's Colonial Shame: Slave-Owners Given Huge Payouts after
Abolition". *The Independent*, 24 February. https://www.independent.co.uk/news/uk/home
-news/britains-colonial-shame-slave-owners-given-huge-payouts-after-abolition-8508358
.html.

National Commission on Reparation. 2013. "Report on the Work of the National Commission
on Reparation, May 2009–October 2013". http://ncr.org.tt/sites/default/files/NCR%20
Report.pdf.

Olusoga, David. 2018. "The Treasury's Tweet Shows Slavery Is Still Misunderstood". *The
Guardian*, 12 February. https://www.theguardian.com/commentisfree/2018/feb/12/treasury
-tweet-slavery-compensate-slave-owners?CMP=share_btn_tw.

Seely, Bruce. 2003. "Historical Patterns in the Scholarship of Technology Transfer".
Comparative Technology Transfer and Society 1 (April): 7–48.

Sen, Amartya. 2000. *Development as Freedom*. New York: Anchor Books.

Shepherd, Verene. 2015. "Reparation & the Right to Development". Presented at the 16th
session of the Working Group of Experts on People of African Descent (WGEPAD),
30 March, Geneva. https://www.ohchr.org/Documents/Issues/Racism/WGEAPD/Session16
/VereneShepherd.pdf.

———. 2017. "What Is in Your Backpack? We Who Believe in Freedom Cannot Rest".
Speech given at the Forty-seventh Congressional Black Caucus Reparations Issue Forum,
22 September, Washington, DC. https://ibw21.org/commentary/prof-verene-shepherd
-speech-congressional-black-caucus-sept-22-2017/.

United Nations. 2001. *Durban Declaration and Plan of Action*. Adopted at the World
Conference against Racism, Racial Discrimination, Xenophobia and Related Violence,
8 September, Durban South Africa.

United Nations General Assembly. 1948. *The Universal Declaration of Human Rights*. http://
www.un.org/en/documents/udhr/index.shtml.

Wittman, Nora. 2013. *Slavery Reparations Time Is Now*. Vienna: Power of the Trinity Publishers.

Contributors

Patsy Lewis is Senior Fellow at the Watson Institute for International and Public Affairs and Director of the Center for Latin American and Caribbean Studies, Brown University, Providence, Rhode Island.

Terri-Ann Gilbert-Roberts is Research Manager in the Economic Youth and Sustainable Development Directorate of the Commonwealth Secretariat, London.

Jessica Byron is Professor of Caribbean Foreign Policy and Diplomacy and Director of the Institute of International Relations, the University of the West Indies, St Augustine, Trinidad and Tobago.

April Karen Baptiste is Professor of Environmental Studies and Africana and Latin American Studies, Colgate University, Hamilton, New York.

Cynthia Barrow-Giles is Professor of Constitutional Governance and Practice, the University of the West Indies, Cave Hill, Barbados.

Roland Craigwell was Professor of Economics, Department of Economics, the University of the West Indies, Cave Hill, Barbados, up to his death in January 2014.

Halimah A.F. DeShong is Senior Lecturer and Head of the Institute for Gender and Development Studies: Nita Barrow Unit, the University of the West Indies, Cave Hill, Barbados.

Hubert Devonish is Professor Emeritus of Linguistics, the University of the West Indies, Mona, Jamaica.

Ronald M. Gordon is Courtesy Professor at the Food and Resource Economics Department, University of Florida, Gainesville, Florida.

Natalie Dietrich Jones is Research Fellow at the Sir Arthur Lewis Institute of Social and Economic Studies, the University of the West Indies, Mona, Jamaica.

Irwin LaRocque was the seventh secretary general of the Caribbean Community (CARICOM) from July 2011 to August 2021.

Jay R. Mandle is the W. Bradford Wiley professor of Economics, Emeritus, Colgate University, Hamilton, New York.

Alain Maurin is Professor of Economics at the University of the French West Indies and Director of the Centre de recherche en économie et droit du développement insulaire (Center for Research in Economics and Law of Insular Development), Pointe-à-Pitre, Guadeloupe.

Tamara Onnis is a course coordinator and lecturer in the Department of Social Sciences, at the University of Applied Sciences, Darmstadt, Germany.

Julia Jhinkoo-Ramdass is an economic consultant with the Caribbean Research Team, Trinidad and Tobago.

The Honourable Justice **Adrian D. Saunders** is President of the Caribbean Court of Justice.

Verene A. Shepherd is Director of the Centre for Reparations Research, the University of the West Indies, Mona, Jamaica, and a vice-chair of the CARICOM Reparations Commission.

John J. VanSickle is Professor Emeritus, Food and Resource Economics, University of Florida, Gainesville.

CPSIA information can be obtained
at www.ICGtesting.com
Printed in the USA
LVHW041753091222
734910LV00005B/391